Sigurd Lewerentz

SIGURD LEWERENTZ
1885 1975

edited by
nicola flora
paolo giardiello
gennaro postiglione
with an essay by
colin st john wilson

Electaarchitecture

Editor
Giovanna Crespi

Copy Editor
Gail Swerling

Translation
David Stanton

Acknowledgments
The authors wish to thank the Museum of Architecture of Stockholm, and especially Bitte Nygren and Lenita Björk; Gunilla Svensson and Lars Berlin, who presently live in the "Black box," Lewerentz's last residence; Francesco Dal Co and the Architecture Editorial Department of Electa.
Our sincere thanks go to Andrea, Matteo and Tomas, for having patiently assisted us throughout our entire stay in Sweden

Distributed by Phaidon Press
ISBN 1-904313-46-9
ISBN 978-1-904313-46-5

www.phaidon.com

www.electaweb.it

First published in English 2002
Reprinted in paperback 2006

Printed in Hong Kong

Contents

Appendices

Sigurd Lewerentz
The Sacred Buildings and the Sacred Sites

Colin St John Wilson

Project for the extension to the Stockholm South Cemetery at Enskede, sketch for the Way of the Cross, 1915 competition.

A Question of Paradox

"It was as if he stood at a slight angle to the world", wrote E.M. Forster of the Greek poet Cavafy; and that image could most aptly be applied to Sigurd Lewerentz. It is said that he could sit for a long time just looking at a common nail and asking himself how many ways it could be used—for "out of the simple question a surprising answer could come". We read also of his instruction to a despairing metal-worker: "All I know is that you are not going to do it the way you normally do."[1]

It is not that we have to contend with perversity; what is at issue for Lewerentz is the search beneath conventional appearance for the shock of a renewed truth. Christian Norberg-Schulz once described the contention of modular space as space without secrets: Lewerentz was able to find secrets wherever he looked because he looked hard. "If you do not expect the unexpected you will not discover it", said Heraclitus,[2] and, in so saying, he pointed to much that is enigmatic in Greek architecture. In the architecture of Lewerentz (above all in his sacred architecture) we are confronted as much with a new interpretation of ritual and symbolic form as with the manner of its making.

But above all we are confronted with a major paradox. Whereas in his early work Lewerentz was a master of the classical language of architecture, in his later work (notably in the churches at Björkhagen and Klippan) he totally rejected that language and yet produced buildings of great authority, propriety and emotional impact. Furthermore, whereas in the case of Asplund, his contemporary and sometime collaborator, this transformation was accompanied by some equivocation, for Lewerentz, the "turn" was extreme, unblinking, absolute. His classicism was more refined, more deeply felt, more original than that of any of his contemporaries; his late work was more austere than any minimalist, more uncompromising than any Brutalist.

The testimony of this man has unshakeable authority, and the grounds for his rejection of the Classical language of architecture must be explored; for his work is the exposition of a profound polemic. Henri Matisse maintained that a painter should have his tongue cut out so that he would be compelled to say all he had to say with his brush. Uniquely among architects, Lewerentz elected that silence.

He was a man of few words; all he had to say was said by the way a brick is laid, a pair of beams straddle a column, a piece of glass is clamped across an aperture in the wall, a path is cut through a forest. What for lesser mortals is called "detail" was for him a means of heightening and transfiguring the mundane, and in that he is of the company of Hawksmoor and Borromini.

The Sacred Buildings

Lewerentz was one of the greatest rarities of our times: a master of sacred architecture. Where others used their skill to make it a little easier to face death, mixing unfocused sentiment with well-focused clinical detail, Lewerentz did not flinch at the tragic sense. By an architectural alchemy of great intensity he fused the simple elements of construction into metaphors of brooding mystery.

Aristotle, in *The Poetics*, assigns unique significance to the ability to invent metaphor: "The greatest thing by far is to be master of metaphor. It is the one thing that cannot be learnt from others and it is also a sign of genius since a good metaphor implies an intuitive perception of the similarity in dissimilars."[3] Lewerentz possessed this unteachable gift to a marked degree. We will see, for instance, how,

Project for a Crematorium at Bergaliden, Helsingborg, study elevation.

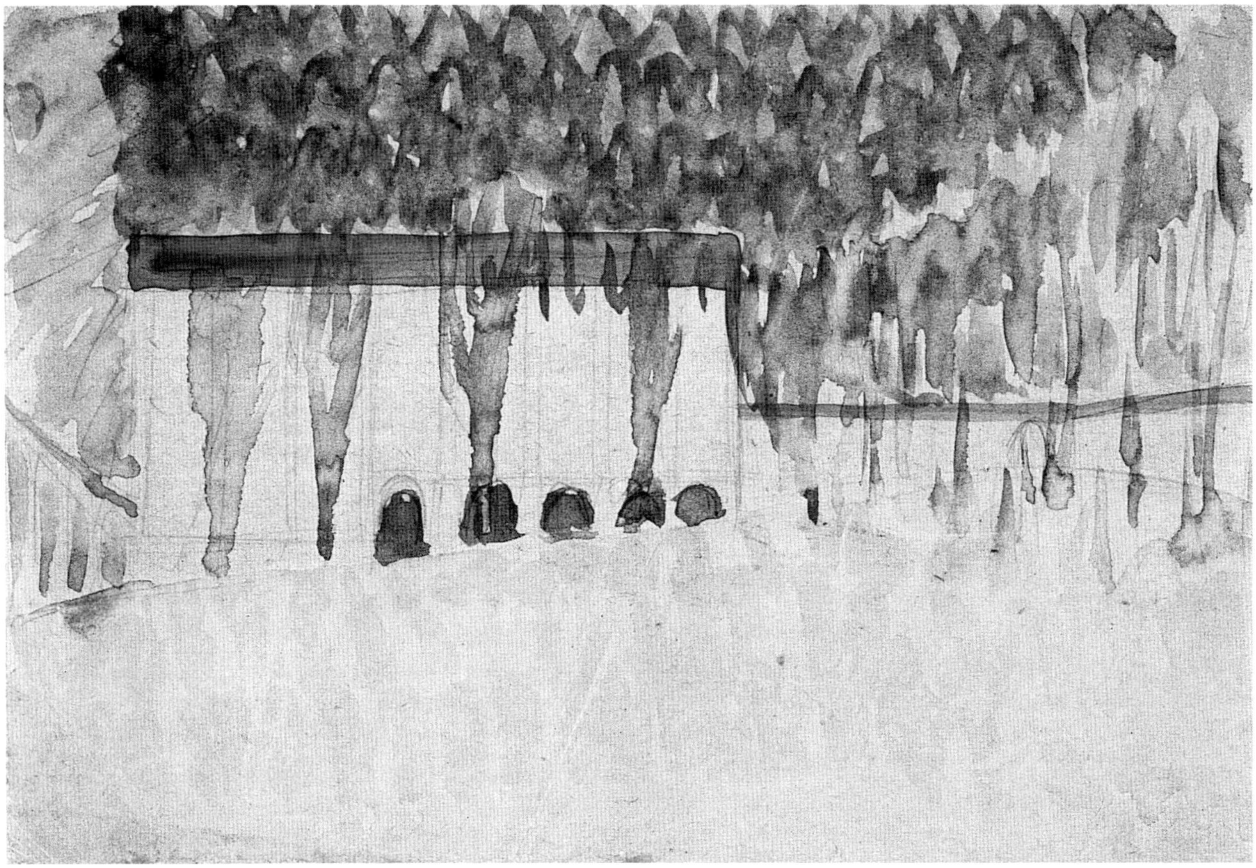

in St Peter's, Klippan, a painfully evolved solution to the need for central support—a "technical" assembly of raw-steel sections into a column and crossbeam, which thrusts into the centre of the Church—irresistibly recalls the central symbols of both the New and the Old Testaments: the tree of knowledge and the cross of redemption. Without any recourse to rhetoric, a way of making has become transmuted into a figure infused with "terribilità".

Such a gift is rare; what is equally extraordinary is Lewerentz's ability to exercise that magic irrespective of stylistic terms. My task therefore is to account for the radical transformation in language between the first neo-classical masterpiece, the Chapel of the Resurrection in Stockholm, and his equally powerful last work, St Peter's, Klippan. A Schinkelesque refinement was abandoned in favour of a poverty of means unique in the history of architecture.

His work is fraught with paradox. He was qualified as a structural engineer and for many years divided his time between conventional practice and the design and production (in his own factory) of standard metal windows, doors and partitions: and these we can see eloquently deployed in his building of 1930 for the Social Security Administration in Stockholm. Yet his later buildings had no windows at all. In addition, in a period increasingly enamoured of high technology he turned towards the masonry of ancient Persia as the point of departure for his last inventions.

It is a pity that his rightful heir and one-time collaborator, the much underrated Peter Celsing, died comparatively young, pre-deceasing Lewerentz himself; but many other architects have responded to his influence,—Klaus Anselm's Konsthal in Mälmo is a case in point. However for the present, Lewerentz's work carries great relevance to any re-appraisal of the classical language of architecture; for the fact is that its most moving and skilful exponent of our time abandoned that language in its entirety—and did so without any loss of power to move us deeply.

In an early project of 1914 in Helsingborg, Lewerentz explored the theme of the cemetery chapel in a profoundly original way. This was in the early days of the practice of cremation, and Maurice Maeterlinck had been drawn in by the town commissioner of Gustaf Schlyter to

Sketch of the overall plan and plans of the ground and first floors.

help formulate a "programme." It was proposed that the mourners should not exit through the door by which they had entered, but instead pass through a progressive "rite of passage", from the chapel where the funeral rites are enacted into a place of memory or celebration and thence out into the graveyard itself by a separate door.

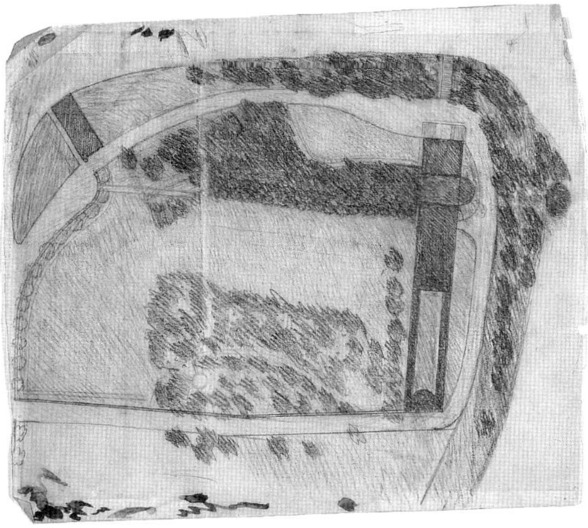

In the case of the Helsingborg project Lewerentz invented an extended narrative in which building and landscape are drawn together in one continuous theme. The sloping contours and presence of water on the site are developed into a moving and lyrical analogue. The water is channelled (as a metaphor for the River Styx) into a dark vault under the entrance façade of the building. In the ceremony itself the mourners move from the dimly lit Hall of Death up a staircase to the Hall of Life, whose high windows receive the dance of sunlight reflected from the waterchase passing beneath. Overhead a choir sings, concealed in its gallery. The mourners then pass into an arcaded cloister, lined with urns and closed at its western end by a memorial pavilion from which, by a small door, they may either walk into a Grove of Remembrance or return to the world of the everyday. The brook that passes like a mill-race beneath the chapel emerges on the far side, renewed as the Waters of Life, in a steep cascade that returns down towards the tree-lined avenue to the south as if struck from the living rock. Classical and biblical metaphors flow together as one.

This rite was not merely the contrivance of a "promenade architecturale", but the enframing and sustaining—through architecture—of a common experience of great poignancy: the necessary acceptance of death, the decent rituals of mourning.

Like so many of Lewerentz's major inventions this project was, alas, never built.

Chapel of the Resurrection

The design, conceived eight years later (1922), for the Chapel of Resurrection in the Woodland Cemetery of Stockholm was executed in full. Here Lewerentz extended his experience of the confrontation with death to a much larger canvas, beyond the isolated building and out into the landscape at its most sublime. The design of the whole Woodland Cemetery itself was won in competition in 1915 in a joint submission with Asplund and went through a number of evolutionary stages that are explored later in this account.

The particular sequence in the plan that forms the approach to the Chapel commences from the raised Grove of Remembrance, a paved square with fixed seats surrounded by elm trees. From this vantage point of rest there lies straight ahead a long pathway cut through the dense woodland forest of tall pines, a thin shaft of light parting the blackness. This is the Way of the Seven Wells, crossed by pathways into the forest, where groups of gravestones are sprinkled at the foot of the trees. Here and there a solitary figure tends a grave. Gradually a white glimmer at the end of the forest path comes into focus, announcing the presence of a tall limestone portico; we are about to arrive at the Chapel of the Resurrection.

The first thing we notice is that the portico closing the view of the forest path is not only disengaged from the megaron form of the

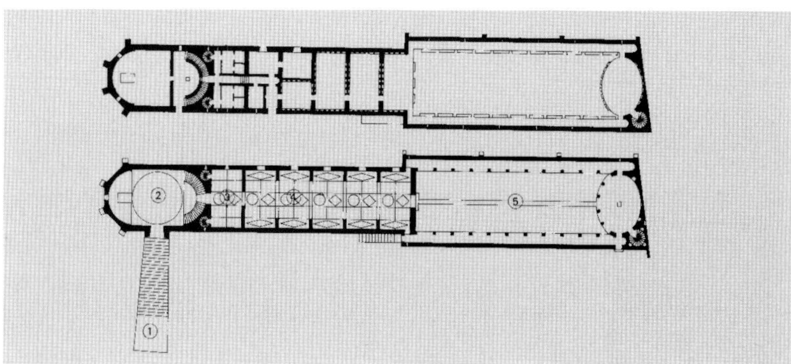

Resurrection Chapel, Stockholm South Cemetery at Enskede, exterior and interior views.

chapel but is, ever so slightly, set at an angle to it. This departure from the orthogonal draws with it the plane of the west gable wall of the chapel itself.

This disengagement is enigmatic. It is a condition present elsewhere in the building at the scale of detail. For instance, just as we see daylight between the roof of the portico and the eaves of the chapel, so too at the eave level of the chapel there is a deep undercut between the roof slate and the stone cornice, as if the plane of slates hovered above the body of the chapel itself.

I know of no precedent for such independence between portico and sanctuary; not even the Erectheion has this freedom.[4] But then, wherever we look in the chapel, things are not quite as we are led to expect. This ramifying strangeness takes hold of the attention in a way that seems to address the visitor with all the intimacy of a personal comment.

The entrance to the chapel stands behind the north-facing portico. The chapel interior is dominated by the presence of a tall aedicular baldachino over the altar, strongly lit from the southern window. The exit is a separate, minor doorway in the west-facing gable. It is clear therefore that Lewerentz is applying the principles of the "rite of passage". The exit opens towards a flight of steps that leads down into a sunken graveyard, surrounded by trees but also flanked along its northern edge by a range of cells in which coffins awaiting burial can be housed. It is in this sunken court that the journey that started at the northern entrance comes to its terminus.

I suggest that the freeing of the portico is to compensate for the weakness that would result from locating it at the far corner of the chapel, a location necessary to the proper sequence of the "rite of passage" procession; for this sequence would clearly require that the entrance door should be located as far away from the east end as possible without actually being in the west wall, which is to be kept as the location for the exit. To have simply attached the portico to the corner of the chapel would have been formally banal.

The "Corinthian" order of the chapel is an original invention in which memories of the Tower of the Winds in Athens are compounded with the Theban bell-capital, which, like the plane of the roof slates, is deeply undercut at the plane of connection to the square abacus. Setting this carved elaboration of limestone against the sheer rendered surface of the chapel, with its plinthless wall, transmits the emotional charge from the whole into the detail of the part.

Although some of the strangeness in this interior is of a conventional mannerist nature—recalling in its distension and structureless "wallpaper" of pilasters the stair-hall of Michelangelo's Biblioteca Laurenziana[5]—the real strangeness lies in that transposition whereby the powerful aedicule, whose presence outside dominates the chapel, is recalled within by the stiff, tall stance of the baldachino. There is something haunting about this insistence, its juxtaposition and transformation that hints at some metaphor we cannot grasp—a

quality to which de Chirico ascribed the status of the "metaphysical".

There presides in both part and whole a Grecian canon of proportion, founded on the square, the golden section and their compounding in the square-root-of-five relationship. The application here is rigorous and confirms my belief that where this is so, the presence of a building becomes charged with "gravitas"; constant relationships are perceived simultaneously or in time, in the way that verse is measured out by rhyme, and this insistence builds up to a persuasive authority.

At about the time of the construction of the Chapel of the Resurrection Lewerentz was also engaged in two major competition projects at Malmö—a new theatre and a project of the Eastern Cemetery (which will be discussed in the section below on the Sacred Sites). They were designs of extraordinary elegance in the manner of Schinkel and their presentation by the draughtsman Artur von Schmalensee is a match for anything in the plates of Schinkel's *Architektonische Entwurfe*; indeed I believe that these projects are equal to anything that Schinkel himself produced; the theatre is richer in ideas than Schinkel's Schauspielhaus in Berlin and the cemetery project would have been the most haunting celebration of morality in our time.

Be that as it may, the drawings, which are now the unchallenged masterpieces of this kind, demonstrate a finesse in the invention and manipulation of classical themes that is truly remarkable. They establish a position of such perfection that the reasons for subsequent rejection of this language must have an exceptional urgency.

Transition

Many others, including Asplund, made the shift shortly afterwards to the "white" architecture of the 1930 Stockholm Exhibition. The building for the Social Security Administration in Stockholm of 1930 was the major work by Lewerentz of this period. However, the austerity of its façade reveals Lewerentz's fundamental kinship to the ethos of Adolf Loos and it is a signal of further austerity to come. The Johanneburg Church project of 1933 for Gothenburg was his most original work during this period

Entrance portico and the access road.

and is discussed below. It is, however, at this time that Lewerentz's final collaboration with Asplund on the last, and most important, building for the Woodland Cemetery took place. The affront, after almost twenty years of profound collaboration, was wounding and perplexing.

Nevertheless the wartime extensions to the Malmö cemetery with the Chapels of St Knut and St Gertrude carried further Lewerentz's "turn", only this time it is not merely a reaction against the classical mode but also against the "white architecture" itself. No one carried that "turn" to the pitch that earned Lewerentz the reputation by the late 1950s of being a godfather to the Brutalists, and which is most dramatically demonstrated in his last two major

Resurrection Chapel, Stockholm South Cemetery at Enskede, plan, north front, cross and longitudinal sections, 1923–25.

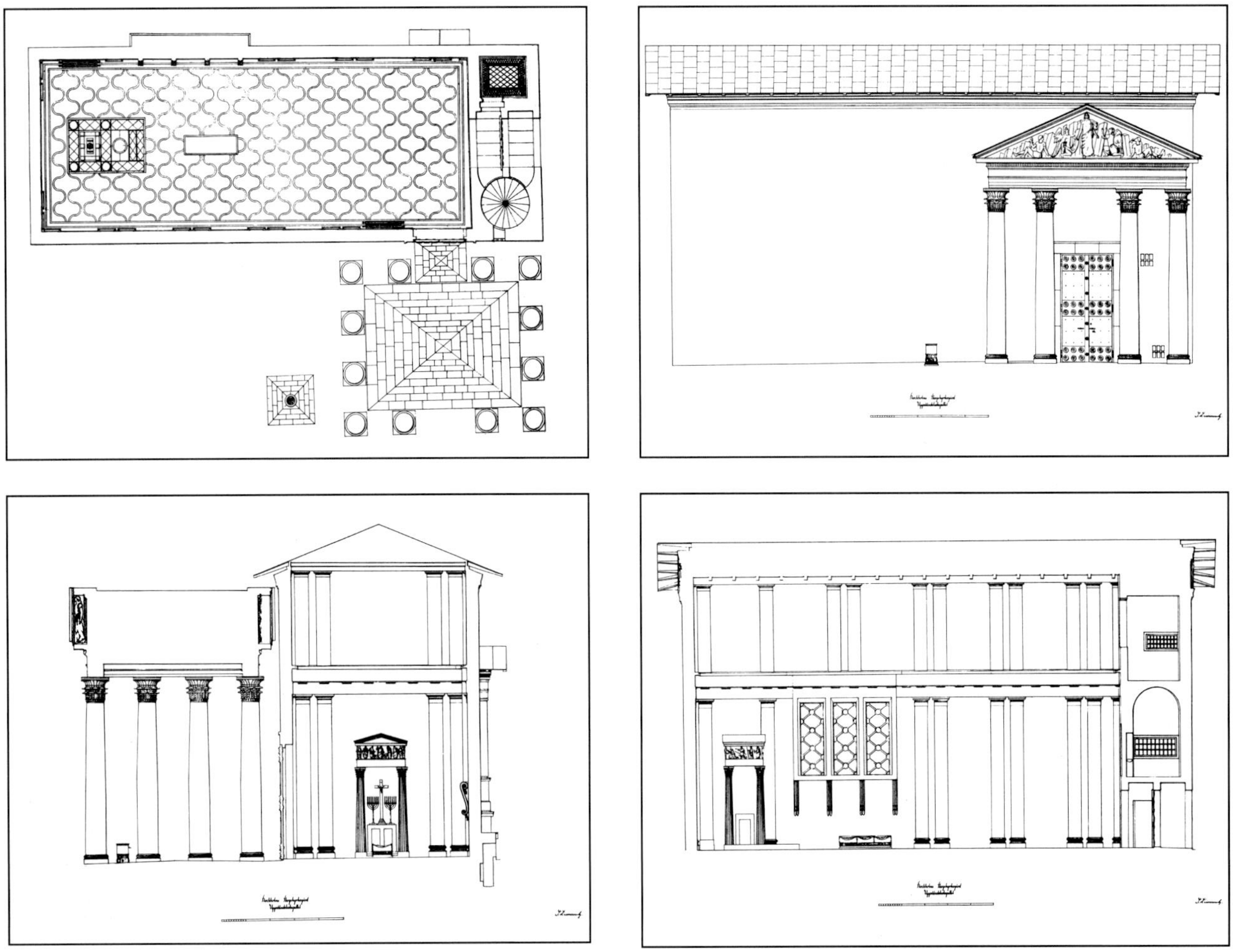

buildings,—St Mark's Church and Community Centre at Skarpnäck (1956–60) and St Peter's Church at Klippan (1962–66). "Swedish grace" was a thing of the past.

Of these two projects it is the Church at Klippan that I have chosen for particular analysis since it carried to a greater extreme the radical paring-down of language which is their common factor. However one aspect of the Skarpnäck development should be identified as illustrative of Lewerentz's unique fusion of metaphysical idea and tectonic practice. The motto that Lewerentz adopted in order to identify his competition project was the word "Mellanspel". We have noted Lewerentz's "elected silence"—his refusal to explain his intentions was proverbial. Nevertheless he does here and there drop a clue that enables us to crack the code of his enigmatic discourse: and in this word we are offered just such a clue. "Mellanspel" is literally compounded of two words,—"mellan" meaning "between" and "spel" meaning "play" and so we are offered the concept of the play generated in the interspace between two structures or two concepts.[6] This perception throws light upon the interlocking pairing of themes at play both between the two structures of the project (Community Centre and Church) and between the whole complex itself and its adjacent suburban residential development,—sacred/profane, new suburb/ancient forest, progressive politics/mythical lake sunk from sight.

In the Church of St Peter, sited on the outskirts of Klippan near Helsingborg, an unprecedented austerity of means prevails. But this austerity is not an end in itself—it is the means by which the tragic aura of the Mass envelops us with a breathtaking primitiveness. Once again there is the element of strangeness that we found in the Chapel of the Resurrection, though it is of a different order. It does not lie in the reinterpretation or distortion of ancient themes; there are no orders, no portico or pediments or symmetry to be subverted, and therefore the building does not lend itself to description in conventional terms.

The building's mystery lies in the discrepancy between its apparent straightforwardness and its actual obliqueness. The harder you look, the more enigmatic it becomes.

The competition design for the Johanneburg Church of 1933, carried out during Lewerentz's "white" period in the 1930s, prefigures a major issue in the design of the Klippan Church. As so often with Lewerentz, the great virtue and subtle originality of his thinking was instantly grasped by the most intelligent of his architectural contemporaries, but was not understood by the members of the jury.

The point at issue is the rethinking of plan-form for the performance of the liturgy. This subject is now well rehearsed and Rudolf Schwarz's *Vom Bau der Kirche* of 1938[7] stands as a remarkable document of exploration at that time. The relocation of the altar was a prime consideration. Instead of being sited at the far end of a linear (basilican) space so that the officiating priest stands between the congregation and the altar and performs the office with his back to the celebrants, the altar was now to be moved into the heart of the congregation. The term that Schwarz used, "the open circle" corresponds closely to the term used by Lewerentz, "*circumstantes*". In this conception, the celebrants "stand round" the performance of the sacraments, which is therefore carried out in full view of the congregation. This re-interpretation of the Lutheran Mass recalls the practices of the primitive church before the time of Constantine, when the sacraments were performed secretly in the catacombs or the family dwellings—in a state of utter simplicity. As we will see his last (but unbuilt) competition project for the Church and Parish Hall in Växjö takes this concept further to the point of actual circularity.

Although at Skarpnäck Lewerentz adopted the linear basilican form, with the church at Klippan he returns to a forceful application of the principle of *circumstantes*.

Just as the Chapel of the Resurrection grew from a reinterpretation of the ceremony of the committal of the dead, so here the new principle of *circumstantes* lies at the heart of a new plan-form.

It shows the altar surrounded (counter-clockwise) by the bishop's seat, pulpit, organ, choir, font, congregation and lay-clergy. The priest's point of entry is immediately from the sacristy to the north; the congregation has two points of entry (from west and south) directly outside, and one (from the north), through a protected entry porch to which is attached a small wedding chapel. There is a bell-tower over the sacristy. The other elements of the church centre—meeting-room, communicants' classrooms, parish council, children's club and pastor's office—take the form of an enclosing L-shape lying protectively to the east and south against the prevailing wind and forming a communal "street-court" as an extension of the meeting rooms and children's club. The children's club, in turn, has its own sunken courtyard at the centre of the "street".

Project for the Malmö Theatre, perspective view of the foyer, 1926 solution.

In proposing the square plan-form required by the principle of *circumstantes*, Lewerentz was confronted by the need to reduce the span of his roof members by some form of intermediate support. In this case, as at Skarpnäck, the roof elements take the form of vaults. But, whereas at Skarpnäck the vaults invariably ran laterally to the nave axis, in St Peter's he ran them along the main axis towards the altar—though they required some form of intermediate support to reduce the length of the span across the entire church (18 metres, approximately 60 feet). This could not be achieved in the masonry structure used elsewhere without massive invasion of the central zone of the church. Lewerentz was thus led to adopt some form of columnar support. At first he divided his space by a pair of columns. Later he proposed a solution that not only reduces the degree of interruption to a minimum but also (as we shall see shortly) imparts a symbolic gesture which is as profoundly apt as it is original. A single column supports a short crossbeam that in turn supports at each extremity a pair of lateral beams, whose outer support lies in the east and west side walls.

At this point we have to note that strange instinct by which Lewerentz, apparently concerned only with a dogged working out of an issue in terms of building construction, in the end arrives at a figure pregnant with symbolic meaning—its form irresistibly evoking the form of the cross with a harshness for which we are quite unprepared. It is almost as if the ancient legend of the Discovery of the True Cross had happened here, and these rough walls had been erected to protect the discovered object. We are stunned by the sheer concentration of means and meaning that transforms a way of building into symbolic statement at a single stroke.

It seems worthwhile therefore to look closely at the building rules that Lewerentz set himself. In the first place we find that the use of brick is subject to three propositions stringently applied in the teeth of commonsense compromise. First, Lewerentz proposes to use it for all purposes: wall, floor, vault, rooflight, altar, pulpit, seat. Second, he will use only the standard, full-size brick; there will be no specially shaped bricks. Third, no brick is to be cut. The only way these conditions can be met is by a very free proportioning in the ratio of mortar to brick; to achieve such jointing (often very large) a very dry mortar mix that included ground slate was employed.

Project for the Johanneberg Church, Göteborg, model.

St Peter's Church at Klippan, exterior and ground-floor plan.

The effect is of a surface in which bricks appear to be embedded in a matrix of mortar rather than laid up in bonded course work of conventional joints.[8] It brings with it memories of ancient brickwork, Byzantine and Persian, as well as the indigenous vernacular of farm buildings.

Heating and ventilation are incorporated in the brickwork such that the cavity walls of the church serve as a plenum, acting through a pattern of open perpendicular joints or through open channels at window sills. The refusal to cut brick produces some startling results; for instance, in the window openings to offices in which the cavity between inner and outer leaf is kept open as just such a channel for warm air, the toothwork of the outer leaf stands exposed. A similar serration occurs at the springing of each vault and at each end of the fissure in the floor created by the font.

Similarly, floor tiles are never cut, whether they be brick or the wider range of Hoganas tiles of different colour and size. Their pattern is frequently eccentric, and width of joint random, but all such work was carried out to the on-the-spot instructions of Lewerentz who apparently spent three entire days a week on the site.

Openings, be they for door or window, are never framed into. Closure is effected by applying an element across the opening to the face of the wall. Thus both door and door-frame, or glazing element, sit on the face of the wall, not in it. The surfaces of the wall and its openings are massively complete irrespective of all trim or services.

As with the Chapel of the Resurrection, we are once again confronted with the unexpected. It were better that nothing be taken for granted, whether it be the detail of the window, vault and door or the layout of the whole. A square plan seems simple enough; but let the floor as it slopes down to the altar swell into a shallow mound and burst open to reveal a well for the baptismal shell, and let a raw steel column crowned with a crossbeam stand like a crucifix off-centre of that space to vie with pulpit and altar as a centre of focus, and a certain drama enters in.

The column itself is not what it at first appears to be; split in two from top to bottom, its twin cross-trees, which are not symmetrical, carry at their extremities yet further beams, which are also split into pairs.

On these beams stand steel struts to support the metal ribs that support the brick vaults at both springing and ridge lines alternatively. Then again, these ribs to the vaults are neither horizontal (they pitch gently to the "centre" of the church) nor do they run parallel but expand and contract as they run from wall to wall. Lewerentz speaks of the vaults as a recall of the ancient symbol of the heavens, but here his treatment of them is strangely moving and

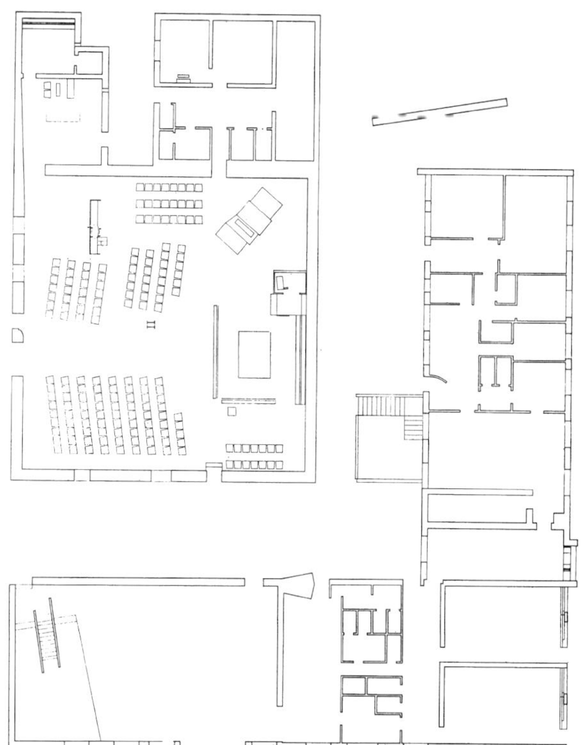

St Peter's Church at Klippan, views of the baptismal font and the central column.

insinuates into the mind a closer analogy to the rhythm of breathing—the rise and fall, the interlocking of expansion and contraction. Lewerentz worked closely with the project engineer and proposed the use of smaller steel sections, paired, rather than large single sections, so that light could shine through the middle of the structural assembly—a theme already explored in the entrance canopies of the Markuskyrka.

To what extent these shifts and discontinuities are brought about for visual reasons or to compensate for the difference in physical performance between steel section and brick vault I do not know. The fact is that a technical requirement is transformed into a haunting metaphor and how this is brought about is unfathomable.

Lewerentz's handling of light deepens this quality. Instead of the coloured radiance of the Gothic or the dazzling luminous white of the contemporary tradition from Bryggman to Leiviska, we are invited into the dark. Enveloped in that heart of darkness that calls on all the senses to measure its limits, we are compelled to pause. In a rare moment of explanation, Lewerentz stated that subdued light was enriching precisely in the degree to which the nature of the space has to be reached for, emerging only in response to exploration. This slow taking possession of space (the way in which it gradually becomes yours) promotes that fusion of privacy in the sharing of a common ritual that is the essence of the numinous. And it is only in such darkness that light begins to take on a figurative quality—the living light of the candle flame or, as at Klippan, the row of roof lights that forms a Way of Light between sacristy and altar.

This invitation to explore is further induced by the way the floor (which is not level) seems to move beneath your feet: at one point as we have seen, the brick surface swells up into a mound and then breaks into a fissure to form the baptismal font—an astonishing metaphor, which hints at the idea of the water of life bursting from the living rock. Then there is the gentle inclination of the floor from the entrance towards the altar, inducing the experience in the visitor of being drawn into a presence. This "movement" in the floor combines with the action of the vaults above, which seems to expand and contract with a "breathing" rhythm to create a certain charge in the air that recalls the interior of St Mark's in Venice. Such space can be activated by the disposition of lights into

the focused spaces of church ritual or can recede into isolated centres of solitary inward focus.

Finally we notice that in his handling of the façades Lewerentz is cryptic to a fault. The only rhetoric left is the peal of the bells. But this too recalls Byzantine practice: just as the rough brick shed gives way to a dark interior shimmering with oriental blue and gold in the tomb of Galla Placidia, so at Klippan, it is within that the building comes to life. Here we have not only a recollection of Adolf Loos but, more aptly, of Le Corbusier, who said of the monastery at La Tourette—the one building that most closely approximates Klippan in its concentration, its passion and its austerity—"... it does not talk. It is on the inside that it lives... that the essential lies".

So to what end did Lewerentz, the most poetic master of the classical language of architecture in this century, abandon that language? As a student of Schinkel, Lewerentz would have been aware of that master's own conviction that the means of architecture would have to be "created anew. It would be a wretched business for architecture... if all necessary elements... had been established once and for all in antiquity"[9] but Lewerentz's concern lay at a much deeper level than the pursuit of novelty.

In a remarkable chapter on Greek architecture in Lisle March Phillips' book *The Works of Man* we read: "Every shed builder who lays a stick on two uprights has mastered the structural principles of a Doric temple: but the Greeks alone have comprehended the inward significance of the act."[10] In Phillips' appraisal of the unprecedented ends to which the pursuit of optical corrections were carried, he advances the notion that what started out as optical rigour became transformed somehow into an ethical obsession: "Visual perception passes into ethical conception. The two are fused together. We think with the eye and see with the mind... A Doric temple is saturated with ideas that were not put into it as ideas at all but by another faculty (that is, sight).

It is, indeed, difficult to speak for a moment of Doric construction without being led insensibly into the language of ethics, for the suggestions of the eye, which that construction everywhere obeys, turn of their own accord into ethical ideas directly they take shape in stone... We find the Doric temple penetrated and, so to speak, suffused with slight imperceptible inflections of line and contour, involving incalculable extra trouble and expense in the

St Peter's Church at Klippan, assonometric drawings of the central column and the roof (graphics by C. St John Wilson).

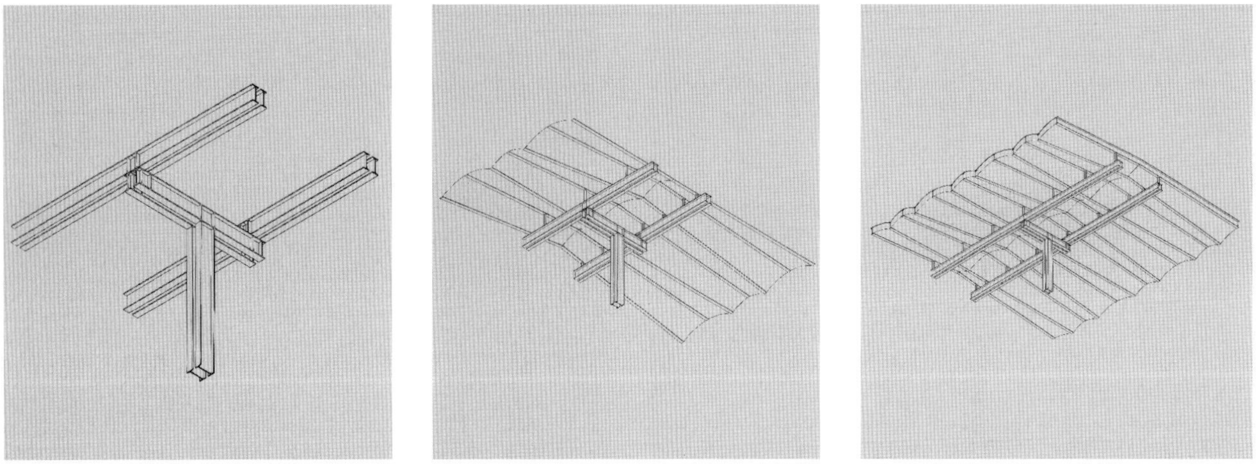

building, and we find that the object and aim of all these expedients is to adapt the outlines of the temple more perfectly and accurately to the laws of sight.

Equal columns which appeared unequal would be made unequal to appear equal. A level floor which looked unlevel would be made unlevel to appear level. Vertical lines which appeared to slant would be made to slant that they might appear vertical…

Nothing in this strange art is what it seems to be. The most obvious facts turn out not to be facts at all. And the closer we carry out examination the more the mystery spreads and deepens. It infects the whole temple".[11]

What we are offered in this description is a search for the truth of a certain kind: "to see with the mind and to think with the eye". In that moment, aesthetics and ethics become one. What was required of the Greek temple was that it would stand as the utterly self-sufficient and visually inviolate sculpture to house and to celebrate a god or goddess. Propriety would ordain which of the prescribed and unchangeable orders should be adopted. Within that symbolism, cosmic order was to be transcribed and embodied as visual order. A building language for the sacred was born.

This insight into a paradox matches very closely the quality of experience provoked by the buildings of Lewerentz. At a time of "isms", of *l'architecture à thèse*, of buildings required to be no more than demonstrations of some narrow issue, here was an architecture of extraordinary directness, utterly transparent in the functions it was created to serve, uniquely concrete in setting forth the substance and the manner of its making.

In developing the design of St Peter's, Lewerentz spoke of two things only: the interpretation of the brief (there was a consultant on liturgical matters, Lars Ridderstedt) and questions of building construction (he and the foreman, Sjöholm, are said to have worked very closely together—often far into the evening planning the next day's work). But throughout the evolution of the design there were endless alterations and on-site revisions. This arduous search reminds me of a statement by the painter Michael Andrews: "Painting is the most marvellous, elaborate and complete way of making up my mind." At Klippan we become witnesses of the extraordinary process by which Lewerentz, at the age of eighty, slowly made up his mind.

An eloquent passage in Heidegger's *The Origin of the Work of Art* describes how a Greek temple "does not cause the material to disappear but rather causes it to come forth for the very first time".[12] Just so at Klippan: brick was never more brick, steel more steel, glass more glass, wood more wood. In that attention to the essential nature of materials there lies a quality of respect that has its own morality. Ethics and technique become one. It is not surprising therefore that the language of classical forms was no longer viable for Lewerentz. For that language was born out of an order of construction, transposed from timber and finding its final and essential refinement intrinsic to stone.

When Lewerentz built the Chapel of the Resurrection, the stonework of the portico was cut from the solid Ignaberga limestone. At that time in Sweden such technology was in no way abnormal; it was not so in 1960. The sort

Building details of the door and window frames.

of equivocation that satisfied a Lutyens—rolled steel columns encased in masonry "orders"—was beneath contempt for a man for whom the spirit of Greek architecture was far closer to his heart than the law. It is perhaps both chastening and reassuring to recall that the very foundation of Western culture is grounded on something that is as simple and austere as it is difficult: the spirit that created the original and imperative ethos of the Doric out of the technology of its day.

There have been those in our time who have sought to revive the notion of "ritual" to give "meaning" to the pursuit of aesthetics, and to reinstate the classical language in order to indulge in the shifts of rhetoric; it is therefore all the more salutary to do honour to the opposite mode, the true and humble process by which a new poetry was hammered out of the endless wrestle with worn-out forms. In doing so it won back a long-lost authenticity and a profound reinterpretation of the place of sacrament.

John Ruskin said: "No one can be an architect who is not a metaphysician",[13] and certainly there is in the "argument" of St Peter's at Klippan much that reminds us of the way in which the philosopher lays down his proposition, brick by brick as it were, each with its own integrity, but nevertheless bonding into a whole wall. Lewerentz was the contemporary of Samuel Beckett and Giacometti, and he shared with them an unflinching acceptance of a deliberate poverty of means. But he did not share their despair. Rather it is as if, like the inventors of the true Doric, he had to find his truth by embracing utter simplicity. "Greece and poverty have always been bedfellows", wrote Herodotus.

When all is said and done, it must also be recognized that St Peter's is an old man's building. Although nearly eighty, Lewerentz spent many days of the week on site interpreting and revising his intentions. While the compression of ideas is enormous, it recalls late Cézanne or the *Rondanini Pietà* on which Michelangelo was working when he died, and which, unfinished and bearing the scars of numberless changes, has the quality of immediacy as if we could still hear the blow of the hammer, as if thought itself were being carved before our eyes. Here too at Klippan, the making and the thought are one.

The Sacred Sites. Monumental Landscapes

Lewerentz's power of metaphorical interpretation was brought to bear with equal invention upon the wider theme of landscape in a series of projects of exceptional beauty of which the Eastern Cemetery project at Malmö was one among many. Here the marriage of building to earth, sky and water sustains a dominant theme across a large range of episodes. This is *l'architecture parlante* on a grand scale. Four examples will suffice to show Lewerentz's range.

In each case, the theme is the elegiac celebration of death and memory in the presence of nature. Adolf Loos wrote: "When we come across a mound in a wood, six feet long and three feet wide, raised to a pyramidal form by means of a spade, we become serious and something in us says: 'Somebody lies buried here'. This is architecture…", and in the same piece: "Only a very small part of architecture belongs to art, the Tomb and the Monument".[14] Whether or not Lewerentz took such thoughts to heart, he did undertake some twenty-eight projects for cemeteries, chapels or churches, one-third of which were carried out —a preponderance in his work the more remarkable when compared to the predominantly secular work of his famous contemporaries. Clearly he was choosing the themes most removed from the everyday and most demanding of metaphoric interpretation.

We saw earlier how Lewerentz was engaged in two major competition projects for the Eastern Cemetery. Of this scheme we have only the drawings, but, executed in the manner of Schinkel, they rival in both form and metaphor anything that the German master ever invented himself.

The scheme encompassed detailed designs for a main chapel, a crematorium and a circular ceremonial plaza. The main chapel took the form of a rectangular cella with two shallow hexastyle and two deep tetrastyle porticoes on a raised podium; the columnar order was Corinthian. The bell-tower was to be located within one of the porticoes. The tripartite crematorium (for which Lewerentz prepared a number of variant solutions) consisted of a central *cella* (for the reception of coffins and caskets and the exhibition of urns for sale) with a conical structure to house two furnaces to the east and a similar structure as a sepulchral chamber to the west. The variants were apparently based upon the Etruscan Necropolis at Tarquinia, with and without paired obelisks. The circular ceremonial plaza was surrounded by a wall broken by four entrance porticoes, with a single column in antis. A small circular chapel also appears in some versions.

Lewerentz's details were very rigorous, his forms very demanding, and when in 1926 the bid for the construction greatly exceeded the proposed expenditure, the project was put off until its resurrection in a very different form much later. However, the drawings, executed by Artur von Schmalensee are remarkably haunting. Modelled on the engravings in Schinkel's *Architektonische Entwürfe*, they equal the work of the German master in the quality of both design and draughtsmanship. Indeed these projects and the Chapel of the Resurrection together form a body of work that makes a unique contribution to the tradition that it salutes. It is significant that in his use of the classical language Lewerentz stayed close to the subject matter out of which that language arose —the sacred, the funerary and the monumental—unlike those who elsewhere have abused it, to lend cachet to such themes as the bank, the lunatic asylum and the house for a stockbroker.

The Woodland Cemetery at Enskede, to the south of Stockholm, is the largest of these projects, and its design evolved through a number of stages, from highly elaborate beginnings to a monumental simplicity. In its final form, it is one of the great epic landscapes of all time; indeed it may be said that in its primal elements—forest, cropped mound, water, low sun—it is the archetypal embodiment of the North, just as the horned mountain, rock and blazing sky of the ancient temple site of Greece is the embodiment of the South.

St Peter's Church at Klippan, details of the floors of the service buildings.

The design is the fruit of a collaboration with Gunnar Asplund that lasted for nearly twenty years, until Lewerentz's shameful dismissal by the Cemetery Board during the evolution of the last chapel group in 1934. While the work was a genuine collaboration, I believe that the greater responsibility for the landscape design rests with Lewerentz—a claim strongly supported by the fact that, of all the buildings on the site, it is his Chapel of the Resurrection that is most at one with the gravitas of the landscape.

The original cemetery design of 1914 won the competition by responding closely to the pre-existing spirit of place (the Nordic forest of tall pines and gravel pits) with the least possible violation of its intrinsic qualities. Conceived in the vernacular of the National Romantic movement, the devices employed for the inhabitation of the forest were numerous and inventive—the Path of the Seven Wells, the Seven Gardens, the Way of the Cross, the Path of Urns—but they were too liberally dispersed, straining to create identity and orientation by episode rather than overall plot. The scheme then underwent a number of stages of development. A stronger and more detailed scheme of 1917 was supplanted a couple of years later by a powerful invention in geometrical order, in which Lewerentz deployed more conventional uses of axis, symmetry and orthogonal grids. In 1922 it too was changed by a sweeping gesture of simplification in which the eastern sector of development was reduced to a straight road running directly to (and through) the portico of a single Chapel of the Holy Cross. From this simplicity, a great drama unfolds.

Opening in solemn mood, a semicircular propylaeum of massive masonry converges upon a narrow Via Sepulchra, whose walls, embedded with columbaria, frame a landscape that is as haunting as it is beautiful. The axiality of approach suddenly dissolves into an apparent irresolution—a device that would be dismissed in conventional Beaux-Arts terminology as an "unresolved duality". To the right, the eye is drawn towards a close-cropped mound that recalls the Bronze Age burial mounds of Agri (known as the Maiden Mounds) and into this is cut a broad flight of steps ascending to a tree-lined platform marked out with a group of stone seats—the Grove of Remembrance. Straight

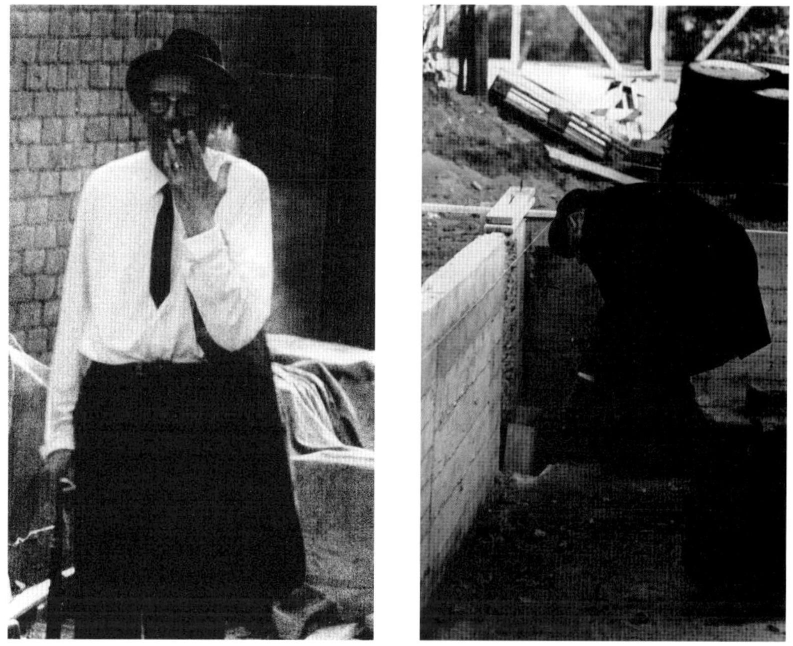

Sigurd Lewerentz at the building yard of St Peter's Church at Klippan.

ahead lies the long dark Way of the Seven Wells, which slices through the dense forest of tall fir and spruce to arrive at the portico of the Chapel of the Resurrection. To the left, the Way of the Cross ascends to the grand portico and impluvium of the chapel group. The Way is firmly defined along one side by the low site wall of the graveyard, but throughout its entire length it is transfixed by the presence of a huge freestanding stone cross. Just as Lewerentz's image of the cross was the imprimatur of the original competition scheme, so the presence of the monumental stone cross silhouetted against the sky gives tragic meaning to the whole landscape. This decision was made by Lewerentz. Asplund had toyed with the idea of placing there an obelisk and he resisted to the end Lewerentz's insistence on the sterner and more tragic form of the Cross. But what of the centre? Bare sweep of the plain, a sheet of unruffled water, a glimpse of dark forest beyond, huge clouds piling up in the sky—this "biblical" landscape is shot through with a very modern disquiet, a focus on the void.

Stuart Wrede[15] has traced one element of the chemistry of this haunting place to the Romantic landscapes of Casper David Friedrich, and there is no doubt that a source of inspiration lies there. But this is no painting. It is a world that you walk into—plain, mound, water and dark forest. Death in the hubbub of the city is different. Compare this place with the Modena

Eastern Cemetery at Malmö, perspective study of the main chapel, c. 1923.

Cemetery of Aldo Rossi. There all is geometry and the melancholy of repetition, of the pathetic mass-produced columbaria in metal racks, row upon row. Here, where the headstones stand between the trees in the silence of the forest, the rhythm of the seasons mediates a very different mood.

The second example of Lewerentz's mastery of landscape is the design of the Rud Cemetery in Karlstad of 1917. This scheme is small, but none the less offers a dramatic composition of great power. Once again, a heavily wooded landscape is the basic theme, but this time focused on an artificially formed valley below. In a recall of the Helsingborg prototype water cascades down a central flight of steps that leads down axially from the square necropolis above, enclosed within a high wall of pruned trees. Here nature is strictly marshalled into a geometry of the sublime in which the imagery, with echoes of Italian rhetoric, is of a more conventional kind. The view from the valley up the cascade to the tall cleft in the trees is carried off in the high manner of Boullée. Unfortunately,

this design was never carried through to completion.

Lewerentz's other major built landscape design was the revised version of the Eastern Cemetery at Malmö of 1943 with the chapels of St Knut, St Gertrud and St Birgitta, the circular plaza of remembrance and the bell-tower. The landscape competition is utterly different from the Rud or Stockholm schemes. Here there is little enclosure; all is exposed along a ridge that runs east-west at an upper level the full length of the site. The first chapel (St Birgitta), a traditional Nordic burial mound and a bell-tower are distributed along the northern part. At the western end, the twin chapels of St Knut and St Gertrud were added to an existing crematorium.

The landscape is remarkable enough—laid out like the excavation of a Hellenistic city—but it is around the forecourts and porticoes of the two chapels that the visitor is arrested by certain unfamiliar traits. The ground surface is raked gravel. The imprint of footsteps disturbs the even grain spread out to receive the ritual procession of mourners (this is no place for tourists). Stone slabs are laid in the raked gravel, whose plane of arrival is warped up to meet the threshold of entry. Overhead, the portico takes the form of a sequence of discreet monopitch canopies—an aura of the shrine sites of Shinto is provoked by this play of roofs and raked gravel "landscape". A shared instinct for the irregular rhythms of nature prevails, together with a reverence for the simple shifts by which they are manifested.

The Crisis of Classicism

It has become apparent in recent exhibitions and publications that the one original contribution during this century to the classical language of architecture lay in certain austere monuments of the Nordic Classicists;[16] and in that achievement, Lewerentz was an undisputed leader. It could even be claimed that some of his work enlarged our understanding of the original Greek. This is a large claim, which I base on T.S. Eliot's celebrated formulation in "Tradition and the Individual Talent" of the relationship between novelty and tradition as a reciprocal exchange—a two-way relationship in which not only is current practice influ-

Study perspective of the main chapel.

enced by the past, but the past is "if ever so slightly altered" by the introduction of "the really new".[17] It follows from this formula that a simple test can be devised. On the one hand, it is axiomatic that the new, in so far as it derives from the past, gains in status. But what is difficult is to repay that debt, and I suggest that the failure to do so—the failure, that is, to deepen our understanding of the past by a contribution in the present—is the mark of kitsch. For it is the mark of kitsch that it borrows indiscriminately, but never honours its debts.

Lewerentz, by his neo-classical work, has "if ever so slightly" altered our perception of both classical and Byzantine Greek architecture: both the Erectheion and Hosias Lukas take on an extra depth in that historical perspective. How, then, could such a master come utterly to reject that language, and then go on to make equally powerful and equally mysterious buildings out of that rejection?

Modern architecture is a critical movement; that is, it is founded upon a criticism of life, and therefore by definition contains a large component of self-criticism and polemic. The debate is fuelled as much by this internal criticism as by external criticism. The possibility of a revival of classical forms exists only as an episode within that debate; it does not exist as an alternative source of authority. It is to be entertained as one influence among many, within a debate whose terms are forever in movement. It is in this sense that Nordic Classicism (whose formal roots lie in the works of Boullée and Ledoux) has differed from the Beaux Arts or revivalist nature of classicism elsewhere. For in Scandinavia, classicism was not merely an escape from National Romanticism, but a step

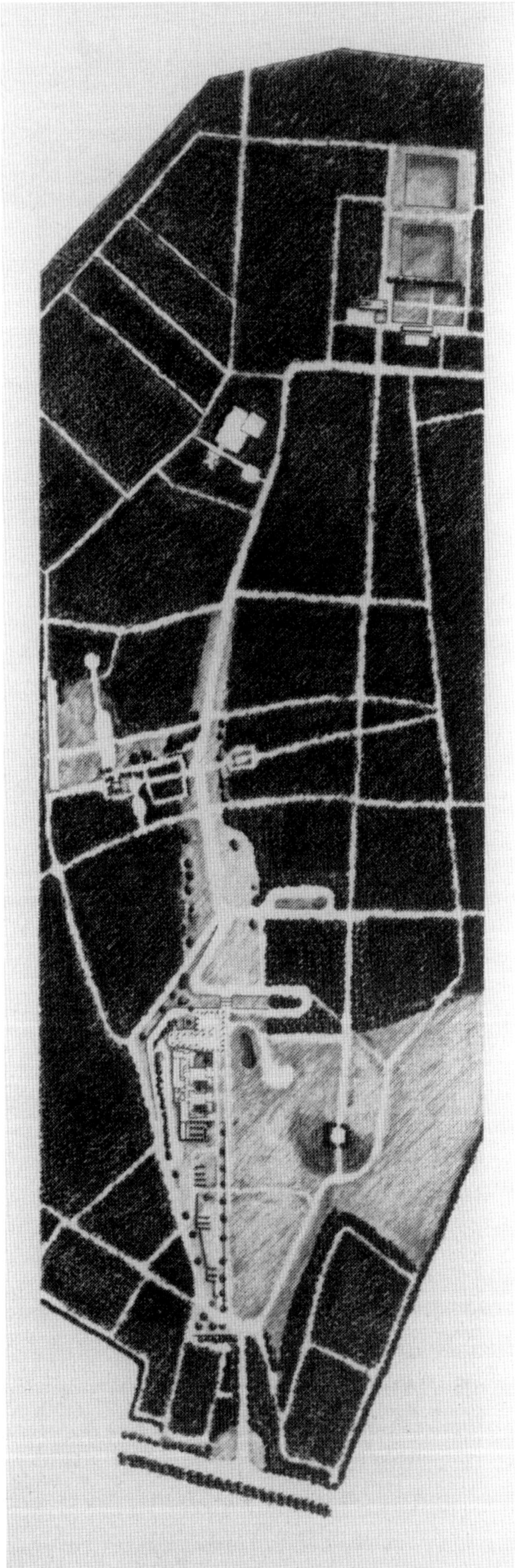

Stockholm South Cemetery at Enskede, plan of the final version (redrawn and finished by C. St John Wilson).

towards Modernism. There was not a shred of nostalgia about it—it was for the most part forward-looking, not a style but an escape from "the Styles". Far from wishing to turn the clock back, there was a feeling that through a return to the true origins (not the Beaux Arts but the purgative spirit of the Doric Greek), a new start might be made. The aim was not revival, but renewal.

Lewerentz had made a contribution of complete authenticity to a programme that lay close to the meaning of the Classical origin—the sacred and the funerary—and within a building method that lay equally close to its origin inspiration—masonry. But from now on, both programme and technical possibility were to be utterly changed. The old language could no longer take the strain.

The "Turn"

The architecture of the chapels of St Knut and St Gertrud marks the moment at which Lewerentz spoke out with a voice entirely his own. Up to that time, his invention had gone into the manipulation of a received language, be it neoclassical or, from the time of the 1930 Stockholm Exhibition, Rationalist. But at this point we can speak of a "turn" or fundamental shift in his work. One of the perspective studies is already a minimalist abstraction of Classical elements. Then quite suddenly, forms are invented and materials put together in ways that had never been tried before. And yet (and this is the most extraordinary characteristic of his late work), this newness reverberates with remote affinities to Persian antiquity and to the early Byzantine. The spirit of that which is most ancient hovers over structures of perplexing novelty. Lewerentz never spelt out the ethos that bound these themes together, but clearly there is an affinity with just such values as were spelt out by Adolf Loos.

As to that new programme to which his friends in Sweden responded with the manifesto *Acceptera*—the broad social and technological revolution of our time—Lewerentz made little direct contribution. His building programme was still in the realm of the sacred. What is remarkable, however, is that even there he found the classical language no longer able to carry meaning as before. So what is at issue in his late

View of the landscape.

buildings is not the inadequacy of the classical language to deal with functionalism, but rather the exhaustion of its powers to deal even with its original province—that realm of building that Loos defined in terms of "the tomb and the monument". In that exhaustion, it had become a language that can only tell a lie. Another truth had to be explored: a secular truth, to exist in parallel to the sacred and to be evolved through the same rigorous search. The fin-de-siècle had made many efforts to obscure the issue by compounding secular needs in a fancy dress borrowed from the language of the sacred, and to that form of aestheticizing pretension a growing disgust began to be voiced: "We have had enough of the extraordinary: what we need is the self-evident" was a typical cry. So the classical sense of truth as a reality to be dug out from the world of appearance—a stripping bare, an absence of rhetoric, an illumination—was revived.

It is an idea that is both very old and also very new, in the true tradition of Modernism. One of its clearest expressions lies in James Joyce's use of the words entelechy and epiphany in forming his own working method. The word entelechy in Aristotle's usage relates to the condition in which a potentiality has become an actuality by achieving a perfection of form. And Joyce uses the word epiphany to denote those moments of showing forth, in which a remark or gesture becomes a sudden revelation in depth of a state of affairs hitherto concealed or unacknowledged—a reality that lies beneath the veil of conventional discourse, the small talk of partly living, suddenly acquires a shape and therefore an identity. The same terms are used by Heidegger, again with insistence on the roots in Greek thinking, in explaining the meaning of truth as revelation (*aletheia*), the laborious uncovering of that which lies concealed: light and attention are directed upon a problematic area until a form of language permits at last the recognition of a true state of affairs and the possible terms of its embodiment. It is in its failure to respond to

Stockholm South Cemetery at Enskede, view.

this test that the capacity and propriety of the old language came into question.

Lewerentz both in his buildings and in his mastery of place, of that "Topos" in which building and nature and symbolic narrative are locked together in one inscrutable gesture, has conjured up a world that is as ancient as it is modern and in whose spell we enjoy at last the conviction that "the really new" has been presented to our view.

Afterthoughts and Forethoughts

To understand how Lewerentz's work was perceived during his life-time it would seem that we have to penetrate a protective screen against the outer world that was drawn down in Sweden after the death of Asplund in 1940. Except for some diplomatic skirmishing by Markelius in the CIAM Congresses of 1929 and 1931 it would seem that after the one brilliant set-piece of the 1930 Stockholm Exhibition Sweden withdrew from the theatre of polemical "isms", movements and counter-movements prevailing elsewhere. It seemed to be a retreat from the brave new world of the Exhibition into a genteel compromise that the *Architectural Review* described as "The New Empiricism" and which became the butt of Aalto's joke about the man who started from his sleep screaming, "Who will save me from Vallingby?".

And so when Lewerentz died in 1965 something rather extraordinary happened. Glowing appraisals were written by the small group of fellow architects who held him in the highest regard but had nevertheless kept him as a secret from their fellow countrymen as much as from the outside world.

The result was that the obituaries strangely took the form of an introduction to his work for the first time rather than a farewell to a man of renowned achievement. And it is at that moment that sufficient background evidence began to emerge as a corrective to the half-truths of "The New Empiricism".

For one thing it was not for lack of good grounds for provocation that the term "the New Brutalism" was first uttered in Sweden.[18] And when Peter Reyner Banham published his book entitled *The New Brutalism* in 1966 he concluded the book with a brief section on Hard Cases: the Brick Brutalists in which he discussed the work of a handful of architects

Eastern Cemetery at Malmö, Chapels of St Gertrud and St Knut, study drawing.

who shared with Brutalism a deliberate austerity, rigorous geometry, naked exposure of the manner of making and of materials "as found" but departed in significant ways from the canon.[19] Lewerentz was one of these and his Markuskyrka was half drawn into the compass of the canon but released, on reflection, as "other", as "an enigma" that "poses a question but illuminates no possible answer".

Quite rightly Lewerentz was allowed to slip through that net into the deeper waters that were his alone. Right to the end of his long life he sustained his extraordinary powers of poetic invention both in interpretation of subject matter and in the mysteries of "techne".

As to the interpretation of subject matter we note that he took the linguistics of Brutalism to an extreme beyond the daring of anyone else but all for quite "other" reasons,—some of which we have touched upon, but others that still elude us. For instance, it has been hinted that the broken plan-form of the sacred elements in the Markuskyrka complex enacted a play upon the idea of the building as the ruin of an earlier perfectly symmetrical form. Such play engages in an alchemy that the Brutalist canon never dreamt of; and it is precisely that alchemy that weaves the magic ring that encircles the world of Lewerentz. It mattered to him that beneath the Markuskyrka there lay a large lake that had sunk from memory and that the surrounding wood had once been a famous forest. Architecture should be able to deal with ghosts whether they be from the past or offerings to the future.

And the last competition project that he produced would have been the most audacious of all. It was in 1974, the year before he died, and prepared with his young associate Bernt Nyberg for the Parish Complex in Vaxjö. Presented under the competition motto "circondare" it took the theme of "*circumstantes*" to an extreme form,—two concentric cylinders of concrete soar up into the proportions of a tower with light-shafts between and an oculus at the top containing a reflecting device that would direct a living shaft of light down upon the altar. It was rejected by the jury which took fright at the "overwhelming scale".

Whatever material Lewerentz chose,—stone, brick or concrete "Form" and "Matter" were one. And it is in his use of brick in his last two major buildings that so much of his thought is condensed; we are brought to reflect upon the extraordinary significance that he attributed to this humble element just at the moment when "progress" was universally believed to lie in emulation of the frame and glass box fathered by the Lever and Seagram buildings at that very time.

Frank Lloyd Wright may have claimed that in his hands a brick was worth its weight in gold but in Lewerentz's hands it unlocked a whole new world. For him it was accorded a status verging on the sacred, a reverence that we may sometimes accord to the objects of Nature but rarely to the elements of building. In these buildings the essential qualities of brick are made, in the words of the philosopher Heidegger, "to come forth into the Open",—to participate in an act of revelation in which those essential properties, shape, texture and bond "shine forth" as never before.

What then are the elements of brick? Brick is compounded of earth, air, fire and water. Nothing could be more elementary. Nothing could be humbler in substance, more modest in manufacture, simpler in shape, ageless in its use by man.

In "the Age of High Tech" this may sound like a list of limitations. But is it?

Is not the simplicity in the manner of its making the very token of its universality? And

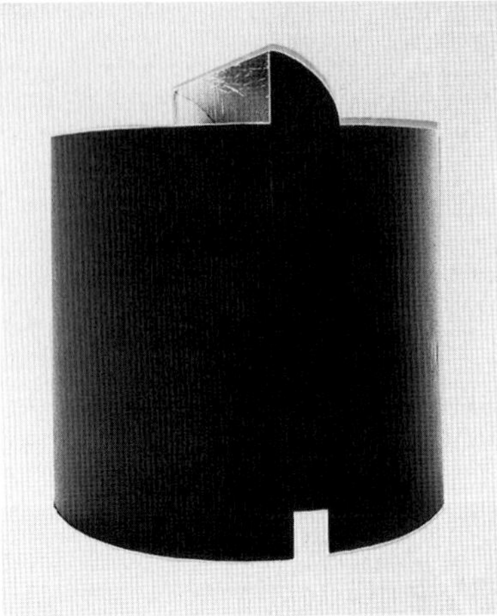

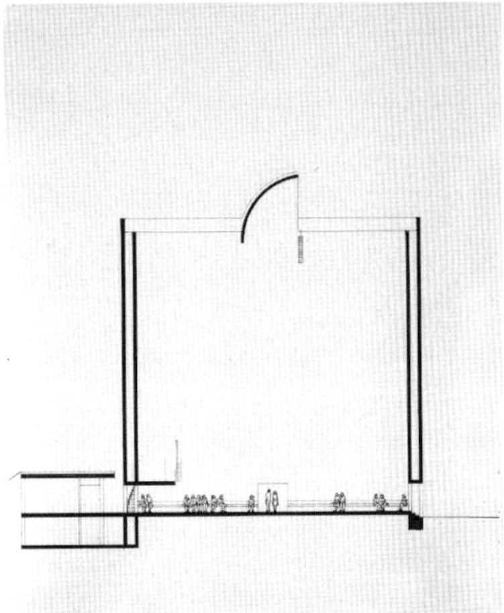

Project for a church at Växjö, model and section.

the rudimentary nature of its shape the key to powers of infinite combination?

And is there not also great strength in the order that the discipline of bond requires of those who practise it? (Brick is not open to the liquid moulding of concrete).

Furthermore it is not only in its shape (whose geometry promotes the combinations and intercombinations of bond) that this virtue lies. More than any other building element brick can be married to every other material whether natural or manufactured: wood, stone, plaster, steel, concrete, glass, lead...

Since it is compounded of natural elements it will respond organically to the processes of nature. There is no other wall material of which it can be said that its appearance is improved with the weathering of time. (This is particularly true in the Northern climate where the proportion of moisture in the air creates a condition that leads to the unpleasant discolouration not only of concrete surfaces but also of many stones).

It would seem that there is nothing simpler than a brick, but then one has to add that there is nothing more mysterious. For of all things made by man, brick retains, even today, some aura of the mythical. For earth, air, fire and water were seen by the ancient philosophers of Greece to be the basic elements of the Cosmos. There is a shadowy connection to those stories of Creation in which the first man was likewise formed from clay.

Finally brick is "arguably the oldest manufactured building element in the history of building". Surely it is the essence of Lewerentz's poetic practice that he could take that which is most simple and most ancient and make of it something that compels us to say that we have never seen anything so rich, so memorable,—and so new.

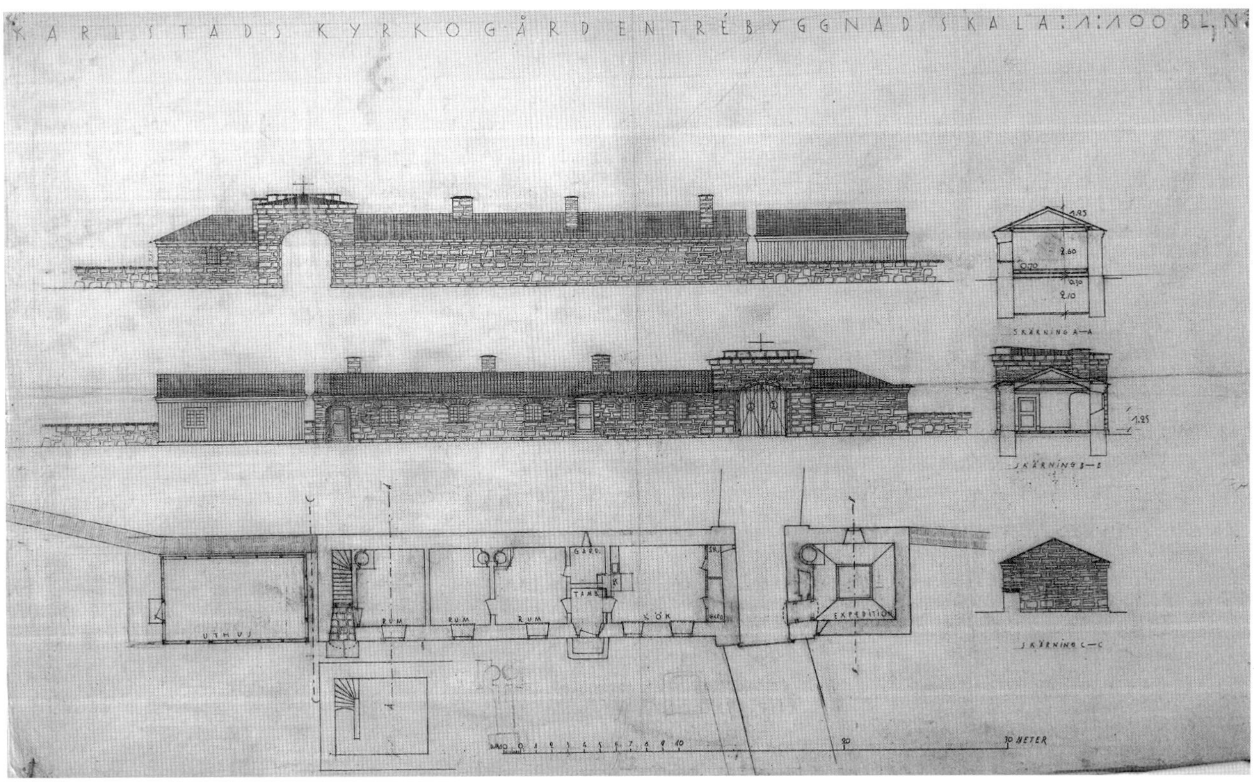

Rud Cemetery, Karlstad, elevations and study plans of the entrance.

St Mark's Church at Skarpnäck, view of the south front of the church.

[1] J. Ahlin, *Sigurd Lewerentz*, Byggeforlaget, Stockholm, 1985 (English trans. 1987).
[2] Heraclitus, Fragment, 18. "The Cosmic Fragments", Cambridge University Press, Cambridge 1978.
[3] Artistotele, *Art of Poetry.*
[4] Ten years later Asplund borrowed the same motif for his version of the large Chapel of the-Holy Cross constructed on the eastern part of the site. This was after Lewerentz had been dismissed from the project.
[5] The intervals between the antae are irregular and their distribution on the north wall is not recalled on the south wall.
[6] I am grateful for this insight to Courtney Danielle Coynz in her dissertation on the topography of the whole complex in her MSC dissertation at Cambridge University 1999.
[7] Published in translation as *The Church Incarnate* in 1958, with an introduction by Mies van der-Rohe.
[8] Lewerentz drew the setting out of every brick at a scale of 1:20 and then demanded that the bricklayers should use neither plumb-line nor spirit level!
[9] K.F. Schinkel, *Tagebucher Briefe Gedanken*, Hans Mackowsky, Berlin 1922.
[10] L. M. Phillips, *The Works of Man*, Duckworth, London 1911, p. 113.
[11] Ibid., pp. 117–18.
[12] M. Heidegger, *Poetry, Language, Thought*, Harper and Row, New York 1971, p. 46.
[13] J. Ruskin, *The Poetry of Architecture.*
[14] A. Loos, *Architecture*, 1909.
[15] S. Wrede, "Landscape & Architecture," in *Perspecta*, no. 20.
[16] "Classical Tradition and the Modern Movement," The 2nd International Alvar Aalto Symposium, 1982; *"Nordic Classicism," 1910–30*, Museum of Finnish Architecture, exhibition and catalogue, 1982.
[17] "Tradition and Individual Talent", in T.S. Eliot, *The Sacred Wood, Essays on Poetry and Criticism*, Methune, London 1920.
[18] See Banham's account of the first use of the term in 1950 by Hans Asplund in discussion with a group of English architects who brought the phrase to England. (*The New Brutalism*, p. 10).
[19] The present author was one of these,—and very happy to share with Lewerentz in excommunication if nothing else.

Journey to Italy

Nicola Flora, Paolo Giardiello, Gennaro Postiglione[1]

The Modernity of Sigurd Lewerentz

A number of black and white photographs in the Arkitekturmuseet (National Museum of Architecture) in Stockholm,[2] are the only evidence of the journey (or journeys) that Sigurd Lewerentz made to Italy towards the end of the first decade of the twentieth century, or at the beginning of the second one, probably during his apprenticeship in Germany[3] or, perhaps, immediately afterwards. These dates have been identified thanks to the explicit reference to "the classical world" contained in the competition project for the extension to the Stockholm South Cemetery, which he prepared together with Erik Gunnar Asplund (who also visited Italy in 1913 and 1914) and submitted in 1915, bearing a motto with a Mediterranean flavour: "the Way of the Cross".[4]

Nothing is known about the length of Lewerentz's journey or where he went, except for a number of places appearing in his photographs. Curiously enough, of the scholars who have concerned themselves with his work, only Luis Moreno Mansilla[5] has paid attention to this important episode in his life. Both Janne Ahlin, the first scholar to devote himself to Lewerentz and his first biographer, and Caroline Constant,[6] who has reconstructed the events linked to the realization of the Stockholm South Cemetery, devote only a few notes to the architect's Italian journey and his unusual decision to document it exclusively with photographs, in open contrast with the usual practice. At that time, in fact, various Scandinavian architects "believed that direct contact with the classical remains was indispensable, so that the study tour of Italy assumed great importance as a formative experience".[7] In December 1913, for instance, Asplund began his wanderings around the Mediterranean, and this, as Luca Ortelli states,[8] had a notable influence on his education and subsequent professional and teaching activity. Asplund's journey, like Lewerentz's, cannot be ascribed to normal academic practice: it was not made possible by an award or a study grant; it took place mainly in Italy and the choice of itineraries was absolutely personal, dictated by omnivorous and unsystematic interests in the natural environment and buildings in a wide variety of styles. However, the real difference between the journeys of Asplund and Lewerentz, whose careers overlapped on a number of occasions, was the way in which they documented them. The former, like many after him,[9] filled more than "three hundred sheets with drawings, sketches, notes, portraits and a wide variety of subjects";[10] moreover, he collected over eight hundred postcards to supplement the photographs he took. According to the available documentation, Lewerentz, on the other hand, did not make a single sketch. The only record of the journey is a relatively small number of photographs, taken from rather odd angles with unconventional framing, which makes it difficult to recognize the subjects.

This radical decision offers the first demonstration of the atypical nature of ther personality of Lewerentz, who was indifferent to the customs of his fellow-countrymen and a forerunner of developments in the cultural climate of his times. Moreover, it hints at his propensity for resolute choices, which is confirmed by the obsessive way in which he devoted himself to his profession—his long experience with the design and production of metal door and window frames attests to this—and the meticulous care he took over the details of his projects.

The decision to entrust the recording of his memories to the camera, a basic tool for "technical reproducibility", is both a sign of his interest in innovatory techniques and a declaration of faith in modernity. Drawing on Walter Benjamin,

Iain Chambers states: "Technical reproducibility implies the shattering of tradition and the secularization of the image."[11] Lewerentz was ahead of his time: he was an exponent of the substantial transformation of the relationship between subject and object to which this quotation refers and he consciously avoided the conventions of his day. Furthermore, his photographs are anything but naturalistic and the way he composes them is the result of his rejection of "transcription" in favour of "representation" of the fragment; they are ranged like the vestiges of a hypothetical map of the memory, a store of experiences that could later be used again in different places and narratives.

Lewerentz's unusual manner of reproducing through fragments is further evidence of his modernity, and it is not difficult to draw an analogy between his technique and the theory of the text formulated by Roland Barthes.[12] In architecture too, in fact, the reading of an artefact entails its deconstruction in order to identify the distinctive elements and compositional logic that allow it to be understood. As in the case of textual analysis, the aim is not to discover the objective meaning crystallized in the work, but rather to produce new meanings, creating a close link between the signification and the use of the work itself.

Lewerentz's works seem to be the result of a similar mental process: the subjects have been chosen with audacity, while, when framing them, he does not seem to have taken into account the fact that he might have wanted to re-use them, so that, in some cases, these pictures do not even seem to be authentic. It is no coincidence these photographs were pieces that Lewerentz would later use to compose the jigsaw puzzles of his projects. For this reason, it is perhaps unnecessary to try to identify the places visited during his Italian journey in the hope of "discovering similarities, hypothesizing influences and reconstructing secret routes in order to demonstrate the closeness of his architecture"[13] to the Mediterranean world.

Lewerentz, it is worth repeating, was in advance of his time: attesting to this is, for example, St Peter's Church at Klippan. The composition by conceptual and concrete fragments, the attention paid to details and their rigorous simplification without losing control of the whole and his mastery of technique all demonstrate his ability to reach the limits of architectural design, where the contradictions and complexity of the project become evident. At Klippan, the use of cavity walls, the application of the windows to the exteriors of the walls, the composition based on the golden section and the decision to use bricks and mortar as the only construction materials all demonstrate that Lewerentz had a rigorous and well-tried philosophy that could be conveyed through the formal language of architecture.

The Photographs of the Italian Journey: the Imprint of a Method of Design

Photographers of the calibre of Cartier-Bresson or Brassäi describe their art as an apparent paradox: that of selecting a fragment of reality, fixing certain limits, but in such a way that the process of selection acts as an explosion opening out onto broader reality, like a dynamic vision that spiritually transcends the field covered by the lens.[14]

Photography used as the page of a notebook cannot be regarded as a speedier and more precise substitute for the sketch or drawing. It is not merely a note collected by a technological tool capable of mechanically replacing the memory or manual skill; even the choice of the composition or the framing involves the construction of a microcosm to be represented within the limits of the field of vision, a miniature world composed of parts extrapolated from the whole, which, when made independent, naturally become separate from the subject from which they are drawn. The photograph is, therefore, an account, inspired by and extracted from the real world: far from being an impartial document, it may be regarded not as the product of a mechanism of objective reproduction, but rather as the imprint of a subjective expressive will and of the concept of design.

In the literary field, in order to explain the structural difference existing between the modern short story and the novel, some critics and writers refer to the distinction between a cinematographic film and a photograph. Although this difference might seem to be closely linked to the size of the image and the length of the episode narrated, authors such as Julio Cortázar, have stressed the total difference between the two art forms: a novel, like a film, recounts, over a long period and in great detail, the plot of a story through which the reader (or film-goer) is taken slowly and with great precision thanks to clear points of reference; on the other hand, the short story—and also the photograph—uses only a fragment of an account (so it should not be merely regarded as the abbreviated form of a longer story) in which before and after, the premises and the consequences are not spelled out, but are left to the reader's capacity for intuition and involvement.[15]

Like the single photograph, the modern short story—although from the structural and compositional points of view it is a complete episode—is, therefore, based on what is substantially an open narrative account, in which there is an implicit invitation addressed to the reader to participate actively and creatively in the story that is only just hinted at. With reference to the use of the camera, in a similar way, when the photograph freezes a clear moment of reality it becomes a memory of what it represents. Often the image, isolated from its context and the sequence of events of which it forms part, assumes a significance that goes beyond mere description, so that it becomes the portrayal of more general sentiments. Photographs of architecture, too, even though taken for documentary purposes, may be subject to this mechanism.

Lewerentz's photographs, taken during his sojourn in Italy, depict the places he visited: Florence, Rome, Tivoli, Pompeii and so on.

Evidently, the number of pictures taken of each subject may indicate the degree of interest they aroused in him. It is not, however, the list of the ancient monuments the architect visited that concerns us; instead, the aspect on which it is worth focusing our attention here is the type of analysis he performs, as documented by the pictures. Lewerentz's photographs, evidently taken with great care, reveal his marked preference for compositions featuring specific parts of the buildings, or else architectural complexes seen in perspective. Among those that have survived, there are not, in fact, overall views of the ancient monuments; the latter are nearly always represented with fragments, using close-ups. The design of the external facing of Florence baptistery, for example, or the strong chiaroscuro produced by the ashlar of the Palazzo Pitti; the rhythm of the columns and shadows they cast in the Imperial Forums in Rome; the fragments of masonry or domestic spaces at Pompeii; the long wall of the Stoa Poikile of Hadrian's Villa at Tivoli—these are just some of the most fascinating and disturbing images that give us a clear idea of the very special way in which Lewerentz observed these vestiges of the past with which he came into contact in Italy.

It should not be imagined, however, that the attitude that these photographs reveal means that Lewerentz was exclusively interested in architectural details and largely indifferent to the overall complexity of the buildings. His photographs do not show isolated structural or decorative details simply for their own sake. The fragments that he captures are pieces of works that become significant thanks to the delimitation of the field of vision and the inclusion or exclusion of the parts—in other words, by virtue of the framing, which is intended to imbue the images with greater pregnancy. These very precise compositions, focusing on the structural details that most interested Lewerentz, allow us to perceive the emotion that the photographer experienced when observing the work, and this is the feeling that they are meant to convey. As Ernest N. Rogers put it, the details represented by Lewerentz "are not considered as independent entities, but as part of a whole" and allude eloquently to the contents of the entire work. So this approach has an implicit desire to consider the constructions of the past not just as objects to be studied and analysed, but rather as living structures that are still able to teach us something and convey emotion, indifferent to the passing of time, but made more fascinating and complete by the processes of stratification comprising them, because "a terminal point does not exist in architecture, there is just a continuous change".

Furthermore, the photographic images constructed by Lewerentz—as has already been noted by L.M. Mansilla—reveal that he has chosen viewpoints very close to his subjects, in the quest for what might be called an intimate relationship with the work being photographed. In other words, he seeks a way of observing it that favours participation rather than contemplation and that, above all, involves the reduction of the distance between the viewer and the subject and brings other senses, apart from sight, into play.

Participation and contemplation are concepts that, in architecture, normally regard two separate aspects of the sensorial and perceptual relationship between the work and the observer: involving all the senses, participation concerns the comprehension of the space in all its three-dimensionality, while contemplation is usually associated with the interpretation of the signals coming from the treatment of surfaces or the objects contained in specific settings.

On the basis of the evidence at our disposal, it is easy to understand that the architecture of the past was observed with great attention by Lewerentz, without his being affected by the current taste, allowing him to appreciate its original spirit. His photographs are not, in fact, the result of a static approach or a "neoclassical" way of looking at things, tending to favour fixed viewpoints, but rather they imply active participation in the many-sided qualities of the subjects observed and a dynamic vision capable of perceiving them in many different ways. The use of close-up, observation through a sequence of structures, the fascination of the materials that change their appearance according to the variations in the light, the impressions caused by the alternation of bright light and total darkness, the possibilities offered by technologies, materials and textures, the different approaches to building, the simplicity of many ancient construction methods and the radicality of the structural decisions of the past are all evident in Lewerentz's photographs, the legacy, one might say, of his Italian journey.

Thus, thanks to this small collection of photographs, Lewerentz was able to take a record of all these aspects back with him to Sweden. What he brought back from Italy did not, however, document a journey, adventurous or otherwise, but the completion of a decisive experience that was to be the premise for his concept of architectural design and a major influence in his projects. Any attempt to understand just how much of the experimental approach evident in the photographs taken during his Italian journey was subsequently translated into specific aspects of his works or influenced his morphological and compositional choices—in other words, the extent to which his modes of photography and architectural design are interlinked and interdependent—can, however, only, be based on fairly subjective hypotheses and comparisons, fascinating and otherwise.

However, having said that, it is undeniable that there is a close correspondence between some of the themes that seem to emerge in the photographs and those that Lewerentz dealt with most frequently in his architectural works. While it is not true that there was a direct transposition of the elements seen in the photographs to the works realized subsequently, the links that a comparison between them allows us to identify certainly played a decisive role in causing simplicity and radicality to be fundamental factors in Lewerentz's architectural designs and aesthetic vision. In his architecture, in fact, every formal element—even those that seem to have been dictated by his personal taste—may be ascribed to the primary forms of the art of building, which Lewerentz displays without masking or superfluous ornament. Even the decorative elements are chosen and used by him in order to exalt the essential values of building on which the formal meanings of architecture are based. This may be noted, for example, in the work he designed in his early period, in which classical forms are still present. But already these buildings—sometimes associated with the Neoclassical style—demonstrate that Lewerentz never adhered totally and uncritically to a particular architectural mode. His works mainly make use of stylistic fragments, signs, or specific forms belonging to comprehensible and codified vocabularies, which, however, Lewerentz assembled in dialectic contrast, or even in collages of rarefied references to earlier styles. This contrapuntal procedure is clearly perceivable in the treatment of the parts of the building in which stylistic references appear, only to disappear when stylistic considerations make way for tectonic ones.

However, even the works of Lewerentz's mature period may be interpreted in the light of what may be deduced from the photographs of his Italian journey. In fact, their sheer radicalness, which counted on the expressive potentiality of the materials rather than on the tectonic ones, recalls the persistence with which the architect attempted to reproduce, in his photographs, the tactile values revealed by the bare masonry of the works of the past, devoid of facing or decorations. The walls of his last buildings, patterns of bricks arranged in a manner that is apparently not tectonic, supported internally by steel and cement evoke the fascination of ruins and what they allow us to observe, and favour expression over representation. It is also worth recalling the window fittings that Lewerentz used after having spent a great deal of time on their design; this provided him with an opportunity to stress the value of simplicity and draw attention to the ways in which he pursued a programme based on the practice of reduction to essentials.

Returning to the comparison made previously between systems of composition in literature (short stories and novels) and the world of images (films and photography), it is possible to identify the ways in which Lewerentz's approach to design led him to use, in the different stages of the project, a precise narrative structure. In the short story, the structure tends, as a priority, to assume the task of expressing the contents through the emotional involvement of the reader. In the contemporary novel, the plot performs a more important function than the style—as happens in architecture, where the functions tend to prevail—while language is subject to the requirements of the narrative. Similarly, in Lewerentz's design procedure, familiar motifs and structures are used in a wide variety of compositions; the architectural language is also simplified, while increasingly rarefied assembly operations are carried out.

With reference to Lewerentz's work, L.M. Mansilla states that "it is difficult to perceive his architecture as a single entity because the individual parts are never seen as a whole, but only partially and from close quarters. The concept of the façade, of the architectural project composed according to abstract rules, whether they be ancient or modern, does not exist." Taking this further, it may be stated that, in Lewerentz's work, the individuation of the significant single component—of the detail, that is—does not involve a loss of control of the whole (which eschews stereotyped forms and familiar, well-established morphological solutions), but rather that the existence of each fragment comprising recognizable stylistic elements is justified by the presence of an underlying theme. For Lewerentz this theme is the compositional structure with which the narrative is woven: the routes planned and the circulation of people, the dimensions and proportions subject to them become the connective tissue attributing meaning to each of the fragments—which are only apparently disconnected—that a "narrator" makes use of to capture the attention of his "readers".

Apart from the frequent use of the golden section or numerical series—that is, the constant use of layouts based on a dual compositional axis—in Lewerentz's work the regulatory system required for the dimensions and form of the building is the result of a design process aiming at make the parts homogeneous without concealing them. These parts are arranged according to logical connections—deriving from relationships that are not fortuitous—that are identified by a personal and refined compositional method. This is based on a single principle—that of the reduction to essentials and the exaltation of the values of economy, regarded as the adequacy of each operation for the specific purpose for which it is carried out—informing every stage of the elaboration of Lewerentz's projects. But, in his architecture, "reduction to essentials" is never the synonym of "simplification" or even "omission" (the elimination of parts essential for the integrity of the work). On the contrary, it is the end of a process of modification, when the work displays its unadorned fullness, having now become the perfect embodiment of economy.

Lewerentz's real contribution to the developments of modern architecture does not lie in his being a precursor or radical experimenter, but rather in the fact that he understood the degree to which it is a manifestation of our times, without abandoning the tradition of which he is the guardian and the principles guaranteeing its future, and without succumbing to fashion or the cult of novelty. The fact that Lewerentz's overriding concerns were simplicity and the meeting of specific needs is evident in his work. His projects always offered solutions that were restrained but geared to the various themes and needs that he had to tackle. The most demanding themes, such as those of funerary and religious ceremonies, or the more worldly ones of the home and workplace, and the values of the community and those of the individual, were treated by Lewerentz with a single conceptual approach that did not, however, prevent him from demonstrating just how many and various were the possible forms of a poetic purpose that had simplicity as its main component.

For this reason, and bearing in mind his well-known terseness, we could dedicate Pablo Neruda's famous remark, "My creatures are born of a long rejection", to Lewerentz; after all, writing, like architectural design, is the "rejection of the intrusive creatures" that one comes across from time to time.

Simplification and Economy: a Stylistic Feature

Lewerentz is one of the twentieth-century architects who has not attempted to construct a theory to explain the principles informing his work or to order his thoughts on the design process. Although he lived in a period in which there was no lack of manifestos intended to support or propagandize the new architectural language that was then establishing itself, he put his trust exclusively in realized projects and construction, the only languages authorized to speak on behalf of architecture. His absolute dedication to the rules of his trade was the result of the constant attention he paid to clarity and his concern with the purity of the lexis of building, which he never abandoned in the course of his long career. In his work, Lewerentz aimed at the most rigorous selection of his means of expression in order to obtain the best possible form of communication. He used forms and materials to achieve transparency in the spatial experience offered by the architecture; he availed himself of the textures of materials and the evocative power of building techniques to turn every building into a metaphor of the world, as Christian Norberg-Schulz put it.

The whole body of Lewerentz's works demonstrates that they tend to draw on a vocabulary of building that is clear but less and less susceptible of reduction because this is the presupposition that allows every building to stand the test of time and survive the changes in taste that the passage of time entails. Because he did not make use of stylistic features, but rather of the procedures of building and design, Lewerentz's forms vary from case to case, although they are subject to a concept of composition and an approach to design that are both absolutely consistent.

Lewerentz did not participate in the search for spectacular effects in which various architects contemporary to him were engaged. He certainly did not aim to astonish and fascinate the public. Reduction to essentials and economy,

the most noticeable features of his projects, are the result of the way in which he related to the setting in which he worked. The natural environment of Scandinavia, moulded by a harsh climate, calls for a rigorous approach to building, which was certainly the case with Lewerentz. At the same time, he demonstrated that he was particularly concerned with the layout of the open-air spaces in which his buildings were sited, seeking to establish a profound relationship with the natural environment that was never mimetic, but rather classical and unrhetorical, reminding us once again of his Italian journey to which reference has already been made.

Stylistic reduction and respect for the economy of the means of expression are the most outstanding features of his work: for example, the layers of mortar, the joints between the materials, the patterns of the brickwork and the swelling up of the floors in the church at Klippan are some of the structural features that he displays in various works of his, all recounting the way in which he carried out this quest. This was intended to renew archaic meanings and symbols (an example is the baptismal font, also in the church at Klippan, where the water drips from a shell), while adopting an architectural language that was anything but naive. The only other twentieth-century architect whose language is comparable to that of Lewerentz, with its masterly combination of archaism and abstraction, is Le Corbusier.

Those who walk along the paths in the Stockholm and Malmö cemeteries, or enter the courtyard of the Social Security Administration offices in Stockholm or the Villa Edstrand at Falsterbo, or, above all, the external and spaces of St Mark's Church at Björkhagen or St Peter's Church at Klippan will immediately notice how Lewerentz's architecture aims to mobilize all the senses, availing itself of repeated contrasts of light, juxtapositions of materials, unexpected inventions, surprising structural mixtures and unforeseeable changes in form that stimulate memory, sight and touch.

All this does not, however, contradict the tendency towards reduction to essentials that pervades all of Lewerentz's work. Although he owned a factory producing the metal window and door frames he himself had designed, in his last works he even went so far as to abandon the use of frames. Rather like what Le Corbusier did in a number of cases, the openings are simply protected by sheets of glass, fixed directly on the brick wall. In this way the thickness of the brickwork is exalted, as may be deduced by observing the solutions adopted in the churches of St Mark and St Peter, and, above all, the flower stall in Malmö's Eastern Cemetery.

The churches at Björkhagen and Klippan seem almost to have been built by the removal of material, by excavation. Monochrome, but never monotonous, the buildings have been constructed with bricks of different colours and sizes (some of them contain small holes to improve their adhesion), arranged according to their textures, as may be clearly noted at Klippan. Varying in intensity and tone, they require—despite what their appearance may suggest—refined, very precise execution.

It is not possible to conclude these reflections on the value of the reduction to essentials that Lewerentz exalts in his architecture without referring to the last masterpiece he realized, the small flower kiosk in the Eastern Cemetery at Malmö, entirely modelled on the golden section. The large sloping roof that characterizes this building favours the entrance of light though the two large windows placed in the upper part of the higher elevation, which is at the rear, where the roof is not visible. On the other hand, the roof projects considerably over the lower front elevation, forming a sort of open portico. Inside the building, the concrete panels are covered with aluminium foil to provide thermal insulation and, at the same time, to reflect the light, diffusing it throughout the interior. Each part of the building is given particular importance. The structure of the roof displays the contortions to which it is subjected when it extends to cover the "portico", the concrete shell displays its nudity, the internal insulation layer is simply nailed to the walls, while the surface-mounted conduits containing the electrical cables describe primitive, brutal arabesques on the walls. This is a composition in which each element becomes pure form: all rhetoric has been abolished and economy appears to be the overriding consideration. Everything here has been reduced to essentials; the work is nothing but the clear composition of the parts, the result of a way of observing the world devoid of nostalgia that Lewerentz adopted from the time of his first journey to Italy.

[1] The three sections into which this essay is divided are by Gennaro Postiglione, Paolo Giardiello and Nicola Flora, in that order.

[2] After the architect's death, the Lewerentz archive, then in Lund, was moved to the Arkitekturmuseet in Stockholm. Lewerentz himself had helped with the reorganization of the documents in the last years of his life. The vast archive was further reordered by the museum staff and outside scholars, such as Janne Ahlin, the author of the first systematic study of the architect, *Sigurd Lewerentz Arkitekt*, Stockholm, 1985.

[3] Lewerentz spent the first part of his apprenticeship in Berlin, in Bruno Möhring's office, during the summer of 1907, returning there the following year after graduating from Gothenburg Technical College. Lewerentz worked for Möhring until early 1909, when he left for his journey to Italy (the only one for which there is any evidence), which concluded in the summer of the same year in Munich. Here the young architect began to work in Theodor Fischer's office, but after a few months moved to Richard Riemerschmid's office, also in Munich. This allowed him to come into contact with the milieu and activities of the Deutscher Werkbund, the association in which Riemerschmid played an important role. In 1911 Lewerentz returned to Sweden, establishing his own practice together with Torsten Stubelius.

[4] Asplund and Lewerentz participated together in the competition for the extension to the Stockholm South Cemetery; their project, which bore the motto "Tallum" and was awarded first prize, contained a visually varied series of ideas that may all be ascribed to the visits the two architects paid separately to Pompeii. The Via dei Sepolcri appears to have inspired the design of a number of parts of the cemetery, such as the Way of the Cross and the Way of the Seven Wells, although it must be stressed that the context in which these parts were used and the overall design of the landscape in the project prepared for the competition appear to be totally imbued with National Romanticism, the movement that had notably influenced the training of the two young architects. See entry 38 in this book.

[5] L.M. Mansilla, "Beyond the Wall of Hadrian's Villa", in *9H-On Continuity*, 1995. The essay, written in 1988, was to have been published in the catalogue of an exhibition devoted to Lewerentz's "classical" period that it had been intended to hold at the 1992 Venice Biennale of Architecture. Unfortunately neither exhibition nor catalogue saw the light of day, and it was necessary to wait until the publication of *9H* to read Mansilla's reflections on the architect's journey to Italy. The essay is published in the appendices of this book.

[6] J. Ahlin's monograph (see note 2) was published on the occasion of the centenary of Lewerentz's birth; it is the only complete publication on the architect, although some of the information is unreliable and the bibliographical details are insufficient. C. Constant's book, *Towards a Spiritual Landscape*, Stockholm, 1994, reconstructs each stage of the realization of Stockholm South Cemetery in great detail and with extensive documentation.

[7] E. Mangone, "Viaggi nel tempo e nello spazio: la stagione del classicismo astratto", unpublished (1997), p. 8.

[8] L. Ortelli, "Verso il sud. Impressioni asplundiane", in *Lotus International*, March 1991, no. 68, pp. 22–23.

[9] Alvar and Aino Aalto, for example, paid their first visit to Italy, in Tuscany, in 1924; the journeys of Pauli Blomstedt and Erik Bryggman, both Finnish, took place in the first half of the 1920s; that of the Norwegian Arnestein Arnberg was in 1910, while his compatriots Gudolf Blakstad and Herman Munte-Kaas set off a few years later to follow in Asplund's footsteps. See Mangone, "Viaggi nel tempo e nello spazio", p. 8 ff.

[10] Ortelli, "Verso il sud. Impressioni asplundiane", p. 23.

[11] I. Chambers, *Paesaggi migratori*, Genoa, 1996, p. 104. Naturally, for this theme, see Walter Benjamin's seminal study: "Das Kunstwerk im Zeitalter seiner technischen Reproduzierbarkeit" (The work of art in the age of mechanical reproduction), originally published in *Zeitschrift fur Socialforschung*, New York, 1936.

[12] R. Barthes, in "Teoria del testo", in his *Scritti*, Turin, 1998, pp. 240–41, wrote: "If the theory of the text tends to abolish the separation of genres and arts, this is because it no longer considers the works to be simple, but as perpetual productions or statements through which the subject continues to struggle: this subject is certainly that of the author, but also that of the reader. Thus, the theory of the text produces the enhancement of a new epistemological subject: reading... Not only does the theory expand the freedom of reading to infinity, but it also stresses the (productive) equivalence of writing and reading ... complete reading is that in which the reader is nothing other than he who wants to write."

[13] Ortelli, "Verso il sud. Impressioni asplundiane", p. 24.

[14] J. Cortázar, *Bestiario*, Turin, 1974, pp. 117–18.

[15] This is what J. Cortázar, *Bestiario*, p. 117, wrote: "In order to explain the specific character of the short story, it is usually compared with the novel, a much more common genre and regarding which there is an abundance of precepts. It is said, for example, that the novel takes place on paper and thus in the time taken for it to be read, without other limits apart from the lack of events to be recounted. As far as the short story is concerned, it starts from the notion of the limit—in the first place, the physical limit, so that in France, when the short story exceeds twenty pages, it is known as a *nouvelle*, a genre halfway between the short story and the novel in the strict sense of the word. In this sense, the difference between the novel and the short story may be compared to that between the cinematographic film and the photograph, in the sense that the film is, first and foremost, more flexible in its organization, recounting fictional events at length, while a successful photograph presupposes strict limits, partly imposed by the reduced field of vision that the lens comprises and also by the way in which the photographer uses these limits aesthetically."

Modern Cemeteries: Notes on the Landscape*

Sigurd Lewerentz

As a complement to the work on the architecture of the Swedish garden, I would like to add some notes on the parish churches, the larger religious communities and, above all, the most modern cemeteries.

The cemetery may, in fact, be regarded as a garden, but of a very special kind, because, as well as possessing the typical characteristics of this kind of open-air space—trees, shrubs, paths and lawns—it is, above all, a monument suitable for a burial ground. The disposition of the graves and the regulation of their design are factors of central importance in the formulation of projects for cemeteries. Today, however, this relationship is disregarded—or perhaps simply underestimated—and so it often happens that cemeteries lack the peace and quiet necessary for places commemorating the dead. But how could it be otherwise, when the usual practice is now that of piling up huge quantities of enormous blocks of granite and other types of rock that stick out of the ground like a forest of stones? The eye does not find peace and the confusion of blocks of stone, large and small, causes distress. We get a very different impression when entering one of our old cemeteries, which are dominated by the remains of stone funerary monuments and horizontal tombstones. In these cemeteries—now, unfortunately, increasingly rare—contact with death is not in any way disturbing; on the contrary, one feels imbued with a feeling of peace emanating from eternity.

Valid solutions have not yet been found to the question of the large cemeteries, which should perhaps be tackled in critically, taking all the different aspects into account. For various reasons, despite the fact that many people believe that a solution is near at hand, this problem has been underestimated, so that it has not been dealt with in the correct way. So long as the tombstones are vertical, not even architects will be able to reduce their impact, gaining space or drawing up projects able to inspire peace and serenity. The tendency today is to build cemeteries in thick woods, or to seek a different way to dominate and surround the site scattered with blocks of stone. Unfortunately, neither tall trees nor hedges are useful for this purpose, although the vegetation could help to create a number of isolated areas with a backdrop concealing the vertical tombstones. Nonetheless, the negative aspects of such monuments, which are so fragmentary and irritating, prevail over everything else: rather than the commemoration of a person, they are the most evident symbol of the struggles and rivalries that characterized those people's lives. The choice of verticality, appropriate for single tombs surrounded by high walls, or else for old cemeteries in churchyards, cannot produce good results if applied to larger areas, as is demonstrated by attempts made up to now. The famous Danish artist and landscape architect Brandt found a single solution to the problem, based exclusively on the capacity of the new generations to rediscover the harmonious, serene forms of the large burial grounds, keeping them alive...

From an architectural point of view it is possible to think of a large cemetery comprising a series of smaller cemeteries surrounded by walls: in this case, the funerary monuments do not disturb the overall effect. This solution is, however, impractical from an economic standpoint because of the high costs that the division of such a vast area would involve. The large cemeteries, in fact, usually consist of plots of land where the vegetation and other features are very specific and difficult to alter. As far as the funerary monuments are concerned, the best ones are those that do not disturb the lie of the land, but are integrated with it. The horizontal monuments deriving from our tradition generally satisfy this requirement and the vegetation growing all around creates a downward thrust, towards the carpet of grass and flowers... From the eighteenth century onwards, those who concerned themselves with the "art of the garden" have stressed the limits imposed by the use of vertical monuments: "The tombs and monuments may become interesting parts of the garden, providing that, when they are being built, a number of norms of moderation and good taste are respected. If the monuments are enclosed in a small area, those strolling there should not be disturbed by their presence. If the dimensions of the monuments are unbalanced, visitors will have a sensation of disharmony from which they will want to free themselves as soon as possible, and the purpose for which the monuments were erected will not have been achieved." In such burial grounds the most important element is missing: an atmosphere of peace and quiet that the surroundings must emit, allowing the visitor tospend a few moments in tranquil silence at the graveside.

There is sense in erecting a monument to commemorate an important event or an outstanding deed, but we seem to have lost our sense of proportion when we build monuments for those who die...

When designing a cemetery, it is necessary, first of all, to provide the shade serving to facilitate orientation. In a garden this could help to draw attention to the lie of the land or the presence of a building, but it must certainly not derive from a funerary monument... For the design of cemeteries with horizontal tombstones, I suggest a burial ground dotted with plaques or tombstones amidst the plants and flowers that are capable of instilling visitors with a sense of tranquillity. The tombstones and sunken burial areas allow the site to be used more economically and the inscriptions can be in front of one other without disturbing the whole, so the number of paths may be halved. The horizontal monuments are less intrusive than the vertical ones and require less maintenance. With the diffusion of the practice of cremation, the number of cemeteries housing cinerary urns will increase; the most significant consequence of this will be the layout of the areas set aside for them and the way these relate to the other burial areas. The horizontal tombstones solve this problem too... As far as the decoration is concerned, there is a wide range of choices ... that is of particular interest to the funerary monument industry...

If we judge the situation with an eye on tradition, we obtain results that enhance the facilities, and come to the following conclusion: the construction of vertical monuments does not allow visitors to experience a sense of harmony in the very place where they seek it. The only cases in which monuments of this kind are justified are those in which they help people to orient themselves. Moreover, whether the graves face east or west or the width of the spaces between them are factors help to create a strong feeling of peace and harmony. The more horizontal monuments there are, the more beautiful and dignified is the whole.

The revival of horizontal tombstones will certainly lead to a revival of the traditional Swedish approach to the design of burial grounds.

* This essay was written by Sigurd Lewerentz in 1939 for a book published by Lindfors Bokförlag of Stockholm devoted to the Swedish, which, however, only came out after the Second World War and without Lewerentz's text. This text, which is incomplete and at times disjointed, is probably the first and only draft of the essay, which was never corrected because it did not appear in the edition published after the war. It has, however, been decided to publish this text here, despite its obvious shortcomings, because it is the only known piece of writing by the architect. In fact, Lewerentz was not fond of writing and his critical output consists exclusively of detailed descriptions that he was required to submit together with the drawings of his projects. His works, on the other hand, are a very complete expression of his approach to architecture.

Catalogue of Works

1. Project for a Naval Museum at Kastellholmen, Stockholm, 1910

While he was studying at the Klara Skola (Free School of Architecture), Lewerentz—like his fellow students—designed a museum for the Swedish navy to be built on the islet of Kastellholmen, one on the many on which Stockholm stands. The theme, which Ragnar Östberg assigned to the students, was based on an idea proposed by an admiral in the navy, who was invited to give a lecture at the school in order to illustrate the principles inspiring it and its contents. The project, which was only outlined by Lewerentz, comprises a large building over a hundred metres in length to be built on the highest point of the island, surmounted by a massive corner tower in which the main entrance-hall is situated. This imposing edifice would have dominated the surrounding area, also because the project provided for the demolition of a number of pre-existing buildings. The project was inspired by the Swedish castles, revealing the interest of Lewerentz in the architectural forms of the National Romantic movement, and, in particular, it was influenced by two of the most important works in this style: Isak Gustav Clason's Nordiska Museet and Ferdinand Boberg's Nobel building.

(P.G.)

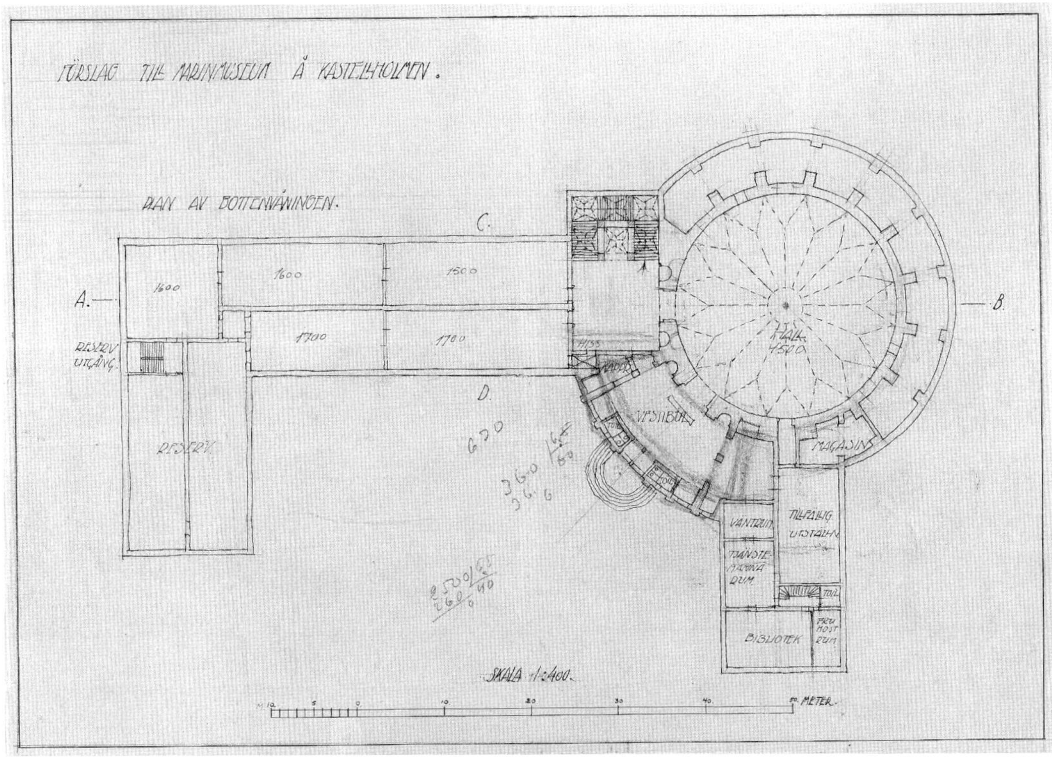

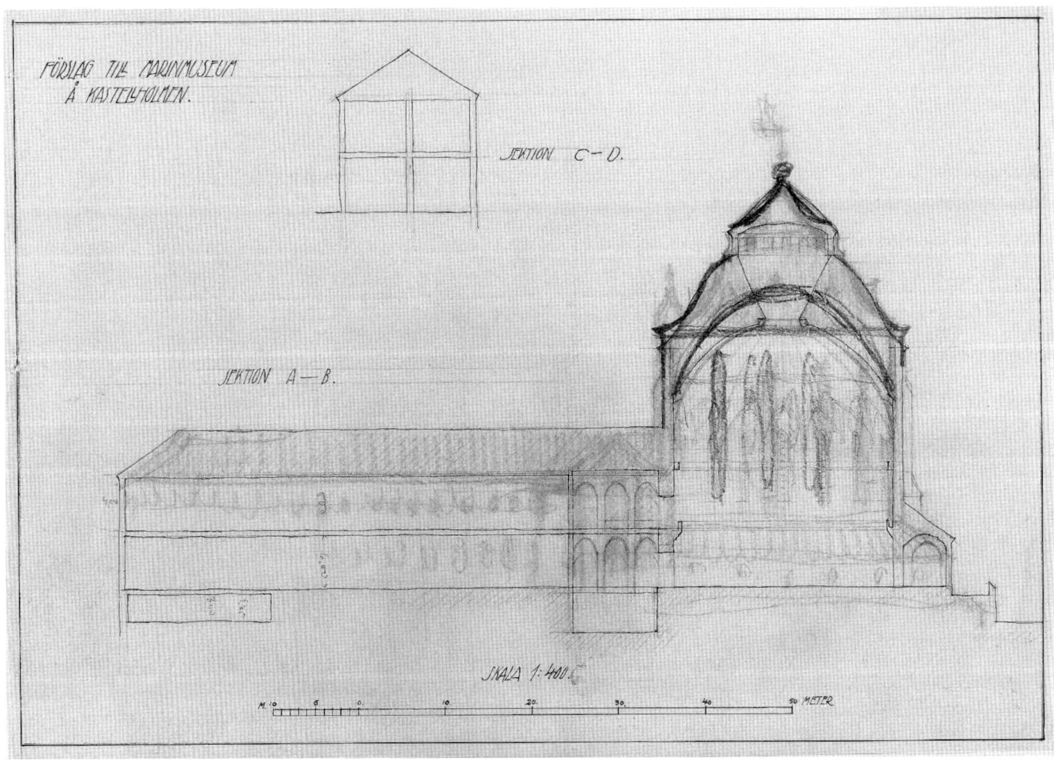

Ground-floor plan.

Cross and longitudinal sections.

2. Project for a Residential Building, Norrköping, 1910–11
(executed when Lewerentz was studying at the Klara Skola)

Perspective drawing.

3. Competition Project for a Mixed School, Nässjö, 1911
with Torsten Stubelius

The project is dated May 1911, the year in which Lewerentz began to work in Carl Westman's office. One of Sweden's leading architects at the time, Westman was an exponent of the National Romantic style that was particularly widespread in northern Europe at the turn of the century. Lewerentz and Stubelius's project is composed of simple buildings constructed in brick and covered by pitched roofs, reflecting the vernacular style. The compositional choices, materials and formal language adopted all attest to the influence of Westman's work, especially such buildings as the Höberga villa at Lidingö and the Röhsska Konstslöjd-muséet (crafts museum) in Gothenburg. Lewerentz shows that from these works, and also from his experience in Westman's office, he has learnt to use materials in an expressive manner and to apply them correctly; not only is he familiar with traditional technologies, but he also pays great attention to the articulation of space.

Bibliography: Ahlin 1985b, p. 29.

(P.G.)

Overall view.

4. Project for the Restoration of the Church of Ytterlänä, Ångermanland, 1911

Interior.

5. Project for Workers' Housing at Eneborg and Pålsjö, Helsingborg, 1911–18

with Torsten Stubelius

In 1907, commissioned by the Helsingborg city council, Stubelius selected the areas in the city most suitable for future residential expansion consisting of subsidized housing for the working classes. Limited in number, the dwellings would mainly have consisted of two-family houses, with the exception of small blocks of flats reflecting the housing tradition of southern Sweden. In 1912 and 1913 Stubelius, together with Lewerentz and the chief engineer of the city, drew up a town plan for the areas chosen—Eneborg, to the south, and Pålsjö, to the north—in which fifteen different housing types were identified; these were a critical reinterpretation of the model of the traditional dwellings of Helsingborg. The buildings are characterized by a very simple design, with details reduced to a minimum and considerable use of prefabricated components, especially for the finishings, in order to safeguard the quality of the project at the construction stage.
To reduce costs, in fact, the houses were to have been built by unskilled workers, which involved the risk that the design specifications would not be strictly adhered to. As in previous works, the two architects used the dark red brick of Helsingborg for the load-bearing masonry, pitched roofs covered with baked clay tiles and external fittings limited in size, painted white. In its general approach, the project resembles one in which Lewerentz had been involved in its early stages: Richard Riemerschmid's scheme for the German garden city of Hellerau (begun in 1909). After the initial phase, work was suspended and it was only in 1917, following pressure from the Egnahemsrörels (Movement for Home Ownership), that a small housing estate was built at Eneborg, making use of some of the designs contained in Stubelius and Lewerentz's project.

Chronology:
1911–13: town plans for the Pålsjö and Eneborg areas.
1916–18: housing estate at Eneborg.

Bibliography: Lewerentz 1926b; Ahlin 1985b, pp. 40–41; Caldenby 1997, pp. 46–49.

(P.G.)

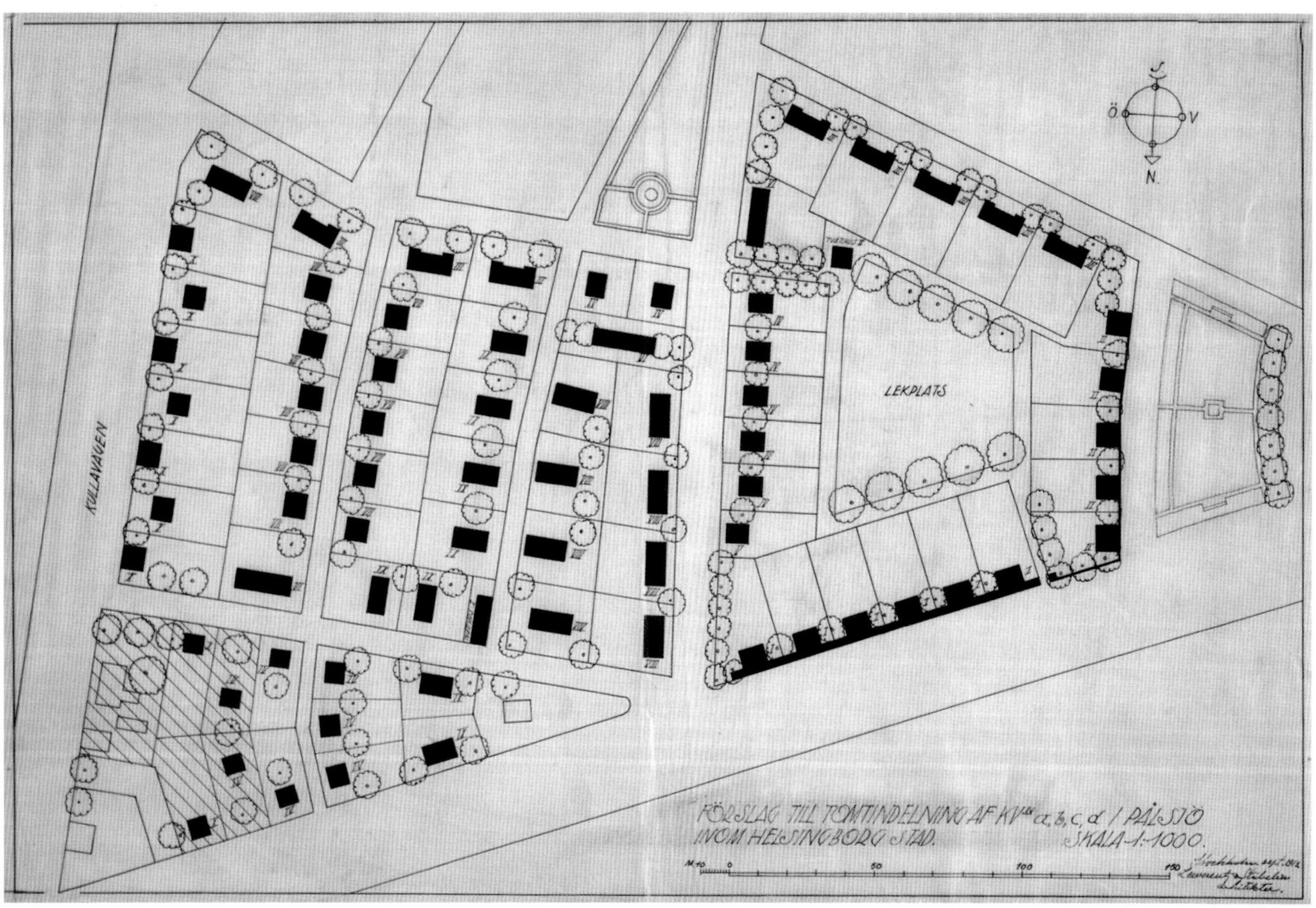

Layout plan, September 1912.

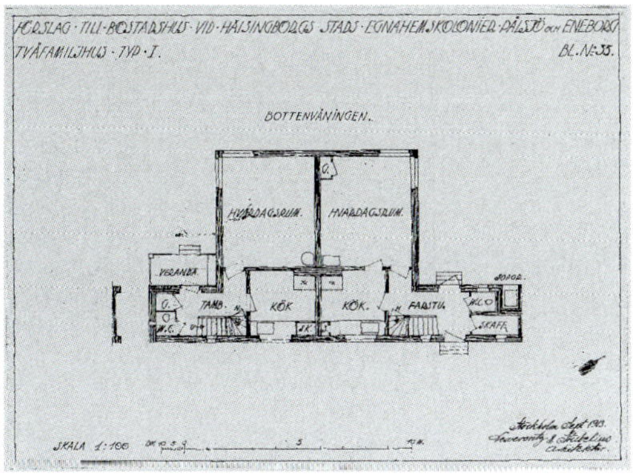

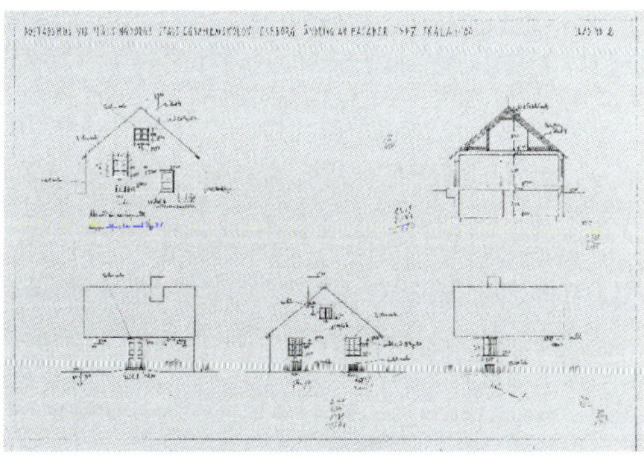

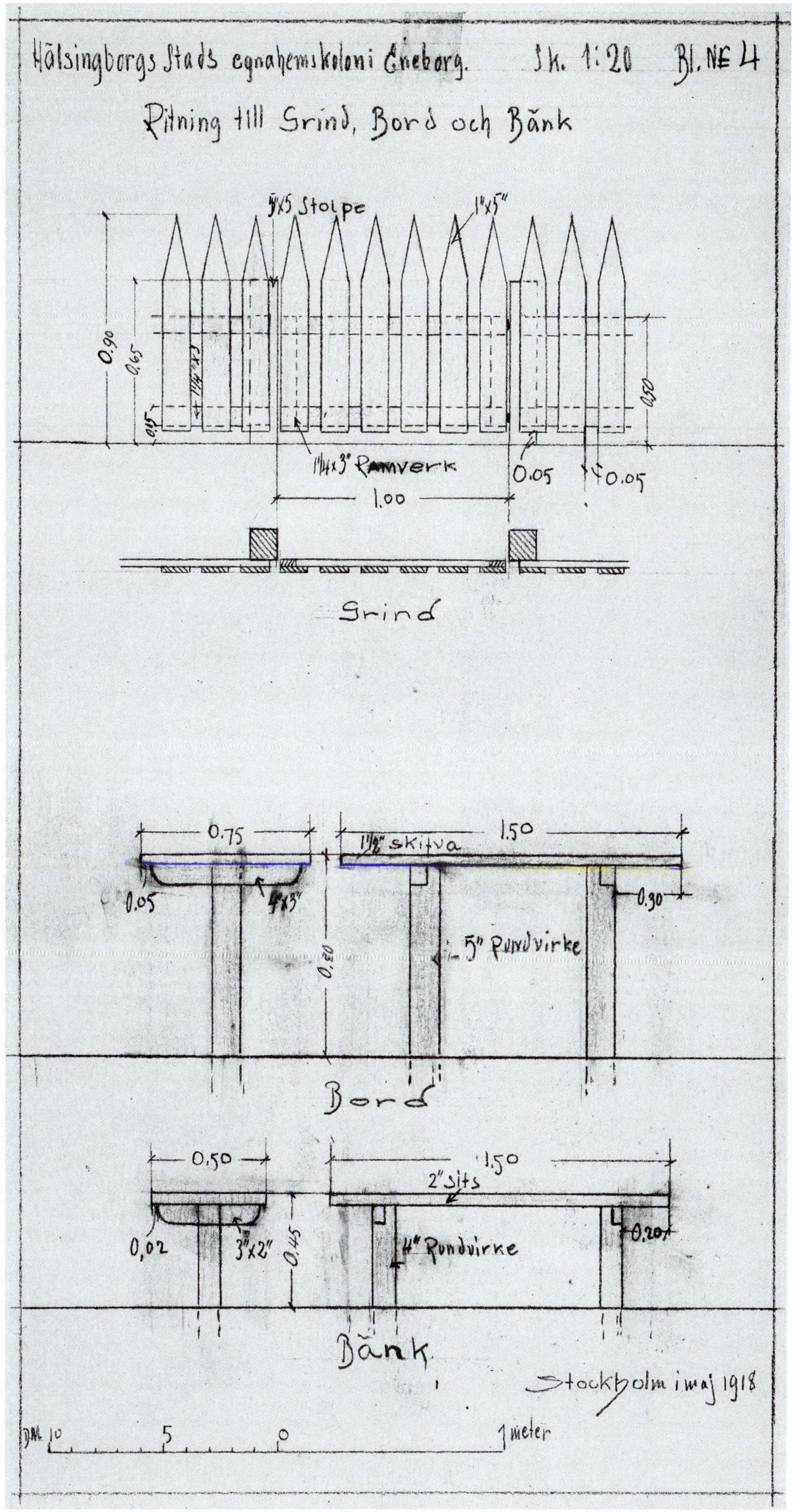

Housing estate at Eneborg, plan and elevation of a two-family house (September 1913) and elevations and cross section of a single-family house (1918).

Detail of fencing and furnishings, 1918.

Housing estate at Eneborg, the façade of a standard house.

Details of the elevations of the houses, 1918.

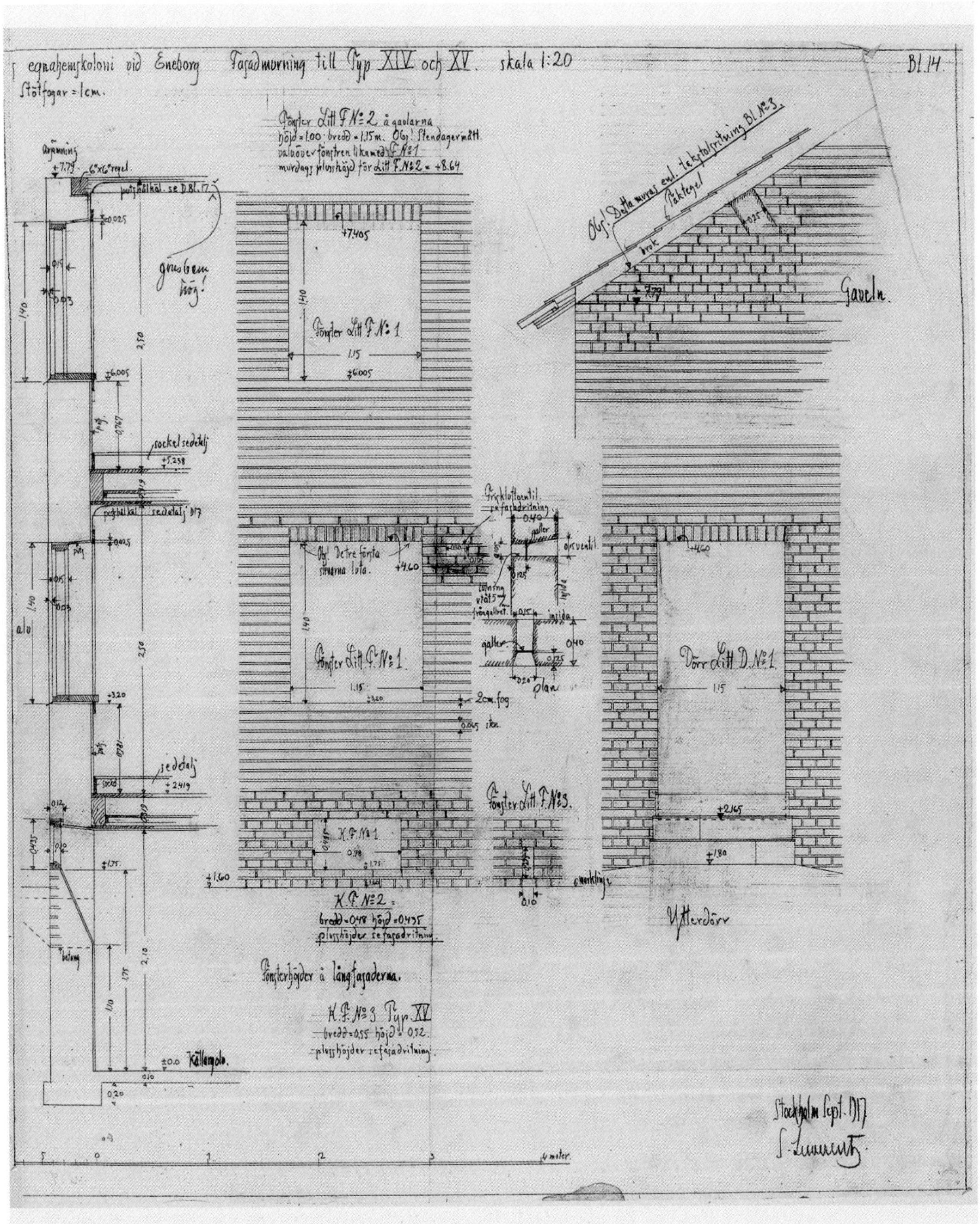

Drawing of the housing estate at Pålsjö, 1911–13.

View of the housing estate built at Eneborg.

6. Working-Class Housing at Karlshäll, Luleå, 1911–13

with Torsten Stubelius

The project for dwellings for the workers of Luleå Träsliperi AB at Karlshäll was the first commission in which Lewerentz and Stubelius were involved in the planning of working-class housing estates. Usually commissioned by the companies employing the workers, dwellings of this kind were financed by the Egnahemsfond (Fund for the Purchase of Houses), a state financial institution which allowed workers to become owners of their own homes by offering mortgages on extremely favourable terms. This social policy had been fostered in Sweden since the beginning of the century by a special association, the Egnahemsrörels (Own Home Movement), founded with the aim of fostering the construction and furnishing of small privately-owned homes. The first housing project at Karlshäll comprises about thirty houses, each subdivided into independent units, comprising two or three dwellings; each house has its own

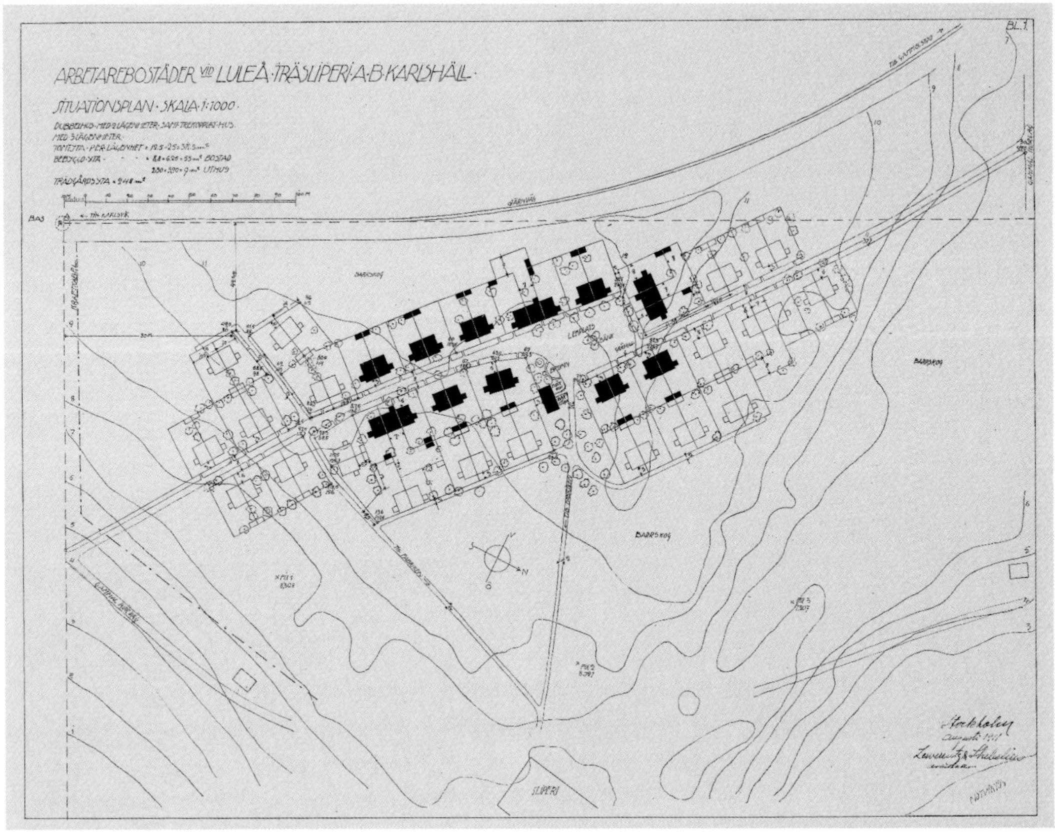

Layout plan.

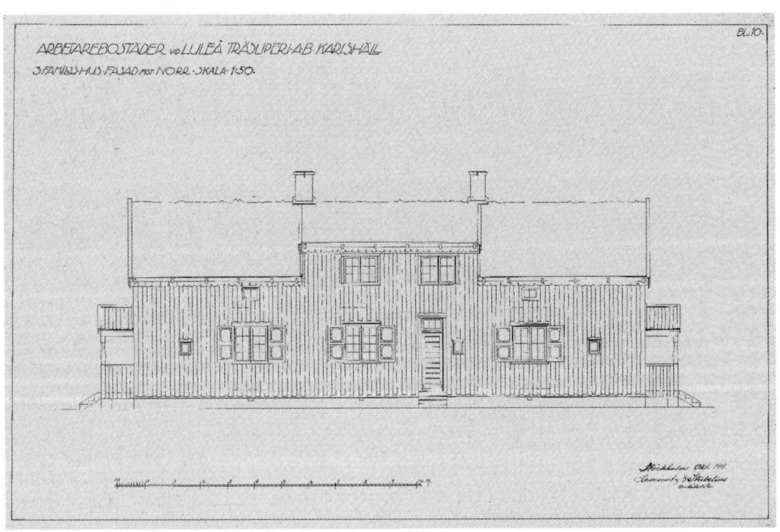

Elevations of the standard houses with two and three dwellings.

garden and all of them front onto avenues ending in squares intended to be places where the inhabitants could socialize. This is where the well was located, in addition to the communal oven and laundry.
The houses, composed of extremely simple forms, with one storey and a habitable attic, have a traditional appearance mainly due to the timber facing of the exterior and the division of the windows into small squares by the glazing bars. An important element in the plan of each dwelling—which is divided into a living-cum-dining-room and bedroom on the ground floor, and attic on the upper floor—is the position of the chimneys serving the fireplaces necessary for heating the rooms on both floors. Thanks to the peripheral position of the access stairway, the room in the attic could, if required, be divided into two dwellings, thus meeting the demand for accommodation for unmarried workers and also providing separate rooms where workers on night shifts could sleep.
The scheme was never completed and only eight of the thirty houses planned were actually built. During the construction stage, moreover, the original designs were considerably simplified, thus notably diminishing the architectural quality of the project.

Bibliography: Ahlin 1985b, pp. 24–25.

(P.G.)

View of completed houses.

7. Furnishings, 1911 onwards

Lewerentz and Stubelius displayed an interest in the design of furnishings from the beginning of the second decade of the twentieth century when, during their separate periods of apprenticeship in Germany, they came into contact with the theories and results of the Deutscher Werkbund and the British Arts and Crafts movement. Thus the two architects were among the first to spread in Sweden the ideas relating to the design of objects, ensuring their presence in all the most important exhibitions of this sector in Europe in the second and third decades of the century. Members of the Svenska Slöjdförening (National Applied Arts Association), they both worked for the Egnahemsrörels (Movement for Home Ownership) and the Förening Verkstad (Association for the Promotion of Furnishing Design), organizations that on various occasions invited the two architects to submit objects and projects.
The activity of Lewerentz as a designer of objects and furnishings for manufacture concluded, however, with his output of the second decade of the twentieth century, when the architecture designed, often in collaboration with Stubelius, lamps for ASEA and Böholmarks, wallpaper for Göteborg Tapetfabrik and furnishings for NK (Nordiska Kompaniet). Subsequently, although he continued to design interiors, he no longer worked on projects for industry, but prepared individual designs to meet specific requirements. In this regard, the production of furnishings for commercial premises—beginning with the fruitful experience with the Stockholm Ljusreklam company, which led to him playing a major role in the Stockholm Exhibition of 1930—accompanied Lewerentz for the rest of his career, to the extent that in 1940 the architect decided to set up his own firm to make metal fixtures and interior partitions so that he could have complete control over the products from design to manufacture.
In addition to his activity as a designer of objects and interior designer, Lewerentz created mechanisms and accessories for fixtures—not only in metal—which he patented from 1929 onwards under the trademark IDESTA, subsequently the name of his factory for the manufacture of fixtures at Eskilstuna. His mechanical designs, as well as his design of details in his architectural projects, attest to the fact that his early training, in the engineering courses at Gothenburg Polytechnic, was anything but academic, and influenced the way the architect conceived his projects and their feasibility.
With the opening of the factory at Eskilstuna, Lewerentz drastically reduced the time he devoted to architecture and design, eventually almost abandoning these activities, putting his energies at the service of his colleagues in the quest for better ways to realize the projects to which the firm was asked to contribute. It was not until 1974 that Lewerentz produced another piece of furniture for manufacture: this was the year in which he designed a chair, of which he only made a few prototypes, with the frame in tubular metal and the seat and back in laminated wood. This strikingly simple object was his last true creation, to which the elderly architect may perhaps have entrusted his spiritual legacy: the incessant desire to ask himself new questions and the never-ending quest for unconventional answers.

Bibliography: Ahlin 1985b, pp. 32–33.

(P.G.)

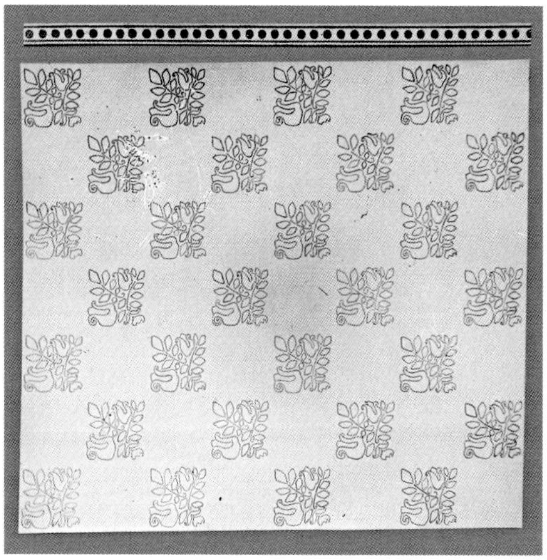

Carpet for Göteborg Tapetfabrik, 1912 (with Torsten Stubelius).

Lampshade for ASEA, 1912 (with Torsten Stubelius).

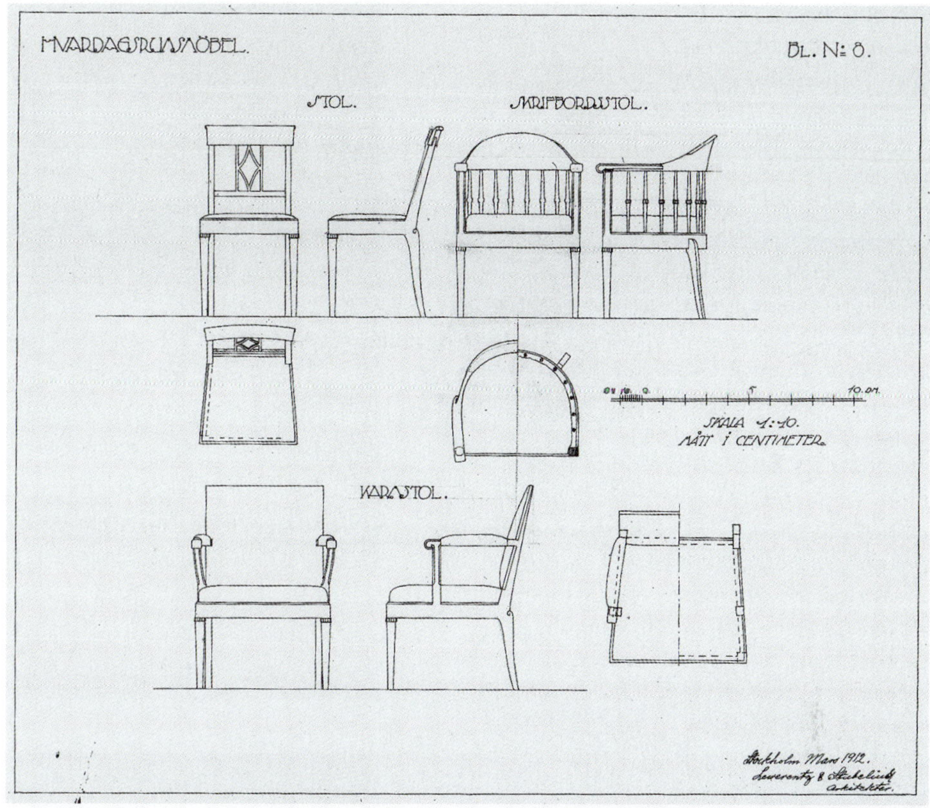

Project for a series of chairs for NK (Nordiska Kompaniet), 1912 (with Torsten Stubelius).

Designs for furniture, 1932.

Chair in metal and laminated wood, 1974.

8. Villa Gustav M. Ericsson, Lidingö-Brevik, 1912
with Torsten Stubelius

The villa for the family of the engineer Gustav M. Ericsson, located on the coast just to the south of Stockholm, is entirely constructed in brick. This splendid work highlights the capacity of the two architects to adapt a building material such as brick not only to the constraints of workers' housing, but also to the expressive power linked to the requirements of clients for whom, as in this case, money was no object. The masterly design of the brickwork reveals, moreover, their adhesion to the National Romantic movement, the style of which characterized the majority of works realized in this period. In particular, Lewerentz, who had recently served his apprenticeship in the office of Carl Westman, one of the leading Swedish architects of the day, appears to have been

Main gate and courtyard.

Front facing the archipelago.

influenced by his master. A number of the features bear a strong compositional and figurative resemblance to the villa in the same area designed by Westman for the art collector K. Fåhraeus to which Lewerentz also contributed. Villa Ericsson is built on a number of levels, the main views being towards the magnificent landscape of the archipelago. The plan is inspired by that of the English country house, giving rise to a series of highly specialized spaces and rooms catering for the varied activities constituting the daily routine of the villa's inhabitants.

Bibliography: Ahlin 1985b, pp. 44–45; Caldenby 1997, pp. 42–43.

(P.G.)

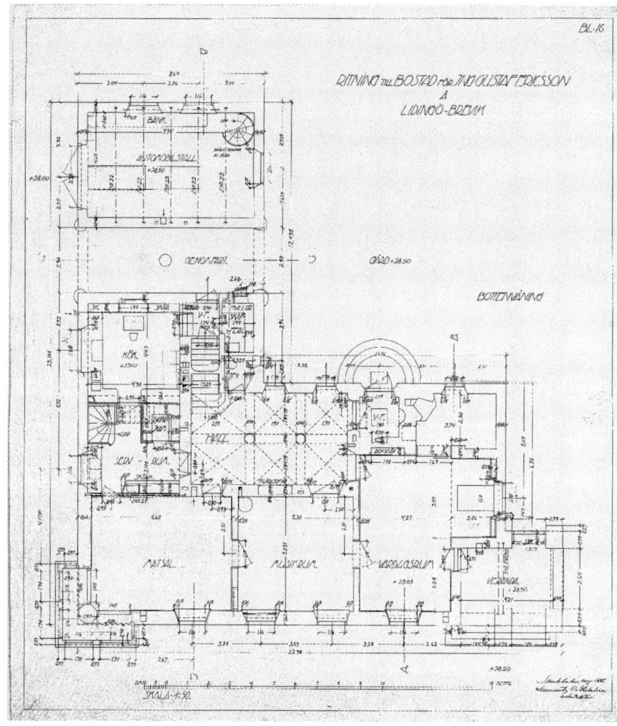

Ground-floor plan, 1912.

West elevation, August 1912.

The drawing-room, kitchen and entrance hall.

Opposite
Sketch of the elevation facing the channel.

9. Boathouse for the Canoes of the City Rowing Club, Stockholm, 1912
with Torsten Stubelius

In 1912, on the occasion of the Olympic Games in Stockholm, Lewerentz and Stubelius were commissioned by the city rowing club to design a boathouse for canoes on a site located by the channel separating the islet of Djurgården from the mainland, in one of the most fascinating spots in Stockholm. By choosing to use wood as the material for the construction, the two architects decided to conform to the traditional building type of the area, totally abandoning the stylistic features of the National Romantic current. Indeed, the construction technique adopted was used to stress the functional nature and simplicity of the small building, without resorting to special formal effects.
The exterior in vertical wooden planks, although painted traditional green, is characterized by the horizontal strip window that, on the side facing the channel, reflects the arrangement of the building's interior. The space for the storage of the canoes, in factm is located on the lower floor. Their length—between 10 and 18 metres—has determined the proportions of the whole building. There are a number of rooms commanding an excellent view of the channel on the upper floor, which overhangs the lower one on the side facing the channel and is reached by a small staircase, covered as in the traditional houses and external to the main volume.

Bibliography: Bartning 1932; Ahlin 1985b, p. 47; Caldenby 1997, pp. 44–45.

(P.G.)

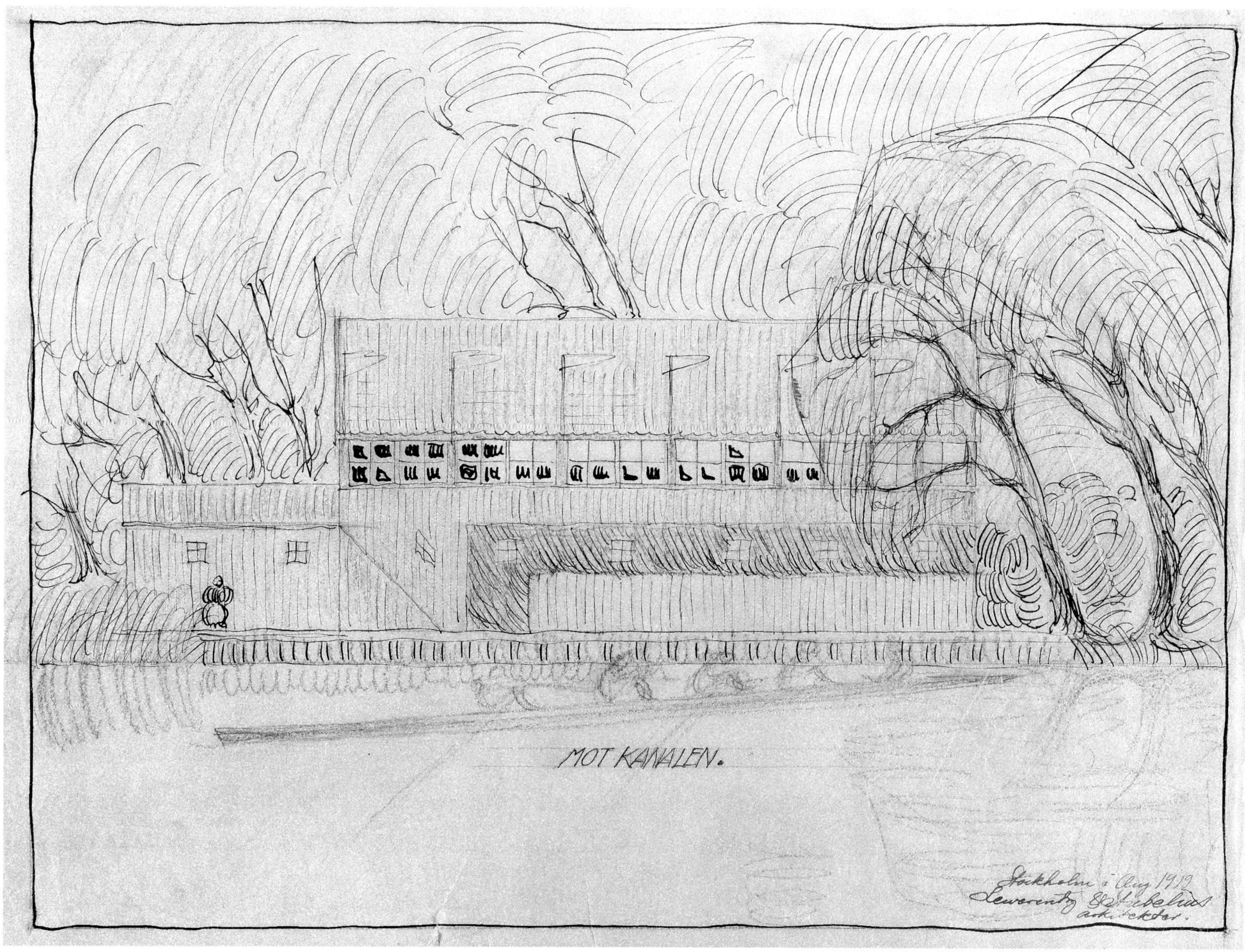

Perspective drawing of the front facing the channel.

Side elevations, final version, August 1912.

One of the sides and the elevation facing the channel.

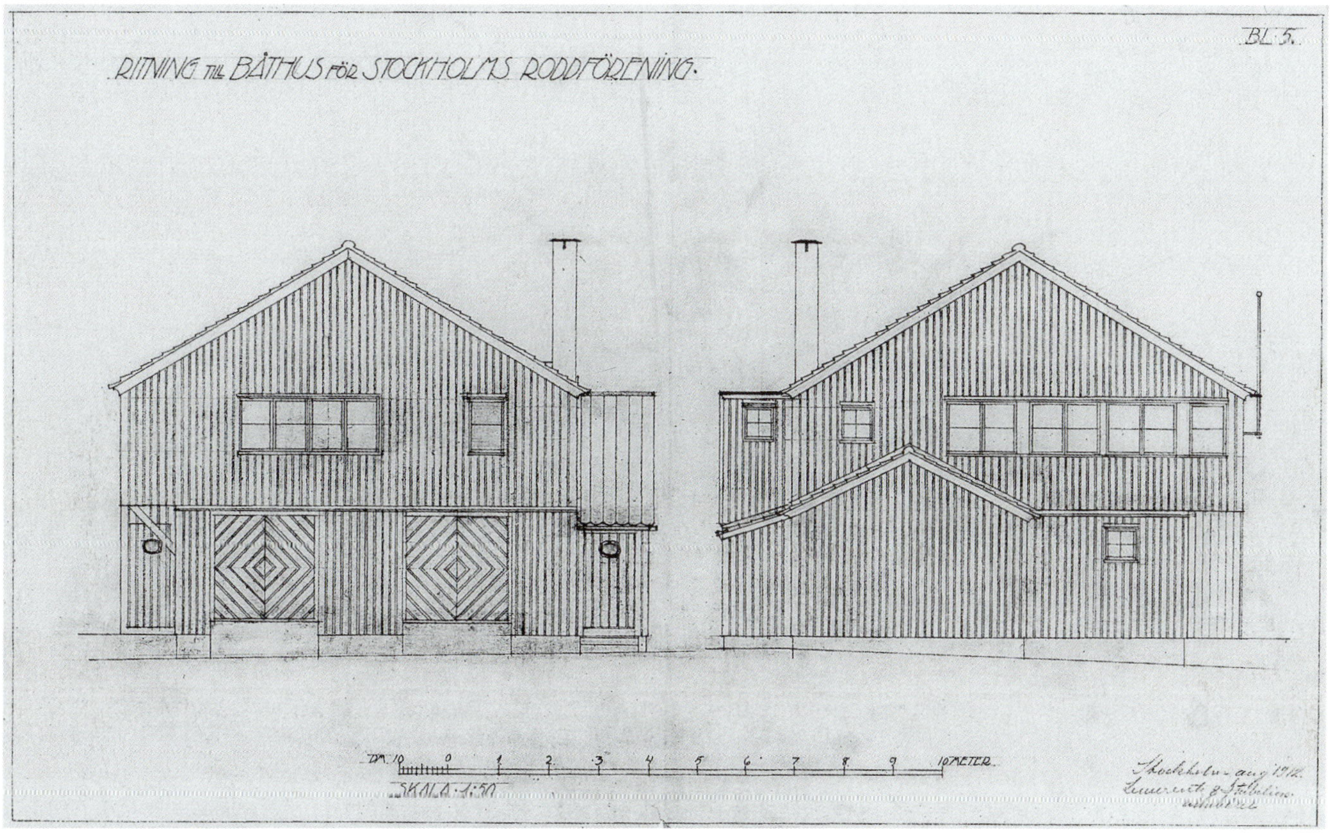

10. Project for Residential Building, Norrköping, 1912

11. Project for Managers' Houses for Sandö Sågverk AB, Sandö, 1912–13

with Torsten Stubelius

In 1912 Lewerentz and Stubelius designed houses for the managers of Sandö Sågverk AB at Sandö, none of which were ever built. Comprising both one- and two-family dwellings, the houses are externally very severe, as are other similar buildings designed by the two architects in the same period. The buildings, characterized by very compact forms, have a simple facing in vertical wooden planks, with just the hint of a pediment over the lintels of the windows, which, reflecting a local tradition, are the main decorative feature.

The care taken over the interiors and their dimensions, on the contrary, clearly reveals the social class of the inhabitants of the houses, the managers of Sandö Sågverk AB. The houses are, in fact, spacious and, on the ground floor, in addition to a large living-cum-dining-room and a smaller room, there is an entrance hall, a number of service rooms and a pantry, forming a link between the kitchen and the other rooms. On the upper floor there are four bedrooms, one of which is very large, while each dwelling has its own garden.

(P.G.)

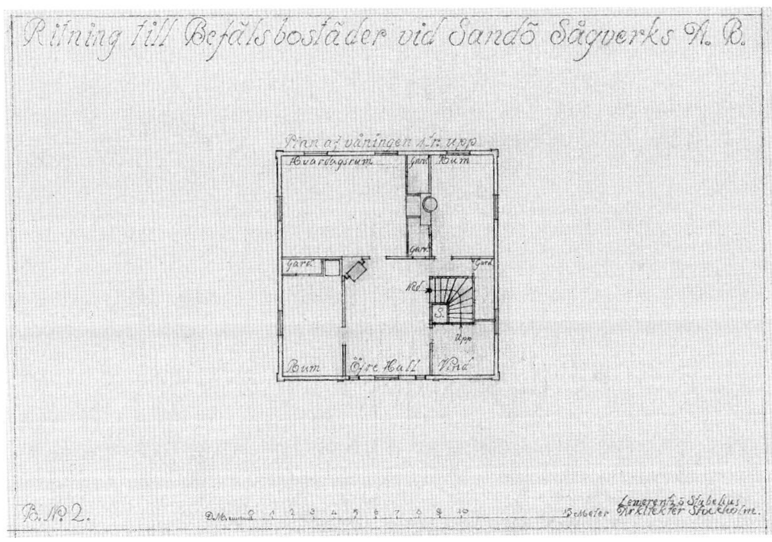

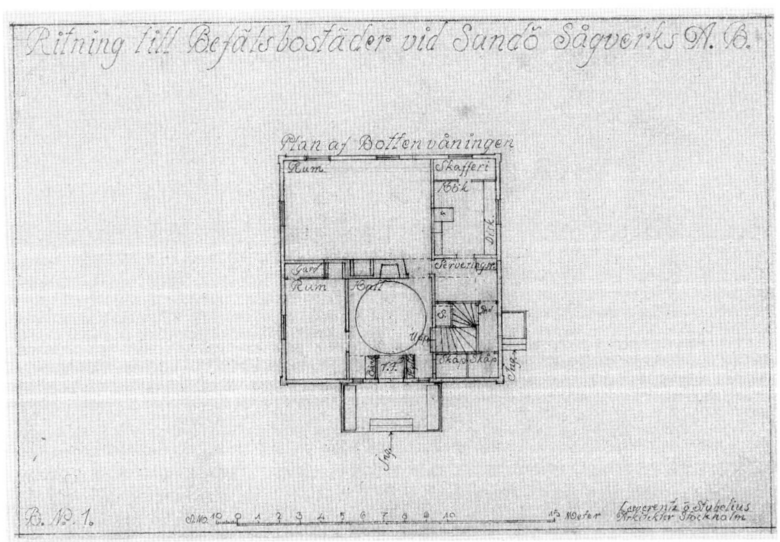

First and ground-floor plans of the houses.

Elevations of the single-family houses.

Ground-floor plan of the two-family houses, with layout of the garden.

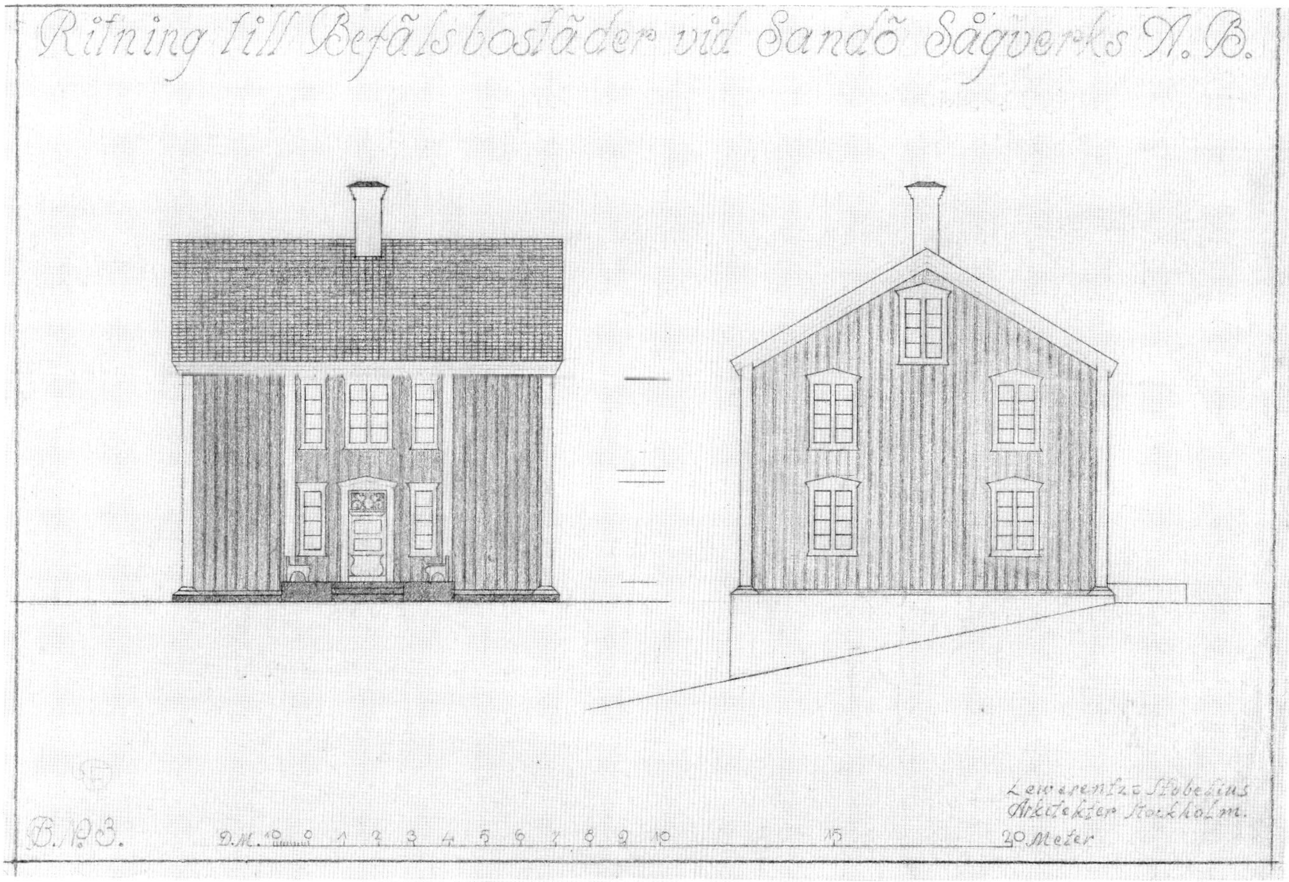

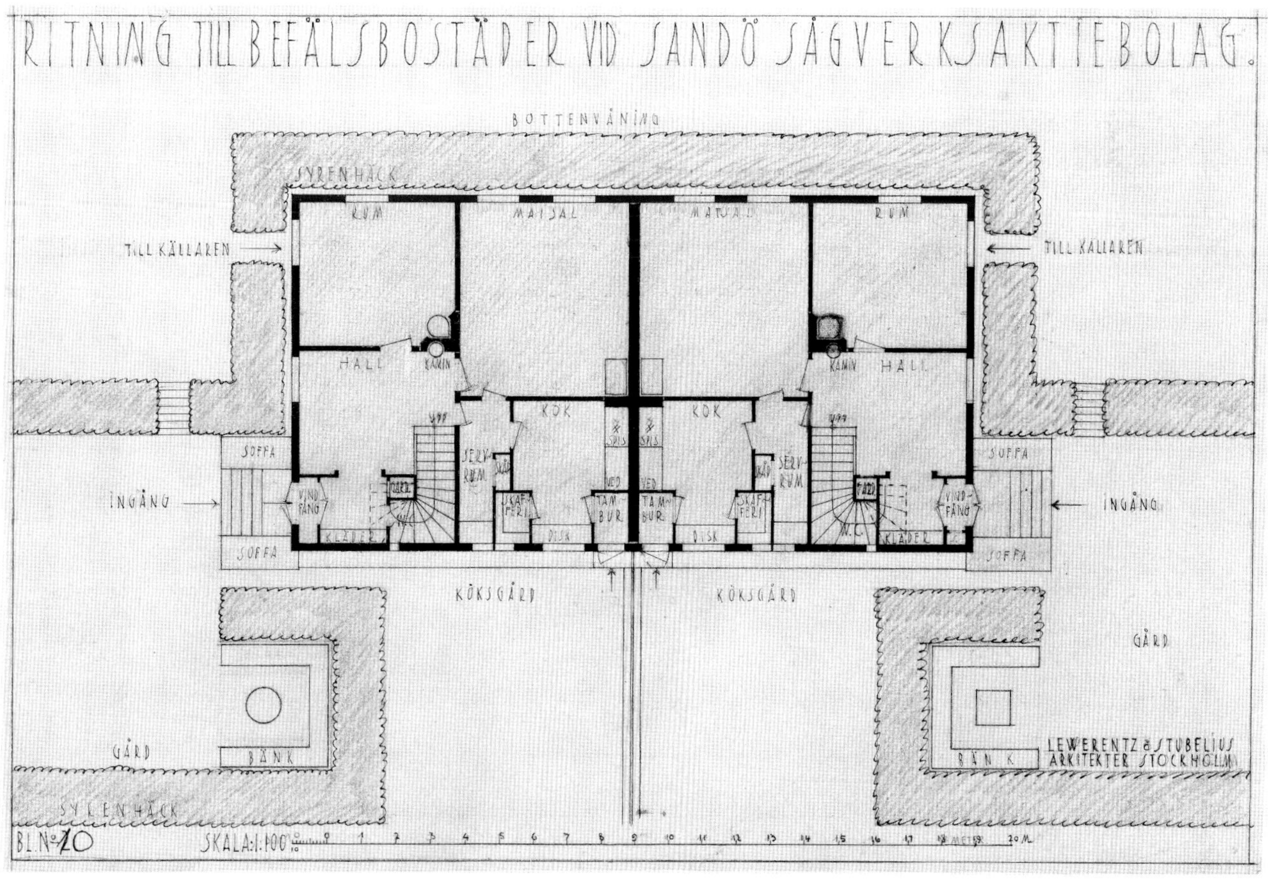

Elevation of a two-family house.

12. Workers' Houses for Skånska Kolbrvtnings AB, Nyvång, 1912–13
with Torsten Stubelius

In 1912 and 1913 Lewerentz and Stubelius were commissioned by Skånska Kolbrvtnings AB to complete a housing estate for workers at Nyvång that had been started in 1910. The two architects envisaged two-family houses and terraces of three houses for the workers and single-family houses for the managers. The project required the use of the traditional forms and materials of the local houses, so that in the plans the rooms are described with archaic terms typical of the rural culture of the area. The construction of about fifty houses, which began in 1914 under the supervision of architects employed by the company, was not totally faithful to the project.

Bibliography: Ahlin 1985b, pp. 32–35.

(P.G.)

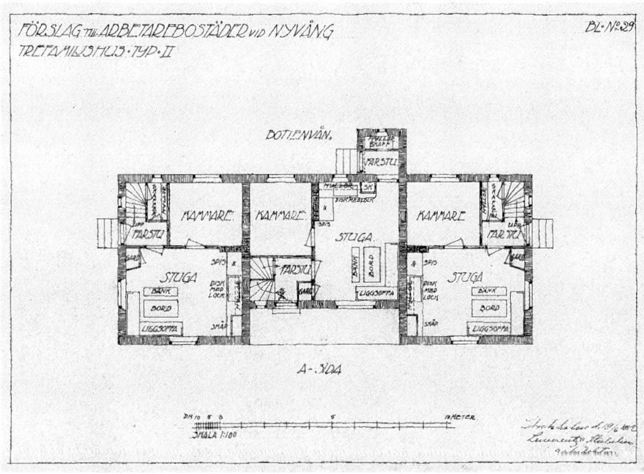

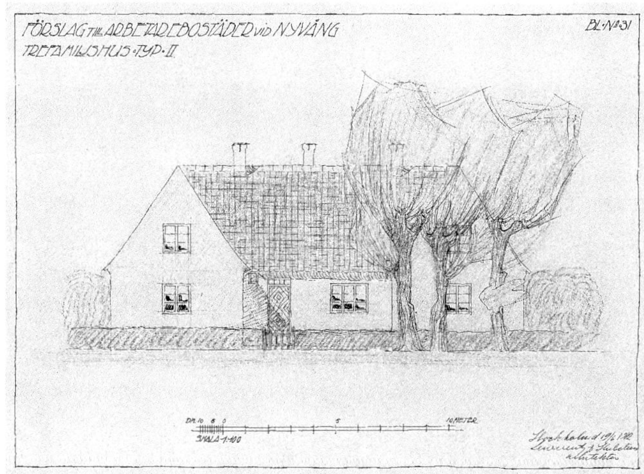

Plan and sketch of a two-family house, type II.

View of the square.

13. Competition Project for a Primary School, Kalmar, 1913

motto "Per"

In 1913, with a project bearing the motto "Per", Lewerentz participated in a competition for a primary school in Kalmar, to be built in a new quarter in the old part of the city. Despite the positive opinion of the critics and its publication in the journal Byggmästaren, the project did not win. The element in Lewerentz's project that differed radically from the others submitted is the distributive plan, arranged around a central corridor, flanked by the classrooms. The simple and austere aspect of the exterior also distinguishes it from the other projects, which were more closely linked to the contemporary styles.

Bibliography: Almqvist 1913; Ahlin 1985b, pp. 94–95; Waern 1996, p. 219.

(P.G.)

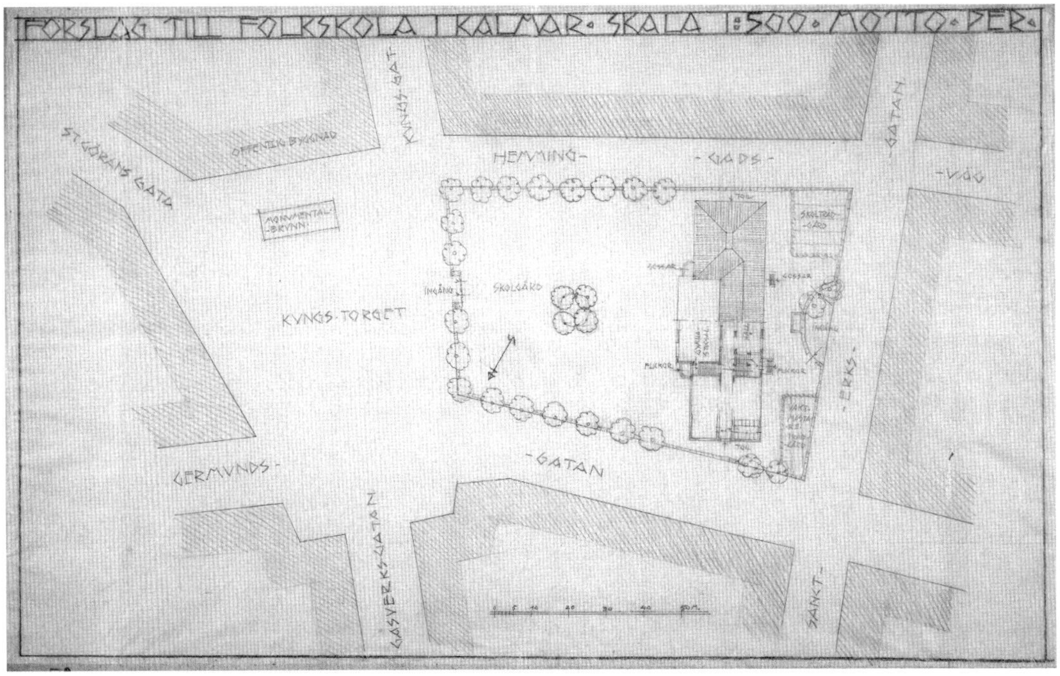

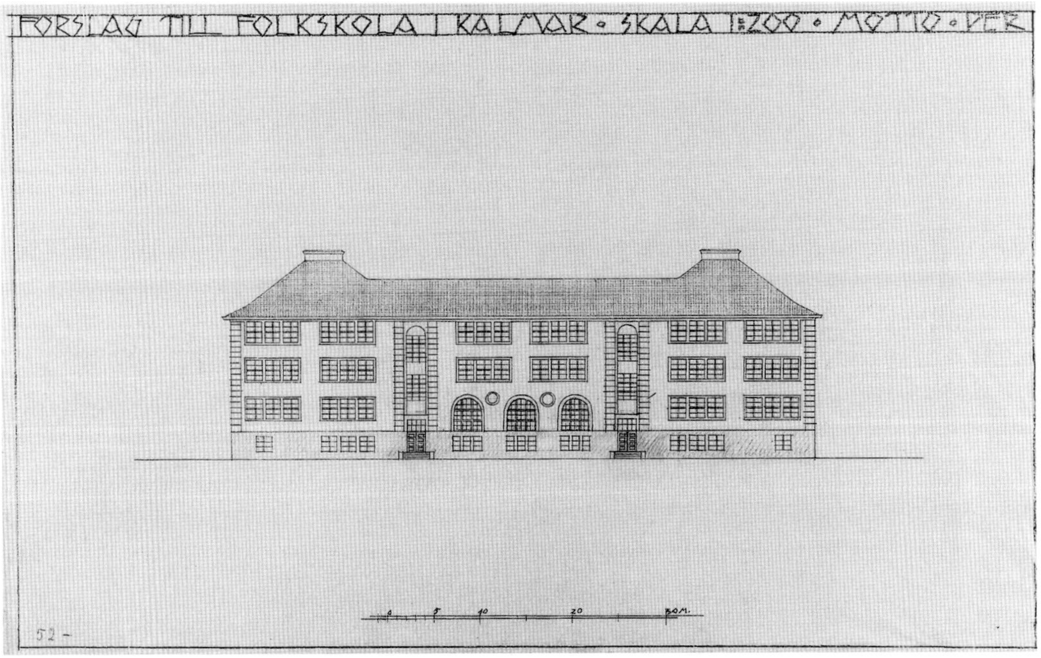

Layout plan and main elevation.

14. Competition Project for the Liljevalch Art Gallery, Djurgården, Stockholm, 1913

motto "Sun"

The programme of the competition for an exhibition building at Djurgården, Stockholm, required a large hall for exhibitions and a series of twelve smaller rooms with direct access from one to the other. The project submitted by Lewerentz, which was perhaps prepared in a short time and bears the motto "Sun" (represented by a symbol, not the written word), consists of a very simple scheme in which the rooms are arranged around a rectangular courtyard. Starting from the large hall, which occupies the whole of one of the shorter sides of the courtyard, they continue along the whole perimeter of the building. At the end of the courtyard opposite the main hall there is a circular space to be used as a cafeteria. Reflecting a style that is more evidently modernist, the disposition of the volumes on the exterior differs in height and form according to the nature of the spaces located below them, the purpose of this being to illuminate the interior adequately.

Bibliography: Waern 1996c, pp. 223–34.

(P.G.)

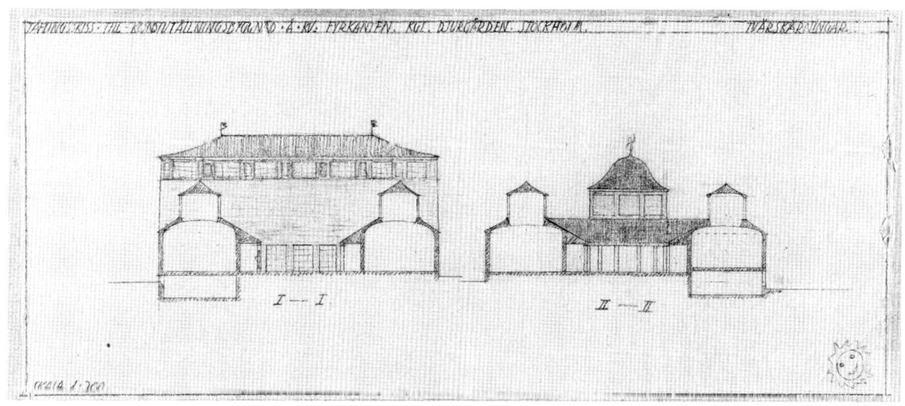

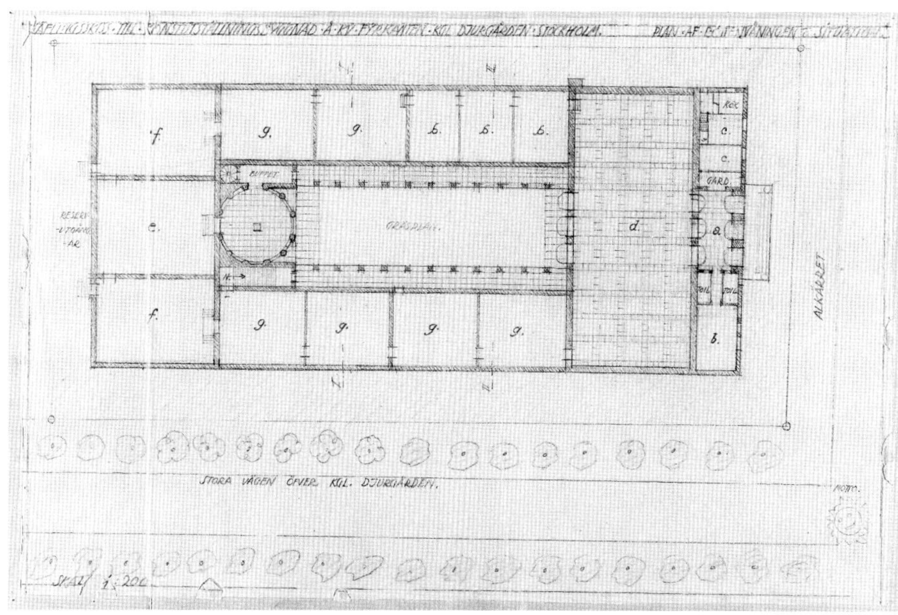

Sketch of the project, sections and plan.

15. Renovation of the *Corps de Logis*, Ånhammer, 1913
with Torsten Stubelius

This renovation project, like others of this kind, mainly consists of the maintenance work that old buildings frequently require: consolidation and functional adaptation of the rooms in the basement; replacement of the wooden planks on the exterior of the building where they have been damaged; repair of the windows and external doors, and, if they are no longer functioning, the replacement of the frames with new ones reproducing the original design; lastly, the upgrading of all the systems of closure. Similar work is carried out on all the interior fixtures. Moreover, the work usually comprises the conservation of the roof through the replacement of damaged elements, whether they be wooden planks or metal sheets—often in copper—and the upgrading of the building services to the new requirements, which sometimes involves the redistribution of the internal spaces and the choice of finishings.

(P.G.)

16. Restoration of the Church of Bro, Uppland, 1913

The project mainly consists of the renovation and maintenance work needed by the old building: a new arrangement of the parvis; cleaning and conservation of the masonry; replacement of the damaged metal elements in the roof. The work was not limited to the exterior, but also involved the interior of the church. Here Lewerentz replaced the whole of the paving, using different materials to distinguish the various parts of the building: stone for the altar and the area where the organ was located and wood for the nave containing the pews.

(P.G.)

Study drawing of main elevation.

17. Holiday House for Olle Hjortzberg and Project for a Housing Scheme at Kummelnäs, Värmdö, 1913–14

with Torsten Stubelius

Although the holiday house for the painter Olle Hjortzberg, who taught at the Fine Arts Academy in Stockholm, constructed in a particularly beautiful part of the archipelago on which the capital is situated, was presented as a joint work by Lewerentz and Stubelius, it should probably be attributed mainly to the latter. A number of the decorative details are, in fact, all too similar to those typical of the holiday homes that, like this one, overlook the bustling channels in the area. The interior is decorated with representations of flowers and birds executed by Hjortzberg himself. In the same period the two architects planned a housing scheme on a site near Hjortzberg's property. In this case, Lewerentz and Stubelius proposed much simpler buildings, without any stylistic elements or historical references, based on the use of standardized elements in order to limit construction costs.

Bibliography: *Sommarstugor vid Kummelnäs* 1914; Ahlin 1985b, p. 42.

(P.G.)

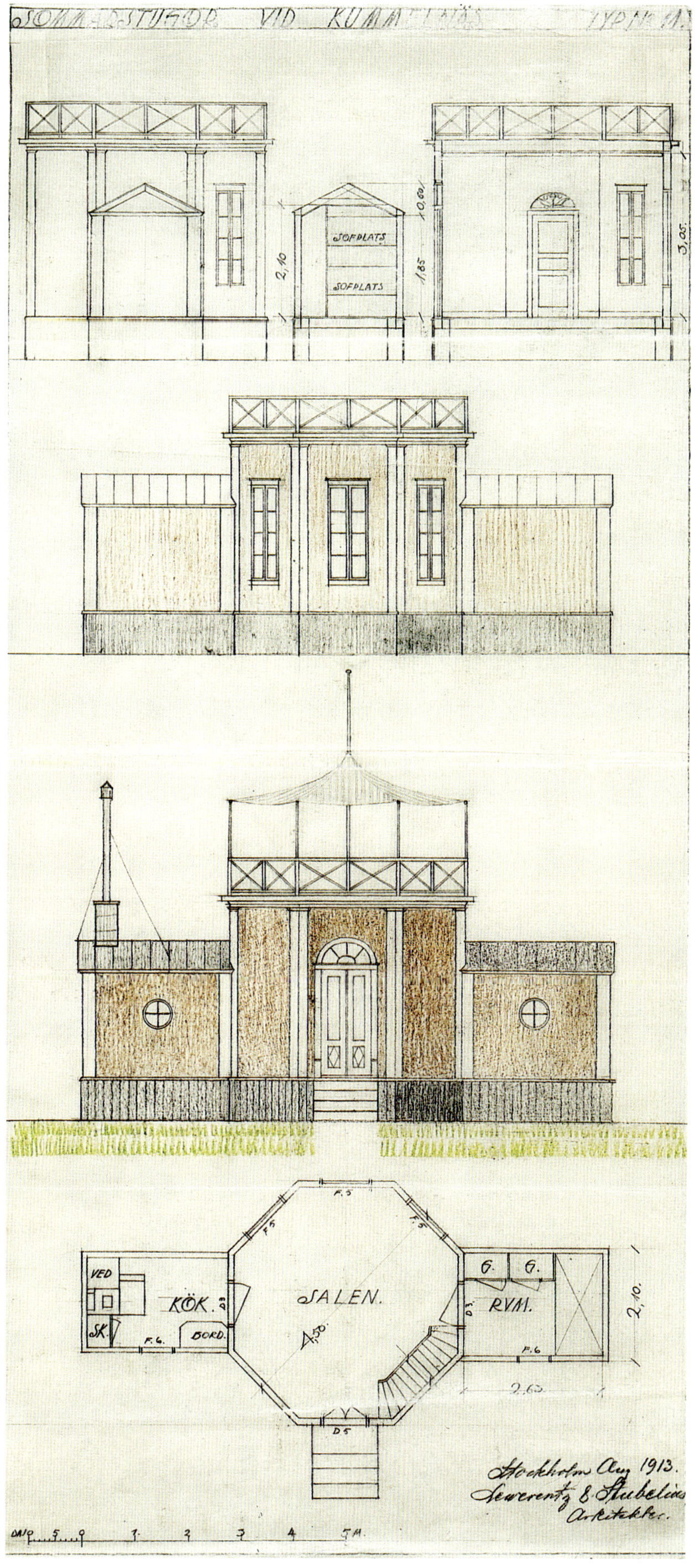

Studies for elevations and plan of a holiday house, 1913.

Hjortzberg House, exterior.

Elevations, plan and section of a standard house, 1913.

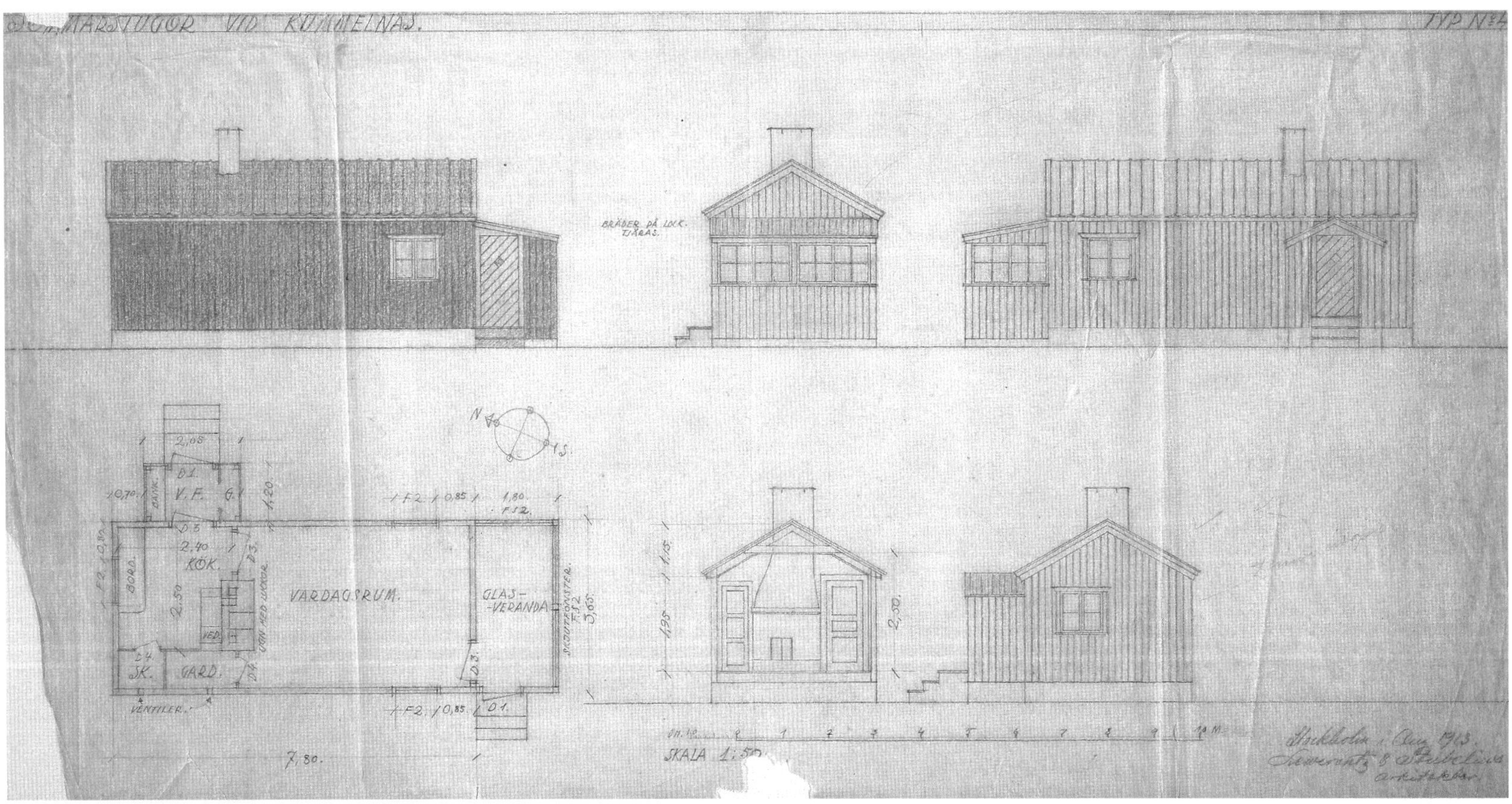

18. Renovation and Extension of the Axel Wallenberg Villa, Drottningholm, Stockholm, 1913–14
with Torsten Stubelius

The intervention of the two architects involved the renovation of the villa and the construction of a service building in which the salient features of traditional Swedish architecture are evident. Consisting of an elongated parallelepiped covered with a pitched roof and faced with vertical wooden planks, this building displays, in a simplified form, the features of the Neoclassical style recurrent in Lewerentz and Stubelius's output of the second decade of the twentieth century.

Dating from the nineteenth century, the villa required above all to be adapted functionally to the requirements of the Wallenberg family, although the renovation work also comprised the decorative features and all the internal finishings that the two architects skilfully adapted to the current style.

(P.G.)

View of exterior.

19. Project for the Extension to the Baltic Separatorer AB Factory, Södertälje, 1913–14
with Torsten Stubelius and Industribyrån AB

In 1913 Lewerentz and Stubelius were commissioned to plan an extension to the Baltic Separatorer factory, situated in the industrial area of Södertälje. A building with three storeys, which were to be devoted respectively to production, assembly and laboratory research, was to be constructed on a surface area of about 2,000 square metres. As in other similar circumstances, the project focused on the main façade, since the general layout was linked to the type of production and the equipment required for this purpose. At an angle to the sides of the site, the long façade is resolved through the use of a classical division: pilasters in brick, with the capitals just hinted at, are surmounted by a wide pediment bearing the firm's name. Subsequent drawings reveal the architects' intention to abandon the excessively imposing style of the first proposal in favour of a simpler manner.

(P.G.)

Study drawing of the main elevation.

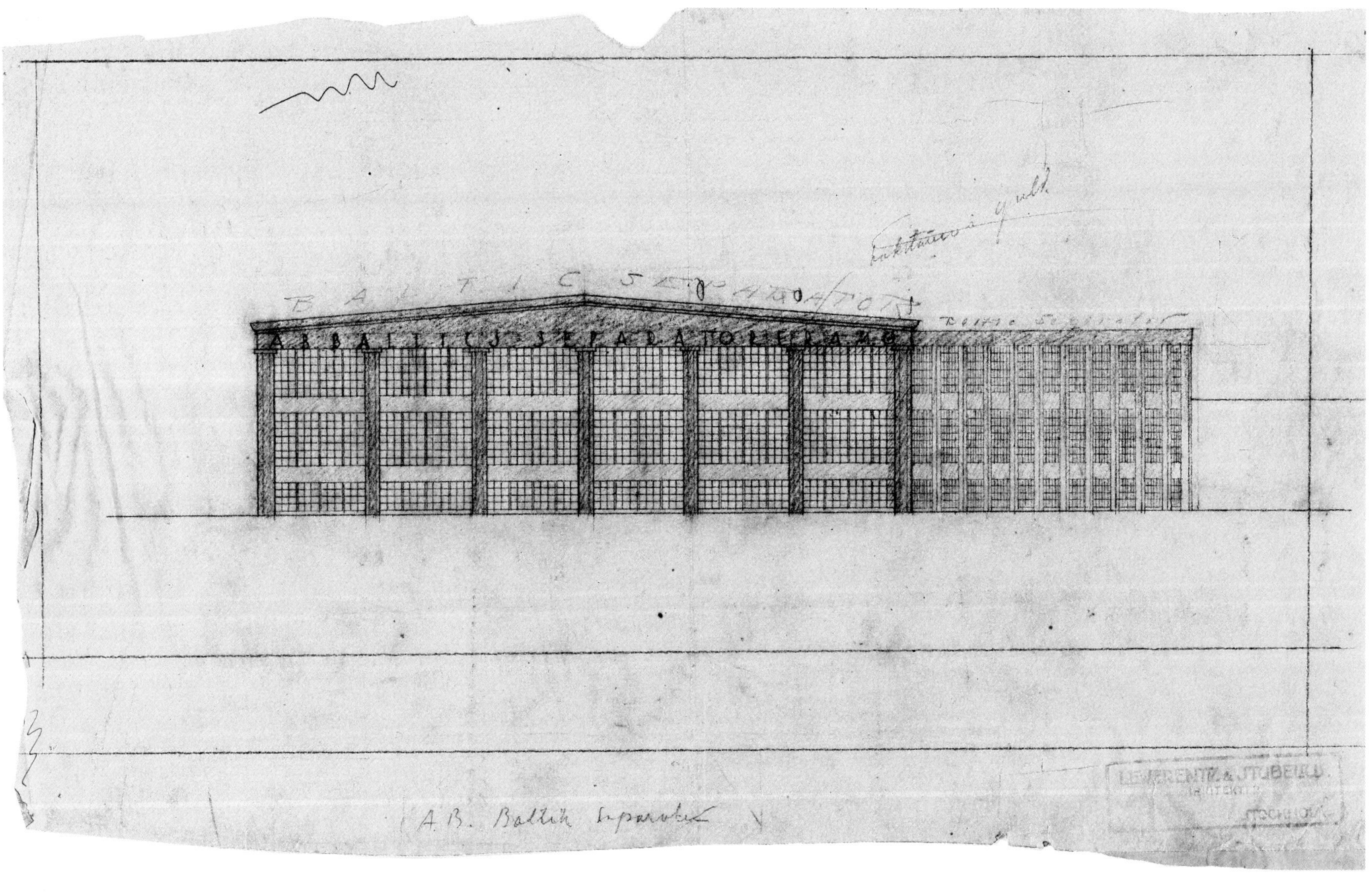

20. Conference Hall for Färe Glasbruk, Sibbhult, 1913–14

with Torsten Stubelius

Commissioned by Färe Glasbruk (glassworks), Lewerentz and Stubelius designed a building intended to house a conference hall and library. The proposal provides for a simple block with a rectangular plan, onto which is grafted, towards the end of one of the long sides, a smaller building containing the kitchen and service areas. The conference hall, which is the equivalent of two storeys in height, is reached by a small entrance hall that also leads, up a short staircase, to the library. The building's exterior is extremely elementary and appears as a rectangular block constructed in wood, divided up by simple square windows and surmounted by a very large tiled roof that seems to oppress it. Lewerentz and Stubelius also designed a number of glasses for Färe Glasbruk.

(P.G.)

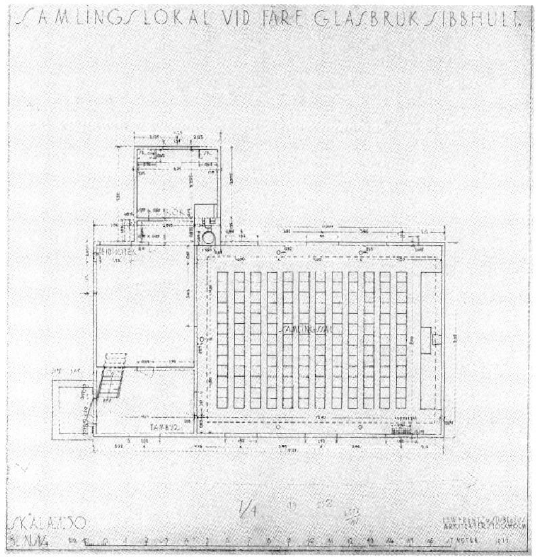

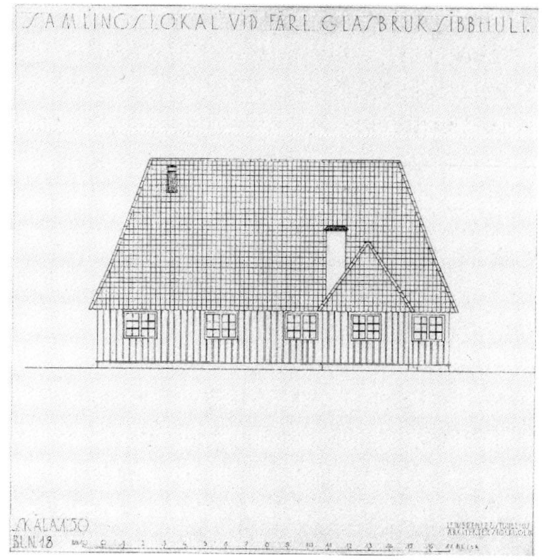

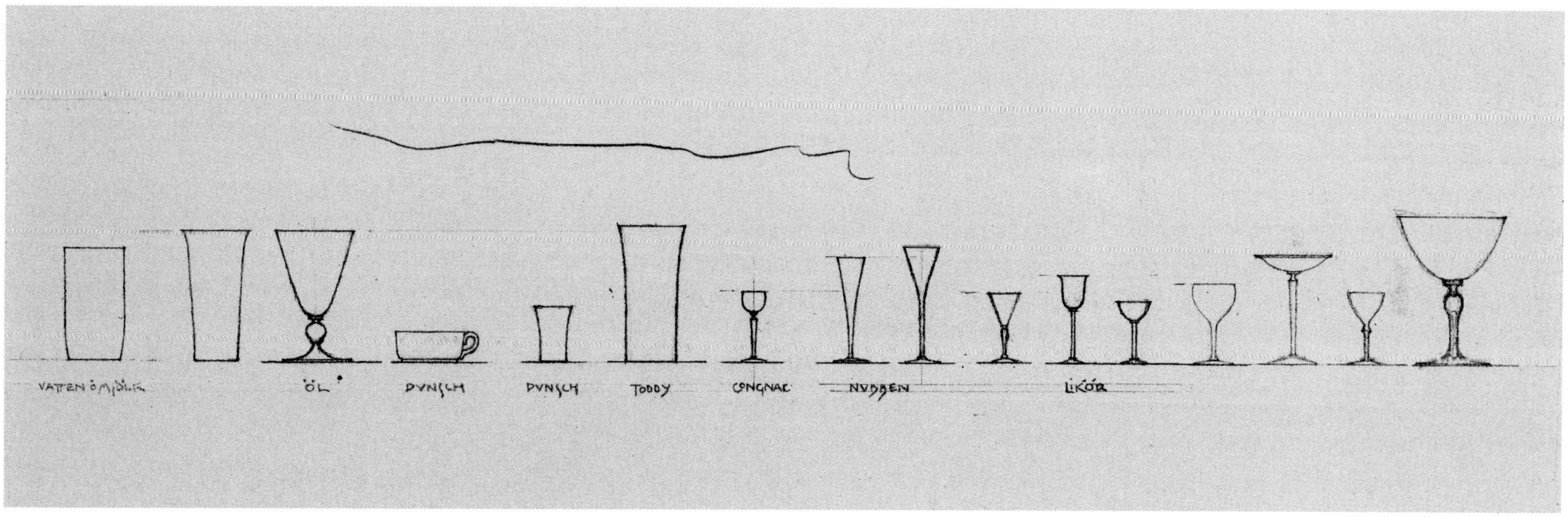

Plan of ground floor and elevation.

Glasses for production by Färe Glasbruk.

21. Projects for Tombstones and Funerary Monuments, 1913 onwards

At the beginning of the twentieth century there was an intense debate in Sweden about cemeteries. Concerning the problems relating to their development and the proposals for new facilities, it was also the result of a desire to find ways of reorganizing the existing ones, in the hope that the intervention of private individuals would be more carefully controlled and become more uniform. The design of each tomb, in fact, had become a practice devoid of rules: tombstones and funerary monuments were produced without any artistic value in materials that were alien to the country's traditions (Carrara marble was the most widespread), the only aim being, where possible, to make them stand out from the others.
In 1914 the city of Stockholm introduced an obligatory review of this design practice in an explicit attempt to harmonize each monument with the tone and general aspect of the cemeteries, so that tombs considered to be out of keeping would have to conform to the new requirements or else they would be modified by the authorities responsible. The subordination of the rights of private individuals to the broader demands of the decorum of public property was—not surprisingly—much criticized and even considered to be a restriction on the freedom of aesthetic expression. In this period of great transformation, many architects and artists, including Lewerentz, took an interest in the question, in an attempt to find a form capable of reconciling individual freedom with the cultural and expressive aspirations of society. Both alone and with Torsten Stubelius or Erik Gunnar Asplund, Lewerentz executed numerous designs for tombstones and funerary monuments and chapels, many of which involved the use of the country's traditional materials—grey and black granite or grey limestone—with simple lettering (Lewerentz took particular care over the letters used in the inscriptions) and austere stylistic features, reduced to uncluttered, rigorous classicism.
In 1919, during their collaboration for the construction of the South Cemetery, near Stockholm, Asplund and Lewerentz won a competition organized by the cemetery board for the preparation of standard designs for the tombstones to be used in the new burial areas. In cemetery projects, Lewerentz always paid great attention to the question of the tombstones, giving instructions to be followed for their installation: for instance, he suggested that they should be placed horizontally on the ground, in contrast to the custom of erecting, in an excessively visible manner, the tombstones vertically over the graves.

Bibliography: Ahlin 1985b, pp. 51–53; Caldenby 1997, pp. 102–103 and 110–111.

(P.G.)

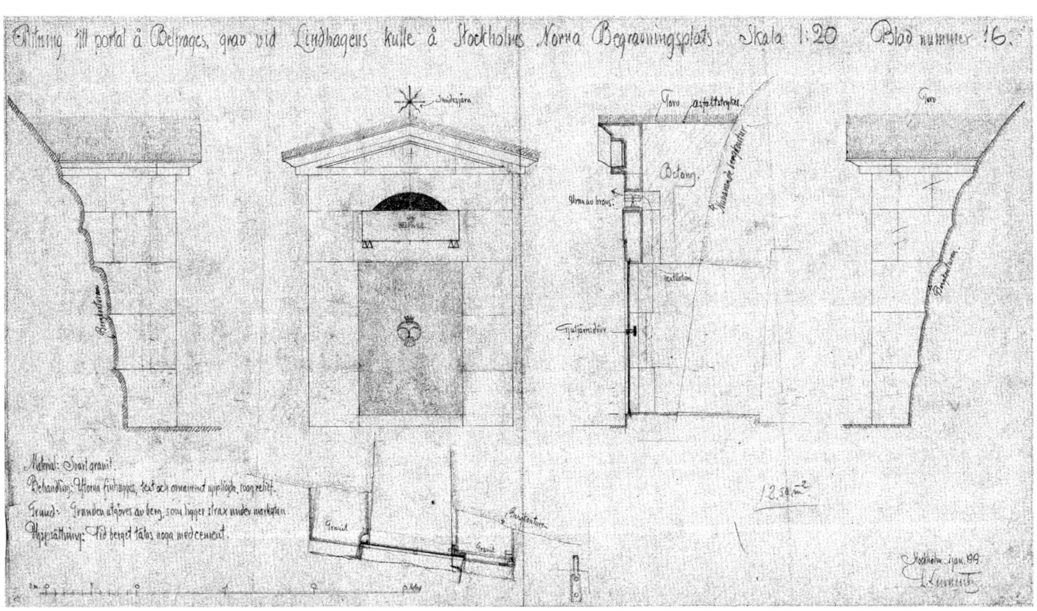

Project for the tomb of L. Forsber, Stockholm, 1915.

Elevation of the tomb of the Belfrage family, Stockholm, 1919.

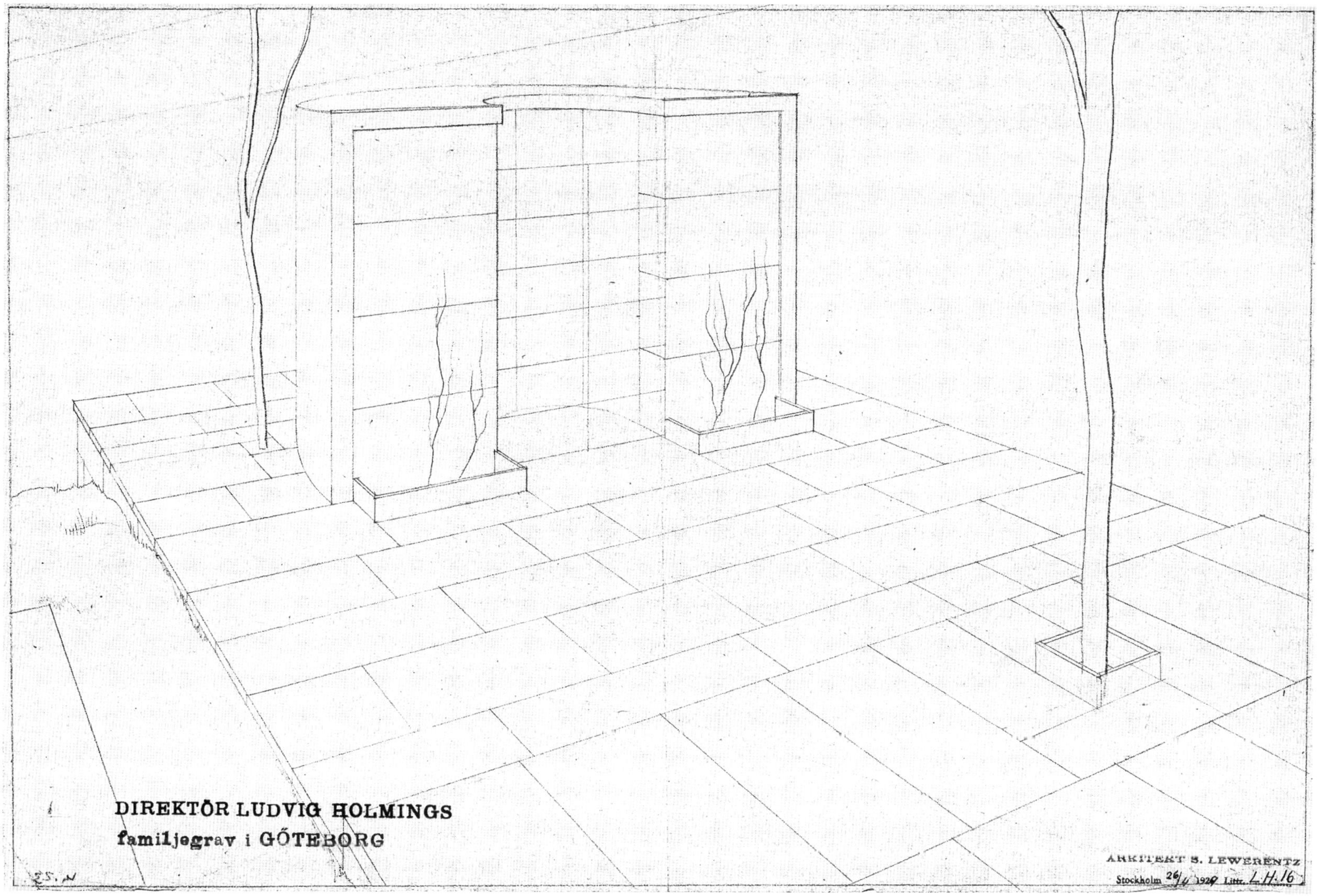

Project for the tomb of the Holming family, Gothenburg, 1929–30.

Project for the tombstone of Nils and Maria Cronstedt, Stockholm, 1916.

Tomb of T.A. Berben, Utterö, Stockholm, 1920.

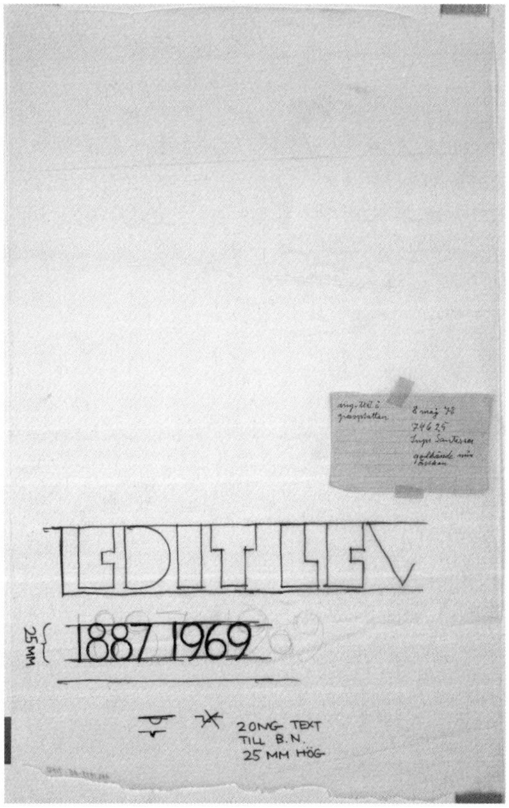

Tomb of the Malmström family, Stockholm, 1929.

Detail of the project for the tombstone of M. Tisell, Stockholm.

Study sketches for the tombstones of Edit and Sigurd Lewerentz, Utterö, 1929 (?).

22. Villa Ahxner, Djursholm, Stockholm, 1914

with Torsten Stubelius
extension and renovation of attic, 1926–27

In the introduction to his project for the Villa Ahxner, published in the journal *Teknisk Tidskrift* in 1919, Lewerentz recounted that the form of the house was inspired by the physical appearance of the jovial client, who suggested that a long, narrow building would make him feel at ease.
In effect, irony apart, the architect was aware that he had designed a low, elongated building in an attempt to give emphasis to the front facing a splendid valley. In reality, the main block, with two storeys, is orthogonal to a wing, only one storey in height, containing the dining-room, kitchen and service rooms. The internal spaces are arranged on both sides of the entrance hall—which occupies the whole width of the main block and, on the side opposite to the door, gives onto a small veranda—from which both the living-rooms and the dining-room may be reached.
Thus there are two orthogonal axes, one from the entrance terminating in the small veranda, the other links the main rooms, with all the doors aligned in a sequence, and also ends in a veranda, larger than the other one.
The linear arrangement of this part of this house—which is extremely traditional—allows all the main rooms to enjoy excellent views of the landscape.
The exterior of the villa is austere and simple, and is characterized by the vertical rhythm of the wooden planks, painted grey with some reddish gradations. Only the attention paid to a number of points of the buildings, such as the corners of the main block, where small wooden columns are inserted, or the veranda flanking the dining-room, reveals the restrained refinement of the details. Lewerentz asserted, in fact, that with this building he had demonstrated that it was possible to construct a villa without having to invest large sums of money.

Views of the exterior.

Bibliography: Lewerentz 1919; Ahlin 1985b, p. 43.

(P.G.)

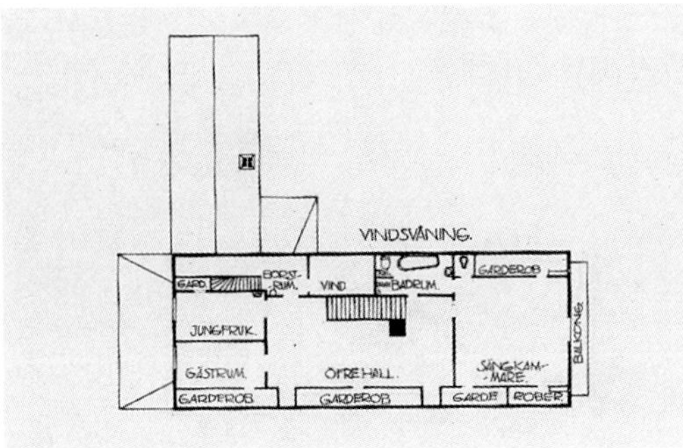

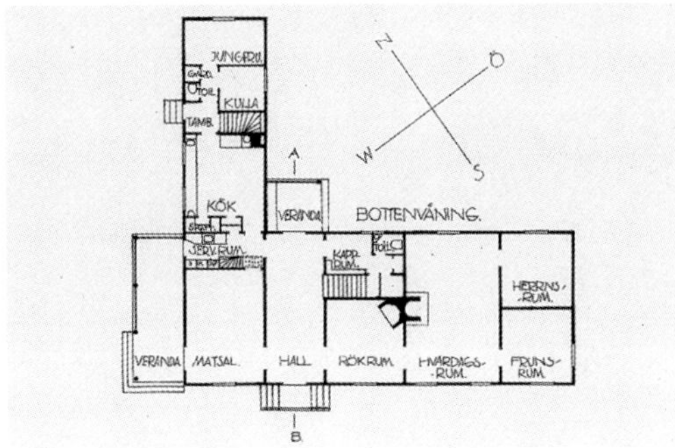

Plans of the two floors and the north-east, north-west and south-west elevations, July 1914.

23. Project for the Villa of K.J. Beskow, Helsingborg, 1914
with Torsten Stubelius

For the family of the engineer Beskow, Lewerentz and Stubelius proposed two versions of the project, suitable for two different sites in Helsingborg. Both versions comprise a square plan, two storeys and a hipped roof. The first version develops the idea of a house in which the interior space surrounds a long hall extending from one side of the building to the other, serving both as a living-room and a passageway. The second version, on the other hand, seeks to give a more precise character to the exterior through the use of stylistic features having Palladian overtones: a Giant Order with Ionic capitals embellishes the main elevation.

(P.G.)

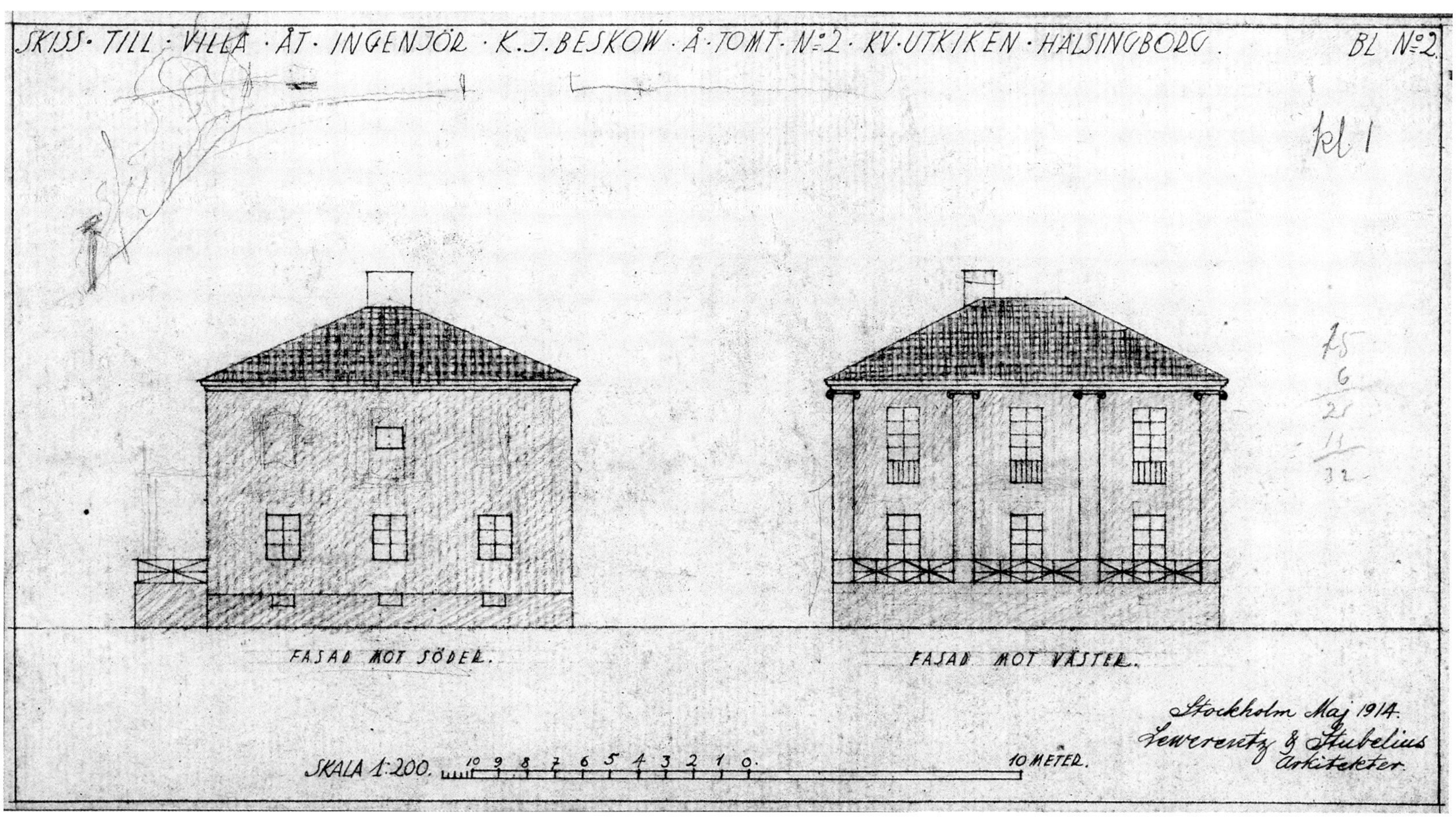

Elevations, second version.

24. Villa Solsidan and Project for a Housing Scheme at Saltsjöbaden, Stockholm, 1914
with Torsten Stubelius

In 1914 Lewerentz and Stubelius designed a villa for the Järnväg AB Stockholm-Saltsjöbaden, the railway company responsible for the development of the area of Saltsjöbaden, in the environs of Stockholm. The exterior of the villa has a very traditional appearance, inspired by the sober classicism that is evident in the villa for Olle Hjortzberg, built in the same year. Two storeys in height, the villa is characterized, on the main front facing south, by a portico with columns that, set forward from the façade, indicates the entrance. The exterior is faced with vertical wooden planks adorned with small volutes, a treatment that makes the whole building uniform without highlighting the internal storeys. This villa is the prototype for a housing scheme that was to have been realized on behalf of the railway company; nothing came of this project, however, and the villa was the only building constructed in the area.

(P.G.)

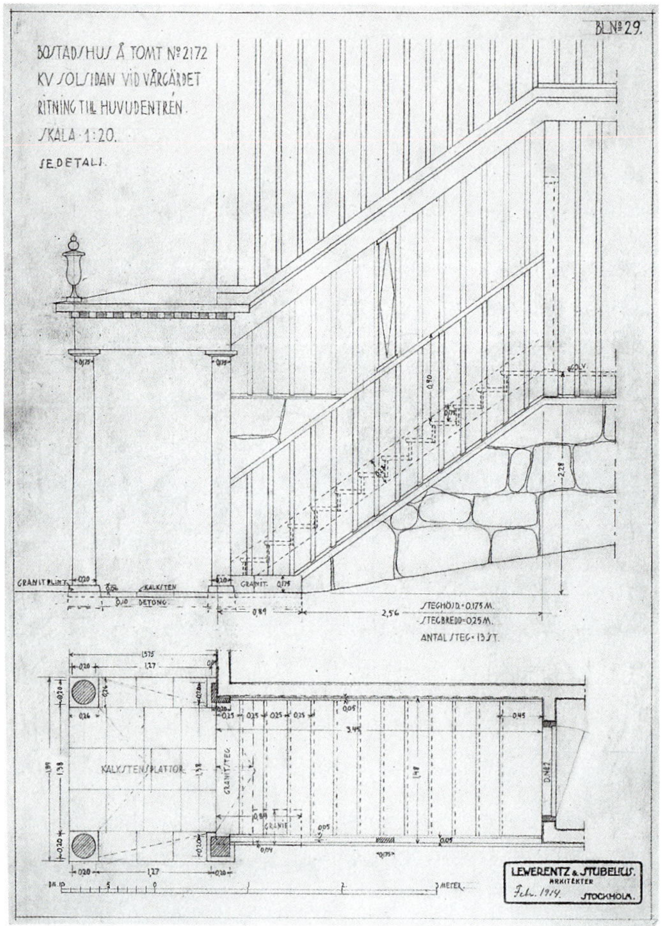

Villa Solsidan, details of the entrance.

Housing scheme in the Saltsjöbaden area, elevation and plan.

25. Project for a Crematorium at Bergaliden, Helsingborg, 1914

In 1914 the cremation board of Helsingborg commissioned Lewerentz and Stubelius to design a cemetery on the hill overlooking the city, next to the Kärnan tower. The programme, formulated together with Gustaf W. Schlyter, commissioner of the board, and the writer Maurice Maeterlinck, sought to give a significant form to the place of cremation, a practice that had started to take root in Sweden in 1883, the year in which the first institution responsible for it was founded.
The central feature of the project is a narrow, elongated building located on the edge of the site and bridging the end of a large pond. The water from this pond, flowing through an arch under the building, descends in a series of small cascades and fountains towards the city. Parallel to the pond is the access way leading, with a ramp, to the first hall of the crematorium, a high space, covered in the central part by a segmental dome, intended to house the funeral ceremonies. With little lighting and mainly closed to the exterior, this Hall of Death is a place with an introversive nature, conducive to prayer and meditation. From here, two semicircular flights of stairs lead to the choir room, where singers and organ are situated in two different galleries. The music from the choir room may be heard in both the Hall of Death and the Hall of Life, to which it gives access. In the latter, the space is divided into five rooms linked to each other and illuminated by a series of windows, the mourners pass as they proceed towards the final stage of the ceremony. In fact, after having crossed the columbarium, an open garden flanked on its long sides by the porticos in which the cinerary urns are kept, this route concludes at the Temple of Memory. Placed at the end of the main axis, which passes through three separate areas, with a parallel alignment on the lower level where the crematorium is located, the Temple of Memory is the place where those who have accompanied the deceased may be reunited once again with their loved one, receiving the cinerary urn to be placed in the cemetery.
As various writers have already pointed out, there are numerous symbolic references in this work: the east-west orientation of the building linking the cycle of life and death with dawn and dusk in accordance with symbology innate in human beings; the presence of flowing water as an image of the origin of life and purification; the orthogonal arrangement of the main routes—that of arrival and the longitudinal axis of the building—which reproduce, in their proportions, the form of the cross. Many of these features were reproduced in the project for the Skogskyrkogården, Stockholm South Cemetery, that Lewerentz produced in collaboration with Erik Gunnar Asplund. It was not by chance that, when discussing the choices underlying the project on the occasion of the presentation of the model of the Helsingborg crematorium at the Exhibition of the Baltic Nations in Malmö in 1914, Asplund and Lewerentz decided to participate in the Stockholm competition together.

Bibliography: Bergsten 1914; Ahlin 1985b, pp. 53–55; Constant 1994, pp. 19–20.

(P.G.)

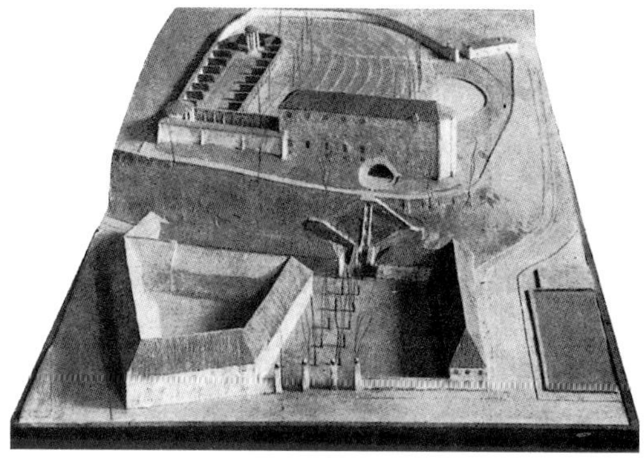

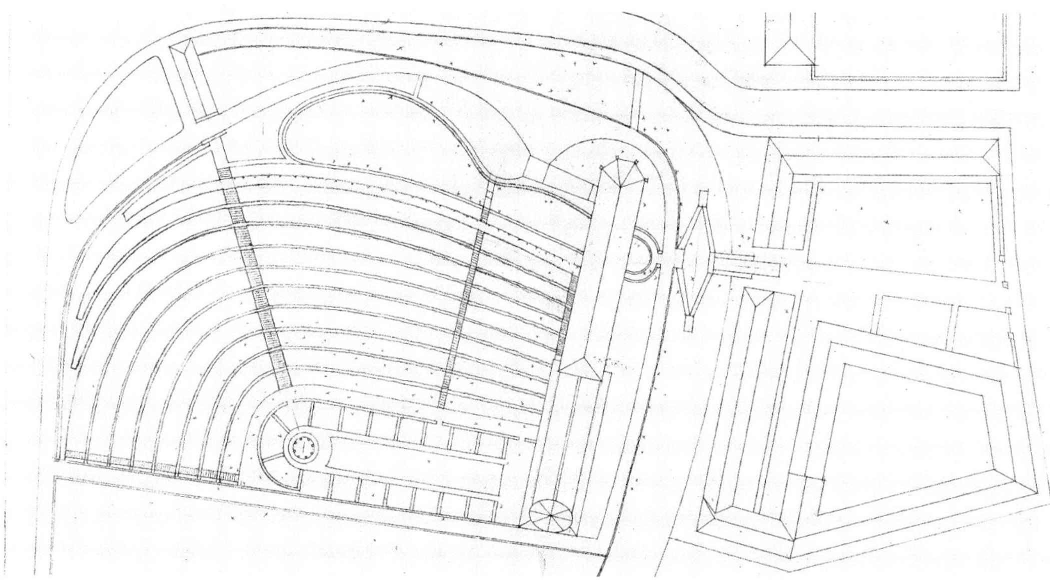

Views of the model and the layout plan.

Study sketch of the layout plan.

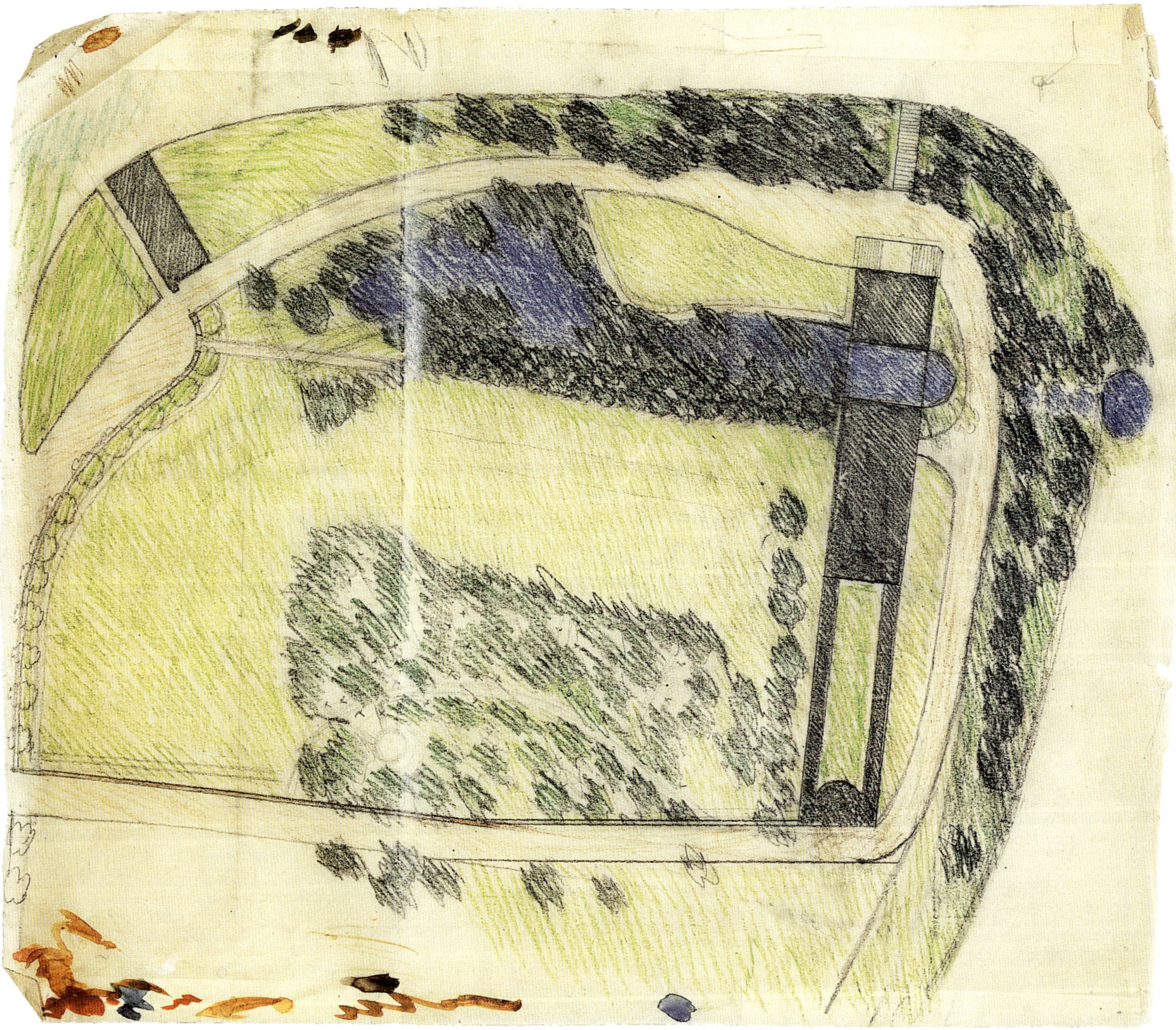

Study sketch of elevation.

Plan of ground and first floors and longitudinal and cross sections.

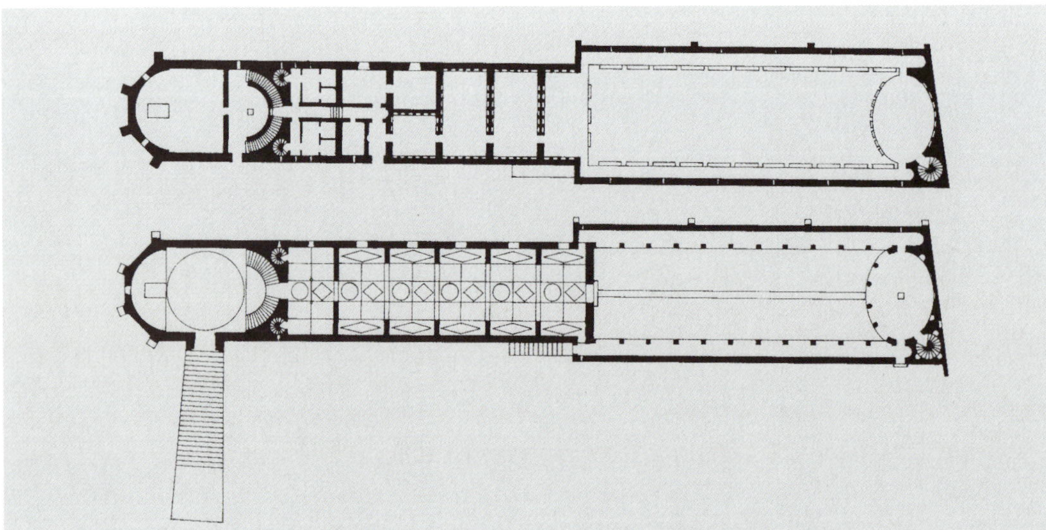

Elevation of the main building.

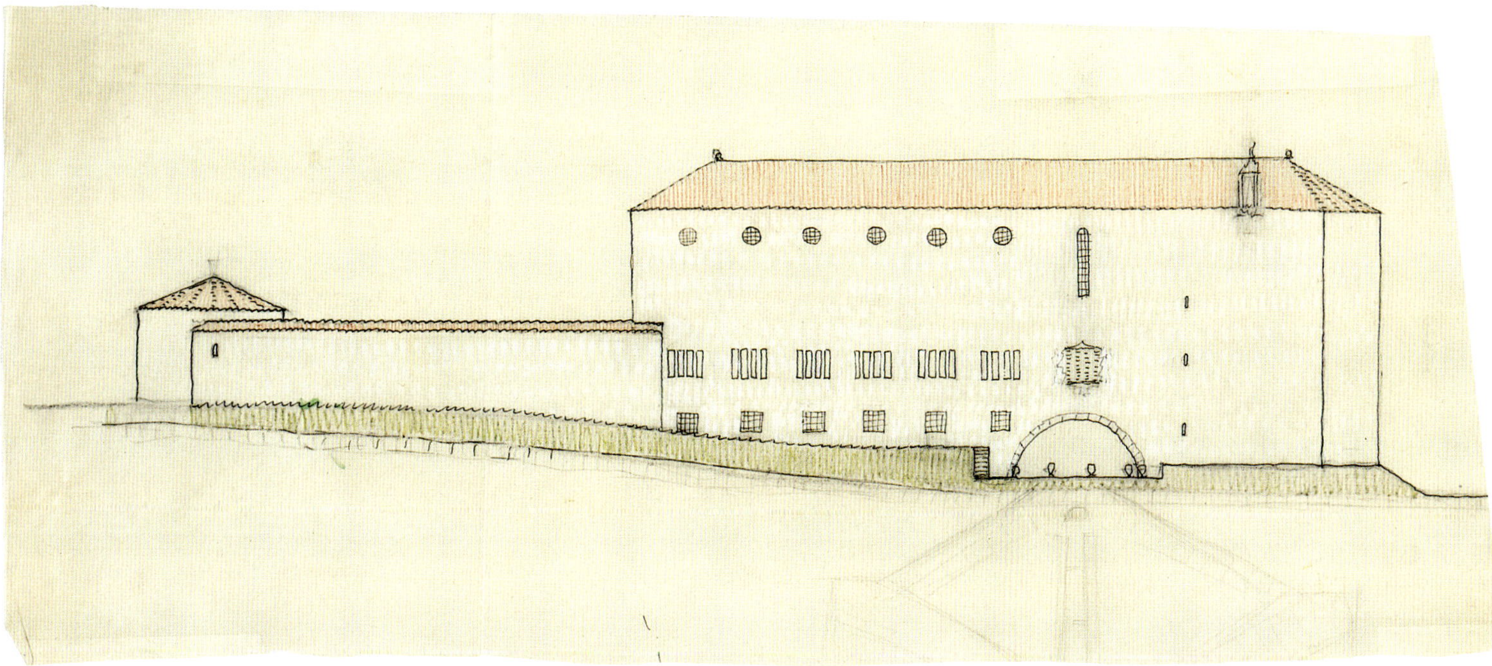

26. Project for a Housing Scheme at Bergaliden, Helsingborg, 1914
with Torsten Stubelius

27. Project for Houses for the Workers and Engineers of Forsbackabruk, Forsbacka, 1914
with Torsten Stubelius

The plots for the houses are located around two internal roads following the lie of the land. A square, at an oblique angle to the orthogonal axes along which the scheme extends, is in contrast to the overall plan, providing, with its narrow, elongated form, a prospect of the River Gauleån. It is also intended to construct, along the coast, a number of communal boathouses, an indoor swimming pool and a workplace for women.

The houses—approximately eighty and divided into three types of various sizes—consist of a wooden structure resting on a low stone base.

(P.G.)

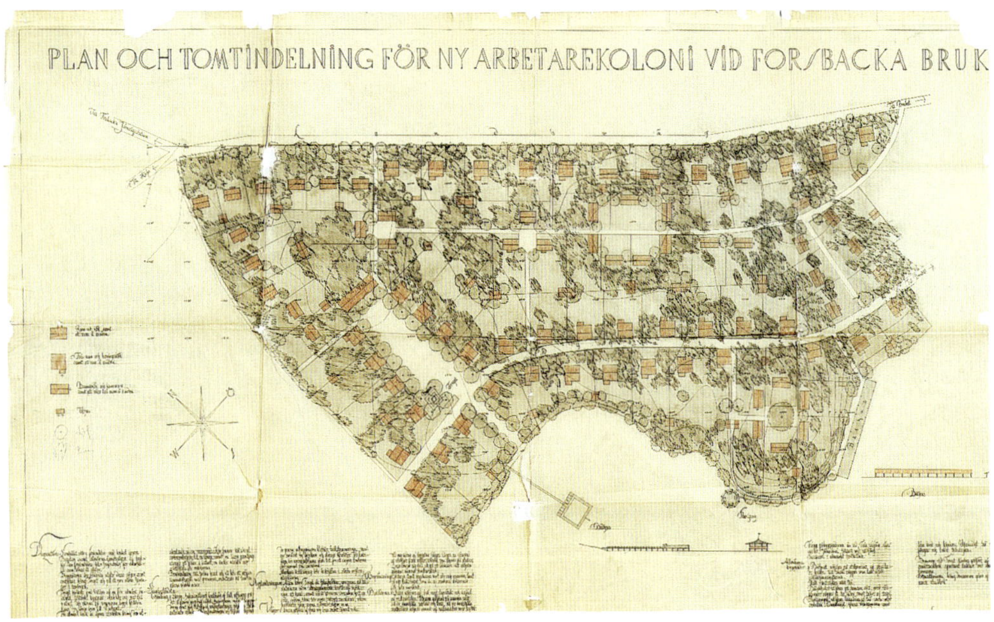

Layout plan.

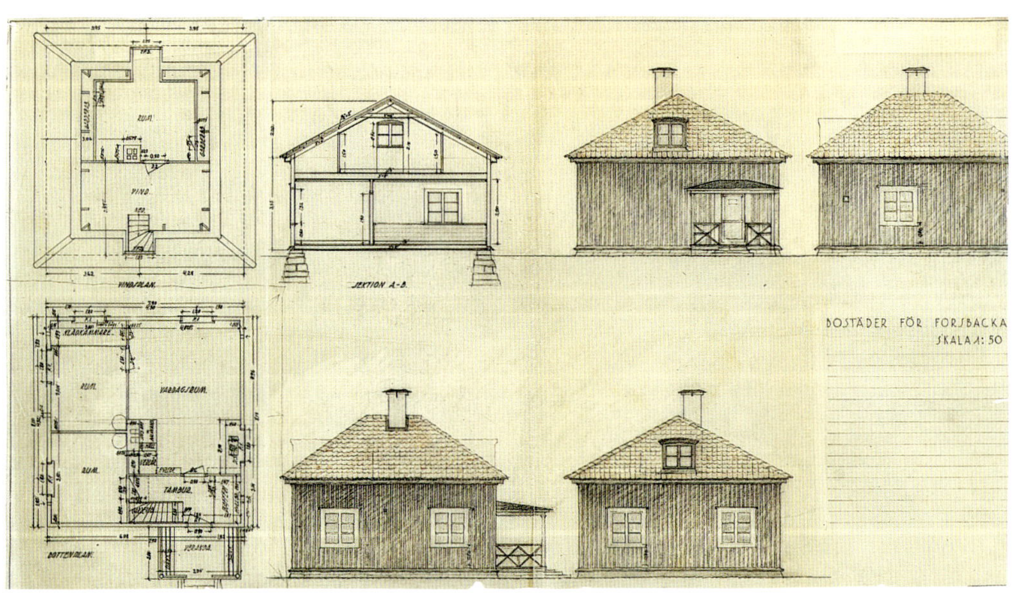

Plans, elevations and section of the housing types.

28. Exhibition of the Baltic Nations, Malmö, 1914

In 1914 an important international exhibition took place at Malmö. Featuring the products and projects of all the countries on the Baltic Sea, it also included a number of pavilions where the works of Lewerentz and Stubelius were displayed. In the one devoted to low-cost housing, the two architects exhibited, on behalf of the Egnahemsrörels (Movement for Home Ownership), a scheme of 1912–13 for single-family houses in the Pålsjö area of Helsingborg and a project of 1912–13 for workers' houses at Nyvång. In addition to these projects of an urban character, in the Svenska Slöjdförening (National Applied Arts Association) pavilion Lewerentz and Stubelius presented a number of glass objects designed in the preceding years for Färe Glasbruk on a stand specially created for the occasion. Lastly, in the Eldbegängelse Förening (National Cremation Association) pavilion the two architects exhibited the model, made in the same year, of the project for the crematorium of Bergaliden at Helsingborg.

Bibliography: Ahlin 1985b, pp. 55, 105, 124.

(G.P.)

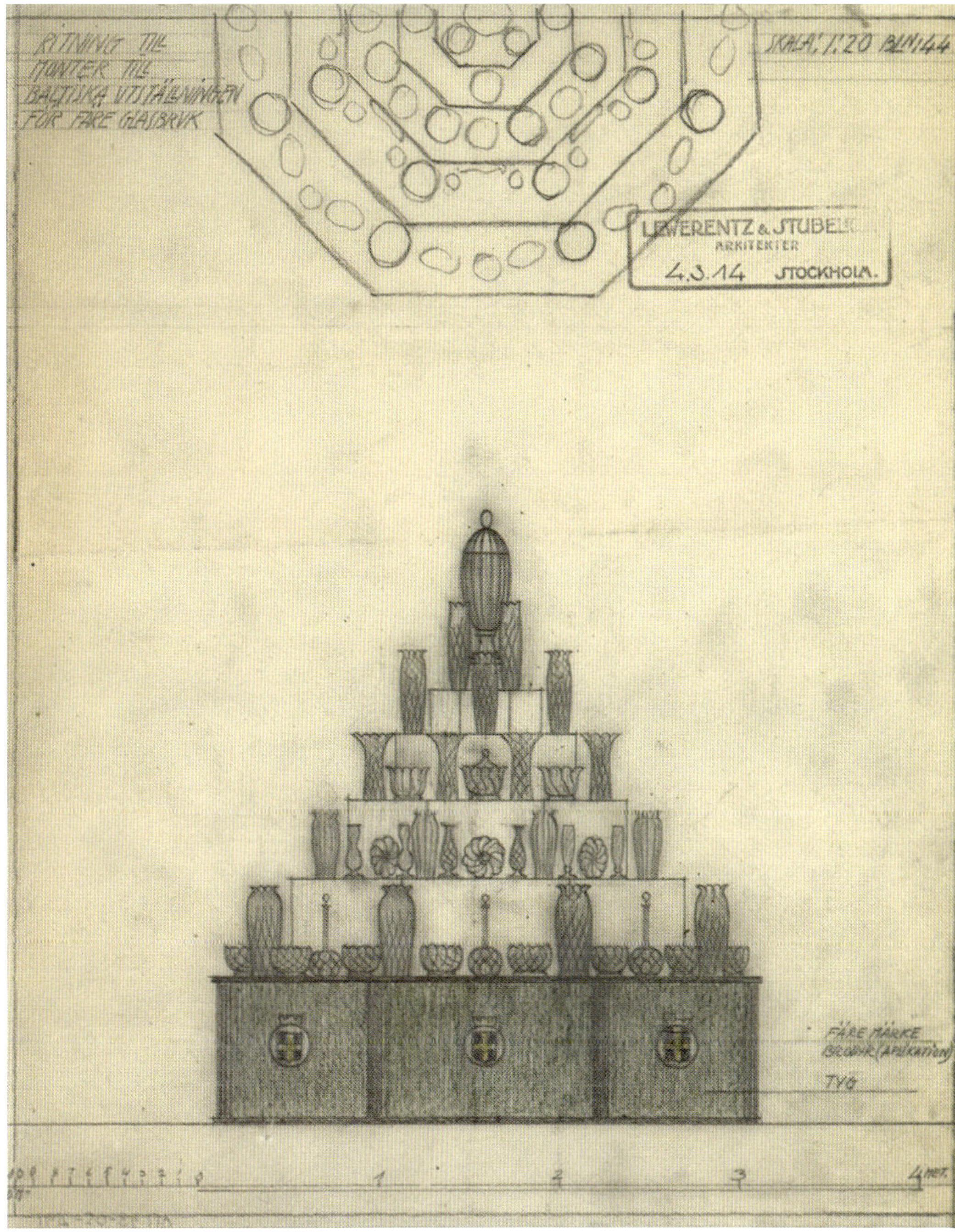

Display stand for glass objects.

29. Summer Restaurant at Pålsjö, Helsingborg, 1914

with Torsten Stubelius

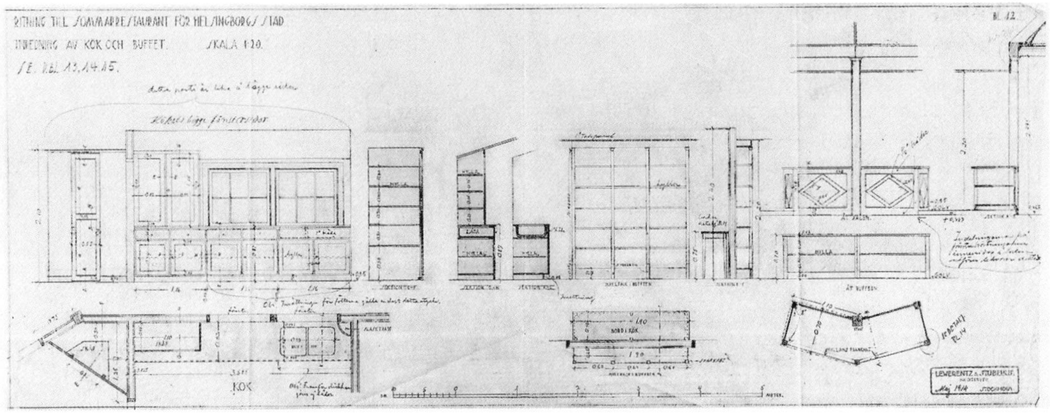

Details of the fixed furnishings and view of the exterior.

In 1914, in the Pålsjöskogen wood, near Helsingborg, Lewerentz and Stubelius built a small summer restaurant. This very simple but charming wooden construction comprises a block with a square base onto which is grafted an octagonal structure with a much higher, pointed roof. Surrounded by slender columns surmounted by stylized capitals, this houses an open dining area. The roof is covered with wooden shingles, while the square block is faced in vertical wooden planks. The whole building is reminiscent of a cabin, or even a tent, ideal for creating an atmosphere conducive to communion with nature.

(P.G.)

30. Villa Ramén, Helsingborg, 1914–15
with Torsten Stubelius

The Villa Ramén was realized by Lewerentz and Stubelius in 1914 on a gently sloping site 1915 overlooking the Sound, a position from which, on clear days, it is possible to see the Danish coast and the city of Helsingør. The villa occupies only a small part of the large site, the rest of which comprises various service facilities and a large garden divided into recreation and rest areas. The building, a parallelepiped surmounted by a hipped roof with sprocketed eaves, is compact and austere, with a regular rows of windows arranged flush with the façade. While the shape of the roof and some of the details on the exterior clearly derive from the building traditions of nearby Denmark, the coloured sketches and the way the volumes are disposed reveal an interest in contemporary central European architecture. The severe appearance of the building is, moreover, reflected by the way the external spaces are arranged; this is intended to provide views both of the garden and the surrounding area.

Bibliography: Ahlin 1985b, p. 46; Caldenby 1997, pp. 54–57.

(G.P.)

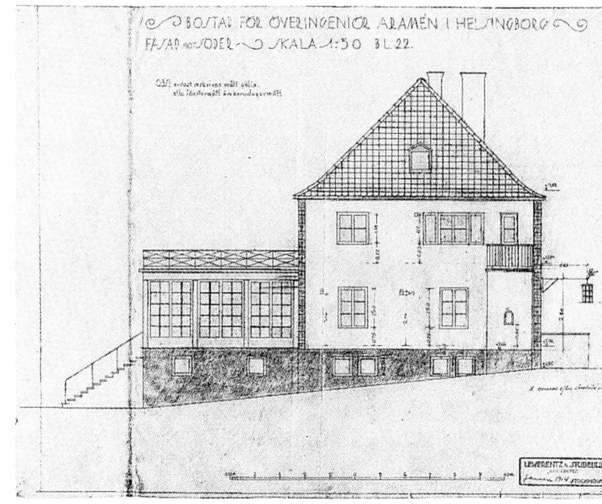

South elevation and layout plan, 1914.

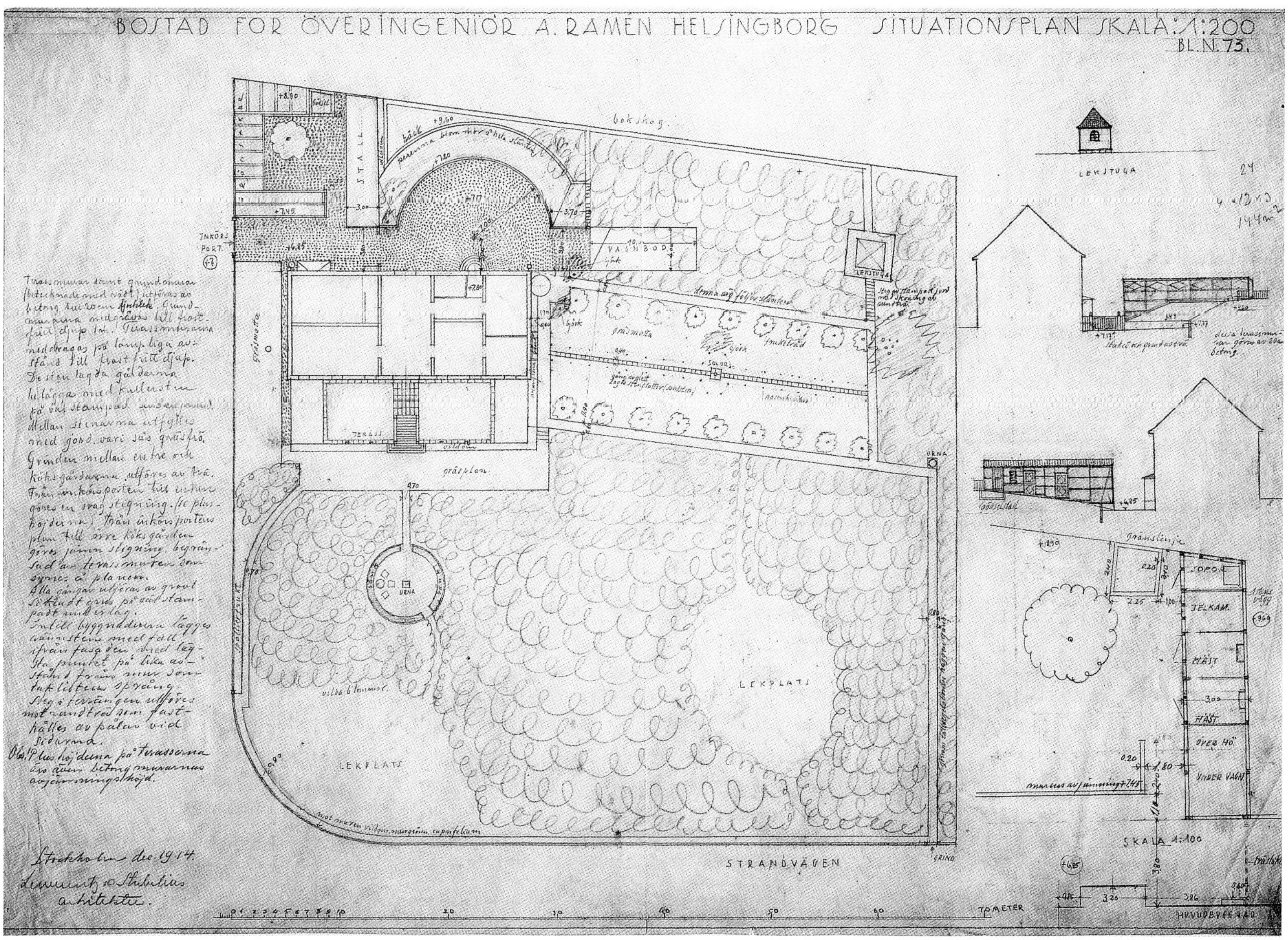

Study sketch
of the forecourt.

Views of the exterior.

31. Forsbacka Cemetery, 1914–22
with Torsten Stubelius

In the first proposals for the cemetery of Forsbacka, an industrial town in central Sweden, the scheme spreads organically over all the available land. The whole of the site, sloping towards the lake shore, is used in Lewerentz and Stubelius's first project, where a layout following the contours was envisaged; extending from the highest area, occupied by a chapel, to the lake below, this also comprised an islet on which a church was planned. In the subsequent project, however, this arrangement was considerably simplified, becoming more schematic and rigid on the slope of the site, although the project that was realized has retained the position of the chapel overlooking the cemetery.

Many versions of this chapel—from 1917 onwards they were signed by Lewerentz—have been found. They all show a building constructed with coarsed random rubble stone blocks, with a double shell and bound with thickly applied mortar, while various versions of the roof exist. The plan of the building is not perfectly square, reflecting the direction of the site boundary and that of the road leading to the entrance, which were not orthogonal. This gave rise to the irregular form of the plan, while detailed studies of the paving have also been found. While the chapel was under construction, in 1919, Lewerentz decided to use stones found locally for both the base and the walls of the small building, manifesting his interest in the texture and overall effect of the structure, thereby aiming to link the architecture to the area through the use of traditional techniques and materials. The church, located on the islet in the layout plan, was never built.

Bibliography: Lewerentz 1915; Ahlin 1985b, pp. 78–79; Caldenby 1997, pp. 58–61.

(P.G.)

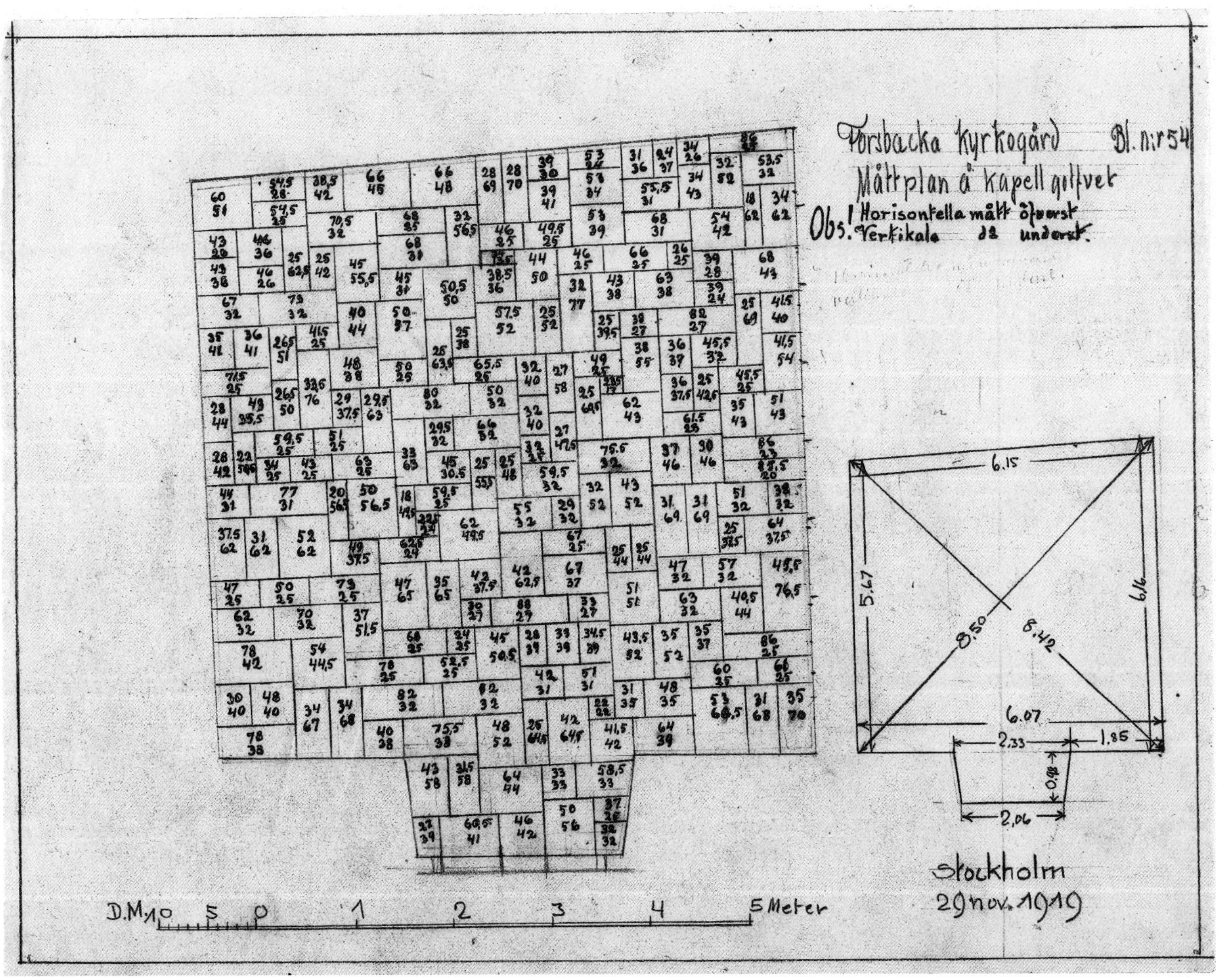

Detail of the paving of the funerary chapel, 29 November 1919.

Layout plan with profiles, December 1914.

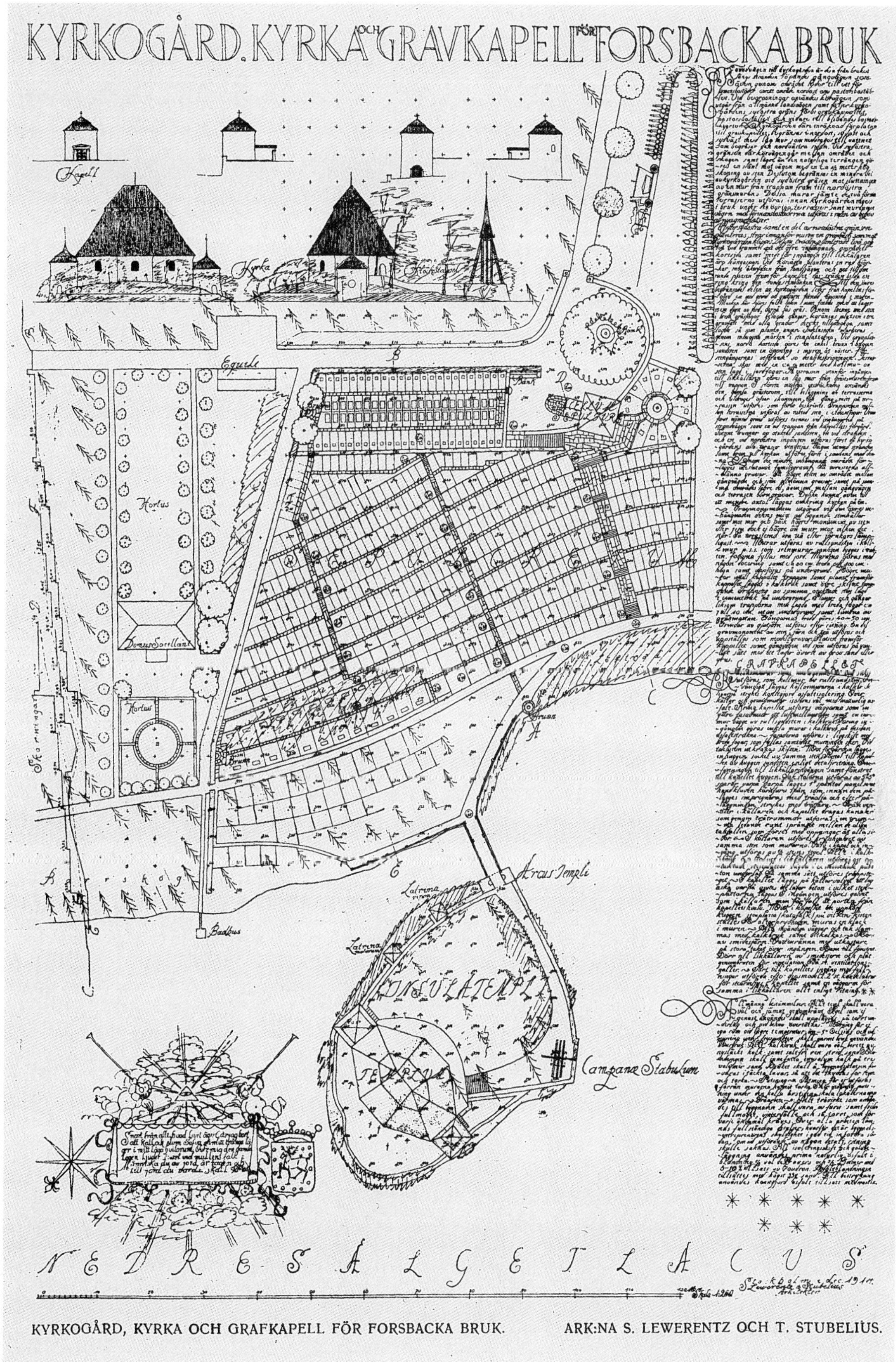

Elevations, plans
and sections of the church
and chapel.

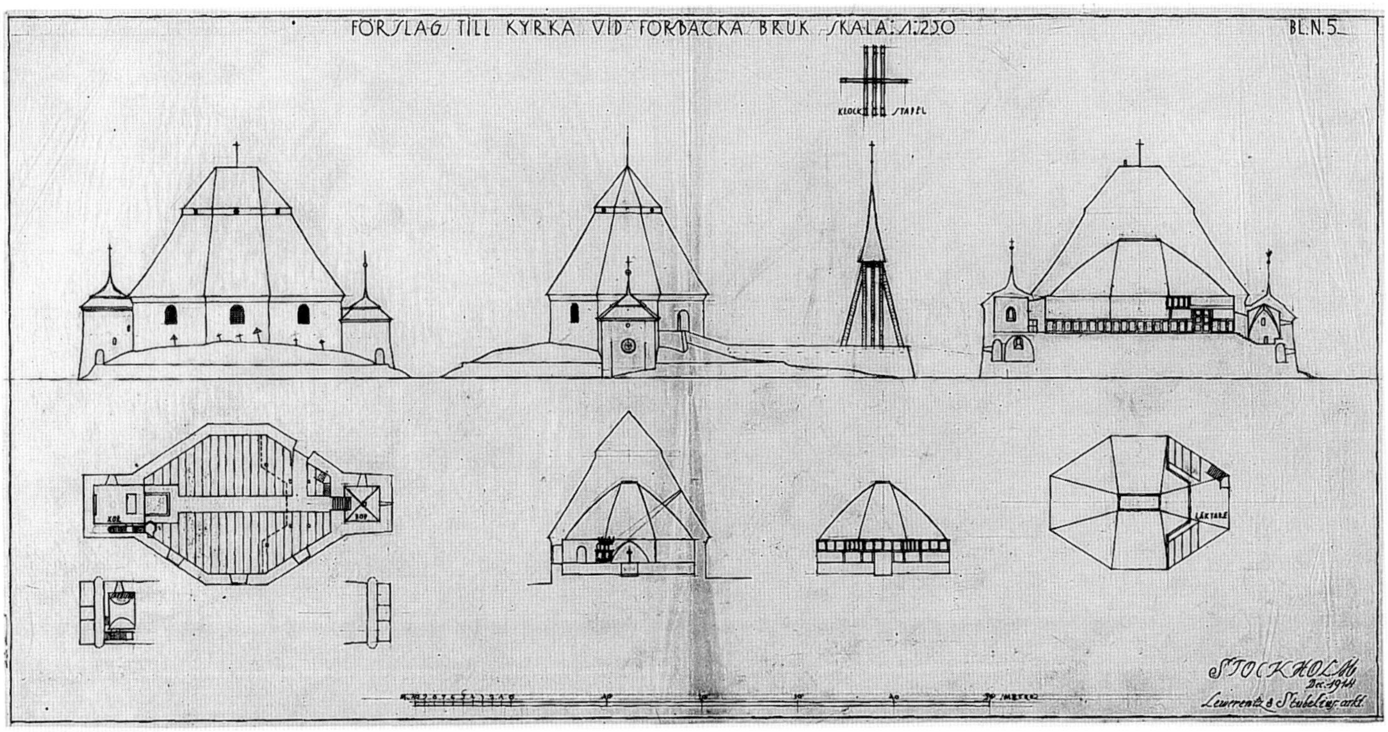

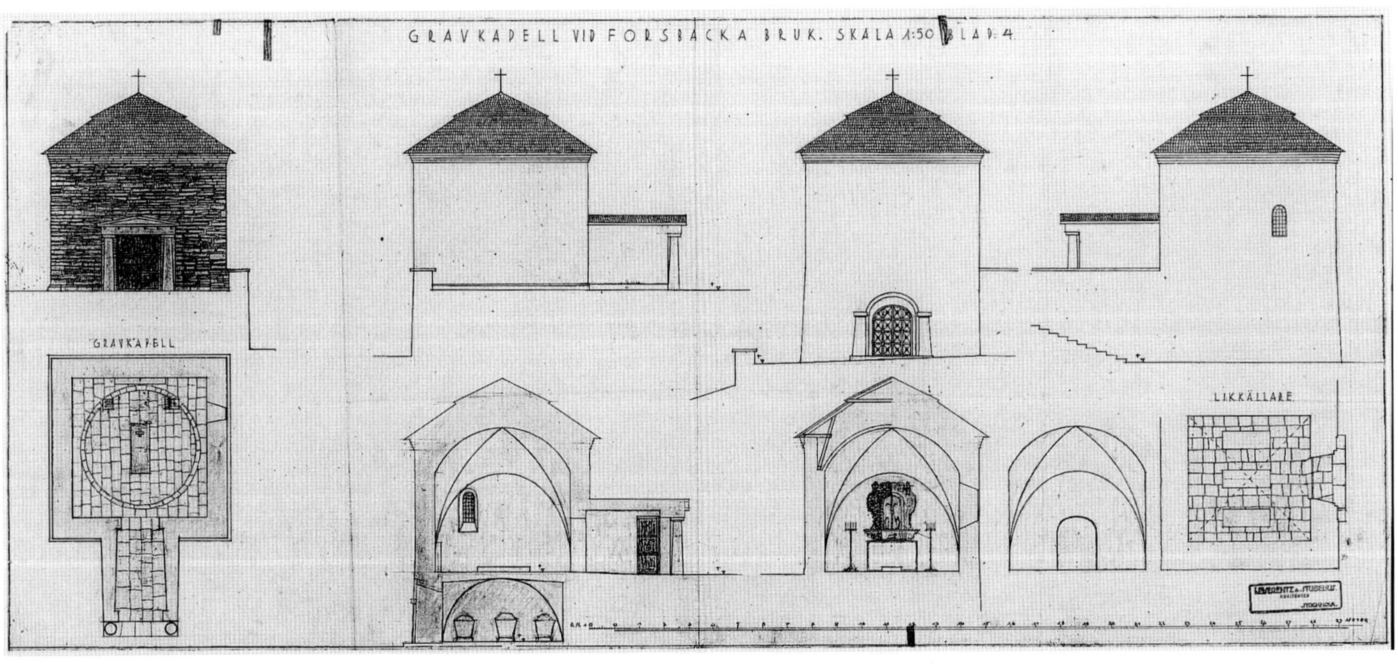

The chapel: different proposals for the elevation, masonry and the form of the roof.

Views of the chapel and cemetery.

32. Project for the Development Plan of Brantevik, 1914–29

In preparing the project for the development plan of Brantevik, a small fishing-port in southern Sweden, Lewerentz began by locating the main square in the highest part of the village, where he sited the most important buildings, including the church, post-office and school. Leading out of the square is a broad tree-lined boulevard, free of buildings and commanding a view towards the sea front and the small harbour below.
In addition, the project proposed the integration between the new and old buildings, which was also achieved through the drawing up of a new map of mobility, characterized by the presence of three main arteries running parallel to the coastline.
On the highest one, which skirts the perimeter of the built-up area, Lewerentz proposed that the new municipal cemetery should be sited close to the main square, but outside the urban area, so that it was, in fact, just behind the church.
Although the details of the project continued to be discussed with the local authority until 1919, it was never realized.

Bibliography: Ahlin 1985b, pp. 48–49.

(P.G.)

33. Project for the Villa of Erick Banck, Helsingborg, 1915
with Torsten Stubelius

The project of the villa for the shipowner Erick Banck at Helsingborg combines a mixture of classical and Baroque stylistic features with a layout that, although traditional, has a number of compositional ideas of a certain interest. On the plan, in fact, one of the short sides is set at a slightly oblique angle, which means that the organization of the rooms has to take this into account. While on the ground floor the effect of this is limited to the internal disposition of the two rooms on the oblique side, on the upper floor a corridor extends along the axis orthogonal to this side, affecting the layout of other rooms.

(G.P.)

Plans of the ground and first floors.

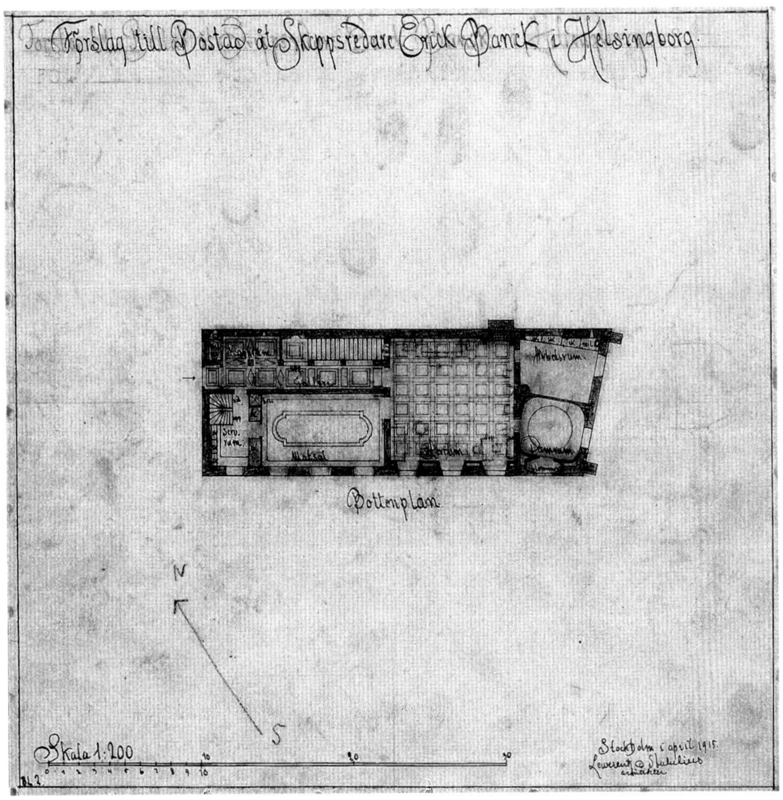

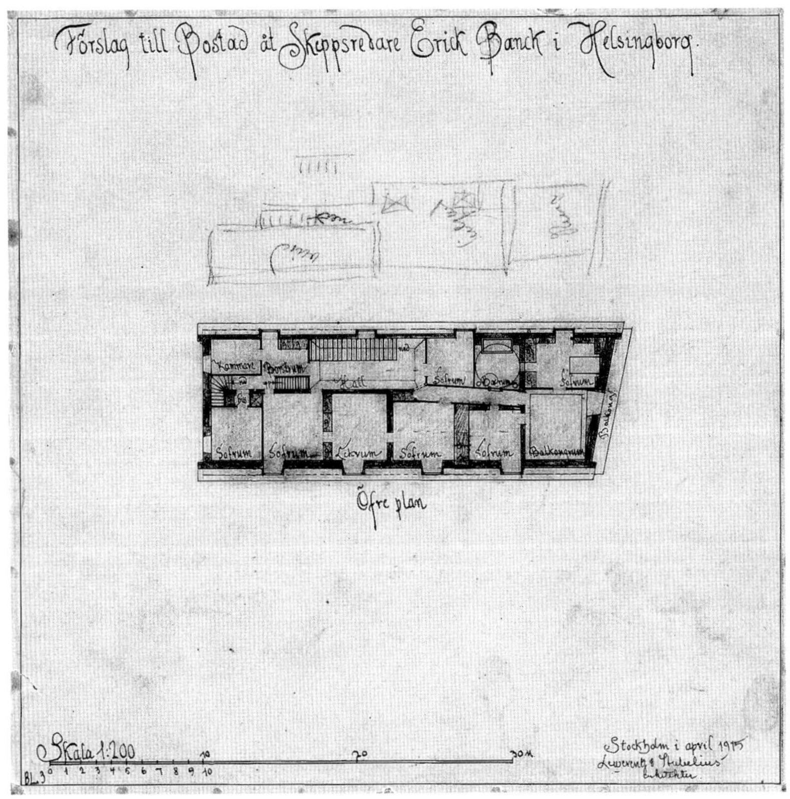

Longitudinal section.

34. Competition Project for Buildings for the Swedish Navy at Skeppsholmen, Stockholm, 1915
motto "till Skepps"

In 1915 Lewerentz participated in the competition for the design of a number of new buildings for the Swedish navy at Kungsholmen, in the central part of the islet of Skeppsholmen, where the headquarters of the navy had been situated for centuries. Already the subject of a competition ten years previously, the site is located in a central area of the capital, just behind the historic island of Gamlasdadt where the royal palace stands. In answer to the request, contained in the conditions of the new competition, to locate the best position, as well as determining their architectural characteristics, for a number of buildings, including a school for non-commissioned officers, two barracks and a refectory, Lewerentz responded by proposing a row of buildings extending to the west of the imposing Orthodox church, parallel to the Tyghuset (house of cloth).

Bibliography: *Skeppsholmentäflingen* 1916.

(G.P.)

Sketch of the project.

35. Renovation and Extension of the *Corps de Logis* at Högsbo, Sandviken, 1915

See entry no. 15.

View of exterior.

36. House and Shop in Kungsgatan, Stockholm, 1915

37. Illustration for *Teknisk Tidskrift*, 1915

38. Competition Project for the Extension to Stockholm South Cemetery at Enskede, Stockholm, 1915 onwards
with Erik Gunnar Asplund
motto "Tallum" first prize

In 1914, on the occasion of the Exhibition of the Baltic Nations in Malmö, Sigurd Lewerentz and Erik Gunnar Asplund met in the mock-up of Ferdinand Boberg's Baltic Temple, housed in the pavilion of the Eldbegängelse Förening (National Cremation Association) designed by Gustav Schlyter. When the two young architects discussed the themes raised by the exhibition they were near the model of the crematorium of Bergaliden at Helsingborg, designed by Lewerentz (in collaboration with Torsten Stubelius) and, according to contemporary accounts, it was here that they decided to participate together in the competition for Stockholm South Cemetery, beginning a professional relationship which was to produce one of the most important and complex architectural works of the twentieth century.
The competition was announced in 1914, but the reasons underlying it date from an earlier period: it was in April 1905, in fact, that the cemetery board of Stockholm informed the municipality that the extension to the city's cemetery had become a matter of some urgency.
In reality, the phenomenon of the overcrowding of the existing cemeteries, together with the need to establish suitable rules for the location and organization of areas for burial, was a problem that had beset Europe since the eighteenth century. At the same time, in Sweden, a debate began regarding the practice of cremation, considered to be one of the possible answers to the problem of overcrowding in the cemeteries. In the period 1882–83 the Eldbegängelse Förening was founded: this was a private association that did not have to face the strong opposition of the Church, as happened in the countries with a stronger Christian tradition. It is no coincidence that the custom of cremating the deceased formed part of the rites of Nordic peoples of the Bronze Age, for whom fire purified the soul, unlike the Christian culture, which with particular reference to the stake and the symbolism of hell regarded fire as an essentially negative phenomenon. Gustav Schlyter, the commissioner of the Helsingborg cemetery board, who was interested in a secular revival of cremation, in the early years of the twentieth century laid down guidelines for the construction of the new cemeteries, seeking to persuade the public to take a positive and serene approach to death, and stressing the profound civil, democratic and egalitarian significance of this practice.
In this context, the director of the Stockholm cemetery board, K.G. Hellström, made sure that the project for the new Stockholm South

Layout plan, preliminary sketch for the 1915 competition (S. Lewerentz and E.G. Asplund).

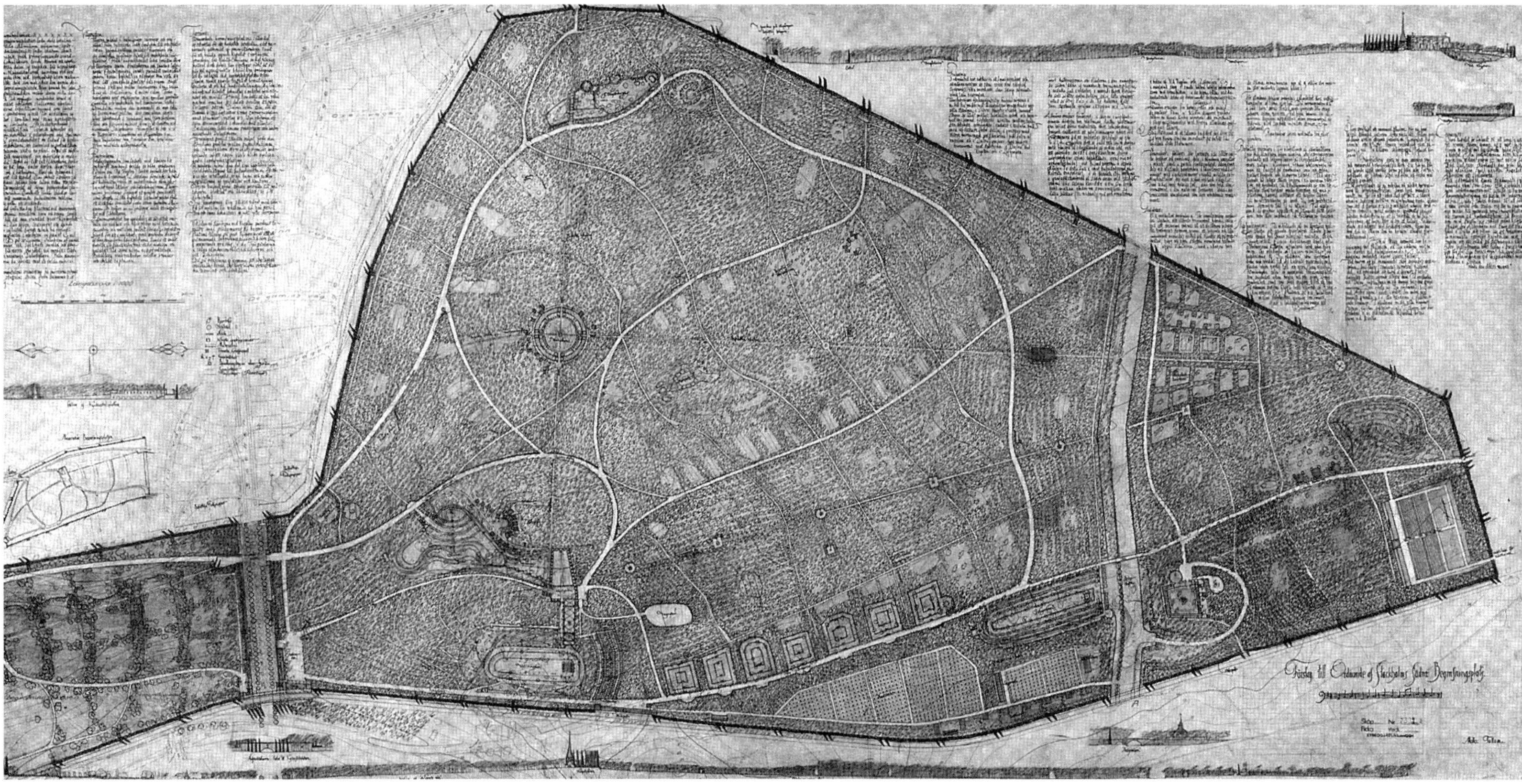

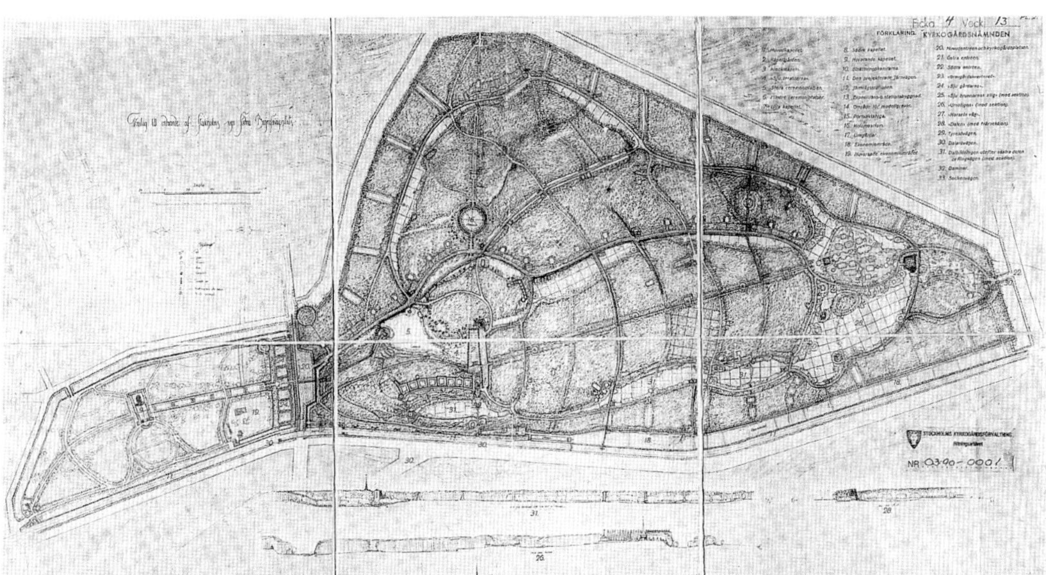

Layout plan submitted to the competition, 1 May 1915 (S. Lewerentz and E.G. Asplund).

Variant of the layout plan, 4 December 1916 (S. Lewerentz and E.G. Asplund).

Cemetery was the result of a competition, international on the recommendation of the municipality, open to architects, artists, landscape architects and others interested in the problem.
The site chosen, about fifty hectares in size, just to the south of the existing cemetery, at Enskede, in an area set aside for the expansion of the city, was mainly wooded, with a low hill dominating the whole site, and was well served by both the road and railway systems. The competition, the first international one in that period in Sweden, was announced in September 1914, with the closing date fixed for the following May. The conditions were published in both Swedish and German, highlighting an interest in what was going on in Germany at the time. They reflect, in fact, the criteria used for contemporary schemes in Germany for the organization of cemeteries, stressing that the site should be laid out, without sacrificing the artistic quality of the new development, so as not to alter in a significant manner the character of the landscape. Inviting the participants to prepare a project in which visitors would be able to orient themselves, thanks to the clarity of the layout, which should provide extensive vistas, the competition programme stated that the whole of the site available would be used, allowing the graves, chapels and other important buildings to be integrated with the existing natural features.
Among the fifty-three participants, some groups came from Germany: these also included those to whom the second and third prizes were awarded, demonstrating the expectations of the jury, which regarded Gunnar Asplund and Sigurd Lewerentz's project, denominated "Tallum", as the one that most forcefully managed to conceive the new cemetery as the inseparable unity of architecture and landscape, as well as of religious character and the primitive Nordic spirit.
"Tallum" sums up the changes and expectations to be found in a society poised between tradition and modernity, attentive to variations in style and its way of life, but, at the same time, anxious to reaffirm ancient principles of settlement, still alive in the nation's culture. It was no coincidence that, despite the uniqueness of the site characterized by forest, other new cemeteries were based on this example in an attempt to identify the sacred values with those of the place itself, combining the profane and the primitive with the fascination of modernity and an ancient sense of the sacred, thereby making the theme of death more acceptable and comprehensible to individuals.

The Competition Project, 1915

"Tallum" differs notably from all the other projects submitted to the competition: Asplund and Lewerentz's proposal seems to give the right answer to all the requests contained in the programme, rejecting, however, any preconceived formalism, and avoiding any schematic and predictable layout. Within an area completely covered by trees, the two architects planned paths freely following the relief of the site, linking significant and fascinating places. The clarity

Study sketch for the Way of the Cross, 1915 competition.

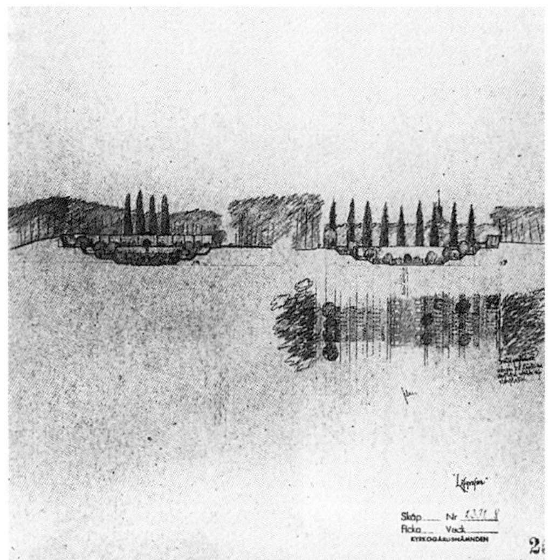

Study drawings for the layout of burial areas.

Study for the burial area in the woods, photomontage.

required by the competition conditions was not banally interpreted with axes and prospects cutting across the site, but rather through the disposition of features that, like stones left in order to find a path one has already walked along, follow each other in sequences rich in symbolic meanings. From the entrance, located on the road dividing the new development from the north cemetery, a number of paths branch out, some narrower, others slightly more evident on the continuous carpet of grass flooring the woodlands as they follow the curves of the contours in a quest for effects of light and shade that, amidst the tall trees, continue to change according to the time of day. Some of these paths suddenly become more prominent, clearly the result of man's intervention: these are routes having a stronger ritual significance linking important points.
Buildings as such are reduced to a minimum and, with the exception of just a few, such as the crematorium tower, visible from the entrance, they reveal themselves little by little. Sign of human presence, are, however, the natural features that have been redesigned and organized in accordance with precise rules. Although harmonizing with their setting, they evoke either archetypal memories, such as the family tombs consisting of earthen mounds like primitive graves, or classical symbols such as the Way of the Urns or the forecourt of the chapel where busts alternate with soaring trees. The whole scheme is interspersed with a number of places having a more secular air, closer to pagan ritual, and others intended for a more monumental representation, obtained by the free use of architectural elements forming part of a classical language. Although there is never romantic or decadent complacency, at times the two architects make use of the *mise en scène* and the construction of fragments of landscape aimed at highlighting parts having a particular significance. The most emblematic place is the main chapel, inspired by Lewerentz and Stubelius's project for the crematorium of Helsingborg. Located near the top of the low hill near the entrance, it may be reached by a path called the Way of the Cross that follows the contours of the land and is marked by a long row of trees. Standing in the lee of one of the sides of the hill, the building extends westwards towards the rise where, conforming to the existing topography, there is a large open area from which it is possible to reach the crypt. The chapel is constructed on an east-west axis and, in front of the entrance, at the east end, there is a forecourt; intended for the burial of famous people, this may also be used for open-air ceremonies. On one side of the Way of the Cross lies the "valley", a place for open-air ceremonies, with a catafalque in the lowest part and seats for the mourners along the side of the hill. The slope linking this place to the chapel garden is divided into seven terraces where chapels and tombs are located. The rest of the scheme extends over the whole available space, comprising various places intended for different functions. Those of particular importance include: the long rectilinear axis called Seven Wells, which, in the subsequent versions, acquired greater importance; the series of Seven Gardens; and the area for family tombs. The jury only raised two objections to the project: the excessive "monotony" due to the fact that there were no clearings in the wood, thus preventing the creation of an alternation between light and shade, which led to fears that an excessive sense of oppression would be caused in the longer processions; and the entrance, which was well sited with regard to the existing north side, but not sufficiently highlighted.

Proposals for a New Version (Revision of the Project)
On the basis of the jury's recommendations, in eighteen months the two architects prepared a new project in which there were a number of evident variations, although these respected the original spirit of the scheme. The revision of 1916 comprised three treeless areas, in contrast to the dense woodland covering most of the site, and the introduction of a wide monumental entrance, while it was also intended to redesign the front facing the road of the north cemetery. Although still based on gentle curves, the layout of the paths and roads appears to be more rigid and orderly; in particular, the secondary roads divide up the burial areas in a more uniform manner. The perimeter is redesigned by inserting a service road around the edge, while the road running across the cemetery in the first scheme, dividing it into two parts, has disappeared.
This version, moreover, seeks to incorporate the principles established by the cemetery board, according to which the design of the individual funerary monuments had to

Woodland Chapel, views of the exterior (E.G. Asplund).

Resurrection or South Chapel, plans, projects of June and September 1922.

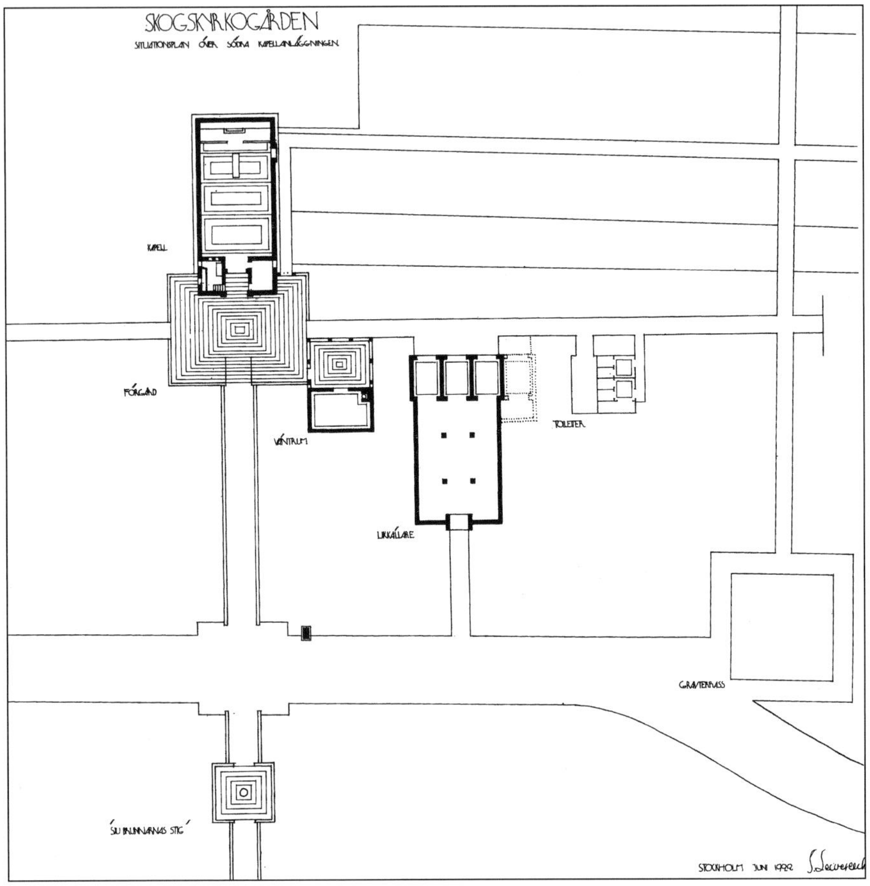

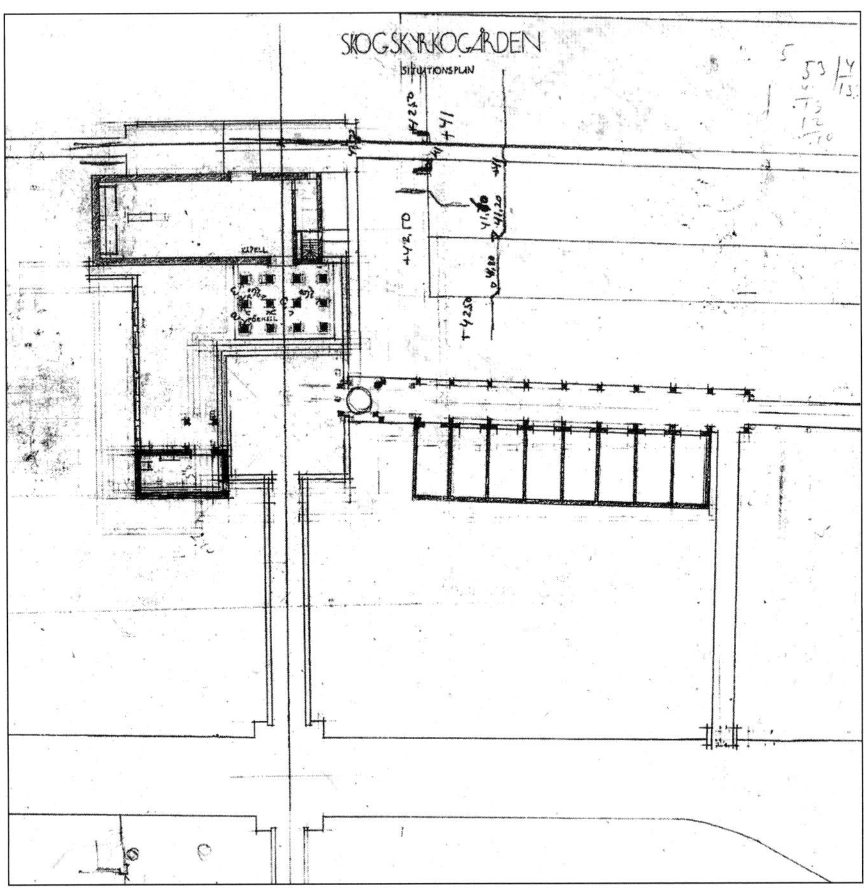

Resurrection Chapel, drawing of the complex, 1923–25.

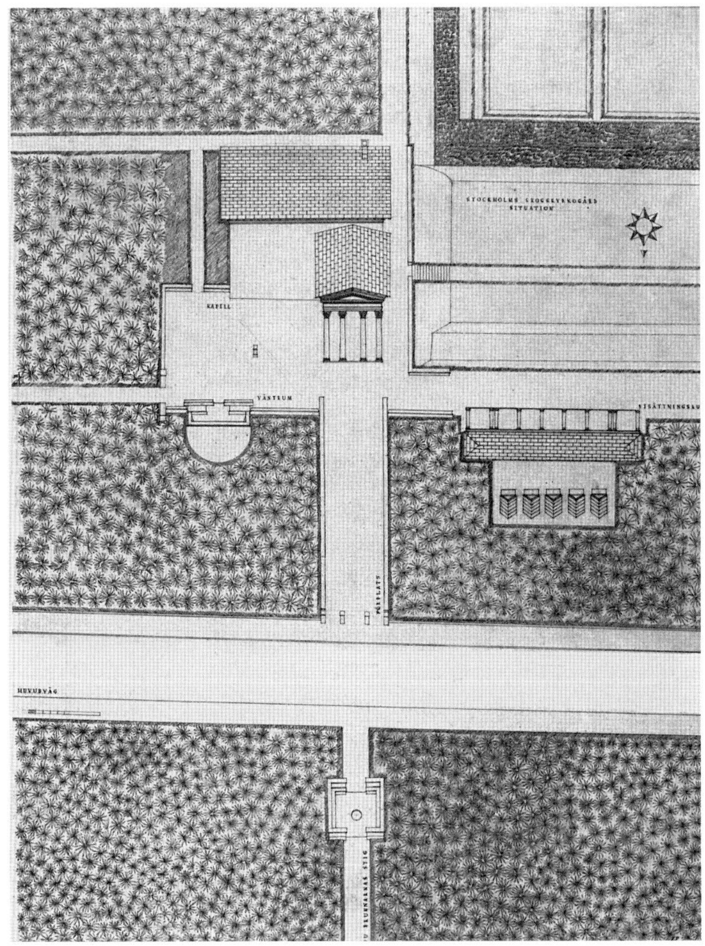

Waiting-room.

The block containing the mortuaries attached to the Resurrection Chapel, details of the portico and general view.

Resurrection Chapel,
plan and west elevation,
1923–25.

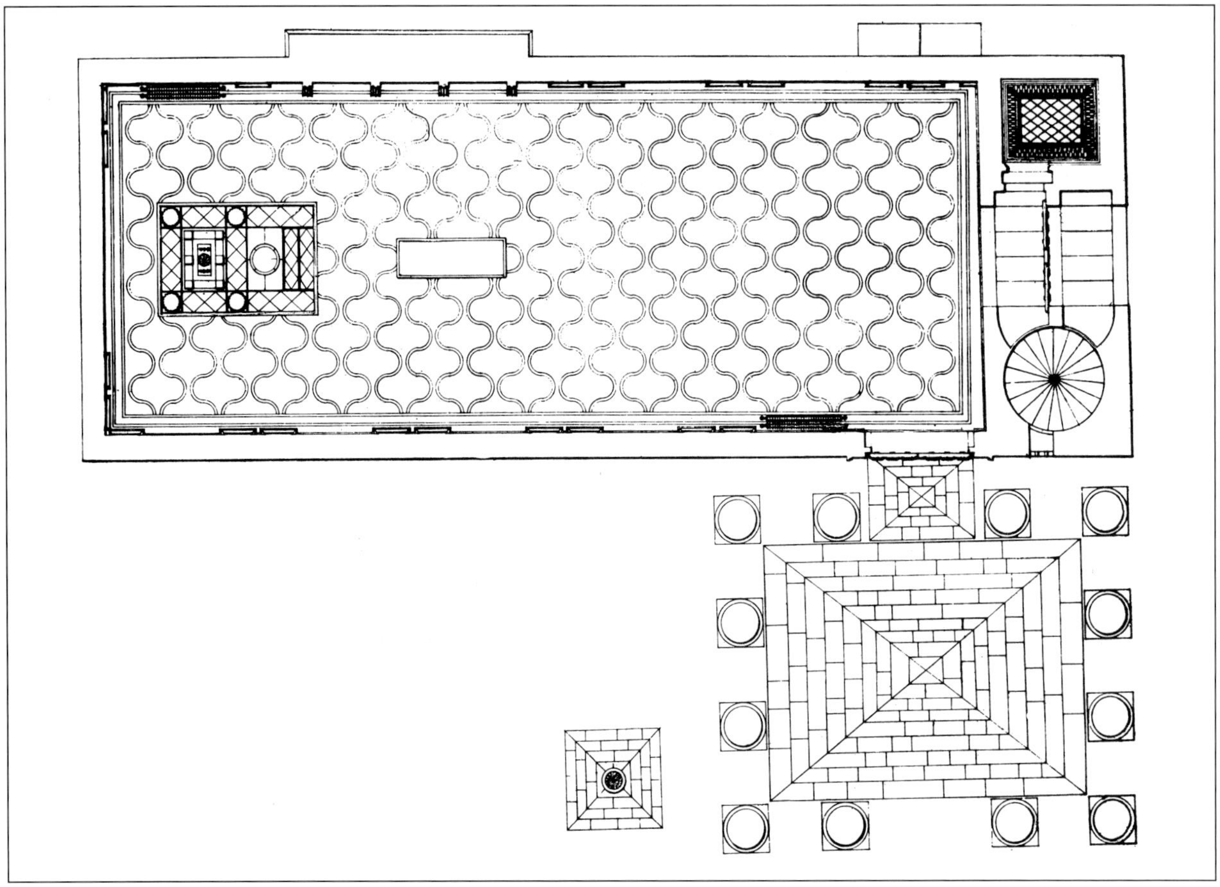

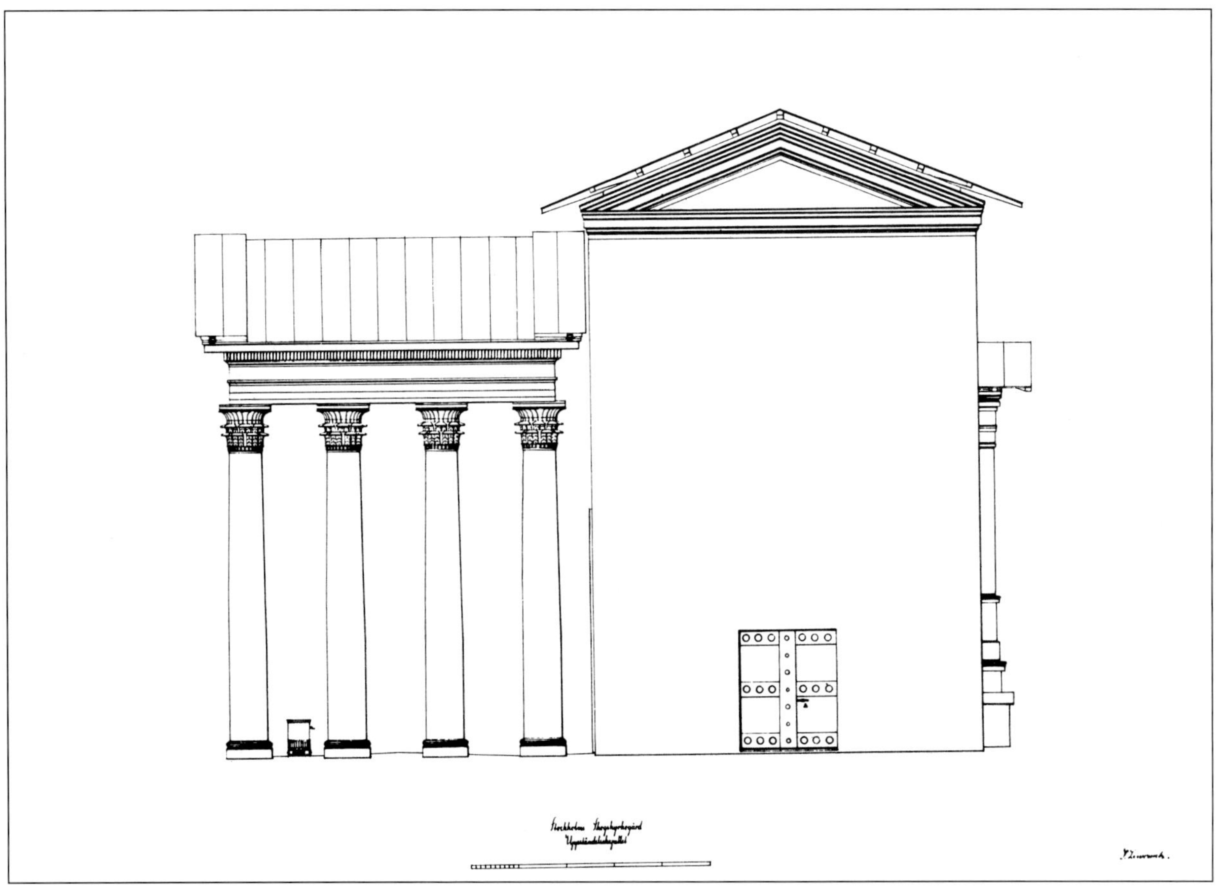

Longitudinal section and north elevation.

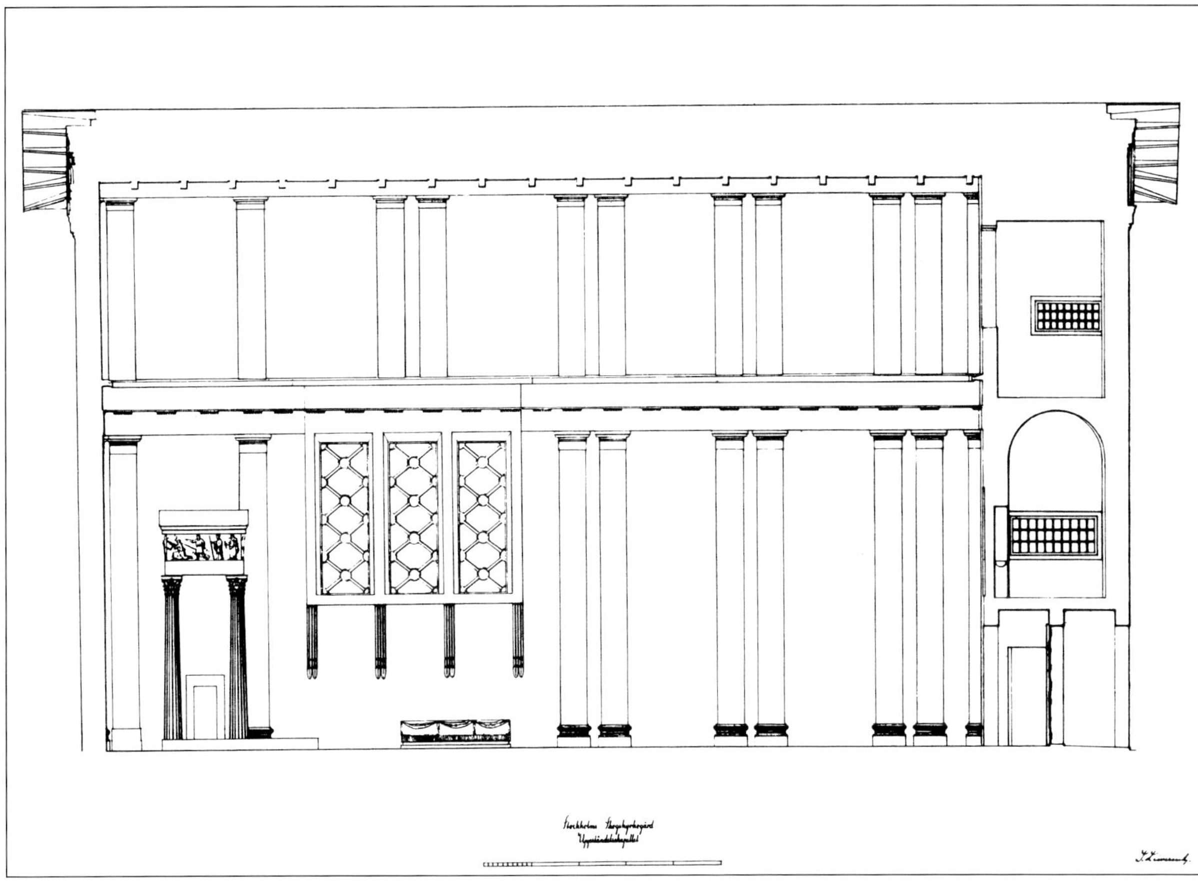

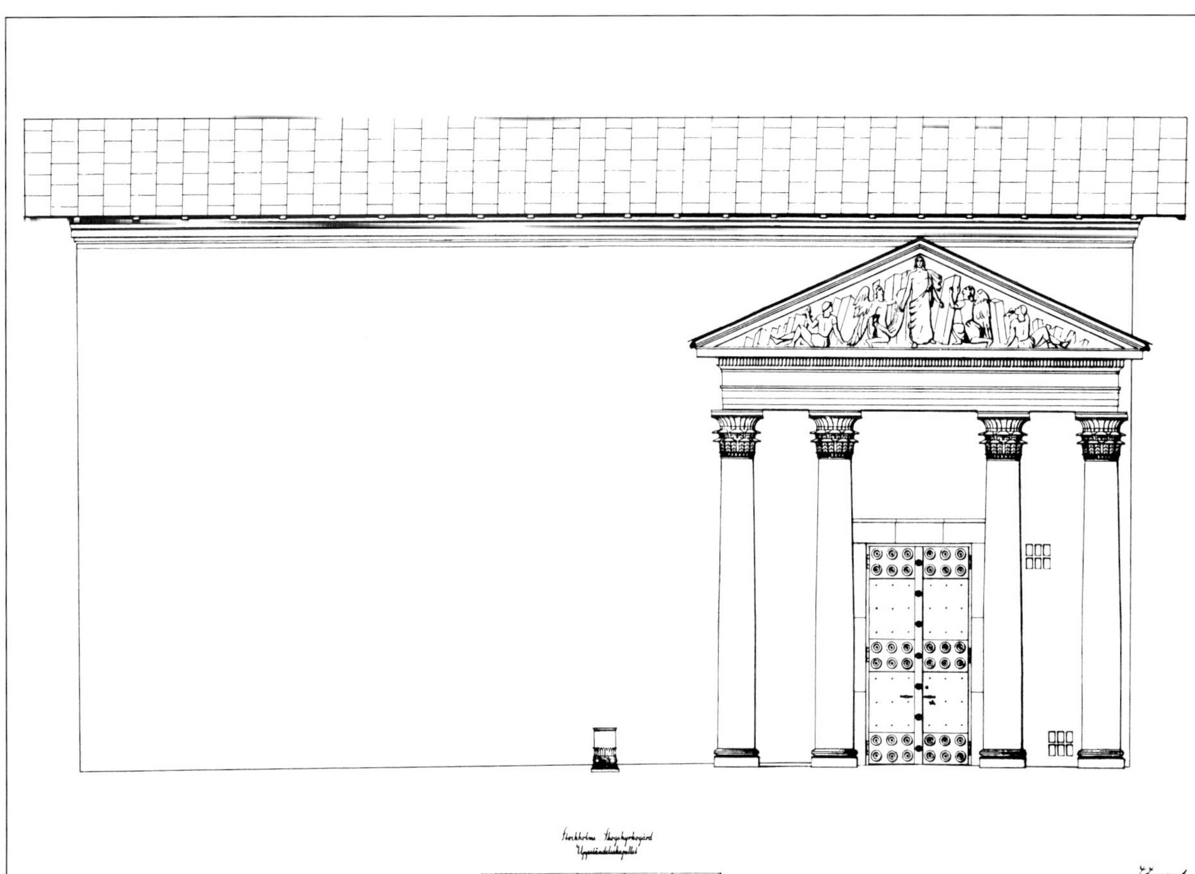

Resurrection Chapel, cross section and south elevation, 1923–25.

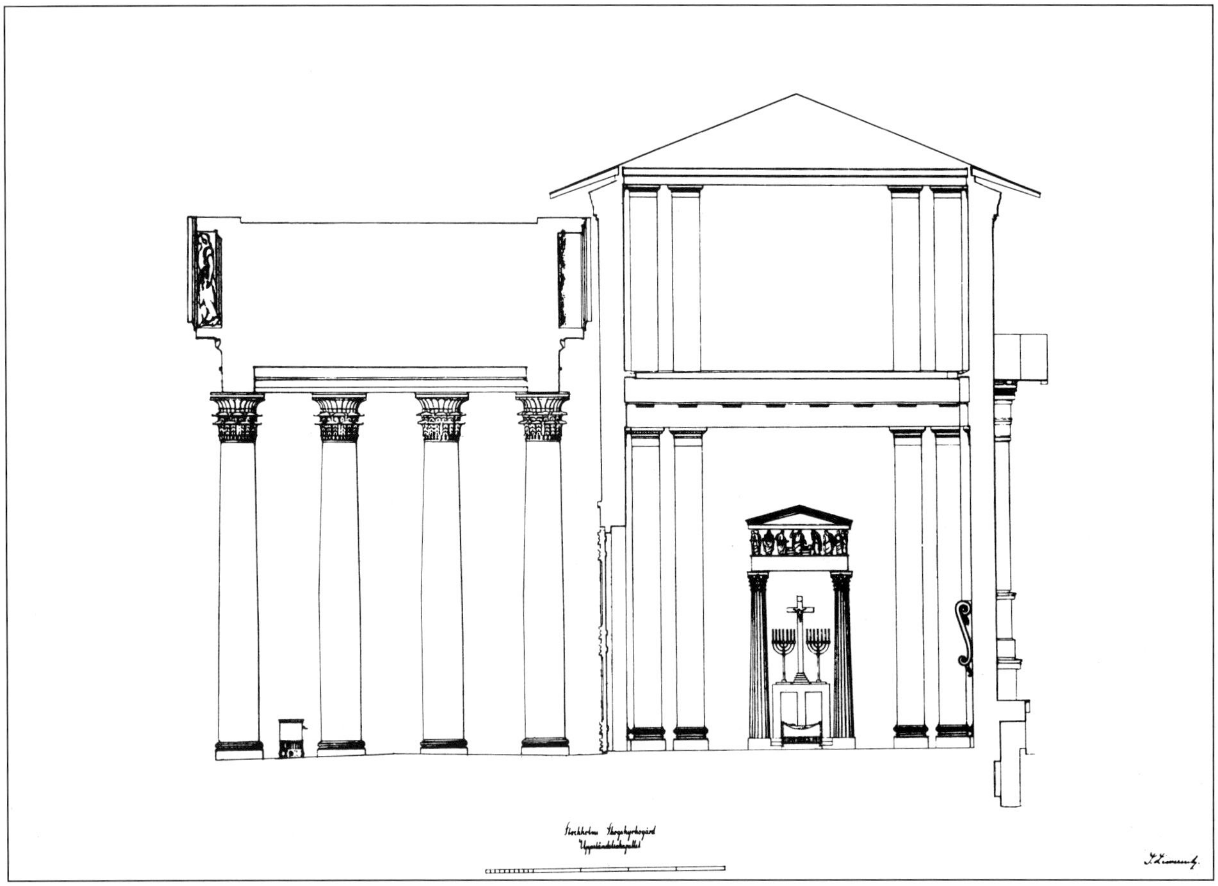

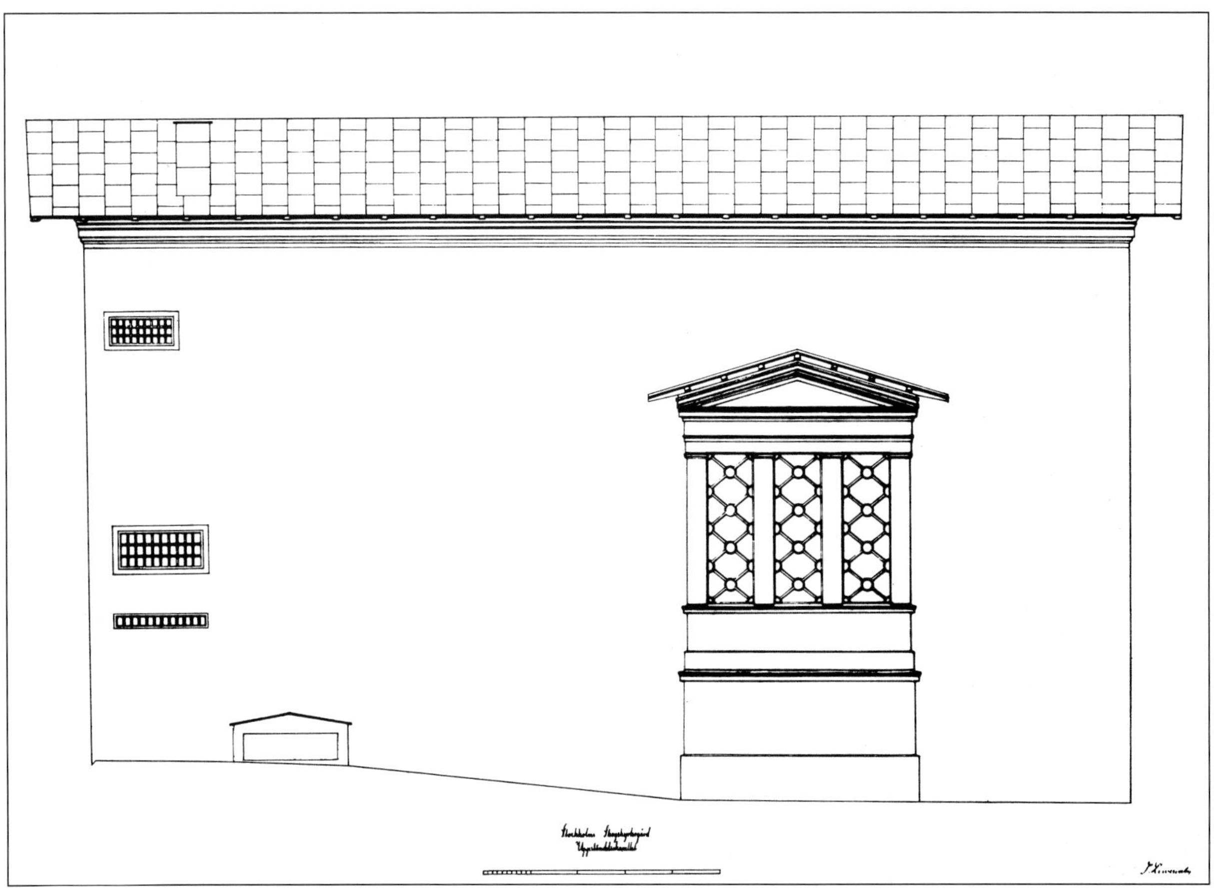

conform to the tone and general aspect of their setting. The decision to impose an organic sense of place on the character of each tomb arose from the need to create order and restore quality to the practice of designing funerary monuments, a theme that Lewerentz and Asplund worked on as consultants in 1916; they were then the winners of a competition announced in 1919 for the design of prototypes of tombs. In 1918 the cemetery board asked the two architects to examine the theme of the entrance and design a small chapel, which was to be realized in a short period of time. Lewerentz devoted himself to the study of the entrance, exploring, for the first time, the theme of the exedra on the principal road from which an oblique axis branched off. In this scheme the compositional structure comprised a series of features to be observed in a sequence, but not from the planned rectilinear route, which culminated

in the small chapel designed by Asplund. The latter, however, having just got married, left for his honeymoon in Denmark, postponing the beginning of the study. On his return, in agreement with the authorities, it was decided that the site Lewerentz had chosen on the rise, at the end of the entrance road, should be set aside for a more important chapel, to be constructed in more durable materials, and the small chapel would, therefore, be built on a more marginal site, leaving it to commune with nature without making its presence over-obvious. It was from these premises that Asplund's celebrated Woodland Chapel was born; this was consecrated, together with the cemetery, in September 1920. Between the 1918 version, in which, among other things, the pathways are more clearly distinguished from the roads, to that of 1924, in which the buildings constructed so far: the Woodland Chapel (1918–22), the service buildings designed by Asplund (1922–24) and the Resurrection Chapel (1921–25) with adjacent services were inserted, various proposals and studies were made. In particular, these regarded the theme

Views of the exterior and portico.

Resurrection Chapel,
view of portico.

Detail showing that the portico is set at a slight angle to the chapel.

Resurrection Chapel,
view of exterior.

View of interior.

Resurrection Chapel,
sketch of the interior
of the sacristy, 1923–25.

Detail of the altar.

Resurrection Chapel, views of the interior and the officiant's room.

of the entrance, the problem of the boundary wall, the siting of the main chapel and the hierarchy of the routes.
In the first version of April 1920, the entrance was followed by a route dotted with features linking it to Asplund's chapel, while in the following version, also of 1920, which was much more solemn with a Neoclassical tone, it was connected for the first time to the Way of the Seven Wells, which, through the main chapel, forms a network of routes linked to each other. Subsequent versions, dated 1923 or 1924, show, through sketches and coloured views that it was not yet possible to give the entrance area its final layout. It was only in 1931, when three consultants, Sigurd Curman, Lars Israel Wahlman and Ragnar Östberg, were asked to give an opinion, that a decision was finally made.
The 1932 project gave a definitive face to the whole of the most northerly part of the scheme: the entrance was inserted in accordance with the recommendations of the three consultants; the road follows a route that is independent of the straight path, which, no longer on the same axis as the entrance, leads to the free-standing portico of the crematorium and the main chapel; lastly, there is the arrangement of the hill with the Grove of Remembrance, a sort of pagan temple from which the Way of the Seven Wells starts and which commands a view of the crematorium and the area in front of this intended for open-air ceremonies.
In the following years the different characters of the two architects emerged: Asplund was more intuitive, faster and better organized; Lewerentz much more reflective, methodical and always in search of the best solution.
It was perhaps these differences that led to the end of the collaboration between the two when, in 1935, the project for the main chapel and crematorium was entrusted to Asplund, while Lewerentz was commissioned to deal with the general aspects and the landscape design. In 1940, shortly before the death of Asplund, the main chapel with the adjacent crematorium was inaugurated; from then onwards Lewerentz continued to work alone on the cemetery.

The Resurrection Chapel (1921–25)

In 1921, a few months after the consecration of Asplund's Woodland Chapel, the cemetery board commissioned Lewerentz to design another small chapel, similar in size to the one just completed but, unlike it, closely correlated with the general plan. With the new chapel, therefore, an attempt was also being made to solve the problem of the Way of the Seven Wells at the end of which the building was to be located. This pathway, present in all variants of the project produced by the two architects, only found its identity becoming the main north-south axis around which the whole of the central part of the scheme was arranged with the studies of the

Sketches for the furnishings.

View of the entrance
to the cemetery, 1924–31

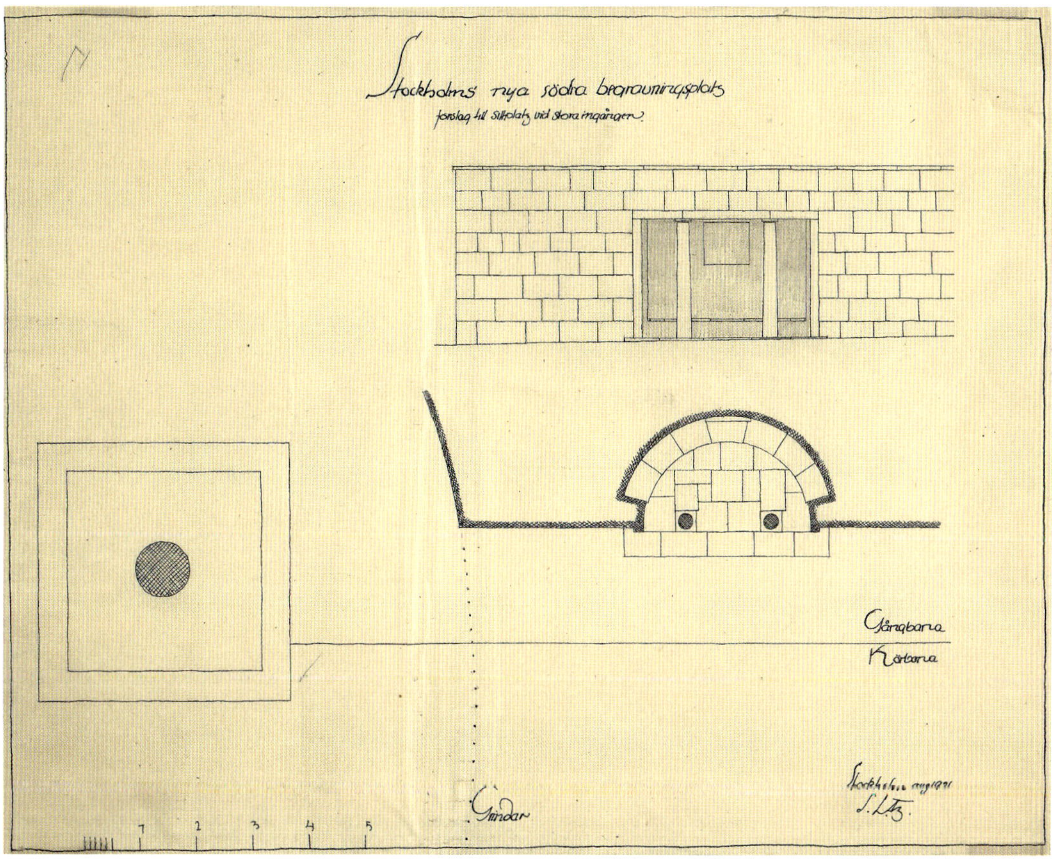

Elevation and plan
of the waiting-room at
the entrance, 1924–31.

The fountain at the
entrance.

entrance made in 1921. From June to September 1921 Lewerentz submitted three versions of the chapel, which raised a problem of a theological nature: the presence of just a catafalque, without an altar, in a structure devoted to cremation. This controversy delayed the approval of the project, so that the architect proposed, in subsequent versions, that there should be both an altar and a catafalque, in an attempt to settle the dispute. In 1922, as a result of pressure from the authorities, Lewerentz was asked to continue with the project, although on this occasion even less time was available. In June he submitted a new variant in which, on the axis of the north-south path and with the service buildings, he located an area of reception and meditation in front of the chapel. Lastly, in September of the same year the definitive version was produced, in which the chapel was oriented along the east-west axis, as is customary with Christian churches, and as Schlyter himself recommended. Originally known as South Chapel, the building only became the Resurrection Chapel in May 1925, when the tympanum over the entrance was embellished with a frieze. Lewerentz's chapel project comprises a number of parts: the chapel itself, the separate entrance portico, the semicircular waiting-room and the service block, with the mortuaries. Together they form a number of significant places that are in harmony with the landscape and the surrounding tombs. The entrance to the chapel, stressed by the dodecastyle portico, is on the same north-south

Service buildings, exterior (S. Lewerentz and E.G. Asplund).

Main chapel and crematorium, elevations and section, 1930 (S. Lewerentz and E.G. Asplund).

axis as the Way of the Seven Wells.
This disposition is, however, in contrast with the rectangular plan of the chapel, which extends asymmetrically along the east-west axis. At one end is located the altar with the catafalque, at the other end there is another door, through which the mourners proceed after the ceremony towards the burial area. This intersection between two orthogonal axes gives rise to an decidedly unconventional internal layout: those entering the building through the portico and the heavy entrance doors will find that their attention is immediately attracted towards the east where the altar is located by the anomalous position of a large window on the south wall, the only source of light in the chapel. This arrangement is, in effect, an invitation to turn towards the altar on the longitudinal axis, that is so as to be able to participate in the ceremony. Lewerentz's total freedom in his design is underlined by his audacious manipulation of the established language of architecture. Although adopting fragments belonging to the classical vocabulary, he subordinates them to the particular sense with which he seeks to inform the work.
In other words, he avails himself of the reassuring presence of what are apparently familiar forms in order to convey new contents. An excellent example of this is the disposition, inside the chapel, of the coupled pilasters, which are not placed symmetrically opposite each other, but serve to indicate how the space should be used.
Similarly, on the exterior, elements characterized by stylistic features, such as the portico, contrast with structures in which the geometric aspect and use of materials is paramount, as in the tall, elongated volume of the chapel and the semicircular one of the waiting-room. In the two subsidiary blocks, in fact, the references to the classical world are not to be found in use of stylistic elements, but rather in the way in which the internal and external space is structured.
The closed semicircular waiting-room is reminiscent of the open-air places for waiting and meditation located on the Via dei Sepolcri at Pompeii, while the elongated block of the mortuaries provides a covered walkway leading towards the adjacent spaces, rather like a stoa.
The area at the side of the portico, characterized by the large blind wall of the chapel and the small well, located on the axis of the first intercolumniation of the portico itself, is the place where the mourners wait before the ceremony begins. Since this is on the north side, it is mainly in the shadow of the chapel, contrasting notably with the interior of the building, which is always bathed in light.
There are, furthermore, many references

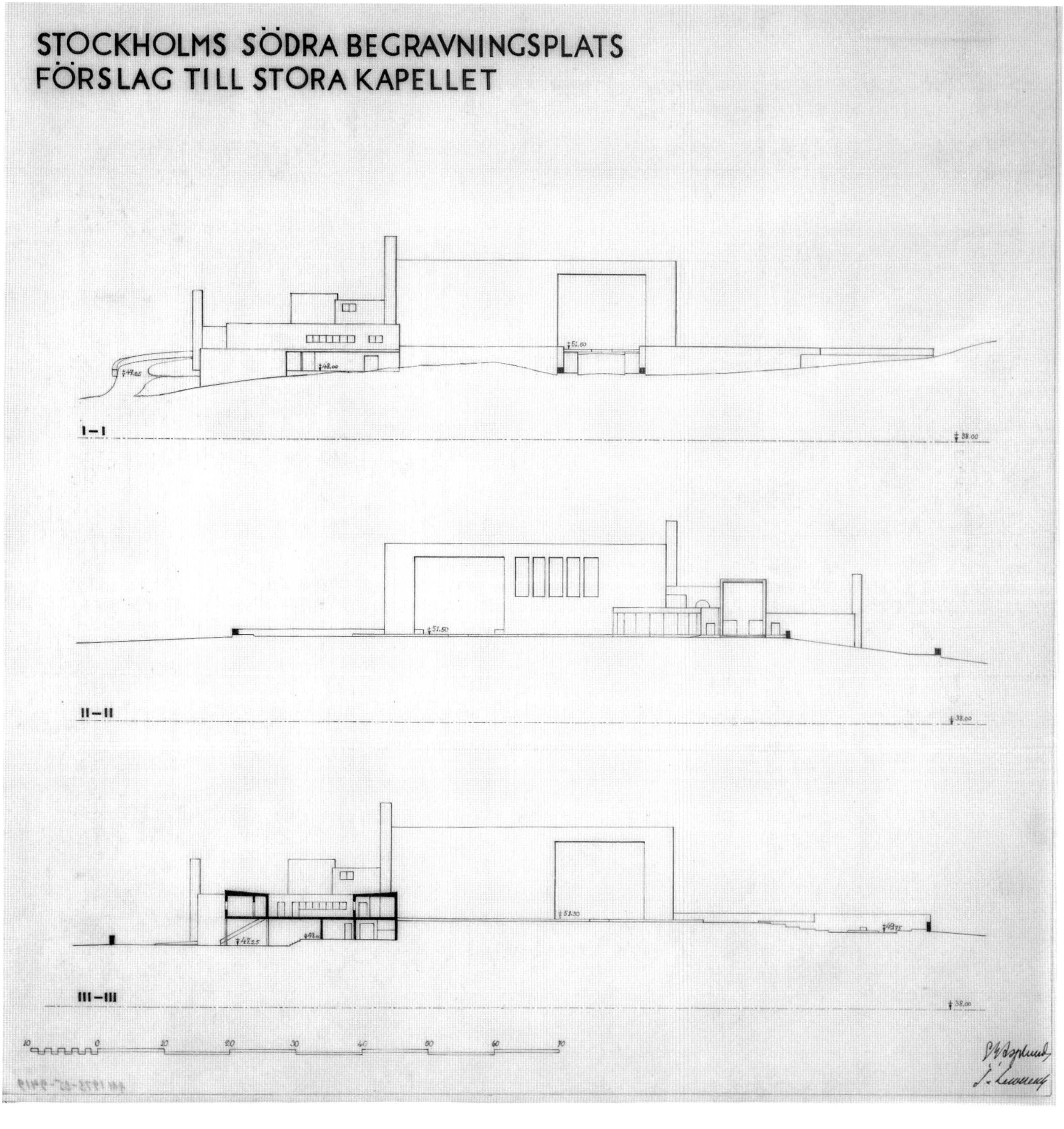
STOCKHOLMS SÖDRA BEGRAVNINGSPLATS
FÖRSLAG TILL STORA KAPELLET
I—I
II—II
III—III

Perspective drawing
of the main chapel
and crematorium, 1930
(S. Lewerentz and
E.G. Asplund).

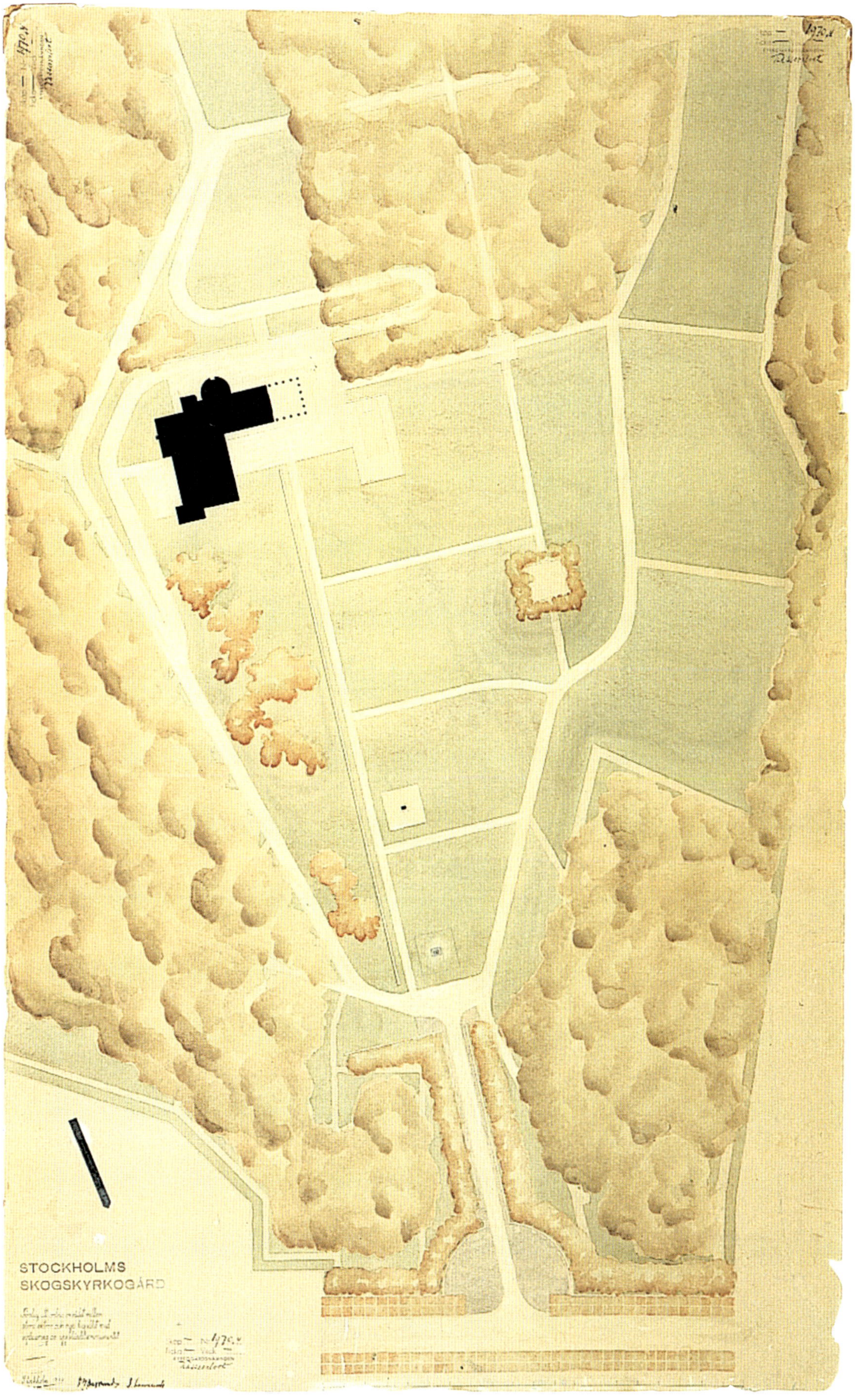

Part of the layout plan
with the addition
of the main chapel, 1932
(E.G. Asplund).

Hill of Remembrance, plan and perspective drawing (1937–40).

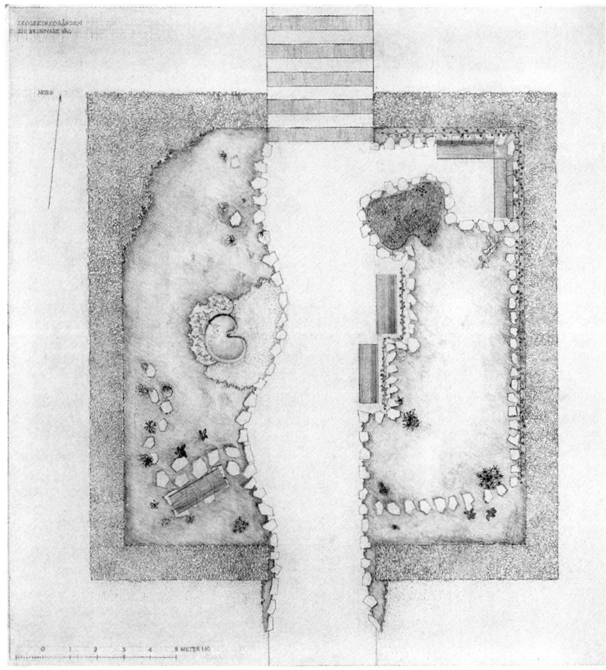

Hill of Remembrance.

Way of the Seven Wells, perspective drawing (c. 1930) and view.

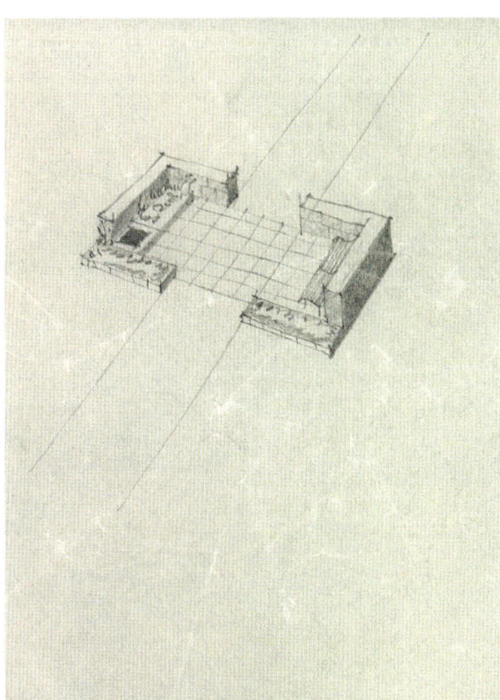

to the harmonies and numerical systems on which the composition of the work is based. What really matters, however, is that these complexities, the result of in-depth studies, although reflecting the evolution of the architect's ideas, in reality give rise to a totally legible whole, the contents of which may be easily discerned by everyone. The work constructed uses the morphological, stylistic and material potentialities of the built form to best advantage, realizing an organic whole in which even the smallest detail contributes to expressing its various meanings.

Lewerentz's Last Works in the Cemetery
From the 1950s onwards the cemetery board again availed themselves of Lewerentz's services, asking him to design a number of additions to the works already completed in the cemetery. In particular, he was consulted for the realization of a pedestrian entrance, with a gate, in the west fence (1951–56), while he was also commissioned to design additional service blocks behind the Resurrection Chapel (1952–61) and a Grove of Remembrance near the main entrance (1958–61). These projects were tackled by Lewerentz after so many years had passed with the same dedication as always; through what are often very evident stylistic juxtapositions, they demonstrate how architecture is able to adapt itself to variations in taste if it is based on principles typical of a sound, timeless approach to construction.

Chronology:
1915: competition projects submitted.
1915–19: first period of revision of project (various alternatives).
1918–22: Woodland Chapel (Asplund only).
1919–22: Resurrection Chapel (various versions), waiting-room and mortuaries (Lewerentz only).
1920–23: various schemes for main entrance.
1922–24 service buildings (Asplund only).
1923–25: Resurrection Chapel (final version, Lewerentz only).
1924–31: various schemes for main entrance (Lewerentz only).
1928: Hill of Remembrance (final version).
1930–34: project for the main chapel, the crematorium and the entrance area.
1934: studies for the access to the main chapel (Asplund only).
1935–40: crematorium and main chapel (Asplund only).
1937–40: proposals for finishings (Lewerentz only).
1939–40: final version of the access path to the crematorium and location of the cross (Asplund only).
1952–61: service buildings for the Resurrection Chapel.
1958–61: Grove of Remembrance.

Bibliography: Blanck 1915a; Blanck 1915b; Lewerentz 1926c; Markelius 1926; Zevi 1943; Porphirios 1983; Ahlin 1985b, pp. 56–67, 111–23, 168–70; Treib 1986; Ortelli 1989, pp. 55–60; Bedoire 1990; Santi 1990, pp. 164–71; Porro 1992; Constant 1994; Johansson 1996; Caldenby 1997, pp. 66–73.

(P.G.)

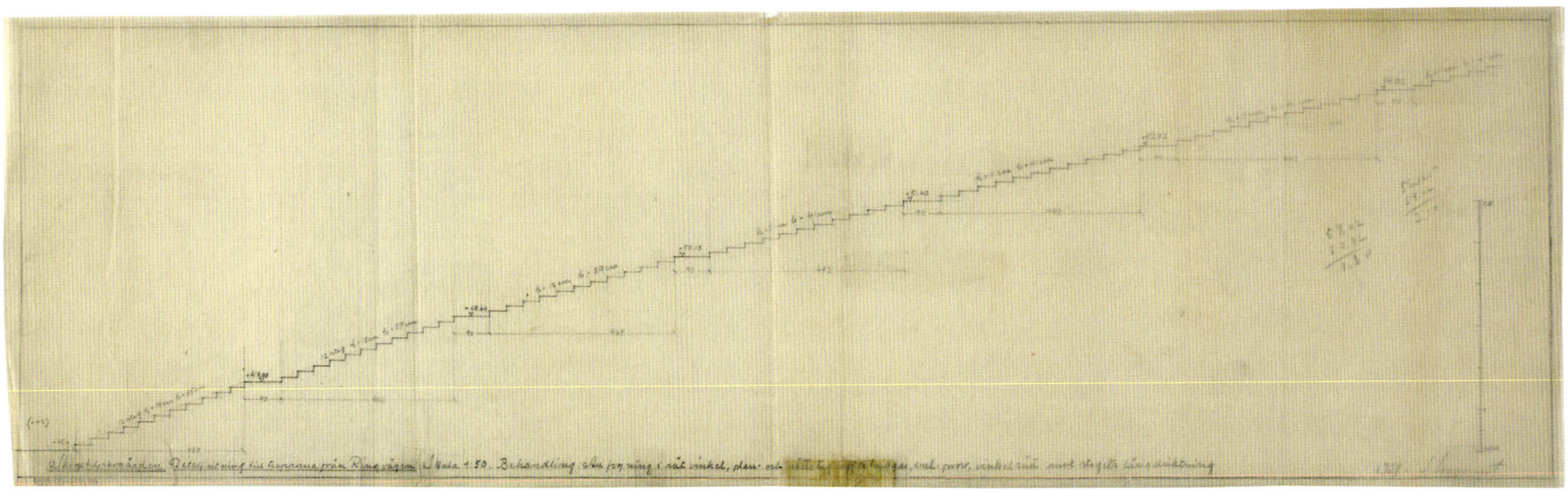

Hill of Remembrance, section of the flight of steps, after 1932.

Main chapel and crematorium, site layout, 1940 (E.G. Asplund).

View of the flight of steps leading to the Hill of Remembrance.

Views of the main chapel and crematorium.

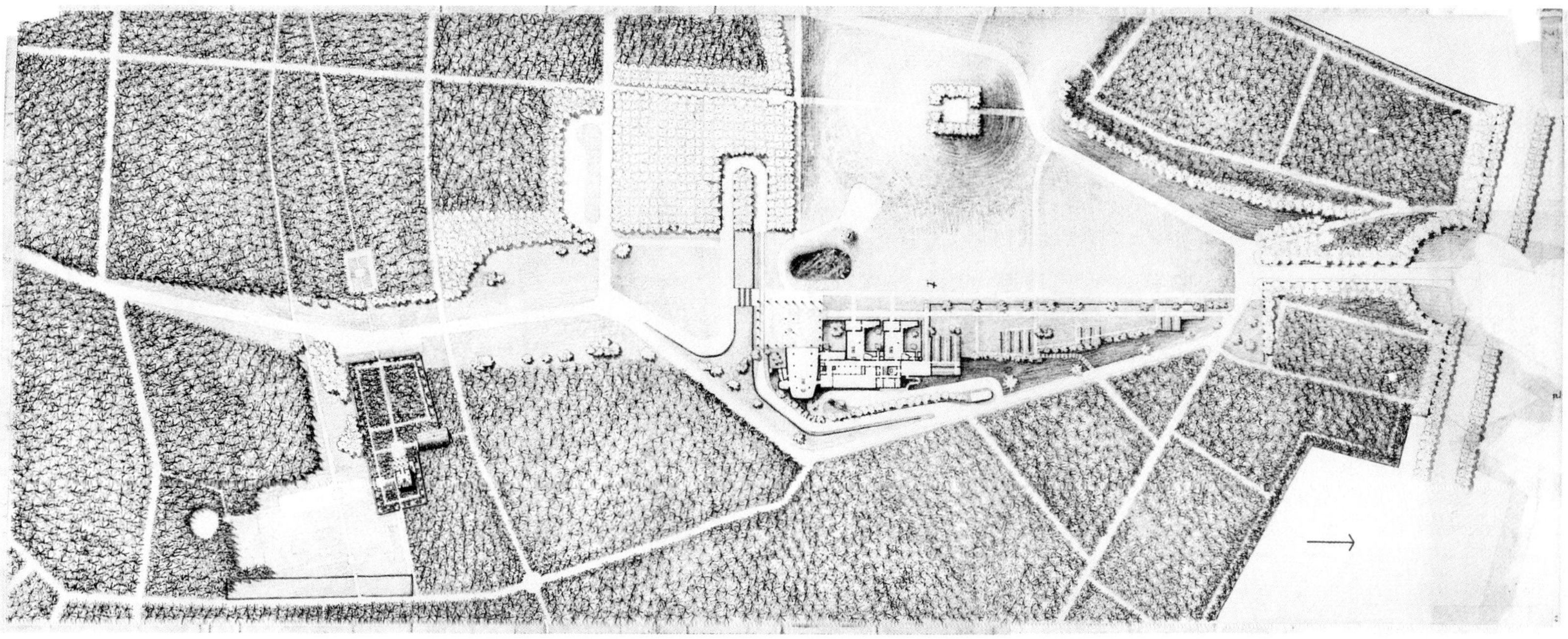

Views of the landscape.

Views of the landscape.

View of the flight of steps leading to the Hill of Remembrance.

Service buildings for the Resurrection Chapel, details.

Place of Remembrance.

39. Valdemarsvik Cemetery, 1915–16

In 1915 Lewerentz and Stubelius's office was commissioned to design a new cemetery at Valdemarsvik, to be located on a long, narrow site in the lee of a wooded hill flanking a small valley just outside the built-up area. Although the preliminary project, which was only partially built, appears to contain a large number of features, overall it is very simple. Clearly, it was intended to construct a fragment of the natural environment dense with significant features where the architecture provides a support to the new design of the environment. In the first version, a small circular chapel appears in the highest part; from this, along small winding paths, it is possible to descend to the area set aside for the tombs, crossing a portion of the hill where stone tumuli dating from the Bronze Age are to be found. In the lower part, the cemetery is arranged around a longitudinal axis along which the burial sites stand at regular intervals. This route, planned to descend first and then to rise slightly towards the end, terminates with a space devoted to open-air ceremonies, as in Lewerentz's project for the Malmö Cemetery.

Layout plan and profiles of the site.

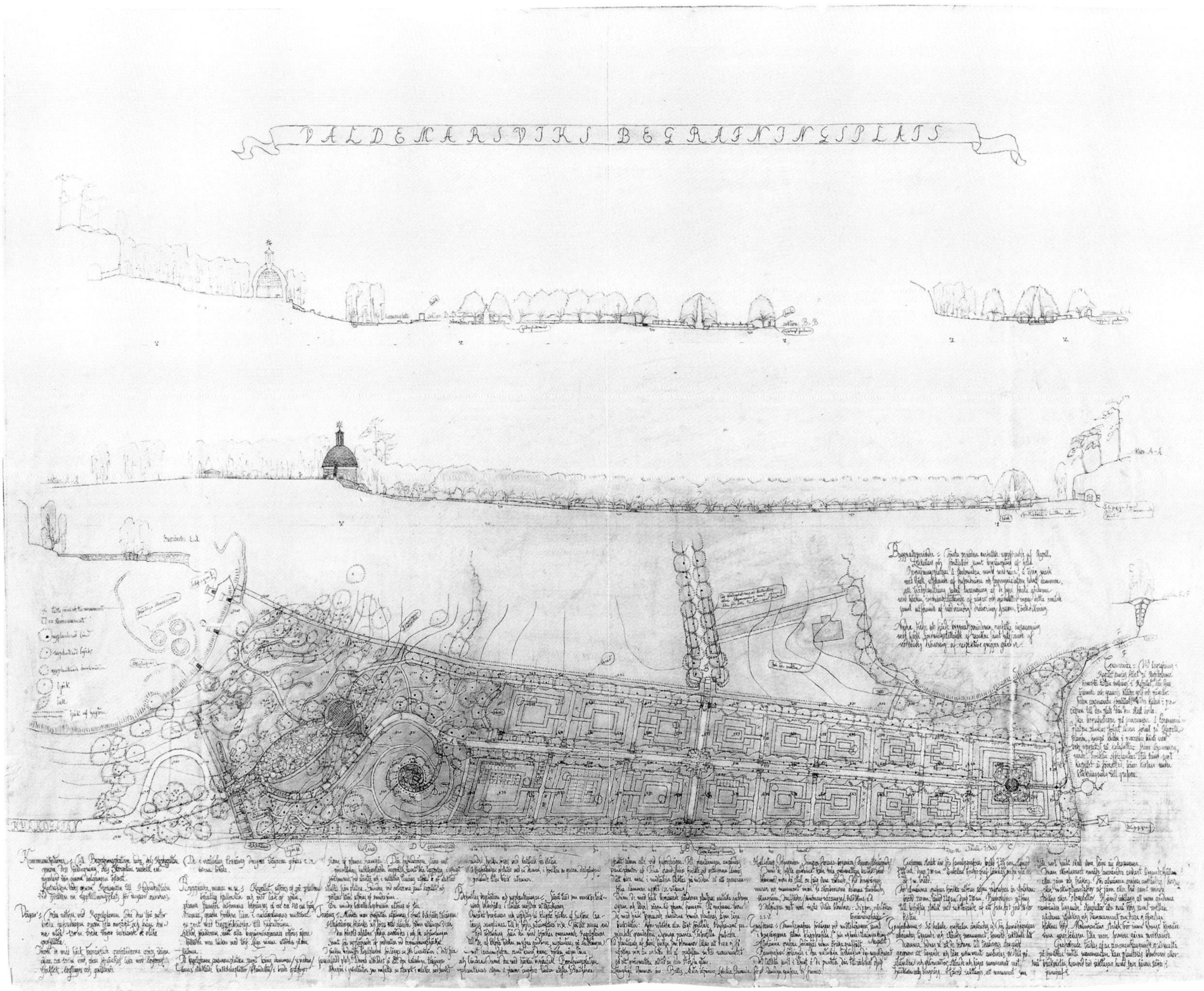

From this space, an axis orthogonal to the principal one leads to a small pond, surrounded by linden trees, into which a stream flows.
The fact that the vegetation is an integral part of the scheme is one of the most interesting aspects of the project. The detailed description of each tree or plant, and even the colours of the flowers, emphasizes that, to all intents and purposes, the natural element is one of the materials with which the project is constructed. Just like stone, wood and gravel, tree trunks, leaves, petals and blades of grass all help to obtain the effect desired by the architects. This effect is not intended, moreover, to be fixed and stable in the course of time, but is constantly changing, like nature itself.
After many variants had been proposed, the cemetery was constructed in the spirit of the initial project, but with some simplifications: features such as the square for open-air ceremonies, the pond and the chapels built into the hillside were eliminated, while, albeit with some modifications, the circular chapel was realized in the original position. Built in local stone, it is covered by a soaring roof in wood—made with over 15,000 shingles—that, constructed on a dodecagonal base, ends, as an octagon, in a spire surmounted by a star. In accordance with the original idea, the chapel is linked to the paths that gradually descend towards the burial area. The access to this area is marked by a sort of rampant arch under which visitors are encouraged to pass and on which a cross is located.
All the details of the interior of the chapel are carefully designed, including the furnishings and the liturgical vessels used during the most important ceremonies.

Bibliography: Ahlin 1985b, pp. 74–76; Caldenby 1997, pp. 62–65.

(P.G.)

Details of the chapel.

Model of the scheme.

Chapel, elevations, plan and sections of the final version, c. 1917.

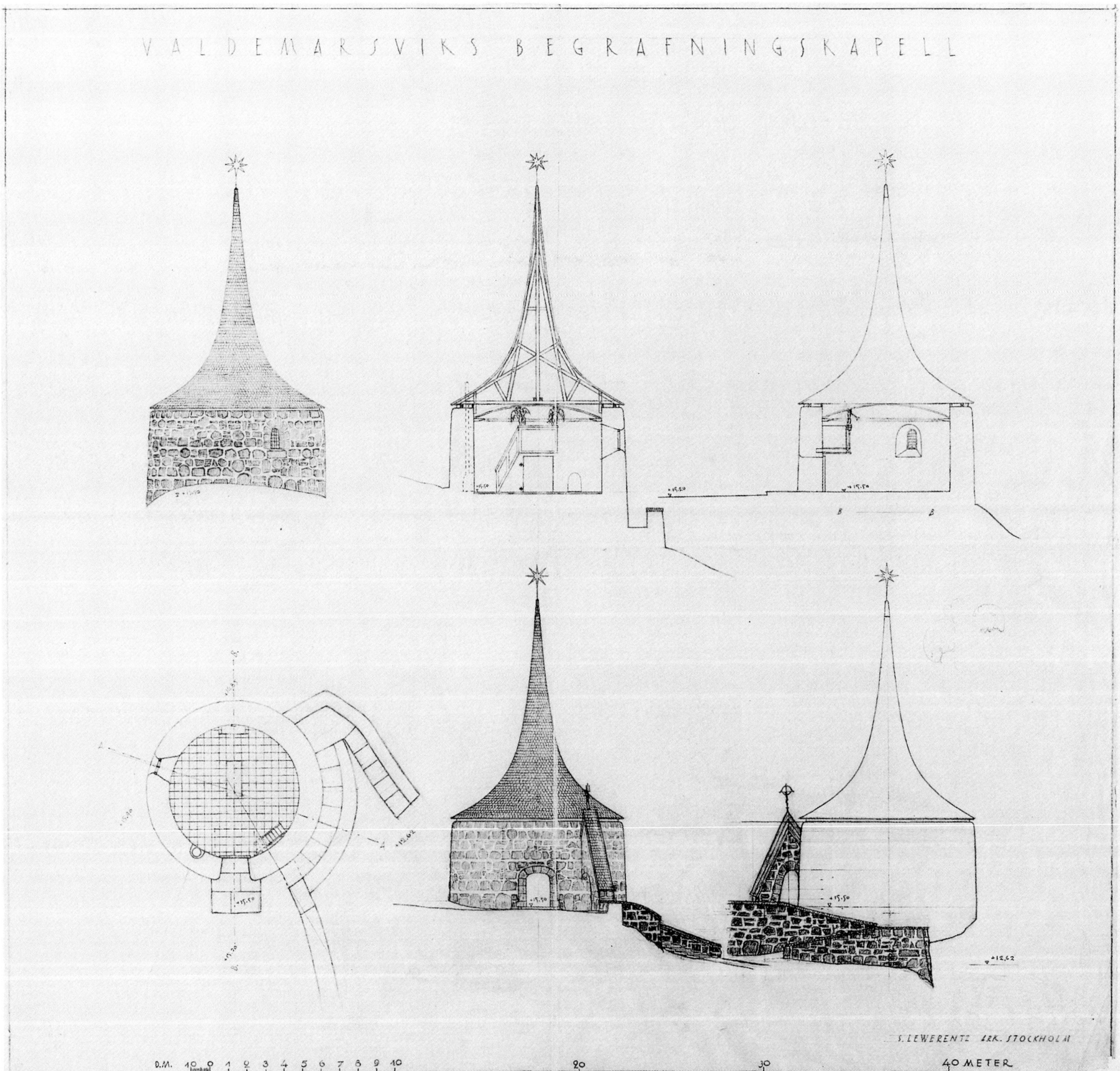

Chapel, elevations and section of one of the intermediate versions.

Chapel, view of exterior.

40. Works and Projects for Marma-Långrörs Sågverk, Marmaverken, Söderhamn, 1915 onwards

partially with Torsten Stubelius

In 1915 Lewerentz received a commission from Marma-Långrörs Sågverk AB, a company concerned with the working of wood on the River Ljusnan, in the Hälsingland region. From 1915 to 1920, Lewerentz, partially with Stubelius, designed a housing estate for the firm's employees near the Marma factory, where houses of various types were planned, from single-family dwellings for the administrative staff to spartan two-storey buildings for the workers, although only part of the project was built. Subsequently Lewerentz designed a housing estate for workers at Vallvik and an extension to the nineteenth-century power station for the sawmill at Långrör, for which he planned a block consisting of a simple building in bare brick: neither of these, however, was realized.

In 1927 the architect was asked by Marma-Långrörs Sågverk AB to give an architectural finish to the exterior of a new sulphates factory that the company had commissioned from a Stockholm engineering firm. Since the internal distribution and the layout of the complex was indissolubly linked to the system used for working the sulphates, Lewerentz's intervention was limited to the design of the façades, which he modified by making use of the structure proposed by the engineers. Along the external walls, in fact, there is a plinth in reinforced concrete that the architecture exploits, leaving it exposed and placing on it a face in brick and limestone. Furthermore, the space between the pilasters on the façade is stressed by the rhythm and size of the openings placed all around the complex.

Lewerentz also intervened in the design of the roofing, which he suggested should be flat, so that the problem of providing adequate lighting for the interior could be resolved by adding a number of monitors (rectangular glazed structures forming continuous lantern lights). After completing the industrial complex, which was made famous by the brick chimney added by the architect—at the time the highest in Europe—Lewerentz was commissioned to design another housing estate for workers at Marmaverken. The new sulphates factory, in fact, attracted further manpower to the area, increasing the need for housing; moreover, the new industrial complex was partially constructed on a residential area Lewerentz's project of 1915–20, described at the beginning of this entry causing the demolition of numerous buildings, so that it was necessary to rebuild elsewhere.

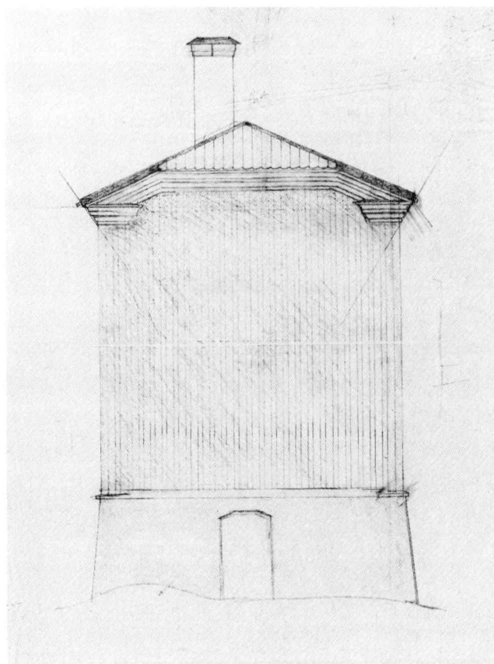

Study elevation for the housing estate realized 1917–20, with Torsten Stubelius.

The project for the new houses involved the construction of two parallel terraces, located on a road inside the industrial area, with large courtyards separating the units.

Chronology:
1915–16: project for workers' houses, with Torsten Stubelius.
1917–20: realization of workers' houses and project for houses for engineers, with Torsten Stubelius.
1927 onwards: industrial building for Ljusnans Sulfatfabrik and workers' houses.

Bibliography: Ahlin 1985b, pp. 49–50, 1641–67; Constant 1994, p. 123.

(G.P.)

Aerial view of the workers' houses.

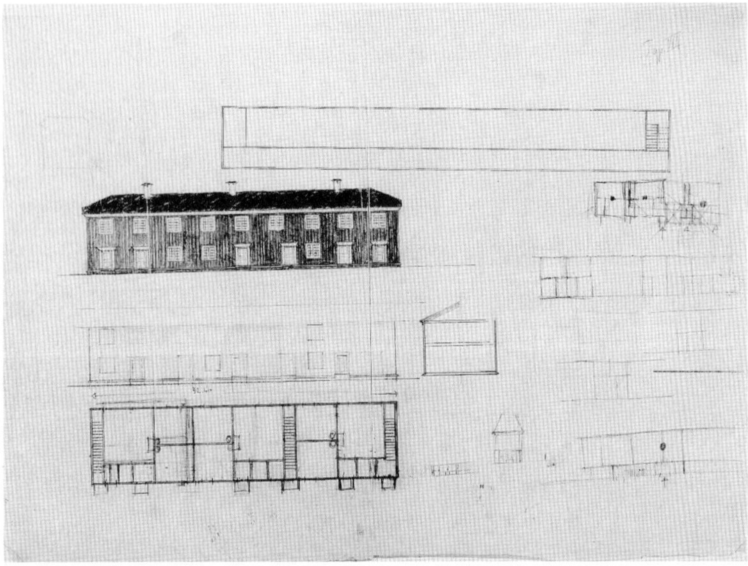

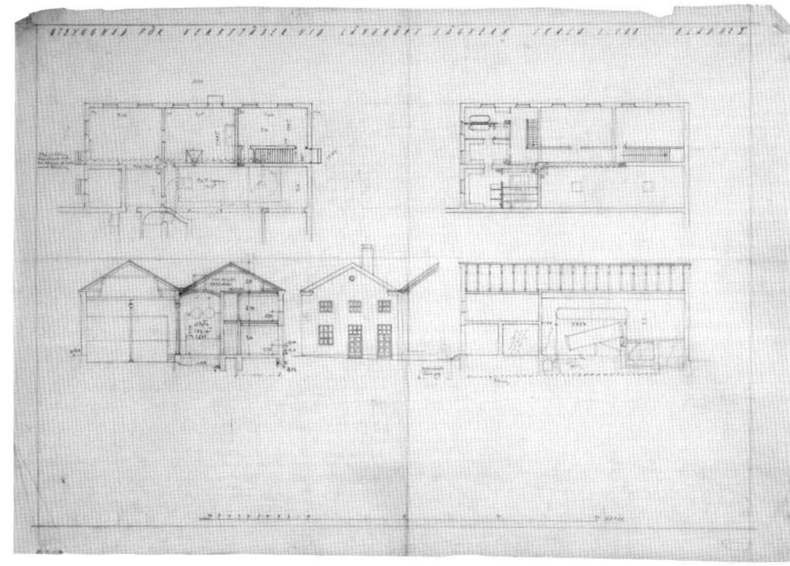

Elevations, plans and sections for the housing estate of 1917–20.

Office buildings, plans, elevation and sections.

Ljusnans Sulfatfabrik, axonometric projection, 1927.

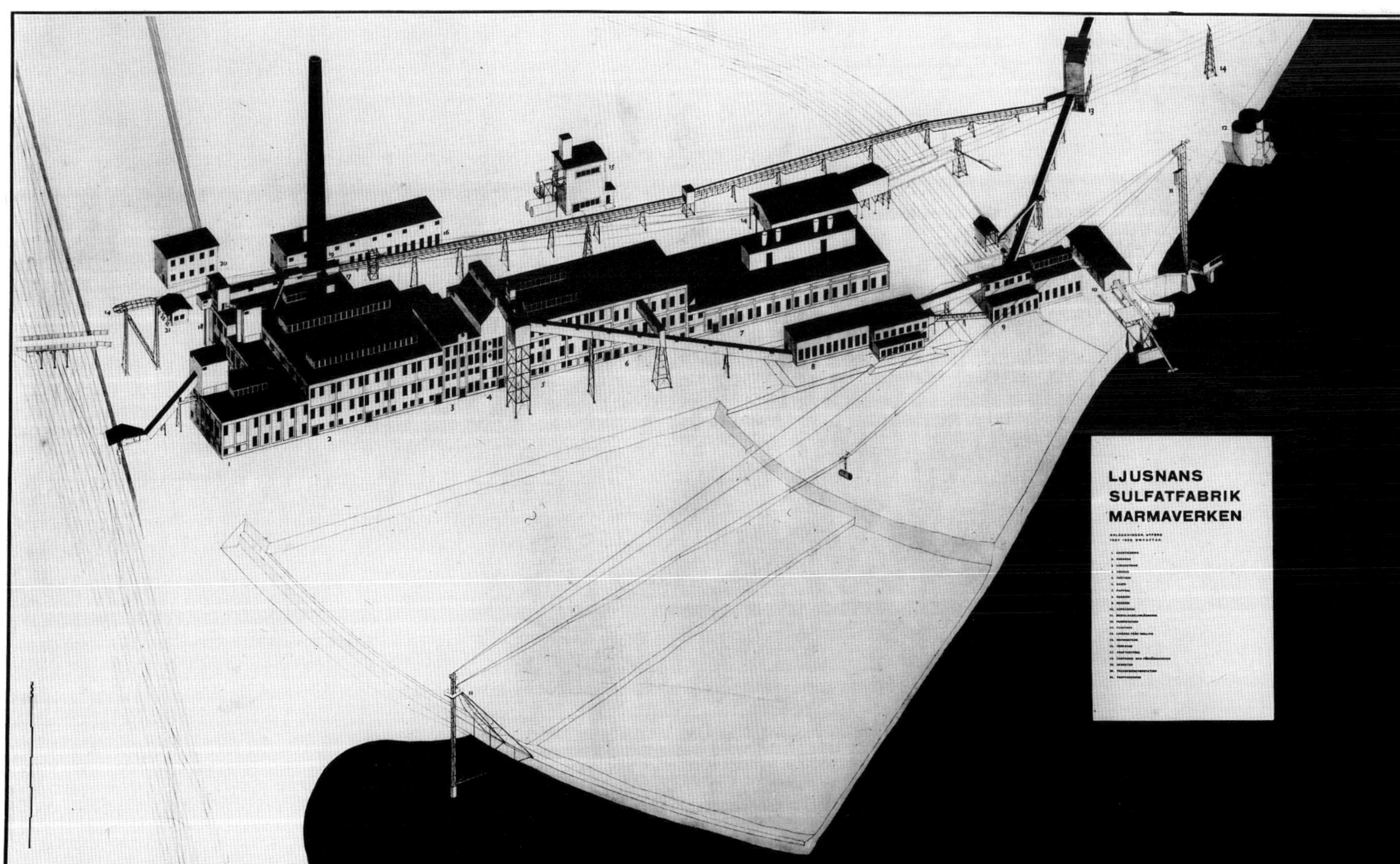

41. Rud Cemetery, Karlstad, 1916–19

In September 1916 Lewerentz was commissioned to design the new cemetery at Karlstad, which was to be constructed in the forest of Rud on a site with an irregular shape and a very uneven surface. Because of the urgent need for space for the graves, the work was divided into four stages in order to speed things up, with the completion of the first part by the spring of 1918.

Despite the irregular form of the area available, Lewerentz proposed a project centred on a single north-south axis. An avenue lined with birches leads to an oval space where the entrance to the cemetery stands: this is an arch in a long, narrow building, placed like a wall to block the view of the interior. This solution was strongly opposed by both the cemetery board and the local people, who, even after a number of changes had been made, continued to reject Lewerentz's project. Having passed the wall-like building, which also contains the custodian's house, offices and storerooms, visitors continue along the path following the principal axis, crossing a large open space—a sort of artificial valley—where the path divides into two symmetrical arms, while the principal axis continues to a small oval pond. Water flows into this from a cascade, on the same axis as the long path, which penetrates a sort of curtain of pruned firs, parallel to the entrance wall. This screen of trees is flanked by an east-west path—orthogonal to the one from the entrance—leading to the funeral area to the east and a chapel to the west. The realization of the project was delayed considerably due to the numerous modifications made at the request of the Karlstad Cemetery Board, which did not approve of many of the choices made by Lewerentz. Despite the variations made while work was underway, the project was completed, but some parts—the most controversial ones—were later demolished. Like other smaller schemes, the Rud cemetery demonstrates that, in his projects, Lewerentz took a particular interest in the natural environment and landscape. The modification of the relief, the use of trees as architectural screens and the discreet insertion of small features serving as a focus of attention, are recurrent themes in the architect's work.

Bibliography: Ahlin 1985b, pp. 80–83; Constant 1994, pp. 119–23; Caldenby 1997, pp. 74–77.

(G.P.)

Study elevations, plans and sections of the entrance building.

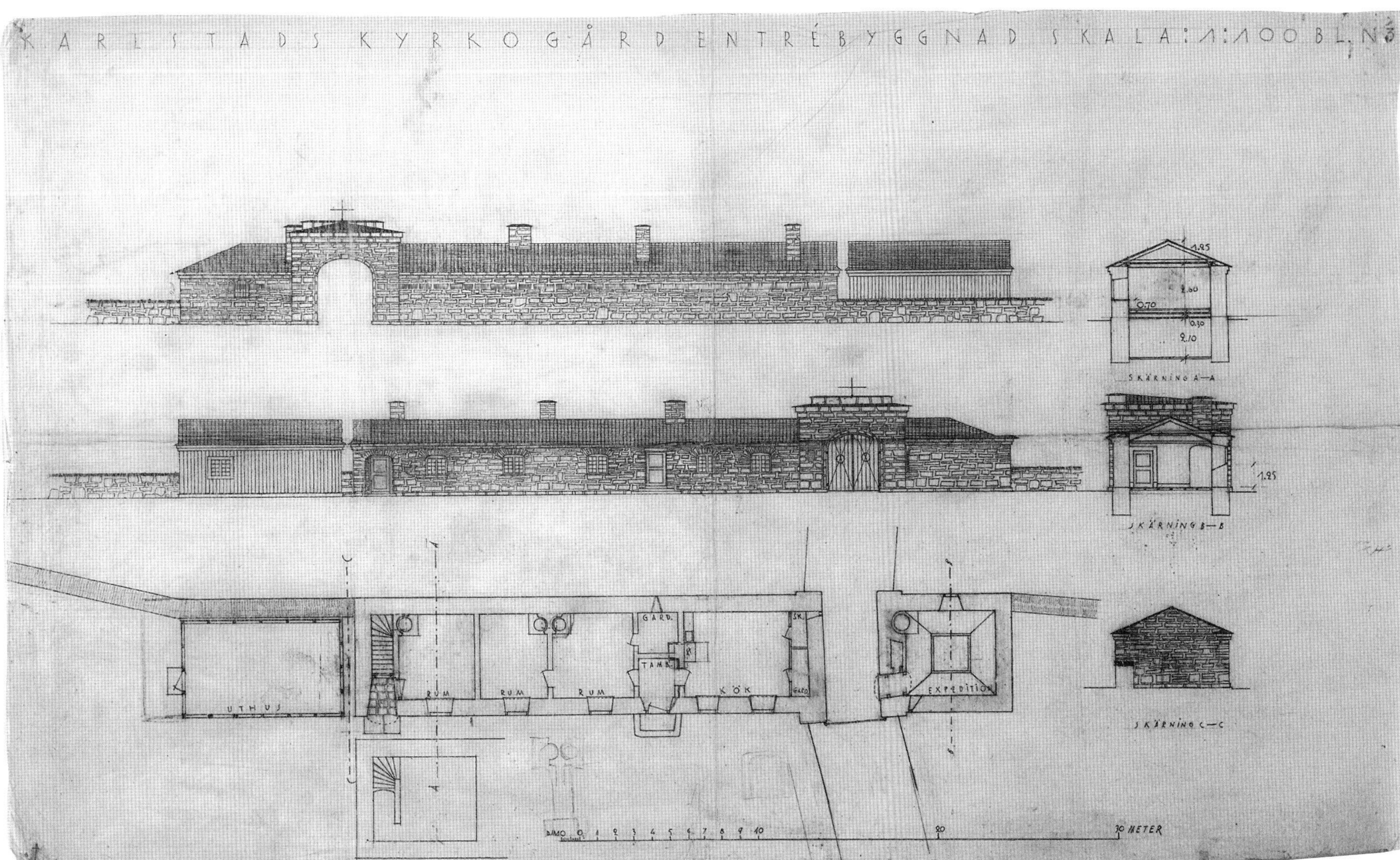

Layout plan and profiles
of the site, October 1917.

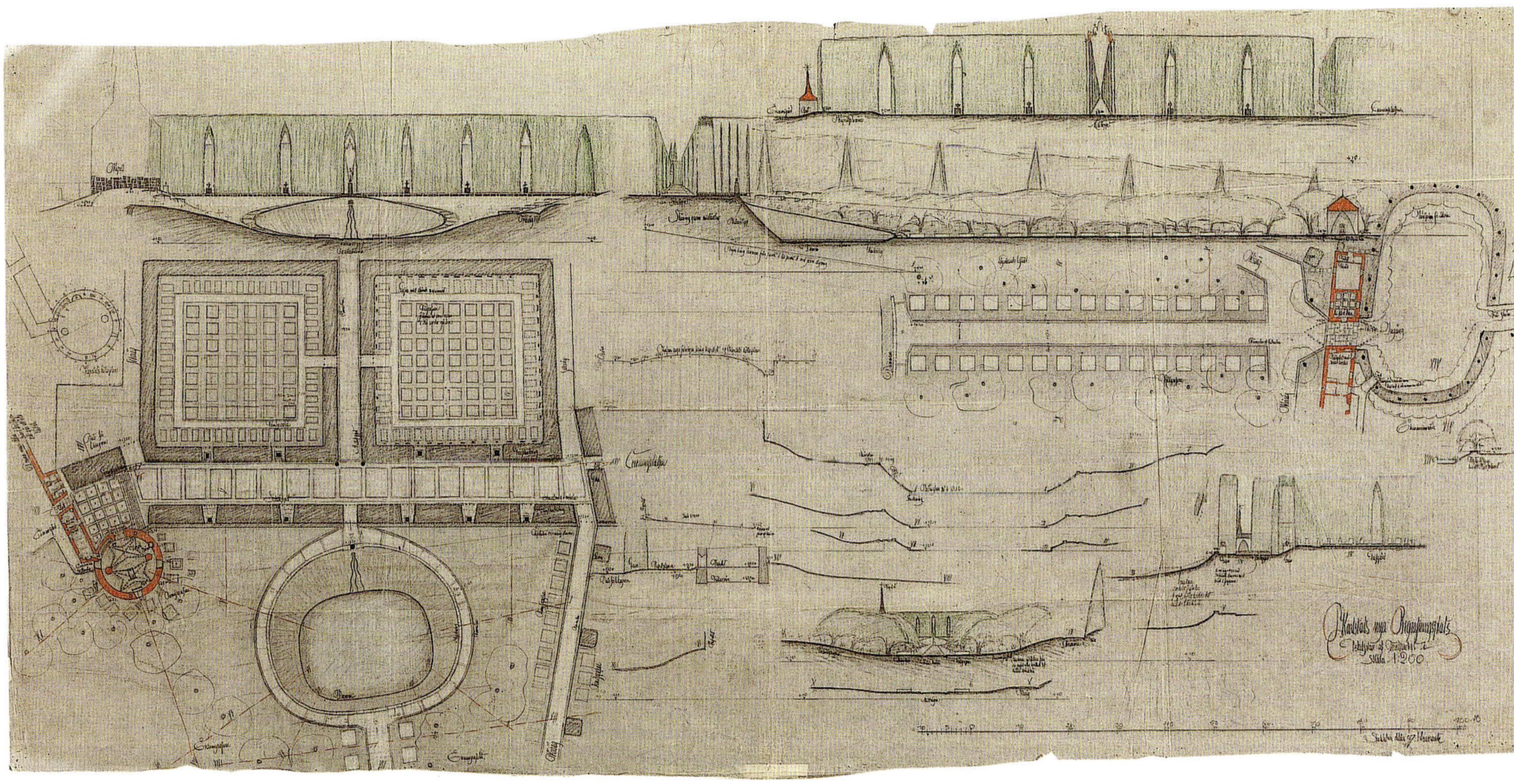

View and perspective drawing of the entrance.

Study sketch of the
funerary chapel, c. 1916.

42. Competition Project for the Eastern Cemetery at Malmö, 1916 onwards

motto "Ås" – first prize

The Competition, 1916

The competition for the extension to the Stockholm South Cemetery of 1915, which Lewerentz and Asplund won, was the first of numerous competitions and projects for cemeteries in Sweden, the concrete result of the debate about the problem of burial grounds that had been going on in the country since the beginning of the century. The story of the cemetery complex of Malmö—even more than that of Stockholm, which was also a long one—is significant because, extending over the whole of Lewerentz's career, it was a project for which he alone was responsible. The constant of the whole project was the need to create spaces where people could undergo a difficult experience, the ritual of separation from a loved one, in the presence of the natural environment, which manifests itself through the artifice of the architect who orients and moulds space, making it recognizable and measurable.

The motto of the competition, "Ås"—meaning ridge—sums up the organizers' intention to turn a fragment of nature into an element that separates and limits, generating new symbolic values with the least possible transformation of the site, in accordance with the conditions contained in the programme. The ritual value of the route along the ridge was a concept that remained unaltered in the different stages of the cemetery project, the development of which spanned the architect's professional career, from the beginning, when he won the competition, to the realization of the flower kiosk, the last work to be completed by Lewerentz.

The Main and Small Chapels, 1920–24

Immediately after winning the competition in 1916—unfortunately nothing remains of the drawings prepared for this—Lewerentz produced a new project (c. 1918–20) in which more attention was paid to the requirements of the cemetery board. The

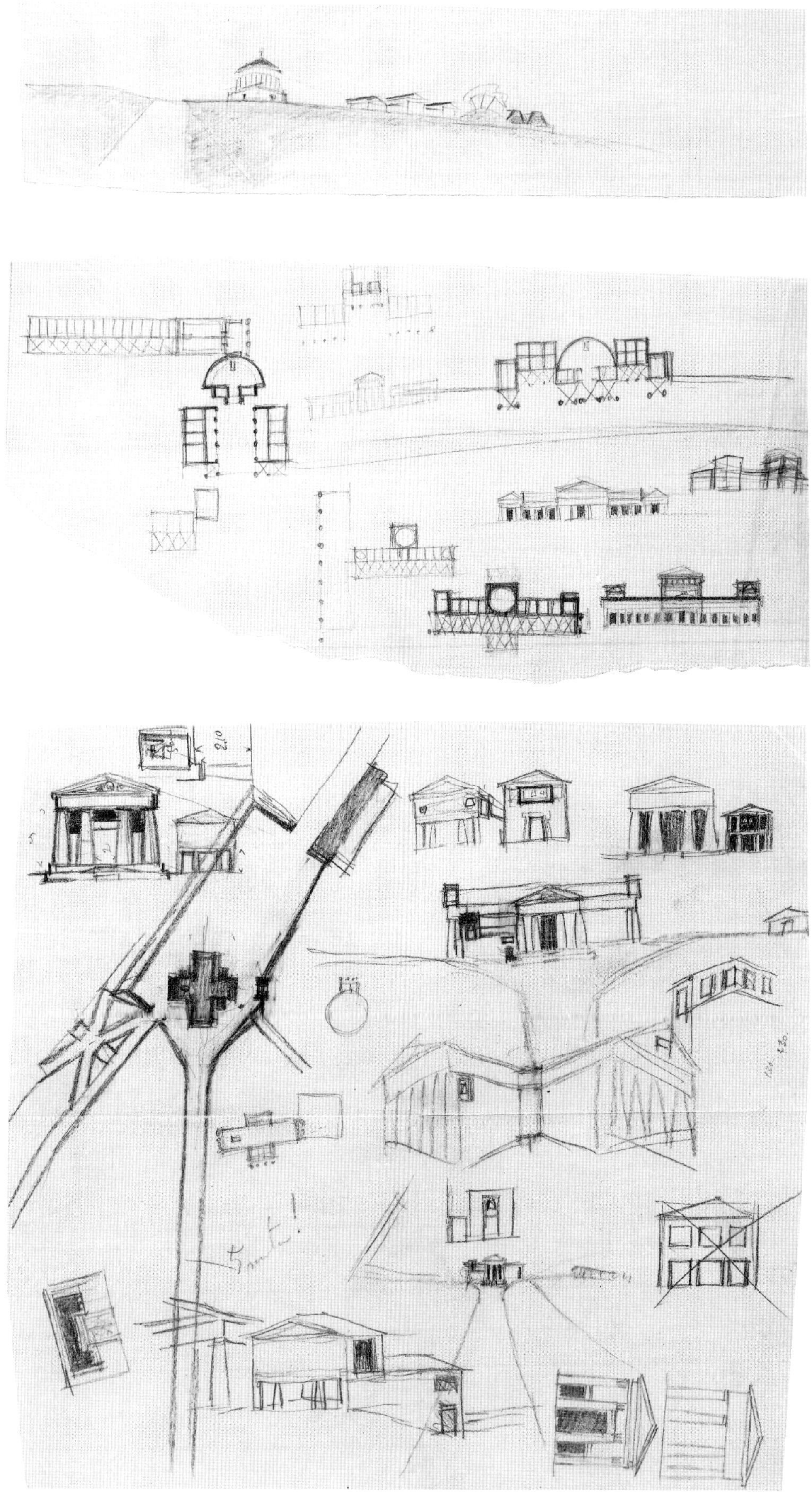

Study sketches for the positioning of the buildings on the site, c. 1916.

Perspective drawing
of the main chapel,
1918–20.

The road running parallel to the ridge that divides the site in two.

The open-air ceremonial area and the ridge that plays a central role in the layout of the site.

Layout plans, 1918 and 1919.

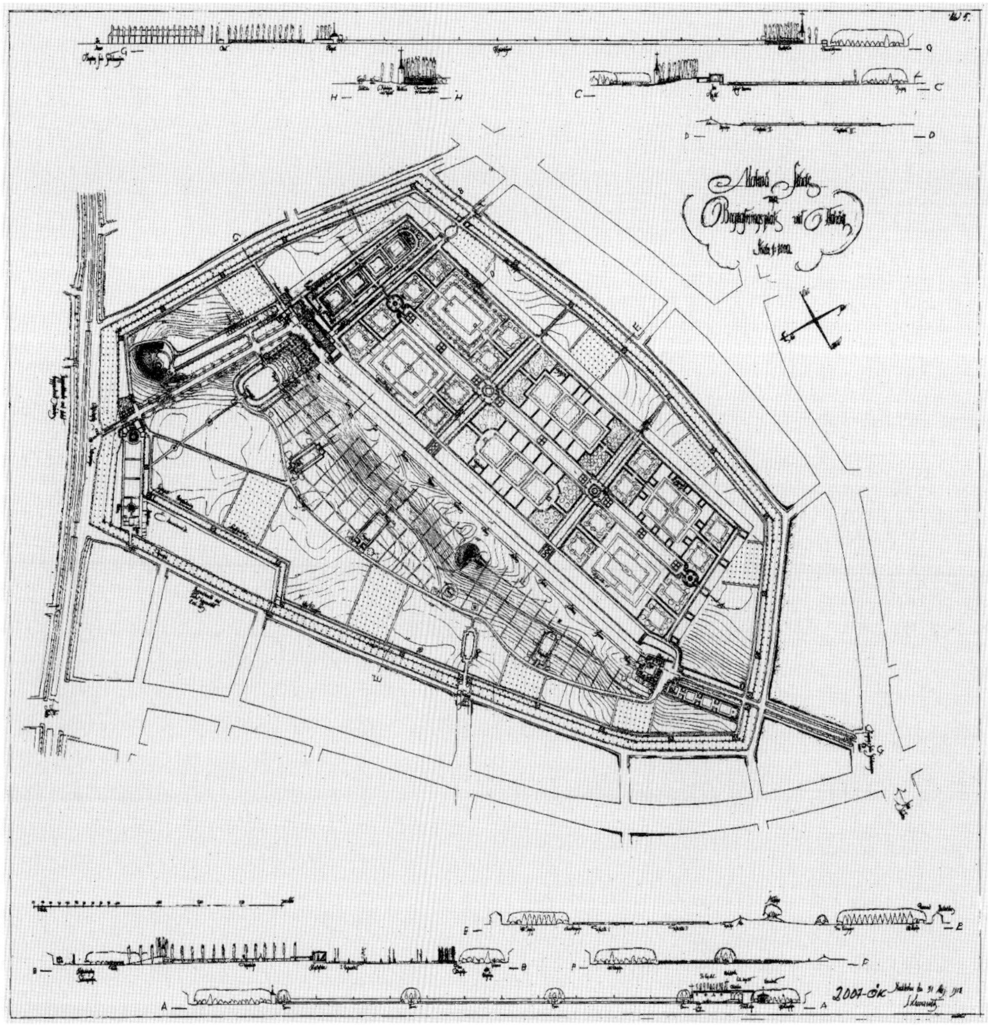

plans—especially in the design of the main chapel—display the influence of the project of 1914 for the crematorium of Bergaliden. This general layout, together with the design of the individual parts, was modified and elaborated in the bird's-eye view drawn in 1923 by Artur von Schmalensee. Still faithful to the concept of the competition project, this version contained an internal road along the ridge: crossing the site from east to west, it constituted the most significant element in the design of the landscape. The ridge, which points towards the city centre, commands an excellent view of the cemetery, where there is a tumulus dating from the Bronze Age, attesting to the fact that, even in ancient times, this was an area dedicated to the burial of the dead. Fully aware of the specificness of the site's characteristics, Lewerentz based the general layout directly on its relief. Starting from the main entrance in Solierupsvägen, a path crosses an open-air ceremonial area to the internal road, dividing the cemetery into two separate parts; along this road Lewerentz located the different buildings; of these, the main and small chapels, since they are placed at the ends, form the most important elements of the composition. In this proposal, the crematorium, with the adjacent chapel and service spaces, is sited on the road parallel to the ridge, as may be observed in the study perspective drawings (1923–24) in which the different buildings are related to each other, in order to impart an austere character to the surroundings. It is above all the crematorium—with the imposing roofs in the shape of truncated cones of its three buildings and its entrance colonnade—that gives a monumental character to the long promenade along the ridge, interrupting the central prospect linking the two chapels. At this stage, the main chapel is the most important building in the cemetery and, in the 1924 version, is still built on a cross plan, but the porticos are less prominent here than previously and the colonnades are positioned close to the boundary walls, their design marked by sophisticated Neoclassicism displaying Schinkelesque influence. However, the small chapel, which even in the subsequent versions maintains its initial circular plan, is characterized by the colonnade surrounding it.

Crematorium, 1923–36

In addition to the modifications to the general design of the cemetery in 1923 and the changes to the project for the main and small chapels, numerous variations were made to the plans for the crematorium complex. These continued to be made until 1936—that is, after the realization of the building itself in 1931—coinciding with the commissioning of Lewerentz to design, in a single complex, the chapels of St Gertrud and St Knut and the extension to the previous crematorium. Due to their very special function, the crematorium buildings form the hub of the cemetery complex and the architect was concerned with their design over a very long period: from the 1916 competition until the construction of the Chapel of Hope in 1956. The most important stages in this process originated from the project of 1923, in which

Small chapel, section, study plan (1920), elevation and plan (1925).

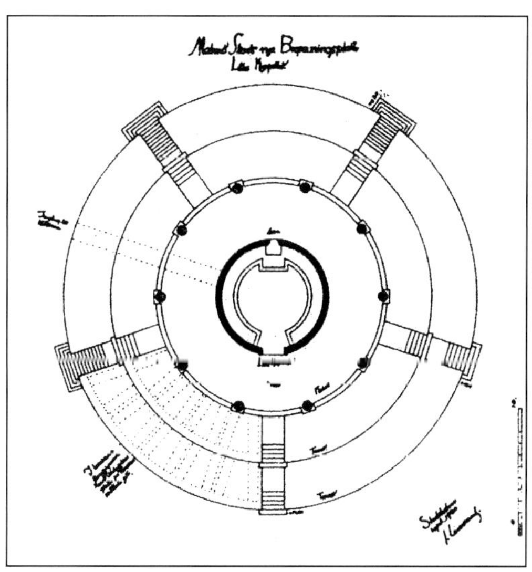

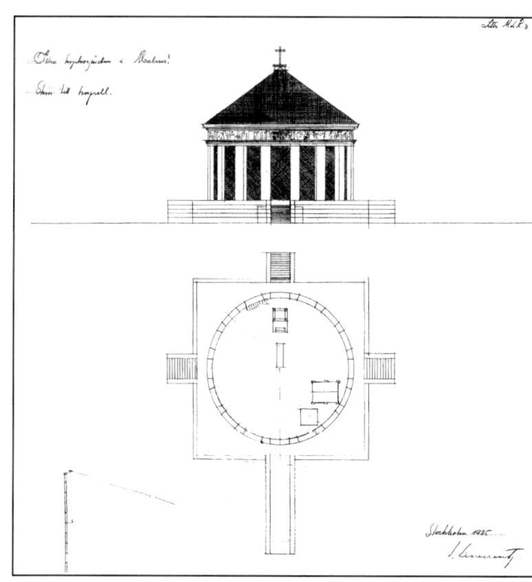

Main chapel, plan and section, 1924.

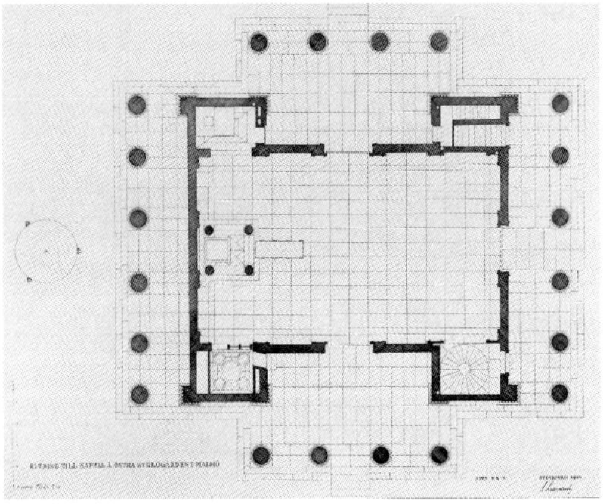

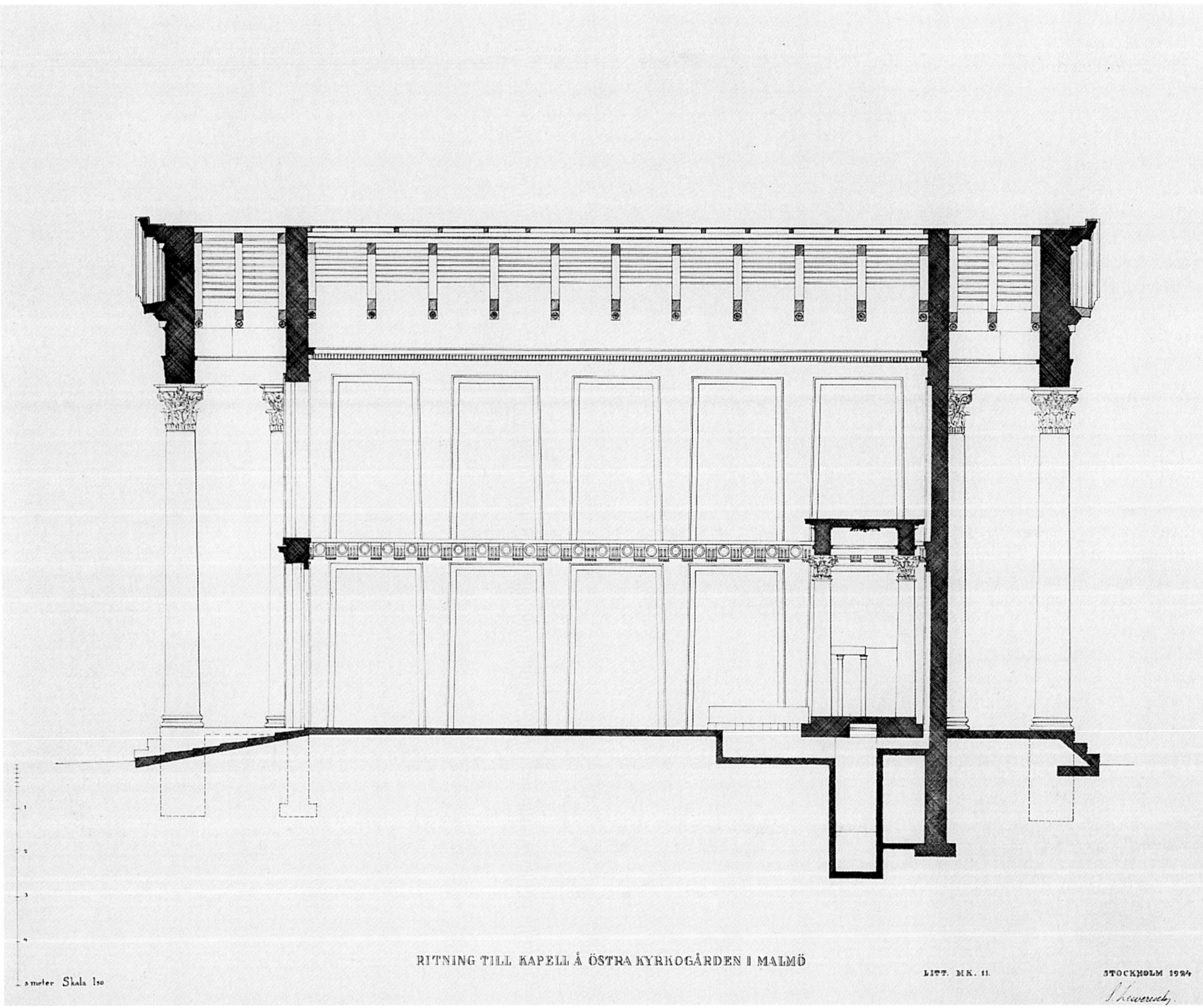

Lewerentz presented the first proposal for a complex with a monumental character extending along the principal road of the cemetery. It is comprised of three buildings placed next to each other: constructed on a square plan, each one has a roof in the form of a truncated cone.
The access to the three buildings, linked to each other by service passages, is through a portico—deep or shallow in the different versions—leading to the central building. Although maintaining the symbolic and monumental form of the building with the conical roofs, in the new version of 1928, the crematorium was smaller in size—with two, not three, buildings—and, above all, its location was changed. Subsequently Lewerentz decided not to intervene in the ridge and gave a new role to a longer road lower down, where both the funerary chapel and the waiting-room are located. The new axis is reached, as previously, by a path that divides the open-air ceremonial area into two parts, linking the main entrance to this space where the most important buildings of the cemetery are situated. The crematorium is located on a path orthogonal to the principal road; in front of this is a large burial space bordered by a double row of trees. Later subjected to successive reductions in volume, the crematorium appeared, at the end of the 1930s, to be a very simple building, in which a chimney with a pronounced conical form was the only reminder of the earlier design. In this period, in fact, the advent of Functionalism in Sweden involved Lewerentz too, as his participation in the Stockholm Exhibition of 1930 clearly indicates, and the crematorium also bears witness to this. However, the crematorium, with the adjacent chapel, immediately proved to be inadequate for its purpose and the architect began to work on a plan for its expansion that coincided with the elaboration of a more general scheme comprising a project for two chapels and an extension to the service rooms of the crematorium.

The Waiting-room, 1922–23, and the Funerary Chapel, 1923–26
Represented in Artur von Schmalensee's engraving of 1923, the waiting-room, together with the service buildings—also shown in the same drawing—was the first nucleus of the cemetery to be constructed.

Main chapel, perspective drawings, c. 1920 and c. 1923.

Main chapel, perspective
drawing, c. 1923.

Bird's-eye view of the site,
c. 1923.

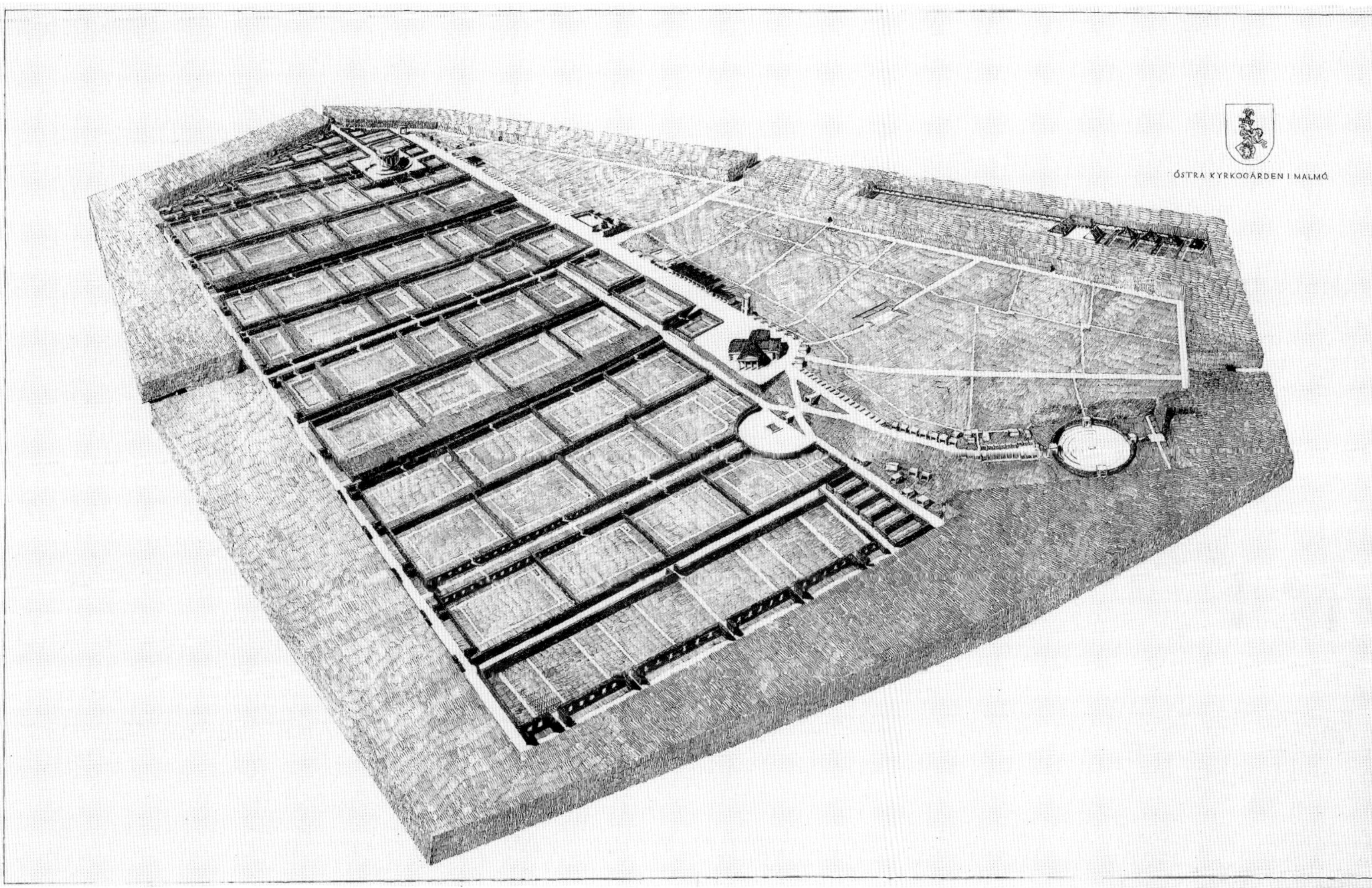

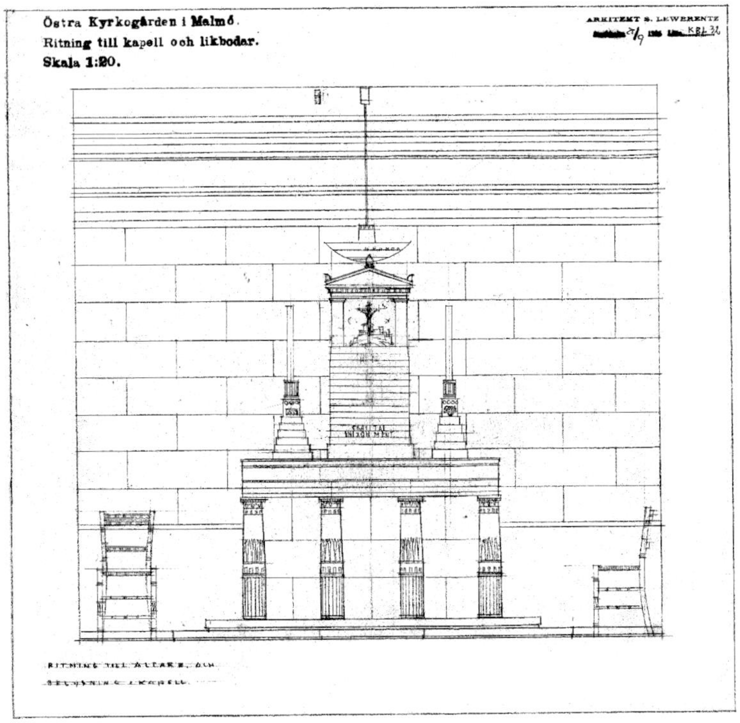

Funerary chapel, internal elevation with the altar, perspective drawing of the colonnade and detail of a column (1925).

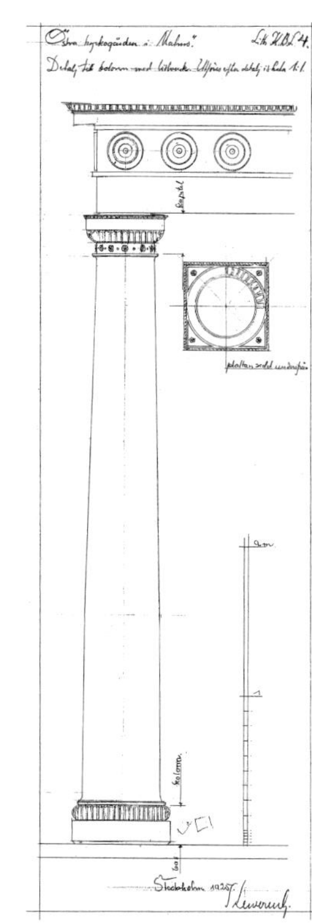

The first work on the project, however, involved exclusively the movement of earth necessary for redesigning the landscape of the area, with the aim of highlighting the qualities present. The funerary chapel (St Birgitta), on the other hand, is located in accordance with instructions differing from those contained in the 1923 project. The building stands on a road located below the principal one, not far from the waiting-room. In this way, Lewerentz abandoned the initial proposal that all the most important buildings should be located on the principal road, and began to produce a less rigid plan, with the most significant features spread out over the whole area of the cemetery.
Both buildings are characterized by a colonnade on their main façades and the unusual choice of inserting them into the ridge dominating the site, creating a contrast that emphasizes their role and dimensions. The two buildings are thus only clearly visible from below and close at hand, as their copper roofs and the earthy tones of the stucco make them indistinguishable from the surrounding landscape, of which they have become part. Together with the Resurrection Chapel in the Stockholm South Cemetery, these two buildings are the main testimony to the period in which Lewerentz interpreted the Neoclassical tradition in architecture in an independent and critical manner.

Chapels of St Gertrud and St Knut and Bell-tower, 1935–43; Extension to the Crematorium, 1955–56
The inadequacy of the first nucleus of the crematorium obliged the cemetery board to undertake an extension to the service rooms and the construction of two chapels. The first projects for the twin chapels of St Gertrud and St Knut, produced in the second half of the 1930s, clearly revealed the influence exerted by Functionalism over Lewerentz. Towards the end of the decade, however, the alternatives that came off his drawing-board attested to the fact that he was progressively abandoning the Rationalist style in favour of more complex forms and less direct references. By 1940 his designs demonstrate that this transformation had already taken place, allowing us to identify the beginning of a process that was to continue without interruption until his death. The adoption of simple geometrical forms, as well as more complex ones, was combined with a careful study of materials and building techniques, and their inherent nature: and these reflections then contributed to his intense work on architectural design.
The façades of the twin chapels are placed at right angles to the old entrance to the

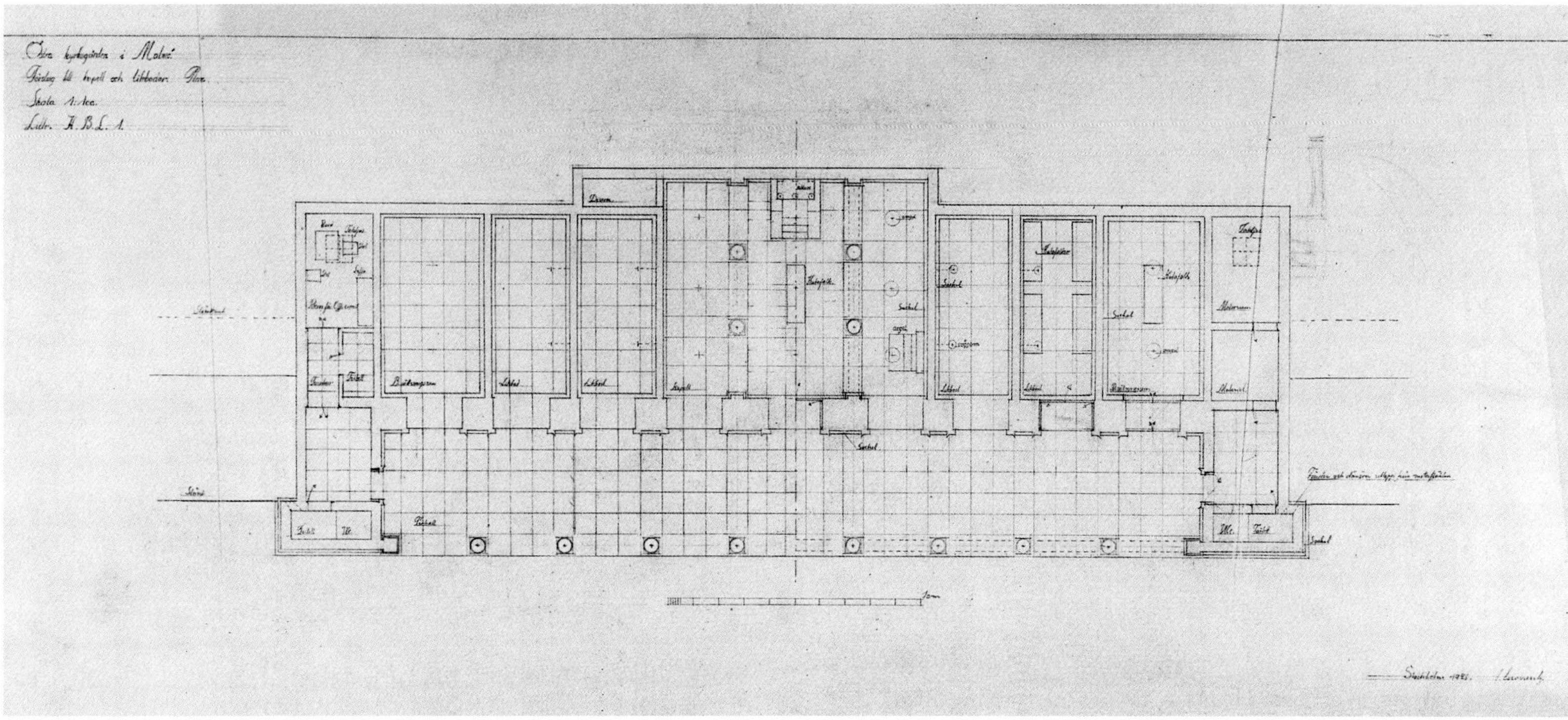

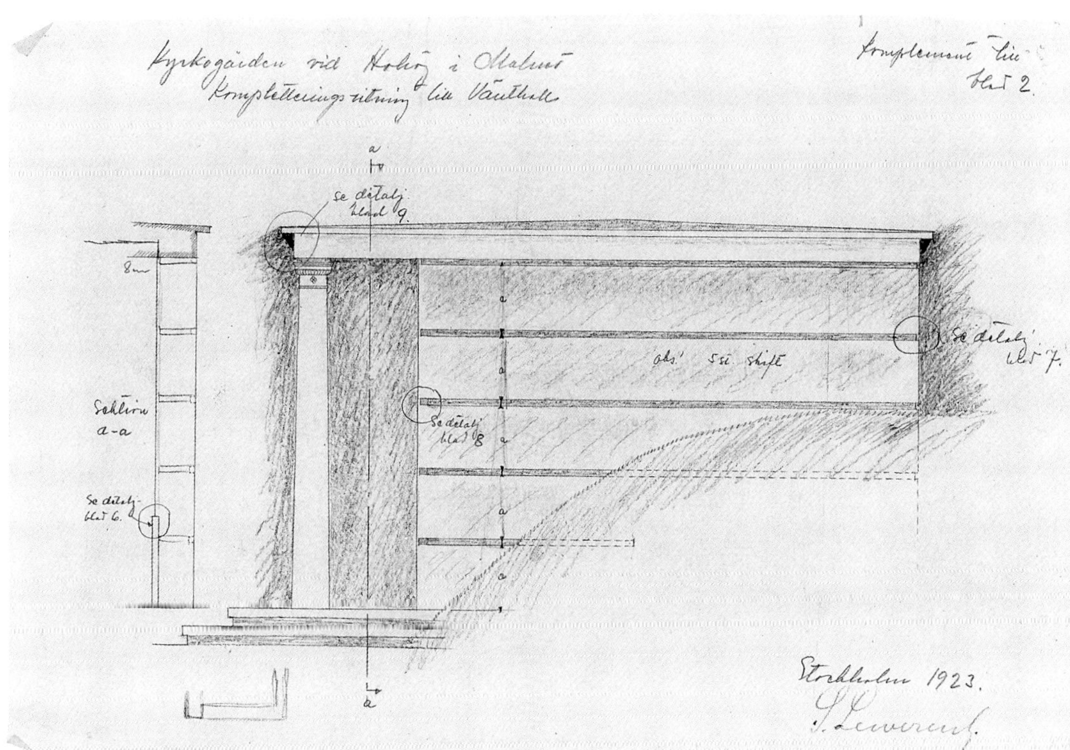

Ground-floor plan.

Waiting-room,
side elevation, 1923.

Funerary chapel, view of the building inserted in the ridge.

cemetery: the design of the landscape defines, through the introduction of imposing tree-lined avenues, the new access directly from the principal axis of the cemetery with a solution that gives compositional balance to the hemicycle onto which the funerary chapel, St Birgitta, fronts. This is what Lewerentz himself wrote in the journal *Byggmästaren*: "The chapels, each with 140 seats, have an organ loft just above their entrances, which thus become large halls. The waiting-rooms flank the latter. Between the two chapels are located the service spaces, linked to the crematorium below by a lift... The crematoria are fitted with the most up-to-date equipment, and great care has been taken to ensure that the ceremonies can take place simultaneously in both chapels without either of them being disturbed by the other or by the technological section. On arrival at the crematorium for the ceremony, the coffin is removed from the hearse in the west area, where the reception space is located, placed on a special trolley and taken through a service corridor to the mortuary, which is at a lower level. Before the funeral service, the coffin is taken into another room, where it is decorated before being placed on a special platform located under each of the chapels—which lifts it up to the higher level. At the end of the ceremony, the coffin is sent down below again, placed on a trolley and taken to the crematorium where it is burnt. The ashes are collected in an urn, which is then placed temporarily in a niche prepared beforehand in a special room, from which it will be then be removed for burial... The chapel walls are faced with bare yellow Lomma bricks internally and Gropptorp marble externally... The foundations are in concrete. The columns of the portico are faced in Ekeberg marble and fragments of the same stone are used as an aggregate in the concrete. The chapel roofs, the ridge-pieces of which come from Töreboda, are made entirely of wood and are covered externally with asbestos cement tiles, while the wooden frame of the portico roof is faced with Ekeberg marble. The chapel floors are in terrazzo in the corridors and parquet under the seats. The areas surrounding the catafalques are floored with Brunflo limestone. The bell-tower has panels framed by a structure consisting of beams and pillars in bare concrete, which is also the material used for the cross surmounting it, while the infilling panels are in Ekeberg marble." In 1955 a new extension to the crematorium commissioned from Lewerentz regarded the original chapel of 1931, already included in the general redesign of the previous years. The interior of the chapel (called "Chapel of Hope" after the extension) was completely redesigned, with a facing of wooden planks that wholly covers the walls and ceiling, and it was enlarged with the addition of two rooms, one for the organ and the other for services, the latter with a separate entrance. The architect seized the opportunity to face the exterior of the old stuccoed building with the same stone as that used for the facing of the twin chapels of St Gertrud and St Knut, giving a sense of continuity to the structure. The new service entrance is characterized by a canopy, which, on one side, almost touches the ground. The main entrance was also redesigned: an imposing single wall made of wooden boards, very dark in colour, separates the interior of the chapel from the exterior, allowing the light

Interior.

to filter into the building through a number of glass elements inserted in the wooden structure.

Flower Kiosk, 1968–69

This small building is the last of the series of projects that Lewerentz realized in the Malmö cemetery over a period of about forty years. The comparison of this final building with the first Neoclassical chapel of 1923, in the lee of the ridge, illustrates the way the architect progressed from one stylistic form to another in his long career: reflecting his ceaseless quest for simplicity, it appears to be projected towards the future. A clear-cut concrete building, with a surface pattern deriving from the formwork, it has a sloping roof with a wide overhang towards the south that shades the flowers in summer and shelters the customers in the winter, when the flowers are protected by the large window. Devoid of a frame, this is simply held by metal plates against the concrete, using a system already tried out in St Peter's Church at Klippan. The two large windows on the north side allow indirect light to enter; this is diffused internally by silvered sheets, which, together with the surface-mounted electric cables and fittings, are the only "decorative" elements in a space where the flowers and the light are the sole protagonists. The crowning achievement of a life spent searching for forms that could not be further simplified, the flower kiosk attests to design skills capable of heralding tendencies that manifested themselves shortly afterwards, the final work of a master that asserts itself with the force of silence.

Chronology:
1916: Lewerentz wins the national competition.
1918–20: projects for the general layout of the cemetery.
1920–23: realization of the service buildings.
1922–25: realization of the open-air ceremonial area (1922–23) and the waiting-room (1922–23), modified in 1958.
1923: project for the general layout of the cemetery.
1923–24: elaboration of the project for the main chapel.
1923–25: elaboration of the first project for the crematorium (version with three cones).
1923–26: realization of the funerary chapel (St Birgitta) and mortuary.
1928: project for the general layout of the cemetery.
1928–29: elaboration of the second project for the crematorium (version with two cones).
1931–36: final version and realization of crematorium (1931–32), with adjacent chapel (1935–36).
1935–43: project for and realization of the bell-tower, the twin chapels of St Gertrud and St Knut and extension to the crematorium.
1955–56: Chapel of Hope, the enlarged version of the crematorium chapel.
1968–71: flower kiosk (1968–69) and custodian's house (1969–71), adjacent to the cemetery complex.
1972–74: projects for the gates (in 1973 the gate of the new main entrance to the cemetery was installed next to the flower kiosk).

Bibliography: Lewerentz 1928a; Jacobsen 1945; Lewerentz 1973b; Nyberg 1976; Ahlin 1985b, pp. 68–73, 124–27, 184–89, 235–37; Constant 1994, pp. 115–19; Caldenby 1997, pp. 78–83, 136–45, 176–79; Postiglione 1998.

(N.F.)

Waiting-room, the building inserted in the ridge and the column at one end.

Funerary chapel, the colonnade.

Crematorium, plan, section
and elevation, 1924.

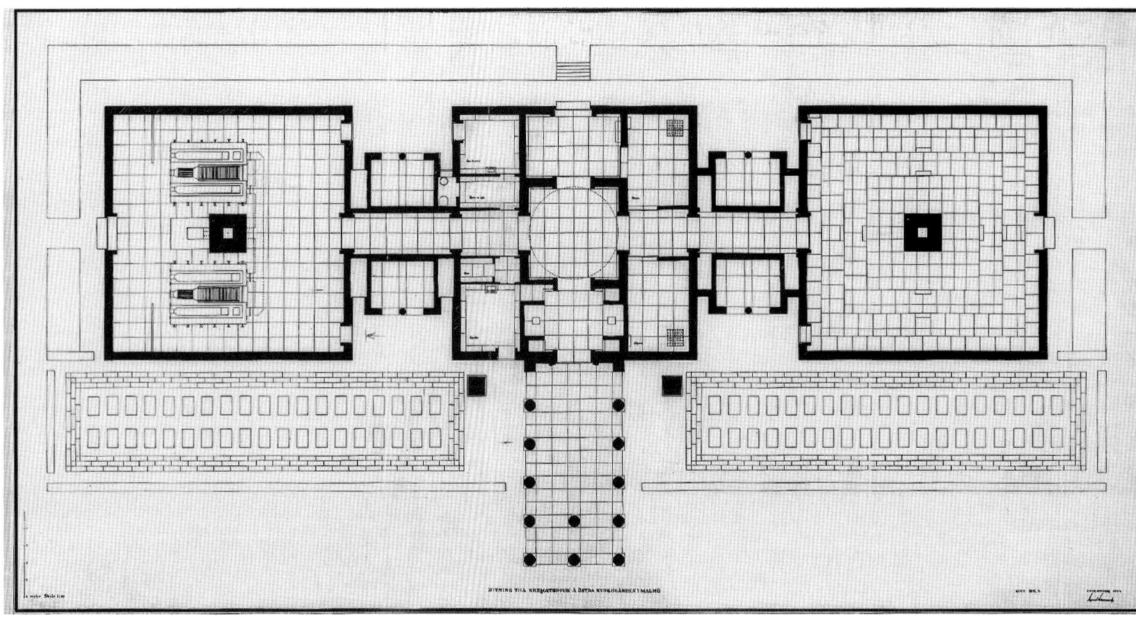

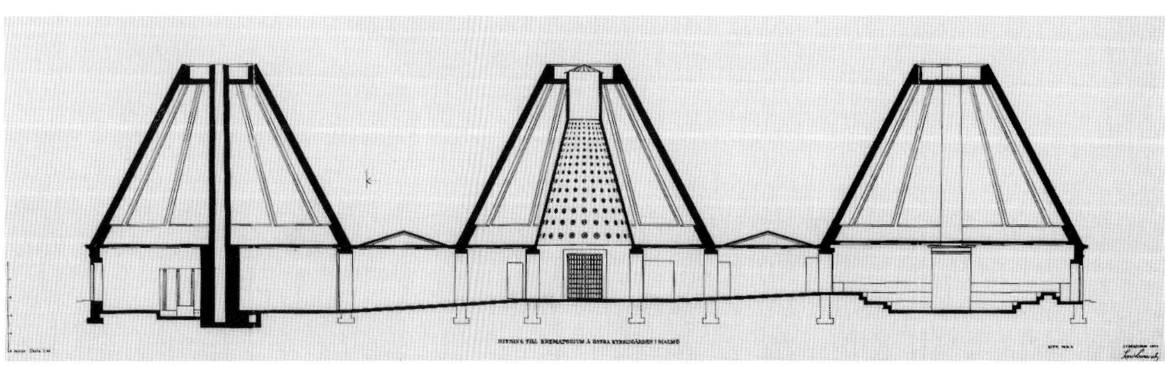

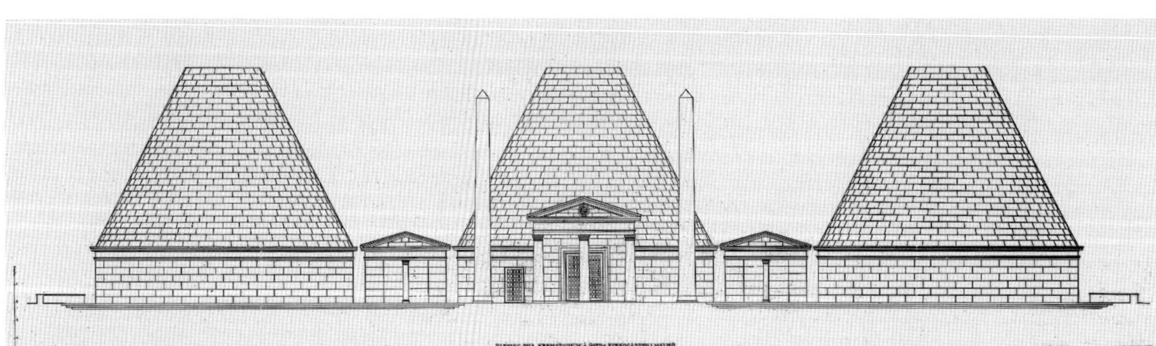

Perspective drawing, 1924 version.

Crematorium, perspective drawing, 1930.

Perspective drawings, c. 1930.

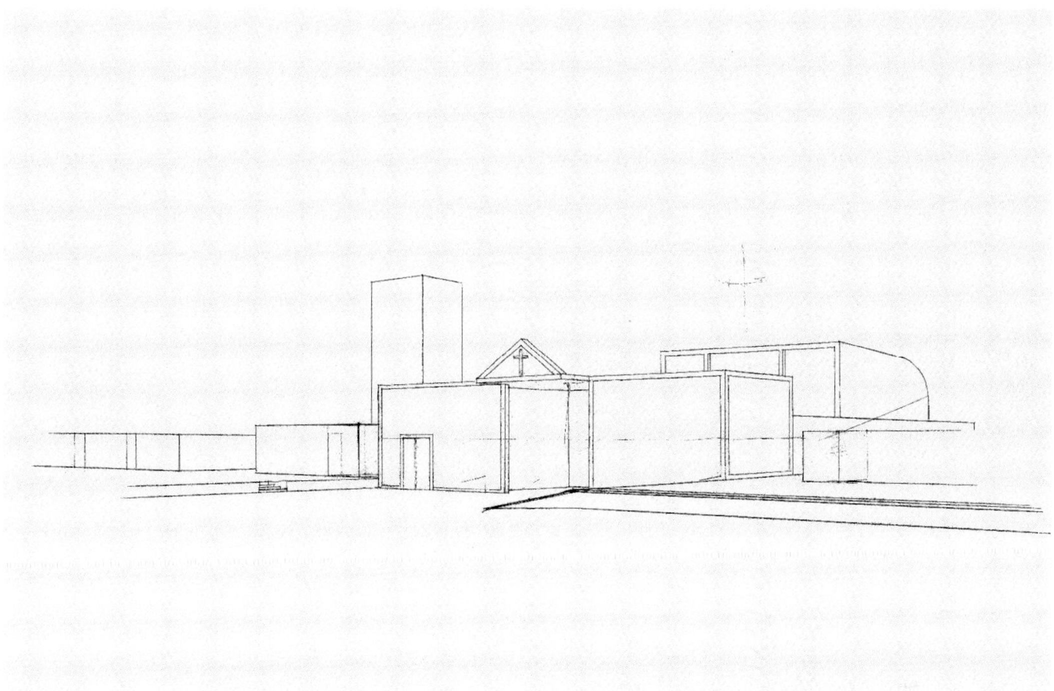

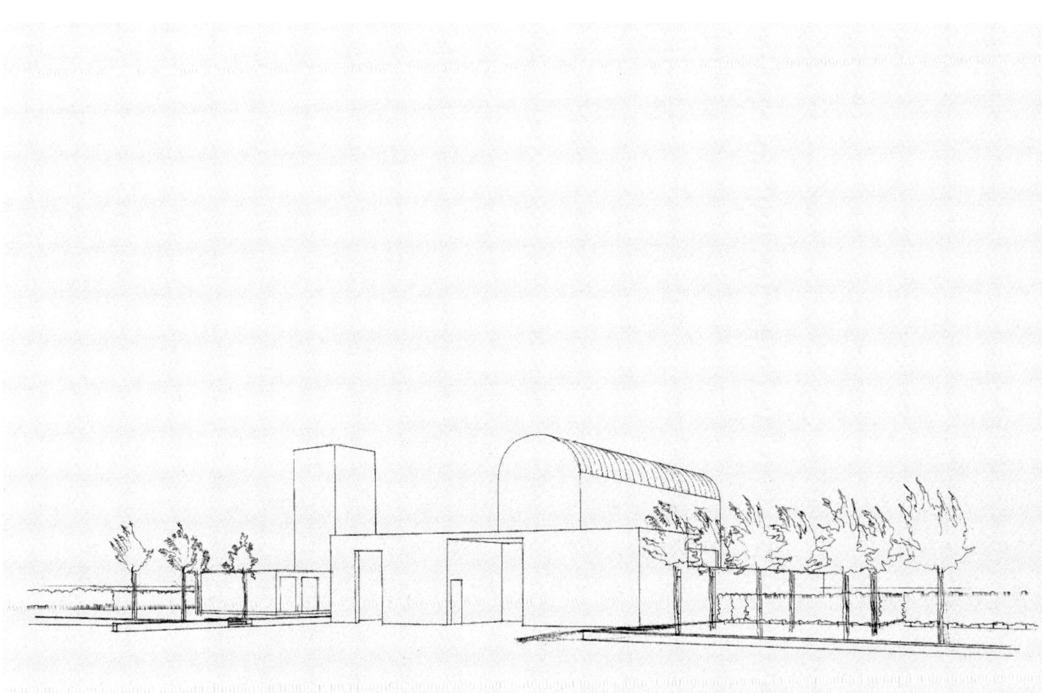

Crematorium and chapel, elevation, plan and view, 1931–36.

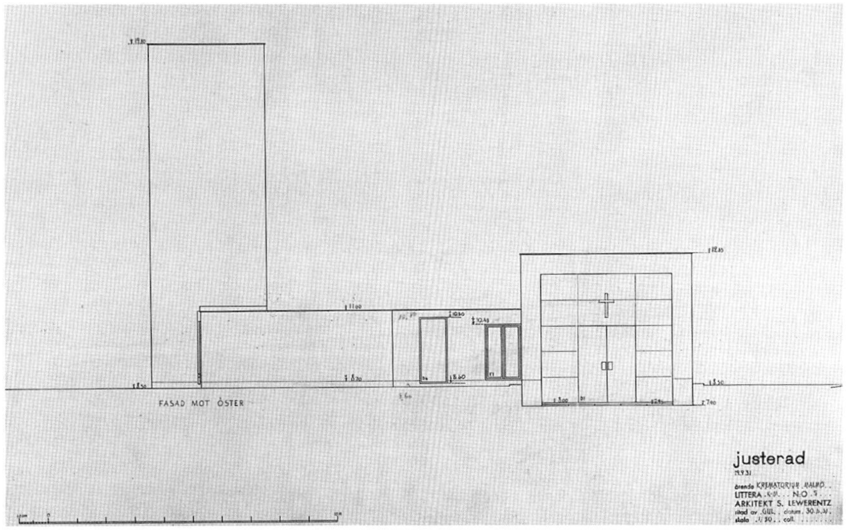

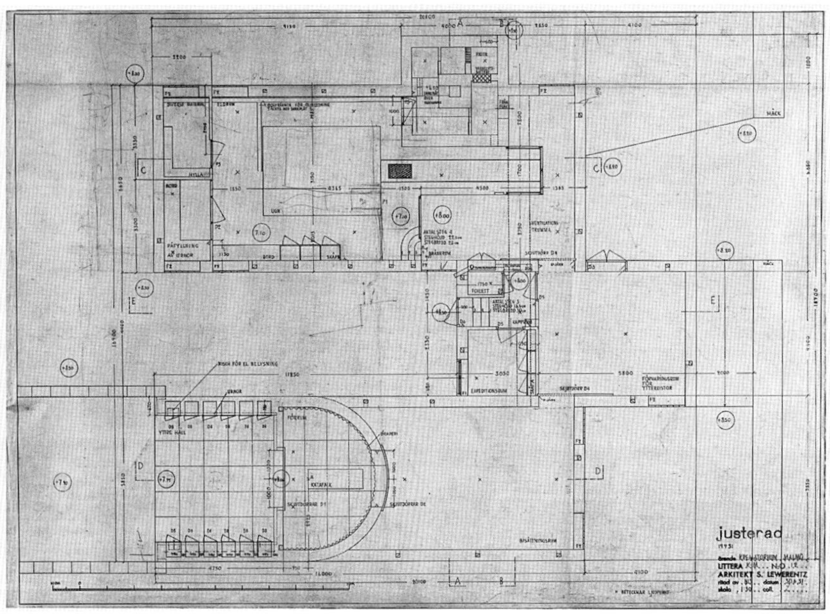

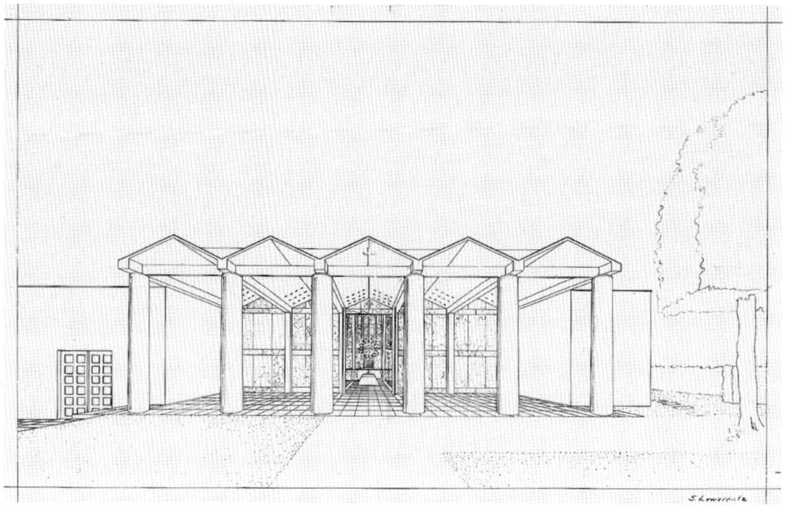

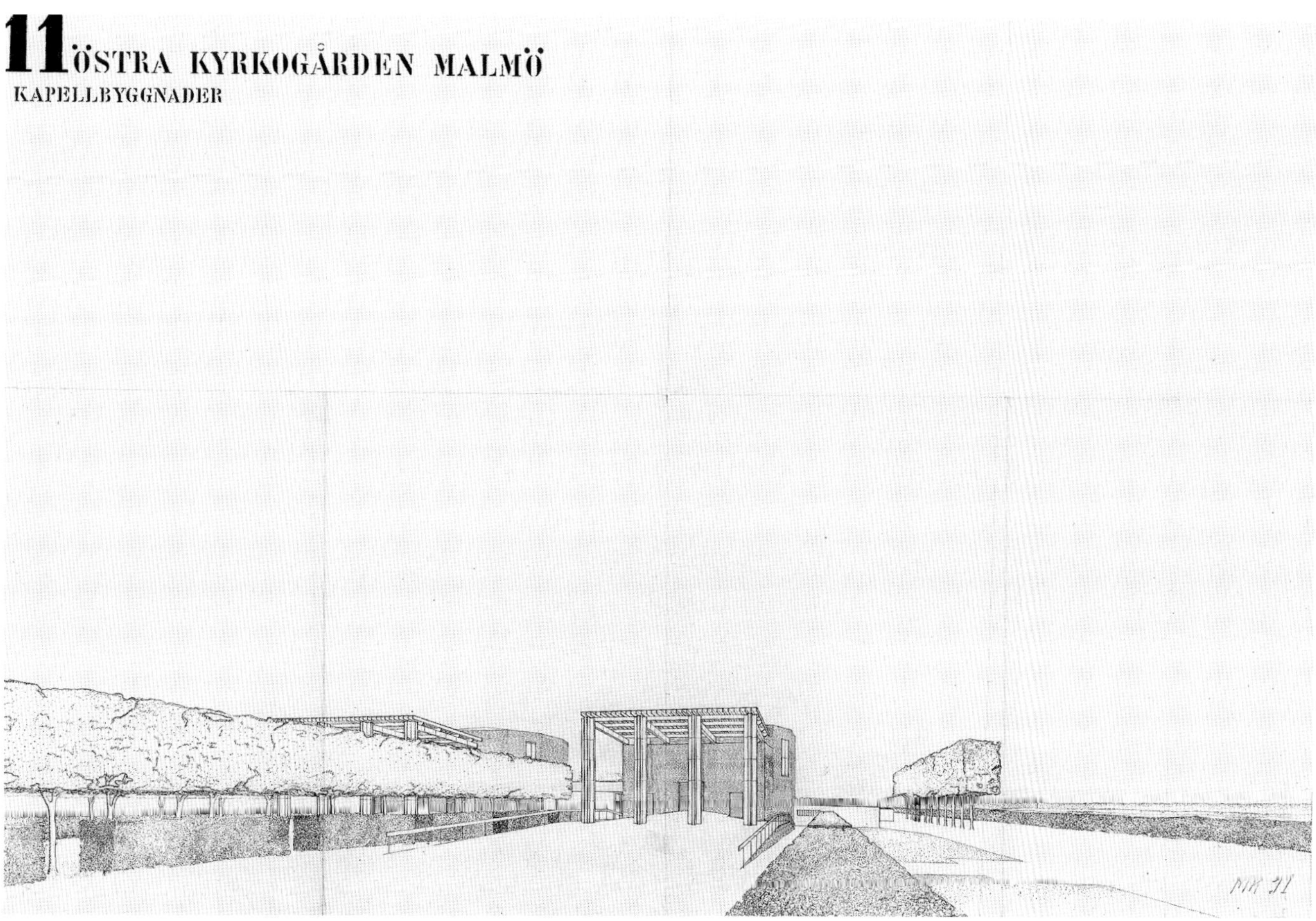

Twin chapels of St Gertrud and St Knut, perspective drawings.

Chapel of St Gertrud and crematorium, side elevation, 1941.

Chapels of St Gertrud and St Knut and crematorium, plan; the walls not blocked in show the pre-existing crematorium.

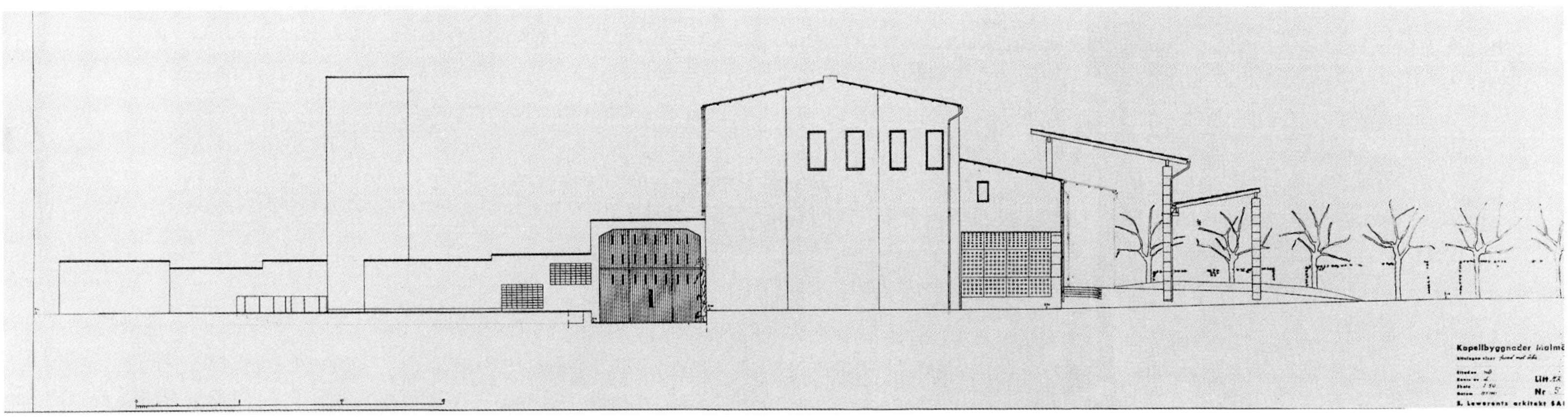

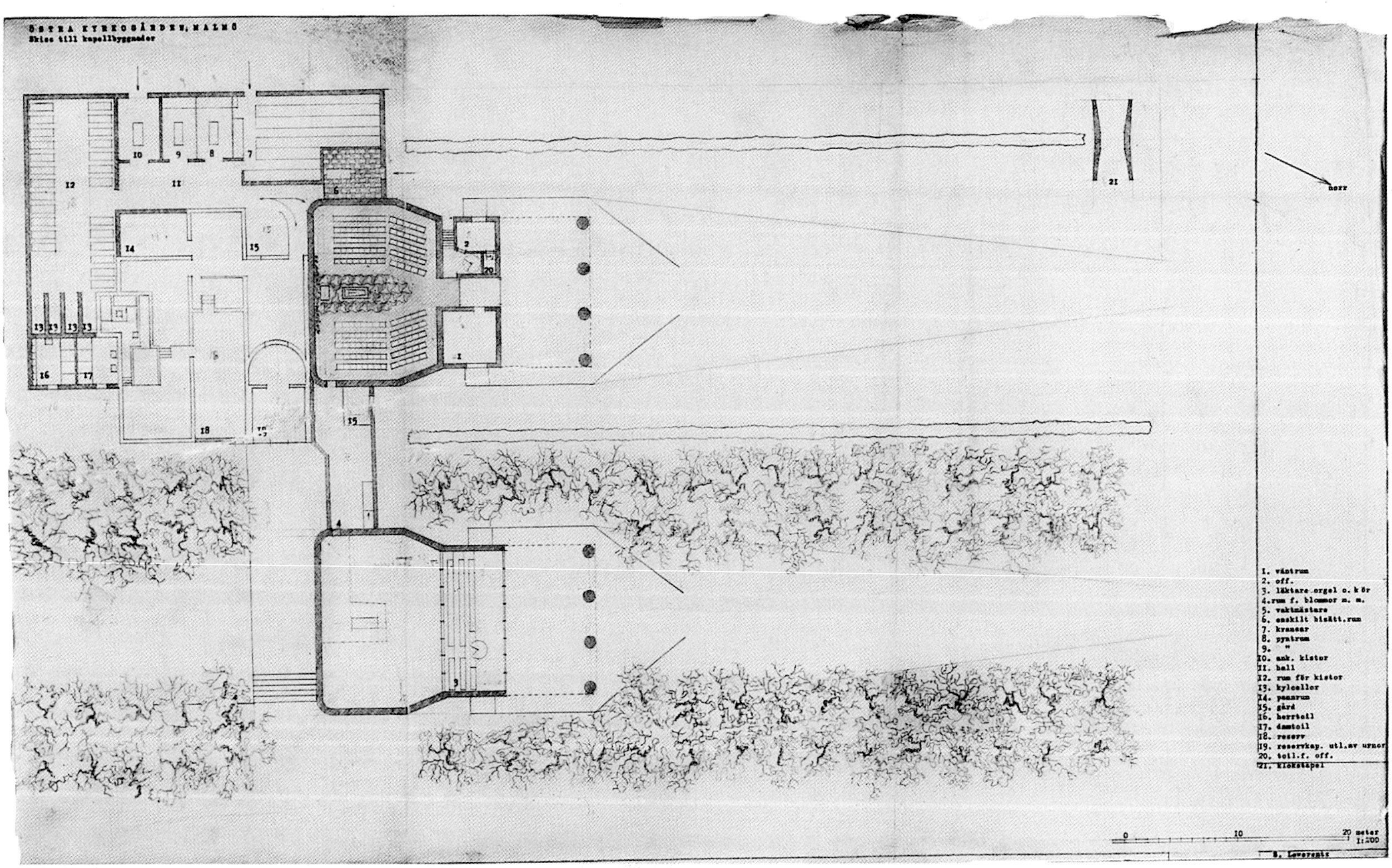

Chapel of St Knut, details of the flooring and sections, 1941.

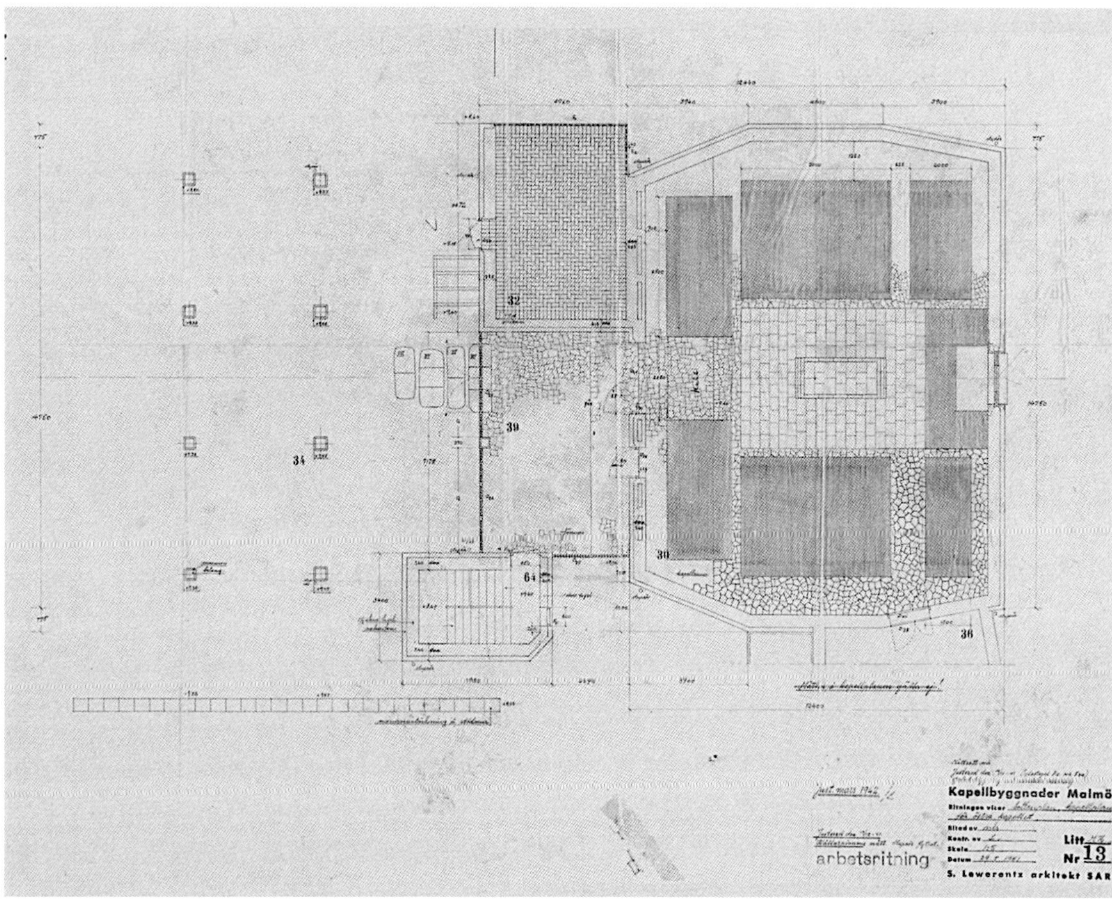

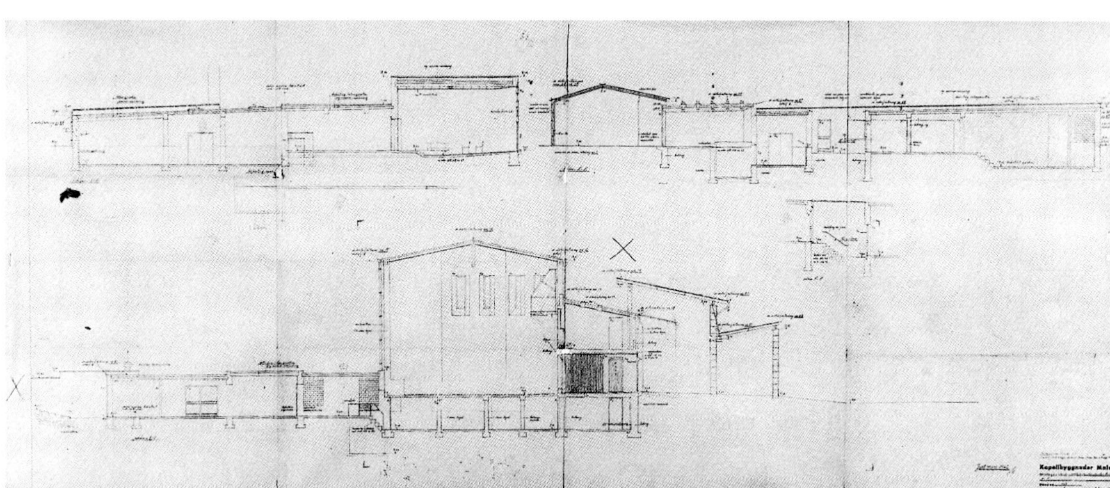

Chapels of St Knut and
St Gertrud, exterior views.

Chapel of St Knut,
the double colonnade
of the portico and details
of the portico and main
door.

Chapels of St Gertrud and St Knut, details of the sacristy and main door.

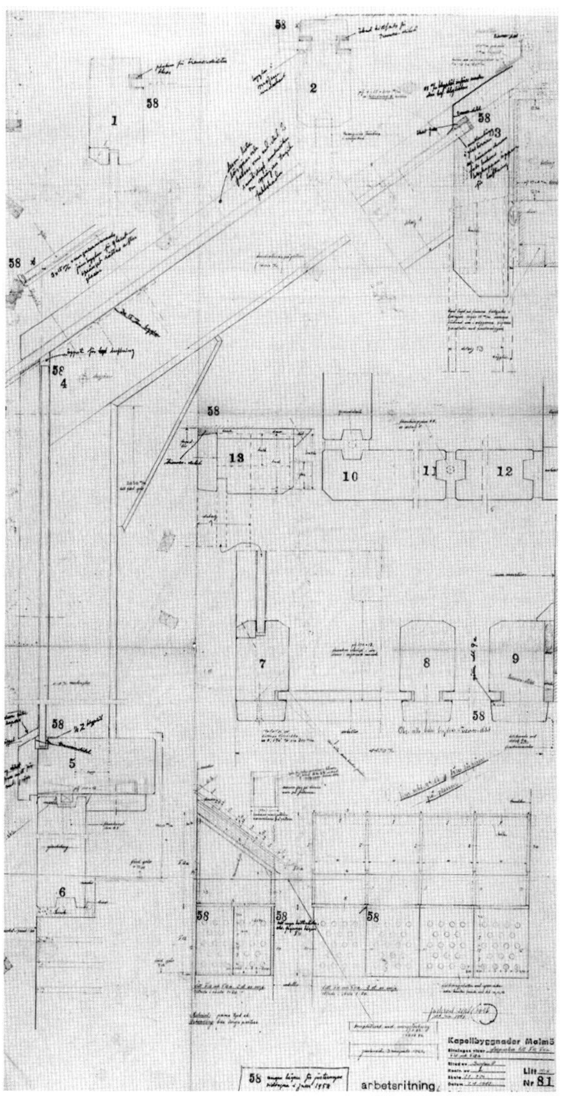

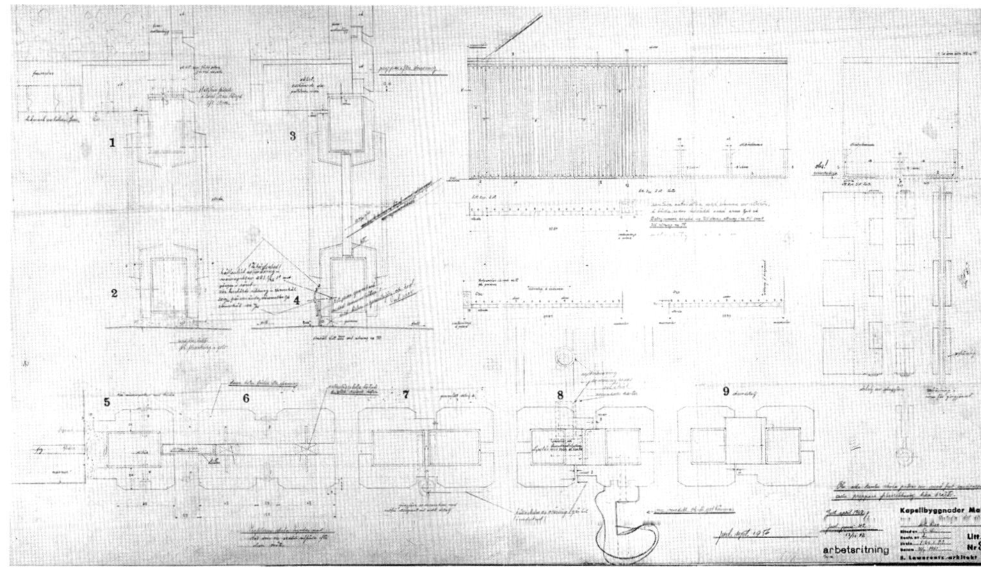

Chapel of St Knut, interior.

The handrail
of the staircase
leading to the choir.

Extension to the crematorium, views of the Chapel of Hope.

Chapel of Hope, side elevation, plan (1955) and detail of the main door.

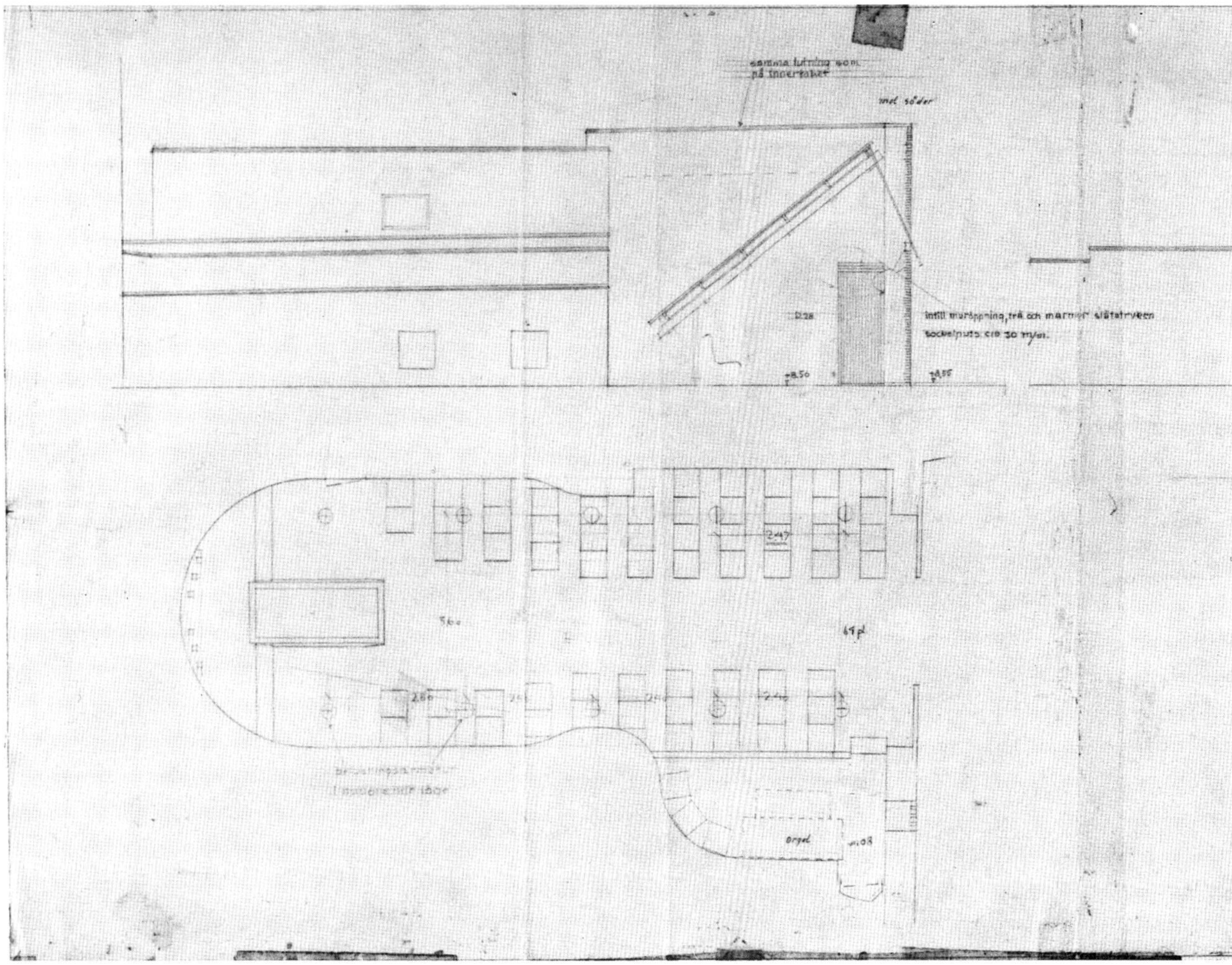

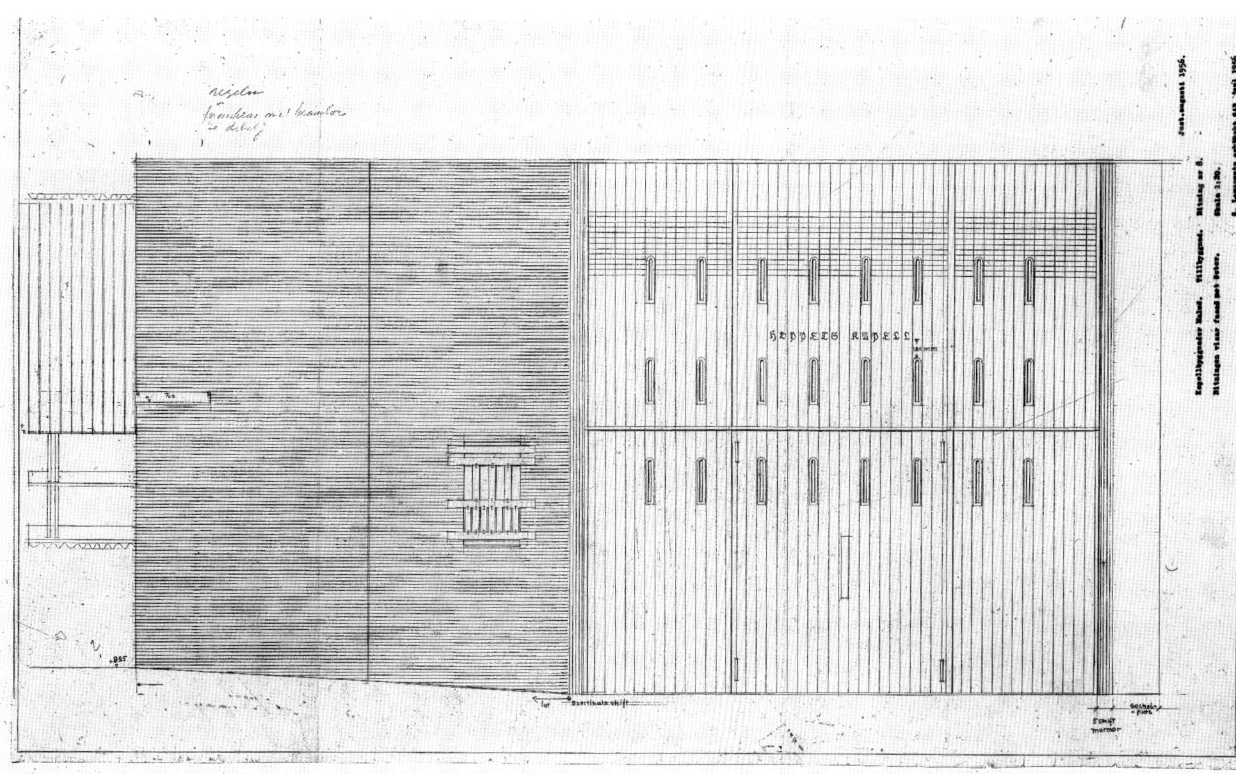

Chapel of Hope, details of the main door.

Extension to the crematorium, service building.

Chapel of Hope, interior.

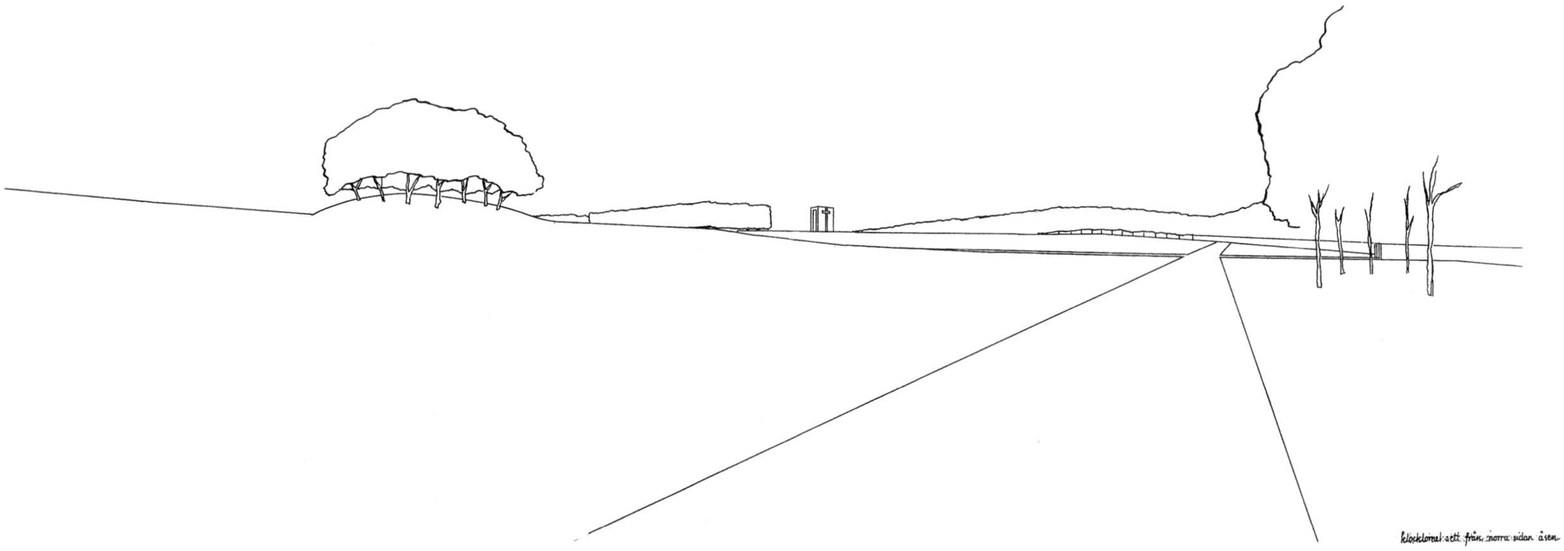

Perspective drawing of the landscape.

Bell-tower, perspective drawings.

Skizz till klockstapel.

Bell-tower, perspective drawing, plan, elevations and study sections, 1936.

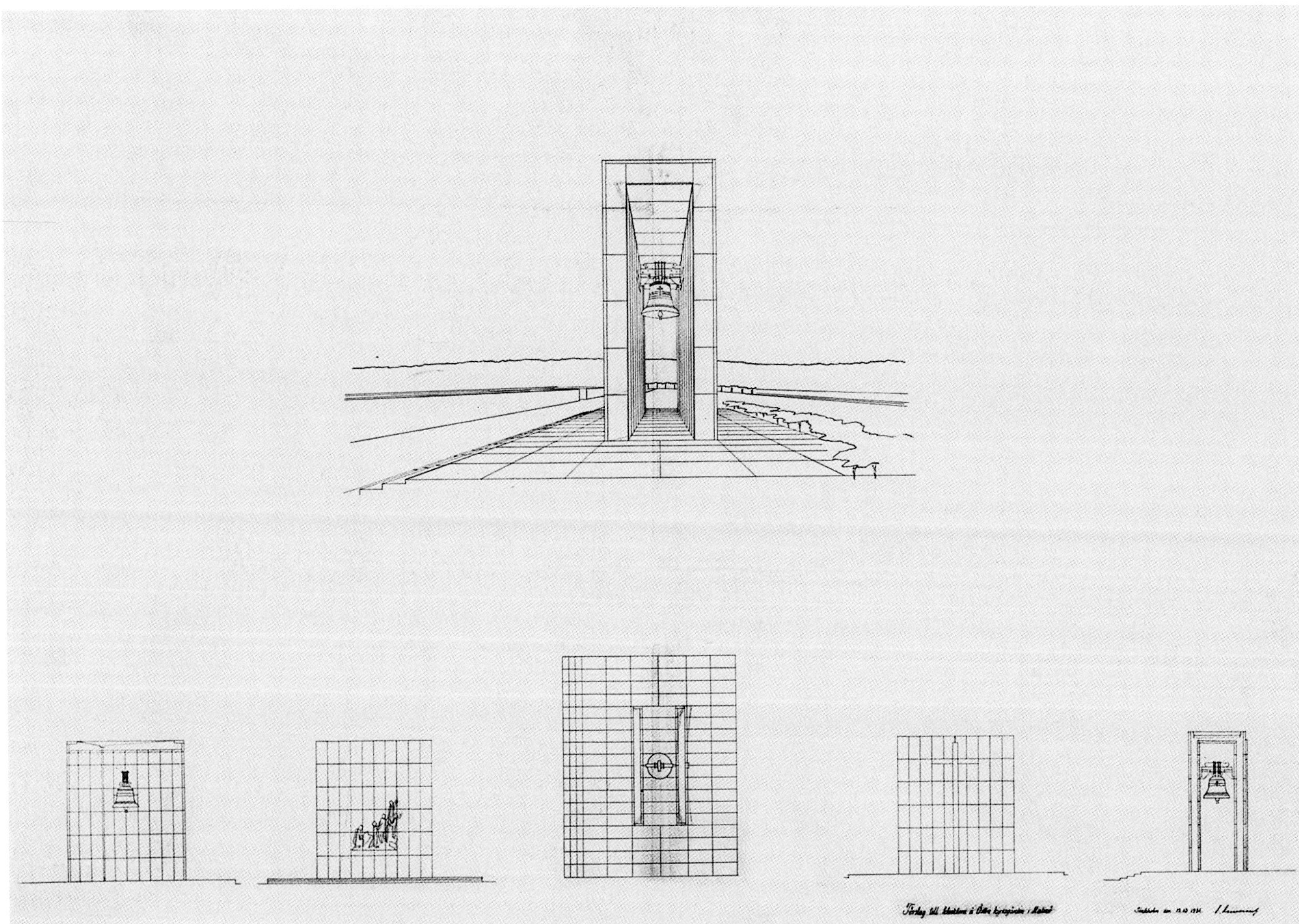

The bell-tower in 1943.

Custodian's house.

Flower kiosk, west front,
in 1969.

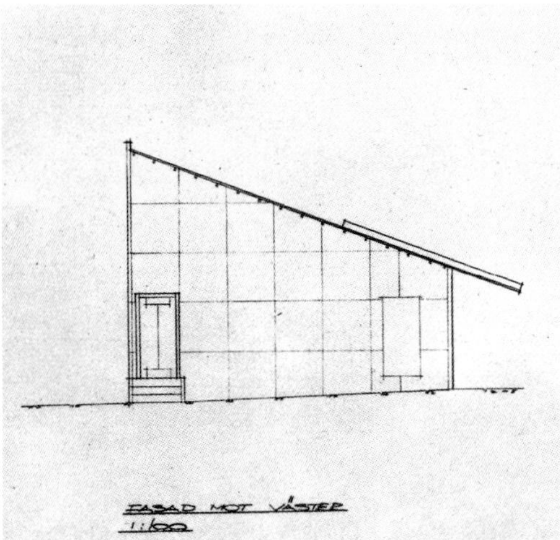

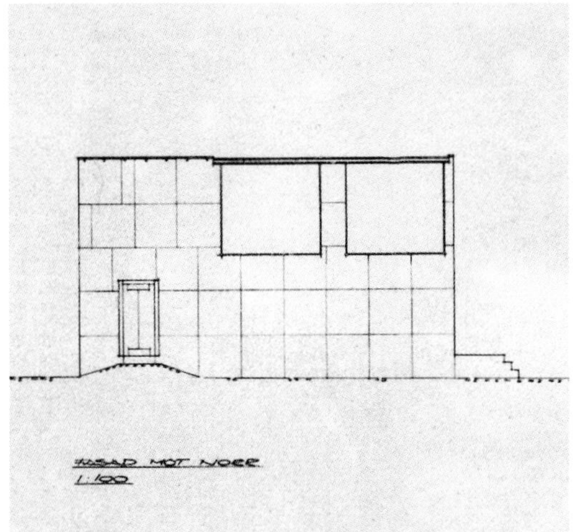

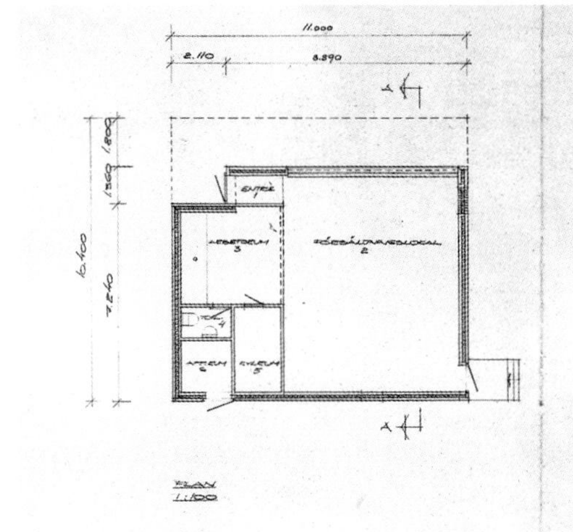

Flower kiosk, elevations, plan and view of the south front.

Detail of the lighting installations.

43. Project for the Cemetery of Nynäshamn, 1917

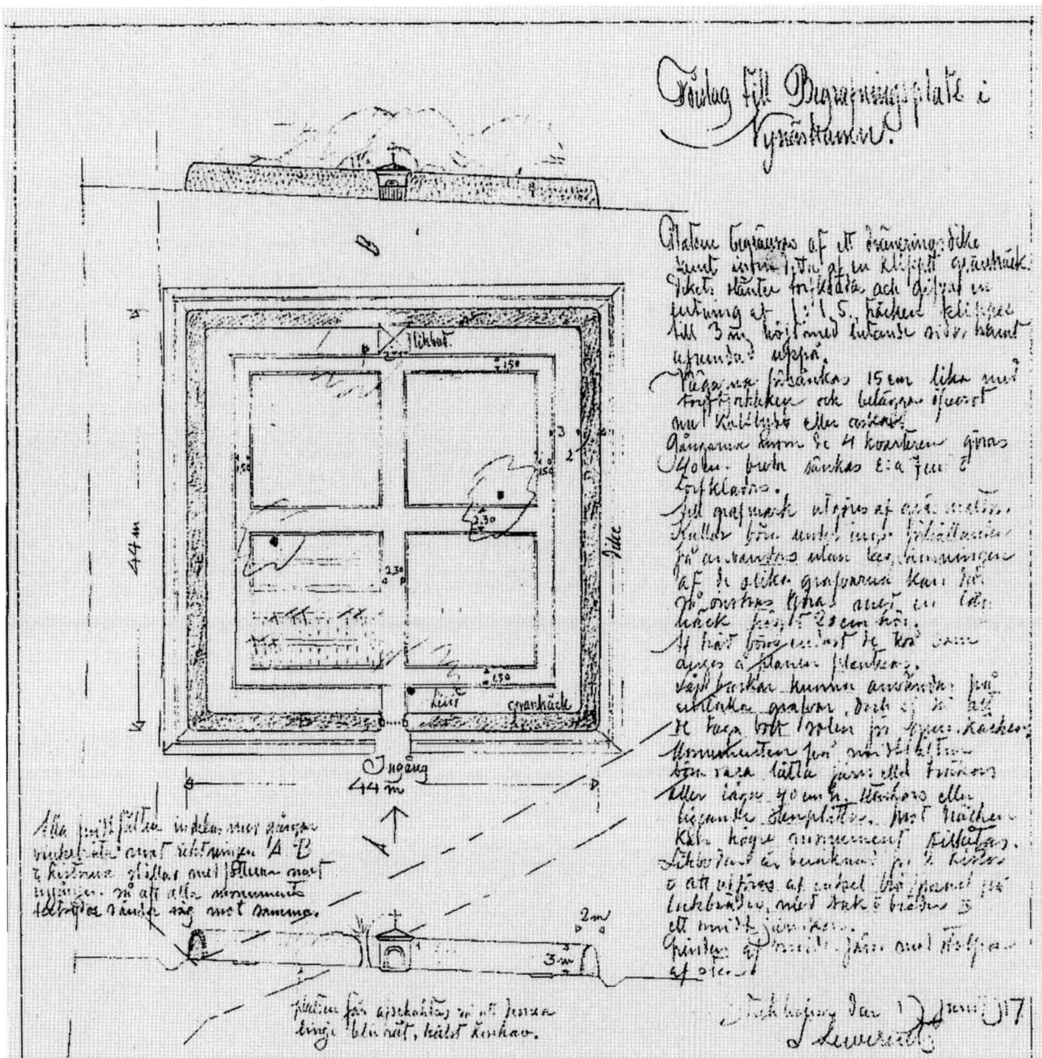

Layout plan.

44. Project for Workers' Houses at Öjervik, Rottneros, 1917

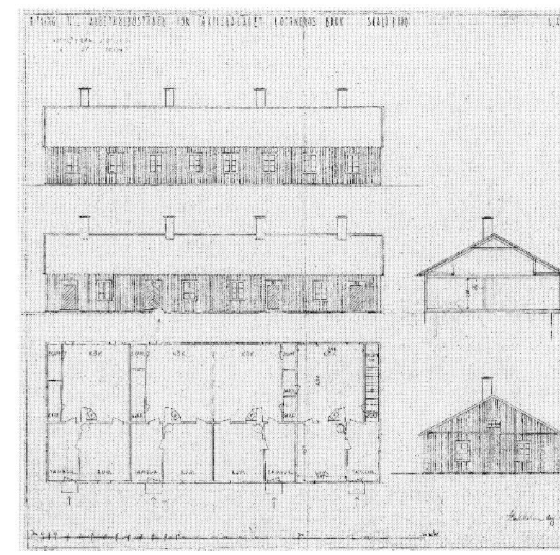

Elevations, plan and section.

45. Renovation of the *Corps de Logis*, Rottneros, 1917

See entry no. 15.

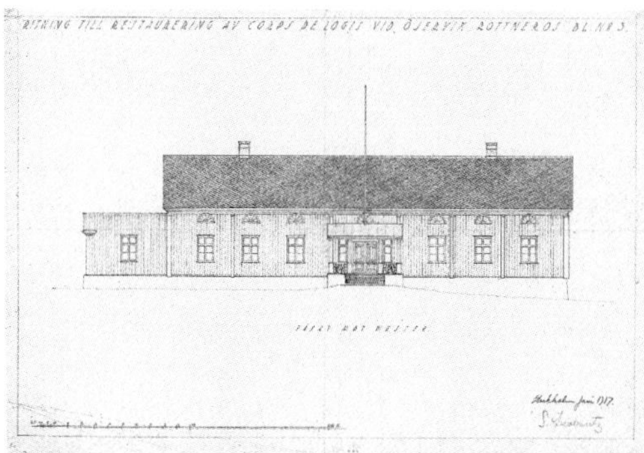

Elevation.

46. Renovation of the *Corps de Logis*, Öjeby, Rottneros, 1917

See entry no. 15.

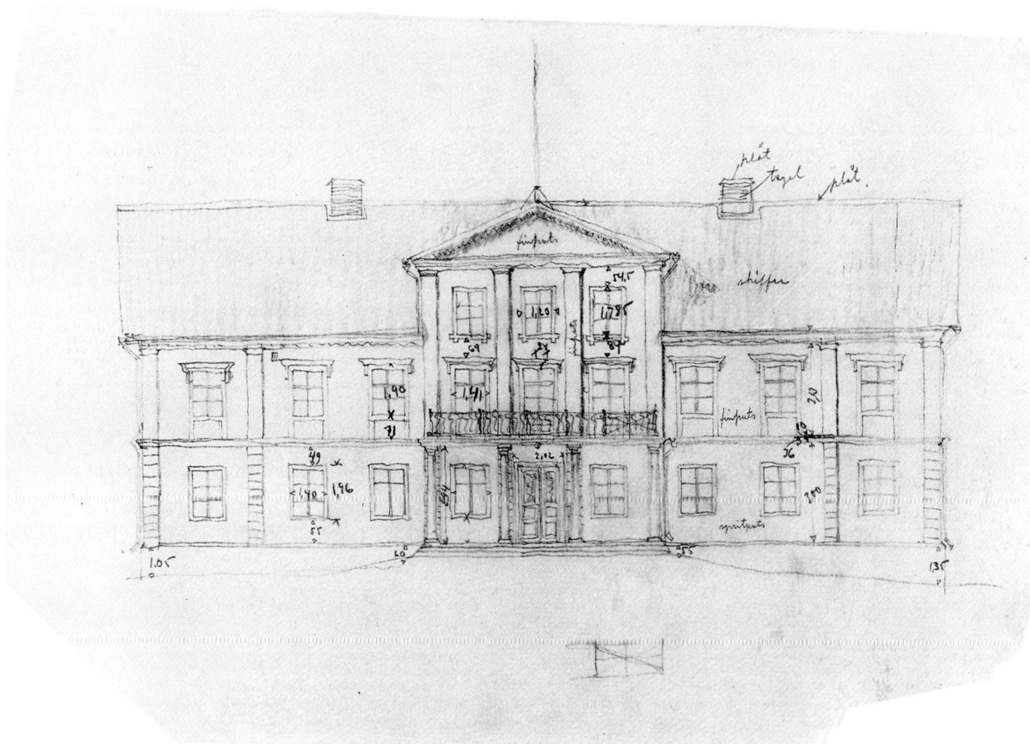

Study sketch.

47. Competition Project for the Reconstruction of the Götaplatsen, Gothenburg, 1917-18

first competition, motto "Skåll", 1981 – citation; second competition, 1918, with Turre Ryberg and Ragnar Hjort.

The competition programme required a monumental square to be laid out in the south-eastern area of the city, at the end of the main street, Kungsportsavenyn. It was to contain a theatre, a concert hall and an art gallery. The conformation of the site, on a gentle slope with a steep rise at one end, suggested that it should be organized symmetrically, with the two theatres at the sides and the gallery forming the backdrop to the deep perspective. In Lewerentz's scheme there is a square, partially occupied by a garden in the form of a trapezium, with the longest side nearest the rear of the square. The theatres are located at the sides of the square, while, at the back, the architect has inserted a series of buildings, fanning out up the steepest part of the slope, apparently arranged symmetrically with respect to the principal axis. Emphasized by stairways and fountains, serving the different terraces on which stand the buildings intended to be used for housing, the main street continues along tree-lined avenue, thus extending the axis of the scheme beyond the square.

Paying particular attention to the urban design aspects of the scheme, Lewerentz focused on the general layout rather than the architectural quality and finish of the buildings. Although it was highly praised in some quarters, the project was criticized by the jury because it did not respect the conditions contained in the programme. Since the competition came to nothing, another one was organized, with the participation of the group that came second—comprising E. Torulf, S. Eriksson, A. Bjerke and R.O. Swensson—and the winners, Ragnar Hjort and Ture Ryberg, who decided to involve Lewerentz, forming a new group of architects. Lewerentz's contribution is quite evident since the new plans submitted to the competition maintained many of the ideas contained in his previous scheme, especially the trapezodial square, with the shorter side near the lower end, and the general layout of the scheme, which was arranged

symmetrically on an axis that, rather than passing though a building, continued along a tree-lined avenue, stressing the fundamental importance of perspective in this project. Once again the jury was unsympathetic to Lewerentz's ideas, and the project was rejected. Despite this, the winning project was not realized and it was not until the 1930s that the square was finally completed. In the meantime, however, the question of the urban renewal of this important area of Gothenburg continued to be the subject of intense debate, and Lewerentz's second project was again presented in the 1920s as the only concrete solution to the problem.

Bibliography: Götaplatsen 1918; Friberger 1927; Ahlin 1985b, pp. 99–104; Waern 1996.

(G. P.)

The model for the first competition.

Perspective drawing for the second competition.

Opposite
Eskilstuna Cemetery, layout plan and bird's-eye view of the project prepared for first competition.

48. New Layout of Eskilstuna Cemetery, 1918.

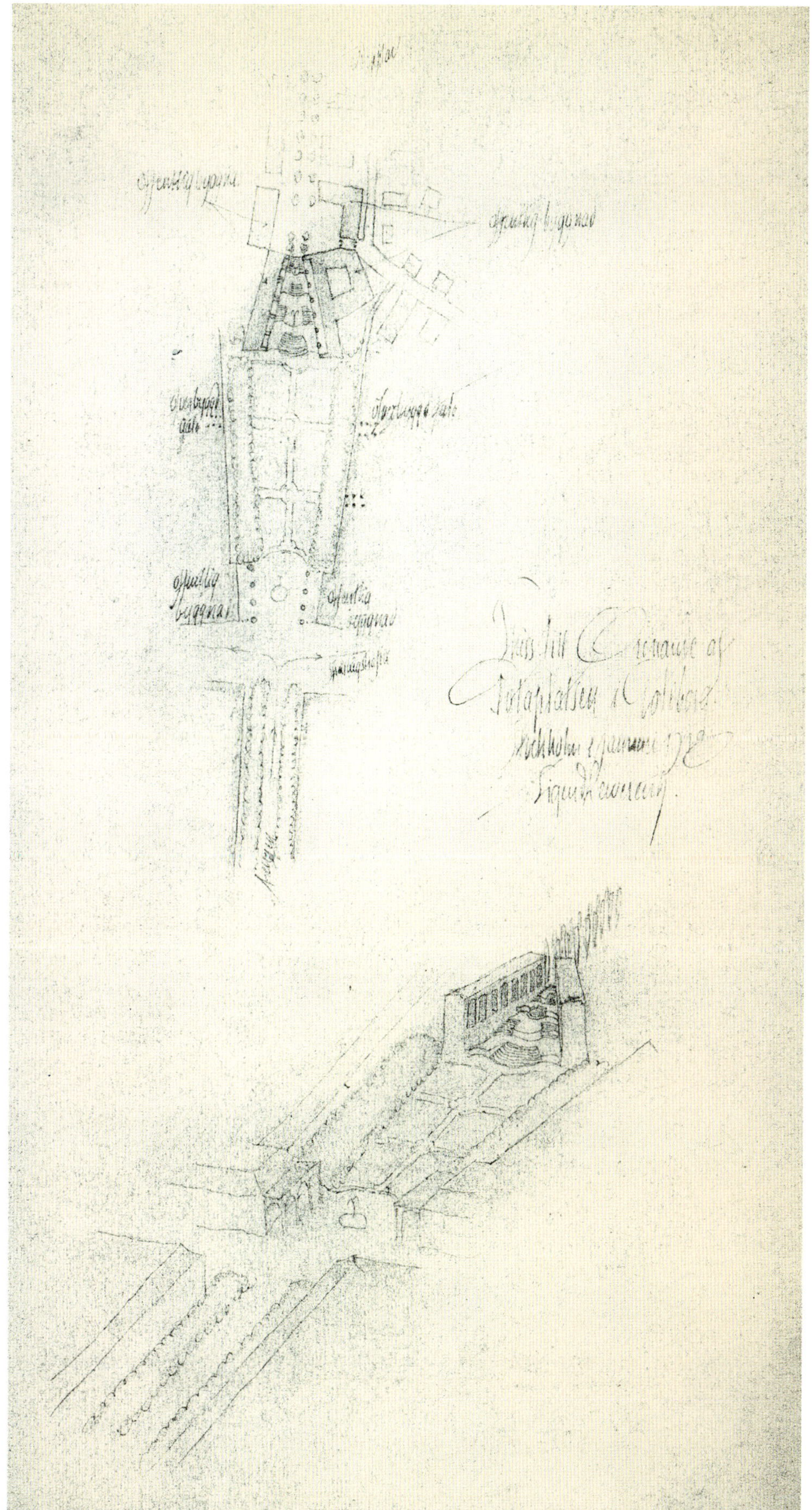

The new layout proposed by Lewerentz for the parish cemetery of Eskilstuna, a small town not far from Stockholm, provides an appropriate and efficient answer to the need to give the network of internal paths and the burial areas a distinct identity, paying particular attention to the design of the landscape, thus allowing the architect to mitigate the ugliness of the existing structures and to give greater character to his scheme. In such cases, Lewerentz began with an analysis of the state of affairs from which the objectives to be pursued in the project usually derived. This is what he wrote in his outline of the project:
"The main observation that one can probably make with regard to the visual impact of the existing cemetery is that it has developed in a chaotic manner; there is a lack of the peace and serenity that usually reign in these places. The reason for this is due to the fact that enormous monuments are located along the paths without the necessary setting; in order to obtain this, the burial areas should be surrounded by thick hedges about a metre in height. The project for the screen of vegetation with the hedges should—over and above the aesthetic and economic aspects—prevent the construction of other monuments with the same criteria. Moreover, in all likelihood, as far as the planting of the larger areas is concerned, this may take place along similar lines to those already adopted, while the burial areas should be surrounded by trees of the same species that has been adopted hitherto, the cedar...
Within the hedges surrounding the burial areas, flowering trees, smaller in size, and various species of shrubs may be planted.
A smaller bulk would also be more suitable for the tombs along the main paths; in order to obtain this rapidly, it is necessary to plant ivy and honeysuckle."
The outline continues with instructions regarding the dimensions of individual tombstones, which were to be placed horizontally (except for the family ones, which could be placed vertically providing they were not excessively large), the materials to be used for the crosses and the type of ornamentation to be used on the tombstones.

(G.P.)

49. Extension to Sundsvall Cemetery, 1918

Involving the rearrangement of a number of plots in Sundsvall Cemetery, the project constitutes, to a large extent, the natural complement to the site's character.
A new network of principal and secondary paths is laid out, defining the areas where the tombstones are to be placed.
As is usual in Lewerentz's cemetery projects, these are to be positioned horizontally, or vertically only if they are not very high, because they have an enormous impact on the character of the place.
The planting of trees along the main paths is not continuous, but is interrupted in the final part of the site to provide a view of the surrounding area; moreover, the rows of trees and the burial areas guide the visitor towards the existing chapel, the principal building in the cemetery.

(G.P.)

50. Competition Project for the Urban Design of the Area around the Saltsjöbaden Station, Stockholm, 1918-19

motto "Tre" – second prize

In 1918 the Järnväg AB Stockholm-Saltsjöbaden—the railway company for which Lewerentz, together with Stubelius, had worked in 1914, when they designed a single-family villa at Saltsjöbaden—organized a competition for the urban design of the area around Saltsjöbaden station. According to the programme, the area was to contain the new station and the adjacent square, a hotel, a restaurant, a shopping district and a road and rail system leading to the islet of Restaurantholm.
Lewerentz's project—which received the second prize, even if, in the opinion of Carl Westman, one of the members of the jury, it should have been awarded first prize—was particularly commended for the way in which it took the natural environment and character of the area into consideration.
The fundamental principle of the project involved the distancing of traffic and the built-up area from the area facing the sea, which was laid out as a park and left free for bathing activities. All the other buildings necessary to meet the requirements of the competition programme, which envisaged a fairly intense level of construction on the site, were located in the area to the south of the railway. The complex extended over the site in total harmony with the topography and character of the area, becoming an integral part of it.

Bibliography: Asplund 1919; Ahlin 1985b, pp. 96–99.

(G.P.)

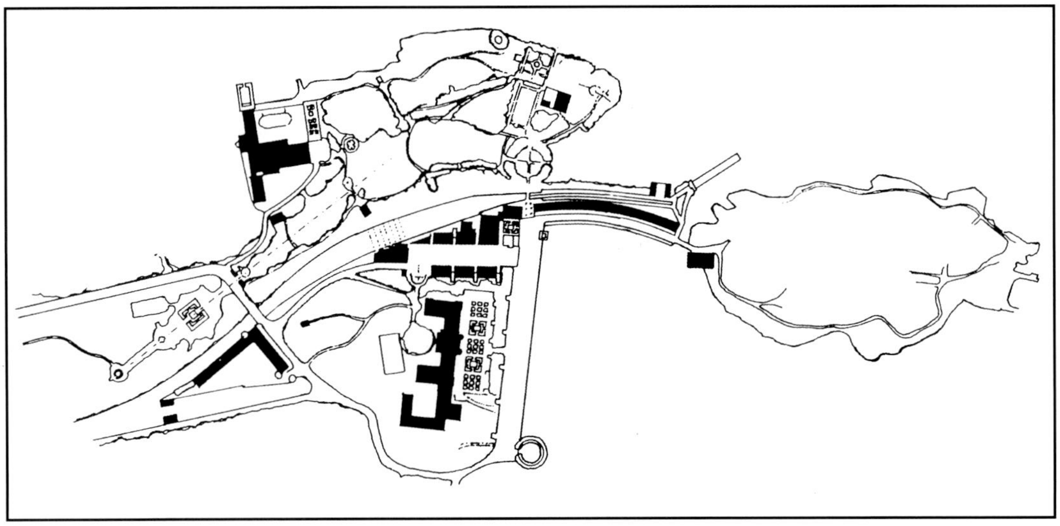

Layout plan.

51. Project for a Cemetery at Pålsjö, Helsingborg, 1919–20

There is a lack of drawings attesting to the work carried out by Lewerentz at Pålsjö, where he produced a project for the local cemetery, with a chapel, crematorium and service buildings. However, from the tone of the letter signed by a number of members of the cemetery board, dated 12 April 1920 and sent to the town council, it may be inferred that the project satisfied the requests contained in the programme:
"The project presented by the architect Sigurd Lewerentz meets this requirement [of the board], obtaining the best possible answer in the debate about the new layout of the cemetery. The project that the architect has submitted to this board provides an effective solution to the question of the crematorium: each building, with a backdrop of trees, is part of a significant architectural and artistic whole."

(G.P.)

52. Wallpaper Factory at Undersås, Gothenburg, 1919–20

In 1919 Lewerentz's father-in-law, a wallpaper manufacturer, asked the architect to design an industrial building, with an adjacent block of workers' flats, in the industrial area of Gothenburg, near the church of Örgryte. Lewerentz's project comprised a large block containing the printing machinery and a two-storey building where the storerooms, packing equipment and the offices would be located; facing the main road, this would incorporate the factory's principal entrance. Next to the industrial complex, Lewerentz also sited a three-storey residential building, intended to house the workers and their families.

(G.P.)

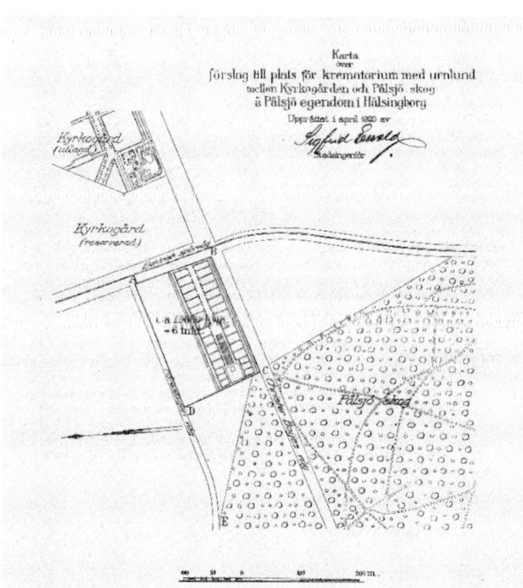

Layout plan.

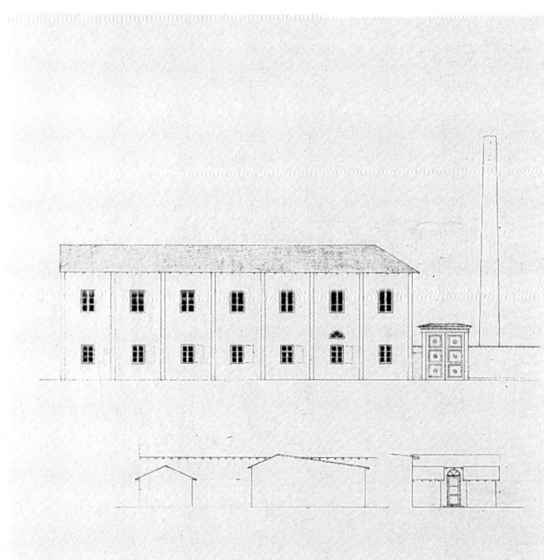

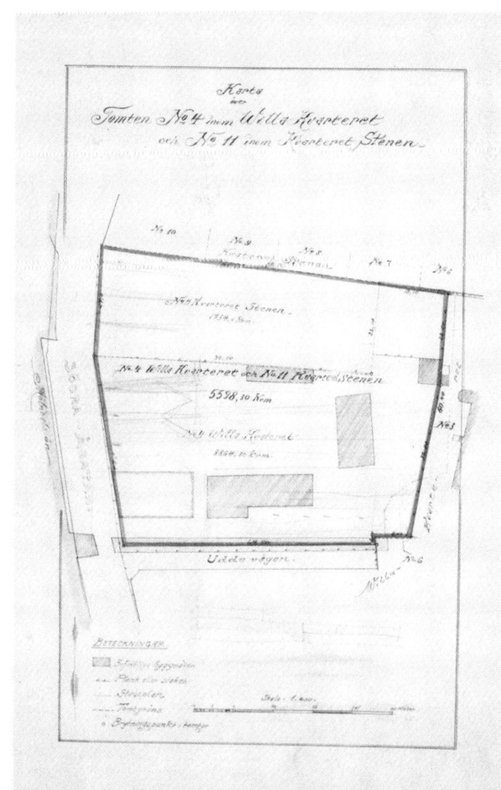

Elevations and layout plan.

53. Extension to Stora Tuna Cemetery and a Cemetery with a Chapel at Kvarnsveden, Borlänge, 1919–24

In 1919 the parish of Stora Tuna, a small town in northern Sweden, near Borlänge, asked Lewerentz to produce a dual project: the extension to Stora Tuna Cemetery and the realization of a new cemetery at Kvarnsveden, a small village just to the north. The project for the extension is based on a very simple layout: two avenues, orthogonal to each other, separate the four burial areas. Bounded by hedges three metres in height, these areas contain the individual graves, while a wide strip, encircling the new site, is intended for the family tombs.
The project for a new cemetery at Kvarnsveden is more complex and of greater interest. The site available, which has the form of a considerably elongated trapezium, is divided into two parts oriented in different ways. The southern section was arranged orthogonally to the axis passing through the entrance—the continuation of a pre-existing external axis—which leads directly to the portico, supported by four rows of four columns, of the main chapel, which, in accordance with tradition, is oriented in an east-west direction, and the long avenue that, leading to the main entrance, separates the two parts of the cemetery.
The northern section, on the other hand, is arranged according to the terraces with their orthogonal geometry, but its orientation follows that of the longer sides of the site, without being set at angle to them, as is the other section.
Thus the internal space of the cemetery clarifies both the general system of reference—external and ritualized—and the internal contingent one, allowing the absoluteness of the first section to conform to the requirements of the site actually available. This dual tension appears to be the core of the project, revealing one of the most typical characteristics of Lewerentz, who was capable of mediating between the absolute and fortuity. In this perspective, the resemblance between the chapel at Kvarnsveden and Asplund's Woodland Chapel in Stockholm South Cemetery—which has often been stressed—appears to be of little account. The Woodland Chapel, where the single-cell building concludes with a dome, is a terminal area, not one of passage, which is what the barrel vault of Lewerentz's chapel clearly seems to be, as it links the structure with the rest of the cemetery complex of which the chapel itself constitutes a part. Another interesting element is the belfry. Situated to the north of the chapel, it is oriented on the same axis and is built on a cross plan that has the same dimensions as the interior of the chapel, indicating, with the greater cross section of one of its two arms, the north. Fragments of a roof, with the same slope and the same materials as the huge slate roof of the chapel, cover the belfry. Its archaic and unemphatic appearance, deriving from its function and the symbolism linking it to the proportions of the chapel, made it difficult to understand and accept. Shortly after it was constructed, in fact, the local community replaced it with a more traditional belfry. Subsequently, a crematorium and mortuary, designed by other architects, were added to the chapel, totally altering its original appearance.

Bibliography: Lewerentz 1928b; Några kapell och staplar 1928; Ahlin 1985b, pp. 84–87; Caldenby 1997, pp. 86–87.

(P.G.)

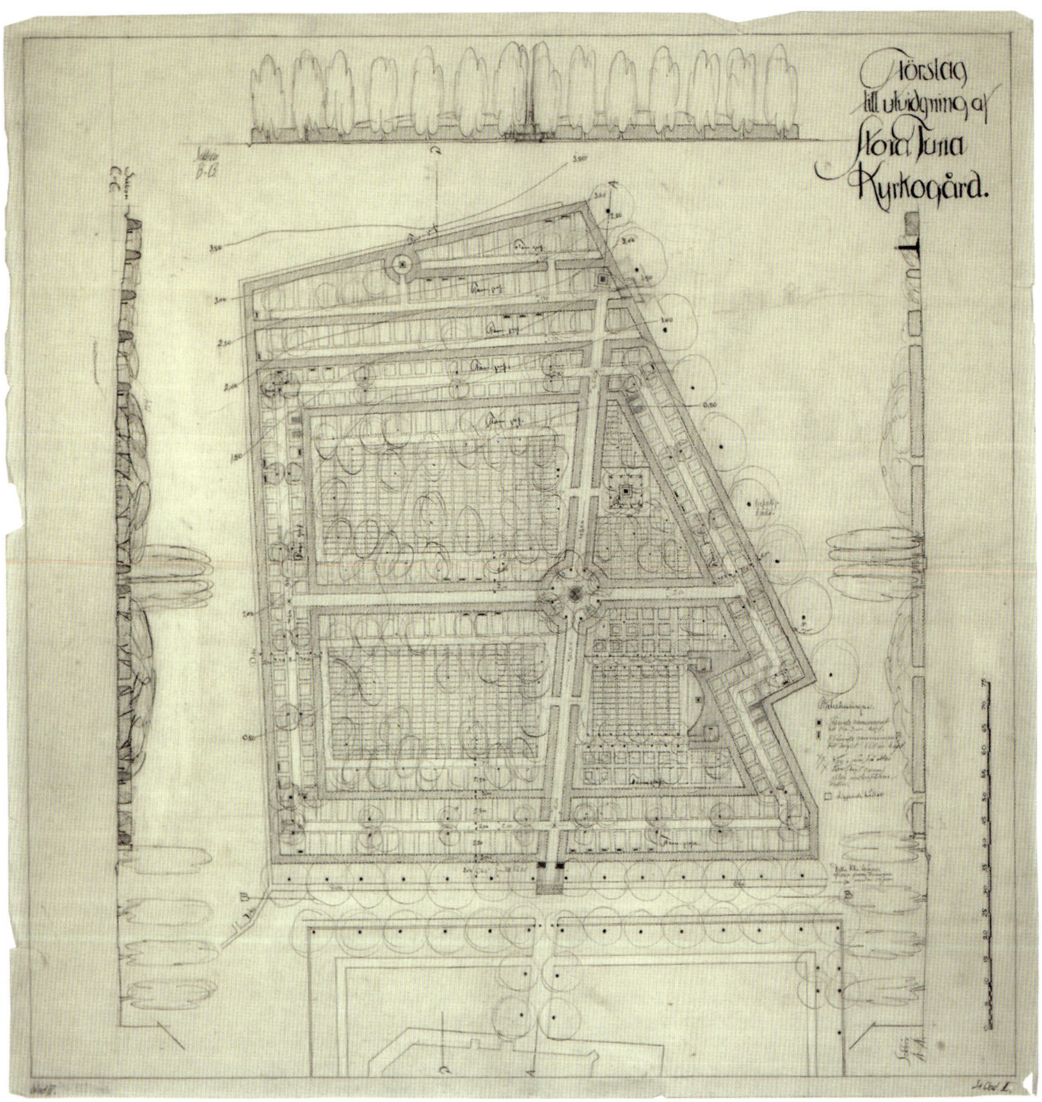

Stora Tuna Cemetery, layout plan.

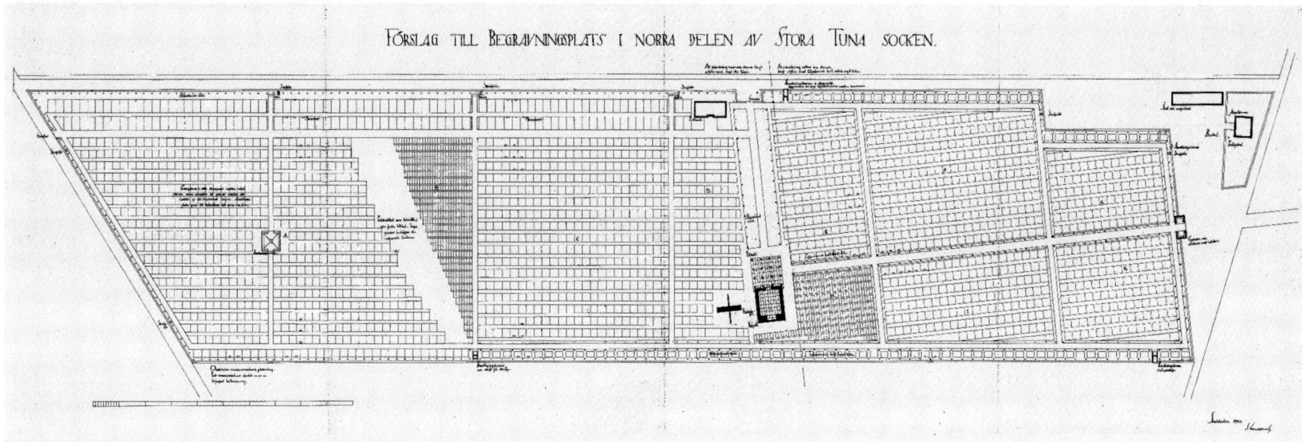

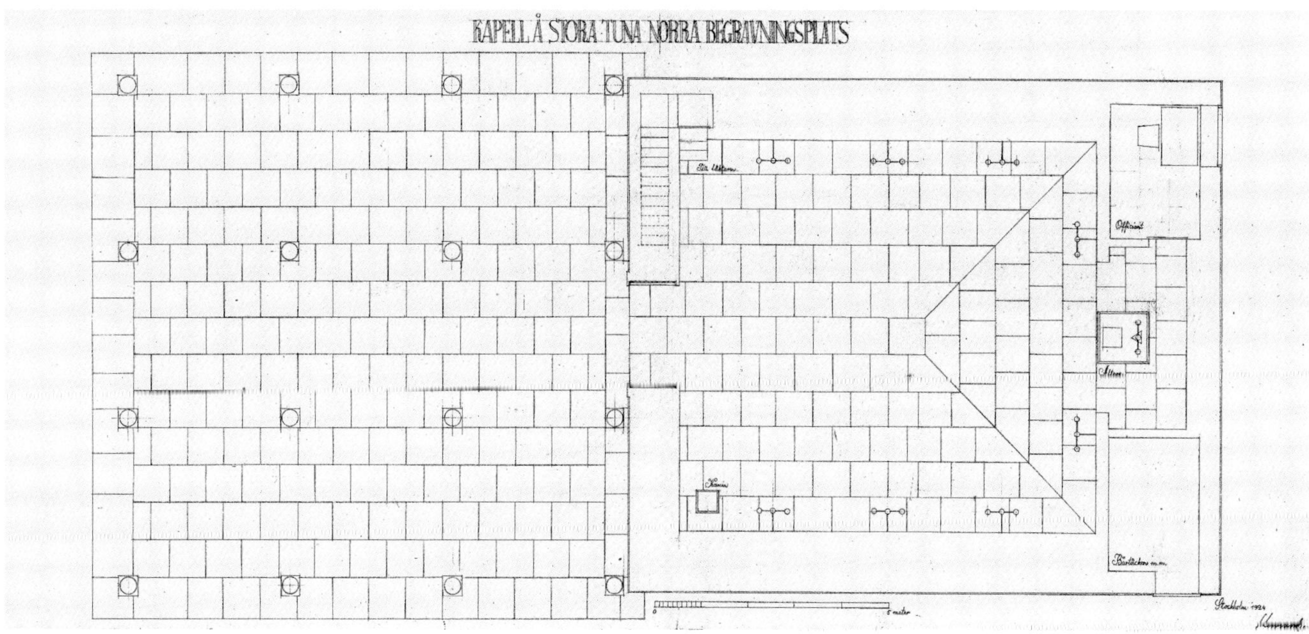

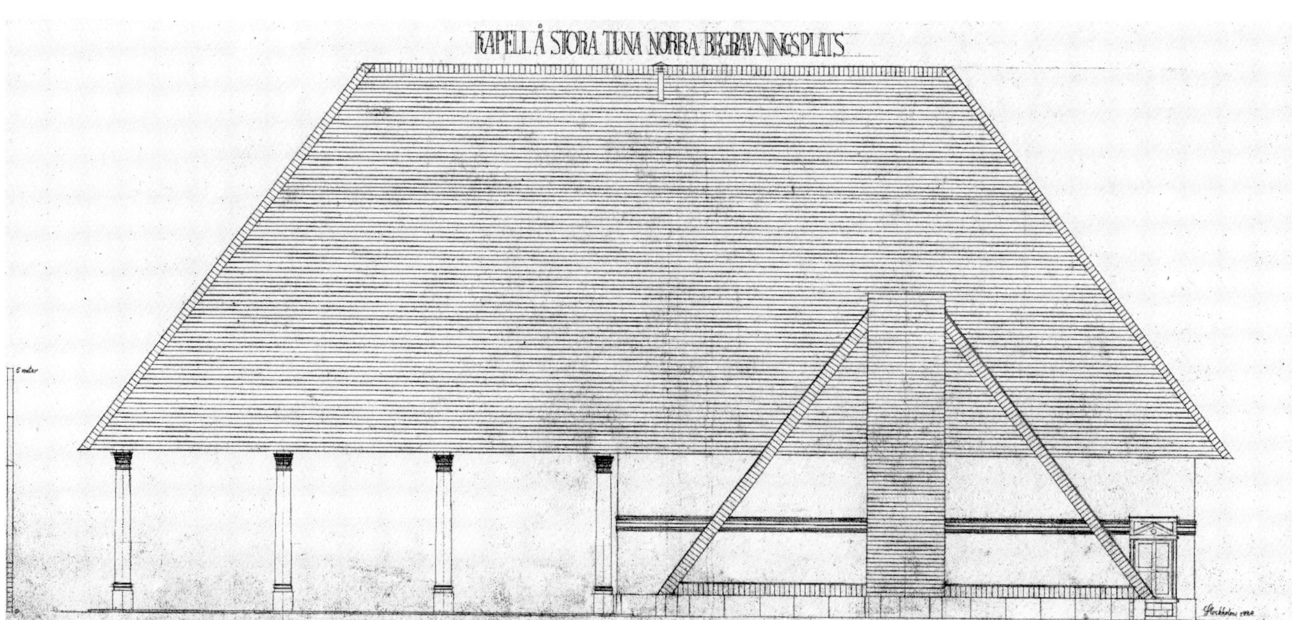

Kvarnsveden Cemetery, layout plan, 1924.

Kvarnsveden Cemetery, funerary chapel, plan showing flooring, and north elevation, 1924.

Kvarnsveden Cemetery,
funerary chapel, interior.

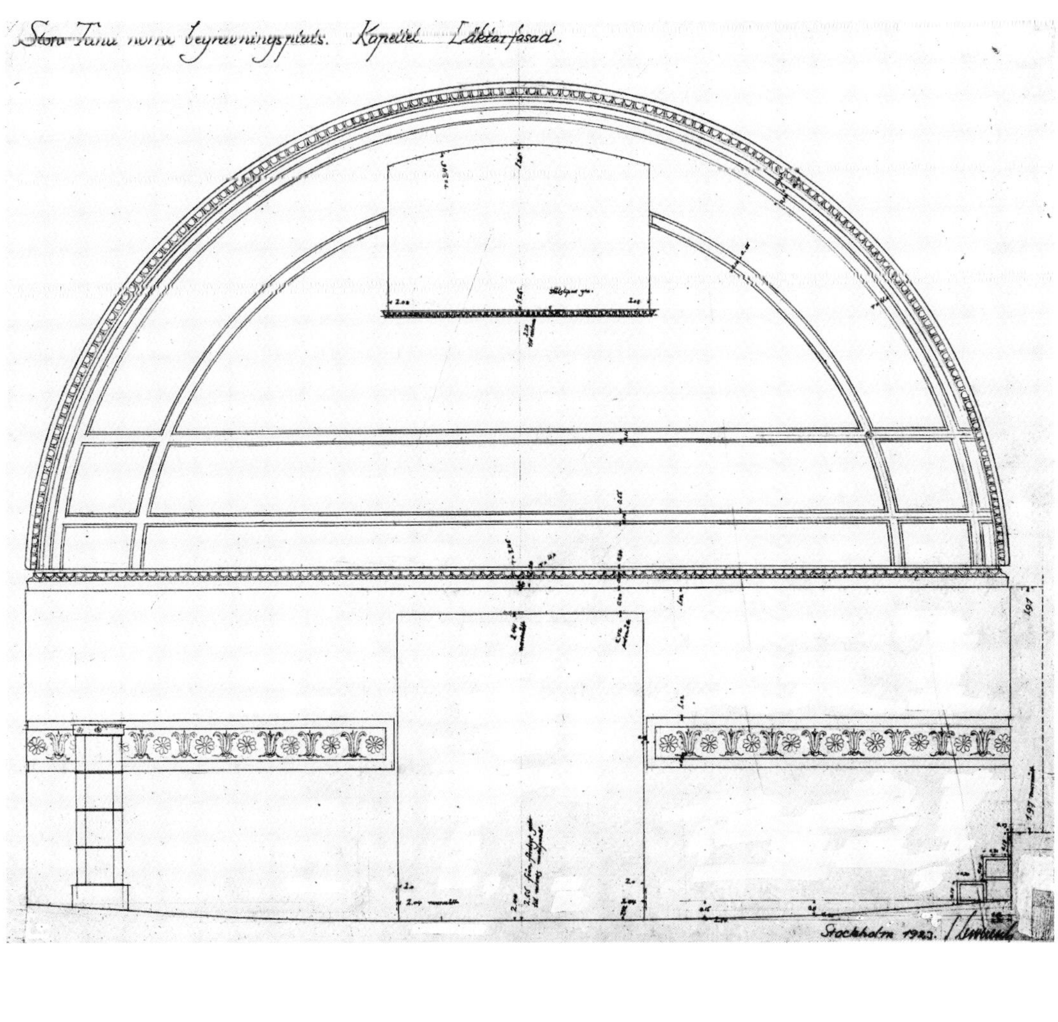

Interior and cross section.

Kvarnsveden Cemetery, the funerary chapel under construction.

54. Förening Verkstad Exhibition, Djurgården, Stockholm, 1920

In 1920 the Förening Verkstad, an association of artists and architects who all felt the need to produce objects with simple, well-defined forms, made its first public appearance at the Liljevalch Gallery, at Djurgården. The members of the association comprised some of the emergent architects of the day, such as Erik Gunnar Asplund and Hakon Ahlberg and, on the occasion of the exhibition, other young architects, including Torsten Stubelius and Sigurd Lewerentz, were also invited to participate.
For the exhibition Lewerentz designed a very refined domestic interior, a drawing-room with space devoted to music, represented by a grand piano; made to a design by the architect himself, this was the feature of greatest interest in the room. The room, with a rectangular plan, was characterized by the polarity of the two main elements: on the one hand the drawing-room table, on the other, the grand piano. The colours were dark, while the walls were finished with antiqued plaster, similar to Pompeian encaustic, common in Neoclassical interiors in Sweden at that time.

Bibliography: Åkerlund 1920; Bergsten 1920; Wahlman 1920; Ahlin 1985b, pp. 105–06.

(G.P.)

55. Project for a Cemetery at Ljungby, 1920–23

Lewerentz worked on this project from 1920 to 1923; in the following three years the requests by the municipality and the parish of Ljungby for modifications were only partially satisfied by the architect. It was, above all, the position of the chapel, placed by the architect on the main avenue, almost at the centre of the site, that was most strongly criticized by the board responsible for the construction of the cemetery, which, up to 1926 repeatedly asked Lewerentz to locate the chapel elsewhere.
In Lewerentz's project, which had already been submitted in 1922, there is a network of orthogonal paths in the cemetery bordering the six burial areas. The chapel is located on the principal axis, while the building housing the equipment is sited outside the entrance, on the road to Ljungby. The whole burial area is, moreover, separated from the external roads by a thick screen of trees, which gives more privacy to the places intended for meditation.

(G.P.)

The drawing-room designed by Lewerentz.

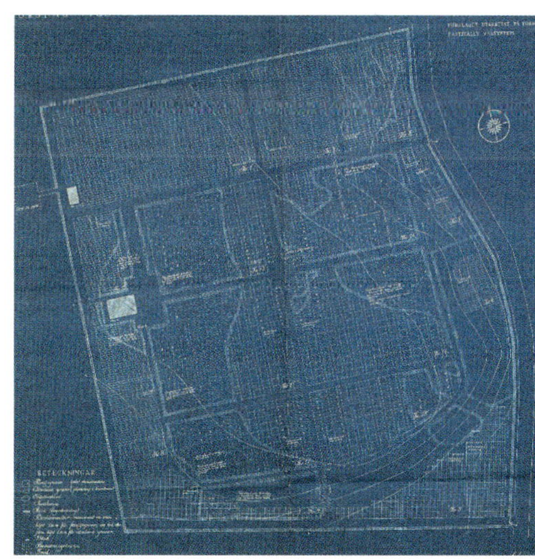

Layout plan.

56. Project for Urban Renewal of the Norrmalm District, Stockholm, 1921

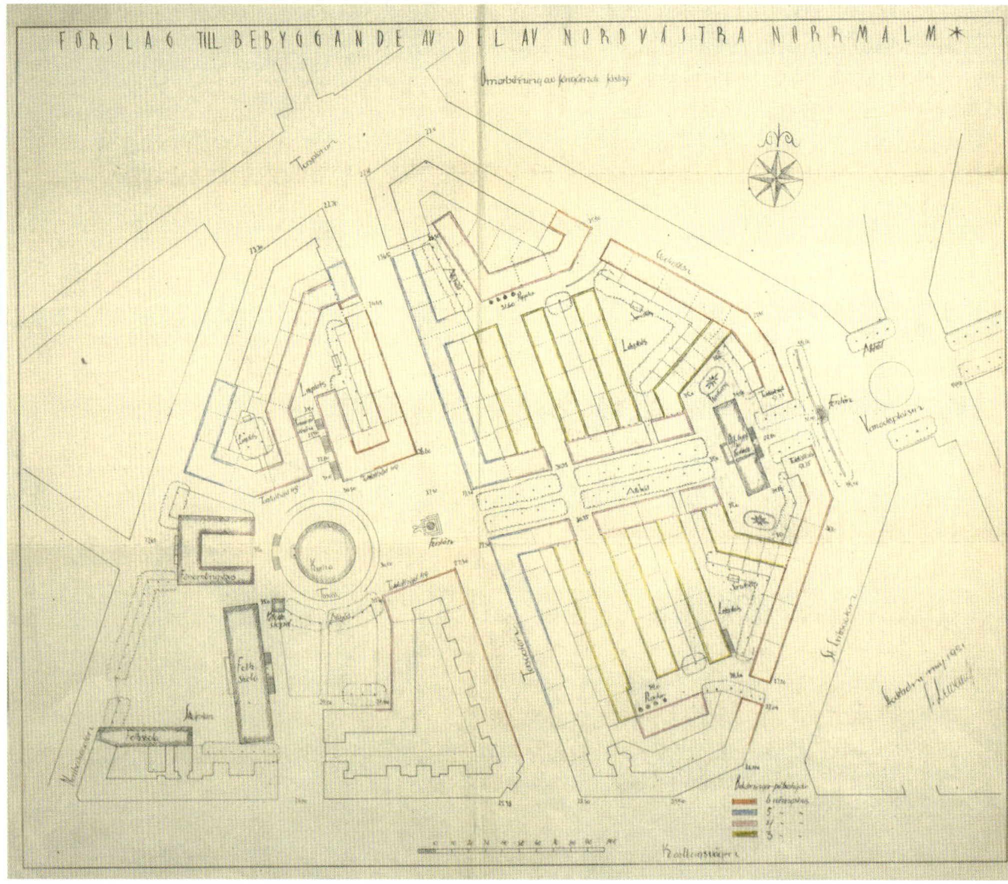

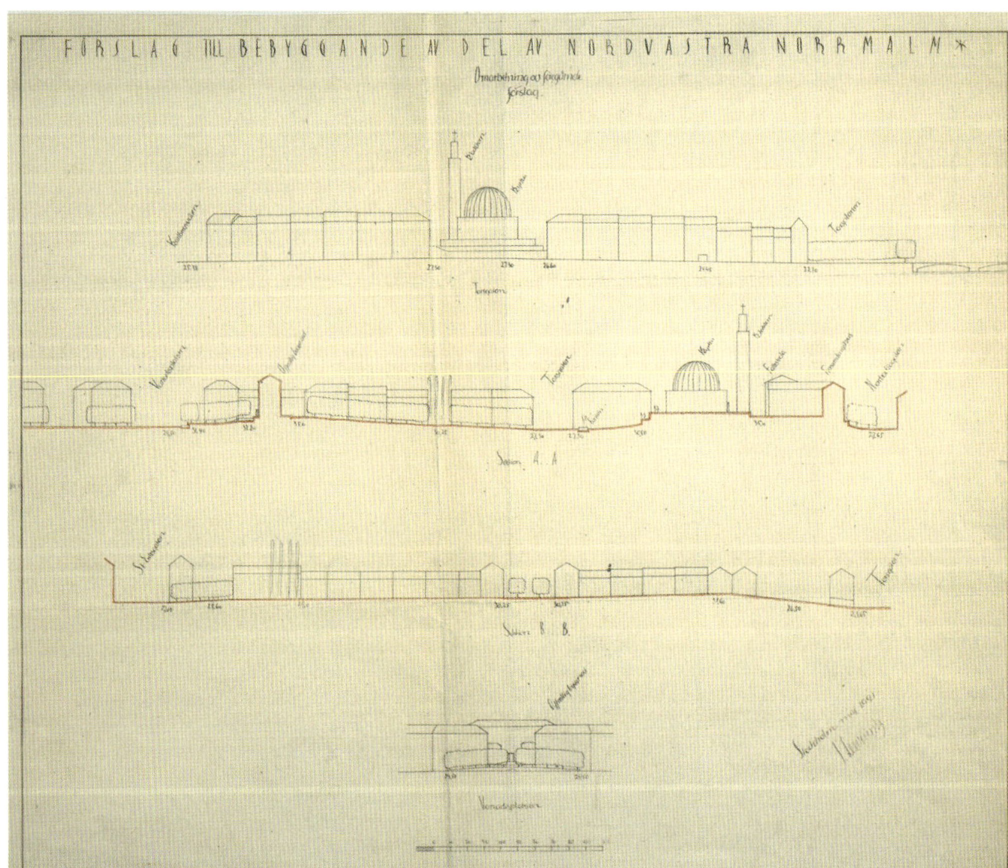

Layout plan and profiles.

57. Project for an Extension to the Långsele Cemetery, 1921–22

Lewerentz produced the project for an extension to the Långsele Cemetery at the request of the municipality, which also required a funerary monument for the family of the benefactor whose munificence made the extension possible. The preliminary project specified that the internal paths would partially be continuations of those of the old cemetery, indicated the location of the burial areas and gave details of the types of trees to be planted and the siting of two small buildings: the benefactor's family chapel and the mortuary.

Bibliography: Ahlin 1985b, pp. 87–88.

(G.P.)

Layout plan and profiles.

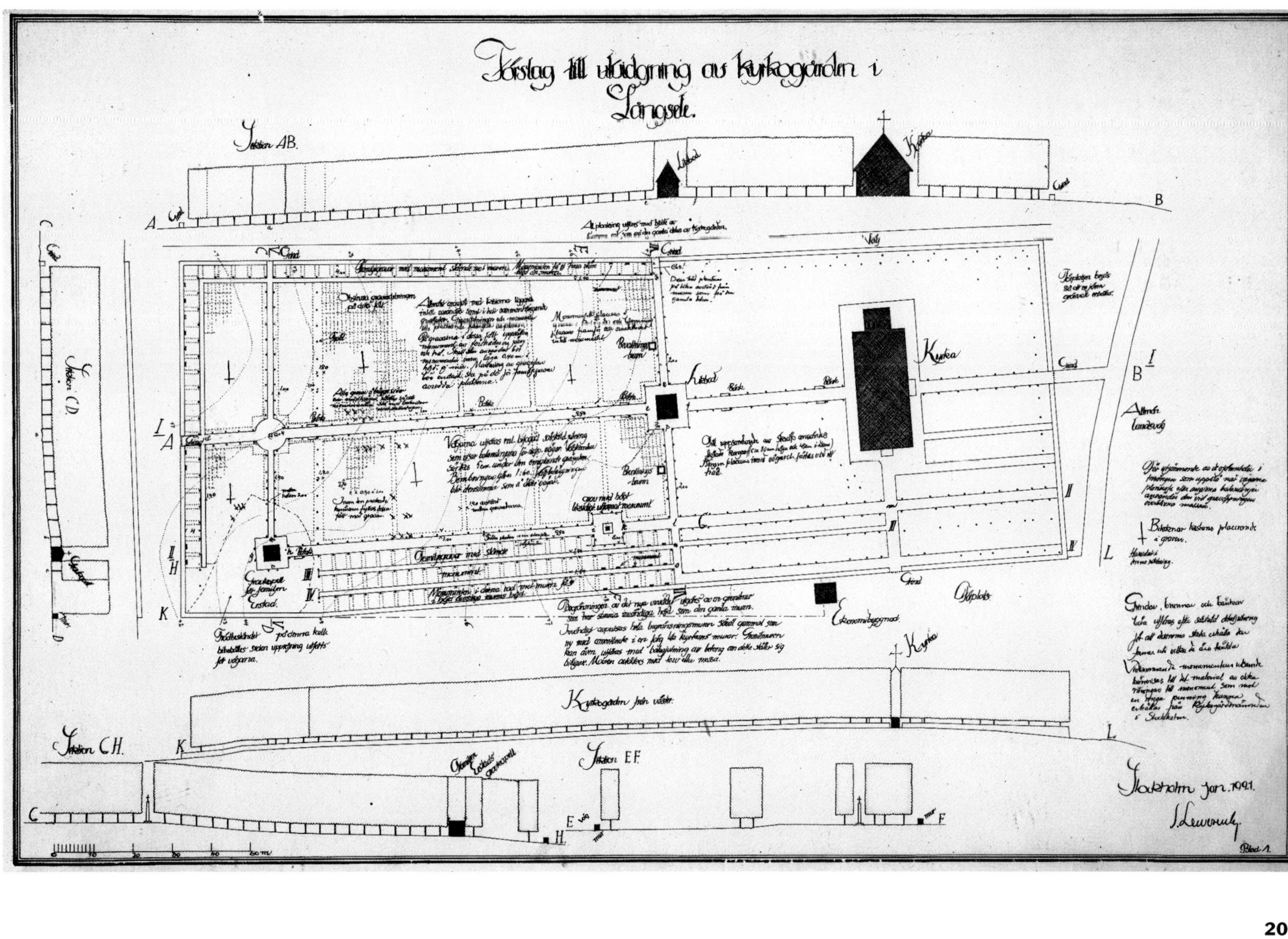

58. Competition Project for Gävleån Cemetery, 1921-22

motto "Efter ån"

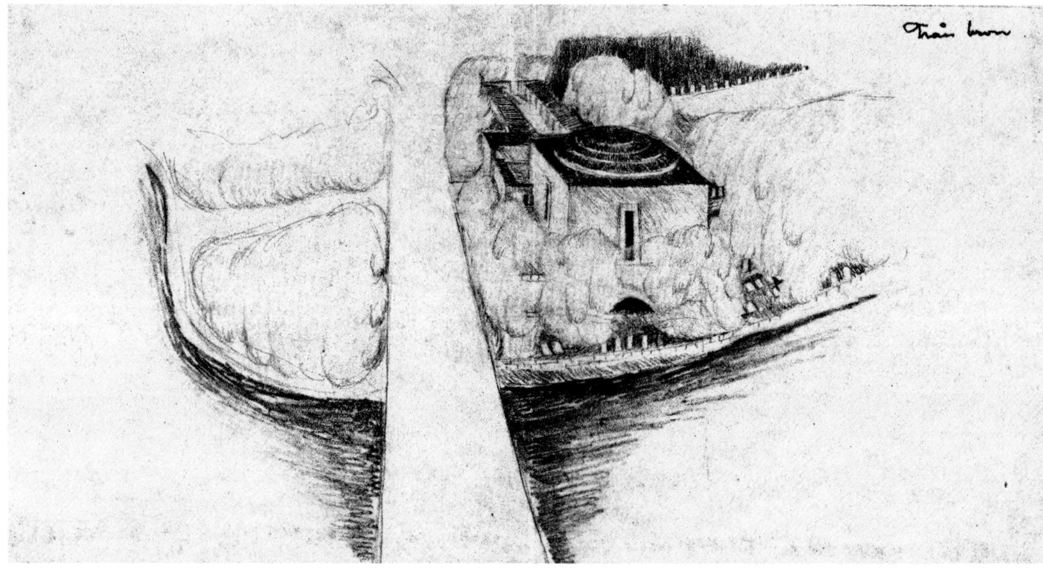

Located just outside the town, the site covers an area of about forty hectares and, along its northern edge, borders on the River Gävleån. As emerges from the competition programme, the position of the main entrance to the south, on the Västravägen, just after the Gustav Bridge, is established by the cemetery board, which also gives precise instructions as to the way the functions should be distributed on the site. The project submitted by Lewerentz respects the conditions of the programme, but interprets them so that they are in harmony with the specific characteristics of the place, as is expressed by the motto "Efter ån" (beyond the brook). In the project he prepared for the competition, the architect not only placed the entrance in the position suggested, but also highlighted its role by locating the chapel next to it and making it the starting-point for the main avenue that crosses the whole of the cemetery. Nearly halfway along this, after running parallel to the river flowing to the north of the site, the avenue widens and links up with the open area in front of the crematorium. After this place, the hub of the whole layout and the network of internal paths, the avenue necessarily becomes rectilinear, which gives it a somewhat monumental character and, to a certain extent, echoes the Way of the Seven Wells in the first project for Stockholm South Cemetery. The avenue then terminates in the "place of remembrance", which may also be reached by various paths linking up with the internal roads in the cemetery. The urns and family tombs are mainly sited in the southern part of the cemetery, which is divided into small plots in the area between the main avenue and the Västravägen, in accordance with a plan that favours privacy and meditation.

Bibliography: Ahlin 1985b, pp. 89–90.

(G.P.)

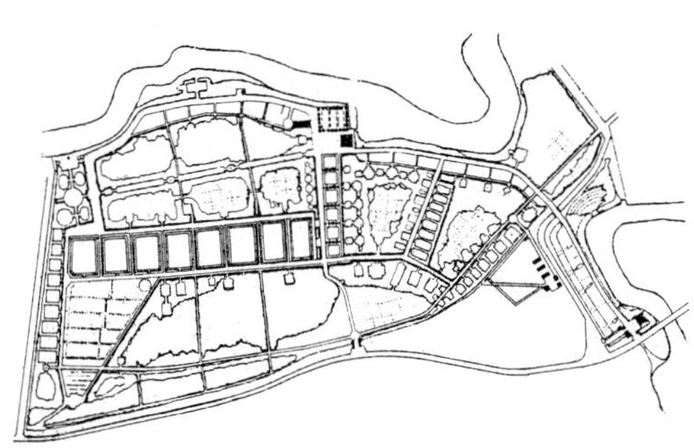

Perspective sketches and layout plan (redrawn).

59. Project for Single-Family Houses at Rostorp, Malmö, 1922

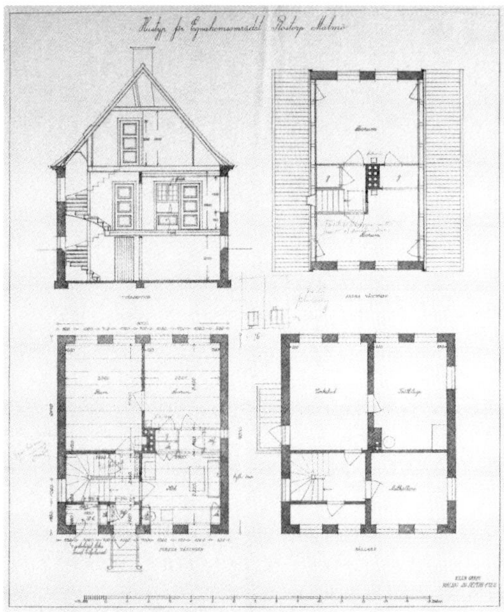

Section and plans of the various floors.

60. Pavilions for the National Exhibition of 1923, Gothenburg, 1922–23

Projects:
Eldbegängelse Förening pavilion
Pavilion for the Förening Verkstad (Association for the Promotion of Furnishing Design), with Melchior Wernstedt
Bedroom in the Förening Verkstad pavilion
Competition for the furnishing of an office for Åtvidaberg, with Osvald Almqvist in the Förening Verkstad section

The National Exhibition in Gothenburg, which opened in May 1923, was intended to be the most important furnishing exhibition of the century, in some respects foreshadowing the issues addressed by the Stockholm Exhibition of 1930. The exhibition was held in an area behind the Götaplatsen that extended from the Museum of Applied Arts to the Liseberg Funfair—inaugurated on the occasion of the exhibition—and was laid out according to a project drawn up by the architect A. Bjerke, who, together with S. Eriksson, won the competition for the Götaplatsen in 1918. Bjerke's project involved the construction of three pavilions behind the museum: the first, containing the exhibition devoted to the applied arts, was designed by Hakon Ahlberg; the second, the one intended for the Förening Verkstad, was the work of Sigurd Lewerentz and Melchior Wernstedt, assisted by E. Wettergren of the Svenska Slöjdförening (National Applied Arts Association) and E. Hald of the Förening Verkstad; the third pavilion, housing the Eldbegängelse Förening (National Cremation Association), was also entrusted to Lewerentz.

The site on which the Förening Verkstad pavilion was to be built was, as Lewerentz wrote in the journal Byggmästaren, located next to Ahlberg's domed hall ... comprising a gently ascending road thirteen metres in width, it borders on a very steep path to the south and a beautiful park to the north, which slopes rapidly downhill... It is, however, very difficult to work on this very narrow site hemmed in between the slopes of the promontory and the ancient trees, without damaging the latter, which, above all, surround the pavilion with the largest number of rooms, influencing the proportions and lighting of the rooms and also the other pavilions and the neighbouring residential areas. It has been decided to build separate pavilions with steeply pitched roofs in order to harmonize the complex with the group of isolated villas with very steep roofs [present in the area]. The longest building was located on the crest of the hill: containing the rooms with the interiors designed by various architects specially invited by the association, it was flanked by an arcade leading towards a small square around which a number of the other exhibition buildings stood.
As Lewerentz stressed in his description, the very uneven surface of the site and the thick vegetation meant that the exhibition had to be housed in a number of separate buildings, so that the small square became the hub of the site. Moreover, in the section devoted to interior design, Lewerentz participated together with Osvald Almqvist in a competition for the furnishings of a typical office to be displayed at the exhibition. Unfortunately, however, these were not selected, although Lewerentz displayed one

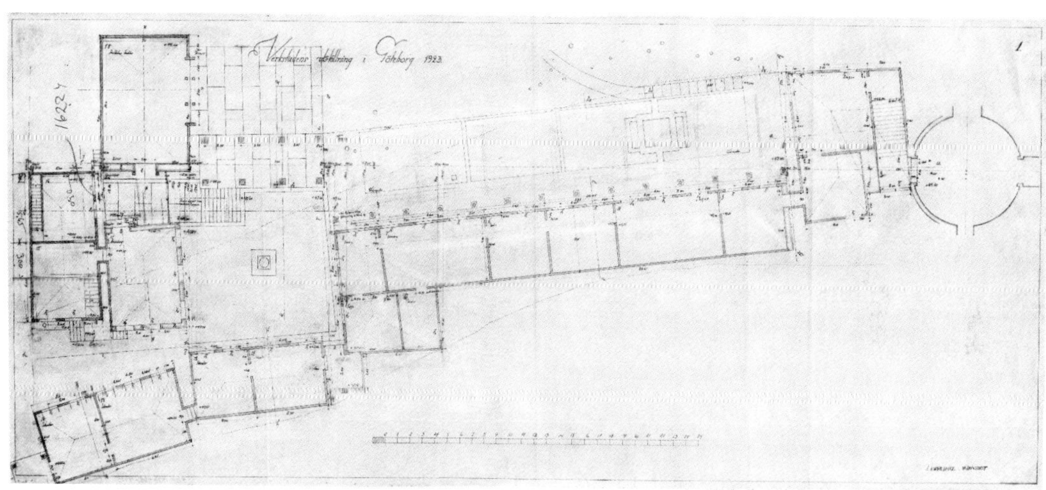

Förening Verkstad pavilion, layout plan, with M. Wernstedt.

of his interior schemes because he was also invited to design a bedroom, which he realized in Neoclassical style.

The Eldbegängelse Förening pavilion, also designed by Lewerentz, was built on the top of the hill, behind the Förening Verkstad pavilion, on a very steep site that the architect adapted by terracing the slope. A flight of steps led up to a vantage point commanding a view of the exhibition area and part of the city. This was overlooked by two small buildings: one sheltered the top of the stairway, while in the other—oriented orthogonally to the first—the architect placed a fountain, which was recessed into the wall and protected by a small loggia. The arch in the wall, through which the water flowed from the fountain, was, in some ways, reminiscent of the design proposed for the crematorium chapel at Bergaliden, where a stream flowed under the building in a vaulted space, with a segmental arch on both the long elevations. The long flight of steps was interrupted by the various terraces, where Lewerentz placed horizontal and vertical tombstones and wall urns.

Bibliography: Ahlberg 1923; Asplund 1923; Blank 1923; Lewerentz 1923; Ahlin 1985b, pp. 106–09.

(G.P.)

Views of the Förening Verkstad pavilion.

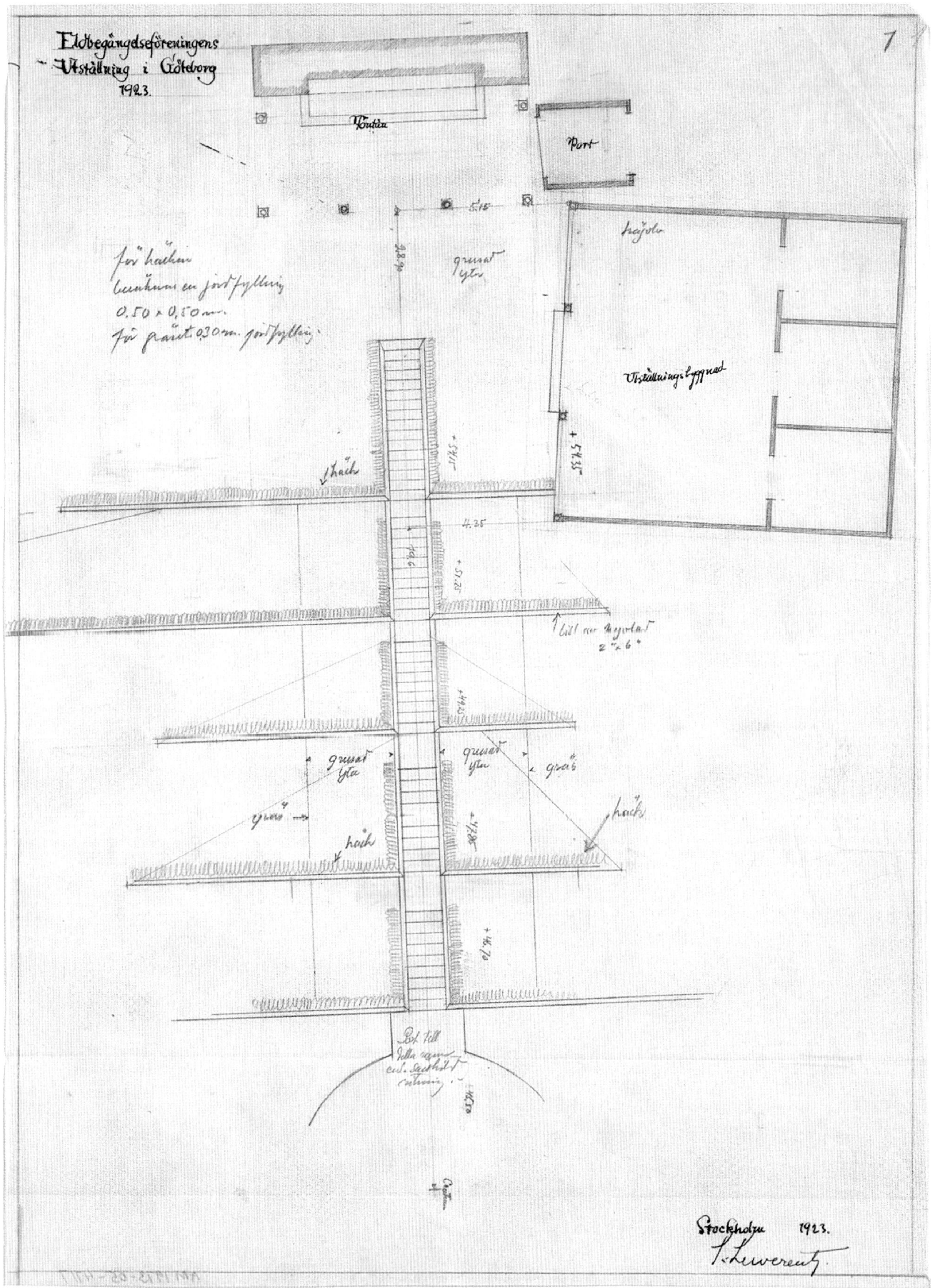

Eldbegängelse Förening pavilion, plan of access stairway.

Förening Verkstad pavilion, study drawing of the bedroom.

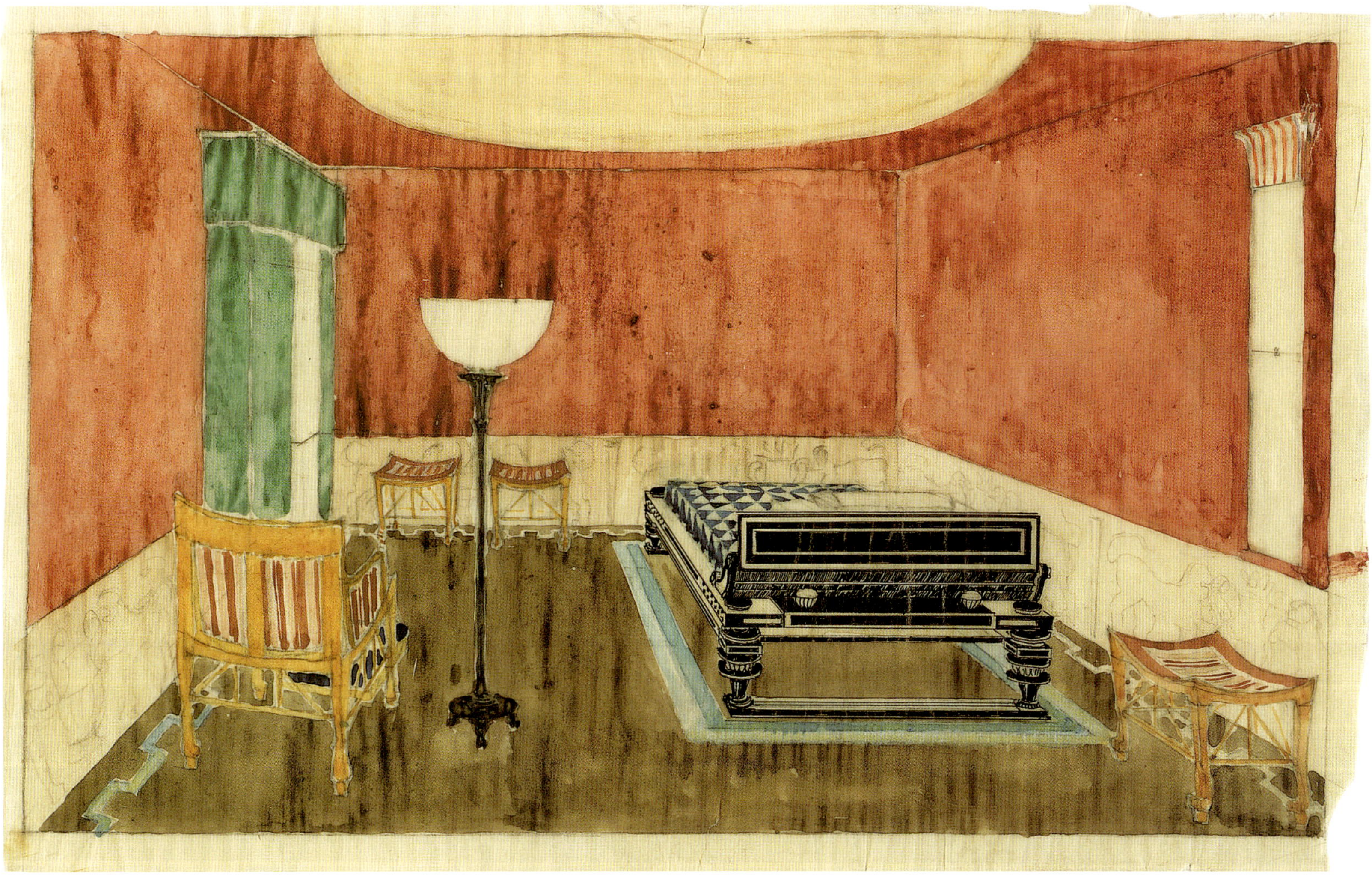

61. Competition Project for Students' Residences and the Students' Union at the University of Uppsala, 1923
with Osvald Almqvist and B. Hedvall; motto "Futurum"

In 1923 the municipality of Uppsala, the seat of Sweden's oldest university, located not far from Stockholm, organized a competition for the design of new students' residences and the students' union. The site selected by the municipal committee—a block known as Ubbo, in one of the historical areas of the city—is characterized by its shape, an irregular triangle, and the presence of a notable difference in level that obliquely divides the area into two parts.

In the project that Lewerentz produced together with O. Almqvist and B. Hedvall, the difference in level became its central element: a long portico crosses the site diagonally on the edge of the steep slope, clearly separating the area destined for the students' residences from the one for the students' union.
The L-shaped blocks of the residences are juxtaposed in order to obtain courtyards overlooked by the rooms, determining the parallel distribution of the buildings, which, thanks to their small scale, are more in keeping with the character of the old city. Indeed, the competition programme laid down that the residences should be limited to a height of two storeys.

The students' union complex, located below the slope and linked to the portico along the top of it by several stairways situated between the buildings, contains, in addition to the administrative offices, a conference hall seating 650, a library, a refectory and other communal spaces. Also for this part of the site, the group of architects proposed an L-shaped plan, similar to the one adopted for the residences, which allowed the different functional requirements to be housed in separate buildings, thus obtaining a very clear general layout despite the high density of the scheme.

Bibliography: Ahlberg 1924, pp. 1–10.

(G.P.)

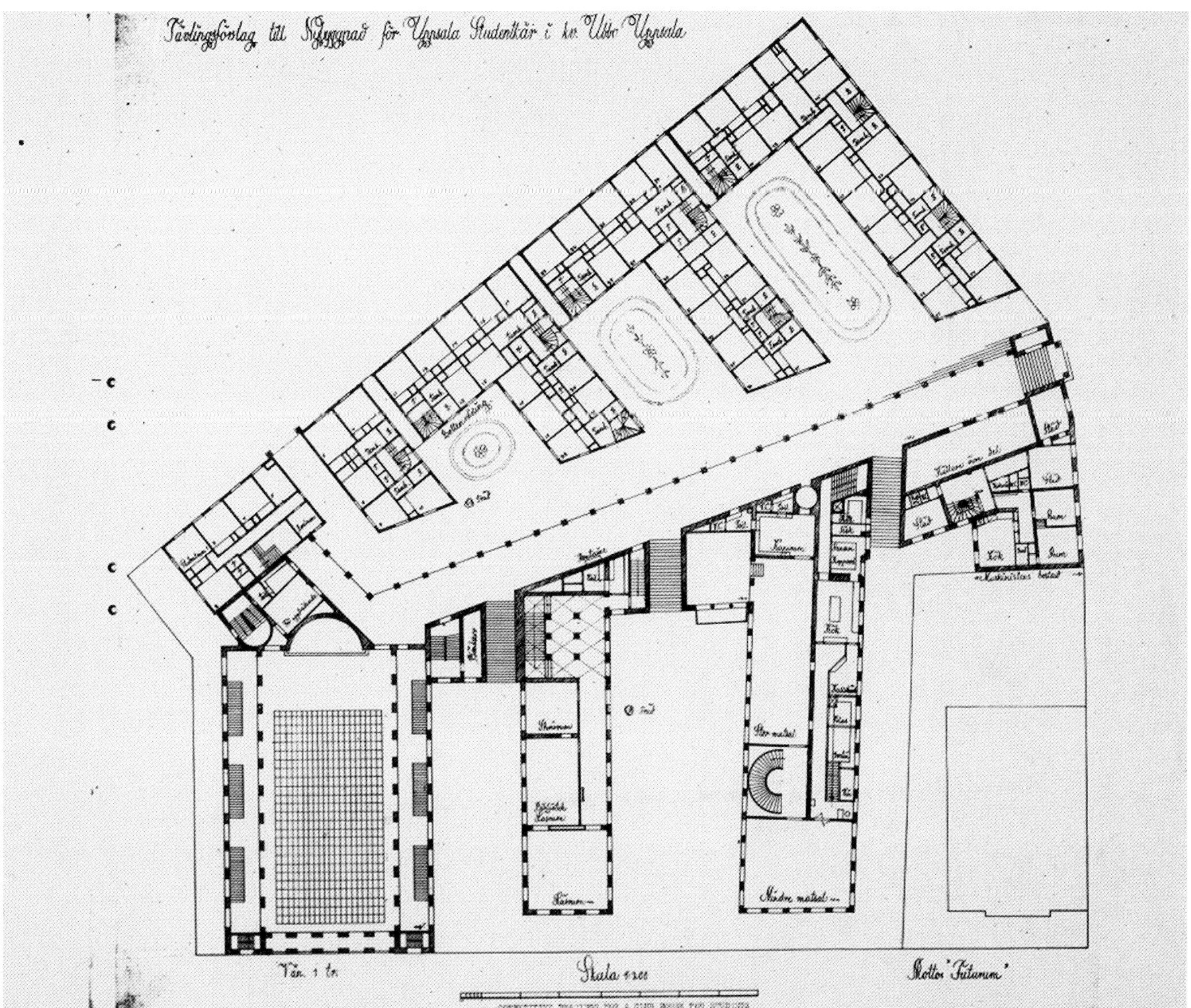

Layout plan.

View of one of the courtyards between the student residences.

62. Project for a Cemetery with a Crematorium, Gothenburg, 1923

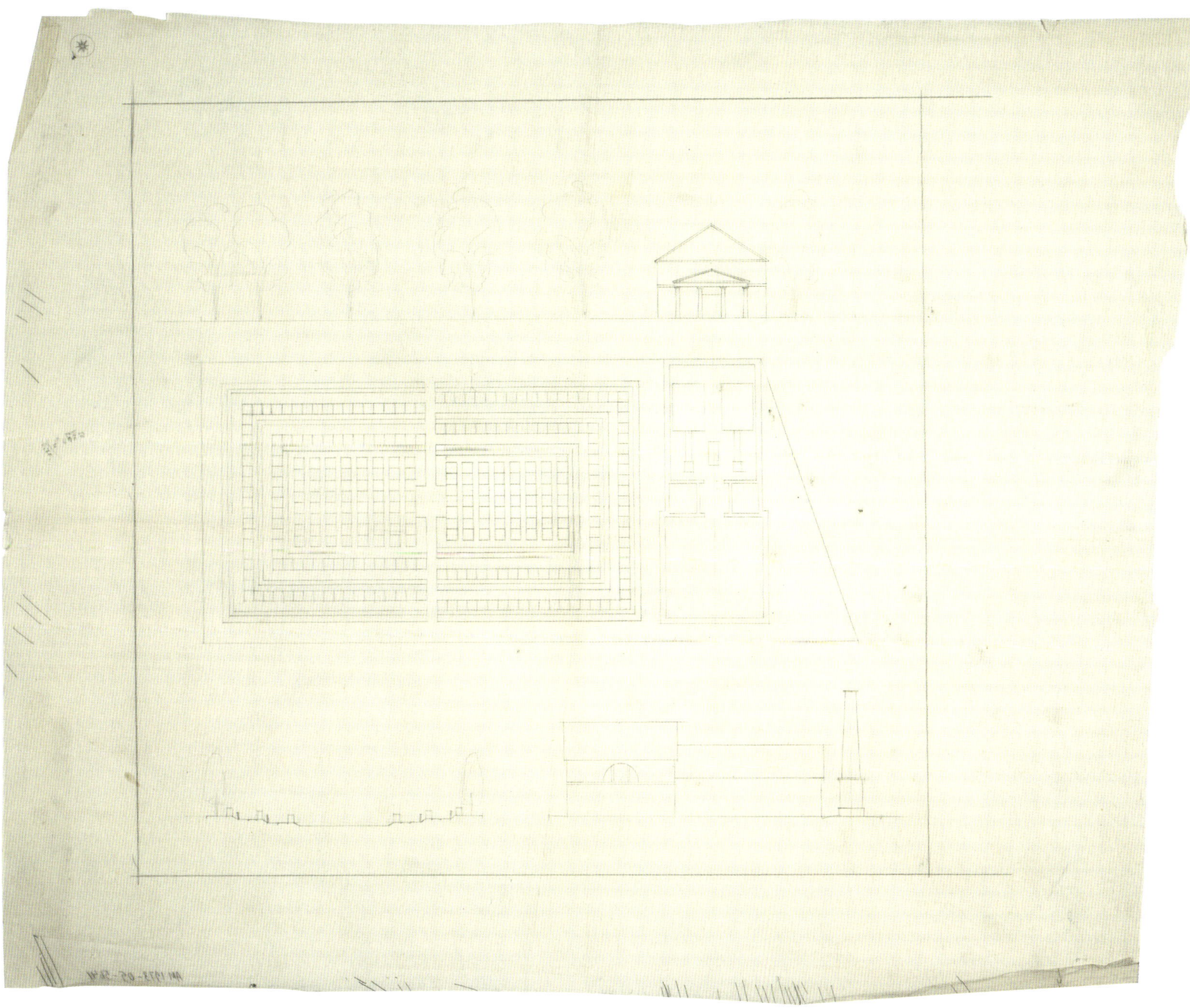

Layout plan and elevations of some buildings.

63. Project (1924–27) and Competitions (1933 onwards) for the Malmö Theatre, 1924 onwards

In 1924 the municipality of Malmö set up a commission to investigate the possibility of erecting a new civic building for theatrical performances and concerts. On behalf of the commission, the engineer E. Bülow Hübe asked Lewerentz to prepare a number of projects for the new theatre that would then serve to check the validity of the programme drawn up by the commission. This required the realization of a single hall seating about a thousand, suitable for various uses (theatrical performances and concerts), with particular attention being paid to the stage and the service rooms, which had to be large enough to store the scenery, as well as providing sufficient space for rehearsals. Lewerentz worked from 1924 to 1927 on three possible solutions. The first involved a single compact building, with a square base, flanked by a narrower, taller construction for the stage. The second proposed a semicircular building for the large hall, leaving unaltered the higher parallelepiped for the stage contained in the first solution, on the opposite side of which was juxtaposed a sort of small temple, serving as the only monumental entrance to the complex. The third solution, chosen by the commission as the scheme on which the competition programme should be based, elaborated the second idea with fewer parts assembled together, but with two different entrances leading to two halls, one for concerts, the other for theatre. The type of architecture proposed by Lewerentz for the complex was decidedly classicizing, displaying the influence—as in the contemporary Resurrection Chapel and, above all, in the project for the main chapel in the Eastern Cemetery at Malmö—of Schinkel, although the individual elements were notably stylized.
In 1926 Lewerentz's project was presented as the ideal proposal for the new civic building, a sort of guide for the commission, which suggested the theatre should be located on one of the sites adjacent to the numerous canals in the centre of Malmö. It was quite some time, however, before the competition was actually announced. When this occurred, in 1933, the

Perspective drawing of the foyer, 1926 version.

commission, deeming that a building of this type required more open space around it, had already found a new site outside the city centre, to the south-west. The competition conditions also required development plans for some of the areas adjacent to the site, as well as a detailed functional programme for the new theatre demonstrating the real capacity of the planned building to become a "total theatre" that, in accordance with the theories current at that time, would be capable of stimulating effective interaction between the audience and the actors.
Lewerentz's project, identified by the motto "43", was the winner. It involved the realization of a complex divided into separate buildings having different functions: thus the clarity of the distribution depended on the spatial articulation. Oriented in such a way that the volume of the hall was on the same axis as the entrance, the structure was divided into three buildings. The largest, having the form of a parallelepiped, dominated the complex; in its centre it housed the stage with the service spaces, while a much smaller construction was placed next to the main block to contain the rehearsal rooms. A separate narrow block, seven storeys high, placed orthogonally to the principal axis, housed the dressing-rooms, costume storage and offices. Lastly, a third block, shaped like a sector of a circle and grafted onto the base of the stage building, contained the auditorium and foyer of a single large hall.
As regards the request for a development plan for the area, Lewerentz proposed a series of buildings in line oriented on the east-west axis, as suggested by the precepts of the new Rationalist architecture.
Because of disagreement among members of the jury, some of whom considered Lewerentz's project unrealizable (although it had been awarded first prize), it was decided to ask the winners of the first three prizes to submit new projects, announcing in 1935 a second competition, which was won once again by Lewerentz.
The second project resembled the previous one in many respects, especially as far as the articulation of the volumes concerned, since this was almost identical. The main changes to the structure were of a technical nature, especially in the auditorium, where special attention was paid to the acoustic problems resulting from the need to use the hall for performances of both drama and music.
Externally, however, the project differed mainly with regard to the new orientation of the layout, which was at right angles to the previous one, and the shifting of the

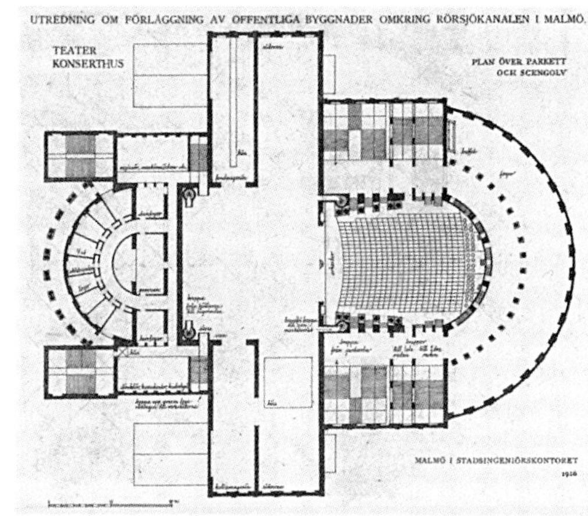

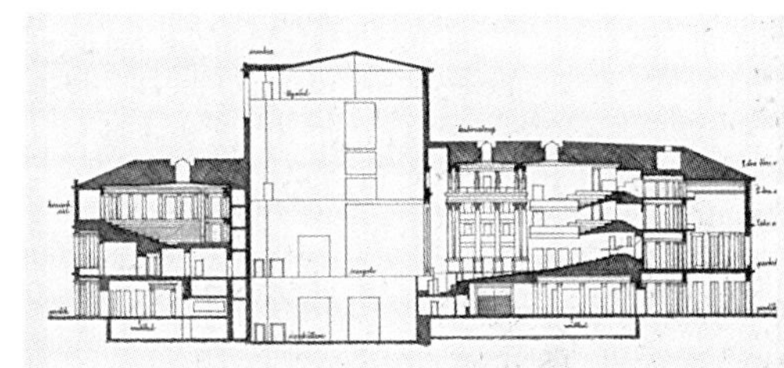

Plan and section.

Aerial view of the site with photomontage, 1924–27 version.

View, layout plan and model, first competition, 1933.

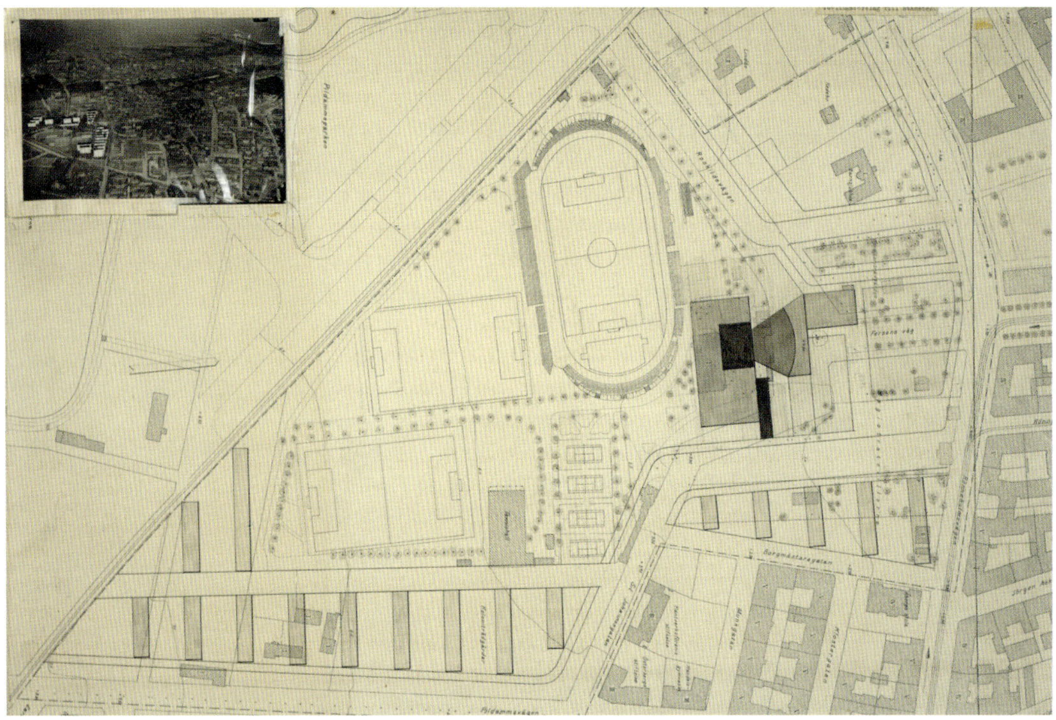

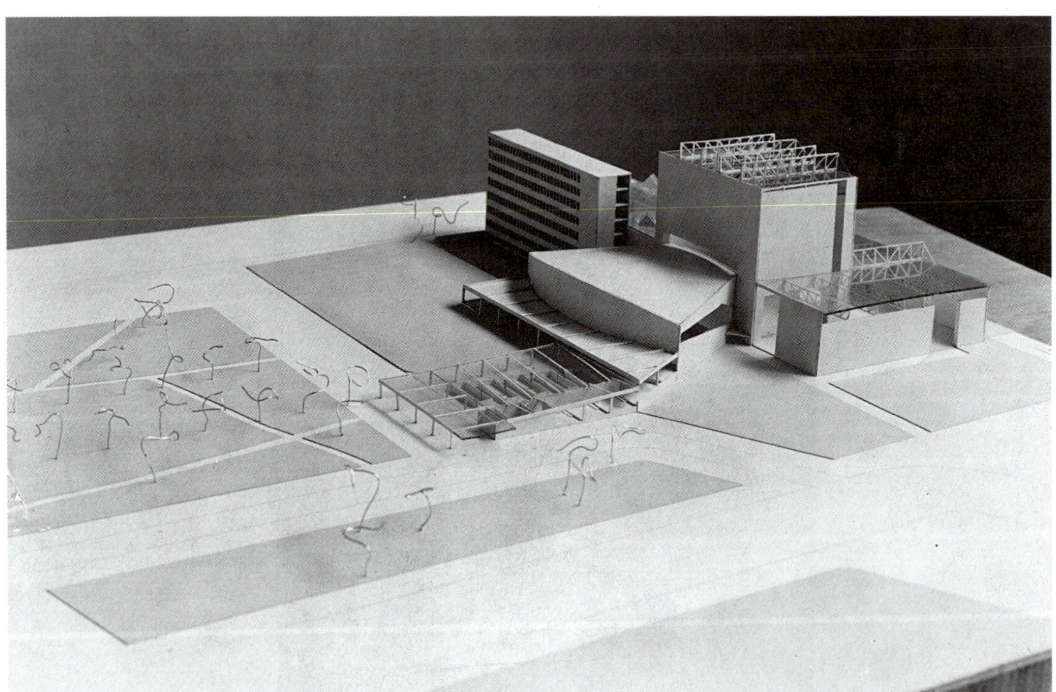

View of proposed theatre,
first competition, 1933.

Side elevations, second competition, 1935.

Study of elevation, final version, 1935–44, with E. Lallerstedt and D. Helldén.

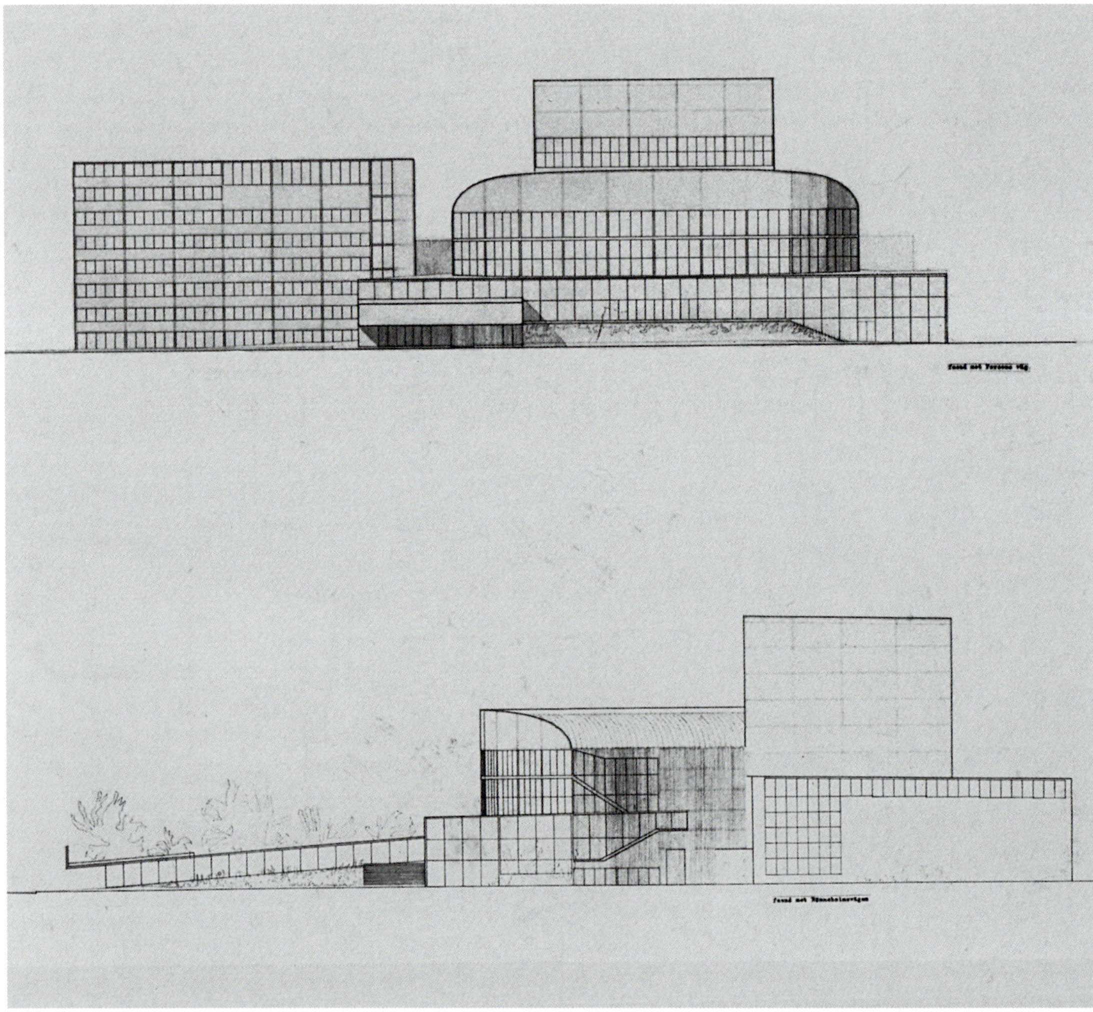

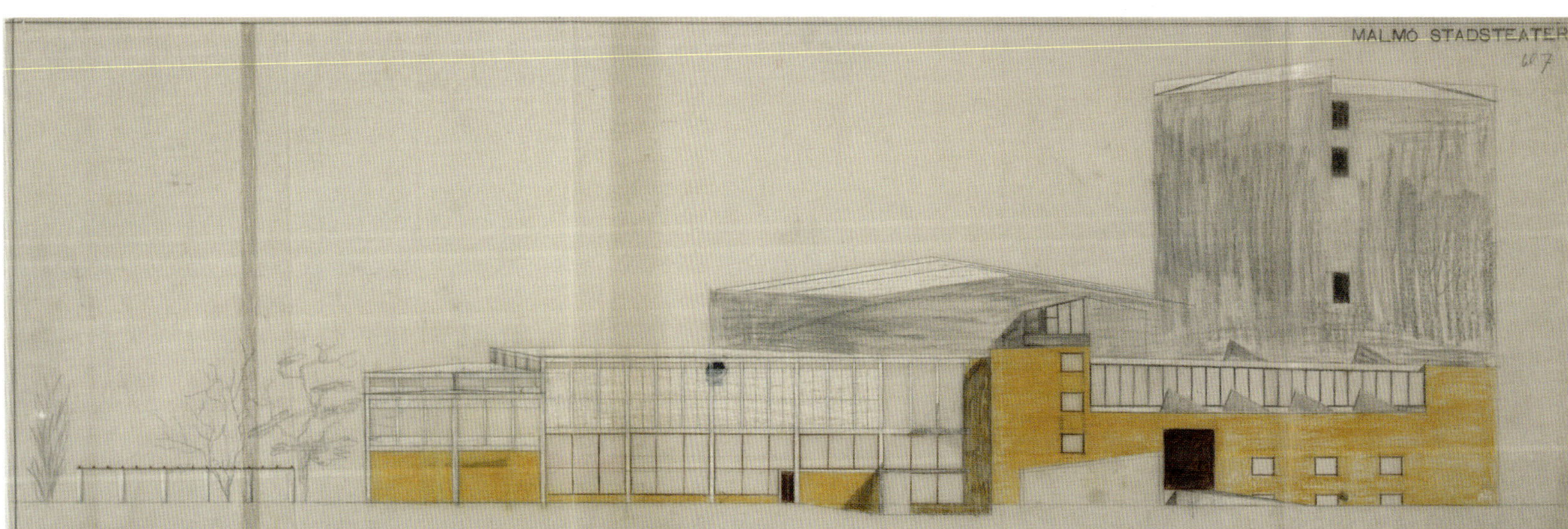

entrance foyer, placed to the left of the entrance axis so that the principal front faced south, improving the internal lighting. The jury, divided as before between the supporters of Lewerentz's project and those in favour of Erik Lallerstedt and David Helldén's project (awarded second prize, as in the previous competition), decided to commission all three architects to design the complex. In 1936 Lewerentz, Lallerstedt and Helldén set up the "Architectural Office for the Municipal Theatre". It took a long time to elaborate the new project, which was only submitted in 1942; this was probably partially due to the difficulty of reconciling the differences in the two initial projects. The building that was finally constructed comprises less articulation of the blocks, with the majority of its functions being housed in a parallelepiped resembling the stage tower in Lewerentz's earlier projects. Adjacent to the tower is a two-storey building in which the auditorium is inserted; this building contains the entrance, the foyers and the service spaces. Lewerentz was particularly interested in the technical aspects of the auditorium, which has seating rising in concentric semicircular tiers and a large proscenium suitable for different kinds of performances. It is designed to be divided by folding walls, creating smaller spaces more appropriate to concerts. The complex

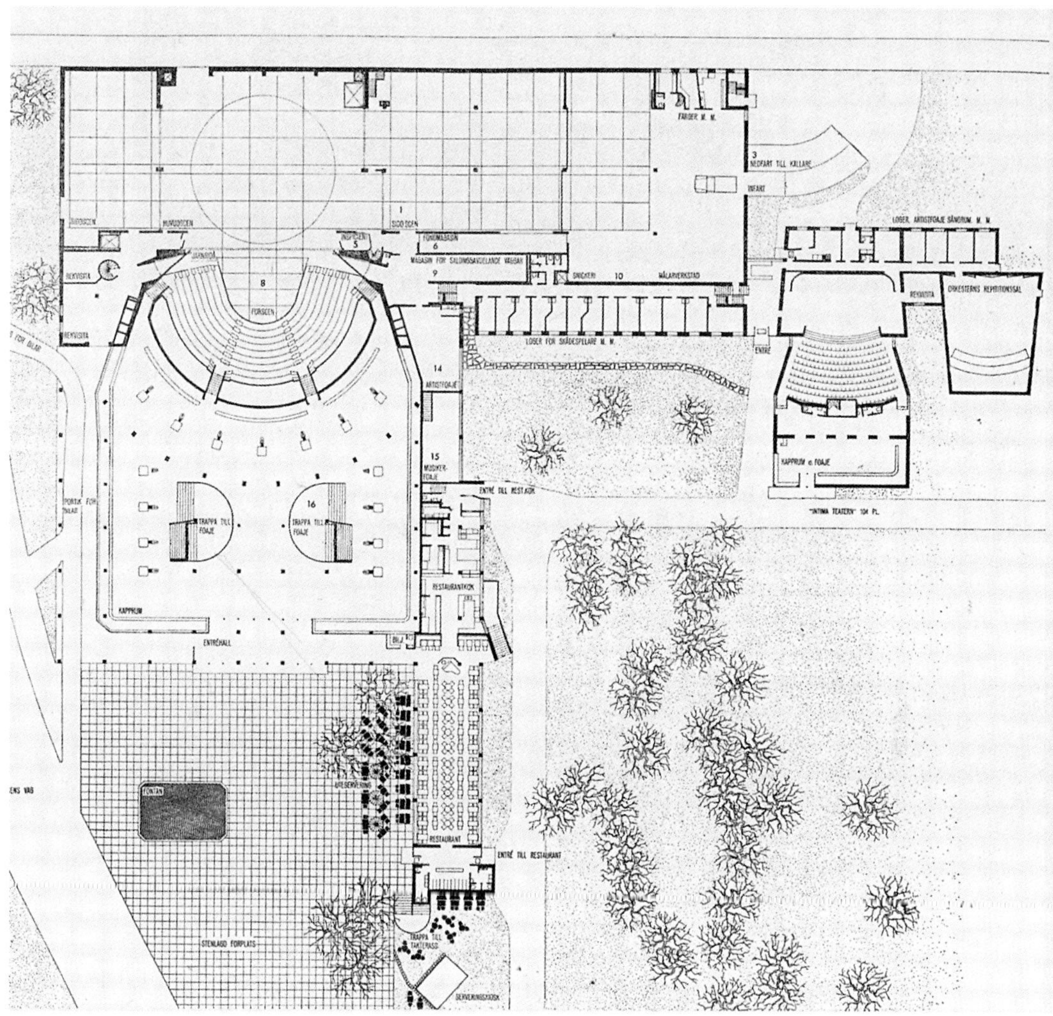

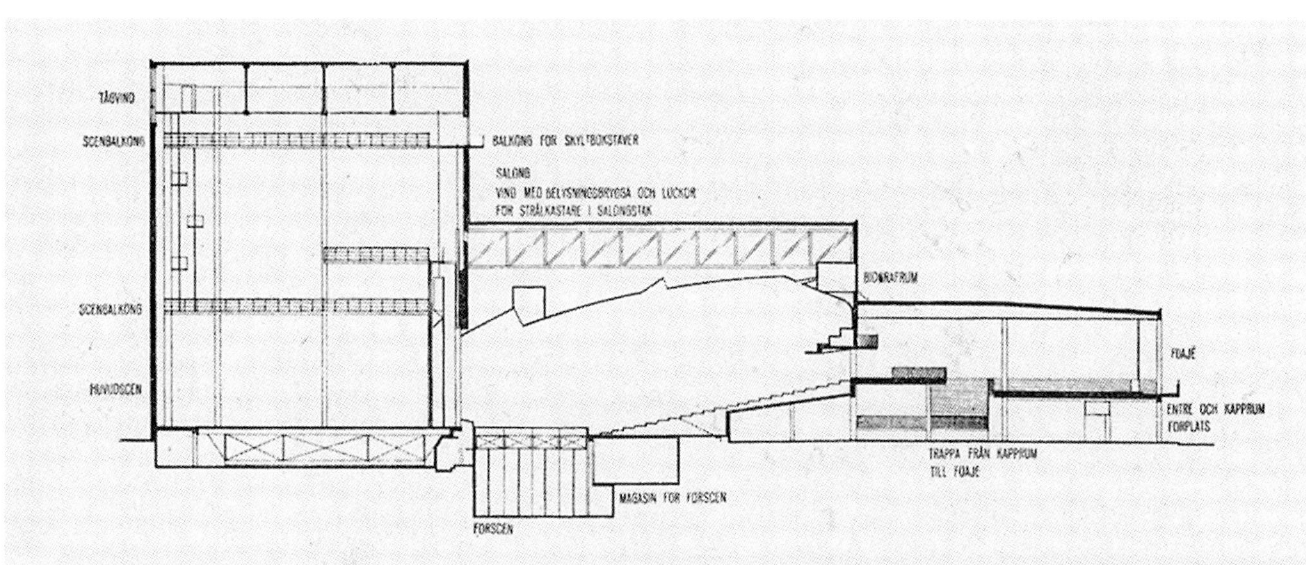

Plan and cross section, final version, 1935–44, with Erik Lallerstedt and David Helldén.

Views of the exterior and the auditorium.

is completed by a small theatre
for rehearsals and performances intended
for audiences limited in size.

Chronology:
1924–27: preliminary projects.
1933–44: competitions.
1933: first competition, motto "43";
first prize.
1935: second competition, motto "1625";
first prize.
1935–44: final version, together
with Erik Lallerstedt and David Helldén.

Bibliography: Curman 1933; Ahrbom 1935;
Malmö stadsteater 1942; Lallerstedt 1944;
Ahlin 1985, pp. 128–31, 176–83; Caldenby
1997, pp. 130–35.

(G.P.)

Views of the exterior.

64. Competition Project for Kviberg Cemetery, Gothenburg, 1926–27
motto "Finis" – third prize

This is what Lewerentz wrote in his outline of the project:
As regards the competition project that has been produced, the author, after having carefully examined the site of the future cemetery and the surrounding area, is of the opinion that, as required by the programme, the following objectives and aspirations may be identified.
The actual conformation of the site seems to express both monumentality and serenity in its profile, making it ideally suited for the intended purpose, without there being any need for radical intervention. The peace and sense of appropriateness that are emanated by this clearly defined place are characteristics that it is necessary to preserve, so that the new project, in its entirety, may be subjected to it, allowing the mass of the hill to have total dominion. Thus, in a wholly natural manner, most of the complex, and also the link with the main road, should be located at the foot of the promontory.
The contribution of the vegetation—a necessary consequence of the division of the site into burial areas, this also separates it from the river, as mentioned previously—is vitally important, so the site may be sheltered from the wind ... as is usually the case around the boundary walls of houses.
A great deal of thick low vegetation, in closely-planted rows, or else scattered in smaller clumps, encloses the site near the boundary walls.
The pre-existing trees should not in any way have to compete with the new arrangement, in the sense that the woods or the trees with thick foliage will be left undisturbed. Right from the main entrance it should be quite evident that the intervention concludes at the foot of the promontory with a more or less open view of the surrounding countryside and part of the city. The area maintains aristocratic isolation in the direction of the river, due to the marked contrast with the residential area lower down the valley; in the direction of Kviberg, because of the extremely open fields; to the north, due to the bare and inaccessible hilltops; lastly, towards the city, because of the division into plateaux, higher up than those of the adjacent urbanized areas.
With regard to the creation of the boundaries of the cemetery, this is of particular importance; as far as the portion towards Kviberg is concerned, this should be extended between the slopes of the hill in the southern part of the cemetery, so that it forms the end of the avenue leading from main entrance at the foot of the promontory...
In brief, the objective described above consists in the fact that the main entrance is located at the end of the mass of the promontory, with the result that the square at the entrance extends along the slope facing the city.
Despite the fact that the general layout was well adapted to the site and the programme, Lewerentz's project was only awarded third prize, probably due to the excessively Neoclassical aspect of the buildings, designed to resemble the temples of ancient Greece.

Bibliography: Friberger 1927; Ahlin 1985b, pp. 91–93; Constant 1994, p. 127.

(G.P.)

View of the site.

65. Furnishings for the Dining-Room of G.J. Versteeghs, Söderhamn, 1927

66. Competition Project for the Urban Renewal of a Block in Jönköping, 1928

with Osvald Almqvist
first, second and third prizes
and a fourth project awarded jury citation

In the competition for the urban development plan for a block on the Strandgatan at Jönköping, Sigurd Lewerentz and Osvald Almqvist were amazingly successful, winning the three first prizes, while a fourth project won a citation.
The three prize-winning projects proposed a similar scheme for the site, located between the Smedjegatorna above and the Strandgatan below, with the buildings disposed parallel to the shore of Lake Munksjön.
In the version awarded first prize, the two architects arranged the buildings along the perimeters of the three blocks in the competition, proposing the creation of a residential type around a courtyard. Although the east-west orientation was predominant, the scheme was very complex from an architectural point of view. Particular attention was paid to the front facing the lake, where heights varying between three and four storeys were suggested in order to maintain continuity with the skyline of the old city, without, however, forsaking an extremely modern formal language for the design of the elevations, almost as if it were intended that the view from a distance should be differ from the one at close quarters.
The project that obtained the second prize was characterized, on the other hand, by the adoption of a rigid north-south orientation of all the buildings, which, although it liberated the two streets leading from the Smedjegatorna to the lakeside, proposed a monotonous solution that lacked any relationship with the surroundings, and denied the buildings furthest from the shore any view of the lake, clearly displaying the influence of contemporary central European architecture.
Lastly, the project that was awarded third prize envisaged the partial rehabilitation of some of the existing buildings on the site, on the one hand attempting a mediation between the new scheme and the older constructions and, on the other hand, maintaining the ideas elaborated in the other two projects.

(G P)

View from the lake.

67. Competition Project for the Katarina Middle School, Stockholm, 1928
with Osvald Almqvist
motto "Aula"

The programme of the competition for the Katerina Middle School also required an urban development plan for Södermalm, a district in the southern part of Stockholm located between the two most important roads in the area: Götagatan and Ringvägen. In its configuration, the project for a residential area and a church formulated by Lewerentz and Almqvist revives a traditional type: the buildings with courtyards open towards the west and the façades along the existing roads reproduce, in fact, the characteristics of architectural styles of the past. However, towards the interior, the articulation of the composition is freer and less tied to the pre-existing situation, becoming wholly modern in the solution proposed for the school. This consists of a long, narrow building, oriented in a south-west-north-east direction, with all the classrooms aligned along the wall facing to the east and served on each floor by a single corridor, in accordance with a principal of distribution favouring functionality and clarity. The simple form of the main building is, however, juxtaposed, at one end, with the block housing the assembly hall and, at the other, with the one containing the offices. As far as the solutions proposed for the façades are concerned, while the classroom windows characterize the elevation facing the school courtyard, the internal staircase occupies the whole of the north end of the building, where there are long horizontal strip windows, which continue along the sides. Otherwise the proposed building is a typically modern structure, both because of the simplicity of the forms and the choice of materials.

Bibliography: Sundahl 1928.

(G.P.)

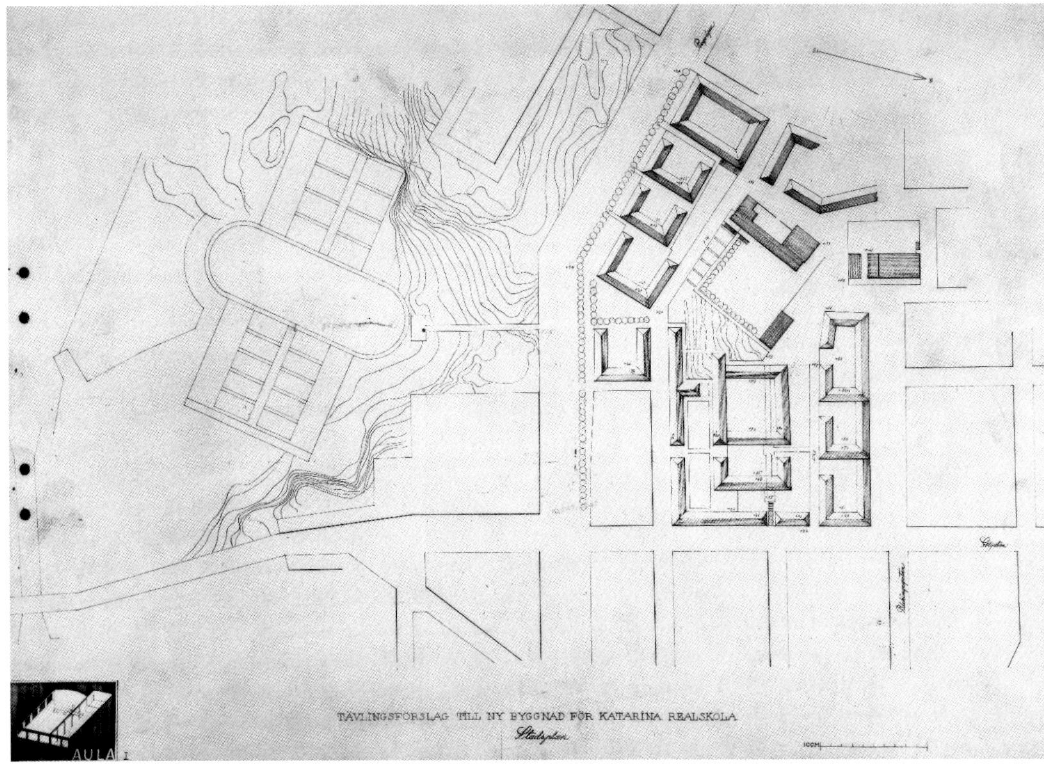

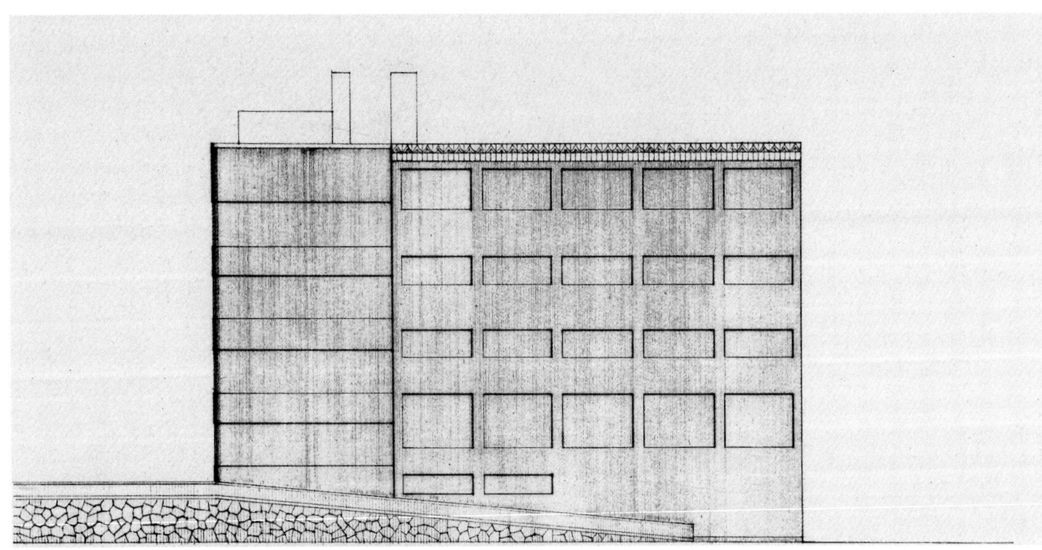

Layout of scheme and elevation of one of the buildings.

68. Competition Project for a Nursing Home and Old People's Home, Uppsala, 1928

motto "Fyrisvalls gård"

As a result of the poor state of the old building serving as a nursing home and old people's home at Uppsala, a competition was announced in 1928 for a new complex on the same site. Besides the renovation and extension of the existing building, the programme required the construction of two two-storey residential blocks to accommodate self-sufficient elderly people and a separate building for the dining-room, lecture theatre and other communal spaces. In addition, there was to be a small building housing the offices, the caretaker's flat and a number of service spaces.

Drawing on the architectural styles of the past, the project submitted by Lewerentz proposed very simple forms for the various buildings, which had traditional pitched roofs, concealing any concession made to the modern style of the period. Even in the general layout and the internal distribution, the architect did not make use of the formal language of contemporary architecture, preferring to resort to more traditional functional types, as, for example, in the residential building, where a long corridor divides the rooms on one side from the communal services on the other, ending in the staircases that, on both sides, link the different floors to each other.

Bibliography: Tävlingen till Uppsala 1928, p. 141.

(G.P.)

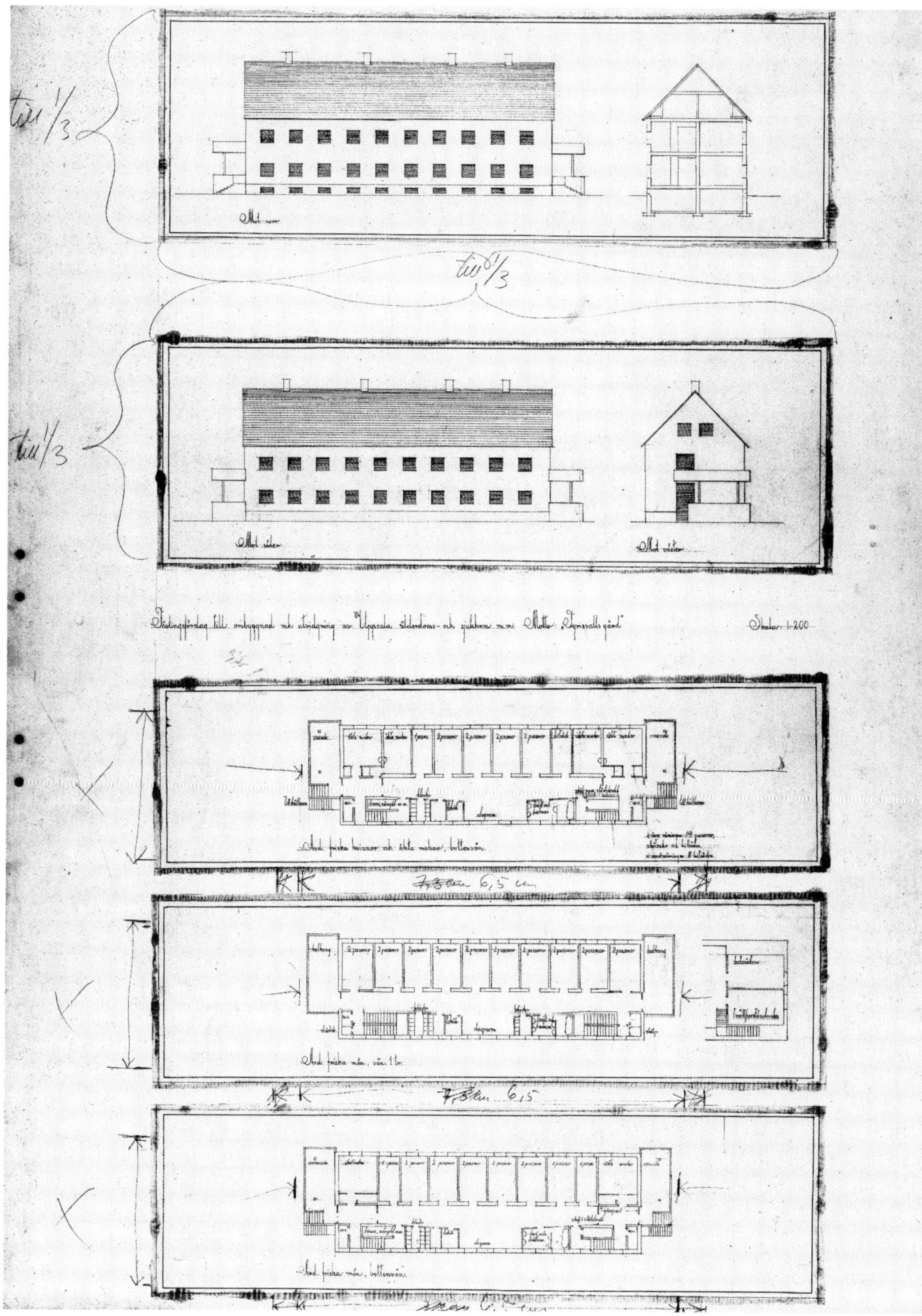

Elevations, plans and section.

69. Competition Project for the Urban Renewal of the Area around Lund Cathedral, 1928

Layout plan.

70. Project (1928) and Competition (1930) for the Office Building of the Riksförsäkringsanstalten (Social Security Administration), Stockholm, 1928 onwards

The project Lewerentz submitted in 1930 to the competition for the building of the Riksförsäkringsanstalten (Social Security Administration) is the elaboration of the programme for a new building drawn up by the architect in 1928 on behalf of the Byggnadstyrels (National Board of Building and Planning). His preliminary project became the basis of the programme of the national competition, which Lewerentz went on to win.

The building, located on a corner site in a block adjacent to the church of Adolf Frederik in the Norrmalm district of Stockholm, is compact and austere, absolutely without any hint of decoration. The setting back of the window- and door-frames and the slight projection of the stone architrave surrounding the main doorway (which serves to stress the grid formed by the surface between the square openings on all the fronts) are the only elements that give substance and weight to a building that would otherwise be totally inexpressive. The building appears externally as a single stuccoed surface from which the openings are cut out, and is surrounded at ground level by a low base and, at the top, by thin coping, both in granite. The six storeys of the building, all housing offices, are completed by two basement floors, used as the archive, and a penthouse, set back from the façade so as not to interfere with its composition; besides further storage space, this contains the employees' canteen. In the centre of the building, an oval courtyard creates a space in which the single continuous elevation assumes a character that is diametrically opposed to that of the external faces. Here, in fact, the rows of windows, separated only by a slender strip of wall, give the building an ascendant rhythm, with rings that are transparent at the level of the corridors and solid at floor level, in marked contrast with the absence of directionality of the external faces.

The courtyard is the central element of the composition, the part to which Lewerentz paid most attention in the different solutions

View of the main entrance
on A. Fredriks Kykrogata.

Elevation on A. Fredriks Kykrogata.

Ground-floor plan.

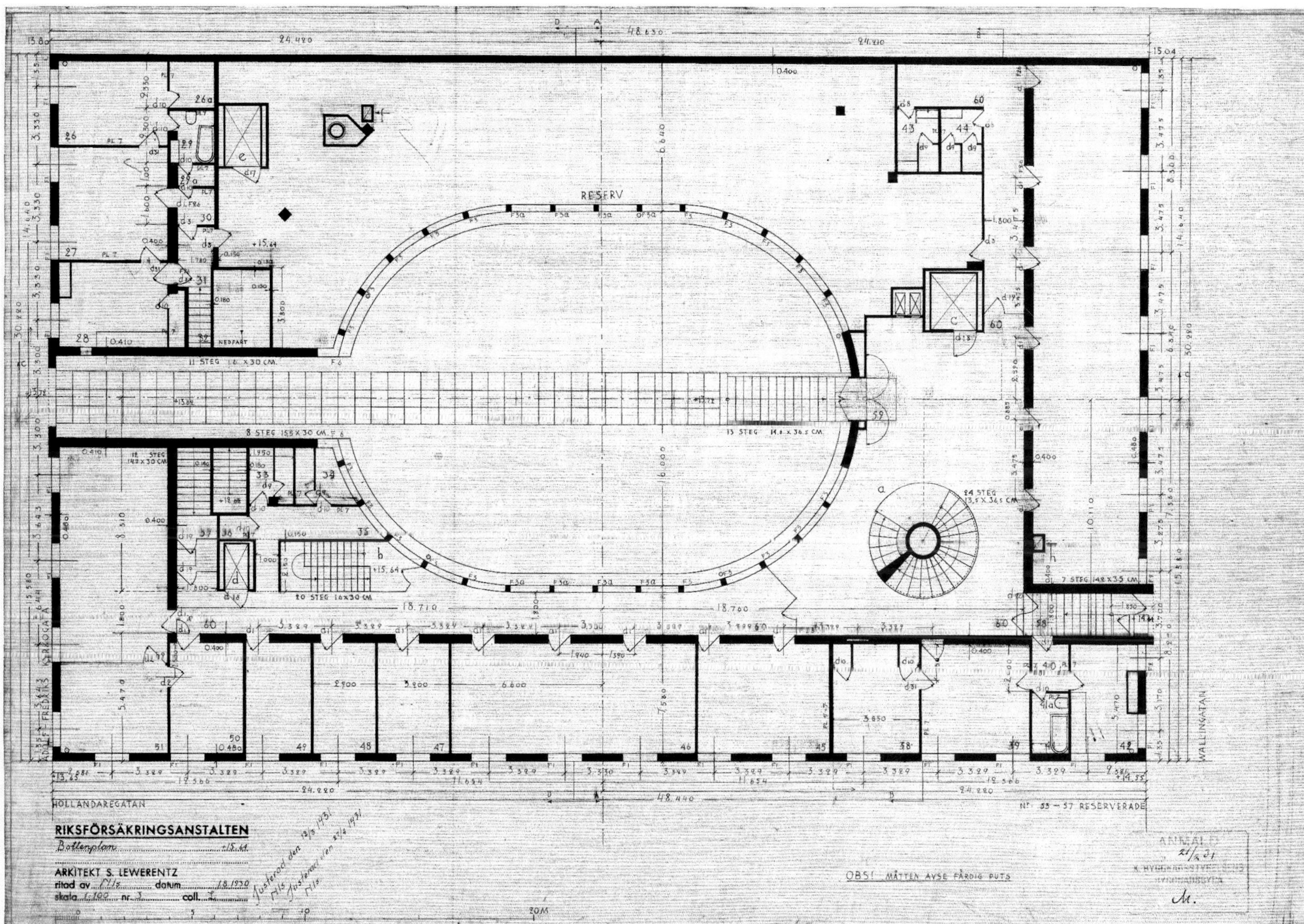

he prepared for the project after winning the competition. Designed to provide light for the rooms overlooking it—service rooms in the narrower wings of the building and offices in the deeper wings—the courtyard was realized with a structure that was externally light and transparent: glass, steel and reinforced concrete. In reality, the whole load-bearing structure of the building was to have been in steel, but the limits imposed by the rather tight budget meant that it was necessary to adopt more traditional systems for the parts where the more modern technique was not absolutely indispensable to the form. Thus the external faces were built in traditional bricks finished with smooth stucco.

On the same axis as the main door on the opposite side of the courtyard, the entrance to the offices leads directly to a large hall in the area between the rectangular external perimeter and the oval internal one. This ambiguous formal structure lends a sense of dynamism to the visual experience of visitors, who on entering the hall, find themselves in an asymmetrical space, dominated by the transparent cylinder of the helicoid staircase that penetrates the whole building vertically, terminating—with its own separate roof—in the penthouse.

In the wing facing the main road, there is a more conventional staircase, also contained in a structure of steel and glass structure produced—like all the internal and external fixtures—by IDESTA to a design by Lewerentz. All the office furnishings were also made to a design by the architect, in wood rather than steel, as was originally planned for purely economic reasons.

Finally, mention should be made of the way Lewerentz used colour in this project. In the interiors, colour is used mainly on the ceilings, as the walls are white, the linoleum floor-coverings are grey and the wood of the furnishings is black. The matt yellow of the public areas (serving to exalt the light reflected by the internal face) contrasts with the glossy blues of the office ceilings, intended to offset the coldness and lack of colour of the dark winter days.

During the 1930s Lewerentz worked on various projects for an extension to the building in Kykrogata, proposing in 1938 that there should be a new independent building in Valhallavägen, although none of these designs was ever realized.

The last of these projects was produced in 1951–52, attesting to the remarkable trust that the insurance institute had in the architect.

Chronology:
1928: preliminary project prior to the competition.
1930: invitation competition – first prize.
1930–32: realization of project.
Not documented:
1933–34: extension project.
1938–39: project for a new building in Valhallavägen.
1951-52: extension project.

Bibliography: Lewerentz 1932a; Ahlin 1985b, pp. 147–50; Wang 1992; Caldenby 1997, pp. 104–09.

(G.P.)

Detail of the entrance on A. Fredriks Kykrogata.

Views and longitudinal section of the courtyard.

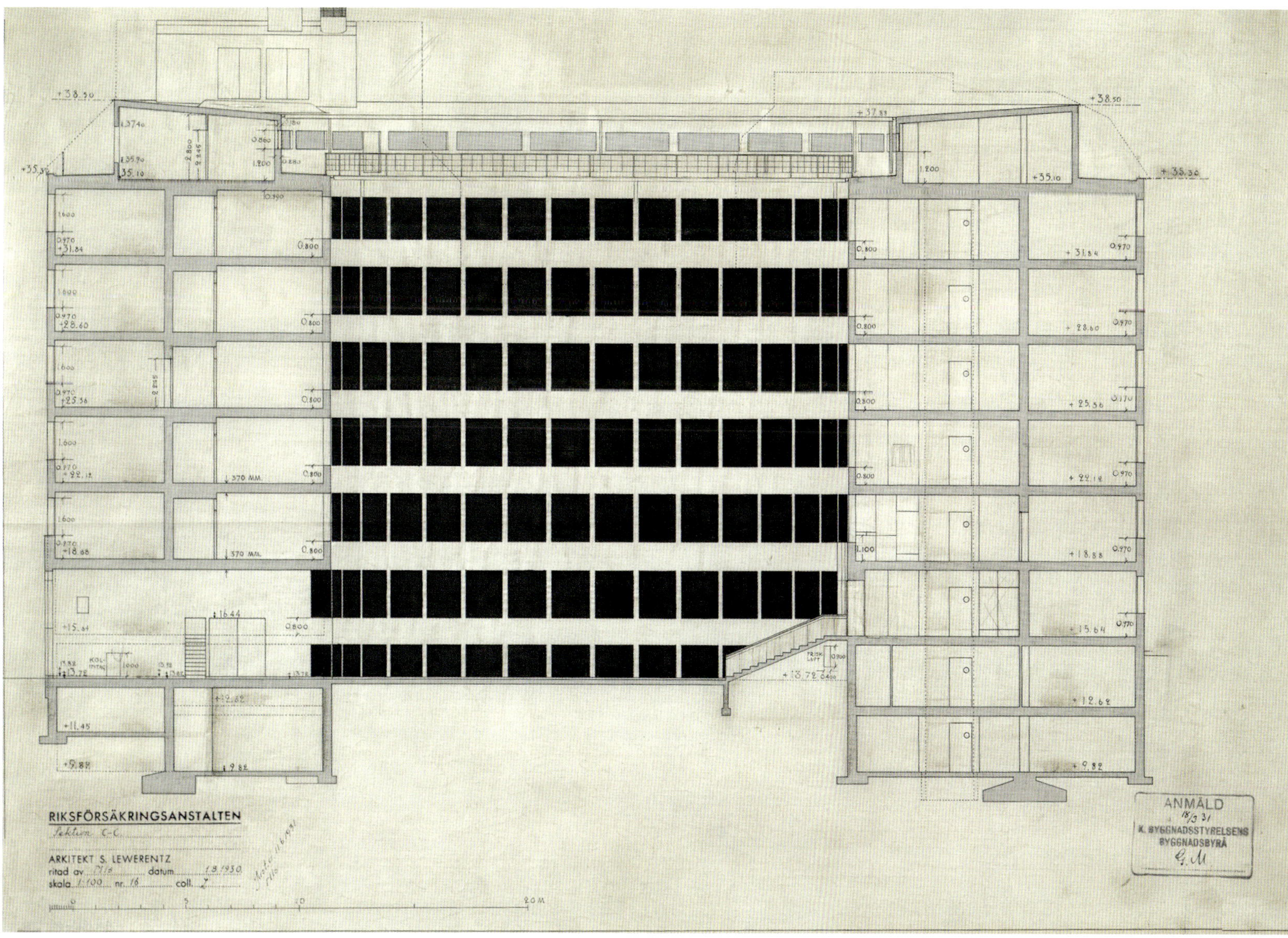
RIKSFÖRSÄKRINGSANSTALTEN
Sektion C-C
ARKITEKT S. LEWERENTZ
ritad av Olle datum 1.3.1930
skala 1:100 nr. 16 coll. 7
ANMÄLD
18/3 31
K. BYGGNADSSTYRELSENS
BYGGNADSBYRÅ

Oval-shaped courtyard.

View of the service staircase and the corridor leading to the offices.

Service staircase, detail of the handrail.

Executive's office.

Details of a clock and the internal door and window fittings.

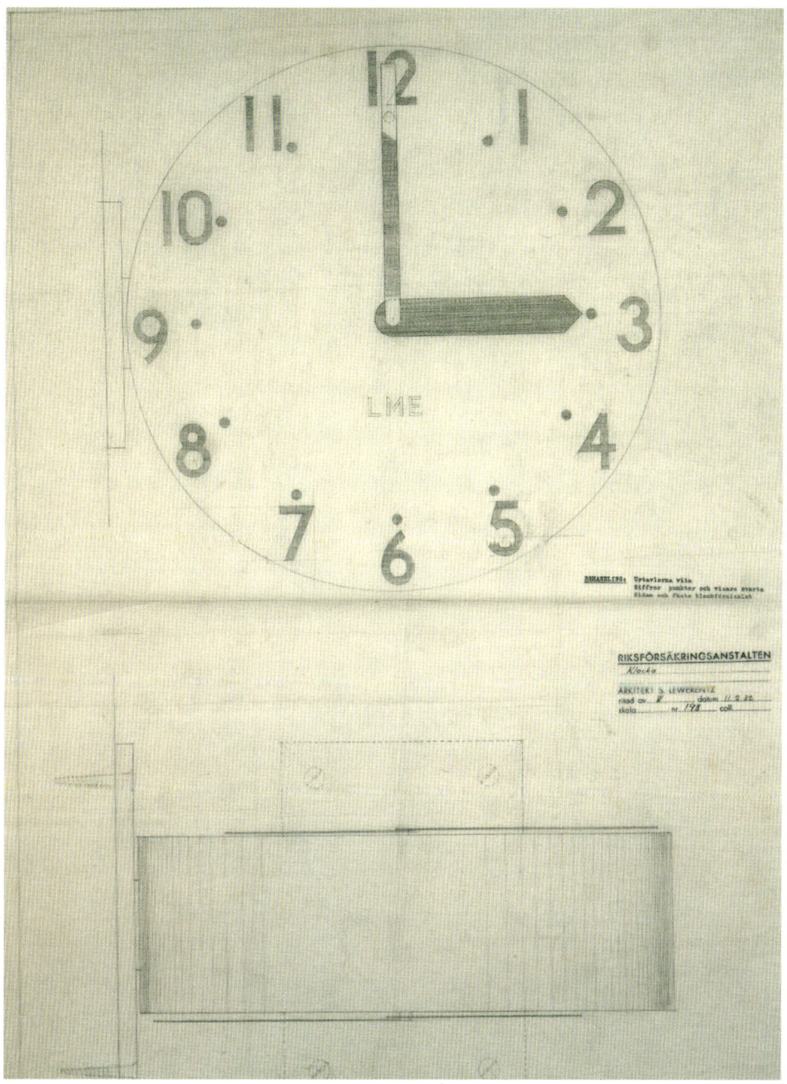

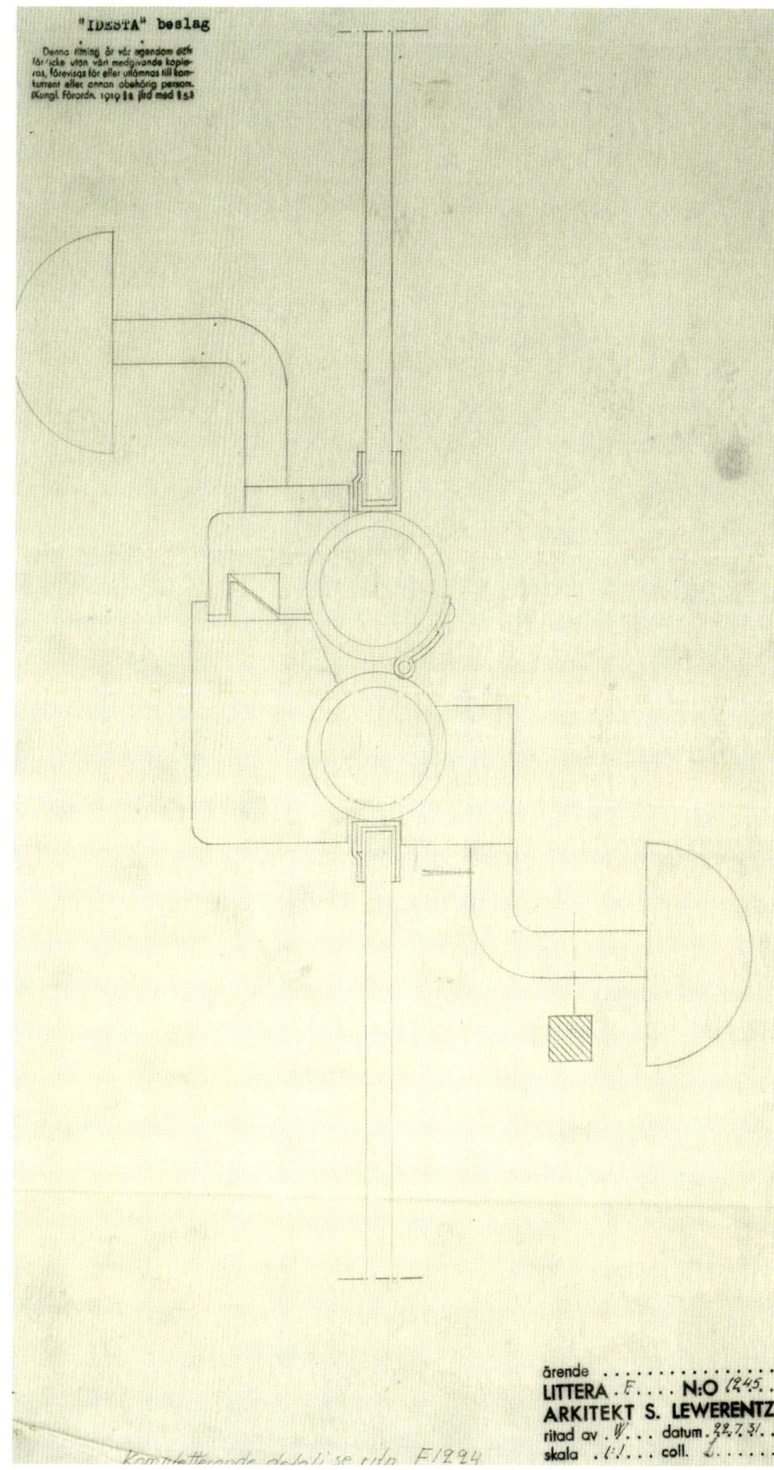

View, plan and elevation
of the main staircase.

Opposite
View of the main staircase.

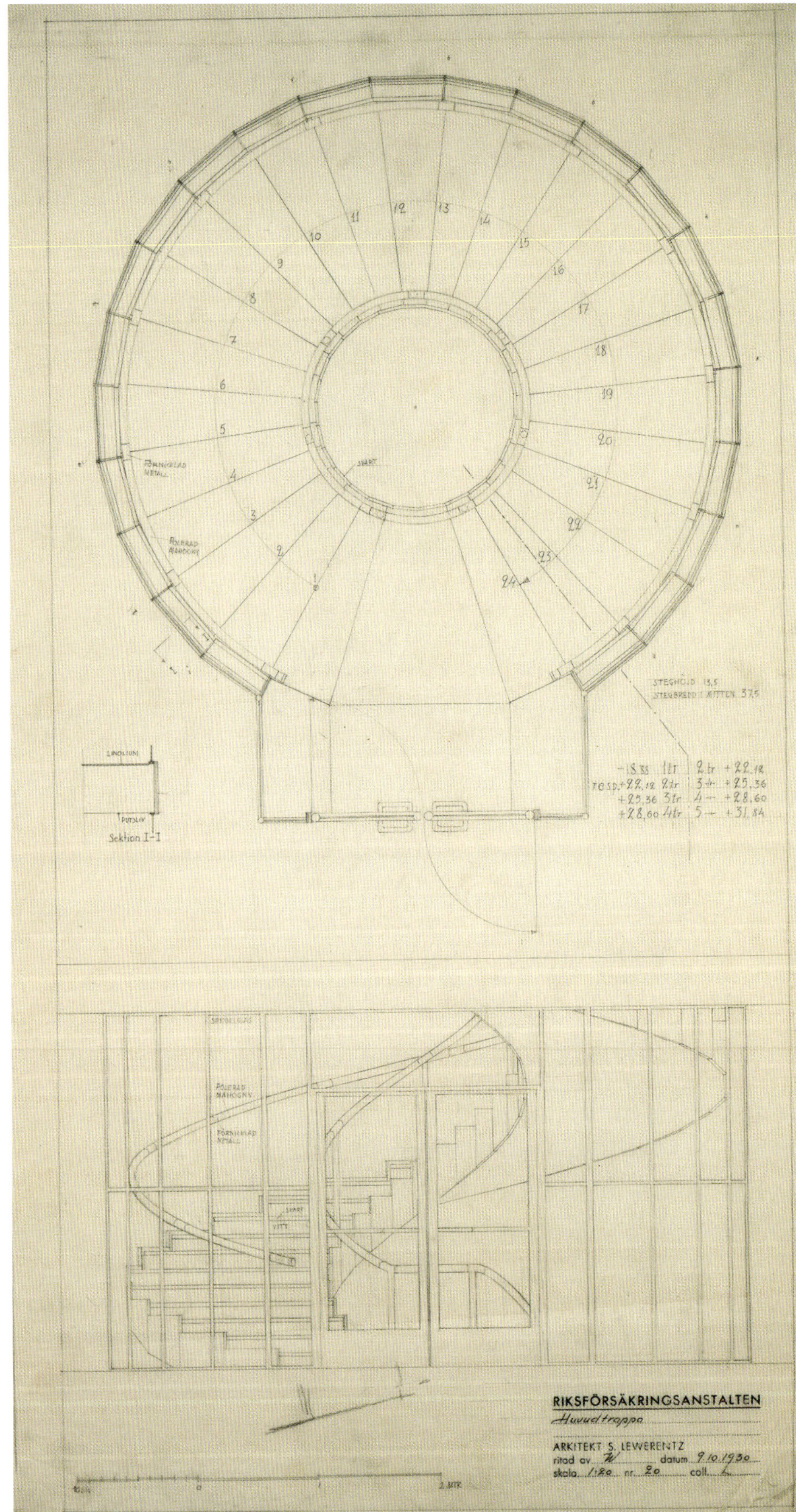

71. Offices for Philips AB, Stockholm, 1929–30

The Philips AB building was constructed in an industrial area in the north-west suburbs of Stockholm, on a site with the shape of a right-angled triangle that Lewerentz planned to use in an intensive manner. The project, which was intended to be built in a number of stages, involves two independent buildings located on the orthogonal sides of a triangle. The six-storey block facing Gävlegatan, the main road, houses the offices, while the other one—situated behind and at right-angles to it—is the same height but has two extra storeys and contains the storerooms, workshops and packing department. The complex is completed by two attic storeys, where the canteen and other offices are located, and two sub-levels, used for conference rooms, storerooms and service rooms. In the centre of the site a sunken courtyard is linked to the main road by a ramp for vehicles. Only half of the office block facing Gävlegatan was built initially; this included the vehicular entrance (still visible today, although the complex has been considerably rebuilt), leaving the low block for the storerooms detached and set back to the north of the site. The building system, with loadbearing external walls in reinforced concrete, gives rise to a rational and rhythmic front facing the road, where only the setback of the windows, arranged so they be opened asymmetrically, and the double opening of the vehicular and pedestrian entrance interrupt the pattern of the large rectangular windows. On each of the solid strips of the façade separating the regular rows of windows are displayed large illuminated signs with the firm's name, deriving from the model that Lewerentz developed in this period with the AB BLOKK company (set up in 1930 with other architects). The Philips offices in Stockholm were the company's first and only important commission.
The open-plan interiors, free from any structural encumbrance as well as from the staircases, which are located in a separate stair-tower on the courtyard side, are divided up by screens in steel and glass and carefully furnished to the architect's designs.
The building was completed around 1950 by the architect C. Tham in accordance with Lewerentz's original project, but in the 1960s and 1990 the complex was rebuilt in order to adapt it to the firm's new requirements, depriving it of much of its expressive force.

Bibliography: Ahlin 1985b, pp. 150–51; Caldenby 1997, pp. 112–15.

(N.F.)

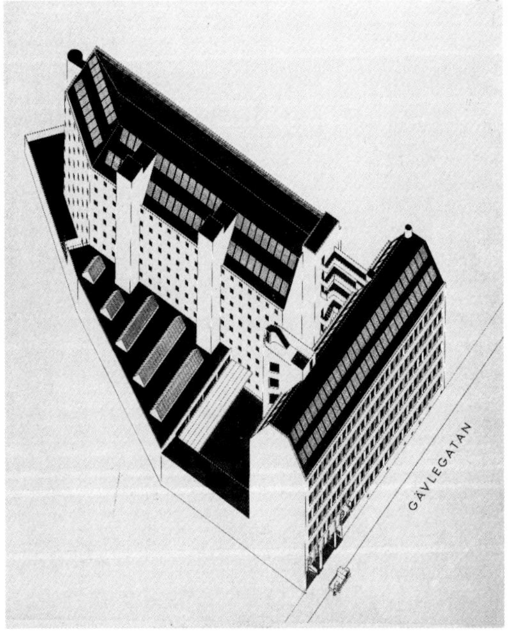

Axonometric projection.

View of the main entrance.

Conference room.

72. Factory Building for Uddeholms Sulfatfabrik at Skoghallsverken, Karlstad, 1929 onwards

The industrial complex of Skoghall, known as Skoghallsverken, located not far from Karlstad, a town on the road from Stockholm to Oslo, near a river, the waters of which had been harnessed for the working of wood. Originally established as a sawmill in 1914, the industrial complex developed in the following years into a paper mill; as a result, factory buildings were constructed, firstly for the production of cellulose, and then, in 1929, for sulphate.
The owners of the paper mill, Uddeholms AB, commissioned Lewerentz to design the external elevations of the sulphate factory, which was to house the packing department and offices, as well as all the processes necessary for the manufacture of paper.
The architect was required to find a solution for all the external faces, despite the fact that an engineering firm in Malmö had already been entrusted with the design and construction of the new buildings.
In his project, Lewerentz proposed that all the external walls should be faced with bare brick, inserting pairs of square windows on each floor between the columns of the loadbearing structure, irrespective of the height of the individual block.
On the east elevation, where the main entrance is located, the architect interrupted the rhythmic pattern of the windows and created a huge opening as high as the building, leaving only the coping and cornice with the task of giving visual unity to the façade. The large window—tripartite also for structural reasons—allows the staircase linking the different floors of the building to be visible.
As a result of the success of his design, Lewerentz continued to work for Uddeholms AB until the 1950s as their architectural consultant for building projects regarding Skoghallsverken.

Bibliography: Ahlin 1985b, pp. 164–67.

(N.F.)

Wooden model and drawing of a proposed extension, 1930s.

Opposite
Drawing of the main entrance, 1929.

SKOGHALLS-VERKEN
ARKITEKT S. LEWERENTZ
Stockholm 22/10 1929 Litt. SKV. No. 17

73. Pavilions and Other Buildings, Furnishings, Objects and Graphics for the Stockholm Exhibition of 1930, Djurgården, 1929–30

The great Stockholm Exhibition of 1930 was the occasion on which central European Modernism finally established itself in Sweden and, more generally, in Scandinavia. Until then, in fact, the new style was not widespread, partly because of the lack of involvement of both industry and the authorities.
Started in the wake of the National Exhibition in Gothenburg in 1923 and the Exposition Internationale des Arts Décoratifs et Industriels Modernes, held in Paris in 1925, the Stockholm Exhibition was organized by the Svenska Slödförening (Swedish Society of Arts and Crafts) under the direction of Gregor Paulsson, then chairman of the association who, from 1927, together with an executive committee, stated that it would be devoted to "applied art, crafts and artistic crafts". The organizers believed that this theme would stimulate the participants to highlight the role and value of everyday implements, a subject about which Paulsson had written numerous articles, assimilating all the revolutionary force of Functionalism.
On the large site selected for the exhibition, located by the sea in the bay of Djurgårdenbrunnsvik, not far the centre of Stockholm, the chief architect, Erik Gunnar Asplund, prepared a master plan in which he laid down the general criteria for the project and the more detailed ones for the buildings he designed. The entrance building and the majority of the pavilions were arranged along a road where the market was to be held; this led to the restaurant designed by Asplund and the area destined for the festivities, in which was placed the advertising mast designed by Lewerentz and erected by Stockholm Ljusreklam AB, of which he was joint owner.
The mast, with its illuminated signs, was the symbol of the exhibition and was designed by the architect so as to be visible from the city. Near the shore, Asplund planned another restaurant with additional exhibition pavilions and the section devoted to the home, to which the organizers paid special attention. Here, in fact, various mock-ups of prototypes were constructed, complete with furnishings and finishings, relating to the theme of the house for everyone, or else, the modern home in general, whether as a self-contained unit or located in a block of flats.

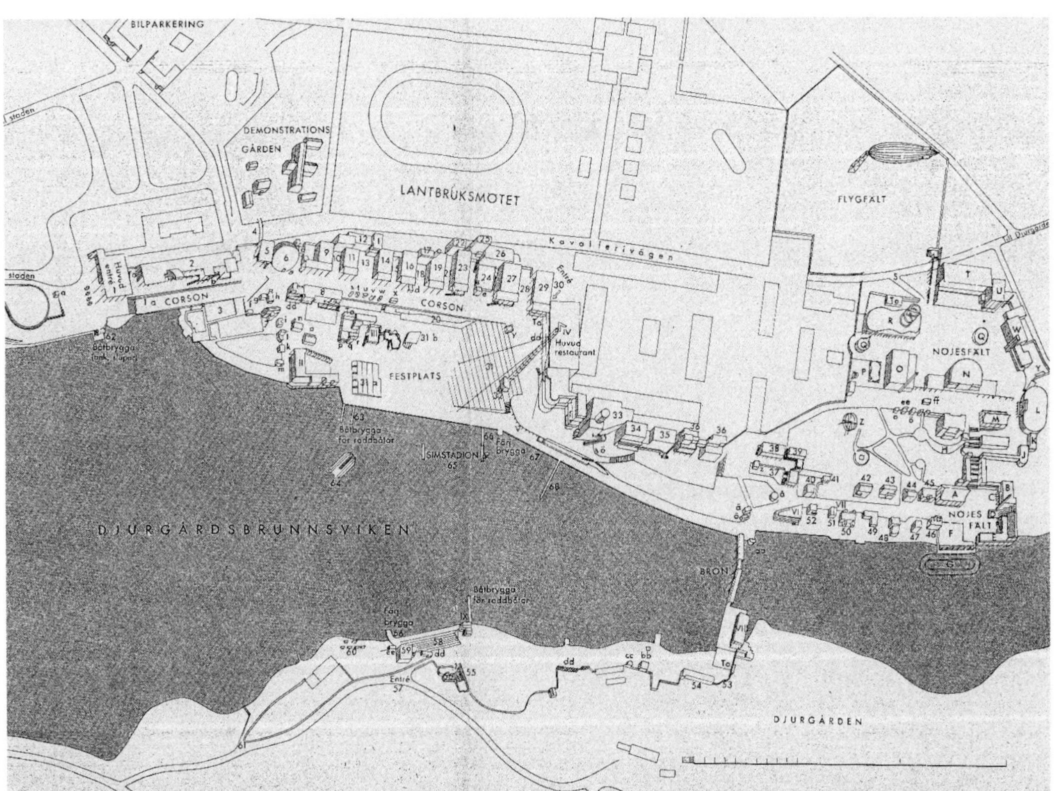

Layout plan (E.G. Asplund).

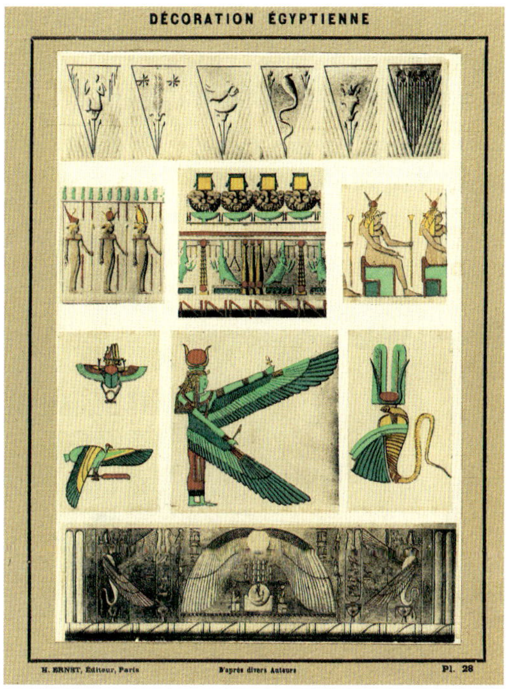

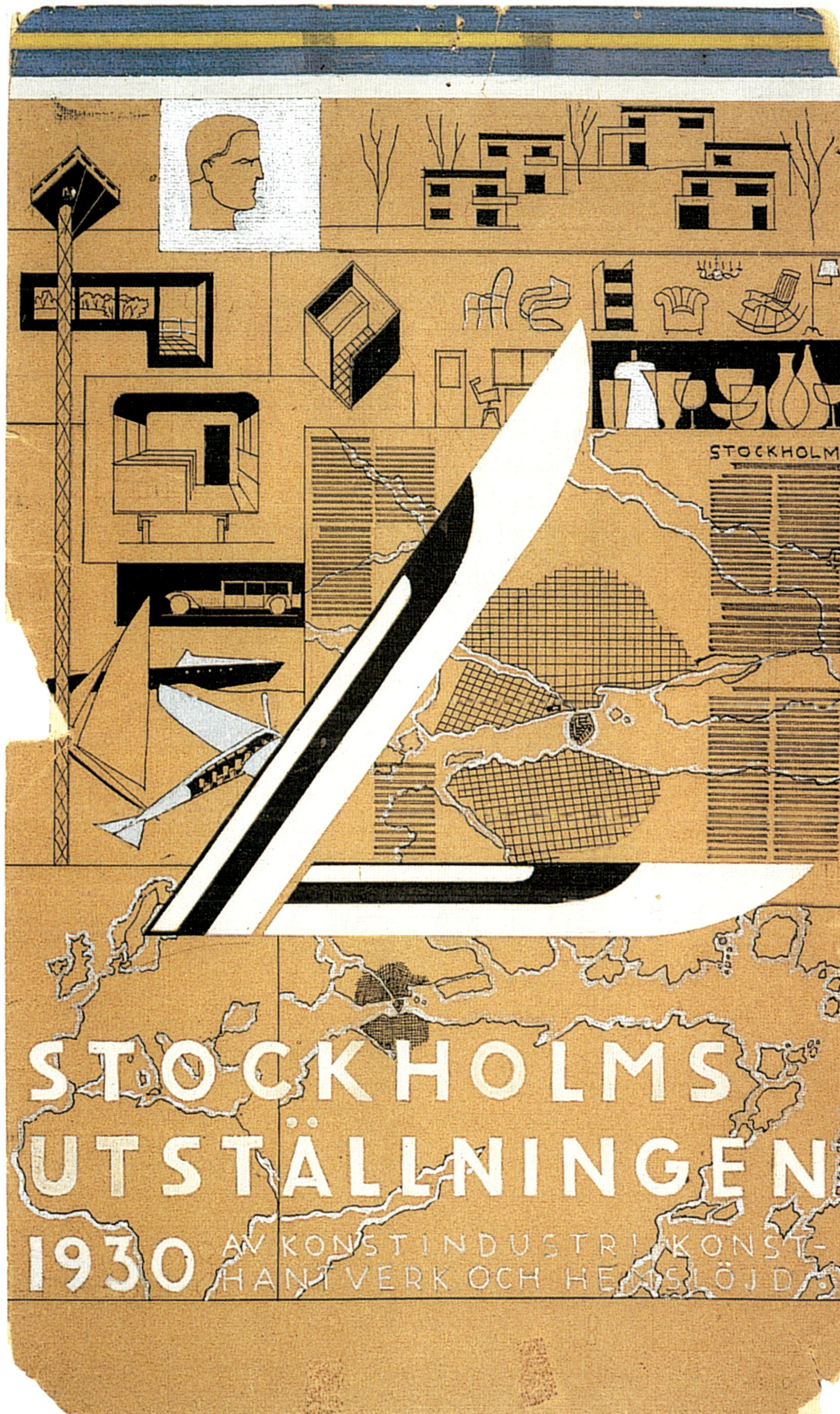

Studies for the exhibition logo and poster.

Study for a wallpaper design.

Exhibition poster.

Studies for the advertising mast.

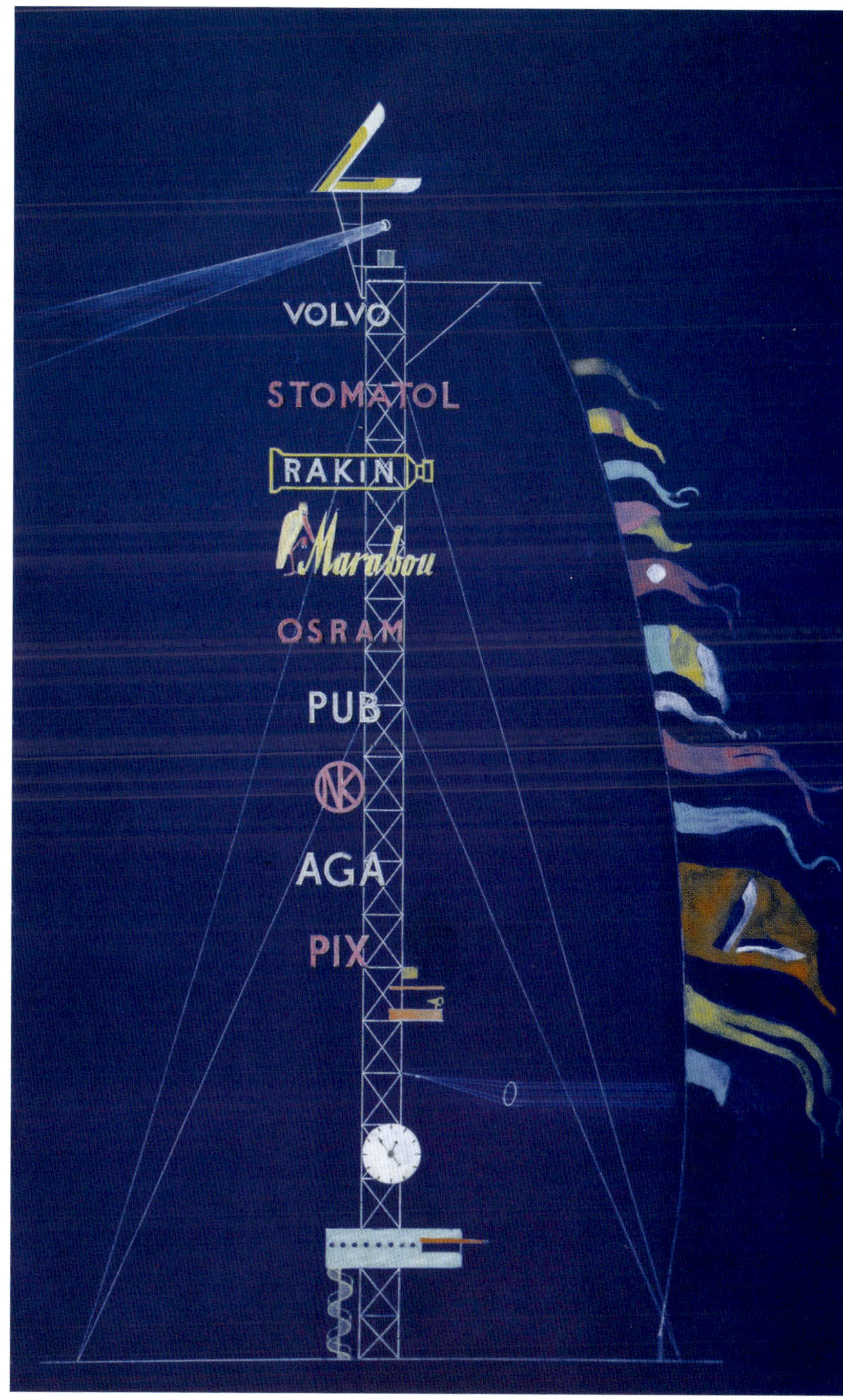

Max Söderholm, bird's-eye view of the exhibition site, gouache, 1929.

The exhibition at night.

E.G. Asplund, view of the square destined for the festivities, gouache, 1929.

The projects realized were chosen in a competition open to a limited group of architects. Lewerentz was one of the few who had two projects realized: a flat and a single-family house ("egna hem no. 47"); of the three projects submitted by the architect, only the one for a terraced house was turned down.
Besides the two homes, Lewerentz also produced a logo and posters for the exhibition, winning an invitation competition organized specially for the purpose. In this he revealed his interest in graphic design and lettering, to which he devoted himself in the 1930s, with numerous projects for the building and renovation of commercial premises that he prepared together with AB BLOKK.
In addition to the works for the exhibition committee, Lewerentz worked on other projects that Stockholm Ljusreklam AB had been commissioned to produce, mostly showcases, display stands and signs for firms, such as PUB and Finbruken, as well as the Gröna Udden café and pastry shop.
The architect also participated in other sections of the exhibition: in the NK (Nordiska Kompaniet) pavilion he displayed refined pieces of furniture specially designed for the occasion, such as a table, a cabinet and an armchair made from precious materials, while his suggested interiors for a General Motors bus were on show in the transport pavilion.

Single-family house no. 47, view of exterior, axonometric projection and plans of both floors.

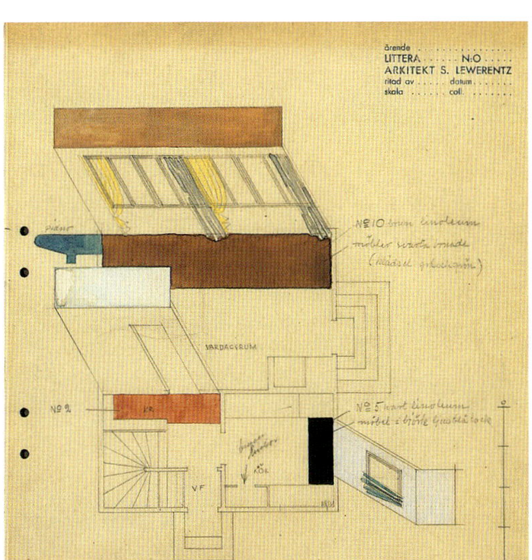

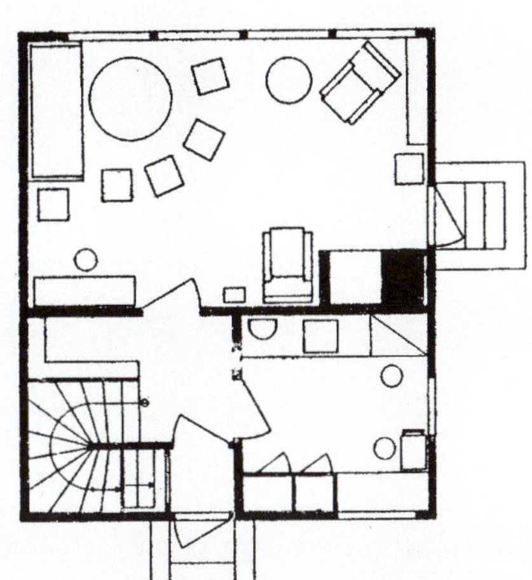

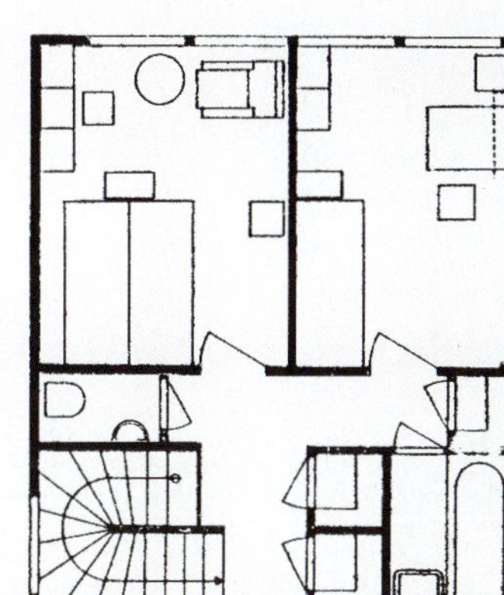

Single-family house no. 47,
one of the bedrooms.

Lágenhet no. 2, plan.

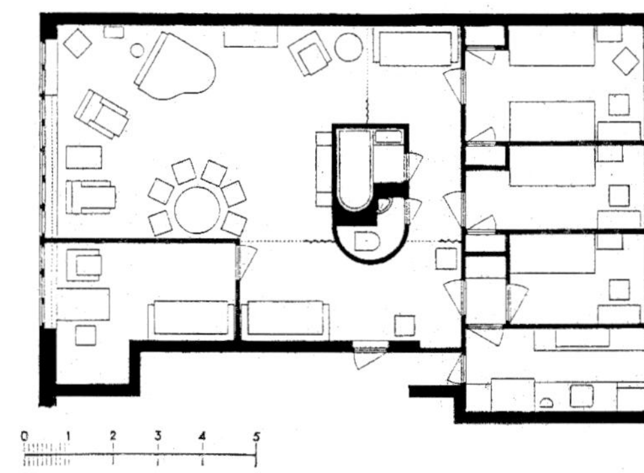

Lágenhet no. 2, view
of the interior.

Lågenhet no. 2, designs for the furnishings.

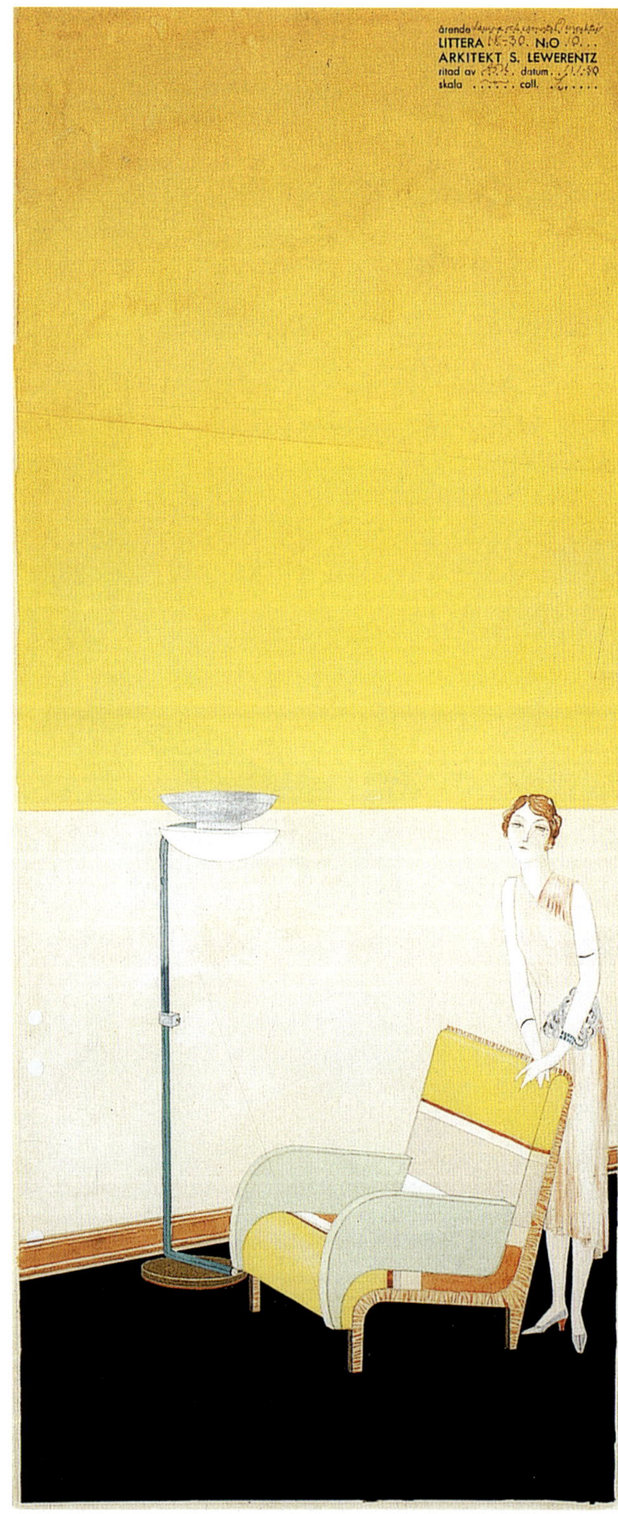

Display stand for the Finbruken department stores, views of the exterior.

Lágenhet No. 2
The solution proposed by the architect referred to a dwelling designed for a multi-storey building fitted with central heating, with its own bathroom and running water, both hot and cold, part of a possible estate constituted by the repetition of the same block a number of times, in conformity with a building type typical of German Rationalism. This flat, intended for a relatively well-off family of three to five people, has a surface area of 93 square metres, and is divided into five rooms, apart from the bathroom and kitchen. The latter, which is very small, is adjacent to the pantry, while the bedrooms, on one side, and the study, on the other, open directly onto the living-room, the flat's hub, which is furnished with a sofa, armchairs, a dining table and a grand piano. The block containing the bathroom stands in the living-room; conceived as an independent structure detached from the walls and with a semicircular wall facing the entrance, this is, typologically, the most innovative element, although it met with a lot of disapproval. The flat is furnished with objects designed by Uno Åhrén that were already being manufactured, with the exception of the wallpaper and the piano, which was designed by Lewerentz, who, with this elegant object, seized the opportunity to experiment with the juxtaposition of stainless steel and wood. The wallpaper—designed by the architect and produced, as on other occasions, by his father-in-law's firm, Göteborg Tapetfabrik—was greatly criticized by many of the committee members, to the extent that it was eliminated. It seemed, in fact, to be a product still linked to the past, in contrast with the modern lifestyles and tastes that the housing section sought to promote.

Single-family House No. 47
In the area devoted to owner-occupied houses, Lewerentz built a small two-storey dwelling, with a surface area similar to that of the flat described above. With a loadbearing structure in wood and a gently sloping flat roof, the building has a very simple form, characterized above all by the arrangement of the doors and windows in the external faces. The living-room and kitchen are on the ground floor, while two bedrooms and the bathroom are on the upper floor; in this case, too, the rooms are furnished with manufactured objects designed by Uno Åhrén and are wallpapered. For this house Lewerentz designed a chandelier, which was installed in the living-room.
In this case, the space is less likely to be used intensely as it is in the flat, allowing the rooms to be more conducive to comfortable living; rather than just being a corridor, the kitchen is a proper room more suited to the preparation of food. Nevertheless, the limited size of the bathroom and kitchen (not only in Lewerentz's project) was much criticized, even before the exhibition closed, by the leading opponents of the new style.

Lewerentz's works and projects for the Stockholm Exhibition, 1929–30:
- standard single-family house ("egna hem no. 47");
- prototype for a flat (no. 2);
- project for a terraced house;
- furniture for the NK pavilion: a table, an armchair and a cabinet;
- display stands for the PUB and Finbruken department stores (with Stockholm Ljusreklam AB);
- showcases and display stands for various firms participating in the exhibition (with Stockholm Ljusreklam AB);
- wallpaper and other furnishings for the houses he designed;
- interiors for a General Motors bus;
- logo and posters for the exhibition (after winning a competition).
- advertising mast (after winning a competition, with Stockholm Ljusreklam AB).

Bibliography: *Stockholmsutställningen* 1930; Ahlin 1985b, pp. 132–41; Rudberg 1999.

(N.F.)

Sign for the PUB department stores.

The Gröna Udden café and pastry shop.

Drawing of a General Motors bus.

Perspective drawing of terraced houses.

74. Renovation Projects Executed by Stockholm Ljusreklam AB, AB BLOKK and AB IDESTA, 1929 onwards

In 1929 Lewerentz, together with the engineer Claes Kreuger, founded a firm specializing in the production of illuminated signs and display stands, with the specific aim of putting his professionalism at the service of the numerous firms that were intending to participate in the Stockholm Exhibition of the following year. This venture lived up to the two entrepreneurs' expectations, and Stockholm Ljusreklam AB realized its most important works on the site of the great exhibition. Some of these were particularly fascinating, such as the advertising mast, bearing coloured illuminated signs, standing in the centre of the main square of the exhibition at Djurgården; located in one of the bays of the Stockholm archipelago, this was visible from many parts of the city. The firm also constructed the display stands for the PUB and Finbruken department stores, many showcases and stands for the principal firms participating in the exhibition, and the Gröna Udden café and pastry shop, a large and very interesting building.

In 1930, as a result of the satisfactory outcome of the exhibition commissions, the firm changed its name to AB BLOKK—the new name was an anagram based on the initials of its partners' surnames—David Blomberg, furniture designer and maker; Sigurd Lewerentz, architect; Axel Olsson, contractor; Gunnar Kocken, captain and representative for the firm AB Byggnadsvaror (the building supplies company owned by Ivar Kreuger); and Claes Kreuger, builder—who were able to deal with all the different stages of the project, from its preliminary design to its realization, on any scale, from that of the object to the urban one. However, AB BLOKK only completed a few works, sometimes contributing to Lewerentz's projects, such as the Riksförsäkringsanstalt building in Stockholm, on other occasions obtaining its own commissions, as in the case of the Philips building, also in Stockholm.

In addition, the firm carried out minor

Renovation of the Diners de Paris restaurant, Stockholm, view of interior, 1930.

Renovation of the Livsmedelsbutik shop, entrance, 1932.

ärende Livsmedelsbutik.
LITTERA ...... N:O .....
ARKITEKT S. LEWERENTZ
ritad av A.G.H datum 10/12/-32
skala coll. L
Denna ritning är Arkitekt S. Lewerentz egendom och får icke utan hans medgivande kopieras, förevisas för eller utlämnas till konkurrent eller annan obehörig person. Kungl. Förord. 1919 § 2 jfrd mod § 5.

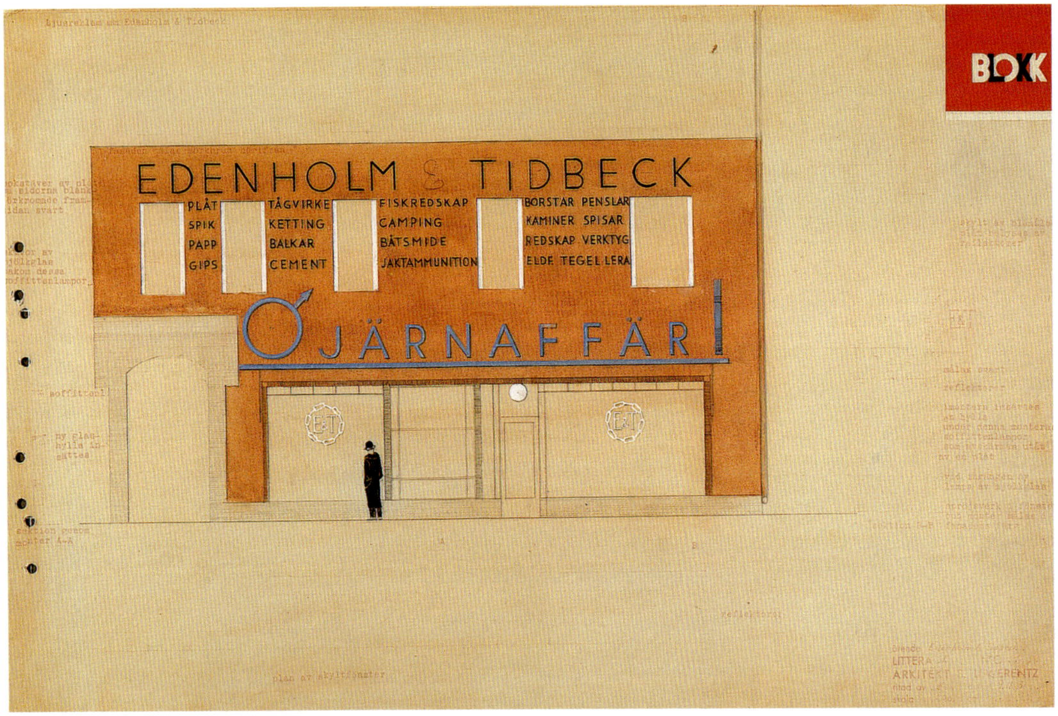

Project for the shop front and sign of an ironmonger's, Stockholm, 1931.

Renovation of the Marabou shop, Gothenburg, view of the entrance, 1929–34.

renovation work on commercial premises, mainly limited to the renewal of the front and illuminated signs. In 1933, however, its disappointing performance induced the partners to wind up the company, which was taken over by Lewerentz, who wanted to personally supervise all the stages in the elaboration and fulfilment of his projects. From then onwards the products made by the firm bore the Idesta trademark, a name that Lewerentz had already registered in 1929 in order to protect his exclusive rights to the manufacture of his own inventions. In the 1930s, although its objectives were reduced in comparison with those at the beginning, AB BLOKK completed a large number of projects, all on a small scale, which dealt with the renovation of commercial premises of various kinds. Sometimes the commissions were very modest and were limited to the renewal of the front, but in some cases the project comprised the whole space and was an example of true interior design. The firm's activity was not limited to Stockholm, but also extended to other Swedish cities and even included, in one case, a project for a shop in Oslo, in neighbouring Norway. Wishing to avoid having to contract out work to craftsmen and other firms, Lewerentz decided to manufacture the metal components himself so he would take responsibility for the whole process, from the design stage to installation, with control over their production. In 1940 he purchased a factory in Eskilstuna, a town not far from Stockholm, where he established his firm making metal door and window frames and partitions, which incorporated AB BLOKK and Idesta. In this period the firm was mainly concerned with the realization of the projects of other architects who availed themselves of Idesta's services because of Lewerentz's excellent reputation. When, in 1956, he decided to move to Skanör, at the tip of the peninsula forming southern Sweden, the management of the factory was taken over by his son, who continued to produce the locks and catches patented by his father and metal parts to special order.

Chronology
1929–30: Stockholm Ljusreklam AB, with C. Kreuger.
1930–33: AB BLOKK, with D. Blomberg, A. Olsson, C. Kreuger, G. Kocken.
1933 onwards: Lewerentz takes over AB BLOKK (with the Idesta trademark).
1940–56: Idesta in Eskilstuna; Lewerentz opens a factory making door and window frames, incorporating both AB BLOKK and Idesta.

Bibliography: Ahlin 1985b, pp. 135–37, 190–93.

(N.F.)

Project for an extension to the PUB department store, Stockholm, view of the entrance, 1930–34.

Filips confectioner's,
Stockholm, entrance,
1930–34.

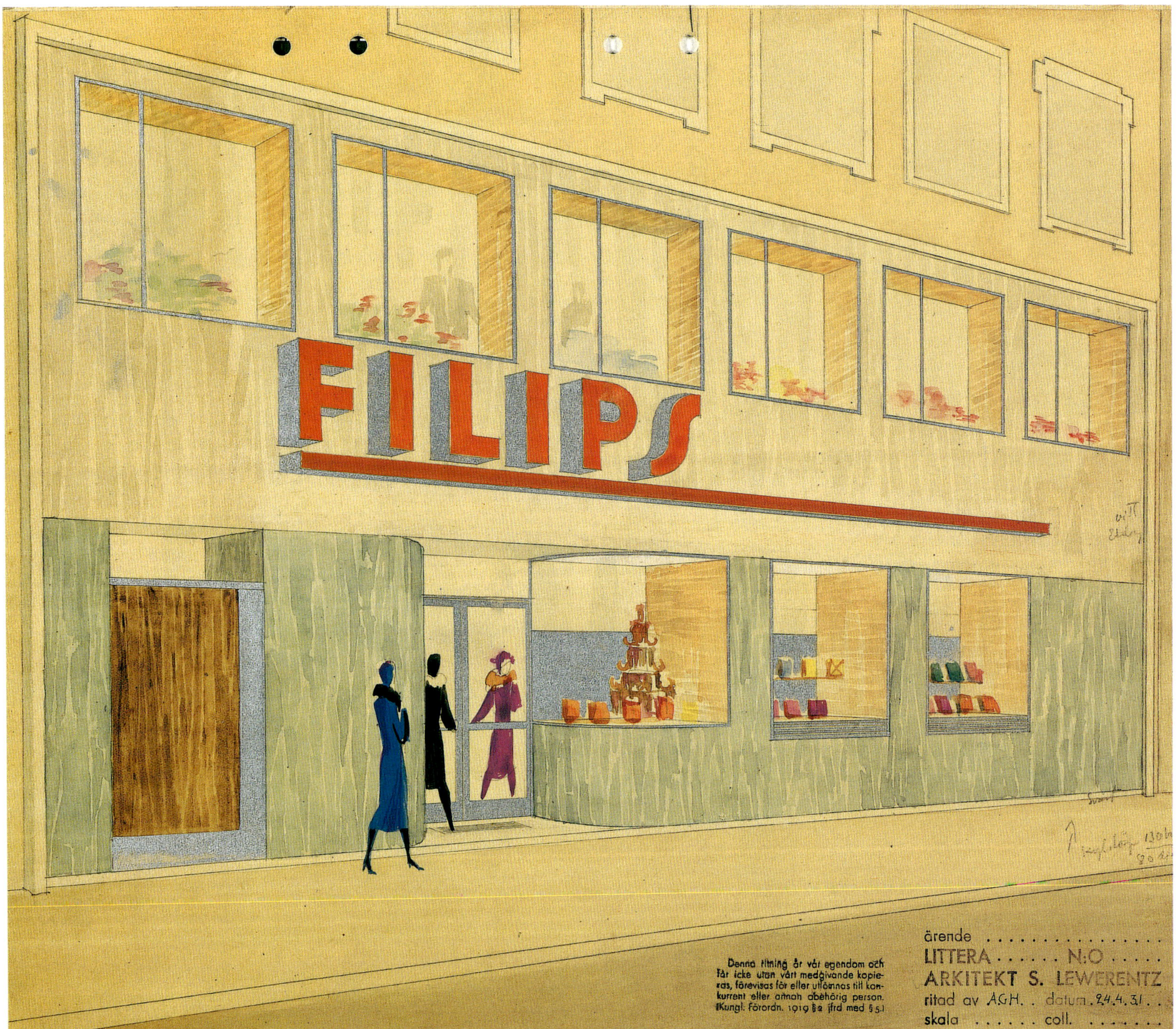

Interior.

Olssons car showroom,
Stockholm, plan, 1932.

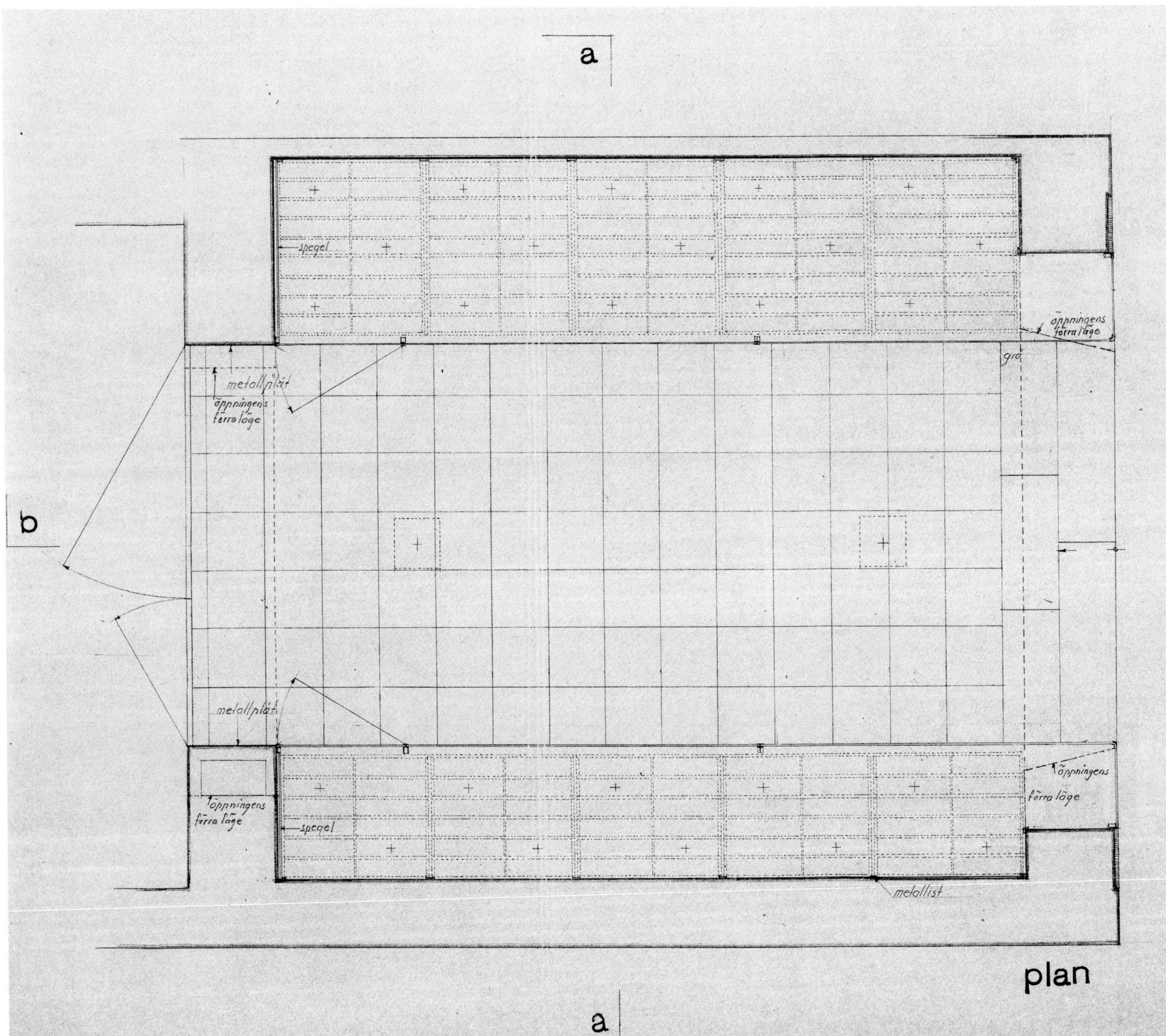

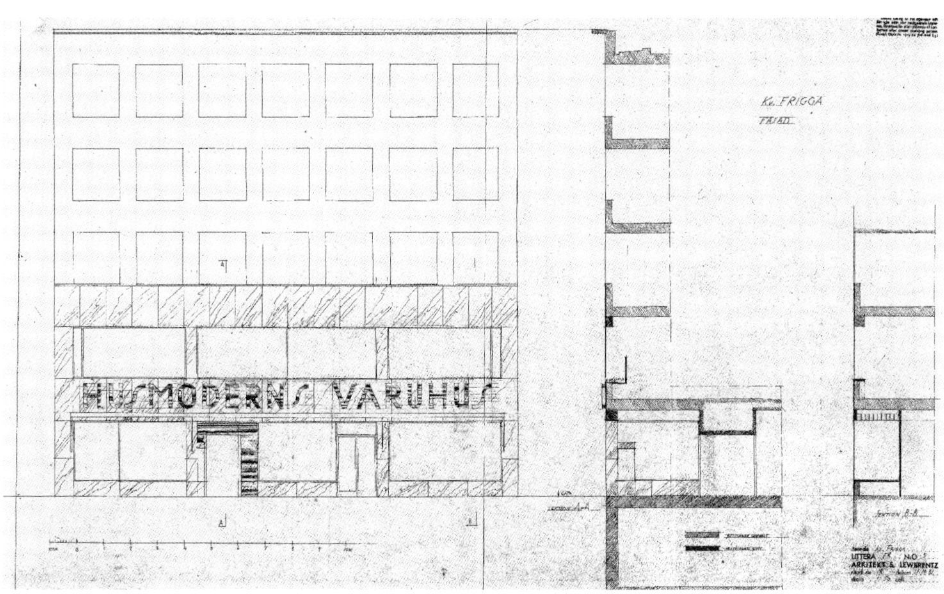

Window of a lingerie shop, Stockholm.

Husmodern department store, elevation and section, 1931.

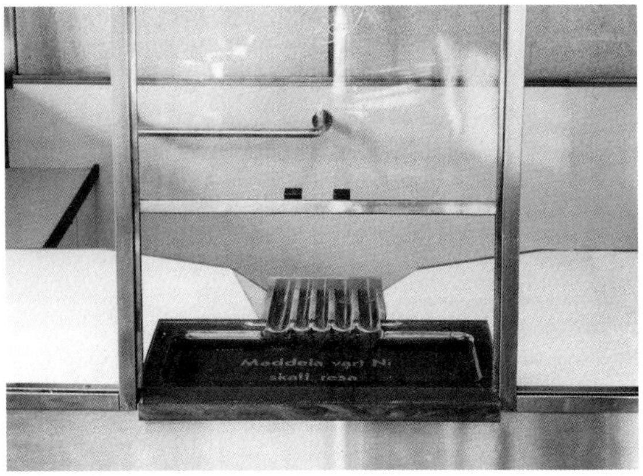

Details and overall view of a ticket booth for the Stockholm underground during manufacture in the Eskilstuna factory.

Manufacture of a partition in the Eskilstuna factory.

75. Projct for a Factory Building for Östrands Sulfatfabrik, Sundsvall, 1930

Elevation.

76. Sigurd Lewerentz's Speedboat, Stockholm, 1930

At the time of the Stockholm Exhibition of 1930, Lewerentz designed a small speedboat, which was built entirely in light mahogany by Gustaf Plym in the Neglinge shipyard. This is what Å. Lovén wrote in the journal *Arkitektur* in 1983:
"[the boat] was eight metres long and two metres wide and had a 120 hp Gray inboard motor capable of propelling it at a maximum speed of 25 knots... The cabin was furnished with a small steel-tube-framed sofa at the back and two armchairs at the front; immediately behind the cabin there was the large motor... With *Ewa*—this was the boat's name—moored at the Kungl. Motorbåt Klubben of Stockholm, it only took Lewerentz five minutes to go from his house at Strandvägen 37 to Persholmsbron, near the moorings of Gruv, on the islet of Utö, where his family owned a former miners' house at Lurgatan... *Ewa* was always kept in a perfect condition because Lewerentz maintained it very carefully. For me, as a young adolescent, it was a great thrill to help 'Uncle Sigurd' to tie up the motorboat... At the beginning of the 1950s *Ewa* was torn from its moorings during a fierce autumn storm at Neglinge and was swept against the rocks."

Bibliography: Lovén 1983; Ahlin 1985b, pp. 142–43.

(N.F.)

Lewerentz's speedboat.

77. Enköping Cemetery, 1930–32

The site available for the realization of the cemetery, just outside the city centre, was flat except for a small hill in the western part. It was here that Lewerentz decided to locate the chapel, which he separated from the burial area by a wide avenue extending from north to south. The cemetery is surrounded by hawthorn hedges, while the internal paths are lined with tall birches. Lewerentz paid particular attention to the design of the small chapel for which he sought—as he usually did in this period of his career—the simplest possible form. In his first solution, he proposed an asymmetric structure comprising the chapel, storerooms and a small sacristy; later this complex was broken up into a series of simple buildings, where each element expressed its function, leaving the reciprocal relationships, the orientations and the dimensions the task of establishing the order and quality of the space. The small chapel that was finally built is a simple volume on a rectangular base; with its stuccoed external walls and, on the north front, a semicircular apse soaring above the rest of the building, it bears no trace of the long design process. The south face of the apse contains a large window that, casting its light directly onto the altar, allows the interior to be well illuminated.
To the west, the complex also comprises a low building, placed orthogonally to the chapel, housing the service rooms and mortuary.

Bibliography: Ahlin 1985b, pp. 144–46; Constant 1994, p. 129; Caldenby 1997, pp. 116–17.

(N.F.)

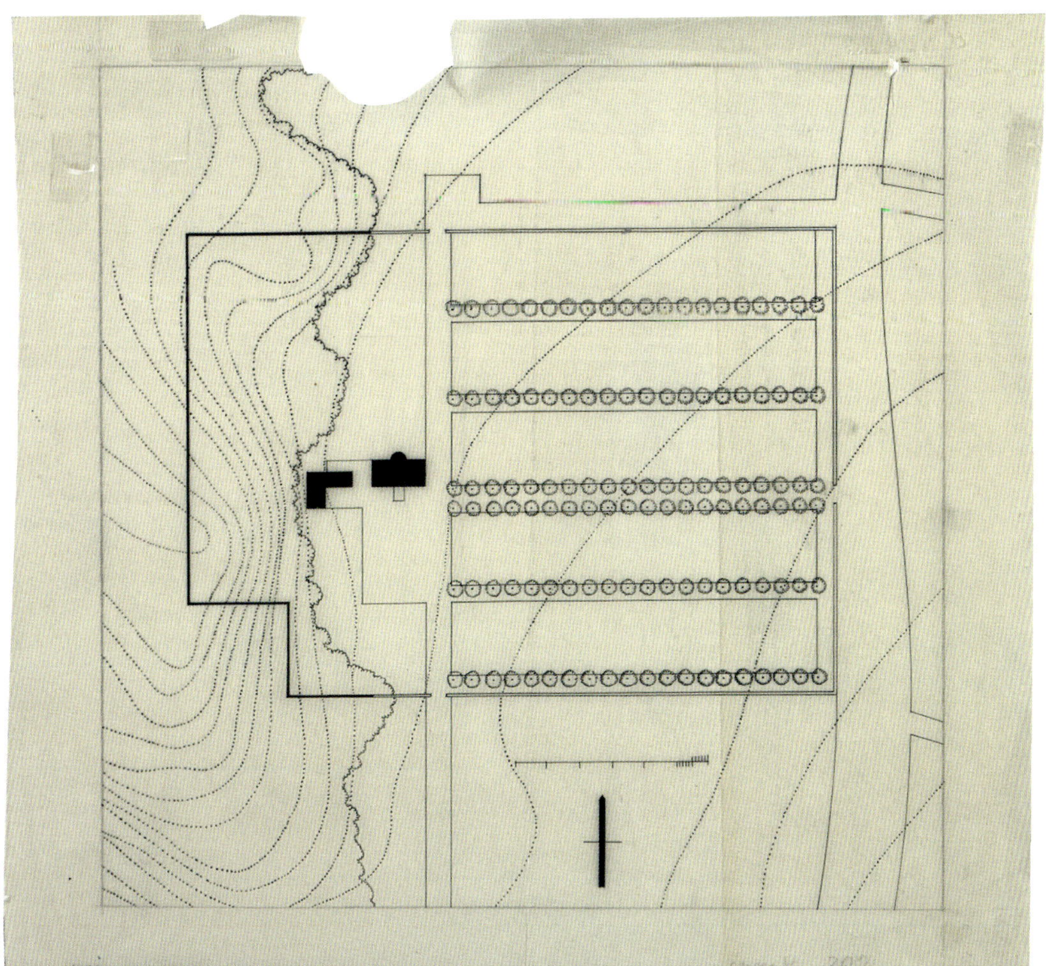

Chapel, rear elevation.

Layout plan with the chapel highlighted.

Perspective study
of the chapel, 1930.

Perspective study
of the chapel, 1930s.

Views of the chapel.

78. Project for a Standard Holiday Chalet, 1931

The popularity of small chalets in the countryside and by the sea was a typically Scandinavian phenomenon in the 1930s, when the propensity of the Nordic peoples for a life in close contact with nature found fertile ground in the new Functionalist ideology. The promotion of a healthier lifestyle, centred above all on the desire to allow the masses to have access to recreational activities and take care of their physical well-being, led to the creation of new building types intended exclusively for leisure purposes.

However, in addition to the buildings for communal use, such as restaurants, cinemas, bathing establishments and so on, small holiday homes became particularly widespread. Here it was possible to spend not only long periods, but also weekends and any other days free from work commitments. Lewerentz, like other architects, produced his own project for a standard house to meet this requirement: laying particular emphasis on simplicity, he proposed a small wooden chalet with a very elementary form and spartan interiors. The project for the chalet was not restricted to the building itself, but also included an enclosed area on one side of it, suggesting that the limited size of the interior was due to the fact that holidaymakers would be spending most of their time in the open air. In 1934 a national competition was organized for the design of a standard holiday chalet; although there are no drawings attesting to Lewerentz's participation, among his documents there is a card bearing the letterhead of the competition on which appear copies of his drawings of the chalet executed some years earlier. It is probable, therefore, that Lewerentz did not propose another version of his project for the competition because he considered the previous one was still valid.

(N.F.)

Study axonometric projection.

79. Competition Project for a Girls' High School, Stockholm, 1931–32
with Osvald Almqvist
motto "Balk"

This is what Lewerentz had to say in his outline of the project: "This building is designed to be built with a steel skeleton and concrete beams and elevations. The window frames are in wood and have a vertical glazing bar in wood too, so that the internal partitions are held in place by the structure of the frames. The staircases and the hall floor are in stone, while the floors of the corridors and classrooms are covered with linoleum... The pillars around the edge of the building's structure are covered with insulation in direct contact with the concrete. The exterior walls are painted with the colours indicated by the letters A, B and C, either directly on the concrete or on the stucco."

Bibliography: Romare 1932.

(G.P.)

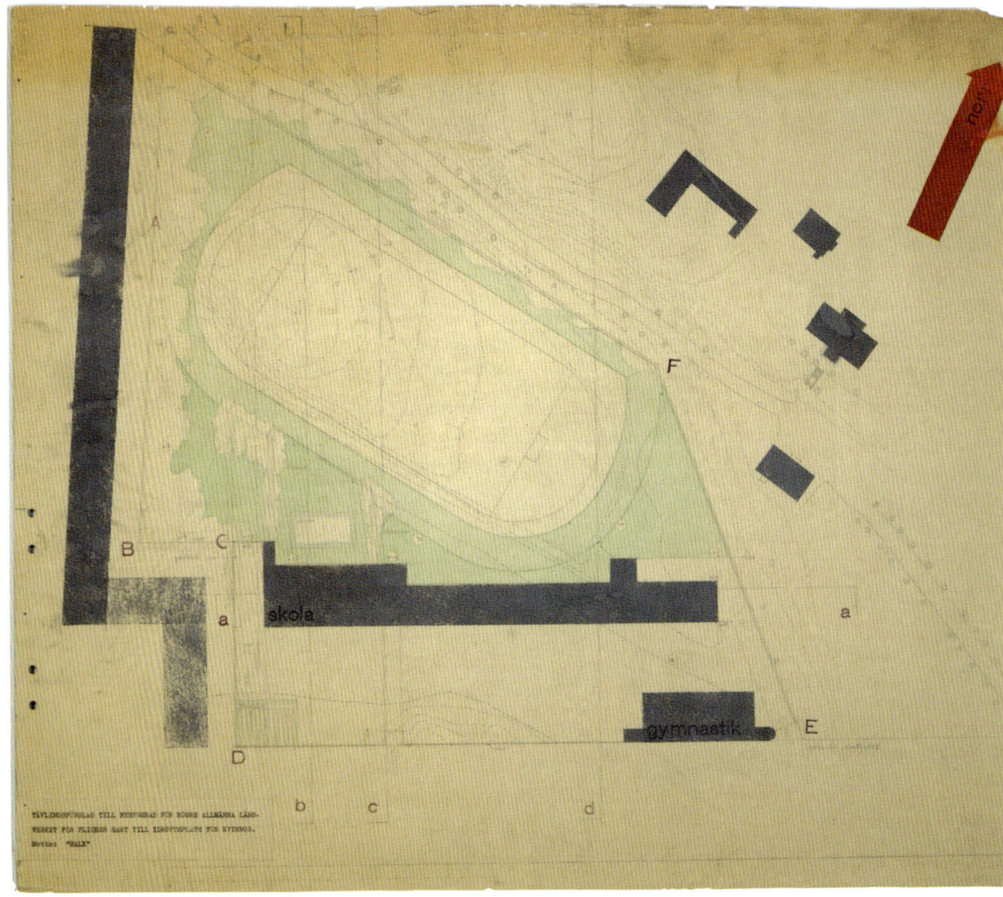

Layout plan and elevation.

80. Project for a Chapel with an Adjacent Crematorium in Djursholm Cemetery, Stockholm, 1932–33

In 1933 Lewerentz submitted to the municipality of Djursholm, a small town on the northern fringe of Stockholm, three different versions of a project for a chapel and a crematorium in the cemetery already existing there.
In the first version, the chapel is sited on the slopes of a small hill in the centre of the cemetery, allowing the crematorium to be built into the hillside. For visitors going up the avenue from the entrance to the chapel, the crematorium is almost invisible, as Lewerentz's perspective studies demonstrate, allowing just the hemispherical shape of the glazed dome surmounting the chapel to emerge. The two side walls extend beyond the entrance, forming an open-air columbarium, a repetition of the arrangement already adopted in the contemporary chapel in Malmö's Eastern Cemetery, while the positioning of the cross echoes that in the project submitted to the competition for the extension to the Stockholm South Cemetery, produced in collaboration with Erik Gunnar Asplund. The coffins are taken from the chapel to the crematorium located below on a platform situated in front of the entrance; powered by a hydraulic mechanism, this allows handling of the coffins to be reduced to a minimum.
In the second version of the project, the two buildings are arranged differently, in this case are close to the cemetery's north entrance, although the internal distribution is basically the same. The chapel still has its square plan, while the columbarium, previously fairly small, now covers a larger area than the chapel itself. The crematorium is still underground, although there is now no relationship with the topography of the site, since it is located in a flat area close to the entrance. Two rows of trees mark the axis leading to the chapel and also give structure to the open space of the columbarium.
On the exterior, a wall progressively increasing in height and curved in the final part leads towards the forecourt, obliging the visitor to take a slightly uphill path beginning at the back of the chapel. The complex also comprises a small building containing the mortuary, adjacent to the chapel's north wall. As in the first version, the essentially horizontal composition is counterpointed by the glazed dome on the chapel and the crematorium chimney. In the third and last version, however, the building is radically different. Again located near the cemetery's main entrance, the chapel is an elongated rectangular building, with a large curved window in the end wall. This design partially resembles that of the contemporary chapel of the Enköping Cemetery, where the theme of the curved wall forming the end of the principal axis is present.

Bibliography: Ahlin 1985b, pp. 153–54.

(N.F.)

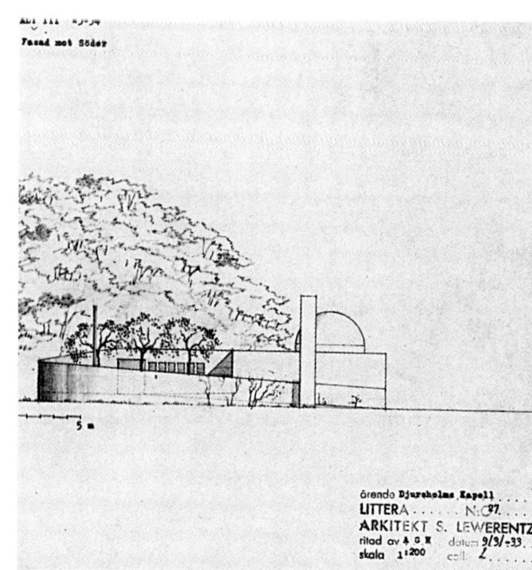

Perspective drawing and south elevation.

81. Competition Project for Malmö City Museum, 1932
with O. Almqvist, E. Wettergren and A.G. Hedberg
motto "Anno 1932" – citation

On the occasion of the transfer of the civic collection to Malmö Castle, a competition was organized for the design of a museum complex that was to house, in addition to the city museum, also the art gallery and natural history museum. The new complex, although constructed in the space left free by the historic building, had to avoid coming into conflict with it, but had rather to perform the task of highlighting its monumentality. The competition jury wrote that the solution submitted by Lewerentz, together with Almqvist and Wettergren, belongs to the group that has concentrated that majority of the rooms in the west area of the courtyard (of the castle), dividing the remaining part between the southern and eastern sides.
A wicket door has been inserted in the main door—(Renaissance, still existing).
In the project the rooms of the art gallery are all located on the ground floor (around the courtyard), with top lighting for the west block ... and side windows in the south and east ones... The drawing of the plan shows very interesting details, such as the entrance hall, and is, on the whole, well conceived. Nonetheless, with regard to the circulation within the art gallery, the fact that visitors start with the 1920s and conclude with the prehistoric section is open to objection. The problem of illumination has been carefully thought out as far as top lighting is concerned, while the wing lit by the windows facing west is rather dark.
The exterior of the complex is particularly interesting because the height of the new buildings has been kept low (and they are not attempting to compete with the monumental building) . . . although the project is technically complex, especially as regards the main block, because of the small courtyards inserted between the different parts of the structure, so that heating and maintenance costs would be high in the completed building.
The overall cubic volume is very large.
As far as the external finishings are concerned, the architects proposed very simple forms covered with stucco, which would be absolutely anonymous, especially for the parts to be built next to the walls of the historic building.

Bibliography: Lindström 1932; Ahlin 1985b, p. 152.

(N.F.)

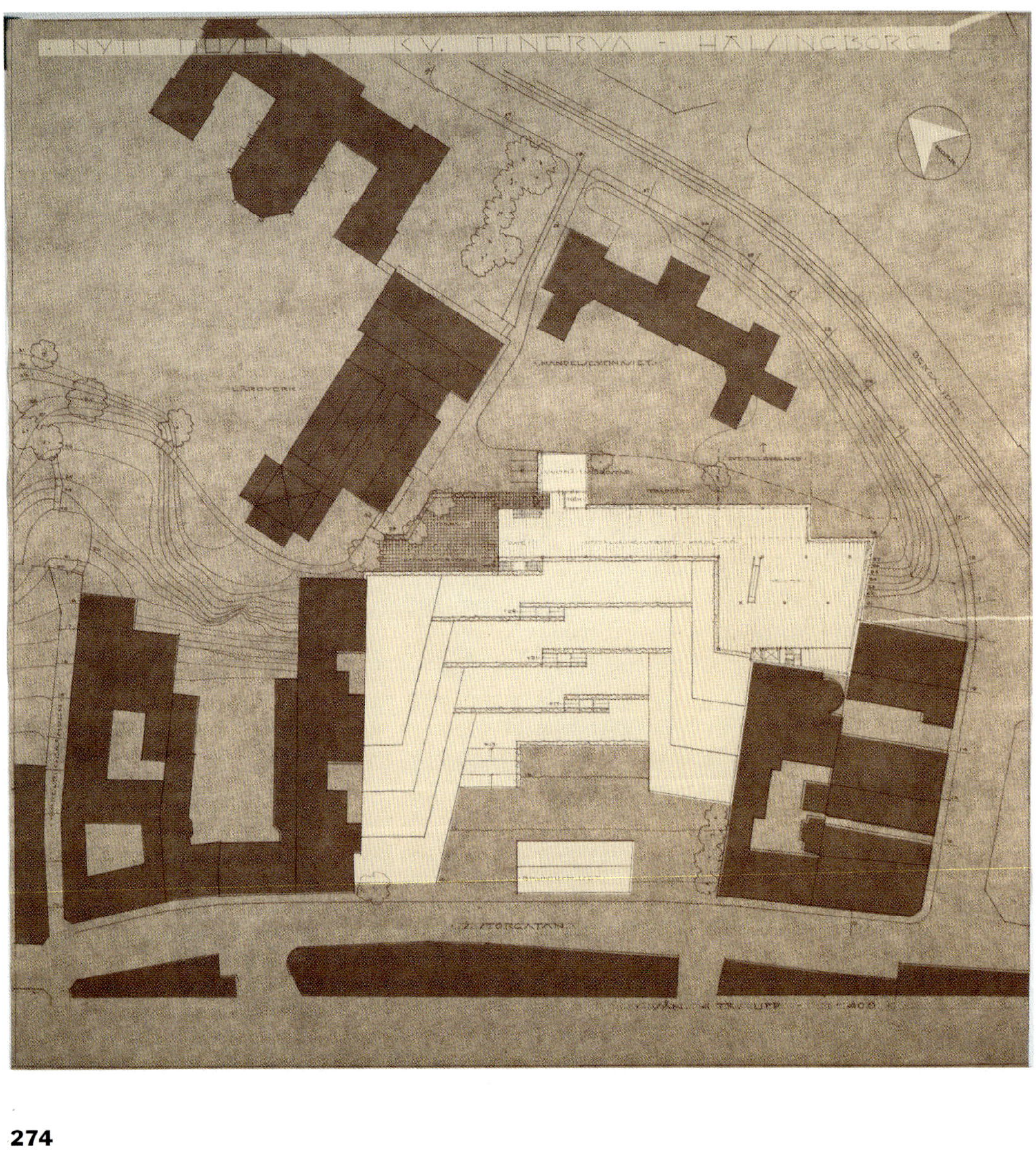

Layout plan

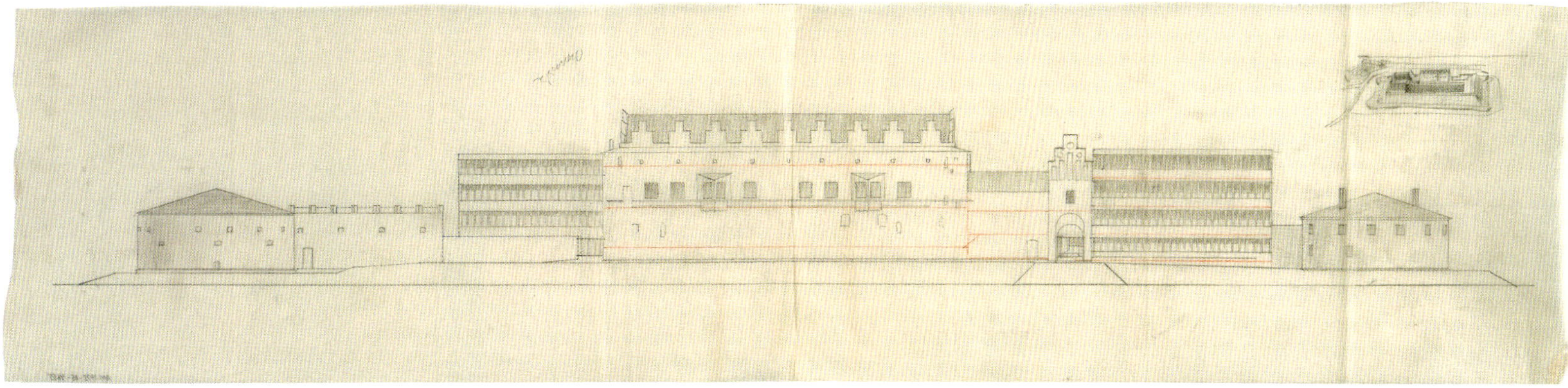

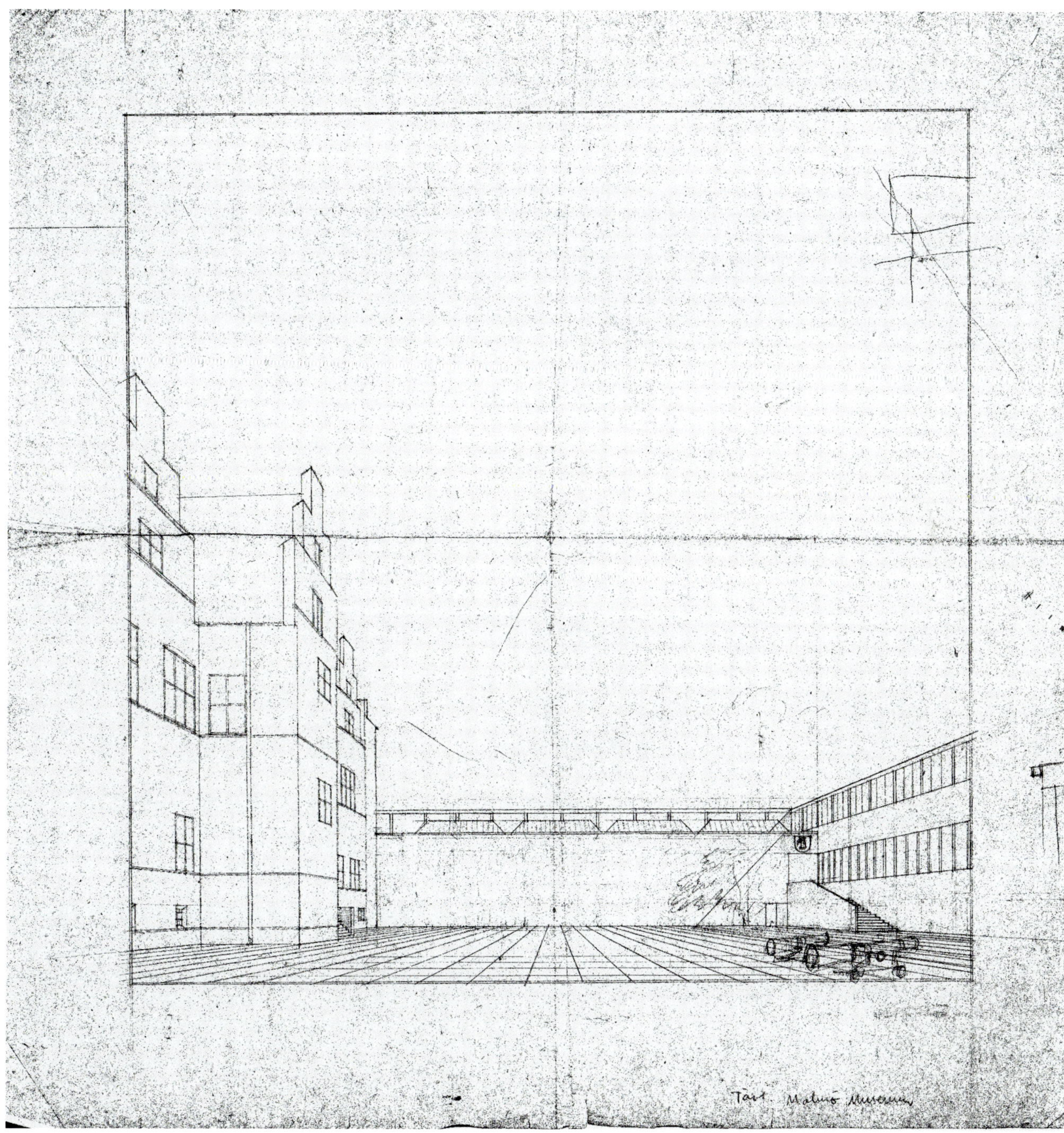

Elevation of the complex and perspective drawing of the courtyard.

82. Competition Project for the Town Plan of the Nedre Norrmalm District, Stockholm, 1932
motto "5881"

The changes in the social fabric of Stockholm, as well as the growth of traffic and commerce and the diffusion of the new Functionalist ideas in the field of urban design, induced the municipality to hold an international competition in 1932 for the transformation of the Nedre Norrmalm district, located to the north of the city's historic centre. The main request in the competition programme was that Sveavägen, an important street crossing the whole of the Nedre Norrmalm district from north to south, should continue with the same width up to Gustav Adolfs Torg, the square overlooked by the Swedish Parliament.
Taking full advantage of the freedom offered by the programme, Lewerentz's project offered a radical solution, totally transforming the whole of the area concerned. Preserving only a few, clearly distinctive buildings, the architect proposed almost total demolition of the existing constructions, which he replaced with modern multi-storey buildings placed in a line, in accordance with the Functionalist tendency then prevalent in central Europe. The buildings again front onto the main street, and are aligned along the perimeters of the blocks, but the parcelization typical of the former arrangement has been replaced by open spaces and other residential buildings placed at an angle to those along the perimeter. In addition, as requested by the programme, Lewerentz extended Sveavägen to Gustav Adolfs Torg, which he expanded northwards in order to allow the street to lead directly into the square.

Bibliography: Olsson 1931; Markelius 1934; Olsson 1934; Ahlin 1985b, pp. 157–61.

(N.F.)

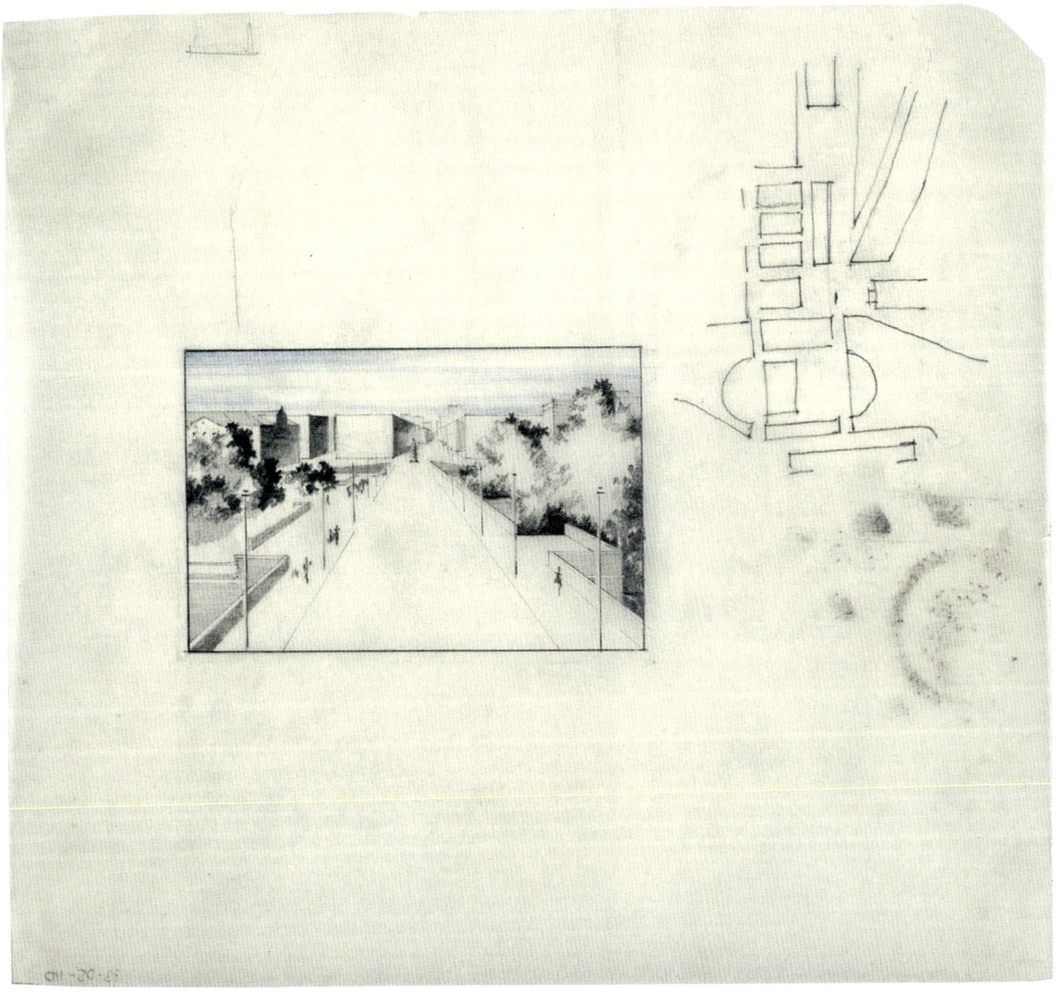

Layout plan and bird's-eye view, study drawings.

83. Furnishings for the Koux Family's Bedroom, 1932

Study drawings.

84. Project for a Power Station at Djursholm, Stockholm, 1933

The short outline of the project states:
The building is to be constructed in concrete with a 1:3:5 mixture, which is a good rule in order to obtain a smooth surface both inside and outside; the external formwork should be made of 1 × 2 rough wood, the frames round the doors are 1 × 1, ... while in the external edge of the roof an element in wood with a regular profile of 1 + 1 / 2 × 3. The pitched roof is covered with tiles in copper sheet blackened through oxidation... The external doors are in rolled iron 1.5 mm thick ... thermal insulation is ensured by loose-fill materials ... and the surface finish consists of a coat of rustproof paint and oil paint as in the sample. The external walls are painted a cement colour or a similar tone according to a sample agreed with the architect.

(G.P.)

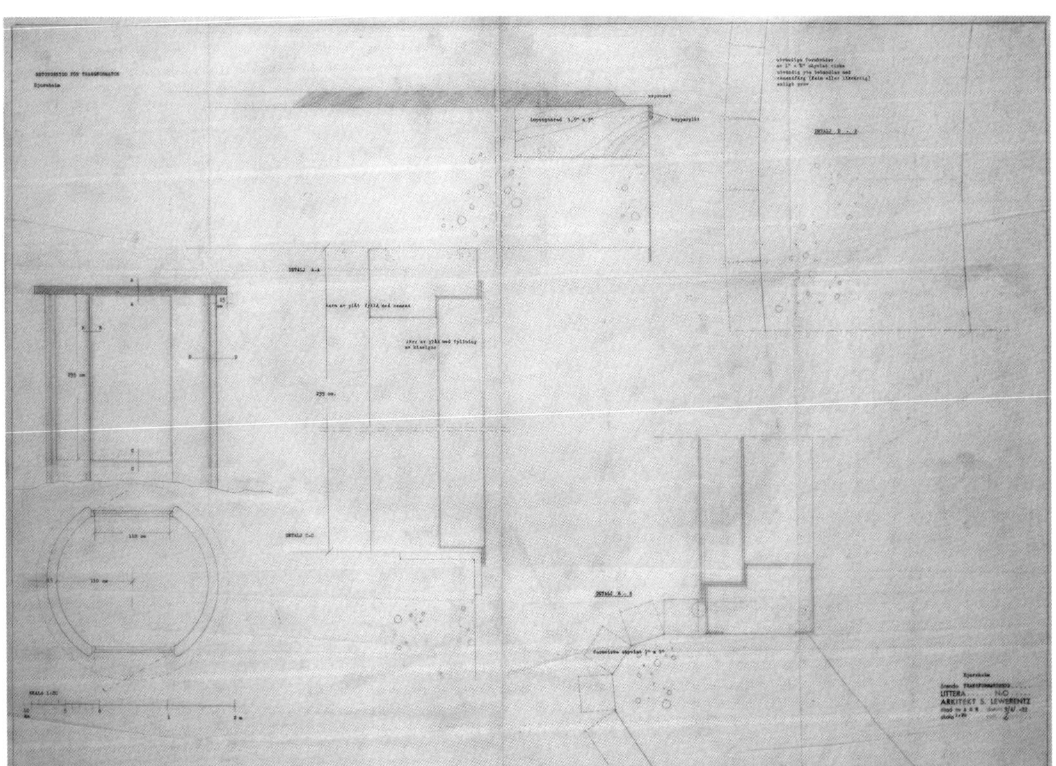

Construction details.

85. Competition Project for the Church of Johanneberg, Gothenburg, 1933–34

motto "Svart och vitt"

Organized for the design of a new church in a developing area in the Johanneberg district of Gothenburg, the competition attracted a large number of architects. Free from any preconceived ideas regarding form and distribution, Lewerentz's strongly innovative approach is wholly centred on the desire to bring together the two main focal points of the Evangelical service: the altar and the pulpit. As a result of this objective, already present in the earliest sketches, the church takes the form of a square with a rounded corner where the altar and the pulpit are located. Consequently, the internal space is organized along one of the diagonals, involving a notable departure from the traditional basilican plan.

The essentially horizontal form of the church—despite the fact that the competition committee was favourable to a more vertical structure—demonstrates that Lewerentz has deliberately chosen to interpret spirituality in a contemporary manner, abandoning verticality, the ancient symbol of transcendence now incompatible with the democratic spirit of modern man. The low building, constructed in yellow brick, is illuminated exclusively by a narrow skylight placed in the centre of the flat roof, which has a strong impact on the interior due to the projecting reinforced concrete beams placed next to it. Lewerentz provided for the other functions required by the competition programme, such as space for the organ, the entrances and the sacristy, by adding subsidiary blocks, constructed almost entirely in steel and glass, to the main church building, the entrance to which is marked by a large, slightly inclined cross.

Resulting from the large, slightly curved concrete beams, the building's industrial overtones, together with its innovative layout, are an endorsement of the positive values of contemporary culture and reflect the changed lifestyle of the people for whom this church is intended. With this project, moreover, Lewerentz is proposing a new type of church conceived as a place where, in a state of total concentration, people may encounter God through the light symbolizing Him and listen to His Word from a new position. This fosters the egalitarian condition of the congregation, which, thanks to the layout, seems to cluster round the altar.

Bibliography: Zimdahl 1934; Ahlin 1985b, pp. 154–55.

(N.F.)

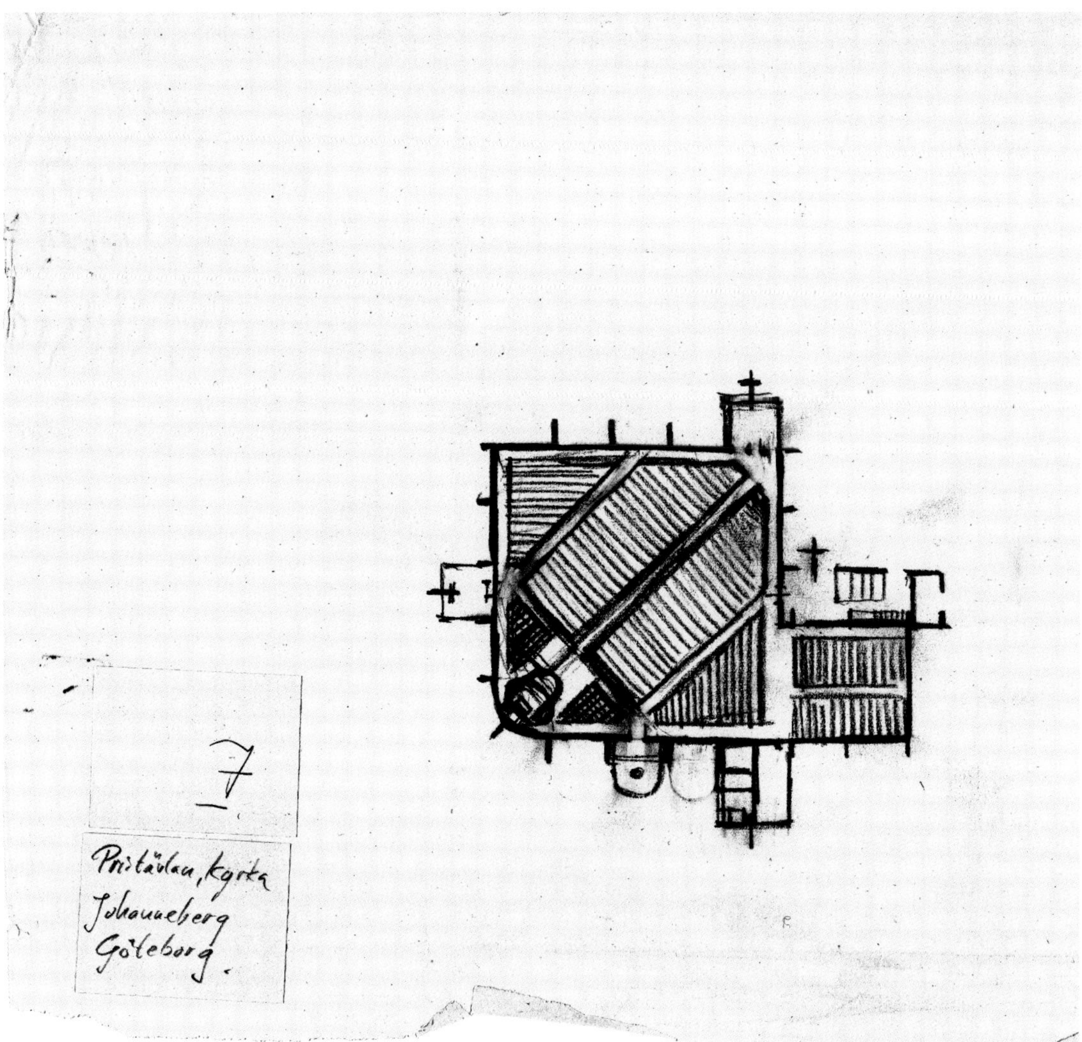

Plan of the church, study drawing.

Elevations and longitudinal section.

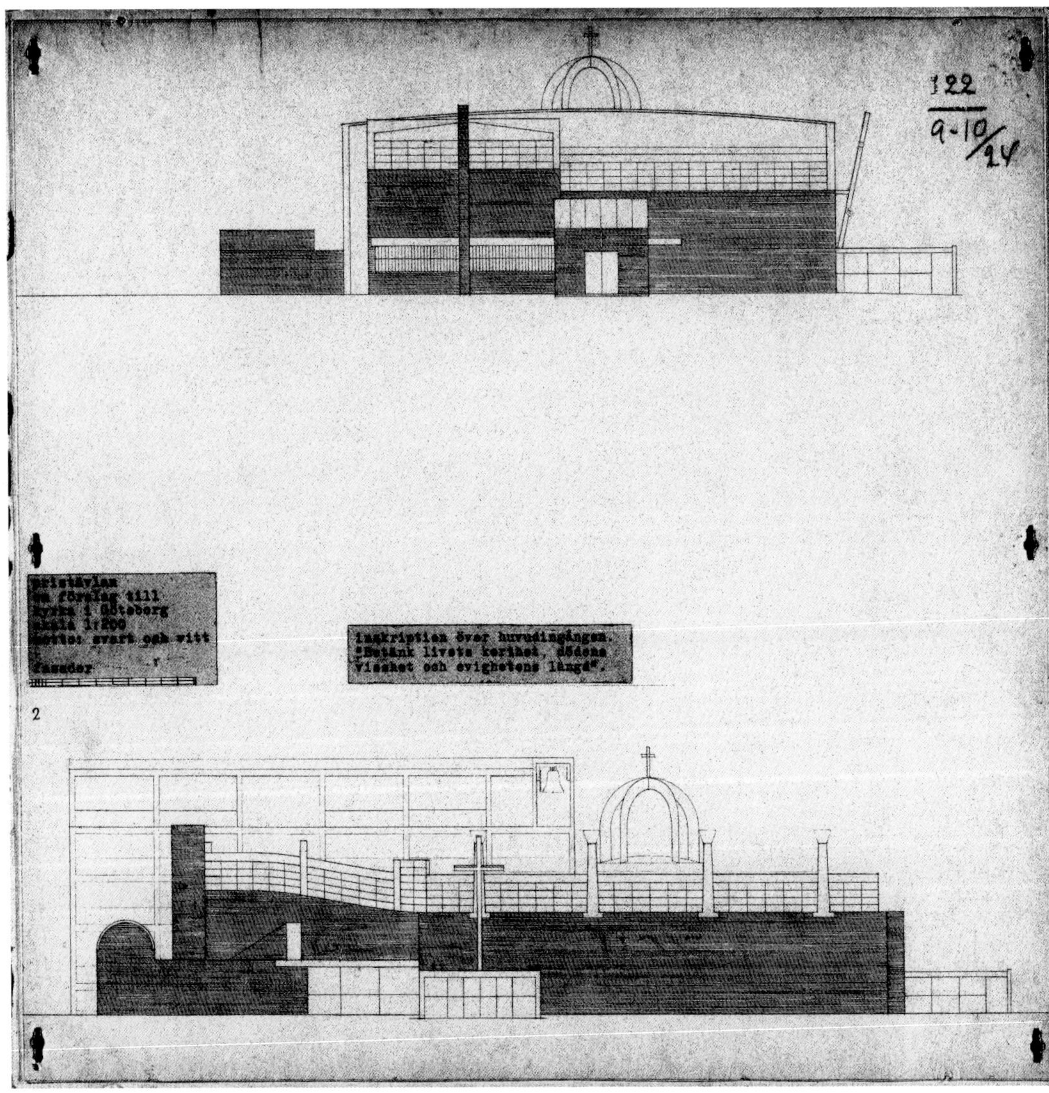

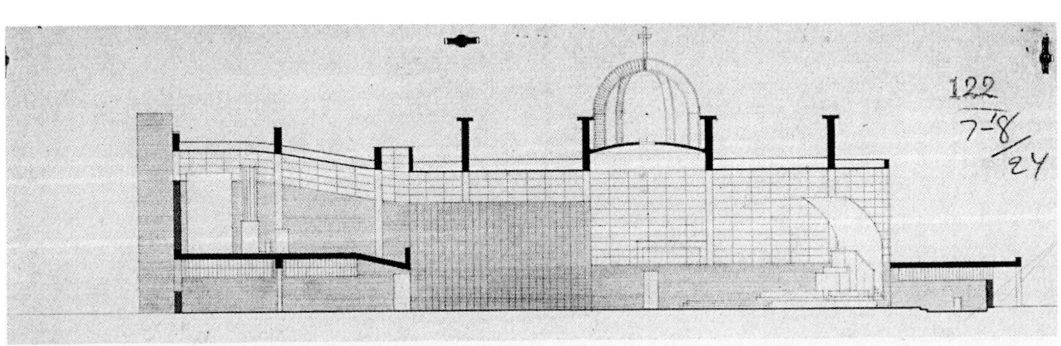

View of the model.

View of the model.

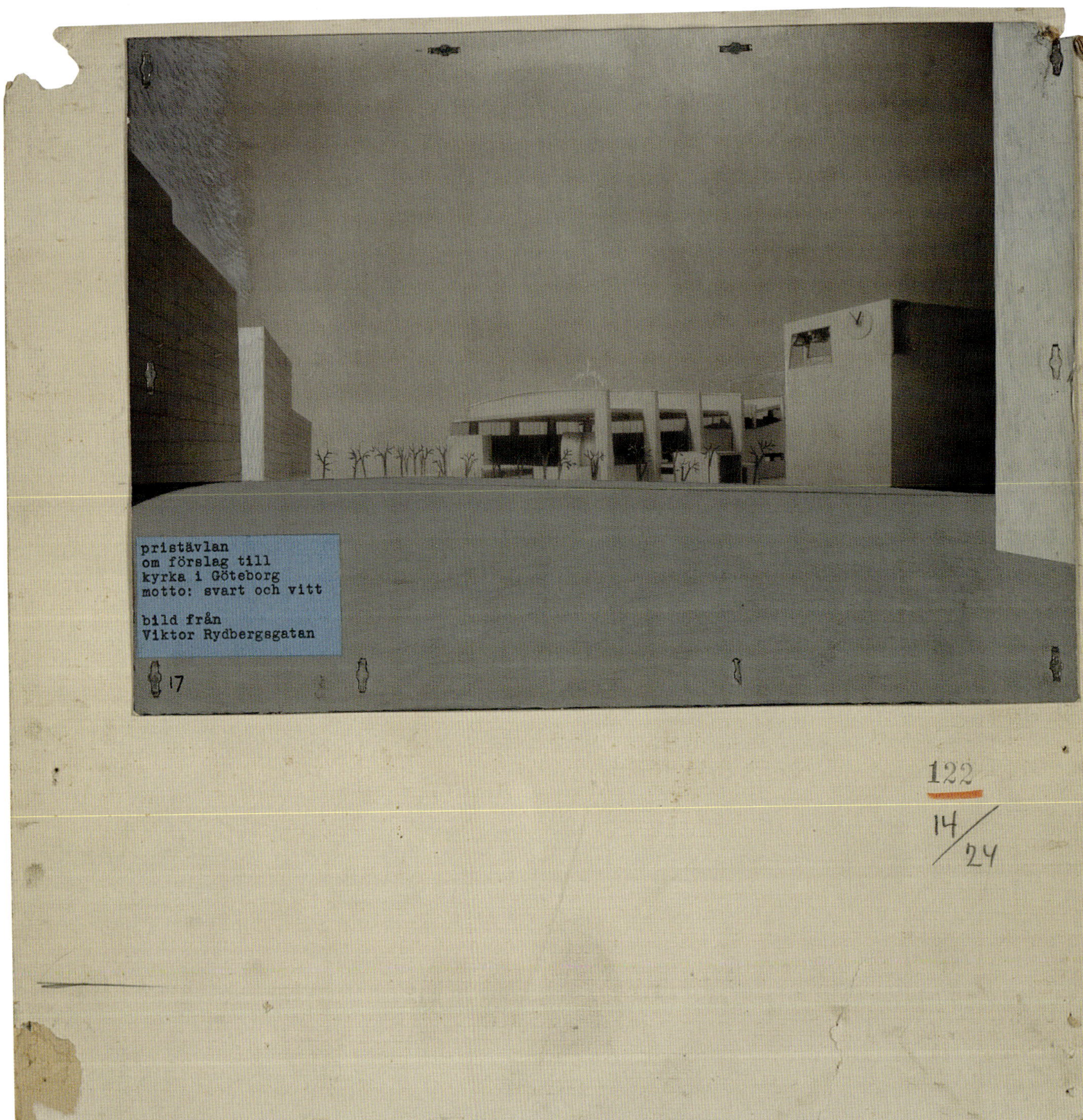

86. Project for a Residential Area at Djursholm, Stockholm, 1933

The study sketches for the project for a residential area at Djursholm, a small town on the northern fringe of Stockholm, show a scheme for single-family houses in which Lewerentz proposes two different building types, although both reflect the principles of the new Functionalist architecture that, after the Stockholm Exhibition of 1930, rapidly spread throughout Sweden: simple forms, large glazed surfaces and a stucco finish for the exterior walls, with no concessions made to local tradition.
The site lies between two parallel roads and the study drawings show both detached two-storey houses and terraced houses, divided by open spaces to increase the privacy of each of the living units, which are presumably intended for middle-class families.

(N.F.)

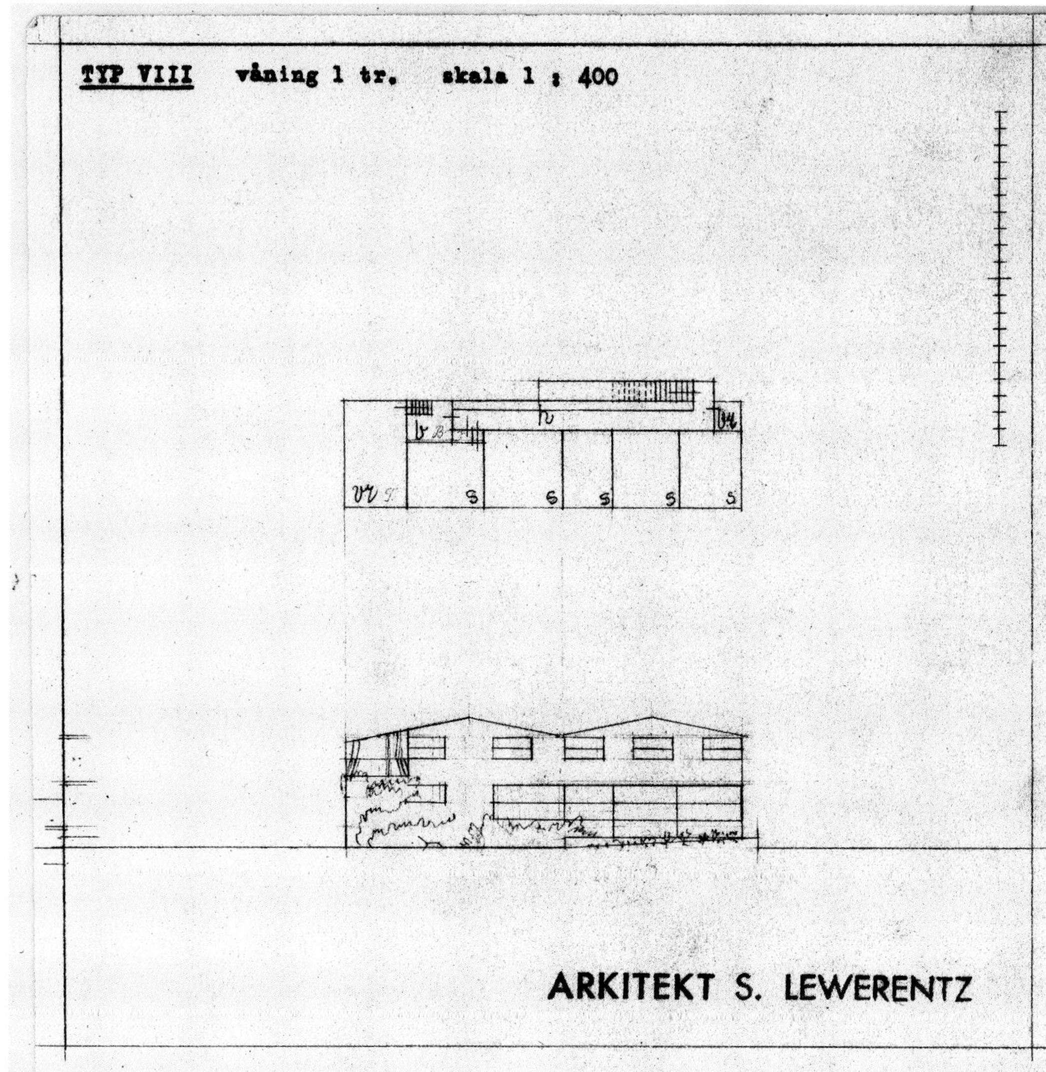

Plan and elevation
of the terraced houses.

87. Project for a Warehouse at Frihannen, Stockholm, 1933

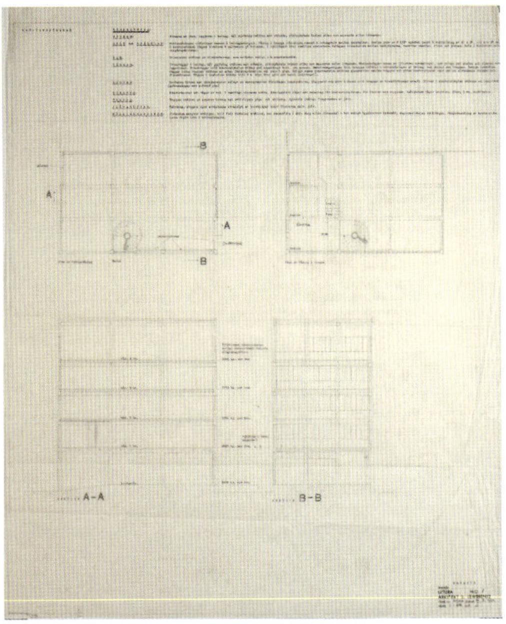

Plans and longitudinal and cross sections.

88. Project for the Division of Land into Plots at Aludden, Djursholm, Stockholm, 1933

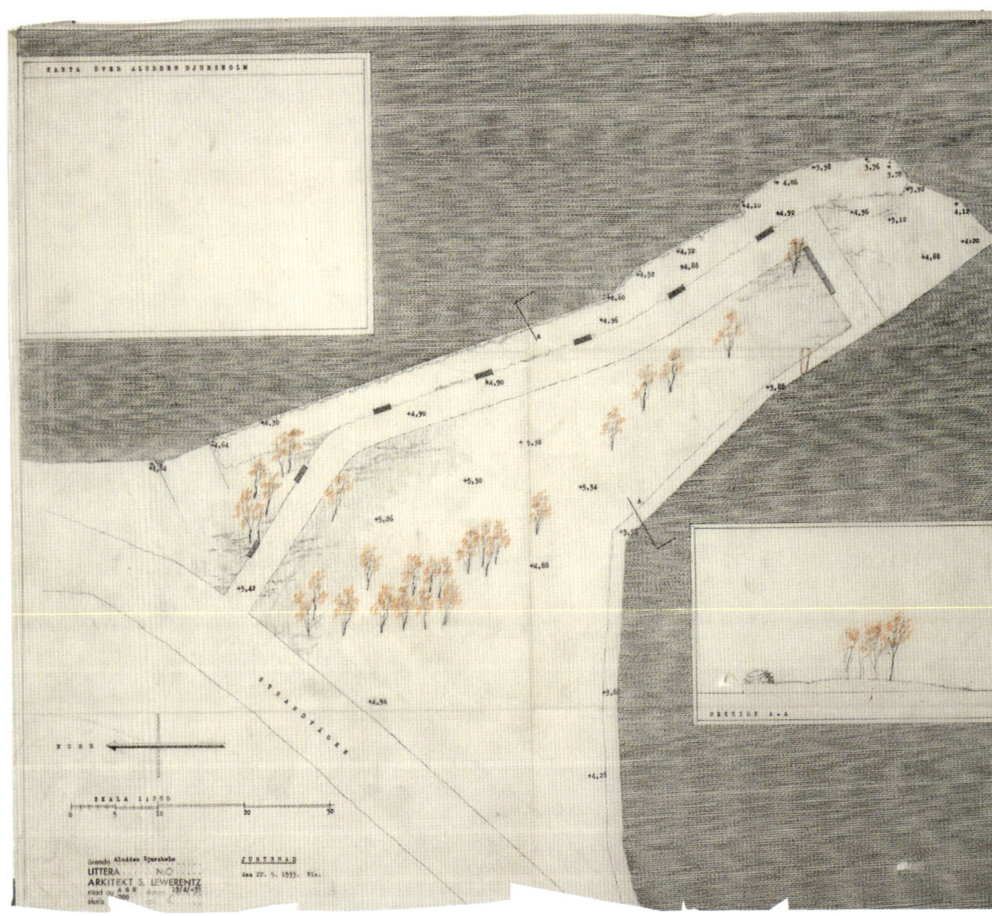

Site plan.

89. Project for Gudmundrå Cemetery, 1933

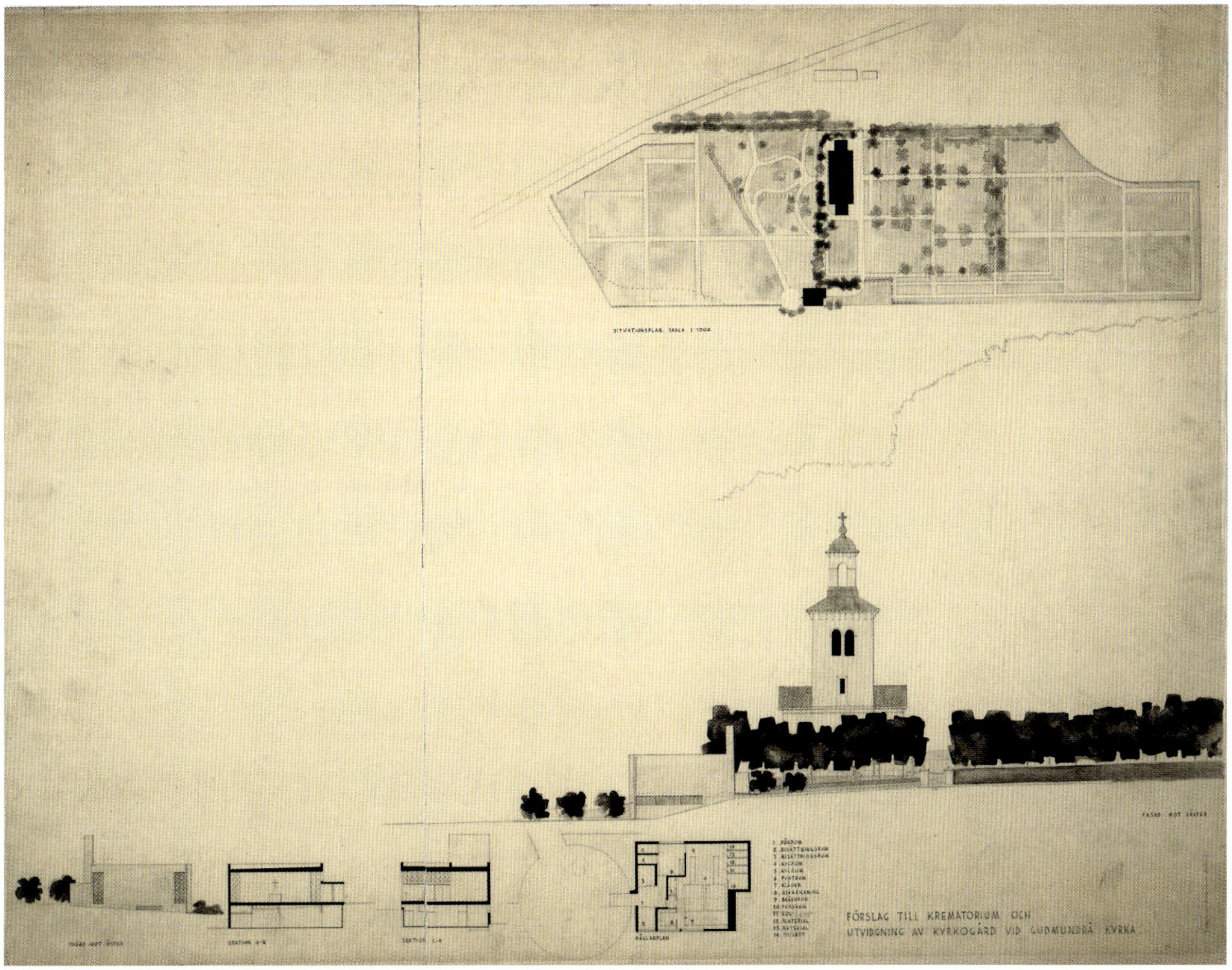

Study drawings, layout plan, elevations, sections and plan.

90. Villa Edstrand, Falsterbo, 1933–37

In 1933 the Edstrand family, the owners of Bröderna Edstrand AB—a firm that, among other things, was an agent for IDESTA's products—commissioned Lewerentz to design a small holiday villa for a site on the outskirts of Falsterbo, a small coastal town in southern Sweden commanding an excellent view of the Sound. In the same year Lewerentz submitted the first versions of his project to his clients; these were all based on the principle that the house should be very small, as they had expressly requested, and, like the subsequent versions elaborated up to 1935, were clearly influenced by Le Corbusier's style, which the architect greatly admired. It was only in 1935, with the penultimate version, that Lewerentz submitted a project that, with its larger size resulting from the changed requirements of the clients, abandons any formal constraints, displaying the fruits of his own poetic research. Leaving no room for pre-established styles and formalism, it is marked by the certainty that architecture is the expression of a fundamental truth. The use of more durable materials suited to the severe climatic conditions, instead of pure but delicate white stucco or the coldness of reinforced concrete, and the need to examine the vital processes at the base of family life—proceeding in the elaboration of the project from the interior towards the exterior, in order to produce a form freed from preconceived schemata or schools—attest to Lewerentz's courage and his conscious acceptance of the premises of modernity, although not necessarily of its now firmly established stylistic elements. The villa is transformed into an elongated two-storey block, located close to the access road, with a closed and compact south-east elevation that manifests the desire to protect the family's privacy, but, at the same time, provides a view from the interior towards the gently undulating meadow and the sea. A special feature of this face is a steel and glass canopy—constructed with elements in the IDESTA catalogue, as are all the window and door assemblies in the building—protecting the entrances to the house and garage, the latter being set at a slight angle to the façade. The first floor of the opposite elevation consists of a long volume interrupted by projecting balconies, which, because the ground floor is almost entirely glazed, seem to be suspended in space. Here a steel structure covers an external space, which is, however, characterized by a strong sense of interiority, as it is sheltered behind, towards the road, by the house itself and, towards the south, on the side facing the meadow, by the slightly rolling terrain. From the ground floor, mainly devoted to service functions and the servants' rooms, a staircase with a very light structure and a distinctly nautical air leads to the upper level where the living-room opens onto a wide balcony. The bedrooms, located on the same side as the main entrance, create a sort of screen separating the domestic activities from the road. In 1944 Lewerentz designed a small extension on the roof consisting of a veranda built almost entirely of steel and glass. Furthermore, in 1961–62 the architect prepared a project for another small house to the north of the site, on the side facing the road, which, however, was never built.

Chronology
1933–35: first stage of the project.
1935–37: second stage of the project and construction of the villa.
1944: extension on the roof.
1961–62: project for another house near the first one.

Bibliography: Ahlsèn 1941; Ahlin 1985b, pp. 171–75; Caldenby 1997, pp. 118–29.

(N.F.)

Axonometric projection,
first version, 1933.

Perspective sketch,
second version, c. 1934.

Elevation, third version,
1934.

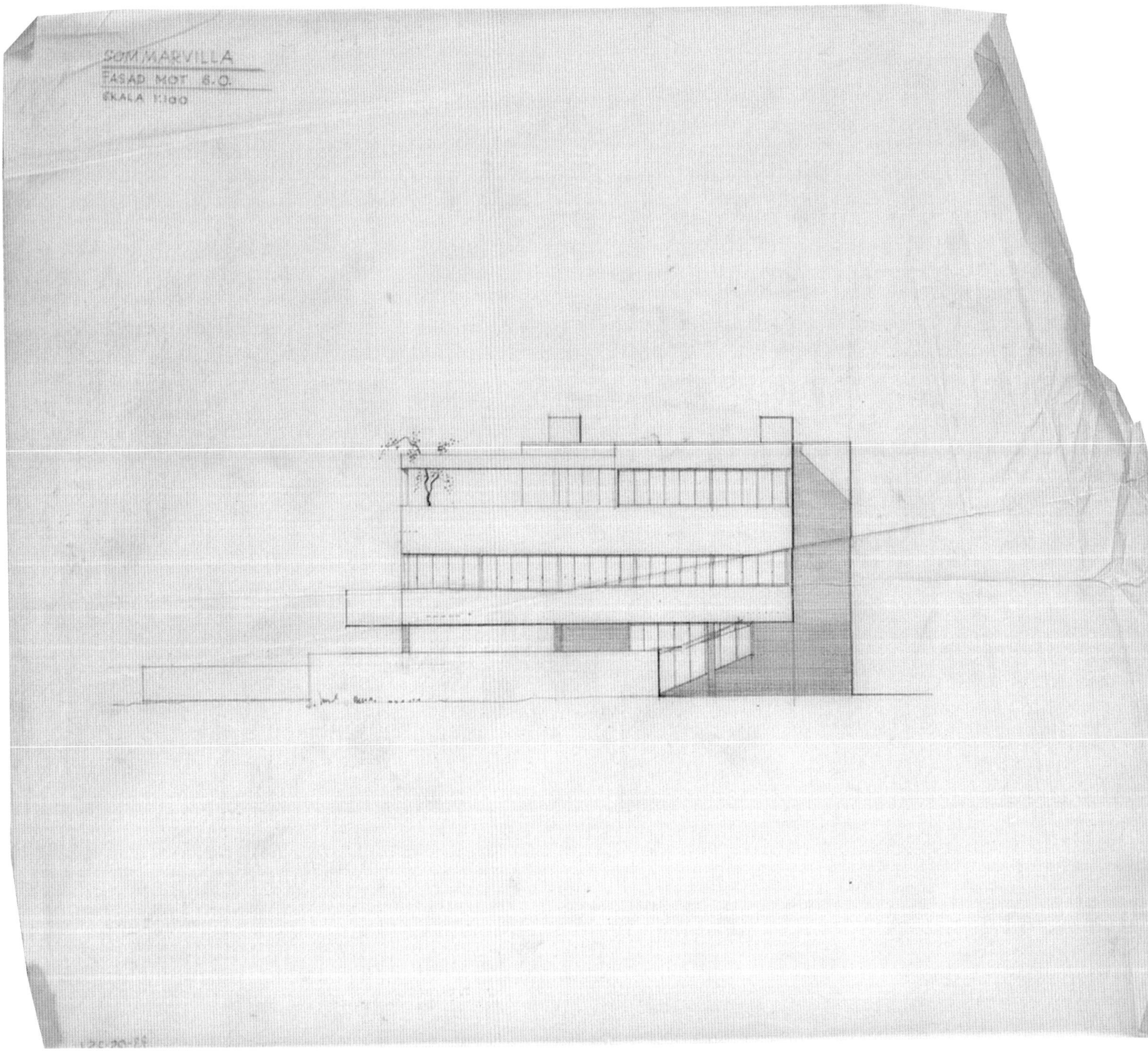

Elevations and plans,
third version.

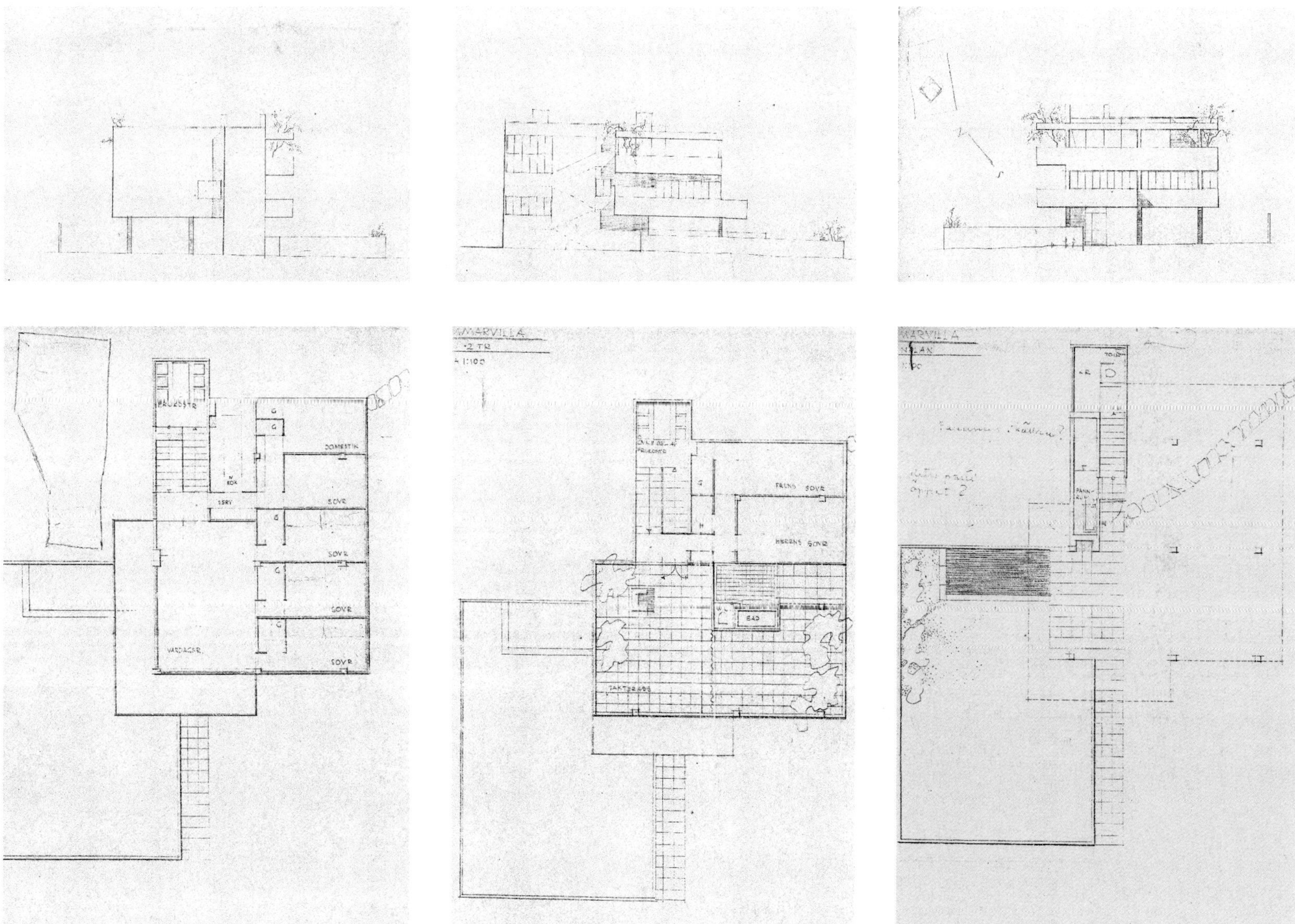

Elevations, fourth version, 1935.

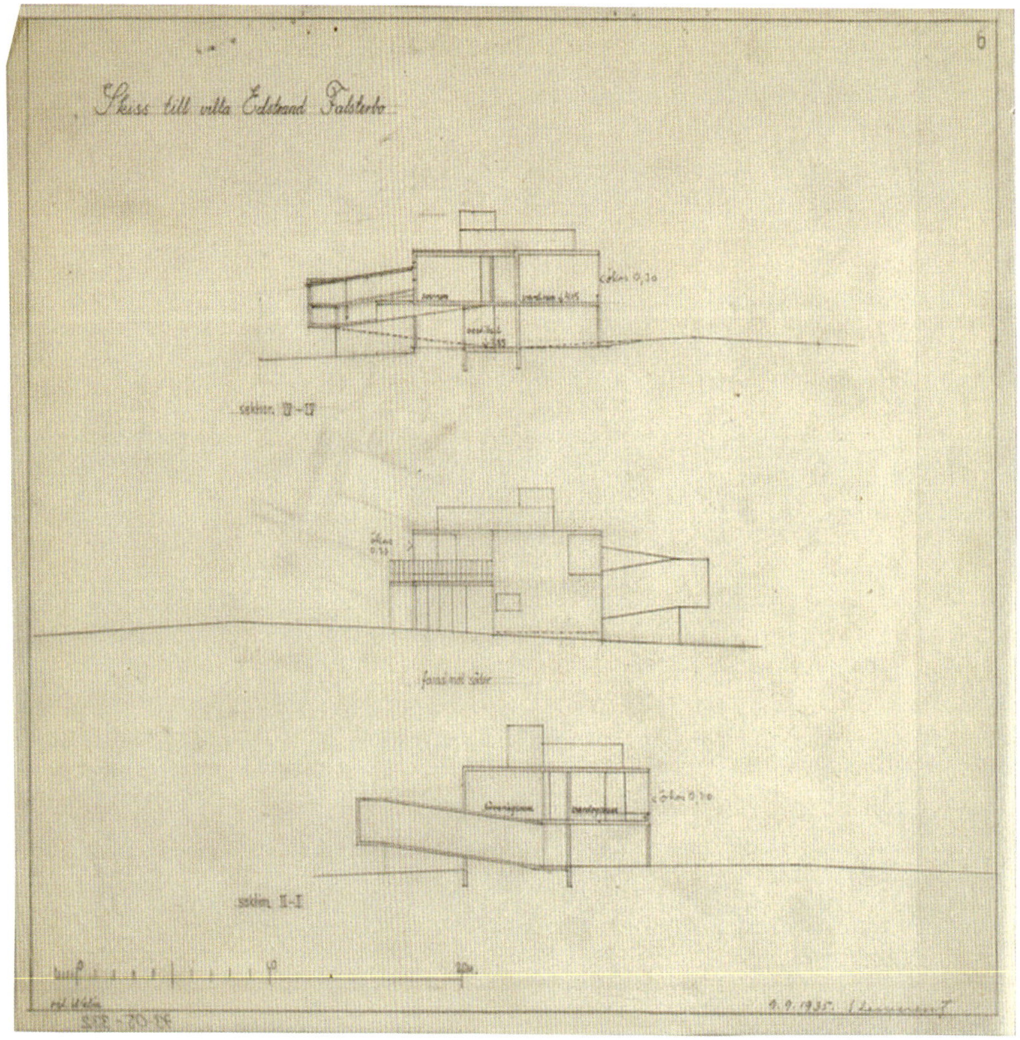

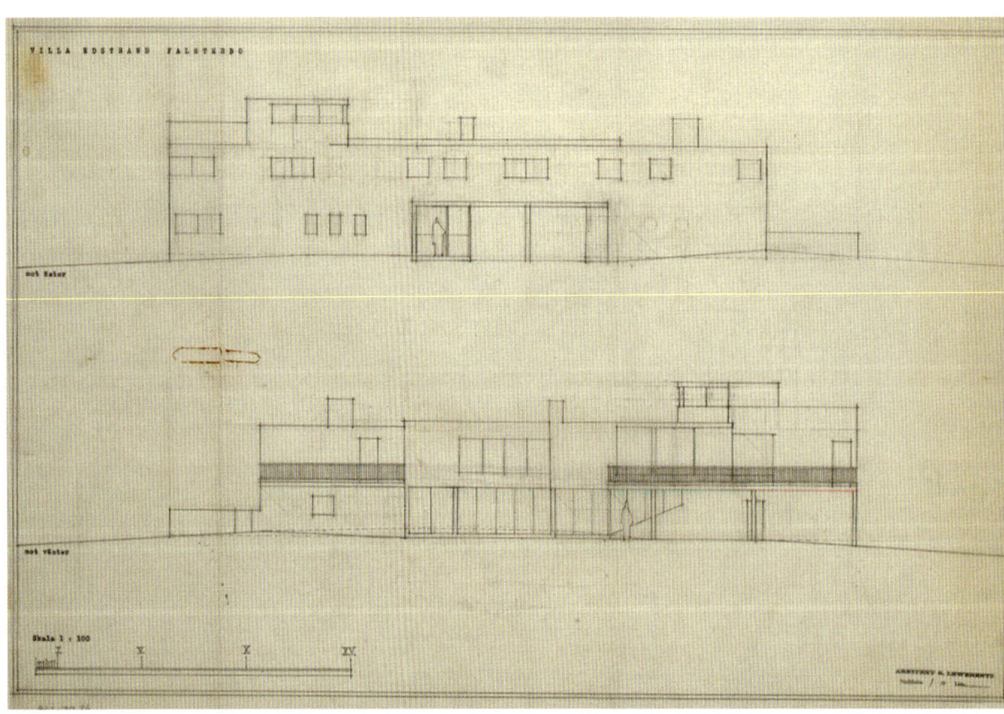

Perspective drawing,
fourth version.

Plans and elevations, final version, 1936.

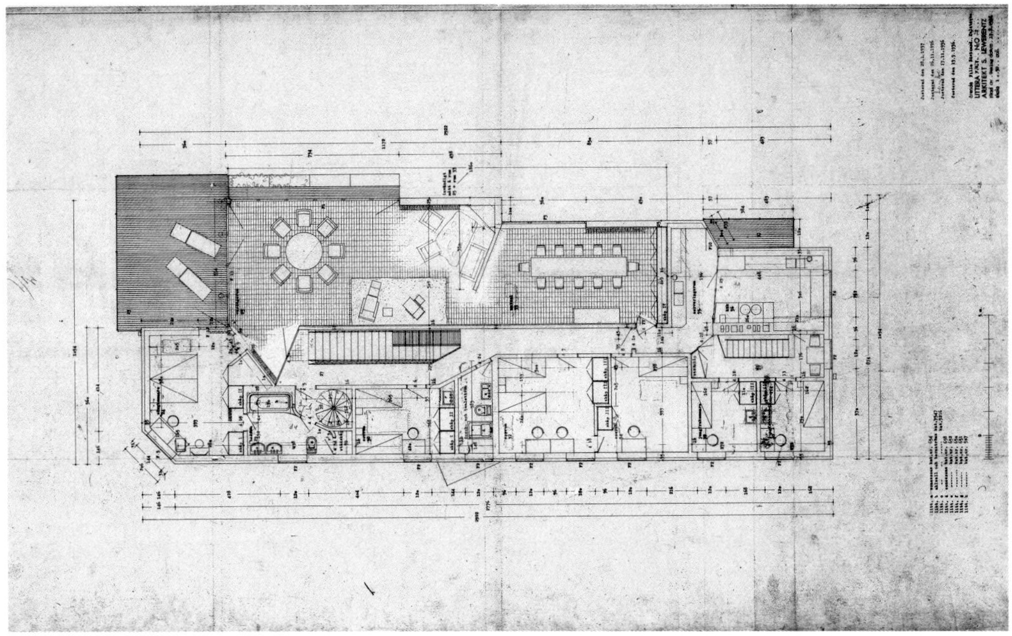

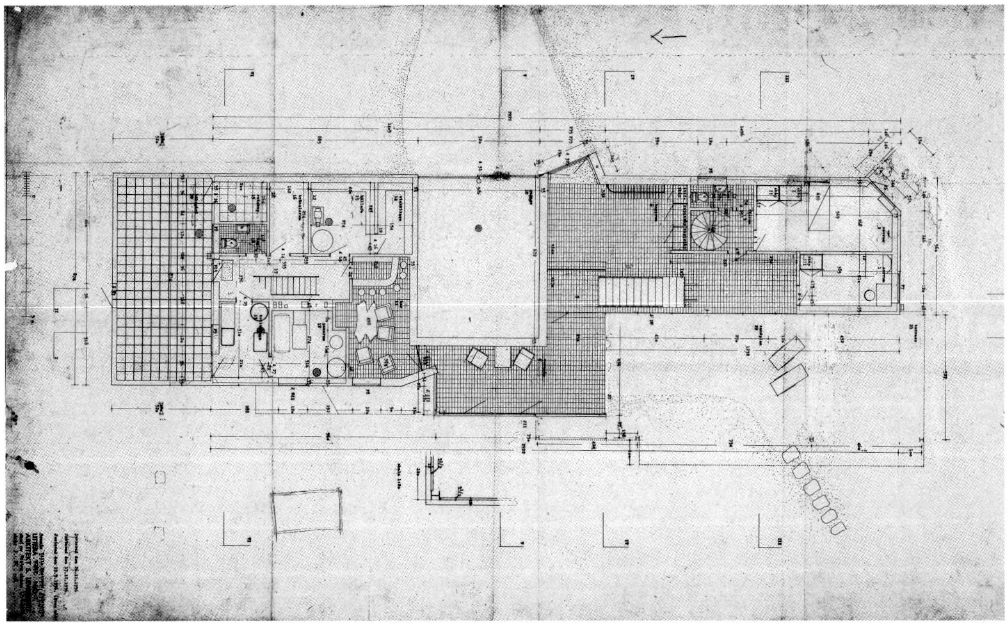

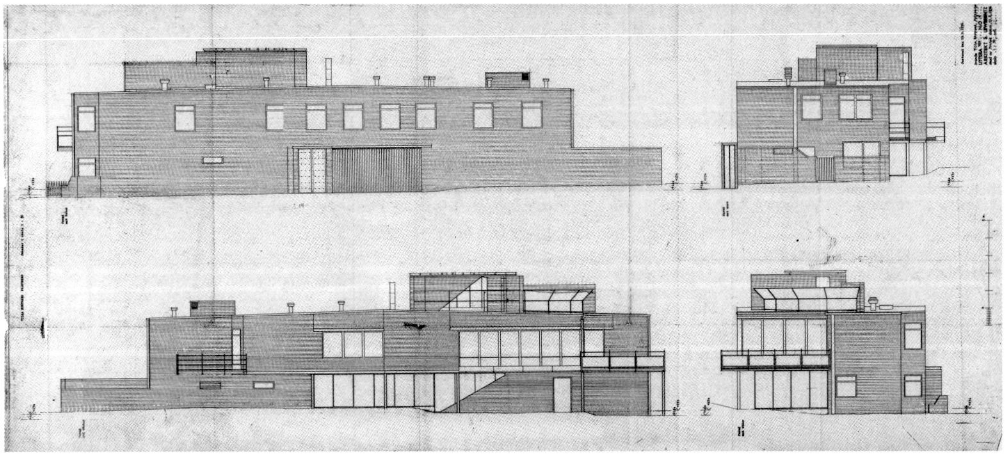

Perspective drawing,
final version.

Views of the exterior.

Views of the exterior and detail of the internal staircase.

Layout plan, project for a second house, 1961–62.

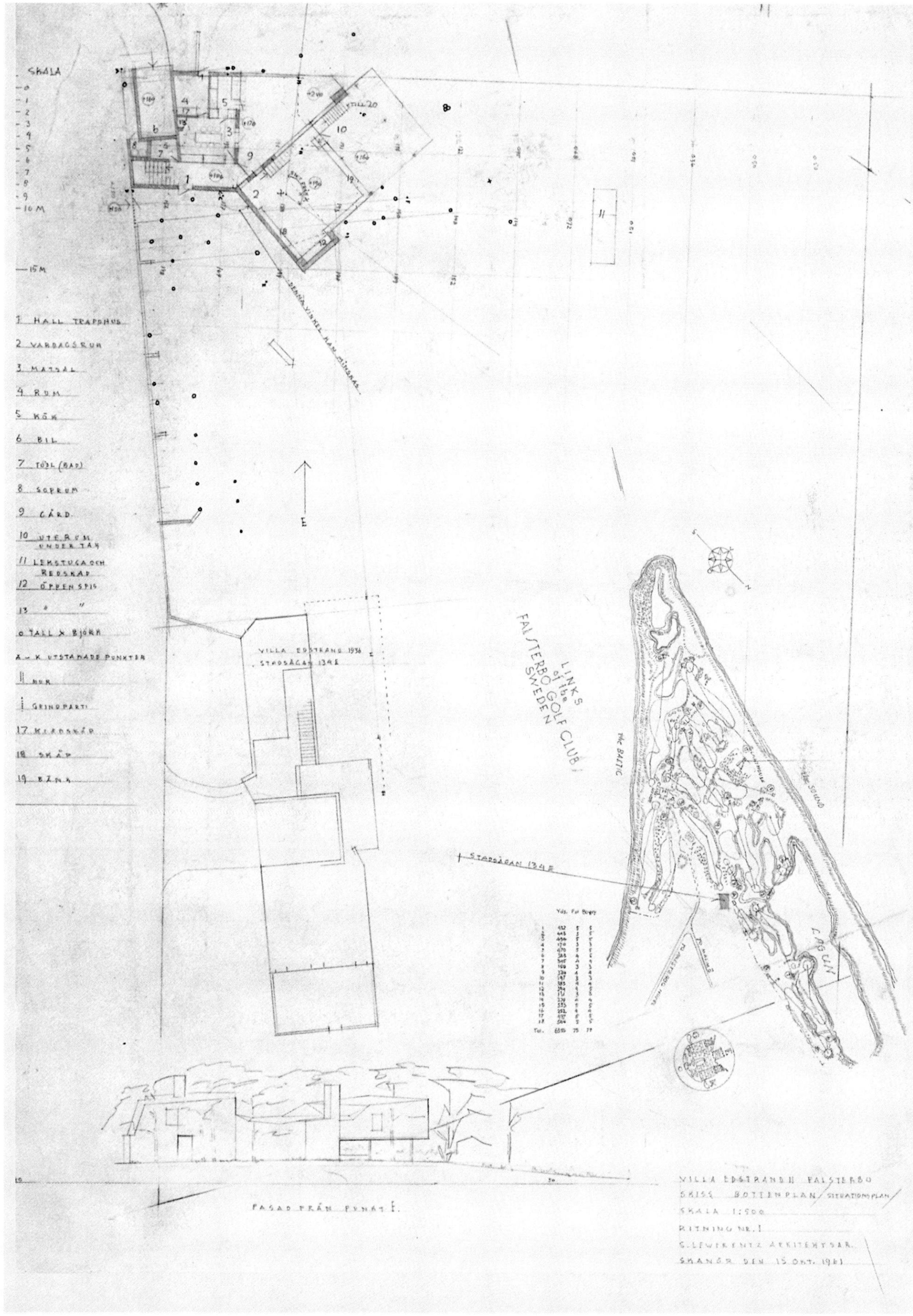

91. Competition Project for Bromma Airport, Stockholm, 1934

citation

In 1934 an invitation competition was organized for the formulation of a project for the new Stockholm airport; besides Lewerentz, Erik Gunnar Asplund, Sven Markelius and P. Hedqvist were asked to participate. The site selected was located in an uninhabited area of Bromma, a suburb four kilometres north of the centre of Stockholm, where the architects were asked not only to design the airport building, but also the layout of the adjacent areas, the runways and the taxiways for the aeroplanes. Their decidedly Functionalist character attests to the architects' awareness of the ideological content that projects intended to meet the demands of this new social function must contain.

As was his usual practice, Lewerentz submitted three different projects, demonstrating that there were a number of possible solutions to the problems posed by the committee. The main project proposes an elongated building linked to a cylindrical waiting-room that is entirely glazed, accessible through an underground passage providing a sheltered route for passengers to reach the centre of the apron, from where they could enjoy an unobstructed 360-degree view of the stationary and taxiing aircraft.

The second project, on the other hand, proposes a raised building under which the aircraft could stop so that passengers could board or disembark easily, even during bad weather, while the third suggests a wholly underground building in which various flights of stairs allow passengers to emerge onto the apron at a point near their waiting aircraft.

Bibliography: *Arkitekttävlingen om flystationsanläggning* 1934, pp. 197–205; Ahlin 1985b, pp. 162–63.

(N.F.)

Layout plan of the main project.

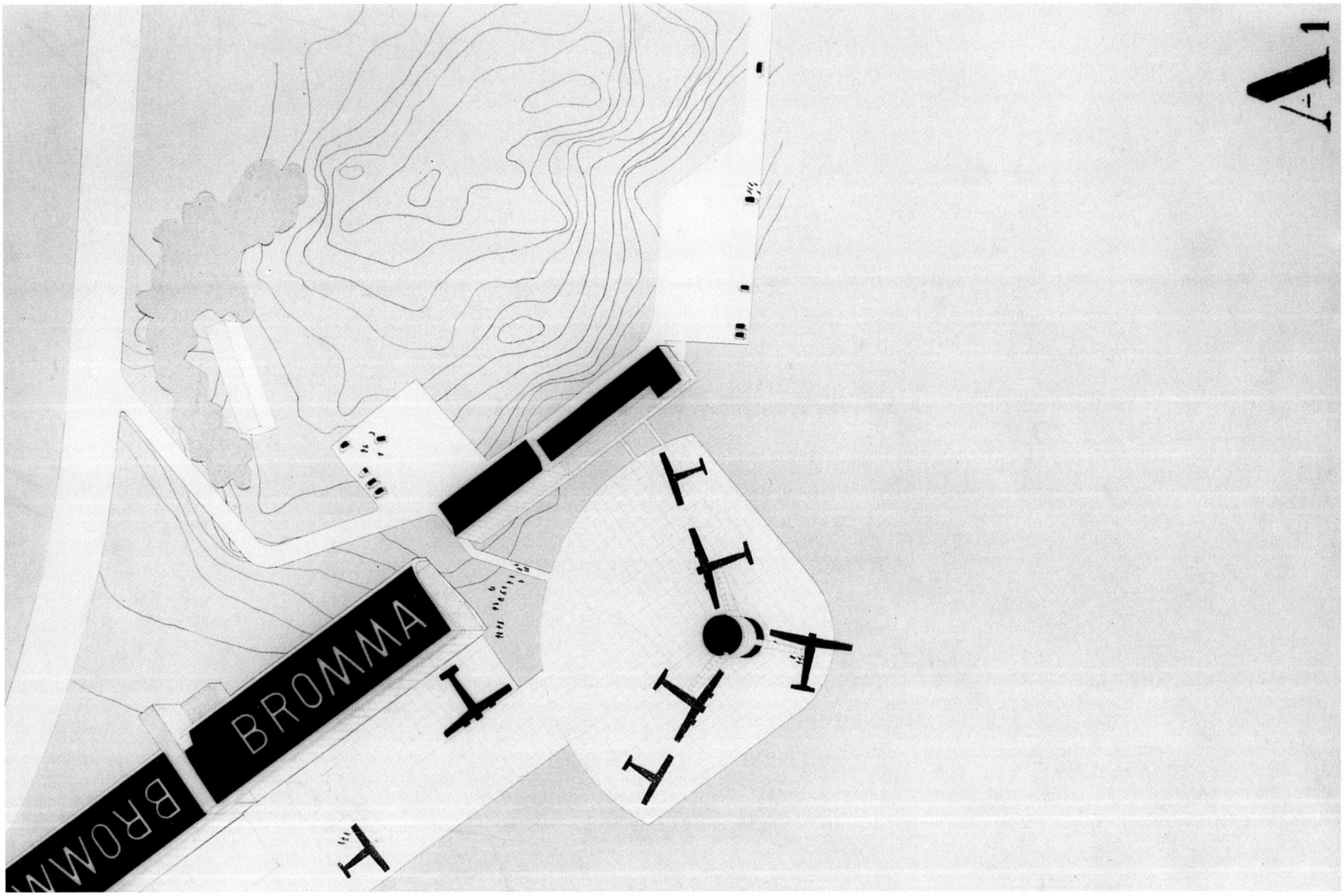

92. Project for Norberg Cemetery, 1934

Lewerentz's project for the rearrangement of Norberg Cemetery was not built, although—as the correspondence between the architect and the city hall demonstrates—the possibility of a commission was concrete and regarded not only the cemetery itself, but also the re-use of a historic building on the site. This is what Lewerentz wrote in 1934: "As far as the possible work in the ceremony hall of the historic chapel is concerned, especially with regard to the display of the urns to be kept there temporarily, I would like to draw a sketch as soon as possible to see whether this solution is feasible. To this end, it is necessary that the drawings of the plan, elevations and sections of this building be sent to me.
As far as the cemetery is concerned, however, it is probable that it will be difficult to place greater emphasis on the principal axis, while the fencing of the site should be carried out properly in the traditional manner. I also believe that the surface area is not large enough to require an additional feature to break its monotony. There is, however, the possibility that a large public monument could be erected in the centre of the cemetery and trees planted around it.
I shall work on this solution and, in a few days' time, I will write again."

(G.P.)

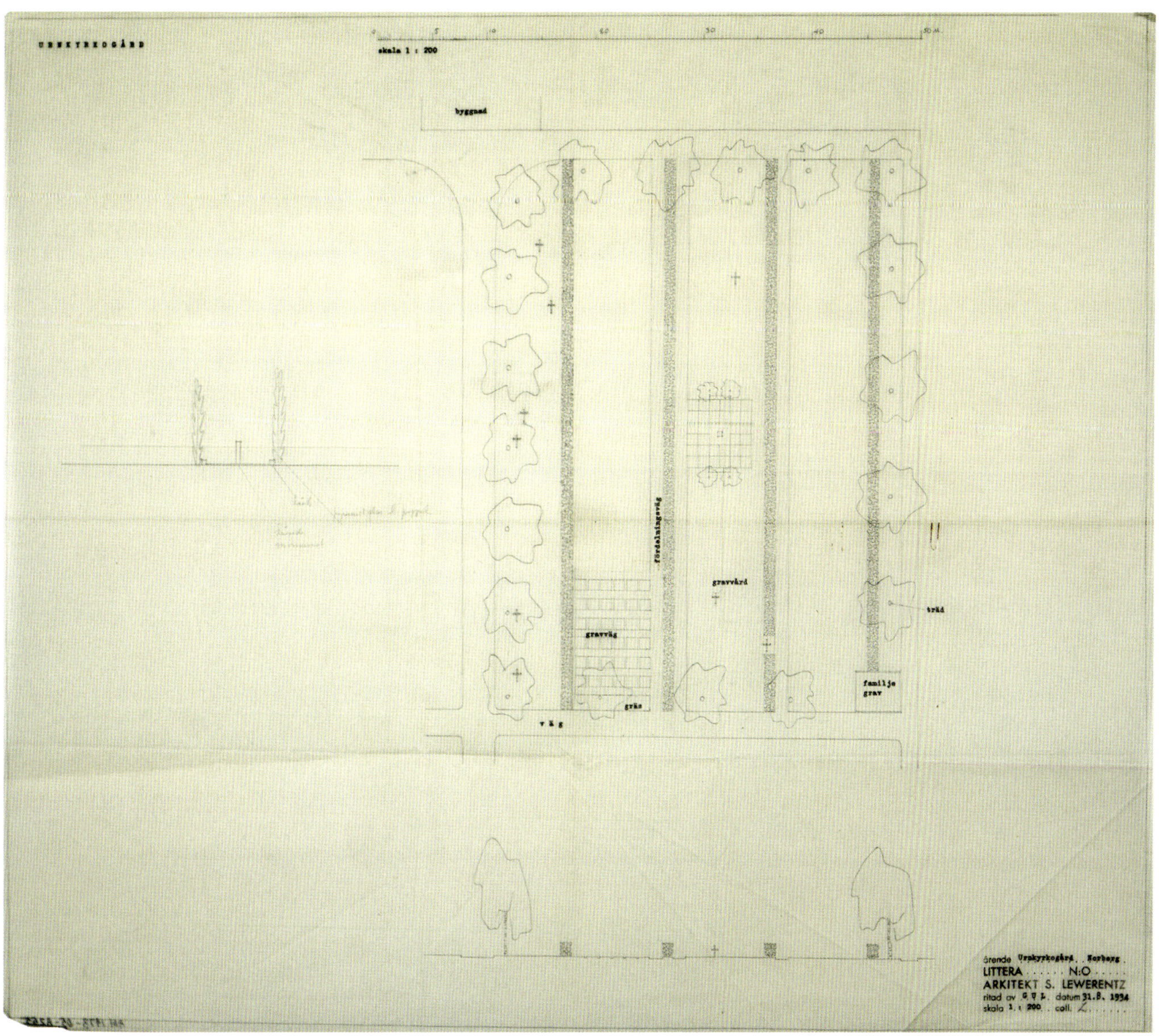

Layout plan of site.

93. Building for Bröderna Edstrand AB, Malmö, 1935–36

The steel merchants Edstrand—for whom Lewerentz was working on a villa by the sea in the same period (see entry 90)—commissioned the architect to design an office building and warehouse at Spadegatan, near the free port of Malmö. For the offices, Lewerentz designed a very simple two-storey structure, completely built in brick on a rectangular plan, with a flat roof; the elevations are characterized by a regular sequence of narrow windows, which thus allow the profile of the main doorways to emerge. The warehouse is more complex and is divided into three sections, decreasing in size in proportion to their respective heights, which meet the need to store steel products of different dimensions. The load-bearing structures and the trusses of the pitched roofs are also in steel, while the soffit is clad in wood. The lower parts of the side elevations of the three sections are closed, with large windows in the upper part, while the front and back are completely open to facilitate access.

(N.F.)

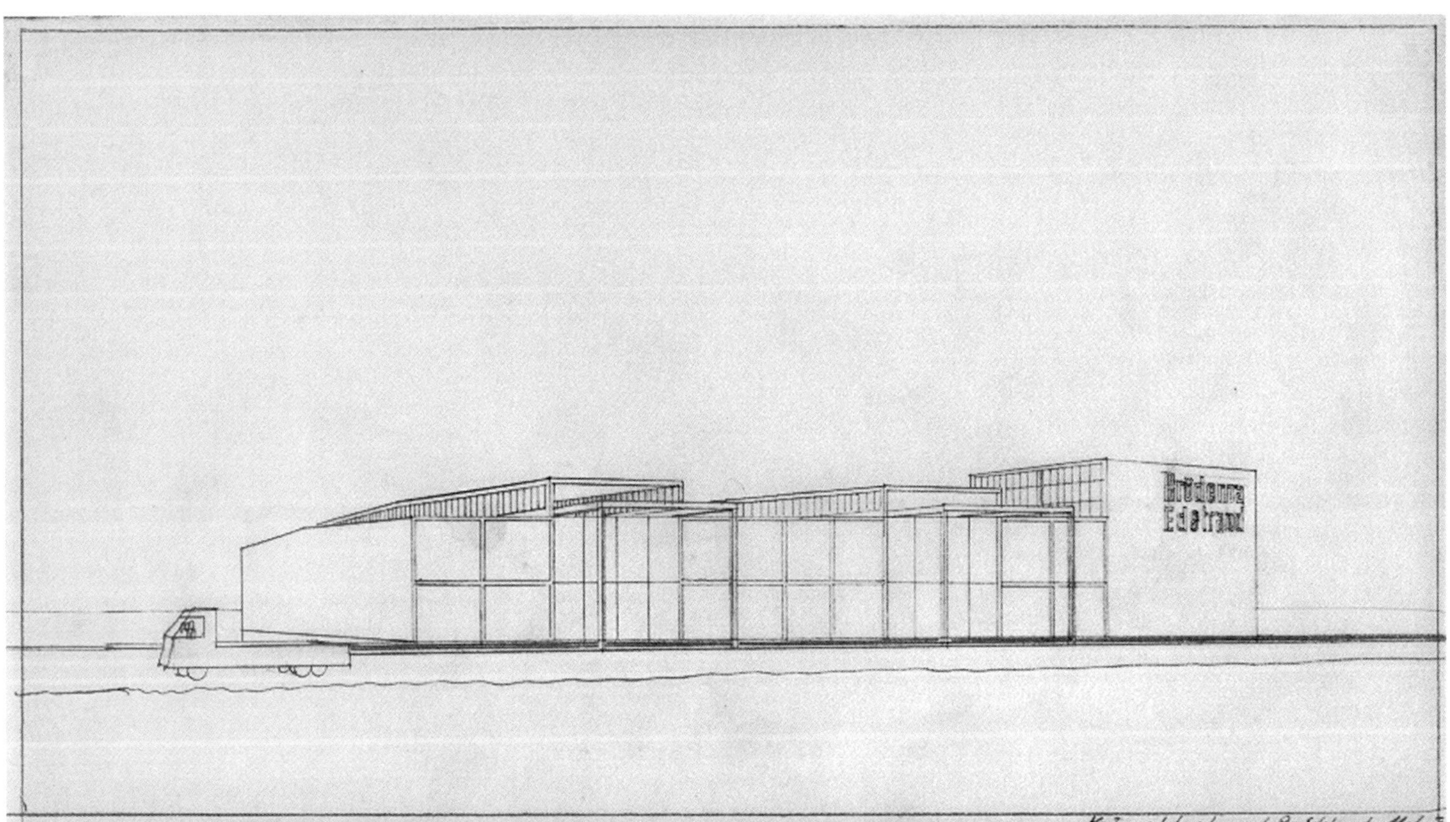

Perspective drawing.

94. Competition Project for an Extension to the Karolinska Institutet, Solna, 1936

with David Helldén
motto "abc"

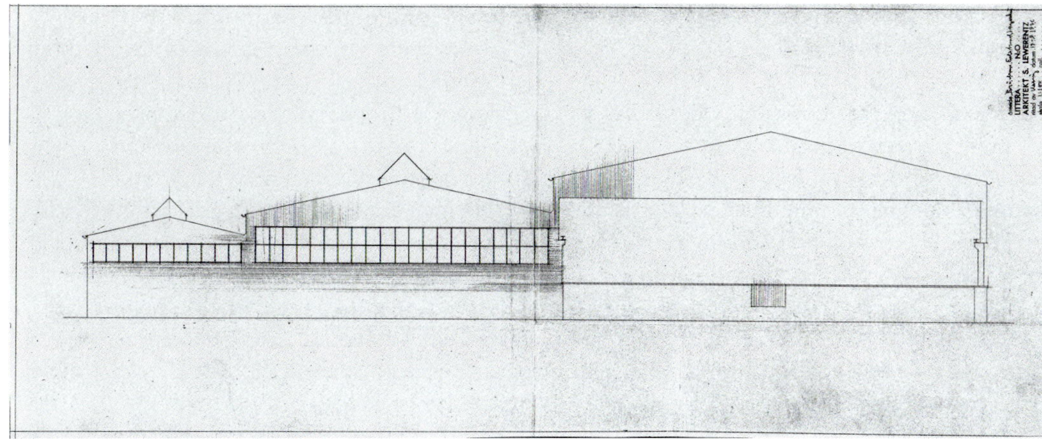

In 1936 the Karolinska Institutet, a medical research institute, organized a competition for an extension to be constructed on a site adjacent to its hospital, the Karolinska Sjukhuset, at Solna. Lewerentz, who had recently started to collaborate with David Helldén on the Malmö Municipal Theatre project, decided to put this partnership to the test by inviting his colleague to participate in the competition.

The project submitted by the two architects proposed the construction on the site of a series of separate buildings, one for each function. Seven blocks house the departments into which the research institute is divided, while the eighth one contains the offices and library; a separate building is occupied by the students' union and accommodation, while the last one is assigned to a chapel with an adjacent mortuary. These buildings, arranged parallel to each other, but diagonally to the perimeter of the site, are oriented north-east-south-west and occupy the whole of the area available. By linking the various blocks with underground passages—a system frequently used in hospitals split up into different buildings—the architects transform the complex into an organic whole, although the blocks above ground level are kept separate.

The internal distribution of the laboratories is simple and rational: the rooms are located along the long fronts of the buildings and are served by a double corridor divided by an empty space from which a continuous skylight provides illumination from above. The largest rooms are placed at the corners of the buildings and the external walls, probably planned to be in brick, are characterized by large windows allowing those working in the laboratories to enjoy an excellent view of the surroundings.

Bibliography: *Tävlingen* 1937, pp. 73–74.

(N.F.)

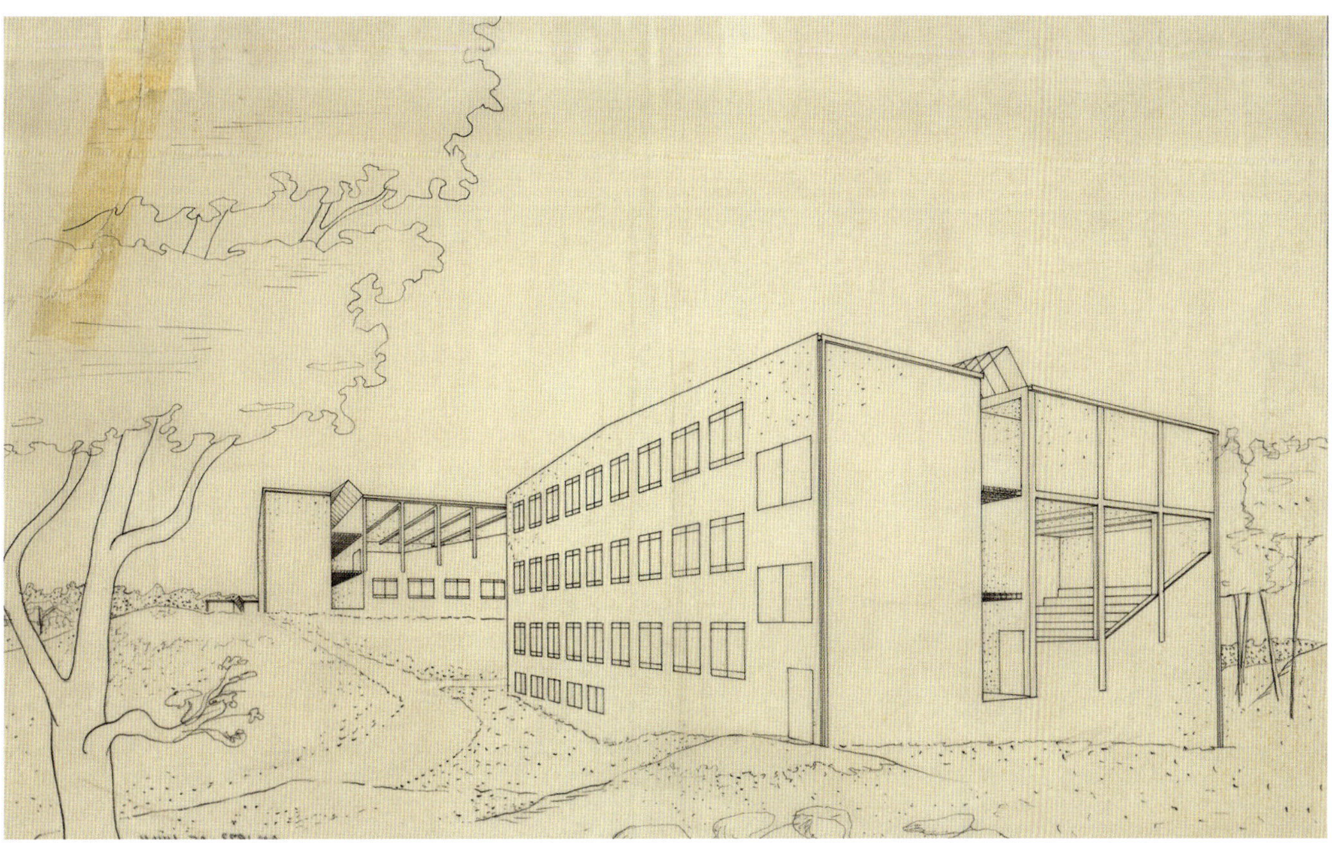

Elevation and perspective drawing.

95. Project for St Sigfrid Griftegård Cemetery, Borås, 1937

The preliminary project for a cemetery at Borås, submitted by Lewerentz to the municipality, consists of a layout plan on a scale of 1:400 and a number of profiles of the site on a scale of 1:200, in which the architect gives instructions regarding the general layout of the principal roads and the location of the area where the crematorium and the service buildings are to be constructed. The drawings also indicate the type of trees to be planted in the cemetery and the arrangement of the tombstones, information that was also contained in the outline of the project: "Except for an area facing the main entrance, the roads through the area in question largely follow the lie of the land. The paths between the tombstones also help to determine the design of the funerary monuments and the planting of trees, which means that the project avoids any possible variation of the existing topography... The articulation of the crematorium, situated towards the rear of the site, with its entrance in the higher part of the land, ... has a notable significance determining a solution that is particularly interesting from an architectural point of view and, at the same time, is an appropriate use of this beautiful site... In order to allow my professional competence to be assessed with a view to a possible commission for the preparation of a more detailed project for the cemetery site and the other necessary work, I enclose information regarding projects of this type I have realized from 1912 onwards."

(G.P.)

Layout plan.

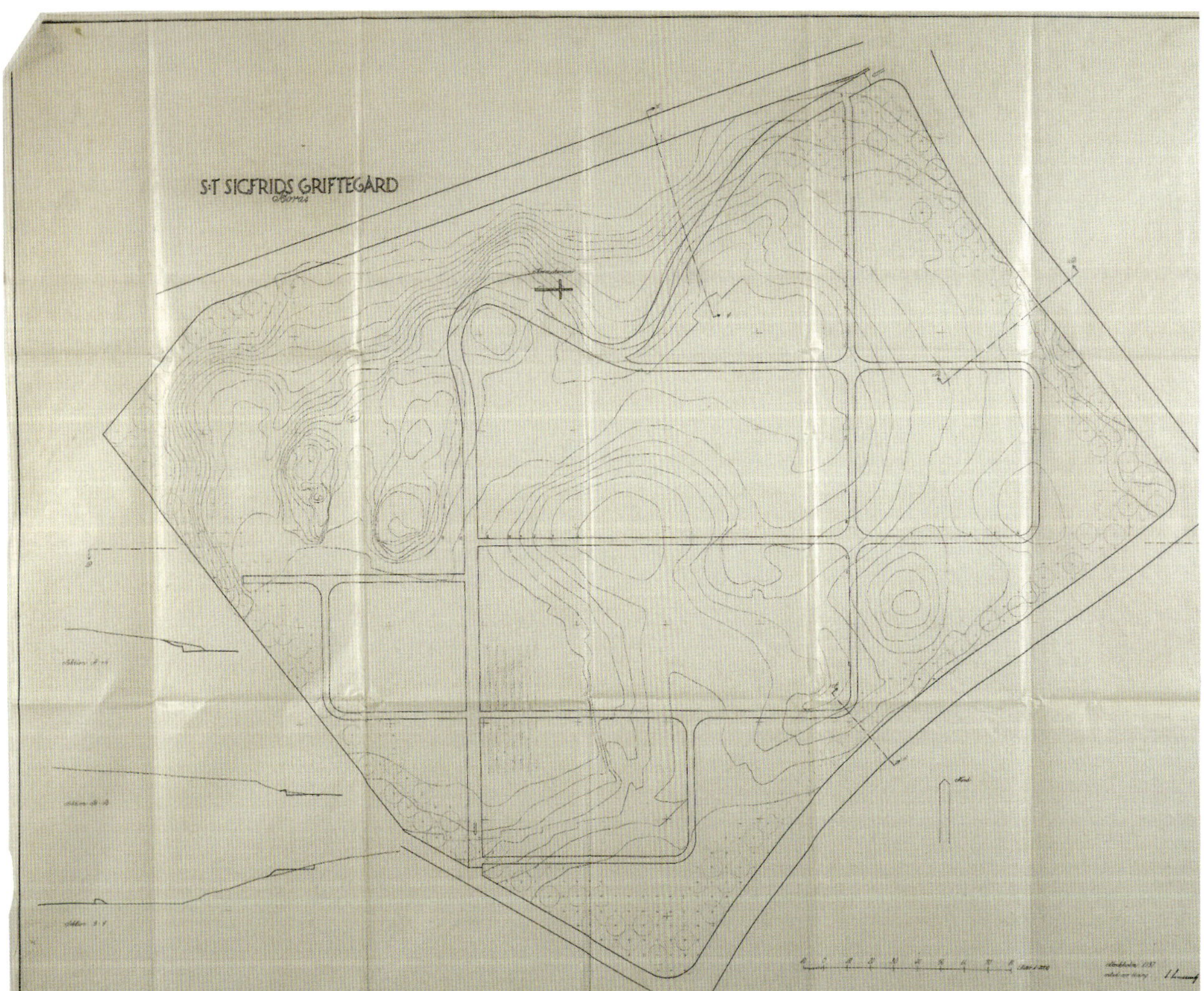

96. Competition Project for the Factory and Offices of Åhlrén & Åkerlunds, Stockholm, 1938
motto "Nu"

Situated in an area between a railway-yard and the edge of the city of Stockholm, the site for the new buildings is strategically placed for a publishing firm like Åhlrén & Åkerlunds. This position, away from the bustling city traffic, allows goods to be received and dispatched without delays.

Lewerentz places the lowest buildings, housing workshops and storerooms in the southern part of the site, where this tapers to a narrow strip, while to the north of this he locates a fifteen-storey office block. The fronts of the latter facing the city are mainly glazed to attract the attention of passers-by to the activity going on inside the building, the ultimate aim evidently being that of inspiring confidence in the firm itself.

(N.F.)

Study sketch and photomontage of the area.

97. Renovation of a Factory, Eskilstuna, 1940 onwards

In 1940, a number of years after having begun to design door and window frames and metal structures for interiors, with the firms Stockholm Ljusreklam (1929) and AB BLOKK (1930–33 with other partners, from 1933 onwards alone), Lewerentz decided to acquire an industrial building in Eskilstuna, a town not far from Stockholm, in order to set up his own factory—incorporating AB BLOKK and AB IDESTA—for the production of frames and metal elements. Deriving above all from commissions received from colleagues who had a high opinion of the architect's technical skills, the products made in Eskilstuna bore the IDESTA trademark, a name that Lewerentz had already registered in 1929 to protect his patent rights. During the sixteen years it was managed by Lewerentz, before being taken over in 1956 by one of his sons, the Eskilstuna factory produced fixtures for such notable projects as Sven Markelius's community centre and Peter Celsing's ticket booths for the Stockholm underground, as well as many other less important schemes. In 1943 Lewerentz himself went to live in Eskilstuna; unable to find a suitable house there, he decided to rebuild the top floor of the factory to accommodate both his home and his office. The rooms were simple and functional: the family's furnishings were sufficient to create a domestic atmosphere. Lewerentz also built a staircase in his flat, leading to the part of the attic he used as his office, where, as was his custom, he painted the walls black and covered the soffit of the roof with aluminium sheets, devices he used years later in his house in Lund and, more significantly, in the flower kiosk for the Eastern Cemetery at Malmö.

Chronology:
1940: renovation of the factory building.
1943: rebuilding of the top floor.

Bibliography: Lewerentz 1948; Ahlin 1985b, pp. 190–93.

(N.F.)

Sigurd Lewerentz (left) in his office at Eskilstuna.

98. Proposed Project for Sködvde Cemetery, 1942

Despite Lewerentz's detailed description, divided into six sections, regarding a possible commission for the realization of a cemetery and sacred buildings at Sködvde in which "The Different Methods for the Conservation of Cinerary Urns outside the Crematorium Chapels" are illustrated, after the *Jordfaastingsakten*, the protocol of the cemetery board dated 26 June 1942 the architect's proposal had no chance of being accepted. The protocol stated: "The board has decided to maintain its position: the project for the new cemetery cannot be realized exclusively using horizontal funerary monuments (as is suggested in Lewerentz's report), but with alternative approaches. If the architect Lewerentz does not wish to accept this request, the board has decided it will revoke the commission and entrust the project for the future cemetery to the architect Sven Ivar Lind of Stockholm."

(G.P.)

99. Competition Project for the Renovation of Uppsala Cathedral, 1947–55

motto "med fasta rötter"

Although the Gothic cathedral of Uppsala was founded in the Middle Ages, numerous alterations and extensions over the centuries have completely changed its original appearance. Thus, in 1946, when a competition for yet another conservation project was announced, the architects were faced with a highly stratified structure. The main problem was the infiltration of water, which, from the roof, penetrated the ancient walls, seriously damaging them, a problem that the committee wished to solve with a project capable of combining the technical requirements with the stylistic ones.
Bearing the motto "med fasta rötter" (with the roots well-planted), Lewerentz's project is characterized by the boldness with which copper flashing is placed along the abutments and buttresses to collect rainwater, which, with the same ostentation is conveyed to ground level by a system of surface-mounted metal downpipes. These conspicuous technical devices, manifested in all their pragmatic spirit are the most original and coherent interpretation of the cathedral's Gothic nature. This architectural style is based on the attribution of an aesthetic value to its most characteristic motifs: compound piers, rib vaults and flying buttresses, which are, in fact, structural elements forming an essential part of the building.
None of the projects submitted, however, satisfied the jury, which, in 1949, decided to hold another competition, although this was limited to those responsible for what were considered to be the eight most interesting projects, including the one by Lewerentz. Continuing along the lines of his previous project, the architect refused to make any concession to the stylistic restoration advocated by the members of the clergy in the jury. In fact, Lewerentz again proposed a solution in which any alterations are made overt by the choice of materials and forms, stressing his belief that the only element of continuity with the past must lie in the capacity of the project to interpret the spirit informing the building's construction. In this case, too, the copper flashing and downpipes are both technical elements, indispensable for solving the problem of the infiltration of water, and features of the overall design of the exterior. In the case of conservation of parts of the fabric that are irremediably damaged, the architect proposes that the new surfaces should be composed of yellow bricks, so

Elevation and model, project of 1949.

Photomontage, project of 1947.

that they will be immediately recognizable and datable.
The project was awarded first prize, although there was considerable disagreement in the jury, where the most conservative members were opposed to the assignment of the commission to Lewerentz. This gave rise to an animated debate that ended in 1950 with the choice of Peter Celsing, an architect who had not participated in the competition. Celsing, however, accepted with the proviso that Lewerentz should also be involved in the preparation of the new project, beginning a period of intense collaboration between the two that lasted until 1955, although they were not able to finally resolve the problem. The vicissitudes of the conservation schemes only ended in 1962, when another architect was asked to prepare a project, which this time came up to the clients' expectations: reflecting the most conservative practice, it involved stylistic restoration. In the five years they worked together, Lewerentz and Celsing produced many study models and photomontages to analyse the impact of the proposed intervention in depth, also with regard to a more general vision, which included the presence of the cathedral in the city's skyline. Nonetheless, the committee responsible for undertaking the work did not consider the various proposals submitted to be sufficiently convincing.

Chronology
1947: first competition,
motto "med fasta rötter".
1949: second competition, first prize,
motto "reflexion".
1950–55: various alternative proposals,
with Peter Celsing.

Bibliography: Reinius 1950; Reinius 1951, p. 67; Lind 1956; *Debatten om Uppsala Domkyrkas* 1947; Ahlin 1985b, pp. 200–08.

(N.F.)

100. Renovation of the North Wing of the *Corps de Logis* at Broxvik, 1948

see entry no. 15

101. Competition Project for Uppsala City Hall, 1949

invitation competition
motto "Miljo" – citation

Probably as a result of his involvement from 1946 to 1955, firstly alone and then with Peter Celsing, in the project for the conservation of Uppsala Cathedral, Lewerentz was invited to participate in a competition for the design of the new city hall for the city. The site chosen for the new building is on one of the banks of the Fyris River, in one of the university quarters of Uppsala, between the castle and the cathedral, characterized by a large number of small historic buildings.
As usual, Lewerentz drew inspiration from the constraints imposed by the surroundings, which were analysed in depth. From the earliest sketches it is evident that he was particularly interested in two aspects: on the one hand, the historic buildings amidst which the new town hall is to stand, on the other the urban landscape of Uppsala, dominated by the castle and cathedral. Thus the architect has designed a building—or rather a complex of buildings—the qualities of which are highlighted in the drawings submitted for the competition. In these, it is clear that his decision to carry out demolition work and divide the town hall into a number of blocks, creating a relatively small complex, derives from his desire to make the view of the castle in one direction, and that of the cathedral in the other, an integral part of the project.
At the same time, the fact that it is split up into a number of blocks allows the new construction to be better integrated with the smaller historic buildings in this part of the city.

The complex, with a U-shaped layout, is generally limited to a height of two storeys, allowing only the blocks housing the most important functions—the municipal hall and the council chamber—to rise above the others. These two blocks are also distinguished by an alternative external finish; the yellow brick planned for the whole complex is replaced with stone and copper, the disposition of the openings stressing their different roles. While, along the whole of the perimeter of the structure, windows are placed with a continuous, asymmetrical rhythm, the walls of the municipal hall and the council chamber are completely blind, with the openings located in the roof itself, which has a different shape here. The interiors, too, have been carefully thought out: the division of the space in some of the rooms is particularly interesting, displaying Lewerentz's special skill as a designer of the metal structures manufactured in his Eskilstuna factory. Partitions in steel and glass allow the rooms to be very versatile, because they can be altered to suit different requirements.
Despite the favourable opinion of some members of the jury, which earned the project a "citation", it was harshly criticized, especially for the excessively industrial appearance of the complex, which did not draw on any earlier styles, foreshadowing the development of the architect's independent poetic spirit, which was later to find more complete expression in the chapels of St Gertrud and St Knut in Malmö's Eastern Cemetery.

Bibliography: Reinius 1949; *Tävlingen* 1949.

(N.F.)

View of the building during the renovation work.

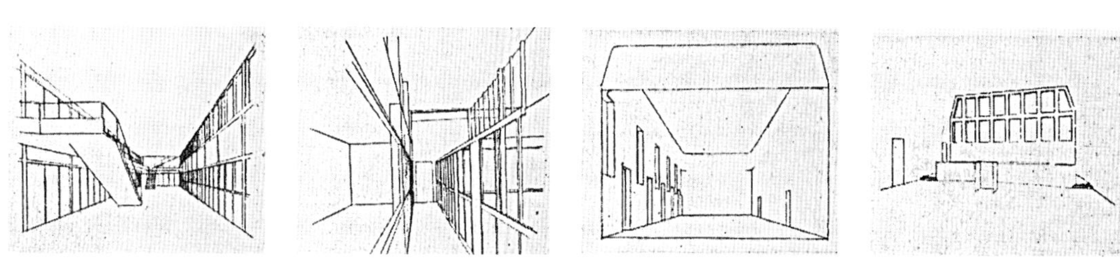

Project for Uppsala town hall, perspective drawings of the interiors.

102. Competition Project for the Interior Design of a Flat, for Svenska Slöjdföreningen, 1949

motto "Rör"

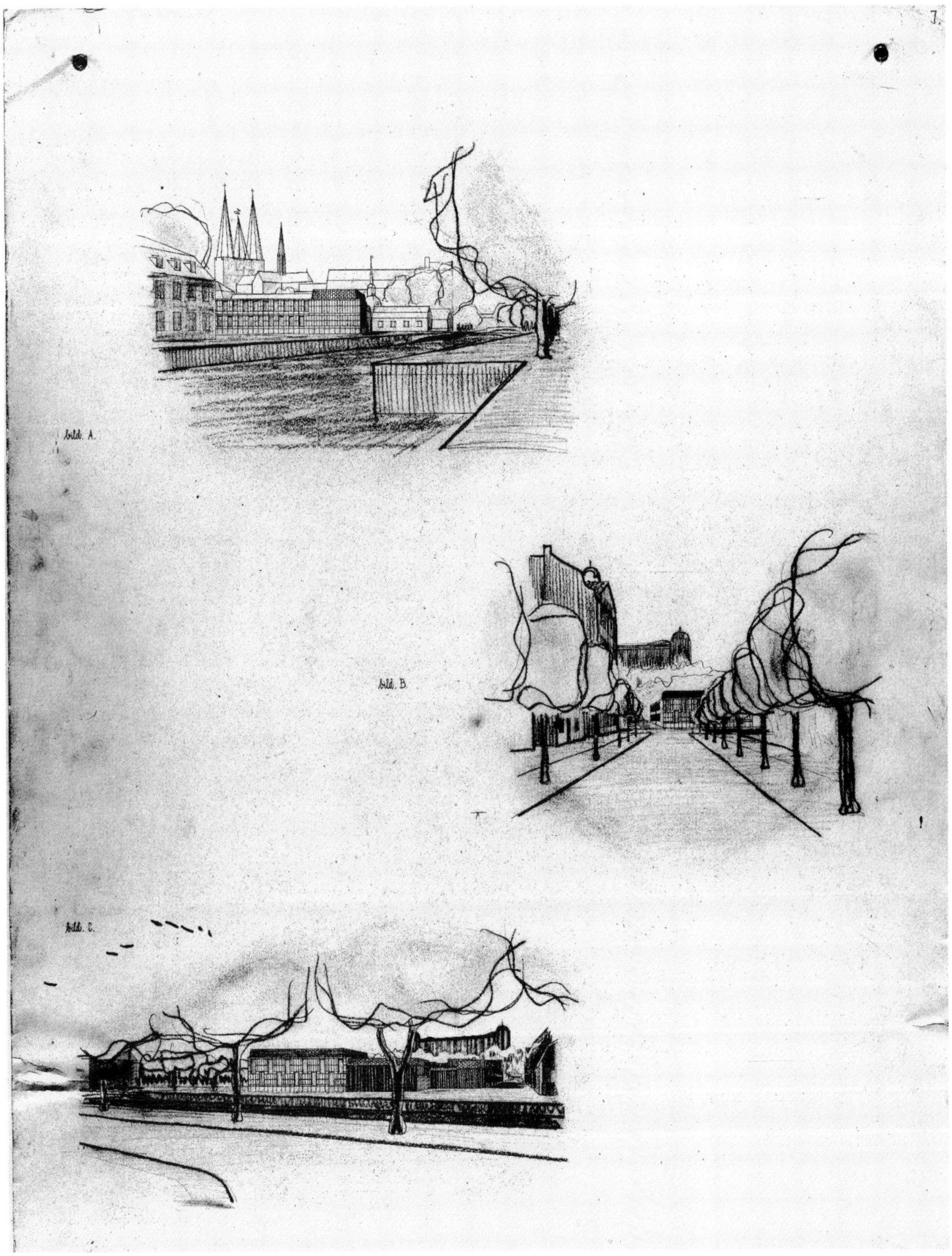

Study sketches
of the complex
in its surroundings.

103. Competition Project for a New Layout for the Kungsträdgården, Stockholm, 1952
motto "Kul"

The Kungsträdgården is one of Stockholm's oldest gardens: originally the Swedish royal family's orchard, in the nineteenth century it was transformed into a public garden. In 1952 the municipality organized a competition for the redesign of the garden with a programme that seemed to be inspired by a typically eighteenth-century layout, centring on a principal axis with a series of ponds and fountains. Although it was greatly criticized for the evident bias of the programme in favour of historicism, numerous architects participated in the competition.
In his project, Lewerentz intended that, in the quadrangular area, there should be a belt of four rows of trees on three sides, delimiting a series of four areas, in the centre of which are placed fountains and ponds surrounded by flower-beds with simple geometric forms.

(N.F.)

Layout plan with profiles.

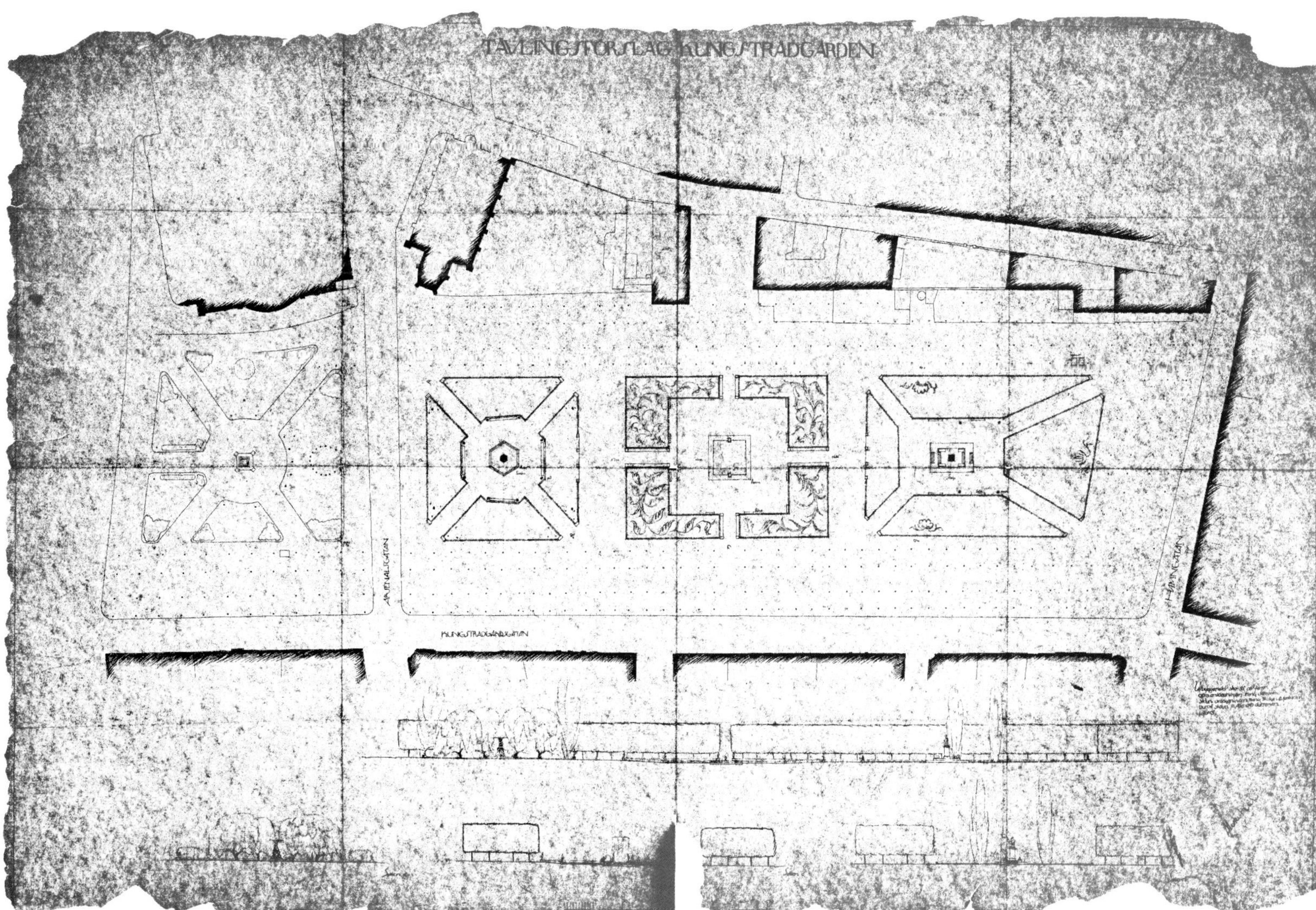

104. Competition Project for the St Mark's Parish Church at Björkhagen, Stockholm, 1956–64
invitation competition
motto "Mellanspel"

In 1955 an invitation competition was held for the design of St Mark's Church for the Skarpnäck parish at Björkhagen, a suburb on the southern edge of Stockholm. In addition to the project for the church, the programme required the design of one building for parish activities and another for offices. The five architects invited to participate in the competition included Lewerentz, whose project was awarded first prize. The project produced for the competition, in which various alternatives to the problems mentioned in the programme are offered, presents a solution very similar to the one that was subsequently realized, except for a number of modifications made by Lewerentz while work was underway and those requested by Nils Roth, a clergyman representing the committee set up to realize the church, who assisted the architect in the stages subsequent to the competition. The changes consisted mainly of a new design for the bell-tower—which had been much criticized from the outset—the enlargement of the building for parish activities to provide space for the instruction of young people, and the insertion of a small pond between the two main blocks of the complex, a reference to the area's history and identity. On the old maps, in fact, the site chosen for the church was called Lillsjön (Small Lake) and, because it was considerably below the level of the surrounding countryside, continued to be marshy, which was beneficial to a birch wood growing there spontaneously. In effect, these constraints on the building's

Layout plan (1959) and view of the model.

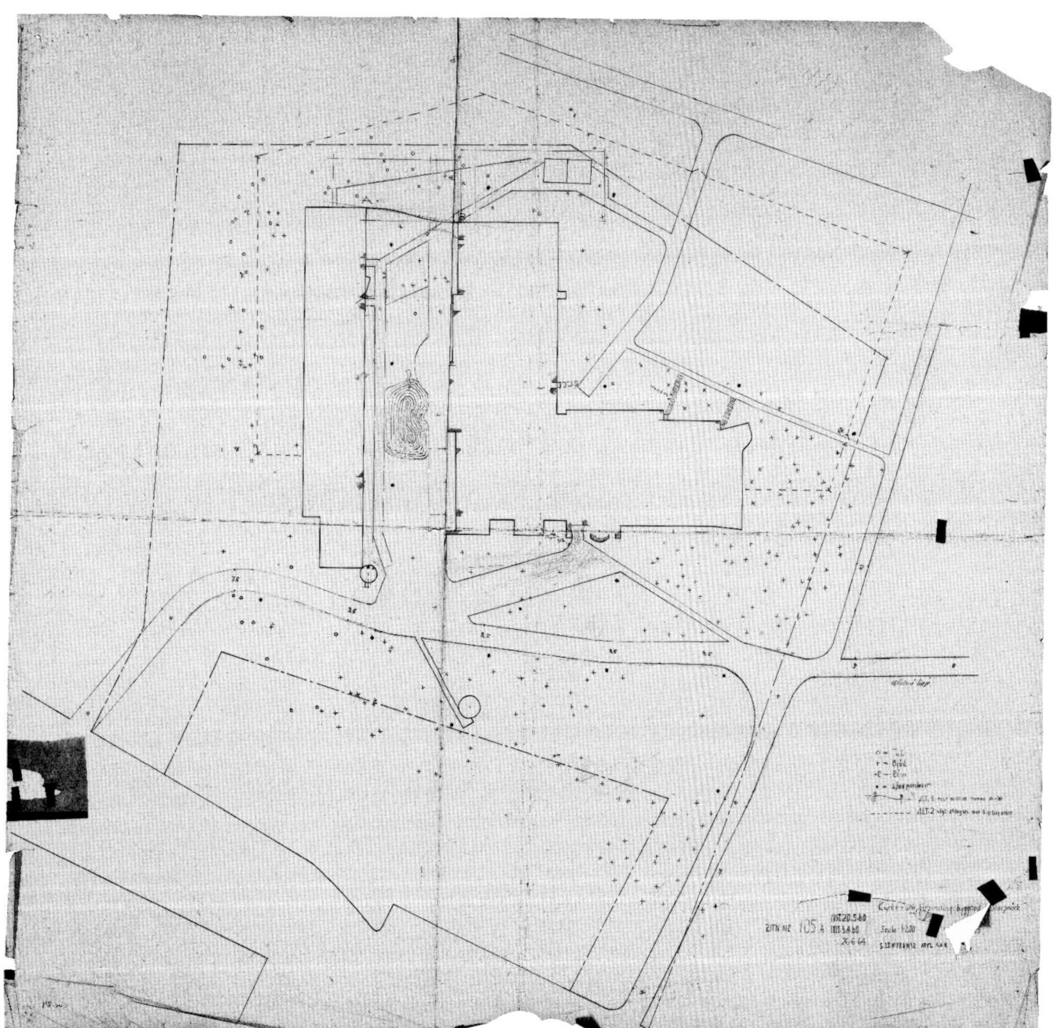

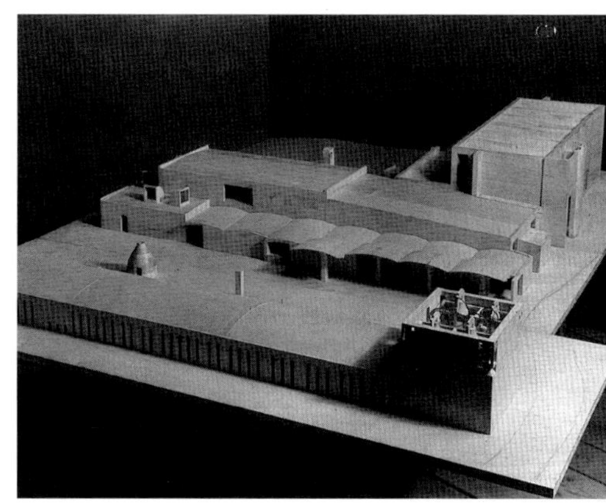

design constituted the starting-point for Lewerentz's elaboration of his project. Two very complex structures face each other, the long narrow space between them forming a courtyard, which becomes an area where various routes intersect and people may sit. On one side the architect locates the elongated office building, on the other the church, with its L-shaped plan, and the parish building, in front of which he places, in the southernmost area, a free-standing porch. Comprising four structures separate from each other, the porch is characterized by roofs having the same curved profile: they are, in fact, fragments of a segmental barrel vault, each supported by a pillar. All the structures are in laminated wood and have a very complex design that tends to divide the elements from each other, generating a stimulating dialectic between the load-bearing structure and the one that is borne. At Björkhagen, Lewerentz, for the first time, uses brick as the main construction element—at Klippan this will become the sole protagonist of the whole structure—especially in the church, where flooring, walls and ceilings are all in this material, while bare concrete, clinker and wood are only found in the other buildings of the complex. Rarely making use of stucco, the architect leaves all the services surface-mounted, transforming them from undesired elements to be hidden under the building's facing into an integral part of the architectural structure. Tubes, draw-in boxes, switches and whatever else is necessary to complete the interiors become an essential part of the design, and through them each space is differentiated. The use of bare brick and the decision to use whole bricks, without ever cutting them, obliges the architect to pay particular attention to the laying of the courses, which have to absorb, through the mortar joints, all the variations of the construction. This determines the texture of the brickwork in which the mortar assumes a similar value to that of the bricks, turning the roles traditionally attributed to the two elements into an ambiguous one. This aspect is stressed by the care taken to ensure that the excess mortar is not removed by the bricklayers, but is left to bear witness to the construction process, thus creating a new conglomerate; rather than brick surfaces, in fact, these seem

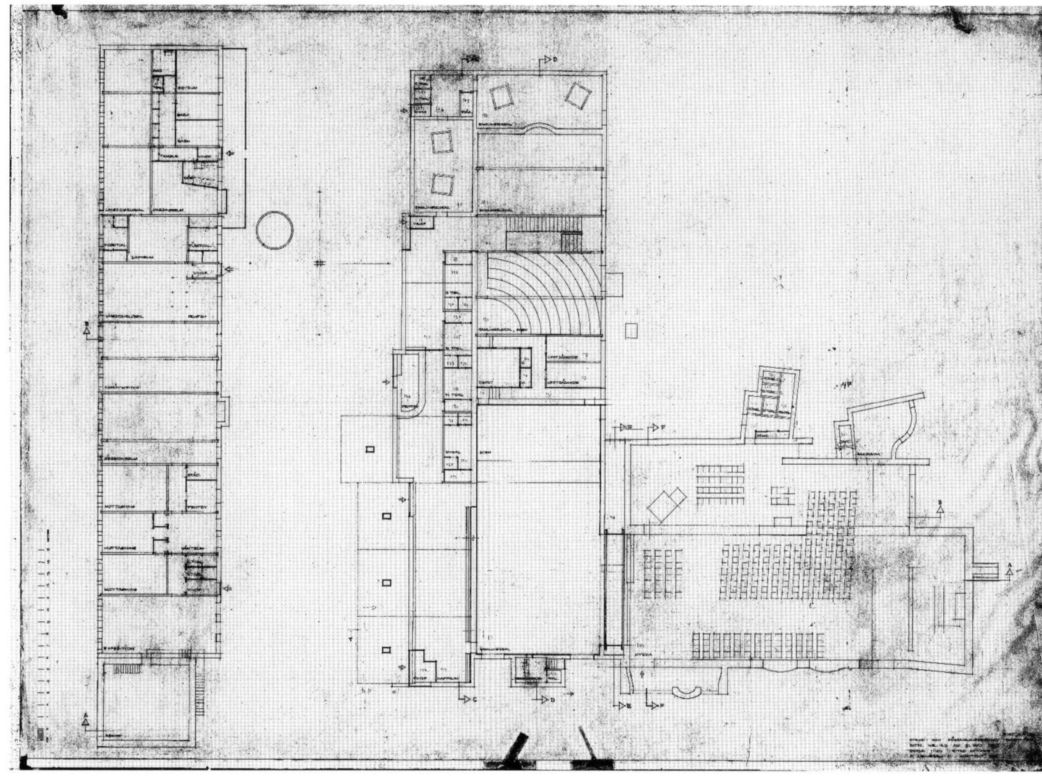

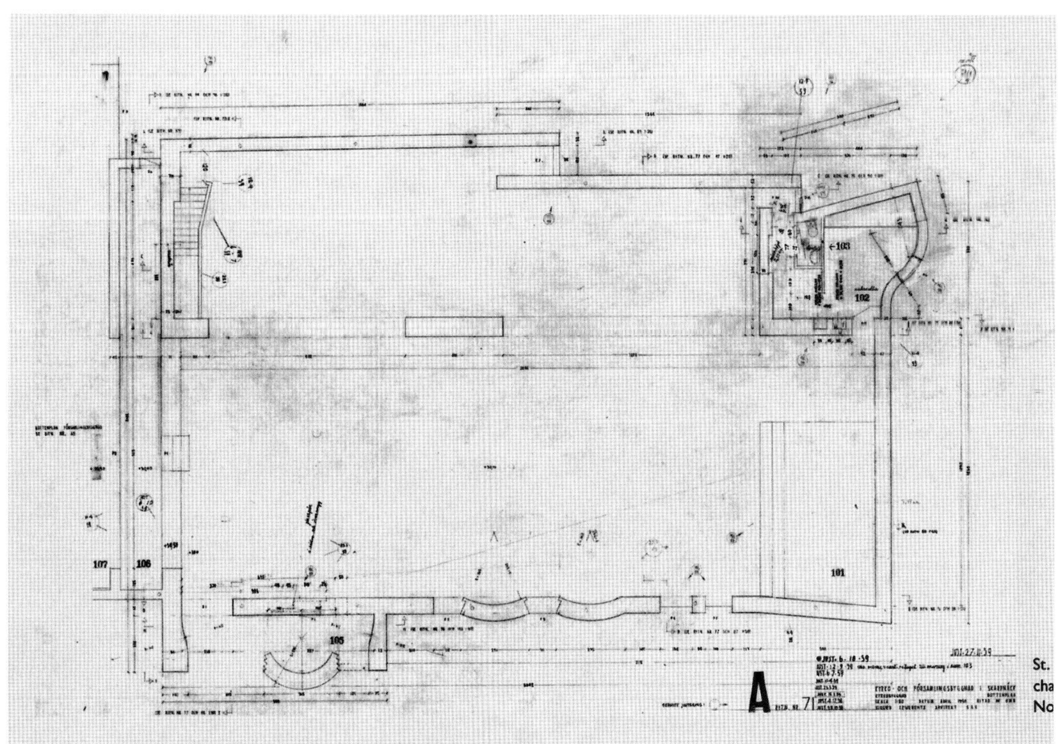

Ground-floor plan, May 1957.

Plan of the church, November 1959.

to be ancient walls, where the bricks have the role of the inert ingredient in the concrete conglomerate, appearing to be submerged in the rough mortar.
It is, above all, on the south face of the church that Lewerentz's skill and inquiring spirit find expression. Appearing to derive from the location of some of the walls inside the birch wood to seal off portions of space that were formerly free, the fragmentary nature of this architecture assumes particular vigour. The wall—or rather what appears to be a single expanse of brickwork—is, however, the result of the juxtaposition of a series of fragments, made evident by large, dark mortar joints running from the edge of the roof to ground level, dividing the façade into a series of vertical bands. Corresponding with the internal use of the space, the divisions fit in with the few openings that Lewerentz places in this façade; highlighting the consistency of plan, section and internal space, they make the arrangement of the functions within legible from the outside. One band corresponds to the entrance area; another two reveal the position of the central section of the church, the part intended for the congregation; another appears to curve slightly to accommodate the pulpit; yet another, with two openings descending to ground level, indicates the presence and size of the transept, which is bathed by the light streaming in through the window, interrupting the obscurity of the rest of the church. The slight angle at which the last band of brickwork is set conceals the holiest part of the church, where the altar and choir are located.
In the first version of the project, in which the outside wall is still formed by a single continuous plane, Lewerentz inclines the apse floor towards the centre, adopting an ancient practice that was intended to symbolize the tilt of Christ's head when he was on the cross. It is likely that what lay behind this early solution was the advice of Nils Roth, the clergyman who assisted the architect after he had won the competition. In the version that was actually built, this device was transferred by Lewerentz to the setting at an angle of the south wall of the apse, the one that is most clearly visible from the outside, offering a fresh interpretation of the very formalized symbolism traditionally found in sacred buildings.

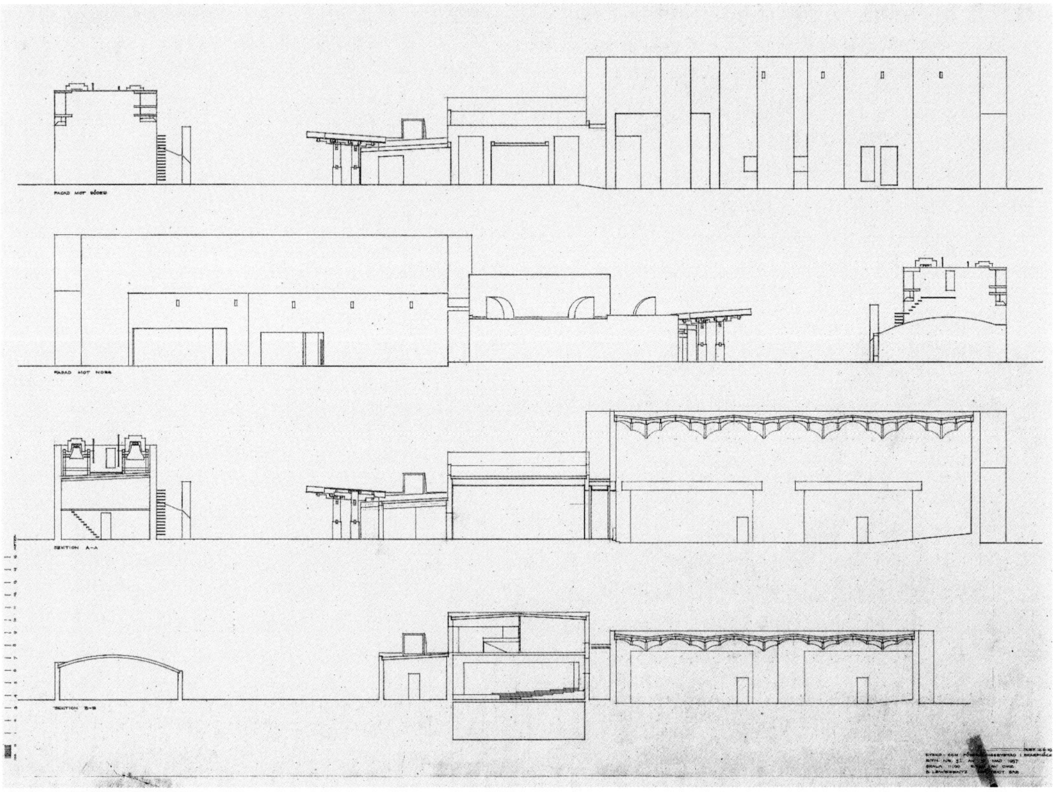

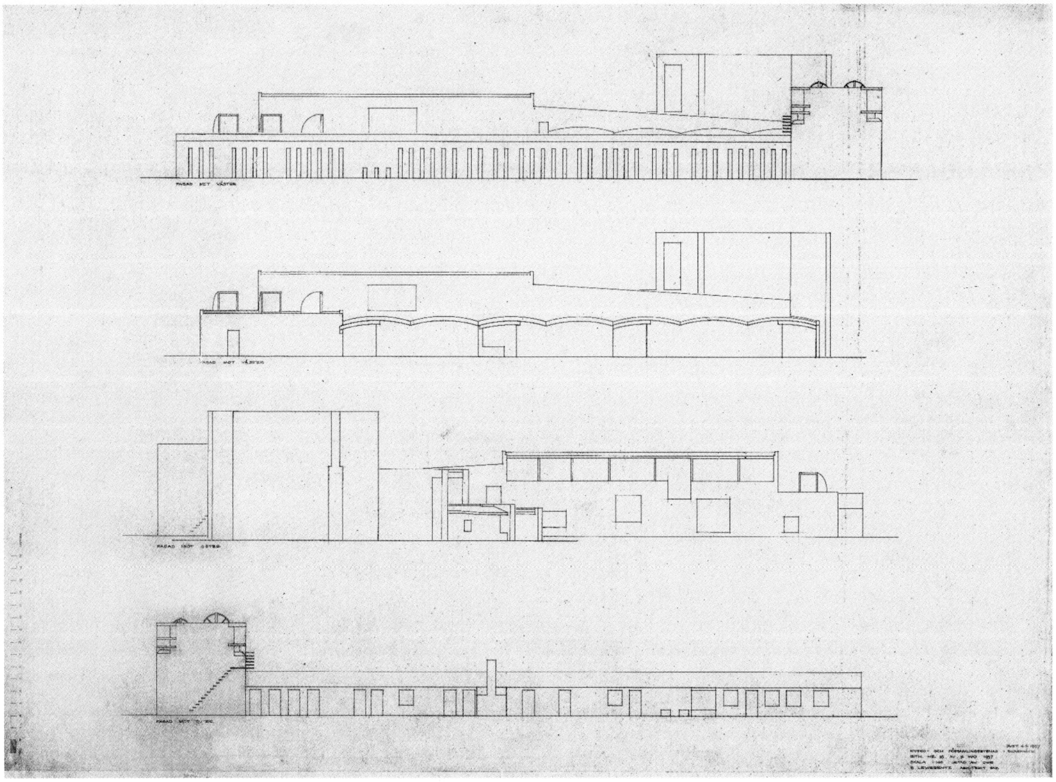

North and south elevations and sections, May 1957.

Elevations of the building for parish activities, May 1957.

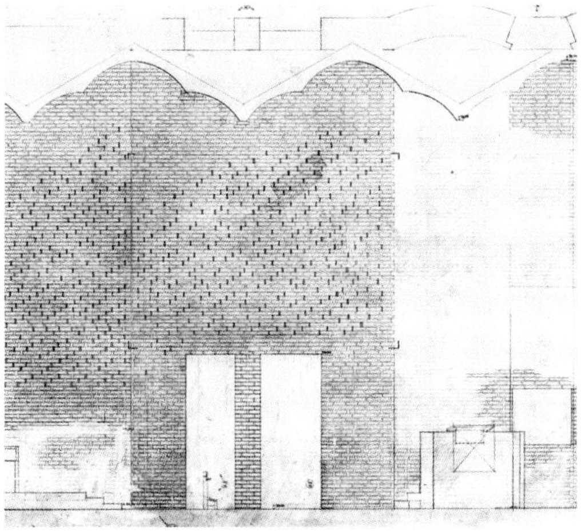

Detail of the brickwork
of the church, April 1958.

South elevation
of the church.

South elevation
of the church.

Nave of the church.

Nave with Barbro Nilsson's altar.

Baptismal font.

The parish buildings are reached by a path through the birch wood surrounding the complex that leads directly into the courtyard flanked by the two blocks into which the complex is divided. On the west side is the elongated office building, while the bell-tower, housing a circular stair shaft in one corner, is adjacent to its south side. The cross, a simple iron structure, is attached to the stair-tower by its transverse piece, as if it were merely a sign, avoiding the emphasis that normally accompanies the choice of its location. The bell-tower is twice as high as the office building; having only one storey, the latter is covered by a segmental barrel vault. Wishing to refrain from using an eaves gutter on the side facing the courtyard, Lewerentz designed a complex system of specially shaped strips of copper laid on the barrel vault in order to channel the rainwater towards certain points of the building, where it can flow away. A number of open downpipes, having a C-shaped profile, without coming into contact with either the roof or the ground, convey the water into the drains in the ground, attesting to the architect's particular fondness for redefining the form and conduct of functions to which, generally speaking, little thought is given, or that are more often simply left to be resolved by the building workers as they see fit. As in the interior, where the services offer an opportunity for giving a new appearance to the spaces, on the exterior the problem of the collection of rainwater is an opportunity for rethinking the built form. Lewerentz focused his attention on the building problem and, refusing to consider the form itself afresh, began using a method at Björkhagen that became a feature of all his subsequent works: he radicalized the contents of the design problems to propose solutions that were as simple as they were innovative and timeless. The way in which he tackled, for the first time here, the design of the windows in the church, bears witness to this. On this occasion Lewerentz decided to analyse in depth the different elements of the building component, focusing on its real needs and ignoring all the possible ready-made solutions. After having managed for many years a factory producing metal door and window frames, and having designed and patented numerous fittings necessary for their use, the architect resolved the same problem by just fixing sheets of glass onto the exterior of the brickwork, with disarming simplicity and in one fell swoop making redundant years of hard work in his Eskilstuna factory. The double glazing and the elastic sealants are certainly the contributions of technology and progress to the project, elements that allowed the architect to formulate his proposal, although the windows of St Mark's—like those

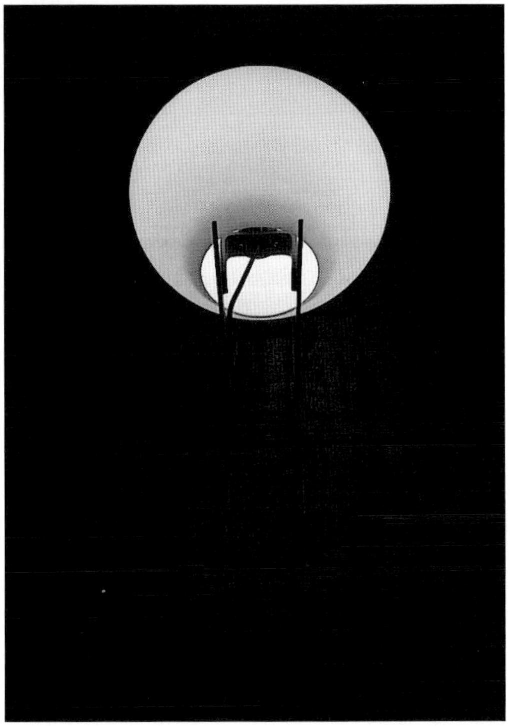

Details of the interior.

South elevation
of the church.

Construction details of the lamps for the interior.

Views of the interior.

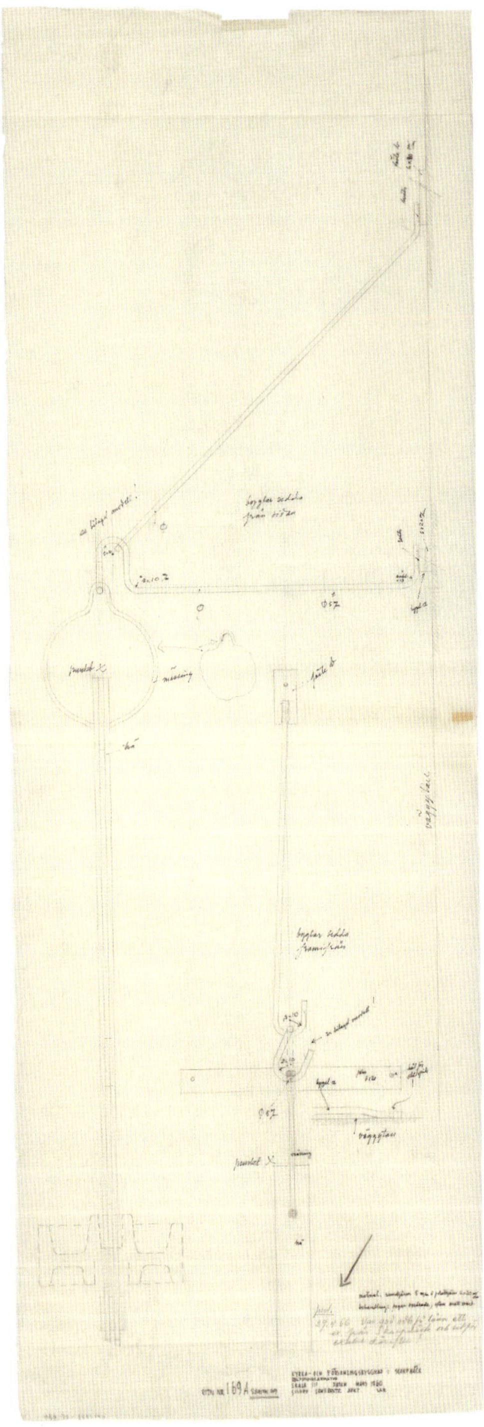

Construction details
of the organ.

View of the organ.

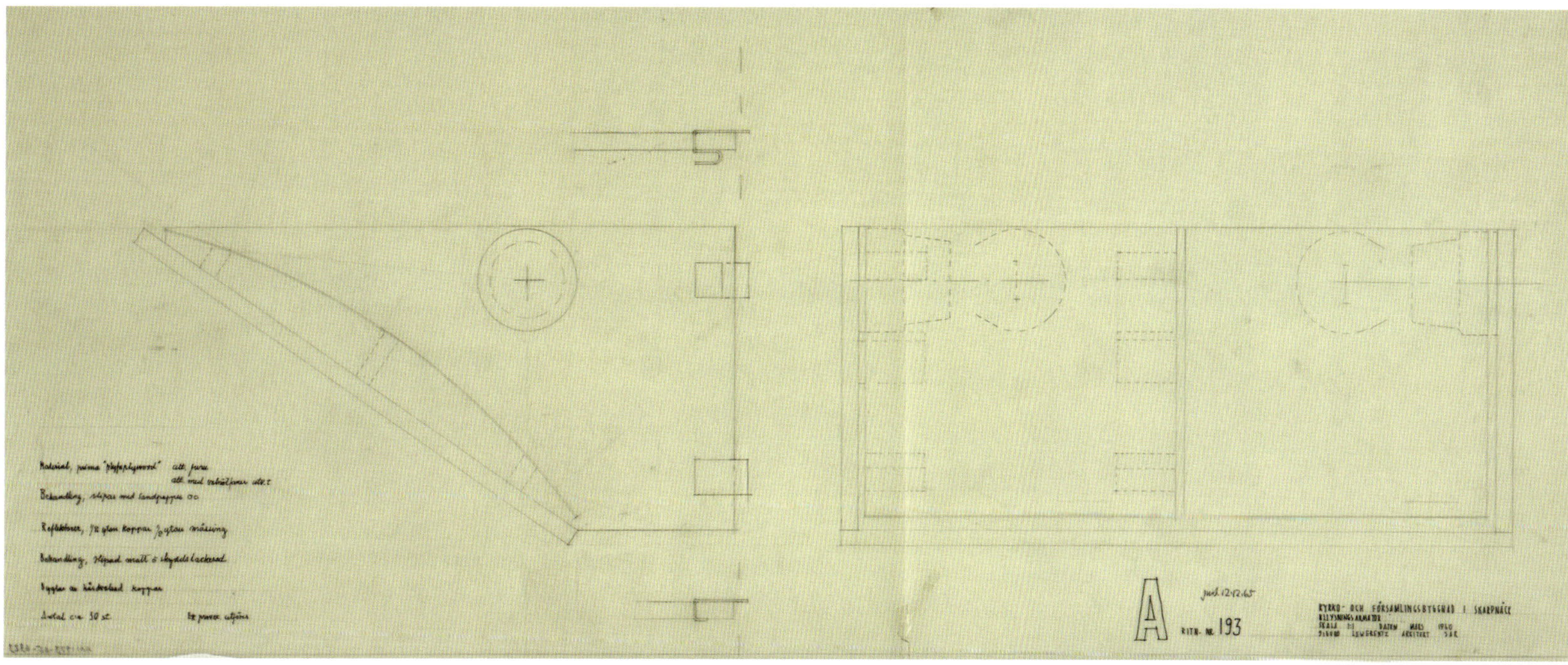

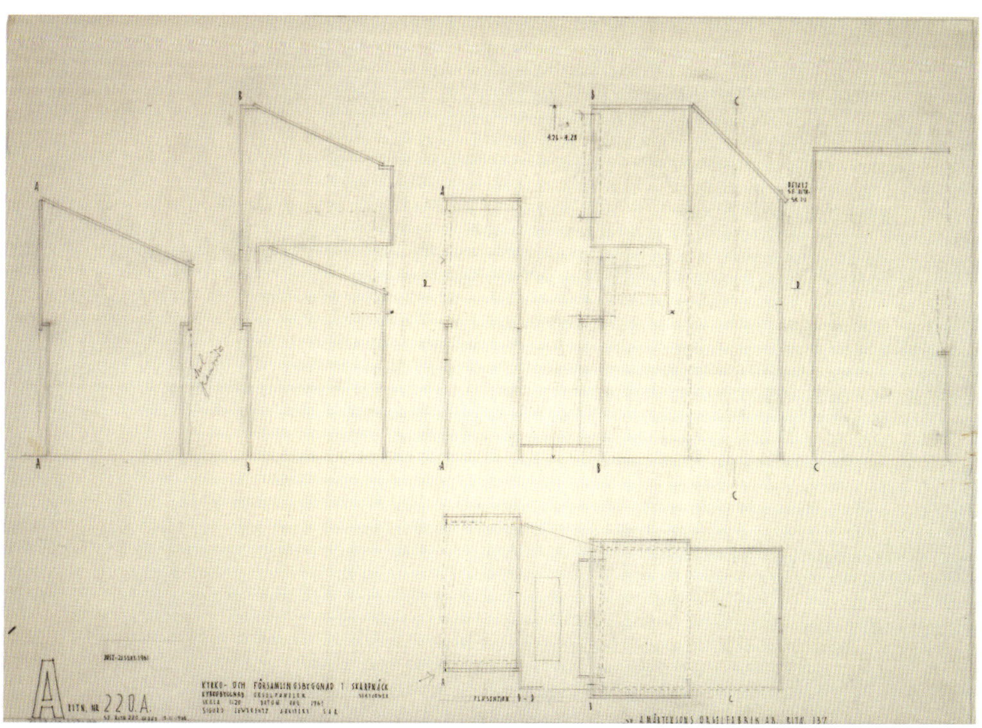

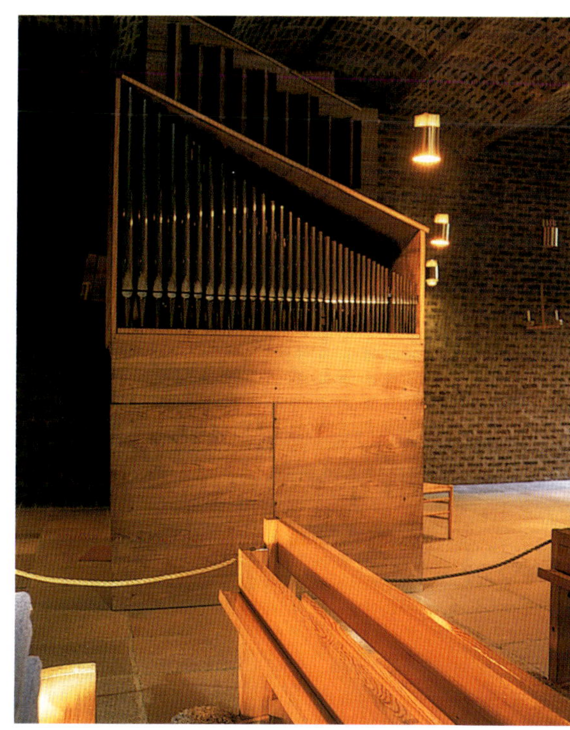

Rear elevation
of the church.

Courtyard.

of St Peter's at Klippan—are anything but technological ostentation.
Lewerentz had, in fact, a rare ability to place progress at the service of the project and its realization, the real focus of his interests, without becoming their victim. The ventilation of the interiors is provided by the forced air system between the two leaves of the cavity wall, which, through a number of openings left in the brickwork, brings the air into the church. The doors and windows are mainly characterized by the absence of any frames, allowing a direct relationship with the exterior to be established, although Lewerentz has placed the panes of glass on the interior. This prevents the interplay of reflections that at Klippan, with the projection of fragments of the natural world onto the surface of the building, deconstructs its unity, creating what is, in effect, a free, abstract composition, based wholly on materials and textures.
Despite the fact that he did not make widespread use of the new type of window at Skarpnäck, which he only installed in the church, Lewerentz also introduced a new system for the installation of the door and window frames, both internal and external, and drastically reduced the number of elements. The architect, in fact, inserted the door leaves and doorstops (or the windows and their outer frames) directly into the apertures in the brickwork, without using sub-frames, staff beads or whatever else had been employed hitherto to allow for the inevitable imperfections in the construction, which, for the first time here, are compensated for by a thick, clearly visible joint formed by a black sealant. Although Lewerentz paid particular attention to different elements of the construction, this does not mean that all the details of the work had already been resolved at the design stage, because the details of the

Opposite
Building for parish activities, view of the entrance.

Construction details and detail of the porch.

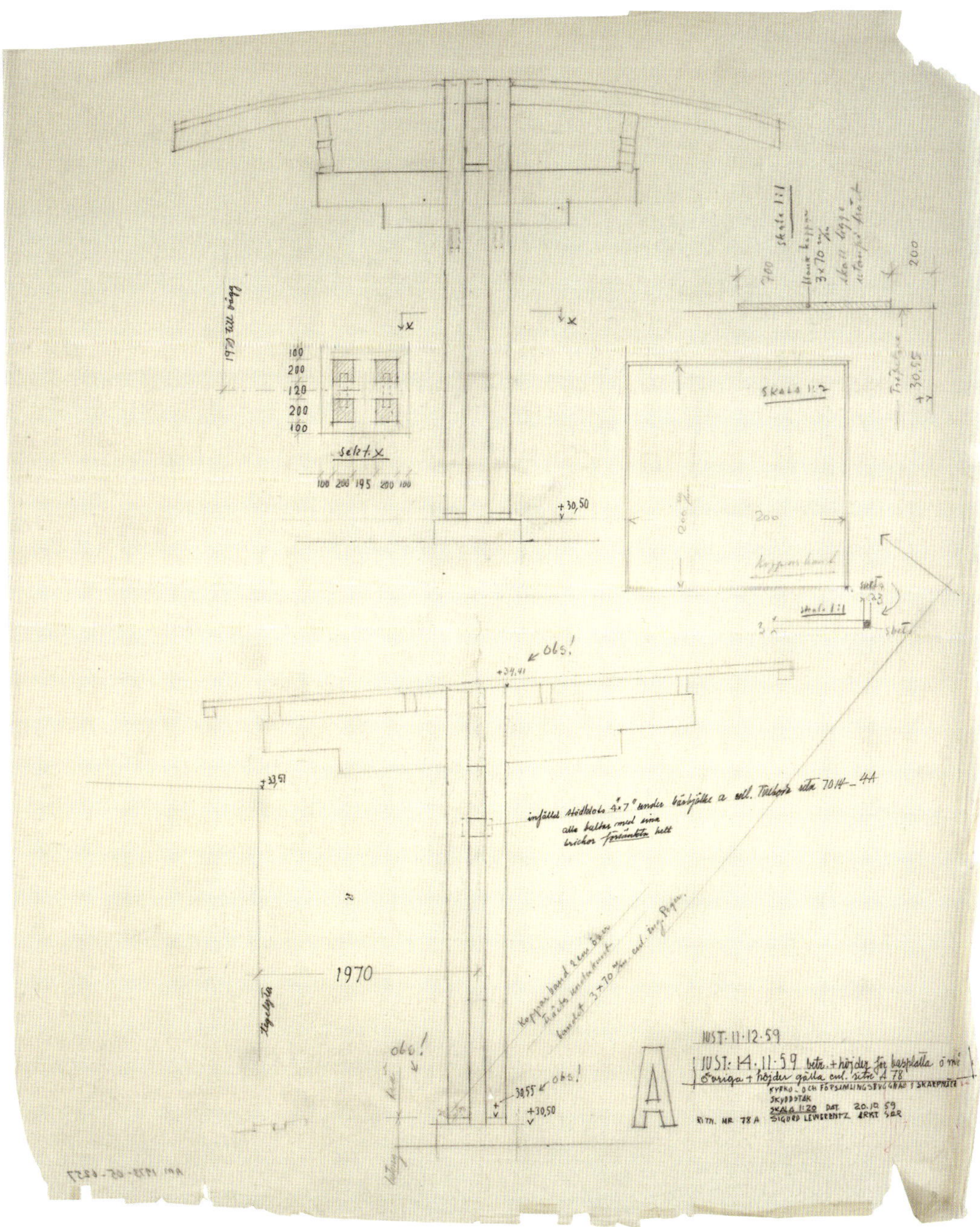

construction are always the direct result of an analysis made of the function, and their role is never independent from the building of which they form part. An overall vision, with the insertion of the work in a more general context, is one of the peculiarities of the work of Lewerentz, who, thanks to his long experience in the design of cemeteries, always elaborated the general and detailed design in parallel, creating a dialectic relationship between the comprehensive vision and specific architectural solutions and finishings.
Each of the blocks at Björkhagen contributes to the overall significance of the work, although continuing to maintain its semantic and compositive independence, which manifests itself in the plan, elevation and articulation of the volumes.
Thus the L-shaped building housing the parish facilities and the church proclaims its distributional and functional layout on the exterior, making physically perceptible the community hall, the section devoted to the parish activities and the one destined for catechesis, and the church, which is itself subdivided into the nave, the aisle and the sacristy. Access to the church, the inside of which is enveloped in almost total darkness, is through a small entrance in the south wall; on the opposite wall two large openings mean that the aisle and the nave form a continuous space, which is stressed by the attention Lewerentz has paid to the lintels. Wishing to keep the surface of the bricks as intact as possible and avoid any visual break between the two parts, the architect has not changed materials, as was planned in the first version, and creates a structure completely in brick, including even the soffit of the roof, which is enriched by the presence of elements in iron and concrete serving to absorb the shearing stress and force of traction.
Also the aisle, like the nave, has a roof consisting of tripartite and splayed vaults, constructed with alternating slopes in order to allow the water to run off.
Placed transversely to the orientation of the church, the vaults appear to be waves pushing the congregation towards the altar.
It appears that, when asked why he had made this choice, Lewerentz replied:

Building for parish activities, construction details and view of the entrance.

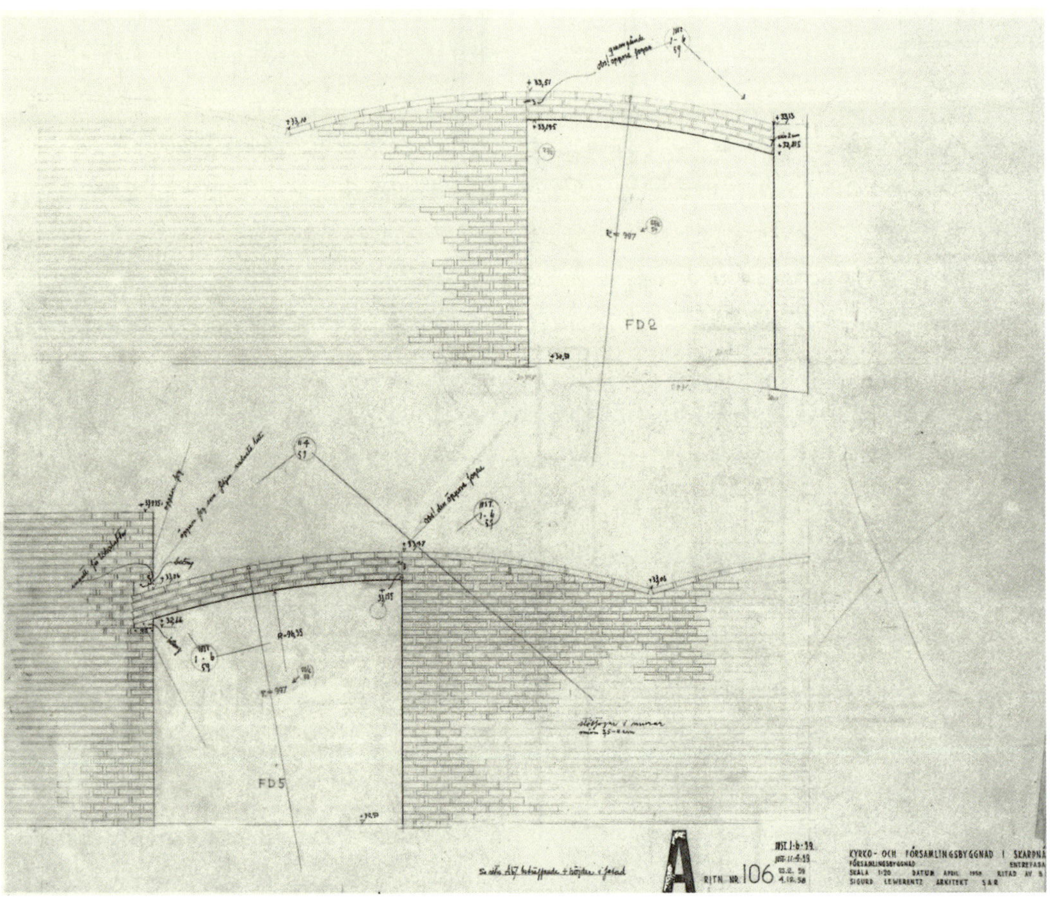

Bell-tower.

Construction details of the lamps for the exterior.

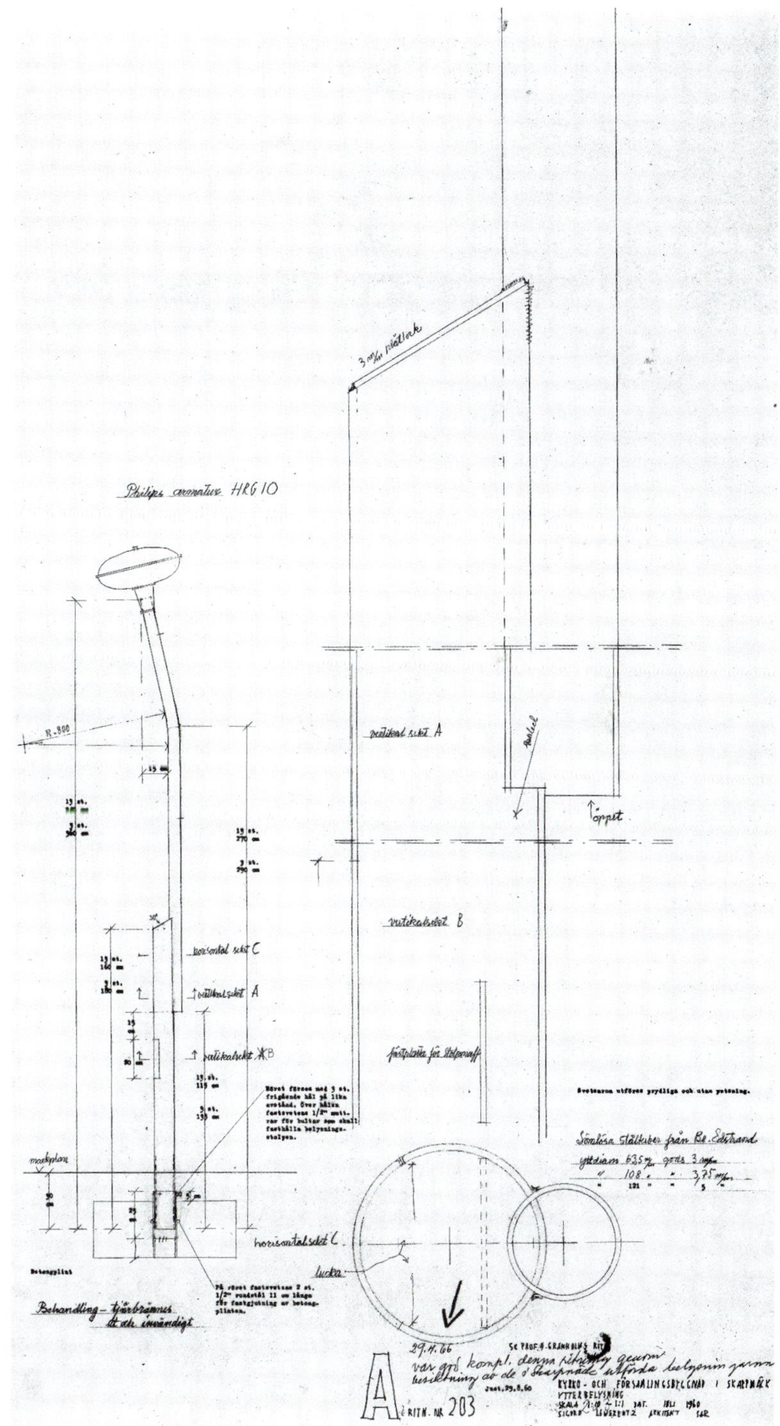

"It's quite simply an aesthetic need!", leaving his interlocutor dumbfounded.
As was the case a few years later at Klippan, Lewerentz has also planned a very large opening, distinct from the entrance, for the exit; this leads directly into the community hall, which, in its turn is linked with the other rooms in the parish building, so that the passage from the religious service to the other community activities is not a brusque one, and takes place entirely within the same building.
The group of buildings, with its very compact plan, only reveals the complexity of its composition in a very partial manner, suggesting that it should be discovered little by little and with use. On the other hand, the intricate dialectic between the part and the whole with which the Björkhagen project is imbued and which is one of the basic elements of its form, appears to reflect the similar dualism, present in Christianity, of the believer and the community, a value on which the teaching of Christ is based.
Probably the decision to use only one material for the construction of St Mark's, the brown Helsingborg brick, also reflects the need to stress the same dichotomy, transforming it into built form, in accordance with a process that tends to obtain complexity without the individual element losing its specific identity. At Björkhagen, as happened later at Klippan, the brick has remained intact in the whole building, without ever being cut to meet the requirements of the design of individual parts, which makes it easy to imagine how hard Lewerentz must have had to work on the building site, despite the fact that he was now advanced in years.

NB Caldenby quotes the motto "Interlude", while Ahlin states that Lewerentz entitled his outline of the project "Interlude"; however, the motto mentioned at the museum is "Mellanspel".

Bibliography: *Arkitektur* 1963; Linn 1965; Sykes 1966; Rappe 1973; Roth 1976; Ahlin 1985b, pp. 209–24; Alenius 1986; Uhlin 1988; Caldenby 1997, pp. 146–63; *Sigurd Lewerentz. Two Churches* 1997.

(G.P.)

Views of the courtyard.

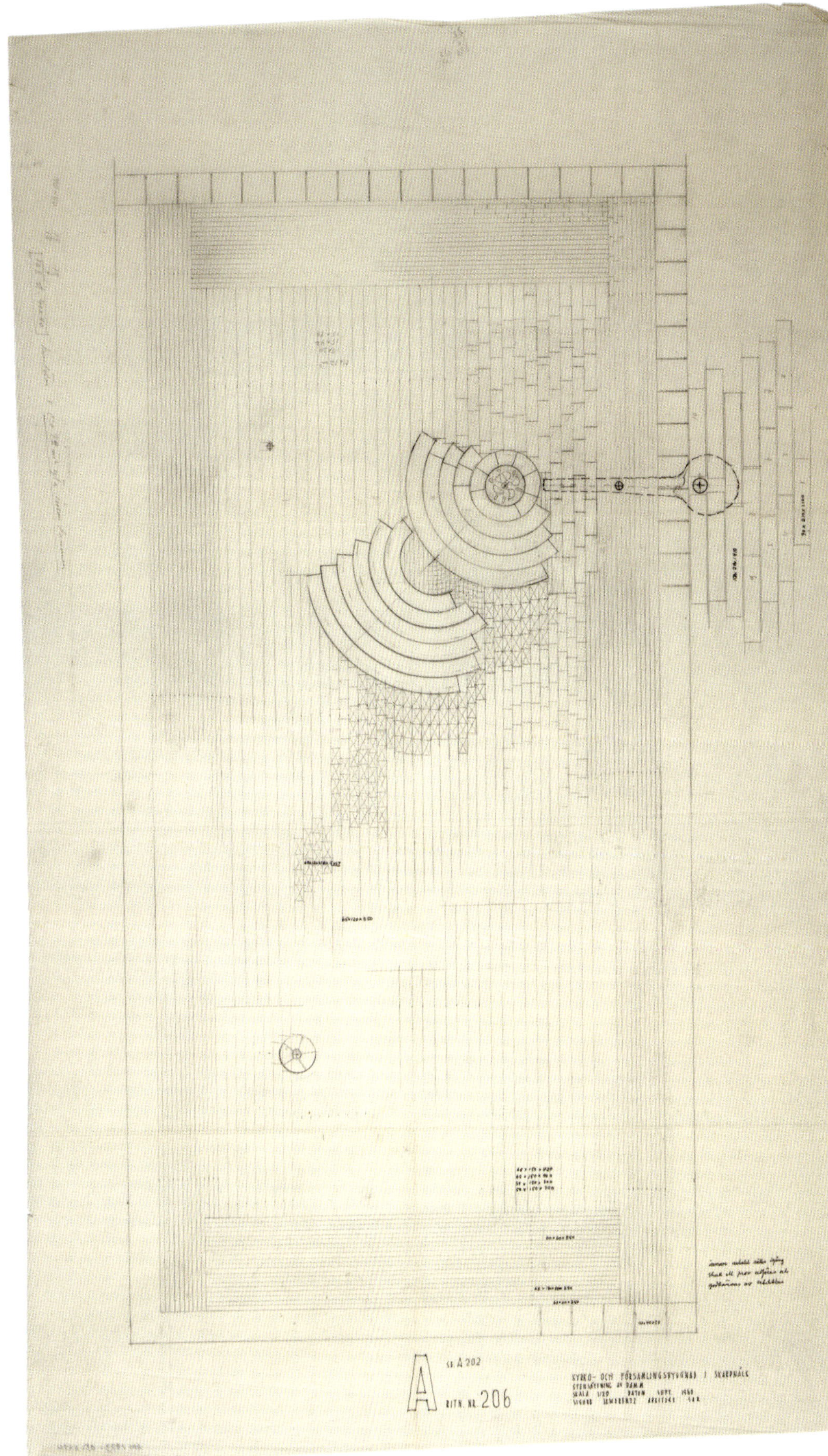

Fountain.

Plan of the basin for the fountain, September 1960.

Construction details and textures of the brickwork.

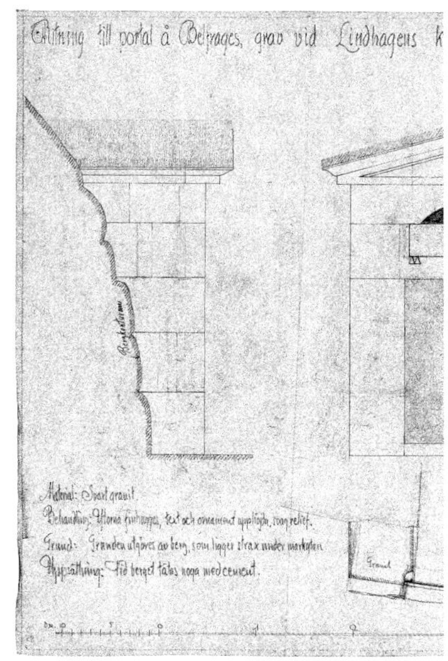

105. Renovation of Lewerentz's House at Skanör, 1956

Living-room.

106. Competition Project for Students' Residences and the Students' Union at the University of Uppsala, 1956

motto "UBBO VI" citation

In his outline of the project, Lewerentz stated:
"Since the density of the Ubbo district should be increased, it is important that the site beyond the boundary of the district towards Odinslund should be kept intact... The students' union is conceived as a single independent building, located near a promontory, with its entrance situated in the area in front of Åsgranden, from where the routes lead to the garage of building C4 and the university office block. The project aims at the future linking of the students' union building with that of the residences, so that there will be a single façade on Odinslund."
The subsequent use of the huge complex for administrative purposes or the renting of office accommodation can only regard the buildings on Slottsgatan. In any case, considerable rebuilding would be necessary for the conversion of the residences into an office block.

Bibliography: *Tävlingen* 1956; Ahlin 1985b, pp. 197–99,

(G.P.)

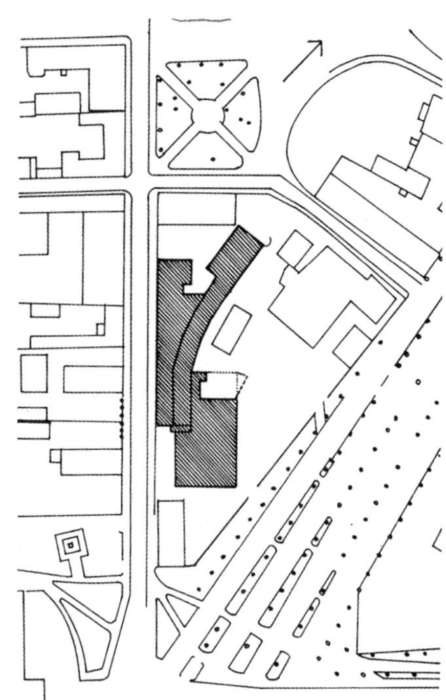

Layout plan.

107. Project for Stadsgård Square, Arboga, 1961 onwards
partially with L. Bergström

The project submitted by Lewerentz to the municipal committee for the redevelopment of Stora Square, in the centre of Arboga, addresses the problem of the renovation of a monumental eighteenth-century building, the Stadsgård, in an unexpected manner. Contrary to the intentions of the municipality, which proposed the replacement of the historic building with a large shopping centre—a form of redevelopment prevalent in the historic centres of Swedish towns in the 1960s—the architect, when redesigning the urban space, makes the imposing edifice the main feature of the square. Lewerentz, in fact proposes its renovation and re-use, assigning a public function with a strong symbolic value—that of the town library—to the *piano nobile*, while he restores its original use, mainly of a commercial type, to the ground floor. In order to highlight the importance of the building and its central role in the rearrangement of the urban space, vehicular traffic and the car park have been moved away from the Stadsgården: a long wall, screened by thick vegetation, marks the boundary between the pedestrian area and the car park, cutting across the whole area longitudinally. This solution also allows Lewerentz to propose an urban space that is more in keeping with the historic building it is planned to re-use.

Bibliography: *Dagens Nyheter*, 8.1.1962.

(G.P.)

View of the model.

Layout plan and profiles.

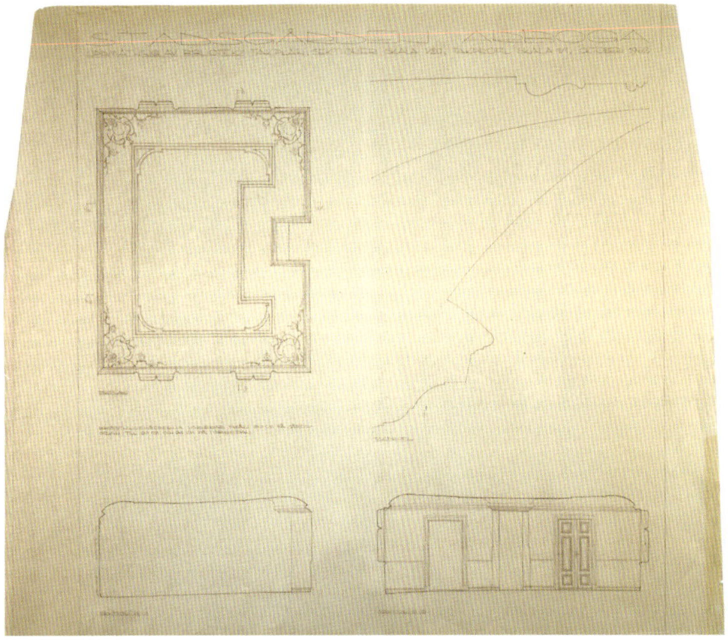

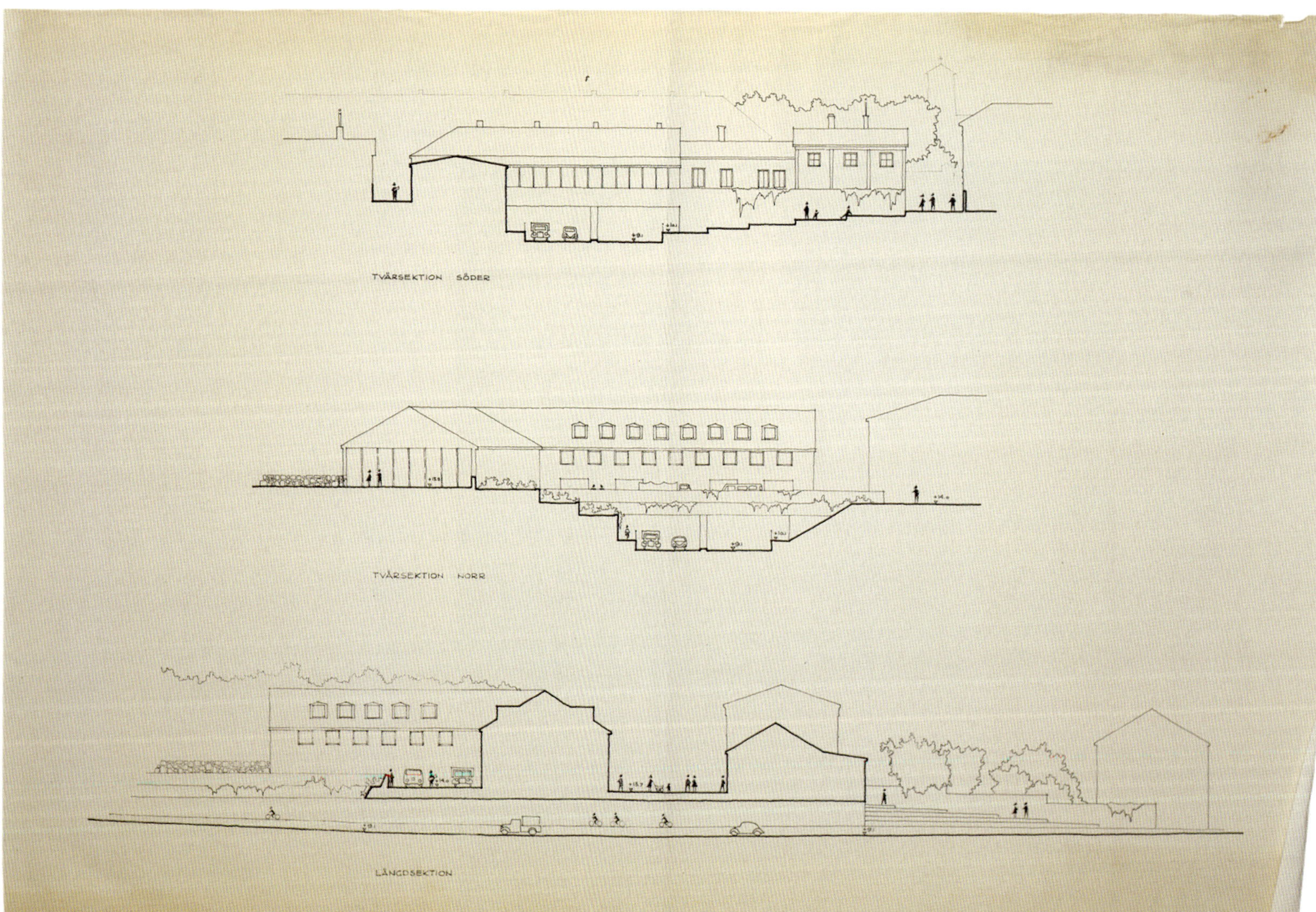

108. St Peter's Church at Klippan, 1962–66

Lewerentz first went to Klippan, a small town not far from Helsingborg, in 1963 in order to visit the site where, a few years later, St Peter's Parish Church would be built. He received the commission, with the agreement of the municipal planning department, from the committee set up to supervise the construction of the religious complex. The architect was assisted by the theologian Lars Ridderstedt, whose official task was to advise him on the project's functional programme and also to help him discover the deep meanings contained in the liturgy. The design of St Peter's is, in fact, based on a careful analysis of the forms of the religious service and a profound reinterpretation of them. The church's square plan, for instance, is the result of the desire to replace the usual basilican plan, which tends to impose hierarchical practices, with a distribution favouring equality between all those participating in the service. In effect, it represents a revival of the coming together, in a circle, of the cenacle—in accordance with the ancient tradition of the *circumstantes*—that characterized the earliest Christian communities. And it is their spirit that the architect allows to live again between the walls of the church: it is, in other words, the primary spirit of a strong, community form of Christianity. Even the darkness enveloping its interior strengthens the primitive atmosphere of this church, avoiding any temptation to historicize it. Only four small windows illuminate it, while two skylights draw attention—with a weak ray of light—to the route the officiating priest takes from the sacristy to the altar. There are no other sources of natural light and the church is mainly illuminated by the candles and a large number of pendant lamps that seem to be floating in the dark. Access to the church is through a side chapel, the entrance door of which is hidden in a narrow passageway on the north side, next to the bell-tower and the sacristy. It is intentionally intimate and informal because it is the result of the observation that usually people arrive in small groups, or alone, and it is only at the end of the service that they head *en masse* for the exit, in this case making use of the wider doors on the west front. Here the architect has laid out a large garden, overlooked by the main façade and embellished with a pond and sculpture.

Study site plan, July 1962.

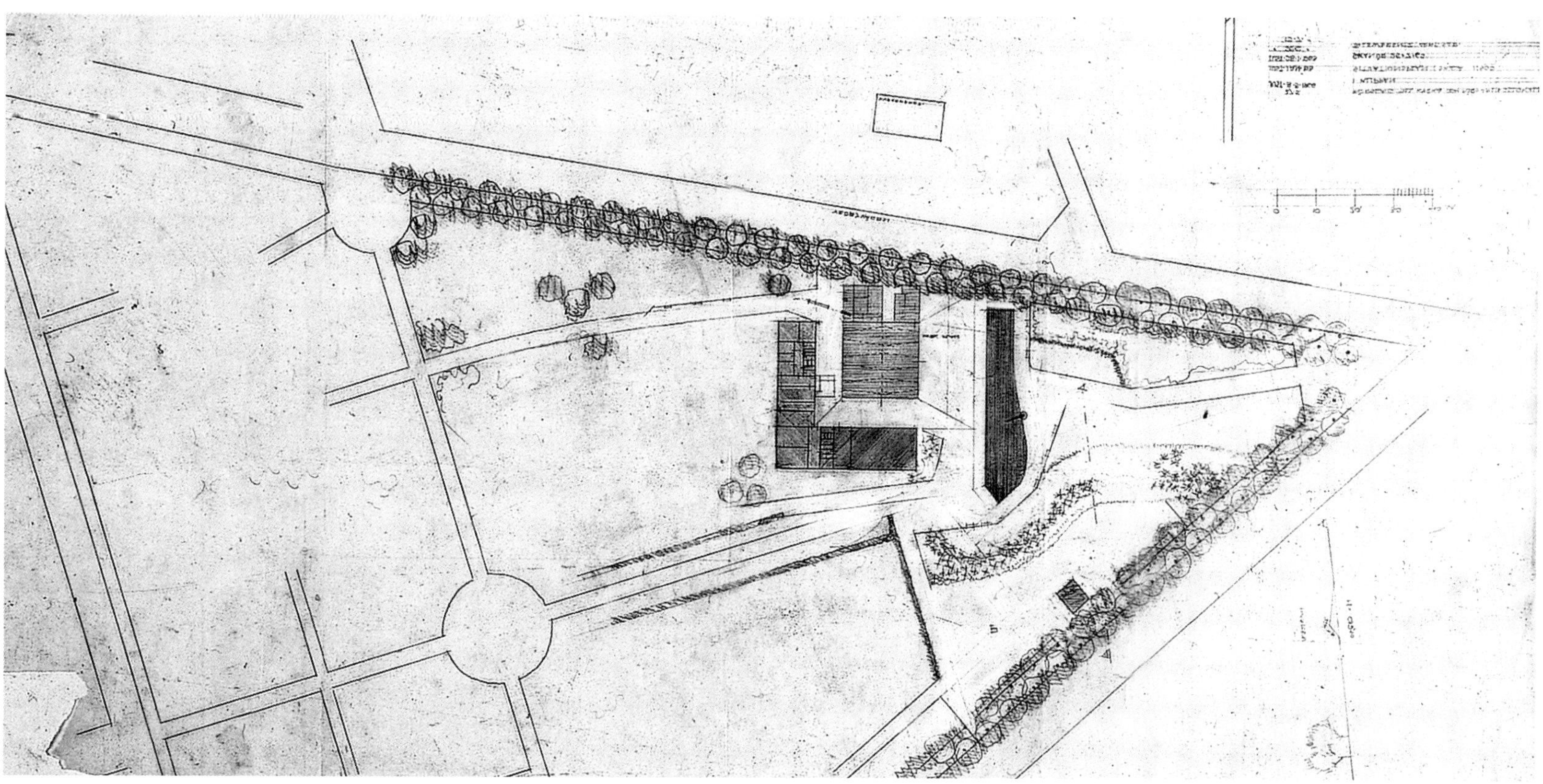

A low building, separated from the church by a long narrow courtyard, houses the parish offices, the meeting rooms and the community hall; with its L-shaped plan, this block forms, together with the church, what is virtually a square plan.
The simple overall layout juxtaposing the two buildings does not reveal the insight and sheer hard work involved in the design of the individual parts. The architecture of St Peter's should, in fact, be seen at close quarters, because this is the only way that it is possible to appreciate the excellence of the design choices and its execution, since in this work Lewerentz has used all the skills he developed during his long career to give a specific meaning to each stage of the process of construction. Consequently the different parts of the building tell the story of the construction, from the moment when the bricks are laid in mortar and when, with a simple piece of sackcloth, the excess mortar is removed by the bricklayers, without further finishing work. Also the work of the blacksmith is impressed in the weld beads that have not been smoothed away, as in the case with the work of all those who have taken part in the realization of the work, both in the church and the community centre. Another example is the design of the flooring and its completion; the fact that the joints between the tiles are slightly in relief is a physical reminder of the pressure exerted on the mortar by the worker when laying the tiles.
All the time taken over construction permeates the building: the frequent visits to the site by Lewerentz and his meetings with Carl Sjöholm, the site manager, stamp the countless modifications made to the project while work was in progress, attesting to an approach in which on-the-spot adaptations to specific requirements had priority over the plans drawn up in the architect's office. The decision to use uncut bricks for the whole building, in fact, involved the commitment to be present every day on site to resolve problems arising there, calculating, in each case, the width of the mortar joint between the courses and allowing it to vary according to particular needs. This is why, in some cases, the mortar, which usually serves to join the courses of bricks, is many times thicker than the bricks themselves, which seem to be floating in it. In these cases the mortar mix is enriched with flakes of slate,

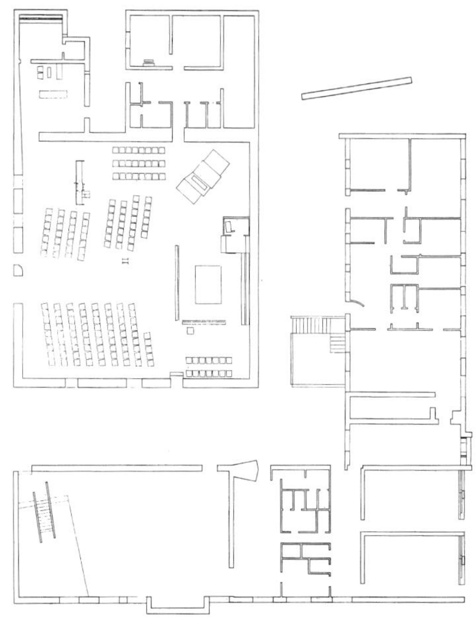

Ground-floor plan of the parish complex (redrawn).

giving it its characteristic rough texture; the slate also serves to reduce as far as possible the phenomenon of shrinkage, which in such conditions may have notably negative effects. On occasion, in order to resolve the problems posed by his refusal to cut the brick, the architect allows the brickwork to, so to speak, fray, giving the work a disquietingly unfinished appearance. This is what happens, for instance, in the church floor near the baptismal font, where a gap in the pattern of the bricks reveals a small pool, an allegorical representation of the Jordan; water drips continuously from the font into the "river", its ceaseless noise breaking the silence of the church. Lewerentz has, in fact, a rare ability to transform what appears to be a straightforward piece of building work into a significant element, subliming technical and functional requirements into fascinating design solutions. This is the case, for example, in the church's interior, of the Cor-Ten steel columns, which, rising like trees from the floor, stretch upwards to support the vaults. The transition from the vertical support to the vaults and the articulation of the metal structure, with its splitting into two to shift the load, gives rise to new symbolic meanings that go beyond merely functional and constructional needs. Not symmetrical, as sound structural logic might have suggested, the column is transformed into a cross to which the architect entrusts the task of supporting—not just symbolically—the church roof. The architect resolved the problem of the external door and window frames by leaving a hole in the brick wall, a simple rectangular space with a soffit also in brick, then applied a thick layer of black sealant on the external edge of the hole, pressing onto this a double pane of glass, just a few centimetres larger, which was fixed to the wall with metal clips. Seen from inside it seems that there is no window, because the frameless glass is practically invisible. From outside, however, the reflective surface of the glass contrasts sharply with the rough texture of the bricks, with no sign of frames, either fixed or movable. Since all the windows are fixed, the ventilation of the interiors is provided by the space left between the leaves of the cavity walls, where the openings left in the inner leaves allow entry of fresh air to the different rooms to be controlled. The placing of the window panes on the external surface of the walls and the absence of frames surrounding the openings make the view towards the exterior from within immediate, eliminating any obstacle between the built space and the natural world, and projecting parts of the exterior onto the reflective surfaces of the windows, creating an unusual blending on the elevations of artifice and nature, brick surfaces and fragments of the sky and trees.

The wooden doors, too—both external and internal—are based on the same principle of constructional simplicity: a frame, in many cases superimposed on the openings made in the brickwork, serves both as the door frame and the door stop; the door leaf, having the same thickness as the frame, consists of four panels of laminated wood mortised into each other with the exposed joints forming a double T pattern. Lastly, a layer of black sealant ensures continuity between the brickwork and the wooden structure.

But the fact that the techniques and technologies adopted when handling the building materials—the bricks, the wood and the metal—does not mean that Lewerentz was an aesthete of tectonics, because this attitude is neither consistent nor all-embracing. The bricks, for example, do not rigorously follow a building design and the arrangement of the courses is not changed in any way where they meet architraves or similar elements. In the same way, the arrangement of the downpipes is also neither schematic nor simplistic. While, in the courtyard, the solution adopted for removing the rainwater from the church roof has produced a decorative motif resulting from the dialectic that the architect has established between the gutters and the downpipes, on the main façade he avoids highlighting the problem, resolving it by inserting the downpipes between the leaves of the cavity walls, leaving the façade completely uncluttered.

Difficult, if not impossible, to classify, the architecture of St Peter's Church at Klippan is that of the fragment and fragmentariness. Not only does it comprise many different facets, but there are many possible ways in which each of these is related to the others. In fact, it is neither possible to sum up this

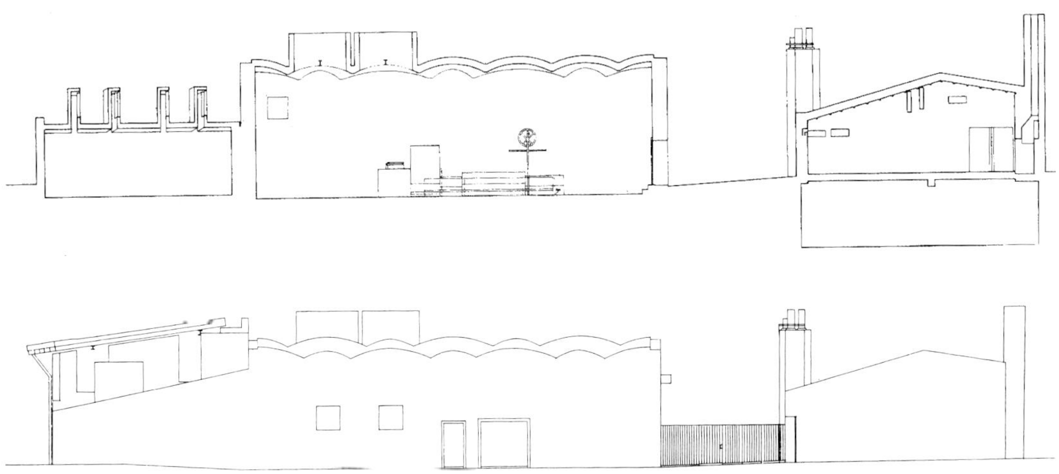

Section (January 1963) and west elevation (redrawn).

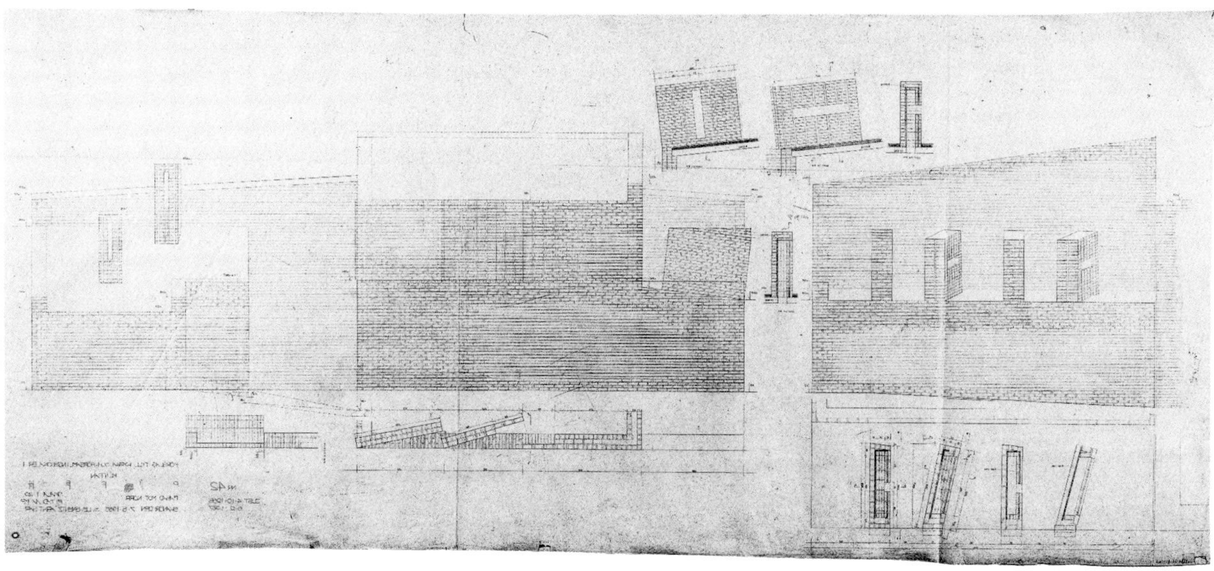

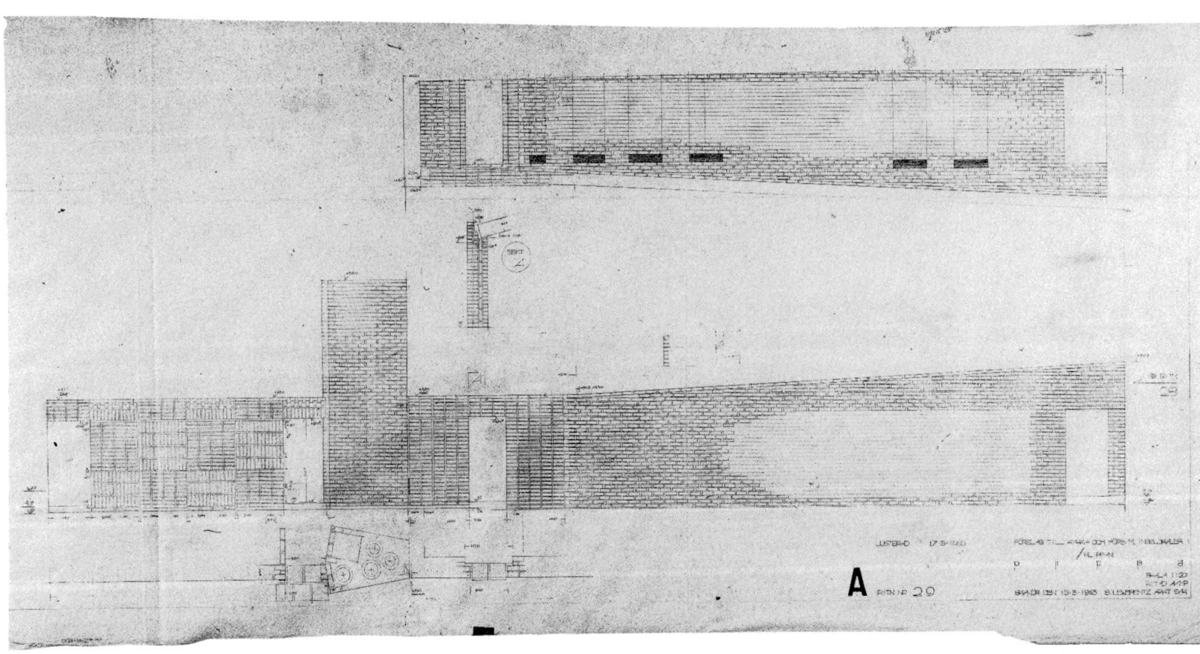

Elevations showing details of the brickwork.

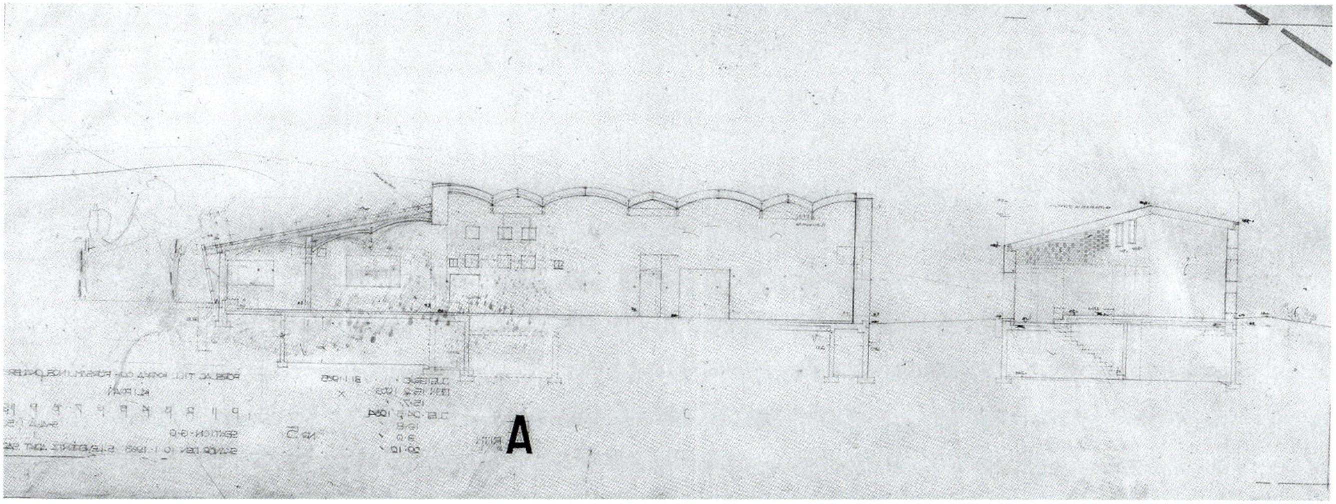

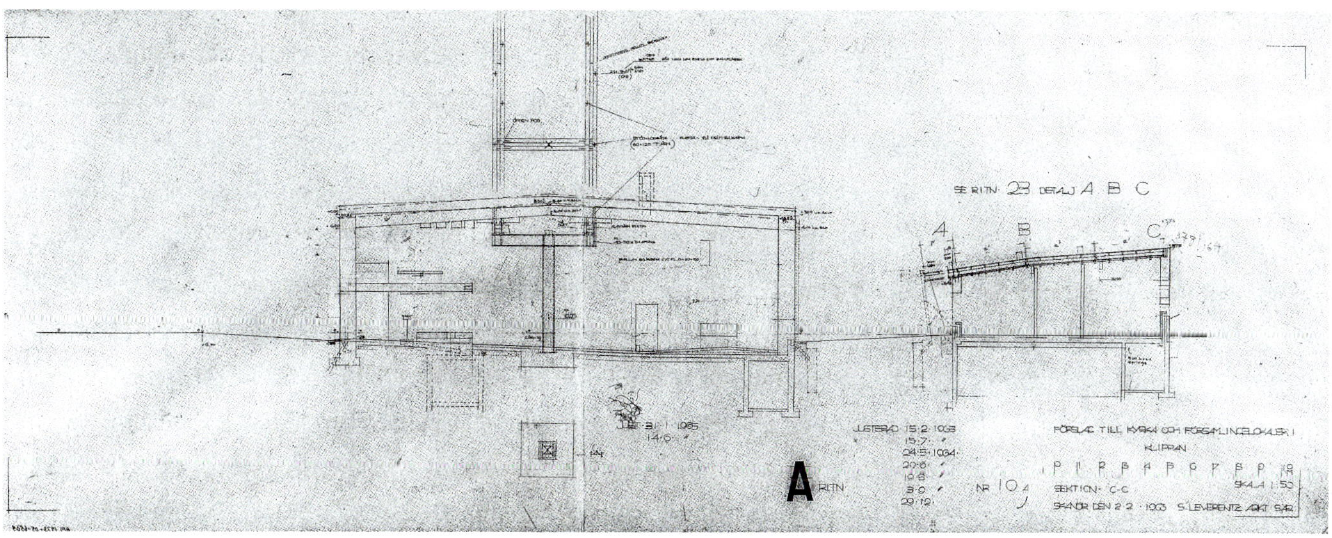

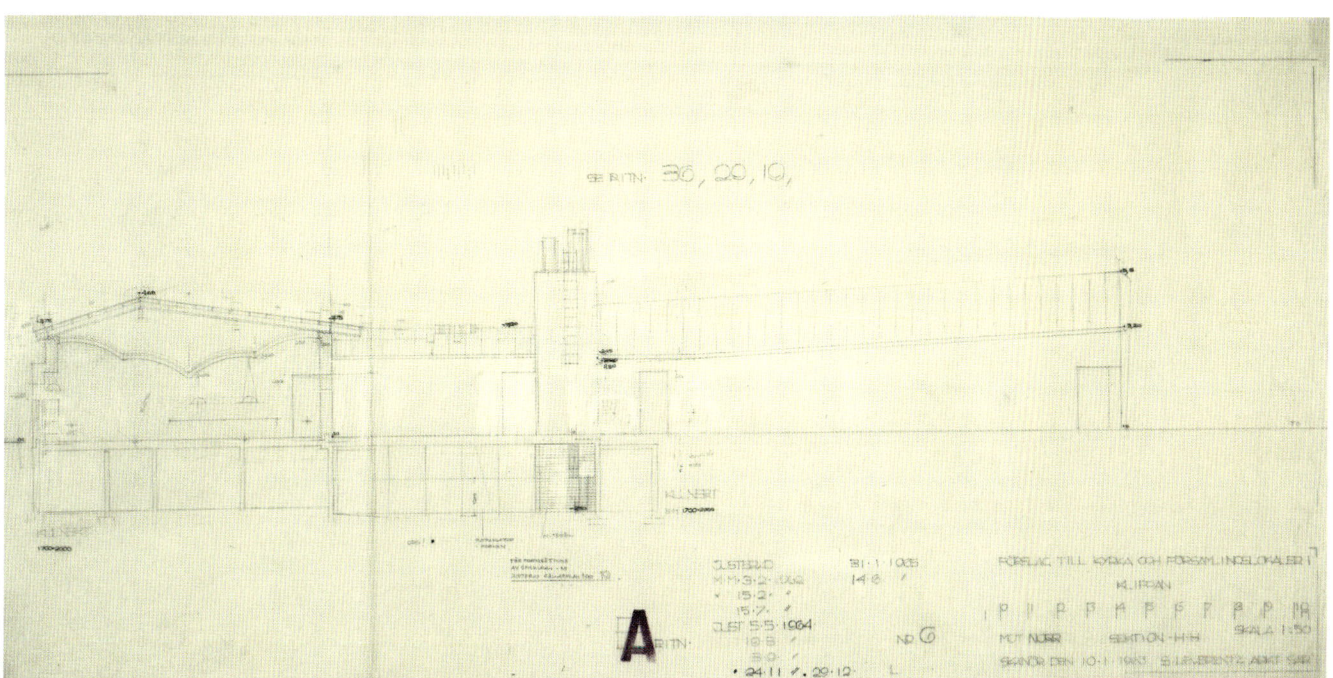

Section of the sacristy (redrawn), section of the church at the point where the altar is located (in the centre is the cross-shaped steel column).

East elevation.

approach to architecture in a few words nor reduce its significance to any one of the themes contained within it. It is only in the physical presence of this church built mainly of one material and in the moving, silent darkness of its interior that a thin, almost intangible thread may be found that is capable of linking together all the single parts of the whole.

Bibliography: Exner 1966; Olsson 1967; Lind 1968a; Lind 1968b; Arlok 1969; Konfeldt 1974; Uhlig 1981; Ahlin 1985b, pp. 225–34; Schöenbenck 1985; Alenius 1986; St John Wilson 1988b; Blundell Jones 1991; St John Wilson 1992; Edman 1993; Dahle 1994; Nicolin 1997; Postiglione 1997; *Two Churches* 1997, pp. 58–92; Caldenby 1998, pp. 165–75.

(G.P.)

Plan of the chapel,
May 1966.

View of the exterior.

Views of the exterior.

The elevation facing the courtyard, the north-east elevation of the parish building and the west elevation.

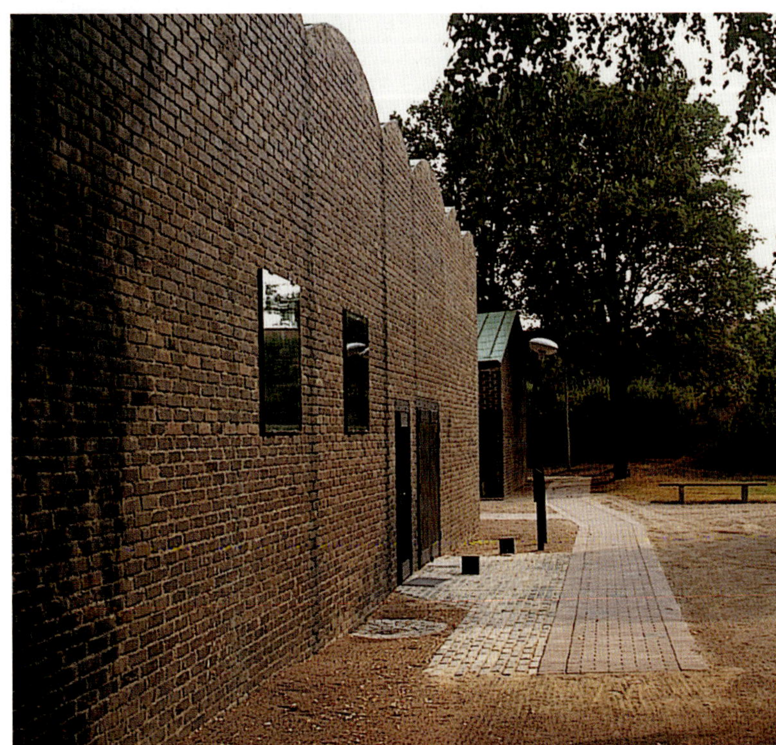

West elevation.

The wedding chapel and
the interior of the church.

Detail of the central column.

The entrance wall
of the church.

View of the altar.

Detail of the central column with the altar in the background.

View of the exterior.

Views of the parish building.

Views of the courtyard and the south elevation of the parish building.

Construction details and details of the door and window frames.

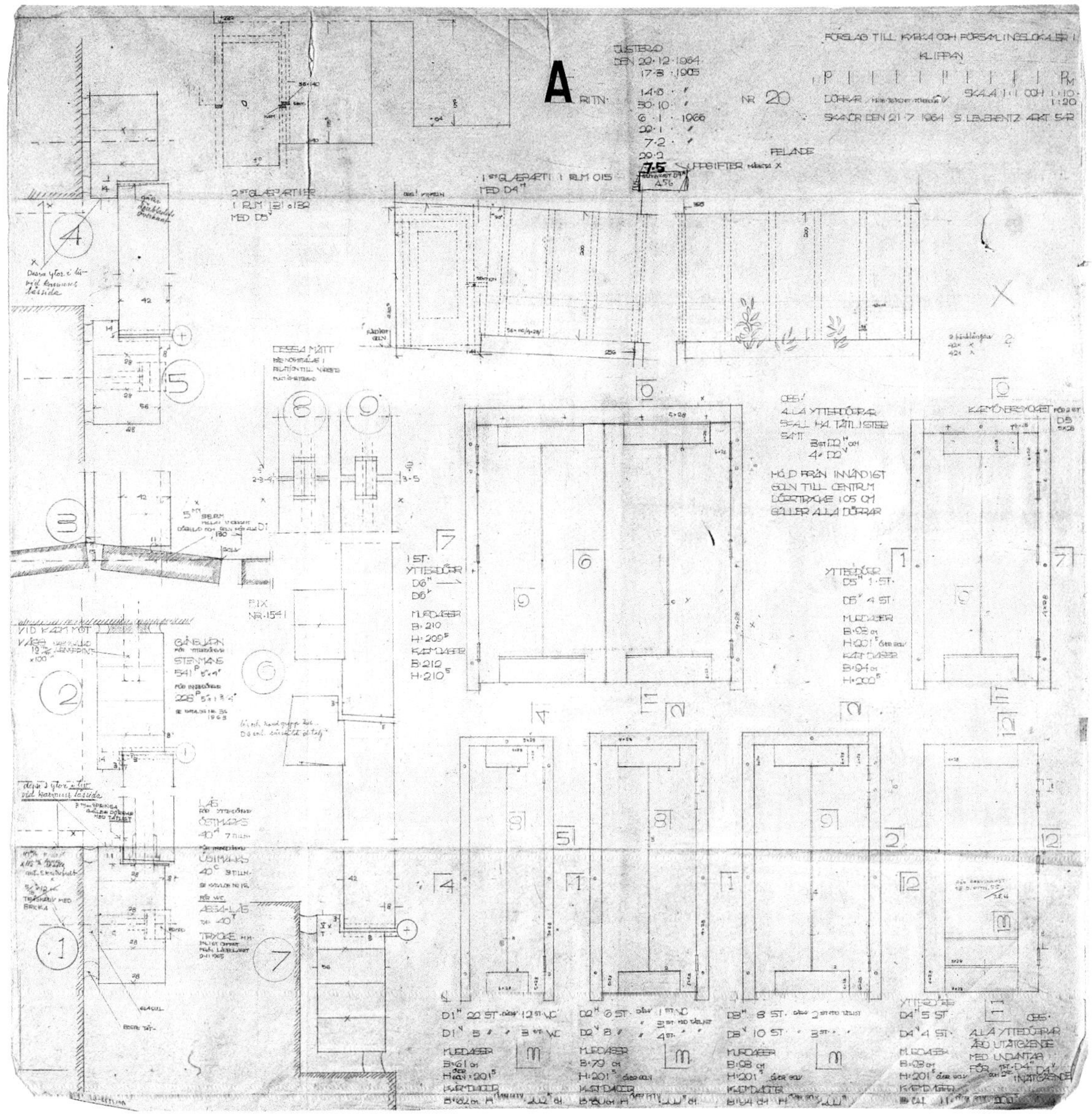

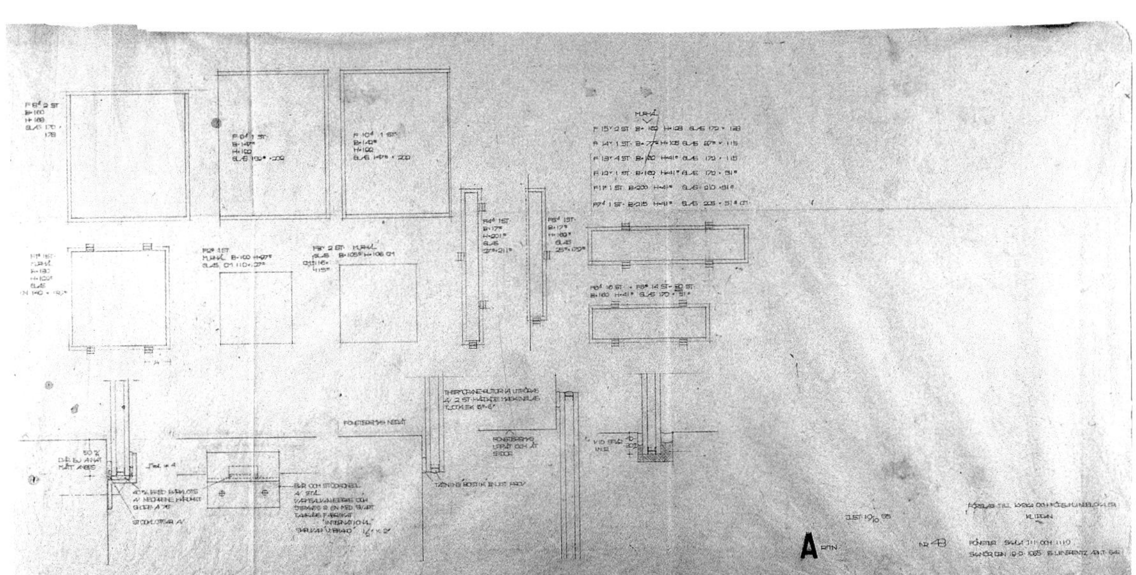

Interior and details
of the parish building.

Details of the brickwork.

Detail of one
of the windows.

109. Project for the Town Plan of Helgeandsholmen and Gustav Adolfs Torg (1962–64) and Competition for an Extension to the Parliament Building (1969–71), Stockholm
partially with Peter Celsing (1962–64)
partially with Bernt Nyberg (1969–71)
motto "Genom samma port"

It was the reform of the Swedish parliamentary system in the early 1960s, which also involved the unification of the two chambers, that inspired Lewerentz to draw up his own project for a new urban layout for the area between Helgeandsholmen—the island where the parliament building is located—and Gustav Adolfs Torg. This project also took into account the fact that the national theatre—the Kungl. Operan—needed to build an extension in the area of Gustav Adolfs Torg.

With these somewhat weak premises, Lewerentz began to work alone as early as 1962 on the general rearrangement of an area in which he was particularly interested, especially because he wanted to create an urban environment more suitable for one of the oldest areas of the city. In the first place the project, elaborated from 1962 to 1964, proposed the construction of two fairly low buildings in the immediate vicinity of the parliament building, concealing its main façade, which in Lewerentz's opinion was too long, giving prominence to just the central part. The different solutions also included the raising of the central part of Riksplan—the square in front of the parliament—not only to strengthen the principal axis of the composition, but also to divert the traffic towards the two sides, thus giving more emphasis to the historic route linking

Study drawing, 1962–64.

Helgeandsholmen to the castle. In his transformation of the square, characterized by numerous small buildings and an intense commercial activity, Lewerentz sought to restore the atmosphere it had before the construction of the parliament building.
To this end, the architect suggested that shops and spaces for street traders should be located on the new level area along the west side of Norrbro. The design of the area, however, was not limited to a new layout for Riksplan, but also extended beyond the Strömmen to Gustav Adolf Torg and the surrounding area, where Lewerentz proposed adding five storeys to a historic building, which he converted into a hotel, returning it to its previous use.
As far as the extension of the Opera in this area is concerned, the architect designed a building that jutted out over the waters of the Strömmen, where he planned to locate, in addition to the service rooms required by the theatre, a café and an exhibition gallery. Thus, the new building assumed an important role in the cultural life of Stockholm.
Despite contacts with the city's technical office and numerous meetings with representatives of the institutions involved, the project was not realized, and it was not until 1969 that the problem, which was now urgent, was addressed again. In fact, this was the year when Lewerentz was invited to participate in a competition, limited to the Nordic countries, for the design of the now indispensable extension to the parliament building on Helgeandsholmen. No longer with Peter Celsing, who was partially involved in the previous project, but this time with Bernt Nyberg, he proposed a new solution for the area surrounding the parliament. Still convinced that the main problem was that of harmonizing the existing building with the urban layout and history of the area, he satisfied all the requirements of the programme by placing four separate blocks, similar to each other and of the same height, close to the three main elevations of the parliament building. Thus screened, the old building considerably reduces its excessive visual impact on the skyline of the island, which—in Lewerentz's opinion—recovers its identity.

Chronology
1962–64: project (with Peter Celsing).
1969–71: competition (with Bernt Nyberg).

Bibliography: Celsing 1964; Ahlin 1985b, pp. 222–24.

(N.F.)

Elevation, engraving, 1969–71.

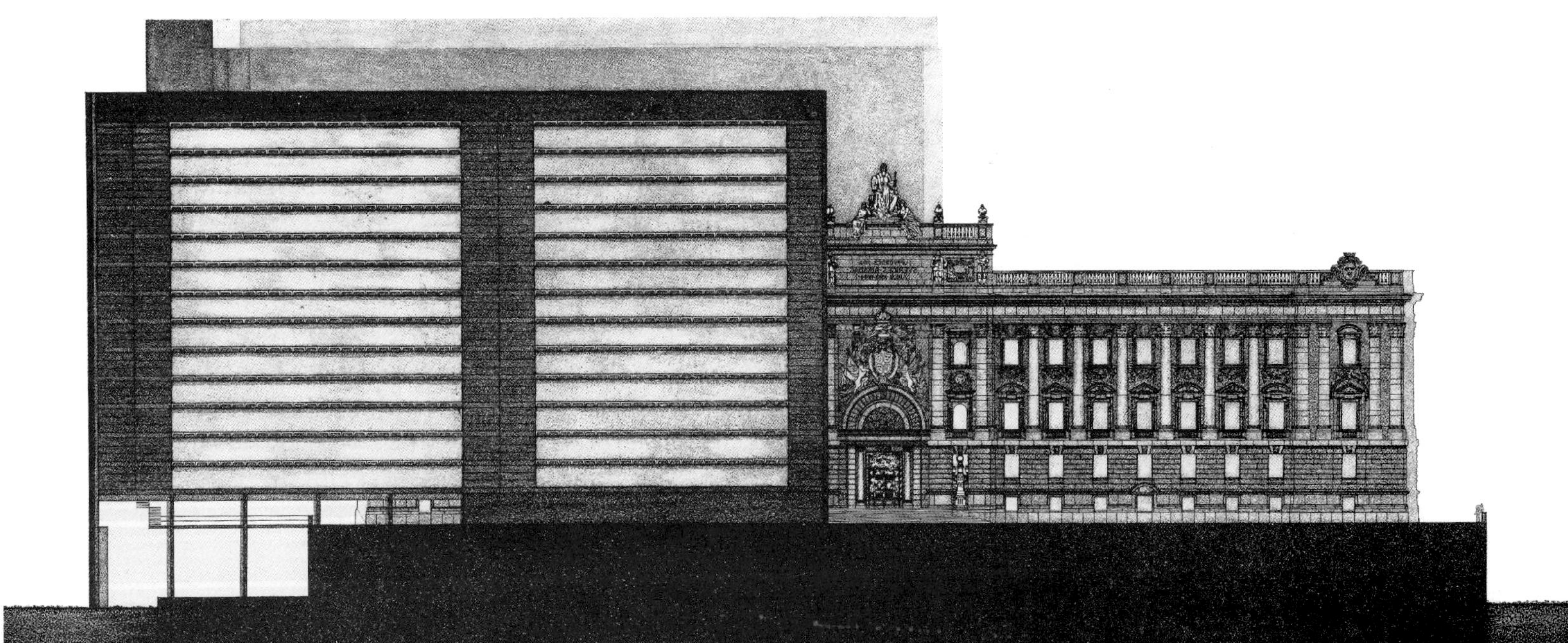

Photomontage, 1963.

110. Competition Project for a Parish Church and Adjacent Buildings at Växjö, 1974

with Bernt Nyberg
motto "Circondare" – citation

Now eighty-nine years old, Lewerentz participated with Bernt Nyberg, his pupil and friend, in the competition for the design of a parish church and associated buildings at Växjö, a town in southern Sweden. Abandoning all traditional forms, the buildings proposed in the project express a clear desire to recount the absolute in the simplest possible way Lewerentz's recourse to the eternal geometric figures of the circle, square and rectangle—independent entities with distinct functional specificity, disposed asymmetrically on the site so as to establish reciprocal relationships and tensions—reveals the extent to which he has now reduced his architectural language to bare essentials, devoid of any rhetoric or formalism.
The church, in particular, with its completely closed cylindrical form, may only be entered through a small opening placed on the same axis as the raised rooflight (having a quarter-circle section, the latter's length is equal to the diameter of the church). The interior consists of a simple space where the altar is the focal point of the service: made sacred by the gentle overhead light, it is a place where the hardness and purity of the materials help to create a timeless environment for meditation. By expressing their individuality, the other two buildings—containing activities linked to the life of the parish and independent of the church—create vibrant tension in the external space, which thus assumes a quasi-urban character. It is, in fact, a sort of courtyard that, conceptually speaking, is reminiscent of the Piazza del Duomo in Pisa.
The project was only awarded seventh place in the competition, demonstrating that it was difficult for the committee to accept it, although they favoured projects that made use of structures and systems deriving from Lewerentz's St Mark's and St Peter's churches. These had now gained wide currency, but were not themselves sufficient to express the need for total silence to which the now elderly architecture aspired.

Bibliography: *Circondare* 1974, p. 19.

(G.P.)

View of the model.

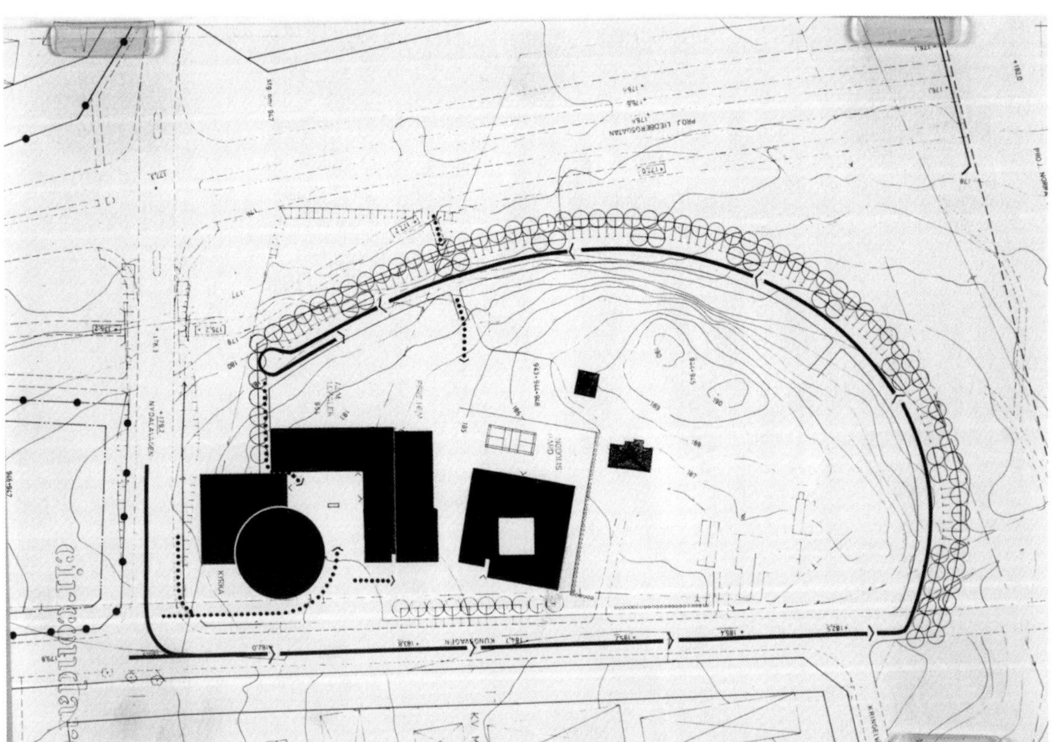

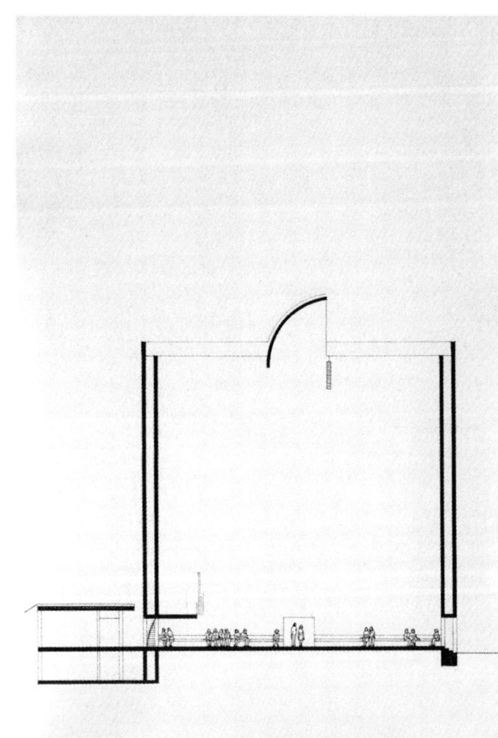

Site plan and section of the church.

Drawing of the interior of the church.

111. Project for Slottshagen, Helsingborg, n.d.
(attribution uncertain)

112. Study for a Column, n.d.

113. Seaside Villa, n.d.

A number of similarities to the Villa Edstrand at Falsterbo (1933–37) suggest that this project by Lewerentz should be dated to the same period. The resemblance to the internal distribution of the second version of the project for the Villa Edstrand may even indicate that these drawings are related to a later version of the same villa.
The layout of the villa, which has three storeys, is organized around the diagonal shift of a rectangle, which, depending on the specific requirements, has different dimensions. Surrounded by a large garden enclosed by a high wall, the ground floor comprises what is probably an area for parking cars and, in the centre, the staircase leading to the residential floor. Supported by pilotis and with strip windows along the whole perimeter, the villa is clearly inspired by Le Corbusier's work. On the first floor, Lewerentz locates four bedrooms, the kitchen and the living-room, while the two main bedrooms are situated on the second floor, where there is a large open balcony divided from the rest of the floor by a curtain.

(N.F.)

114. Project for a Funerary Chapel at Hotagen, n.d.

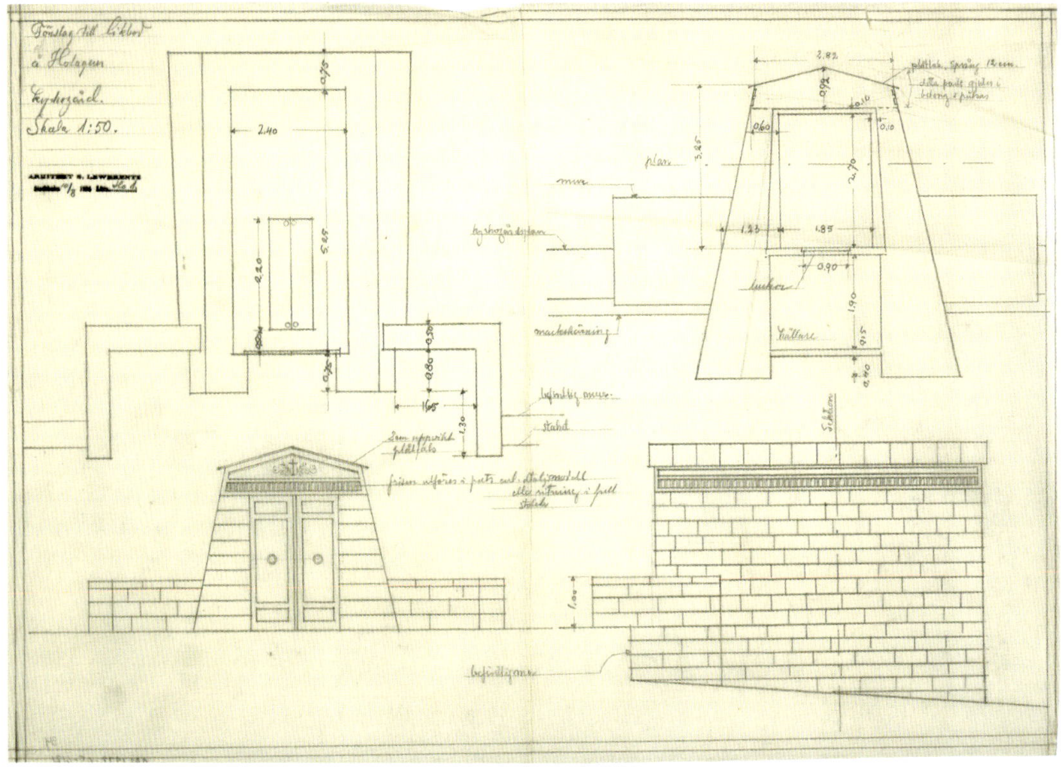

Plan, section and elevations.

115. Project for an Altar, n.d. (second decade of twentieth century)

Study drawing.

116. Lovön Pavilion at Drottningholm, Stockholm, n.d. (second decade of twentieth century)

View of the pavilion.

This small pavilion, located in the royal garden at Drottningholm, the holiday residence of the Swedish royal family, has a wooden structure and is closed on three sides, while the roof imitates the style of Chinese architecture. Inside the building, a large circular mirror placed in front of an opening of the same size creates an interplay of reflections and symmetries that alters the observer's perception of space. In the 1930s the end wall was decorated with a painting of a garden pavilion set in a Chinese landscape.

Bibliography: Caldenby 1997, pp. 84–85.

(N.F.)

117. Project for the Interior Design of a Cinema, Stockholm, n.d. (second decade of twentieth century)
with Torsten Stubelius

This project for the interior design of a cinema at number 7, Stora Vattugatan, a street in the centre of Stockholm, involves the replacement of all the internal and external window and door frames, the painting of the rooms, a new lighting system and the renovation of the entrance hall. In their introduction to the preliminary project—nothing of which, unfortunately, has survived—the architects describe the work to be undertaken: "The walls, including the mouldings and the central panel, of the entrance hall, should be made of pine. In the entrance area and the projection room the floor should also be in pine. A part of the loadbearing frame of the highest floor ... should be made with a framework of joists covered with flooring consisting of 1½-inch boards. In the projection room, furthermore, another floor should be built for the equipment. On the lower part of the front facing the street there will be a single revolving door in pine, with three glass cases for the display of posters. The seating will be of just one type, with folding seats in pine. In the hall, as well as in the cinema itself, the skirting board is in pine..."

(G.P.)

118. Competition Project for the Bekå Department Store, Malmö, n.d. (1930s)

Elevation of the department store.

Appendices

edited by Gennaro Postiglione

The Resurrection Chapel

Sven Markelius

In the plans for the Enskede Cemetery three separate spaces were provided for chapels. E.G. Asplund completed the Skogskapell, the Woodland Chapel, in the autumn of 1920, and a short time later he finished the Resurrection Chapel as well, to a design by Sigurd Lewerentz. The only project not to have been built is the one for the third space, the largest of all, intended for the cemetery's principal chapel and located on a slight slope, opposite the main entrance and closely linked with it from the architectural point of view.

The Resurrection Chapel is located in the southern part of the cemetery, on the boundary which runs through much of the wooded area, and it is designed in total harmony with the surrounding architectural landscape.

The path planned at this point will naturally be bounded by the large area set aside for the chapel and closely linked to the architecture that characterizes the entrance to the cemetery: this path represents the natural point of departure for anyone heading for the Resurrection Chapel. The area, which is connected with the central part of the cemetery, constitutes the route of access to the other chapels and houses, in addition to the Resurrection Chapel, two more buildings of a distinctive character. The first of them contains five mortuary chapels and the second a small waiting room. The juxtaposition of the buildings and their architectural forms appear well suited to the requirements of the geographic location and the aesthetic intention, and are at the same time traits characteristic of the architect's work in general. The most notable feature of the building is its relative elevation, something that was intended to create a contrast with the existing Woodland Chapel. It is interesting to note how this contrast, perhaps not entirely deliberate, is in harmony with the natural elements that characterize the vegetation and the lie of the ground. Asplund wanted to build his chapel right in the middle of the wood, sensing that, through its limited elevation and exteriors that almost vanish amidst the dense and tall pines that surround it, an architectural unity endowed with force and agility would be created. The Resurrection Chapel represents the culmination of this architecturally formal environment, surrounded by the wood in a natural way and connected with a number of areas of regular shape intended to house tombs. The chapel stands among the tombs which, owing to a natural depression in the ground, are situated at a lower level than it is. As a result the chapel, ringed by trees, stands out from its surroundings.

The peculiar design of the building, with an asymmetrical atrium, is in part motivated by the underlying intention: its principal lines can be traced back to the requirement, already mentioned at the beginning, of maintaining a style in keeping with tradition. Thus the construction of the monumental atrium becomes a natural consequence of the desire to emphasize the main entrance on the grand avenue of access and to delimit the cemetery with rich and precious architecture. So the chapel is, as might have been expected, very tall and has a length that is visibly greater than its width: proportions that are reminiscent of traditional churches and that give the rooms inside a highly original character. The white stuccoes of the walls are studded with figures in soft and contrasting colours, indigo for the ceiling, black for the crucifix and the few chairs and a delicate, rust red for the altar. The floor is decorated with designs in white marble and mosaic. The illumination of the room is of great interest, with light entering through a single large window set in the south wall of the building. At the time of day when funeral ceremonies are usually held, sunlight falls on the bier and altar, attracting attention to them. In a similar manner, the position of the organ and the choir show that the aim of the architectural composition is to give greater expressiveness to the ceremonies. The singers in the choir and the music of the organ are heard from above, through holes in the walls: the location of the organist and choristers in a position where they are not visible from the main room is carefully designed to avoid giving mourners the impression, inappropriate in these cases, that they are in a concert hall. Thus the musical accompaniment at funeral ceremonies is clearly conceived as a secondary factor.

The sacristy and the mortuary chapel, situated close to the entrance on the left, both demonstrate the care that has gone into their location, which has an appropriate intimacy that contrasts with the more official character of the main room. The first room is painted a pale violet colour, dotted with the silver, white, black and gold of the furniture and other fittings. The particular position of the second room, smaller and more secluded, helps to create a calm and meditative impression that is well suited to its function. In this room too, designed to offer a moment of privacy to the distressed mourner, the architect has given proof of his singular ability to find means of expression suited to the creation of a particular atmosphere. The ceiling and walls are covered with grey velvet, part of which is draped. The floor is decorated with a mosaic of white marble.

The building, thanks to donations from the Eva Bonnier Fund, has been embellished with a precious work of sculpture, Ivar Johnsson's group *Kristi uppståndelse* (*Resurrection of Christ*), set in the tympanum of the atrium. The group, which consists of the figure of Christ in the middle, flanked by two angels, occupies only the central part of the tympanum and therefore conveys a sense of incompleteness. It is worth mentioning here the desire of the architect and the sculptor to complete the group with two reclining figures that would have filled the lateral parts of the tympanum. On the tabernacle, set above the altar, a fine stucco frieze by Karl Dahlquist represents scenes from the Bible.

To formulate an overall judgement, it can be said that the building's role is perfectly reflected in its artistic completeness and in the architect's ability to create forms that are well-proportioned and elegant, but at the same time grave and solemn. The melancholy atmosphere of the place never becomes depressing and the fullness of expression never lapses into sentimentality. The form speaks a pure language, in which the clarity is not lost in the confused murmurs of a setting of mystical nature. In its completeness, this form constitutes a precious contribution to our more modern architecture, and

one to which it refers in its most artistically elevated moments. And I am not referring here to those stylistic elements that are closely related to the Greek, classical and in part Egyptian tradition. These are no more than superficial and petty details, although expressed with a beguiling delicacy, which do not invalidate the overall value of the work. Its fundamental value lies in the extreme coherence of the architectural solutions with the atmosphere of the sacred place. This work will unquestionably outlive the classical style from which it takes its inspiration.
(from *Byggmästaren*, no. 20, 1926, pp. 233–37)

The Church at Klippan

Sven Ivar Lind

As soon as it was finished, the church of St Mark for the Skarpnäck parish at Björkhagen was considered to be Sigurd Lewerentz's masterpiece in the area of church design. But if the first reaction was positive, later judgement was less so. The quantity of works created by the architect is limited, but their quality is undoubtedly remarkable. The various works present different characteristics and what unites them is neither form, nor a typical approach, nor the repetition of a particular motif.
In the history of art and in the art of our own time it is possible to recognize highly personal languages and identify the master or the pupil. The gallery owner and sometimes even the critic do not find such a language very interesting. In fact, it is not this that gives a work its vitality. The personal style can have a certain weight, and therefore be of value in any form of communication, but it also entails limitations and risks.
An eminent critic has recently written, on the subject of another contemporary master, that the architect was able to create a world of his own through a rich production characterized by a personal touch, from the drawing of the plan down to the smallest detail, utilizing in a brilliant manner the formal means at his disposal, the undulating line and the fan shape. Yet it is not in the language of form that we find the roots of Alvar Aalto's power. The more personal and original the language, the more recognizable it is. But this represents a risk for the work, which can turn into an enclave closed off to reality: a private area inside a public room. Artists run the risk of being encapsulated or rejected as something extraneous to the body of the society in which they operate.
A formal style can become a handicap that the artist has to overcome, or it can represent a mask through which it is necessary to bring out the expression. The architect's purpose is not to create a private world. Pupils acquire the language of their master, but they cannot possess his mastery of it. This, in fact, does not involve controlling a technique, a material, a body of knowledge, but controlling ourselves. It is for this reason that the master is his own best pupil.
"By dint of constructing", says Eupalinos, "I am convinced that I have constructed myself". A form of expression, a technique or a formal solution to a problem can be defined as masterly. Once created, it can be possessed or utilized by all, with or without mastery; mastery does not necessarily follow form.
In the works of Sigurd Lewerentz we seek the architect's personal style in vain. Obviously this does not mean that recognizable forms, materials and ways of using them do not reappear, as in his last designs of churches: the characteristic Helsingborg tile, the iron girders, the vistas in concrete. None of this is personal and the techniques used are not new. The method and the creative process are apparently characteristic, but in reality it is a question of something more profound: what commands is the creative gene.
Lewerentz's expression is harsh, devoid of sentiment and functional. Yet all this prose of the object functions as poetry. How can this be so? We are no longer able to endure orators, visionaries and aesthetes. Everyday objects, on the other hand, such as Tessenow's towel rails and wash basins, can evoke fresh air and gurgling water on a sunny morning. Too sophisticated a style makes even the clothes we wear every day look ugly. An ordinary message dressed up as eloquence becomes ridiculous. But what happens when the language of the everyday is raised to the level of poetry and experiments with imposing and penetrating force? When poetry makes its way into a grain of sand or a simple metal tube? The artist, an observer of reality, may be able to mediate and pass on the intensity of his impression to the gaze of observers, bringing them into direct contact with reality, in a gentle or brutal way. Observers, revealers, have to respect reality in order to be able to discern other concepts or ideal visions. To do this, they must have a great deal of patience, critical capacity and passion.
"Accepting existing reality: only in this way..." Such an argument invites misunderstanding. The artist will find the reality behind its conventional image. Passionately, patiently, he has to look at and question everything, to be at one and the same time sceptical and open-minded: doubting ready-made formulas, staying open to all possibilities, trying things out over and over again. Such an attitude frees him from prejudices, doctrines, the system and routine and leads to a supreme, although uncomfortable, liberty. It is not big or small questions that are required to assume this stance. Everything is essential, but each thing is located on a different rung of a ladder, like the universe and the atom, the organism and the cell, the whole and the detail, even though they are all indissolubly bound together.
What is primary and what is secondary depends on the point at which the observer finds himself, the place he is coming from, paradoxically free from analysis of flows and any coordinating plan. For such a passion, work is a door opening onto reality and reality is the great illusion.
In the churches at Björkhagen and Klippan, dating from the same period, the same technique was applied but different solutions were devised for a single problem. The Klippan church is not a repetition of the Björkhagen church. As at Björkhagen, the building is divided into two blocks, one subordinate to the other, with a room in the middle, but the relationship between these volumes is different. The two units are blurred and in part richly and freely articulated. Yet the whole is strangely solid, composed and restful. The interior of the church and the secondary parts connected with it constitute its centre. Other spaces terminate at the central part through two sides and form the courtyard. This ensemble is more united and denser than the Björkhagen church. Moving around the four parts of the nucleus, which remain closely linked to the whole of the organization, it is possible to sense the different value and the various nuances.
The angular shape of the courtyard creates an internal area sheltered from the wind, and its two hinges can be perceived simultaneously. The different effect of concave and convex underlines the relationship between nucleus and external part. The architectural pattern is so simple that we always perceive a clear image of the totality and, at the same time, of each part's place within it. This sensation appears evident and natural. However, the simplicity in the pattern underlying the construction has nothing schematic or systematic about it. The church's interior is extremely simple. At Björkhagen there are two pronounced corridors linked by an arch, from east to west. At Klippan the plan is square and the arch connects the south and north sides, while the supporting girder, which creates a T-shape, supports the other two sides, from east to west. The walls stand opposite one another, facing a central point. The solution is of no particular technological interest, but has a clarity that gives it an essentially symbolic significance.
Many of our churches have a chancel in the east, a vestibule on the southern side, a bell-tower with a clock to the west and a sacristy on the north side. The church at Klippan is radically different from this scheme. The building has a central block, which is left empty to the east, south and west, while all the minor functions are located in the northern part. The rooms set aside for young people have a separate entrance from the rest, situated on the ground floor, so as not to interfere with civil activities or religious festivities. The organ has been dismantled and subsequently located elsewhere, leaving a large empty space. Passion and devotion have led the architect to consider all the details, especially in this project, where the details and the whole are inseparable.
(from *Arkitektur*, no. 5, May 1968, pp. 2–13)

Sigurd Lewerentz's Last House

Bernt Nyberg

During the thirties Sigurd Lewerentz, his wife Edit and their three children lived in three different flats in Stockholm and in an old miners' hut at Üto. These and the architect's subsequent temporary homes are worthy of particular attention.

Sigurd Lewerentz never designed a house for himself but, after moving from Stockholm to Eskilstuna in 1943, was driven by circumstances to set up his flat in the attic of the building which was to be used for the production of doors and windows to his patented designs.

In 1958, as a result of problems with his wife's health, Sigurd Lewerentz moved to Skåne. The couple went to live on a typical farm in the area of Mellangatan, at Skanör, part of which had already been converted into a habitation, and renovated it at minimum expense. Lewerentz created a basic studio above the old stall, with aluminium facings, and set up two drawing tables in it. It was in this room that, with the help of a few assistants, he drew up the project for the church at Klippan and completed the project for the Malmö Cemetery (Östra Kyrkogård), as well as those of the two houses in concrete.

The flat at Skanör was similar to the attic at Eskilstuna and was designed entirely to meet the couple's living needs. When Edit Lewerentz died in 1969, many of the rooms were suddenly left empty. Sigurd Lewerentz looked for a new home and in 1970 moved to Lund, where he lived in an ascetic manner until the end of his days. His home and studio at no. 26 Kävlingevägen were fitted out by the owner of the apartment, who worked in close contact with Lewerentz.

The two architects spent five intense years in those rooms, over which time they took part in the competition for the Parliament Building and received new commissions for the Woodland Cemetery (Skogskyrkogård) and Östra Kyrkogård. The project for the church at Växjö stimulated his imagination again, giving rise to surprising and personal artistic solutions. For example, he made use of the designs of some upholstery in the style of the thirties. A model of wooden chair, followed by the model of a table, was created for a young colleague, and both were patented on 14 January 1976. In addition, a competition was held for the decoration of the Klippan church and its parvis. Sigurd Lewerentz, however, was not very nostalgic about his past. Today the archives contain indexes and lists he compiled himself. Most of the work has been done. Pencils still lie on the illuminated table in his room, as if it were just another working day.

(from *Arkitektur*, no. 2, May 1976, p. 2)

Sigurd Lewerentz

Bengt Edman

Almost all the architects who made a contribution to the creation of the Modern Movement—Gropius, Mies van der Rohe, Le Corbusier, etc.—were born around the middle of the 1880s. Sigurd Lewerentz and the better known Gunnar Asplund were born in 1885. Lewerentz lived longer than any of the others: he died in Lund in 1975 and was working up until the end, still attracting a great deal of interest right up to the moment of his death.

Myths and legends have grown up around Lewerentz, certainly not because this is what he wanted, but simply because everything that he did caused surprise by the innovative character of its solutions, and opened up new prospects for the colleagues who followed his work. It can be said that Lewerentz's long life and career represent a piece of the history of architecture—even though he was formally not even an architect but an engineer, something which bothered him at times.

From the outset his training was moulded by his experience of manual work: during the holidays he worked in the forge of his father's glassworks, and quickly learned the art of the blacksmith from the skilled craftsmen there. This practical activity was in stark contrast with his theoretical studies, and it is probably the source of his distrust, expressed on many occasions, of excessive theoretical speculation. The reason for a lack of truth, in his opinion, should be sought in the materials themselves.

The view that Lewerentz's production was very limited, in both quantity and range, is as widely held as it is mistaken. It is true that many of his projects were never realized, partly because of his intransigence with his clients, but there are at least 150 projects, relating to the most varied problems, stretching from chairs to urban development schemes (with a certain predilection for sacred themes) and comprising, among other things, designs for upholstery, a grand piano, industrial buildings, gardens, dwellings and public buildings. On top of all these activities, he ran a factory producing metal doors and windows that he had designed himself.

If in a certain sense his vision of the world was formed while working in his father's forge, Lewerentz was later to explore the world of architecture through a journey he made to Germany and Italy from 1907 to 1910. In Berlin and Munich, working with architects like Theodor Fischer and Richard Riemerschmid, he came into contact with the ideas of the Deutscher Werkbund, which had been set up in those very years.

With Riemerschmid he worked on the planning of Hellerau, a garden city on the British model on the outskirts of Dresden, for which he also designed details for industrial production.

Returning to Sweden in 1911, he opened a studio in Stockholm and started to work as an architect in his own right. The first thing that drew attention to him was a competition project for a crematorium in Helsingborg, drawn up during a brief stay in Lugano.

The project was not realized, but turned out to be important as it marked the beginning of his friendship with Gunnar Asplund. The two architects, then around thirty years old, decided to take part in the international competition for a cemetery in the forest to the south of Stockholm. There has been much debate over the role that each of them played in this celebrated work, but it is clear that Lewerentz's contribution has been greatly undervalued, and it would be worth going into the question more thoroughly.

After a life of relative anonymity, Lewerentz suddenly became very well-known, and not just among architects, at an age when almost all his colleagues had stopped working. The church of St Markus was consecrated in 1960, when Lewerentz was seventy-five, and that of St Peter seven years later.

(from *Spazio & Società*, no. 23, September–December 1983, pp. 98–105)

Classical, Christian, Socialdemocrat Asplund and Lewerentz's Funerary Architecture

Demetri Porphyrios

Asplund and Lewerentz were among the first to awaken an acute consciousness of the aesthetic of absence. Their cemetery designs and funerary architecture testify to a certain symbolist concern with form; indeed a quest for the representational forms of death. In this essay I will discuss first the planning of their Woodland Cemetery in Stockholm and then proceed with an analysis of the Woodland and Resurrection Chapels.[1]

In their winning scheme for the 1915 Woodland Cemetery competition, Asplund and Lewerentz divided the site into a number of densely forested burial grounds that were bounded by serpentine roads and walkways. And while the divisions of the site appear arbitrary, they were not meaningless. Both the character assigned to the burial grounds and the allées proposed serve as dramatic illustrations of the central theme the architects had in mind: to establish a symbolic liaison between nature and death.

The cemetery was conceived as a woodland burial ground; an idea that was current in contemporary German cemetery planning. However, compared with the entries awarded second and third prizes, the winning scheme by Asplund and Lewerentz places an exclusive emphasis on the state of tranquility that nature could be made to evoke.[2] Nilsson/Samuelson and Claesson/Wadsjö opted for the idea of a cemetery in the image of a meandering *city beautiful*. They displaced the suburban typology of the popular at the time *garden city* from the world of leisure and commerce to that of transcendence without the slightest reservation as to the trivialization that such displacement might engender. By contrast, Asplund's and Lewerentz's scheme shows their predilection for the "holy calm", that "blissful liaison" between self and world so much cherished by the romantic consciousness.[3]

The attitude suggested by this mode of experiencing nature is one of subjective containment and withdrawal. The visitor or mourner contributes to his experience which is, in this sense, never objective. Physically, he is very close to nature, almost touching; intellectually and psychologically he is separated from nature by the topography of death. Nature here offers a kind of analogical justification for death: the artifice of nature itself serves as warrant for the mute nostalgia that accompanies death.

At the same time, such mythmaking—the association of nature with death—avoided the sinister iconographies of death so common in the popular imagination of nineteenth-century northern Europe. The terrifying mediaeval mask of death which in the nineteenth century was made to inhabit the picturesque, Gothicized backgrounds of Anglo-Germanic macabre tales, has disappeared. Its place has been taken by a diffuse, yet pervasive, feeling of solitude.

Nothing in Asplund's and Lewerentz's scheme, however, was new; its governing ideas had already featured, though often in tentative and fragmentary shape, in historical sources which the architects themselves so freely acknowledged. The "way of the cross"—the main approach to the crematorium—ascending gradually the hilly terrain and flanked by commemorative stelae, sarcophaghi and monuments, is clearly indebted to the confluent remembrance of the Italian necropolis, the Sacred Way of the Kerameikos cemetery, and the Calvary hill. The seemingly haphazard routes and pedestrian walks crisscrossing the site are certainly motivated by a sort of romantic *Wanderlust* that aims at imprinting on the visitor a variety of vivid, singular and lasting impressions. Finally, the conception of the burial grounds as a forested Elysium[4] designed to console can be traced back to the reforms instituted by the late eighteenth century. And yet, the cemetery plan proposed by Asplund and Lewerentz impressed both jurors and public as a splendid innovation and earned its authors the epithet "masters of the nameless"—*Meister des Namenlosen*; a rare acknowledgement of professionalism in the poetics of death. What lent Asplund's and Lewerentz's scheme the appearance of originality and profundity was the austerity of its formal techniques, the cumulative experience of its unfolding, and the apparent single-mindedness of its authors. By 1940, when the definitive plan around the crematorium was finally drawn up, many changes had been introduced, yet none had disturbed the "holy calm" of the initial plan nor its iconographic mythology.

It would be misleading, however, to suppose that the acclaim the Woodland Cemetery enjoyed, made it into a prototypical example of the genre. Though much of its symbolic imagery was to be utilized in future projects, neither Asplund nor Lewerentz were to resort again to the *parti* of "blissful liaison" between nature and death.

In 1916, only a year after his collaboration with Asplund, Sigurd Lewerentz won a competition for the Eastern Cemetery at Malmö, a project that was never to be realized in its entirety.[5] The gridiron plan of hedged burial grounds is rotated to accommodate both the irregularities of the site boundaries and the small hill one encounters upon entering the cemetery. Prompted by the topography and perhaps still relishing the experience of the plan for the Woodland Cemetery, Lewerentz situated along the base of the hill the main promenade leading from the entry gates to the crematorium. Along this promenade and built into the slope of the hill, the visitor encounters a circular ceremonial plaza, a classical stoa with a chapel and mortuary rooms, and finally the main chapel and crematorium. The conscious disjunction between the geometric order of the burial grounds and the accommodating order of the main promenade, together with the civic solemnity of the ceremonial plaza, the stoa, the chapels and the crematorium, invoke the experience one has when walking along the main streets of deserted cities of antiquity.

A similar, if less dramatic, attitude Lewerentz adopted in his 1923 plan for the Stora Tuna North Cemetery, in Tynaslätten, between Borlänge and Kwarnsveden.[6] Here, the routes connecting the cemetery gates and mortuary rooms to the main chapel are celebrated as planted allées and converge on right angles to the hypostyle portico of the chapel. The burial grounds consist of traditionally aligned graveyards and family sepulchres. And yet, by geometrically disaligning the districts into which the burial grounds are divided while insisting on the meticulous alignment of the grave stelae, Lewerentz manages to impart to the cemetery a feeling of diachrony similar to that experienced in cities that have grown over time. But though urban typologies could not assume a prescriptive role in the design of cemeteries, they were to exert a steadying influence. In his unrealized project for a cemetery in Oxelösund, 1925, Asplund showed a predilection for the walled temenos.[7] The cemetery is bounded by a formal high hedge which describes three geometrically distinct "open rooms." The visitor approaches the cemetery along an axial route that cuts through an informal clearance in the surrounding forest. Upon arrival, one enters a forecourt lined with the sepulchral tombs of distinguished families and citizens and with the main chapel built into the sloping hill. This forecourt leads to a circus-shaped burial ground devoted exclusively to individual graveyards except for the monumental street of family tombs to the east. The crescents have the graveyards of children and the central rectangle those of adults. To the west lies a long and narrow rectangular burial ground with the family tombs. Its two entries are in axis with the adjacent transversal paths and its organization is marked by the lateral displacement between the gridiron of the family tombs and that of the pine allées.

Asplund's originality lay not in his choice of the urban typologies of the temenos, the street or the gridiron plan, but in his subtle derangement of these typologies. A planner's options are strictly circumscribed by *fortuna* and *necessità*; the city of the dead, however, is by definition powerless in the face of these forces: its sole option is that of confronting the reality of urban typologies with the solitude and emptiness of their forms when forgotten by historical time.

I have elsewhere discussed in detail the classico-vernacular sensibility of early twentieth-century Scandinavian architecture.[8] The term *Doricism* I have used has been less of a stylistic label than a description of the primitivist and essentialist strife so characteristic of their work. In conceding that in architecture inspiration can proceed only through distantiation from the model, Scandinavian Doricists abandoned revivalism. What made the rules of revivalism meaningless canons was the trivialization that accompanied the estrangement of style from morality. The almost compulsive reiteration of the "conspicuous conventions" of classicism across the nineteenth century—that splendid age of consumption—suggested to many that such conventions were being devalued through overt sentimentality and false pathos. Thus, by the turn of the century, the conventional language of classicism was generally held to be depreciated. As early as 1906, Tens Norup had commented extensively on the "de-potentiation" of traditional stylistic conventions and the task of Scandinavian architects became the rediscovery of a classicism in which "something fundamental" is given back to form and in which the lost dimension of myth is rekindled.

Hence their nostalgia for an unmodified datum, something "which has not been spoiled," as Asplund said. In fact, Asplund's designs for the Woodland Chapel are eloquent illustrations of this search for an unspoilt classicism. The first project, drawn in 1918, was a curious mixture of a prostyle temple with a temple *in antis*: the distance between the prostyle and the cella was increased to accommodate a vestibule, the organ and ancillary facilities, while two staircases occupied the poché of the *antis*. The classical portico was thus transformed into a loggia. On axis with the entry and in the end of the *cella a baldacchino* mediated between the altar and the catafalque.

The final scheme, though dating from 1918 as well, shares none of the classical aspirations of the first project.[9] In plan, the chapel appears to comprise a hypostyle portico attached to a cella; a *parti* which was to inform also the 1926 chapel by Lewerentz at the Stora Tuna Cemetery. The steep, barnlike roof, however, unifies volumetrically both hypostyle and cella and, in the case of the Woodland Chapel, it allows the cella to develop sectionally into a skylit dome that is supported by a circular colonnade. The catafalque is on axis with the entry and sits near the altar, while a small window illuminates the organ. The circular

colonnade in fluted doric columns makes it clear that the "hall of life" was conceived as a *martyrium*. It was therefore designed on a central plan and, for liturgical purposes, the colonnade of ancient peripteral temples was situated in the interior; a typology to which Ragnar Östberg was to refer again in his "hall of life" for the Helsingborg crematorium of 1920–28.
Apart from this ecclesiastical reference, however, there are no signs that would link Asplund's Woodland Chapel to the stylistic conventions and refinements of classicism. The sources have to be sought elsewhere: in Sebastiano Serlio's house for a farmer illustrated in his *Regole generali di architettura*..., in Andreas Kirkerop's hunting lodge built for the Liselund estate, Denmark, in 1795, or in Christian Frederik Hansen's Gebaur country house of 1806.
And while the first two of these examples point to clear iconographic precedents, the third refers to a source that is more akin in sensibility than in style. In fact, the affinity between Scandinavian Doricism and Enlightenment's predilection for the primitive is quite fundamental: both believed that whereas contemporary architecture had become a species of refined, yet meaningless, embellishment, in primitive cultures architecture performed a necessarily expressive role. And irrespective of whether this distinction needed to be proved, it was considered a ground for asserting the aesthetic and moral superiority of the "homme sauvage."
The enthusiasm for the primitive forest cultures of Scandinavia is indicative of the contempt with which the "Augustan" age of academic classicism was now held. Just as William Morris had questioned the ethics of nineteenth-century industrial capital as a universal morality, so Asplund rejected the false decorum of academic classicism as a universal aesthetic. But if there was no universal criterion of architectural excellence, it was still possible for Scandinavian Doricists to define architecture as an expression of the "unspoilt core" of human existence. Asplund had recurrently criticized the artificiality of academicism which had stifled the originality and spontaneity of his generation. Peasant rusticity, on the other hand, as the youth of Scandinavian culture, possessed a harmony and vigour which was as yet unfettered by the commercialism of the nineteenth-century city.
The affinity between Scandinavian Doricism and eighteenth-century Neoclassicism is not confined to their mutual obsession with primitivism. Both movements were also suspicious of all those preaching for classical revivalism. The same dialectic characterizes both Scandinavian Doricism and Enlightenment Neoclassicism: both appealed simultaneously to primitivism and antiquity, developed tensions with classical revivalism, and launched themselves on the aesthetic of Modernity. These similarities, of course, do not amount to identity. Each movement had its own historical task, defined by its relative proximity to academic classicism.
The progressive architects of the Enlightenment could recognize academicism only in the stifling anachronism of design rules. The *querelle*, seen from a twentieth-century perspective, was not about the propriety of applying anachronistic standards in the evaluation of architecture, but rather about *which* anachronistic standards to apply. In this sense, for the Scandinavian architects of early twentieth-century classicism, the *querelle* was not only impossible to resolve but meaningless. For them, the perspectives of both "ancients" and "moderns" were serious obstacles to an understanding of classicism. For them, the crucial question was not which anachronistic standards to use, but whether to apply anachronistic standards in the first place. The classicism of Scandinavian Doricists, therefore, is marked by a concern for a relevance which seemed to have been lost in the nineteenth-century pursuits for ever more precise historical detail. The habit of nineteenth-century academicism had been that of conceiving the history of classical architecture as a repository of examples for subsequent quotation and use; and its evaluative criteria were based on the proper acquaintance with the minutiae of style that the past could afford. Scandinavian Doricists, on the contrary, could not take antiquity as literally as nineteenth-century antiquarians could: precisely because antiquity had to be wrested from the hands of late nineteenth-century sentimentalism and industrial commercialism.
It is from such a perspective that we should look at the Resurrection Chapel of 1922–25, in the Woodland Cemetery of Stockholm.[10] If Asplund's Woodland Chapel illustrates the period's obsession with primitivism, Lewerentz's Resurrection Chapel describes the period's critical tensions with academicism and classical revivalism. The approach to the chapel is along a Neoclassical axis that cuts through the forested burial grounds. The idea of an axial promenade, perhaps deriving from the Helsingborg crematorium project designed by Lewerentz and Stubelius in 1913, was to feature again in Aage Rafn's project for a crematorium of 1921. In the case of the Resurrection Chapel, however, the visitor, upon arrival, is baffled by the assymetrical disposition of the pedimented entry portico. In fact, the portico is free-standing and (in a way similar to the siting of his chapel at the Stora Tuna Cemetery) stands at the intersection of the axis of the main approach and the route that leads to the mortuary rooms.
The decision to inflect the entry portico to both routes of approach was a later development. The tetrastyle/tristyle portico of the first version frontalizes the portico exclusively towards the Neoclassical axis of the main approach. On the contrary, the portico as built is a double tetrastyle inflecting, therefore, towards both approaches. And though the hierarchical front remains that of the pedimented side of the portico, the pedimented gable of the chapel proper faces the mortuary rooms. This ambiguity is never resolved. Instead, it is intensified by the two entries to the chapel as well as by the architectonic treatment of the "holy window."
Treated as a pedimented tetrastyle portico, this window is made to resemble a miniature temple front that sits on a high stylobate. And yet, its low relief and its relative inaccessibility point to its vestigial role: it is the Holy Window that illuminates the Hall of Life and through which the soul of the deceased ascends symbolically to the heavens.
In direct contrast to the Schinkelesque domesticity of its exterior, the interior of the Hall of Life is markedly somber. The deep sections of the pilasters of the holy window elicit images of steeply tapering dungeon windows and the four volutes that support vestigially the window sill, in their elongated and almost skeletal profiles, prefigure the fate of all earthly concerns. The unadorned walls of the interior are modulated hesitantly by the almost graphic frailty of the engaged pilasters and entablature. Above the entablature the air becomes heavy and dark and the architecture returns to the austerity of exposing the constructional members of the roof—an idea which Lewerentz was to utilize again in his project for the Malmö mortuary chapel of 1926.
The manifest tensions with the language of classicism which Lewerentz explored in his Resurrection Chapel, inform also his 1926 design for the Malmö crematorium. If the Resurrection Chapel stresses the power of unadulterated form and of building technique, the Malmö crematorium stresses the power that form derives from iconography. Funereal iconographic themes from the classical and pre-classical world are subtly interwined with references from the early history of industrial buildings. The tholos of the central conical pavilion alludes to preclassical Mycenaean tombs. The single central column of the pedimented fronts recall the choregic monument of Thrasyllos on the south-east cliff of the Acropolis, later converted into a chapel of Panaghia Spilaiotissa (St Mary of the Cavern). Finally, the conical shape of the pavilions themselves—two of which hide the cremation furnaces and recall Asplund's pyramidal service pavilions in the Woodland Cemetery, 1922—are indebted both to the numerous eighteenth-century projects for pyramidal funerary monuments and to the industrial furnaces of early factories like those depicted by C.N. Ledoux in his designs for the Ville de Chaux. Asplund's and Lewerentz's affection for the metaphysical symbolism of both nature and classical antiquity did not make them pagans; they remained within the Christian fold. Their architecture founded its radicalism in a tenacious ideal: by rediscovering a classicism in which "something fundamental" is given

back to form, they sought an architecture that would enable classicism, Christianity, and social democracy to coexist side by side. They sought for this ideal with all the hesitancy of the pioneer but their ambivalence was conscious and persistent.

[1] For their help and generous response to my promptings for illustrations and material I am thankful to Mr Juhani Pallasmaa, curator of the Suomen Rakennustainteen Museum in Helsinki and Mr Henrik Andersson, curator of the Arkitekturmusset in Stockholm. I would also like to thank Miss Helen Porfyriou for translating a number of articles from Swedish and for her assistance in locating certain bibliographical sources.
[2] For the winning entries of the Woodland Cemetery competition, see *Arkitektur*, 1915.
[3] For a history and description of the Woodland Cemetery plan and its funerary buildings, see the relevant chapters in G. Holmdahl, S.I. Lind, K. Ödeen (eds.), *Gunnar Asplund Architect: 1885–1940*, Stockholm, 1950; S. Wrede, *The Architecture of Gunnar Asplund*, Cambridge, Mass. 1980. Also see the articles by H.O. Andersson, "En del i Naturens Stora Kretslopp," in *Form, Swedish Journal of Design*, 1982, vol. 6-7; B. Johansson, "Skogskyrkogården och den Sanitära Estetiken", in *Arkitektur*, 1982, vol. 2.
[4] For a brief but informative account of funerary architecture in the late eighteenth and nineteenth centuries in France, see R. Etlin, "Landscapes of Eternity: Funerary Architecture and the Cemetery, 1793–1881", in *Oppositions*, vol. 8, 1977
[5] For the Eastern Cemetery at Malmö, see *Byggmästaren*, 1928, pp. 181–88.
[6] For the Stora Tuna North Cemetery, see *Byggmästaren*, 1928, pp. 18–21.
[7] For the plan for the Oxelösund Cemetery by Asplund, see *Byggmästaren*, 1925, pp. 158–59.
[8] Cf. D. Porphyrios, "Scandinavian Doricism", in *Classicism is not a Style*, London, 1982; "Facce reversibili: architettura danese e svedese: 1905–1930/Reversible Faces: Danish and Swedish Architecture: 1905–1930", in *Lotus international*, 16, 1977; see also the relevant notes in my book *Sources of Modern Eclecticism*, London 1982. For a comprehensive catalogue of early twentieth-century classicism in Scandinavia, see *Nordisk Klassicism/Nordic Classicism: 1910–1930*, ed. J. Pallasmaa, Museum of Finnish Architecture, 1982.
[9] Asplund's Woodland Chapel was frequently published in Scandinavian periodicals. See, for example, the articles in *Architekten*, 1923 and 1929. Also see Holmdahl, Lind, Ödeen, op. cit. and S. Wrede, op. cit.
[10] Lewerentz's Resurrection Chapel was published in *Architekten*, 1923. The issue of *Arkitektur*, September 1963, no. 9, was dedicated to S. Lewerentz.

(from *Lotus international*, no. 38, 1983, pp. 59–70)

The Landscape that Can Survive and the Lewerentz Connection

Alison Smithson

The first recognition of a style—the landscape that can survive—is to be found in the commonality that exists in the ordinary language of urban infil, everywhere.

Some sort of dialogue with nature has always been the regenerator of landscape style.

A dialogue with nature in a different geographic location to that which energised the English Landscape Garden Style is one of response to a terrain that in England is barely 2½ degrees of latitude further north; the heartland of the Landscape Garden is the Midlands and that of a natural-seeming-landscape-that-can-survive is in the Pennines and the Cheviots.

Attitudes to a man-made landscape capable of survival evolved in the middle of the nineteenth century, for functional reasons, when the idea of public parks meant that these places had to accept mass use by all classes: an idea so unusual that Olmsted remarked on the good behaviour of working people in Paxton's park at Birkenhead.

The idea taken by Olmsted to New England returned to Scandinavia, where, again, the inescapable characteristics of a geographic landscape, that had to be worked with, resulted in another idea about a dialogue with nature. Undoubtedly, the weighing in favour of Scandinavia taking-over as lead-energy earlier this century, can in part be ascribed to Olmsted who—claiming the purpose of Central Park, 1863, was "To provide for the masses of the city a brief equivalent of a visit to the countryside"—largely accepted the thin-soil he was working on in New York, as the generator of his style. It may even be that the majority of public parks first made in Europe, were on rotten land, unused by virtue of being otherwise unusable... like the Parc des Buttes Chaumont in Paris being old quarries.

Olmsted's knowledge of European public parks, their building, their use; their then fairly short history, meant a return influence was not without meaning.

Add to the thin, Scandinavian-type, soil coverage of New England, a possible instinctive predilection on Olmsted's part—traces of an inherited sensibility—and we have the invention, the landscape that can survive.

With the invention of the motor vehicle, it was the survival capability of the Scandinavian-type nature that became its prime asset.

The style is basically what will survive the passing vehicle; discourage encroachment by the passers-by who are not neighbours, but whom-so-ever the motor vehicle has brought to pass; a means of landscaping that can withstand the ravages of winter and wind in the opened-up city; manage to look presentable with only rational care.

In Scandinavia, at the turn of the century, there came an appreciation of the forest clearing—engendered by nineteenth century prosperity-given-leisure... the concept, and taking, of the long holiday... together with a period of affluence that coincided with the passing, into nursery stock, of so many of the eighteenth and nineteenth century plant discoveries.

The Scandinavians in particular included in the language, the leaf interest of the incredible variety suddenly become available.

Thus, by the 1930s, we came to have a fully fledged landscape that can survive, its attractions underwritten for European Municipalities of that decade of the 1930s and the 1950s—for there was a gap—by democratic socialism and the new-programme social-building-types and the public works. That is, for the period just passing, democratic socialism changed men's minds; for many, like a new pair of glasses, made them see things differently.

The imprint of Stockholm's interchange, 1936 was considerable. This imprint carried over therefore—despite the gap—to when the problem of all Europe was remnant space. All spaces filled by planting were residual, the fall-out of other decisions incompletely taken... taken without a sense of connections; so that, everywhere, to make good, we find Scandinavian-nature-type low-growing shrubs grouped at the foot of slab blocks, ornamenting all suburban junctions, making neat the run-in to all motor-way intersections... on the march, in boxes, down pedestrian malls. But the landscape that can survive can stretch only so far... it can cover; look presentable... but it cannot make meaningful the city pulled apart.

The Swedes are aware, that despite intention, Scandinavian-nature-space, dating from the 1930s and 1940s, shown in the photomontages of that time to be joyfully used by the city dwellers at their leisure, is empty. The success of the city transformation, has removed the old functional underpinning of the shared open space. The dispersed urban densities leave not so many people to sit on the ground. Less crowded houses do not impel people out of doors.

Leisure patterns have changed; bifurcated towards the more structured and the disconnected or apart participation... that is, concerned with listening to, or watching, or working machines. Open space of the social democratic type has been found both too unprivate—that is without obvious connections yet insufficiently public property to be inviting to use well. Paradoxically, the old Swedish private parks are more popular... perhaps exercising a right adds a frisson.

Everywhere we have the decision to make as to what we want places to go as. Open spaces in the city we need to re-tune towards the urban, so that urban sense again flows overall and does not suffer rude, suburban, punctuations.

Outside the cities we need to renew the idea of the enjoyment of the natural; even the idyllic... and possibly even extend our choice into some as yet undefined new-place-for-man-to-be-in-nature.

It is time for a reconsideration, a redefinition... for landscape that is a true extension—in the sense of a limb or a finger—of the aesthetic of buildings that no longer leave remnant space... that is the buildings also reach-out in their aesthetic. A sense of territory underpins civilisation. Disregard that sense and we get a vulnerable society in a vandalised place; a disintegrative attitude instead of a sense of a community-in-a-place; loss of identity instead of natural confidence. Territoriality is part of the meaning of architecture... is part of the aesthetic and intention of the Economist Building; where a sense of progression to the entrance, an attenuated approach, allows a person to leave the city behind to enter another-paced-place, that of work and to enter self-collectedly.

We wrote on the heroic Period of Modern Architecture: "The next collection of the architecture of our own period will be quite different for it will not record 'buildings', but built-places...". In today's invention of building types, the open spaces are a natural part of the structuring of the inside spaces; their use-pattern is one of connection; their function, extending the possibilities of the pleasures of inhabitation, for a society in which "leisure" takes on strange, new meanings.

Second recognition: "the Lewerentz connection" my seeing a language of landscape, shared by architects extending their particular Scandinavian inheritance.

Lewerentz and Asplund stepped out of a neo-classical inheritance; into making something to do with an appreciation of their forests... and undoubtedly, this is being extended, yet again, by Pietila and Erskine; working their buildings into nature.

To make the neo-classical connection clear: Scandinavian Neoclassical is what we call Custom's House neo-classical; clear representative of the style and you can find it in sea ports the world over. The style's importance in this story is that it speaks lucidly of the wonders of the platform that is the made-level surface; the capabilities that build the perfectly smooth ashlar wall (implied if not in actuality); the column that stands for civilization's capabilities and pleasures arrived in yet another place; the pediment of careful completion... with all the overtones of careful order... even if it is the careful, beautifully written book-keeping skills of trade such as Schliemann deployed... a new dawn of everything, as it were rising from the sea: it is these notions and the spirit they represent, that identify the true Neoclassicism.

So Lewerentz and Asplund stepped out to extend this inheritance with its notions of the level platform, that as a master stroke establishes a sense of order ... and this they thought about throughout their lives, working with these everlasting ideas and relating them to the pleasures of the forest floor ... the clearing in the forest and its softly undulating surface ... a sibilant play, like the story whispered in the pine tops ... for this reticence, this understatement, is in neo-classicism: to quote ourselves: "... understatement to the point of anonymity".

My recognition of the extension of the landscape language was in the work of Lewerentz in the cemetery at Malmö, 1926–73. I saw it related to the lines of pollarded trees and clipped beech parterres of Sweden's baroque manors and domestic-scale royal houses; whose inspiration was through trade connections with the Hanseatic ports and the Low Countries when the Baltic was a pond.

In the Forest Cemetery, Stockholm, 1917–40, both Lewerentz and Asplund extended the aesthetic of the forest clearing, remembered with relaxed affection.

Our interest in Lewerentz is his inventing a language we might call trees that became buildings... a grove of column trunks truncated, some still growing, some made building.

Out of the as-found, Lewerentz has trunk columns roofed amid tree-columns standing around in the open. We find variations of light as we move through and around this part built, part still growing forest. Columns are rooted, as by their bases firmly as pine trunks are rooted to the ground to become built-trunks among growing tree trunks; the extra size of these trunks among columns of the forest draw our attention, bring our attention to entrance, form the interlude between the weather outside and the protected peace inside. In this natural-seeming way, the stand of column-trunks ceases to have dominant overtones of classical portico; it is the essential sheltered-clearing that allows entrance, it is the Scandinavian respite before the door.

The walls of the chapel receiving growing shadows, moving in their season; these trees—as detached columns—gather around as column outriders of the building to form the preliminary skin to the outside wall, making little connections, stitching the building into place. This is a trick that Lewerentz carried with him to his last chapel. Around the chapel, the forest floor undulates and stresses the wonder of the flat plane that is respite before entry, and a tongue of the inside floor, as it were, stuck out to get the taste of first snow. Including the pine trunks in his realm ... with column-shafts-that-are-the-built-world, is something Lewerentz invented ... and extended at Malmö ... in this place, Lewerentz includes the clean sharp sand of the lakeshore. Trees ... columns... roofs ...The lean-to sheds that at Malmö form respite before entrance seem Piero della Francesca's Nativity shed built.

Now Asplund at the Forest Cemetery, Stockholm; first the forest is cleared and distanced before the building can begin... here the suavity of clearance is the pause that allows the building in this place. Where the built-respite begins is the first column-trunk at the edge of the clearing. The column'd respite is echoed by a formal grove also at the edge of forest; here the mottled black of the birch trunks seem to have built-in dappled shadows that indicate another idea about edge... dark edge of forest, dappled edge of grove; protection offered by edge of building. In the way the building groups around the built grove that is respite before entrance, a steading is established. Within the column grove, there is light falling, indicating another protected clearing that echoes the greater: illuminates a man-made order on a platform laid down in the greater undulating landscape.

The recognition of what Lewerentz was about was made easy for us by Asplund, who by being revealed to us in a book in the late 1940s, made us aware of a whole other language, rooted in inheritance and springing to life in the 1930s.

You could say there were ready made connections in our experience for my seeing this now-you-have-column, now-you-have-tree; for the column as trunk—the astonishing Bramante column with branch-stumps seen by us in 1951 in the cortile of Sant'Ambrogio, Milan. Myself prepared by a previous discovery in 1949 of a column embossed by heraldic fleur-de-lis. These tree-trunk columns prepared us also for seeing lines of pines in the early 1950s, when in our jeep on the All Roman road in Norfolk; on this dead straight road, lines of pines that are field divides, crest the landscape as the jeep moved past.

Taken together, all these earlier sightings, allowed the insight in Sweden (May 1981); in addition, receptiveness to the message from the two Scandinavian architects was already in our work... we had, in 1975, begun to build our respect for lines of trees in the landscape... in an area, not far from Warwickshire, where there are the traditional black and white inns, manors, farm houses ... timber and plaster in a green landscape with trees. Tree portraits, taken at dusk, to enable us to accurately portray mature hedgerow trees ... you remember our landscape inheritance is 2½ degrees of latitude further north and therefore the landscape-feature-trees of the Midlands and south are wonderful things to us.

These were the site trees around our Lucas H.Q ... Lucas ... a line of trees ... a steel frame; the building steps through the landscape. The size of the mature trees represents the "genius of the place". If we think of the English Landscape as a large garden, undisturbed trees have the ability to transmit, to a new building, an established look, so that the amalgam, building-trees, has already an ageless quality; is already part of a continuum to do with growth and change.

How people arrange themselves to work in the building will hopefully owe as much to the trees as to the structure. The line of the old hedgerow trees laces the built to the ground; lacing, then taken up, as an interplay between a red structure... and a line of trees.

Lines of trees act as dividers to space between wings of the building; a territoriality line is thereby drawn, a natural seeming line, older than the building, an inheritance of space, under, and either side of a tree. These tree-line-penetrations of the building cluster act as natural screen-divisions, more permanent than some internal divisions... tree lines indicating change of pace and mood between departments of the occupying organisation. The interpenetration by the family of trees-of-an-age, integrate man and shelter with landscape as found and the whole mood of renewal of the landscape by the new structure lacing through, is one of reticent manners as in-comer.

Whether we absorb anything of the tree-as-column-outrider in our line of trees ... a steel structure ... lies in our future ... it will show only an appropriate site, an appropriate programme, calls the theme up again.

(from *Spazio & Società*, no. 25, March 1984, pp. 78–85)

On the Centenary of Sigurd Lewerentz's Birth

Stefan Alenius

We walk towards the walls. There does not seem to be any road leading to them. It is not a main façade or a well-defined entrance that has brought us here. Perhaps it is just our dedication and the help of a tortuous path covered with stones that has drawn us to this point, along perhaps with the lure of these extraneous but at the same time obvious walls. They are concealed amidst the trees and with their numerous joints and bluish, grey and pink bricks, the walls look like splotches of colour, almost like birches or the shadows of birches. Why not invert the perspective of time? The older walls have coloured and stained the young wood.

It is only when we have traversed the last section of the path that runs through a courtyard, and reached the construction, that the buildings of the church in the courtyard in the middle of those of the parish become visible and we actually realize how low is the level of this ground. At this moment, it feels natural to stop and look around.

The first thing we notice is the disposition of the two buildings. The administrative section is a long and narrow, single-storey construction with a low-vaulted roof. The building is set in a north-south direction and one side faces onto the light railway that brought us to Björkhagen. This "outer façade" is treated in a different way from the other façade facing onto the courtyard. On the courtyard side the vault of the roof projects outwards. The masonry and the windows are very different on the two façades. The balanced style and striking appearance of the outer side contrasts with the one facing onto the courtyard, which is more restrained and varied. The front that you go past before arriving in the courtyard has an imposing bell-tower, a two-storey-high brick cube.

The other construction is made up of two units. One for the congregation of the parish, parallel to the administrative building and at a right-angle to the church, and the church itself, which is oriented in the traditional east-west direction and forms the other "outer façade" of the whole complex.

The church also presents two different façades. The one facing outwards is the higher of the two. The construction for the congregation which gives onto the courtyard is lower and has a vaulted roof. Unlike the long and regular vaults of the administrative buildings, these are set at a right-angle to the longitudinal direction and emphasize the entrance function. A large wooden roof on the front of the building for the congregation facing onto the courtyard repeats and reinforces this character.

From the point where we stopped it is difficult to imagine the entrance that leads directly into the church through its south wall. In fact it is concealed by projections of the walls and the only thing that suggests the existence of an entrance is the fact that the path keeps going. While the roofs of the entrance into the courtyard resemble the canopies of railway-station platforms, the entrance of the church maintains its original form and grandeur, although it is partly hidden by more recent constructions. One senses the three-dimensionality of this construction. We think about the masonry: no wall in the zone looks like another. The variations from façade to façade are remarkable. Even individual parts of the same façade are very different, but what predominates is coherence. It is the "same" wall that runs along the entire group of constructions. It is a wall rich in variations that renders the work of the masons visible. The result is an old-fashioned, "hand-made" wall. One is reminded of ruins, of the remains of ancient buildings. Only among the ruins of Rome and Hadrian's Villa have I found the same imposing masses of masonry as in the church at Björkhagen. Nature blends with the walls to the point where the "feel" of the walls is impressed on the passers-by, who caress it and run their fingers along the joints. There can be no doubt that Lewerentz wanted to give a character of antiquity, of original walls, to the constructions at Björkhagen. A guiding thread of vitality in his interpretation of the concept of church.

It was there that everything was born! Not in the young and aggressive Roman empire, nor in the more mature and expansive one. In its maturity and its slow decline ancient Rome shifted to the composure of Christianity. Early Christianity expressed itself through a tradition that was still Roman. The basilica with its nave and aisles and the apse of the chancel was adopted by the first Christians.

We see how Lewerentz interpreted the church by giving the greatest importance to the different sources. The theme of the antiquity of the walls is supported by the modelling of the ground. To place the entire complex on the same level it was necessary to excavate the hillside, allowing the wood, situated at a lower level, to penetrate into the slope itself. Where the different levels meet, the masses of earth have been arranged almost like "excavated dikes". It looks as if the constructions have been "dug" out and are located on an "older" stratum of ground. The surrounding constructions, on the other hand, are located on a more recent stratum. The trees have insinuated themselves into the zone of the excavations. The church becomes the most ancient element of the place. The walls inside which the present church is set link the activities of human beings to this old stratum of the ground. It seems as if the old church has preserved its original level from the deposits of time, continuing to dig into the hillside.

We try to follow the trace of this association of ideas as we enter the church, passing through the almost hidden main door on the southern side. Outside we were in the shade of the birch trees, but the passage from light to darkness is really abrupt. The imposing character of the walls outside and the desire to touch them are replaced by the opposite impression: the confines are dissolved in the semi-darkness. The low direct lighting, bulbs hanging from brass lamps, creates reflections on the vaults of the ceiling. Darkness above and warm reflections around the benches on the floor. Space and light become visible. As our eyes grow accustomed to the dark we slowly begin to perceive the weight of the walls and once again the combination of the vaulted brick roof and the tiled floor creates a sense of balance and absorption between light and space.

In the contemplative peace and quiet of this setting we begin to study the structure of the building. There is a nave with an altar at the end, toward the chancel. And there is one, and just one, lower aisle. The corridor and the aisle to the north are united by a large opening. A single sturdy column of brick supports the beams above. Once there might have been more columns. However, it became possible to dispense with these when the wall was united, acquiring solidity and the capacity to support the enormous span. We carry on with our association of ideas. The twin of the large opening on the opposite side was closed when the aisle to the south collapsed and the congregation, in order to preserve the house of God, turned the south side into the new outer wall. Although secularisation has pushed the church into the background, its absence is keenly felt by the faithful, who have taken steps to keep it alive. And this is possible thanks to those who will still find their way there even though the exterior is hidden!

Small openings remain in the outer wall, in particular the clear indication that divides the chancel from the nave: the important mediaeval distinction between choir and church. This deep opening, which reaches as far as the floor, plunges the choir into a more profound darkness. At the same time, it seems as if the trunks of the birch trees come into the church. Nature has taken the place of the missing aisle: it has been transformed into an element in tune with the architecture, with its light, its space and its walls, which seem to underline this essential duality.

It is only when we come out from the back of the church and enter the rooms set aside for the congregation that the "place" of the church's interior is revealed in all its completeness. Here we find again Lewerentz's clear modes of expression: the same walls and the same material reappear. The union of the surfaces of the floor, walls and ceiling stands out, together with the relationships of light and depth. In the part of the congregation, what prevail are bricks, clinker, terracotta, concrete and wood just as they are, without dualities. These rooms do not have the same coherent structure as the church: here the ceilings and the walls are in net contrast. The brick walls seem to have been retouched with modern means for modern purposes. The differences lie in the meanings, the atmosphere and the use. The building is rich in details and variants on the theme. Without being too obvious, the clinker floors form new designs, cheerful in the part for the congregation and more serious inside the church. The concrete or wooden structures of the ceilings indicate a modern adaptation of the requirements of support of the old walls on the part of the churchgoers. The vaulted ceiling of the church rests on metal flanges similar to the old wooden frameworks. The church spreads out from the heavy bottom to become a tall space, again with a sense of absorption. One wall of the choir is inclined inwards. This is an allusion to the mediaeval model in which such an inclination represented Christ's head, tilted on the cross. The benches have all been located in the nave since the collapse of the southern aisle. Hence the central passage has been displaced to the side.

There could be more of these examples, and their interpretations. Anonymous and without pretensions, it is protected by the wood and its custodians. It is not formally linked to the younger constructions around it and has no ambitions to stand out in an age of "transitory" secularisation.

All that has been said about the church at Björkhagen is valid for the one at Klippan as well. In addition to more specific interpretations, we find the same register: bricks, concrete, wall and simple cubical forms. We recognize the calm, apparently modest tone. The materials are the same.

And yet Klippan is another entity, a different construction. Like two twins growing up in different environments, these constructions are formed or deformed by their surroundings. A group of birch trees (typical of central Sweden) gives the church a different appearance than it would have on the southern plain of Sweden.

If we want to use a similar interpretation to that of Björkhagen for Klippan, then we get these impressions: the low building hides from the wind, pressing itself against the ground. The ground becomes the sloping floor of the church. Lewerentz has found an ancient culture to excavate in the ground of Scania. It is as if the church had been kept alive by this ancient base: the roots of the church are in history.

The models, drawings and reports indicate a persistent interest in the elements of the architecture. Lewerentz works with natural and obvious elements. He is the Carl Rydberg of architecture. In the drawings we find the tints, the colours, the movements of the hand and an illusory richness of light, air, drama and completeness. In the architecture these elements become elements of construction, arranged in a natural way and interpreted on the basis of existential qualities. In Lewerentz, the objective is the fundamental.

It would be easy to look at the material, the construction and the building alone. But this evident objectivity would lead us to forget the morphology of the architecture.

In his ordering of the principles of architecture, Lewerentz does not just use positive elements, the objects of architecture. He also uses contrasts, "empty" elements, and out of these he composes the objects, which are hollowed out of the mass—the spaces! Structured air, space and volume.

Obviously, we find the same elements with the same basic simplicity on the outside. Perhaps these characteristics are even stronger at Klippan. The expression of the building touches us immediately, but the attentive observer will not fail to notice the same elementary structure in the spaces as well. These principles form a sort of "original level". From this point of view, Lewerentz reminds us of Louis Kahn, whose work seems to be imbued with the same balanced contemporaneity of space and object.

Look at the façades at Klippan. Don't we find the same motif? With a precise modelling, with the clear-cut openings of the windows, the façades circumscribe the space, which at bottom is the purpose of the construction itself. This is conveyed through the massive masonry as well. The space and the object find a balance and give the walls a sense of transparency.

Let us go inside! The church's isolated column supports, as if it were a hand, the imposing brick vaults with beams. This generates the low and broad structure of the church, with flexibility and clarity. The space and the structure are balanced, in contradistinction and in precision.

In the architecture of Louis Kahn this contradistinction contains a note of theory and pedagogy. Kahn wants to tell us something, wants to be understood. He wants to teach. Lewerentz has chosen silence over words and profundity in execution. Perhaps this is the reason he is so little known, in spite of the magnificence of his architecture. That is how it has been up to now, for everything is there waiting for us...

(from *Casabella*, no. 528, October 1986, pp. 42–51)

The Resurrection Chapel

Luis Moreno Mansilla

The first work by Sigurd Lewerentz (1885–1975) barely escapes the silence that hangs over those architects who, gifted solely with an acute sensibility, make no apparent attempt to translate the fascination of the modern.

And yet, while history, like Saturn, devours its children, contemporary critics are looking back and rediscovering architects like Lewerentz, in whom a lively imagination is combined with a rich heritage of imagination and inspiration. This is a heritage whose roots lie in classical architecture and which constitutes the basis of the nationalisms from which they derive, as a final resource, a fertile, though critical, relationship with the past, and with contemporary thinking. It is from this situation, in which the debate between classicism, functionalism and nationalism unfolded at the beginning of the century, that we can approach the intimacy of the Resurrection Chapel, not so much with the pretence of uncovering its more or less hidden intentions as with the desire to draw attention to the value of such a refined, complex and enigmatic work.

The Resurrection Chapel, completed at the end of 1925, constitutes Lewerentz's best-documented contribution to the cemetery to the south of Stockholm, for which he and Asplund had won the competition years earlier, shortly after the latter's return from a visit to Italy.

Asplund had constructed the Woodland Chapel in 1920 and Lewerentz, as had been agreed, was supposed to draw up the design for the new commission: a chapel situated close to the way of the seven fountains, in the south of the cemetery. The vicissitudes of this commission are recounted in great detail in Janne Ahlin's book *Sigurd Lewerentz, Arkitekt*, published in Stockholm in 1985. The first sketches of July 1921 convey the impression of a chapel-passageway, implying an unusual conception of the rite. The funeral procession was to enter from one side of the chapel and leave from the opposite side, with the emphasis placed on the space traversed rather than on the more orthodox position of the altar. However, the idea appeared too far-fetched to the archbishop of Stockholm and was rejected.

In April 1922, Lewerentz resumed work on the project and the new designs were approved at the beginning of 1923, with a few reservations on the part of the client with regard to the heating and the position of the chapel with respect to the natural light. However, Lewerentz did not accept these objections, thereby adding to his reputation as a man who was fairly difficult to work with.

At the time the work was only studied by a few architects, among them Sven Markelius (who was present at the chapel's inauguration) and Nordenstrom. The latter made a thorough study of the measurements and proportions and analysed the use of the Fibonacci series. According to Nordenstrom, two different series were present, on different bases (8 for the outside and 7 for the inside), with absolutely no connection between them, echoing the distinction between Le Corbusier's blue and red series which characterized the elusive ambiguity of the French architect. In the entrance doorways and the portico, however, both series were used in a subtle alternation. In any case, Lewerentz was irritated when he found out that correspondences had been pointed out which were not part of his intentions.

On the other hand, the report on the project, written by Lewerentz himself, provides no clue that might help in the interpretation of the work, but confines itself to a brief enumeration of the duration of the work, its cost and the artists who contributed to its realization.

A visit to the cemetery, on the outskirts of Stockholm, is a pleasant and surprising experience, largely as a result of the great sense of peace that pervades the place. In Asplund's chapel and crematorium you do not get the bittersweet feelings aroused by a visit to classical ruins, perceived in terms of their remoteness and uniqueness and which runs the risk of turning into a moment of pure contemplation. What you feel here, on the contrary, is a sense of reverence for a beauty that is still possible, that provokes a burst of admiration as well as a responsible desire for analysis.

Even at the height of winter, sunshine contends with shade, through the tall pines, for the dominion of a tranquil site, where the small tombstones set up to commemorate the death of a beloved companion are sometimes flanked by folding chairs of wood and iron.

As we walk along the paths, we leave behind us the iron fountains in the form of Roman basins, which cancel out the centuries and embrace the past, reducing life to a single instant.

Approaching the chapel slowly, we discover an enigmatic building, against the backdrop of a tetrastyle portico of classical appearance.

Arriving from the north, the sun, which can still be glimpsed behind the chapel, casts a permanent shadow on the asymmetrical, austere and polished wall (Lewerentz's collaborators suggested inserting a console in the wall, but the architect rejected the idea forcefully, provoking not just a fierce argument but also the scepticism of his colleagues over his technical abilities. In my view, this absence of ornament was more than justified for reasons that will be analysed later). Behind the portico, a set of blank walls is faced with a copper surface that has a green patina. This facing appears to underline the inexorable passing of time, in the sense that matter has to metamorphose in order to stay alive, just as inert copper comes to life to acquire the patina of eternity.

The path leads into an open space and, entering the portico, we see on the left, among the columns, a fountain of cylindrical shape, the fountain of life, perhaps a baptismal font or the seventh well. It is water that, in its perennial cycle, emerges from the ground, turns into vapour and returns obstinately to fall on the earth as rain.

Let us now put forward a hypothesis of interpretation. The Resurrection Chapel represents an apparently simple iconographic cycle: the portico is an architecture of the past, just as at this moment life has passed, but it is also relevant to the present, as it has been resuscitated from classicism; it announces the refuge of the gods and the passing of that threshold, and leads to a blank wall, mute and sombre. In my opinion this represents death, and the interior of the chapel embodies resurrection. The scheme is debatable but not illogical: life, death, resurrection. Let us go back to the portico. The floor is made up of a central part of pale stone, slightly raised in the middle, constructed out of Ingenberg marble. Consequently, in order to enter the chapel, it is necessary to go up a gentle slope and then down again. Clearly the intention is to make rainwater drain outwards. Yet it also appears to symbolize the life cycle of ascent-descent, concealed behind a functional alibi, or vice versa, and this dual character is a constant feature of the work, which combines intensity and ambiguity, capacity to suggest different contents and to exclude them at the same time from a univocal interpretation. The outer columns stand, on the contrary, on a somewhat less geometrical base of cobbles. This change of paving, from flagstones to cobbled surface and then to the gravel of the open space, is a tragic reminder of the progressive crumbling of life into death. Everything disappears, reduced to dust.

And so we come to the wall, in which the only thing that is visible is a heavy bronze door, opening onto the outside. The resurrection is not a door that opens easily and therefore one that requires personal effort.

But here we come to our first surprise: as we approach, we notice a wedge of light separating the chapel from the portico. This gap, though so small as to seem almost incredible, is clearly visible in the plan. And it can also be admitted that the pediment at the rear contains at least a hint of decoration, which renders more explicit the deliberately fragmentary quality that has been so much talked about. This rear pediment, which no one has seen, symbolizes the other side of life. Life is separate from death, and death and resurrection appear to be two sides of the same coin. Between them, if we draw closer, there is only the light of hope. But we shall come back to this subject.

The chapel, blank and bare on three sides, does not conceal, as might be imagined, a dark room. On the contrary, light floods the room, entering through a large window in the south front, opposite the entrance and at the most distant point. Moreover, the nave in which we are standing has a different orientation, since the side, east-west entrance, and the congregation, gathered in solitude on mournful black chairs, designed by Lewerentz himself, face towards the altar and, beyond it, the east, from where the sun rises each morning. Following an almost Egyptian ritual, the mourners will go out from another door, facing west, to bury the deceased, at the point where the sun dies only to be born again, and then descend the slope towards enormous pine trees.

The water that bathes the floor constitutes a metaphor of the natural cycle of this element and at the same time is a refinement of the crematorium project that Lewerentz had drawn up with Stubelius for Helsingborg in 1913, in which a stream crossed the building orthogonally, entering tranquilly under a vault over which Hades presided, to emerge from the other side in the form of a vigorous waterfall, symbolizing the renewal of life. The floor of grey marble mosaic is not a perfect geometric plane, but undulates gently in a manner that recalls the exterior.

The roofing seems light and almost airy, inasmuch as the walls draw back in a obvious manner, apparent in the plan, and the long but slender roof seems almost unsupported, creating the impression that air circulates between wall and roof, or that the roof is raised above the walls, letting through the air, or perhaps the souls of the dead.

Thus a subtle iconographic cycle is completed: the ancient classical atrium and the roofing marked by the passing of the years suggest the continuous flow of time. At once close by and far away stands the dark wall, death, announced by the fountain of life, i.e. eternity; the chapel is flooded by an inner light, unexpected and profound, in which we identify with the eternal return of the sun, dawn, sunset, dawn.

But let us go beyond this and look at the chapel again, from the viewpoint of an almost exclusively architectural debate over classicism and functionalism. Now we are faced by an enigma. Let us analyse the plan and the longitudinal section. The inner walls are adorned with a double order of columns in relief, made out of stucco, that runs along all four walls in a manner that is surprising to say the least. We notice that the number of columns on the south wall does not match the number on the north one. In addition, the columns are not even set opposite one another, but slightly staggered. On the south wall they pass beyond the large window and their double order is interrupted as we approach the central wall, to the east. Towards the north the double rhythm of the columns is maintained until it disappears abruptly, in the vicinity of the wall with the altar. The latter is decidedly symmetrical, in apparent contrast with the irregularity that characterizes the rest of the complex. Speaking of a work like this, so refined and inspired by the canons of the classical world, it is difficult to attribute the lack of regularity to structural shortcomings on the part of the architect. I am more inclined to see it as deliberate. But why?

Jannin speaks of an abstract subdivision, in which the pattern of geometric relationships is what matters. Thus, on the altar wall, the surface of the lower part forms a square and that of the upper part a rectangle placed horizontally, both disposed according to the Fibonacci series. If we look instead at the areas bounded by the rows of columns, we find a different, almost opposite relationship, between the vertical rectangle at the bottom and the square above. The theme of displacement is to some extent reminiscent of the subtle movements of Villa Snellman, in which a complicated handling of accumulative distortions, probably inspired by Italian vernacular architecture, takes on a greater abstraction, transforming its naturalness into a geometric rule. As early as the twenties, this was used with discretion by Petterson as a way of making the composition vibrate.

It is possible to put forward other, more poetic hypotheses. It might seem, in fact, that the succession of the columns is interrupted to allow a more functional positioning of the radiators, close to the door on one side and to the window and the officiant on the other. In this connection, it should be pointed out that there are two heating systems in the chapel: one consists of the radiators, which Lewerentz describes as independent in his report; the other is the under-floor heating which served the architect as a justification for his choice of a thin mosaic flooring, capable of transmitting heat. Perhaps Lewerentz, without showing it, put functional needs before a more orthodox disposition of the columns, preferring functionalism over classical rules. Could this have been a prediction? Putting aside for a moment the symbolic interpretation advanced up to now, let us place the work in the cultural context of its time. What do we observe? First of all, a classical atrium, a linear and rigorously syntactical piece of architecture, respectful of the tradition of a certain logic of construction, and moreover isolated, separated from the chapel. Separate because the latter was designed on the basis of a very different architectural concept, which excludes any possible link or continuity with the classical atrium. We do not find ourselves, as in Asplund's chapel, in front of the concept of Christian unity, which fuses and separates body and soul into *loggia* and dome. What we are faced with is an attempt at synthesis, already classical in the Scandinavian architecture of the period, between the wall as vernacular architectural element and the *loggia* as classical reminiscence. An attempt, moreover, to force a dialogue between a syntactic architecture with echoes of ancient Greece and another, spatialist one, filled with references to Rome and decidedly modern.

So the architecture of the chapel is one of walls, without decorations on the outside and spatialist on the inside, although without renouncing the ornament of the columns. Even the abstraction is not homogeneous, as it is in the portico. Let us go back now to that decorated pediment at the rear, as if there should be nothing behind, while here there are four distinct walls. Consequently, the decoration is arranged freely, without any syntactical presupposition on the inner façades, in accordance with the particular composition of each part. The walls become independent of the structure represented and the latter is disposed with a rather strained elasticity.

But it needs to be asked whether this structure is figured, is really decorative, or whether we are faced instead with an anticipation of the open plan, in which completeness and structure are about to be dissociated? Nordenstrom explains: "The columns are not in themselves architectural structure". Jannin, for his part, sees in the chapel "an external space, in which the walls are almost immaterial planes".

Let us return to the plan. Is it not true that the walls withdraw as they approach the roof and that they therefore support almost nothing? Does this not mean that they turn into partitions of a certain thickness? Is it not true that the pairs of columns rest almost exclusively on piers that are in the end not so false, by means of architraves which, if it were really just a masonry structure, would make no sense?

In our opinion Lewerentz, caught up in a personal debate between classicism and functionalism, designed a complex work that induces reflection, in which he covertly sought to unite two quite distinct approaches to architecture. Thus the chapel became a polemic and subtle dialogue, in which a masterful work of classicism concealed an exploration of modernity. What we shall never know is whether this work was dictated by an intention that, in the key of an enigma, heralded a then imminent future, or was born instead out of regret over an inevitable evolution.

These notes, which I dedicate to C.P., originated in Stockholm, following a conversation between myself, P. Feduchi, A. Soto, R. García de Pablos and L. Nuñez.

(from *Sigurd Lewerentz, 1885–1975*, exhibition catalogue, Madrid 1987, pp. 27–38)

Sigurd Lewerentz

Janne Ahlin

Lewerentz had a long life—some ninety years and five months, to be exact—and was one of the last surviving members of that generation of architects born in the 1880s who had such an enormous influence on the development of Modernism during the 1930s. He was not in the limelight the way Asplund was, and only much later in life did he enjoy the reputation and standing due to him. Without Asplund's quick intuitive facility, his rise within the profession was slow; but ultimately all the characteristic features of his genius emerged. Lewerentz was the eternal researcher. A continually active worker, he got by on only a very few hours of sleep; it was as if there were a burning fire within him—a fire that also forged and annealed those who worked with him.

One of the founding fathers of early-twentieth-century architecture, he was the very first in Sweden to have close contacts with the recently-established Deutscher Werkbund in Germany (partly because in his youth he had served as an apprentice with various important architects within that movement). Lewerentz made a hugely important contribution to the Classicism of the 1920s, and his works for the 1930 Stockholm Exposition deservedly attracted great attention. However, he then chose the path of a "solitary wanderer" and was "forgotten"—partly, no doubt, due to the difficulties encountered in the designs for the Cemetery in the Wood and the Malmö City Theatre. His reputation spread further afield only after his long work on proposals for the restoration of the Uppsala Cathedral, as a result of which architects were more attentive to his work, raising him to the dangerous position of a sort of demigod. Later he would design two churches that made his name known world-wide. Lewerentz worked on various types of projects: from simple workers' houses to public residences for aristocrats; from factories to churches and burial grounds; from offices to the design of shop fittings; from furniture to urban planning and a whole host of inventive objects produced in his own factory.

He never held a teaching post. Stones, not words, were the constituents of his language.

Working Methods

Lewerentz's sketches and finished buildings reveal that all phases in architectural creation are an act of will; they demonstrate how insidious circumstances can be, underlining the contradictory role of the external conditions within which the architect must strive for, if not clarity, at least coherence of composition. The buildings preserve traces of the work of creation behind them—traces which reveal the struggles that the architect must go through before he can claim that a building is finished. All of this is very clearly legible in Lewerentz's late work. His style changed over time, and yet it is not stylistic differences that are the most important thing to note when studying his creations. Even if there are recurrent themes within them, his buildings are very difficult to imitate, and impossible to re-create elsewhere. Lewerentz had no followers in the strict sense of the word; his method of working made such a thing very unlikely (whereas more or less gifted admirers could launch into imitations of the buildings of Alvar Aalto, Frank Lloyd Wright and Mies van der Rohe).

Unlike certain radical architects, Sigurd Lewerentz was never a visionary who aimed to overthrow the world's existing order; in this sense, one could even deny he was a radical. However, his radicalism lay elsewhere: in the surprising ways in which he confronted the very task of construction. His method of working meant he did not keep a large architectural studio; normally, he worked with only a couple of assistants and a secretary. He wanted total control over the work process, and his assistants were responsible solely for producing the fine copies of architectural drawings, creating models and, sometimes, carrying out on-site inspections. Lewerentz took all the decisions himself and, without a word of explanation, would simply present them to those working at the drawing-boards (what explanations he might give concerned technical and practical problems). In effect, the architect never put his ideas or his aesthetics into words; he communicated them in silence, using energetically-sketched pencil drawings or indications of a particular way in which materials should be treated or employed.

Certainly, this does not mean that he was indifferent to aesthetic considerations. Throughout his life he was fascinated by the mathematical concept of the golden section, and when at home would enthusiastically explain its characteristics to

his family, applying its proportions to those of his own buildings (sometimes using Fibonacci numbers as his units of measure).
Symmetry was another thing that fascinated him—or rather, the ways in which he might work upon deviations from the symmetrical. His drawings show how, through slight shifts and deformations, he managed to imbue the symmetrical with dynamic movement. He was all in favour of shifts away from the lines laid down by the established grammar of architecture, and sometimes used planes resting on circles or squares in order to set up tensions within a closed space.
Another non-conventional element —perhaps the most important of all —was the role played by the direct study and observation of nature. Lewerentz regularly went on excursions around Skärgarden, the archipelago on which Stockholm is built, and made a very detailed study of the district around Utö. The moss, stones and waves of the area could capture his attention for hours and hours, and might then reappear in the choice of a colour or a design feature, in a building or in an object of everyday use. This study of nature was how he escaped from a, perhaps, oppressive workload; and it was not unknown for Lewerentz to become so engrossed that he would even forget the family who were waiting for him.
Clearly, his intense inner life required continual stimuli; the architect simply could not tolerate being inactive. And he felt happiest of all when tackling a practical problem; this was when he felt he was on sure ground. On the contrary, he reacted impatiently to the demands of a social life which left him feeling unsure of himself. There was nothing to be gained from such occasions, which simply robbed him of precious worktime; when obliged to participate in them, he did so silently and grimly. His happiest and most profitable moments were the evenings and nights spent in solitude. The telephone was off the hook; there was no one to disturb him, no one to look at what he was doing or how he was doing it. Then he was liberated from the embarrassment he would have felt if people discovered how much difficult labour and exertion went into the creation of a single drawing; if they had seen how total the darkness before he managed, step by step, to arrive at clarity. It seemed that each and every time, each and every question had to be re-examined from basics if he was to create a new, sharper form. It was as if he knew that by searching long enough in the darkness he would, in time, break through to the light. Sometimes he would dedicate an inordinate length of time to the completion of a simple job; indeed, simply starting a job was difficult enough. The result was that the relations between architect and client could become very tense, and sometimes he might even be sacked from a job, or have to leave a project incomplete. And thence, obviously, would arise arguments about his fee.
Lewerentz made severe demands not only on himself but also on his client and his assistants. He produced an incredible quantity of drawings which he then left for the latter, with orders that they were to be copied out in fine using a sharpened, hard-leaded pencil. To judge the fruits of his nocturnal labours more efficiently, he used to pin them all up on the walls and then go through them; there might be just the slightest difference between one drawing and the next, but for him each variation was relevant. An outsider looking on might well have taken the whole process to reveal indecision on the architect's part.
Lewerentz always made the final choice by himself—something which distinguished him from numerous other architects, who precisely at this moment of decision-making might draw on outside help. In his case, the one person he was listening to was himself. But once the decision had been taken, it was held to like an absolute truth, upon which there could be no compromise.
He might sit for ages simply contemplating a nail, asking what use he could put it to. It obviously wasn't because he was incompetent but because he realised that if you let things take their time, the most surprising answers can emerge to the simplest of questions.
To his colleagues, Lewerentz—especially the older Lewerentz—appeared a rather gauche figure, out of touch with current trends and practises. The truth was, however, that he turned his back on conventional, tried-and-trusted schema to make way for fresh new ways of approaching reality. And one is most sensitive in these matters when the novelty is still a mute form glimpsed in an uncertain light—that is, before the troops of wordmongers have exerted their systematic discipline over the new discovery. Lewerentz chose to hold rather than give his own counsel; and thus an aura of mystery grew up around him.

Background and Early Years

Let us step back almost one hundred years.
Lewerentz was born on 29 July 1885—the same year as Gunnar Asplund and a year after Oswald Almqvist, the colleague he held in highest esteem. His father was joint owner and manager of the Sandö Glasbruk glassworks in Kramförs, and the young boy would grow up in an area where the glow of kilns and the sparks of smithies often played across the small island in the middle of the River Ångermanälv. After primary school, Lewerentz enrolled at Södra Latin Grammar School in Stockholm, but broke off his studies before taking his baccalaureate. He then attended the Chalmers Tekniska Läroanstalt Technical School, where he studied machine technology (perhaps because his father had him in mind as his successor at the glassworks). However, Lewerentz soon changed his course of studies and five years later, in June 1908, took his final exam in civil engineering. Previous summers he had passed as an assistant mechanic in his father's glassworks, but the summer of 1907 he had spent working at the studio of Bruno Möhring in Berlin, to which he now returned for a longer period of apprenticeship. From there he would go on to Munich, at the time considered second only to Paris as the artistic capital of Europe, working first with Theodor Fischer then with Richard Riemerschmid, both important figures in the recently-established Deutscher Werkbund. In Riemerschmid's studio Lewerentz would work on drawings for the housing in the famous garden city of Hellerau near Dresden. He also undertook a long study trip through Italy before returning to Sweden a couple of years later.
At this point Lewerentz intended continuing his studies at the Architectural School of the Academy of Fine Arts, but then interrupted them almost immediately, joining with a group of students who protested against the excessive traditionalism of the Academy's teaching methods; they wanted more realistic courses that reflected the everyday world around them. The result was the foundation of the Klara Skola, which survived a year. The students were there joined by some of the most important architects of the day, who offered their services as teachers; one of these was Carl Westmann, with whom Lewerentz would then work on Villa Högberga in Lidingö, the home of the writer Claes Fähraeus and one of the most important works of National Romanticist architecture in Sweden.
In September 1911 Lewerentz left Westmann's studio to set up on his own with Torsten Stubelius, who would turn out to be an invaluable partner during these early years; he was responsible for the clients whilst Lewerentz worked at the drawing-board. The partnership between the two architects lasted just over five years, but resulted in a wide variety of projects: designs for housing for industrial workers (rarely built), and other industrial designs for lighting systems, glassware, furniture and upholstery. The two architects showed great interest in the design of burial grounds, making particularly in-depth studies of cremation facilities.
The designs and model of the Chapel at the Helsingbord Crematorium were displayed at the Baltic Exposition held in Malmö in 1914. Even though the structure was never built, it is important because it was the basis for the joint work of Sigurd Lewerentz and Gunnar Asplund on the competition designs for the Cemetery in the Woods (the Lewerentz designs served from the main chapel on the raised part of the site). This first victory in an international architectural competition would lead to both men being involved in a series of undertakings that would ultimately occupy them throughout their lives. After winning the commission, the two young architects prepared an overall plan, in which the light, romantic touch of the competition proposal gave way to a more energetic articulation of the site. Existing

gravel quarries were exploited to create hollows, light-filled clearings were made, deciduous trees were planted so that the changing colours of their leaves might underline the changing of the seasons.

A large model was sent up on a trellis table in Lewerentz's studio, and the two architects circled round and round it, immersed in quiet discussion. Up to this point they had worked on the thing together; but given that it was a very complex project, it was only natural that they should end up dividing the tasks between them. Thus Asplund designed the first chapel, whilst Lewerentz worked on the main entrance from Sockenvägen and the link-up with the existing cemetery of Sandsborg, on the other side of the road. Asplund's second job was the service facilities, whilst Lewerentz went on to design the Resurrection Chapel. Subsequently, he would work mainly on the landscaping—partly because he claimed that Asplund wasn't very interested in the lay-out of paths and in the composition of man-made masses and hollows (what is more, this part of the commission was relatively badly paid). The two architects decided on a joint design for the large chapel—called the Chapel of the Holy Cross—and in autumn 1933 presented the Cemeteries Commission with a finished proposal that contained the core of all the future work on the site: the layout of the landscape, the idea of the pairing of atrium and cella, and even the sculptural group of the Resurrection. The drawings, in the Lewerentz archives, are signed by both men. Then, however, events took an unpleasant turn: Lewerentz became directly involved in the disputes within the Commission and, after some hesitation, Asplund continued work on the project alone. The decision led to a break between the two men.

In 1916 Lewerentz, this time on his own, had won another competition to design a cemetery. On a gravelly ridge in the open countryside of Skäne, in the eastern outskirts of Malmö, he set about moulding the landscape, which gradually acquired a character that clearly reflected the influence of his frequent trips to Italy. Visual images of the Classical began to materialise in the Swedish countryside.

Years of Intense Work

Lewerentz's designs from 1920 onwards generally reveal a more programmatic approach. The free, almost nonchalant, use of pencil and charcoal was replaced by more meticulous techniques, with drawings being produced in hand-mixed India ink on carefully-chosen backgrounds. Lewerentz was assisted here by three highly-skilled draughtsmen: Kurt and Artur von Schmaalense and Gunnar Hoving. His source of inspiration was now Schinkel, whose wonderful perspective drawings were studied in minute detail. The influence of the German architect is fairly clear in the proposals for the Malmö theatre and concert hall of the mid-1920s (the stage is practically a copy of that at the Berlin Schauspielhaus).

In the 1930s Lewerentz would further develop the abstract approach of the previous decade, eschewing decoration and gradually dropping the amenities of classicism whilst still maintaining the firm incisive penstroke of his drawings. He was commissioned to build offices, shops and industrial facilities; at the same time he also worked in the field of design, his IDESTA brand patenting special door and window parts in stainless steel. This later activity started in 1929 thanks to the collaboration with the engineer Claes Kreuger, with whom Lewerentz set up two companies: SL Stockholm Ljusreklam and AB BLOKK. The former produced illuminated signs (neon was then a novelty) and display facilities; the latter, an association of professionals from various fields of the building industry—from planning to actual construction—offered a sort of "package bid" for an entire commission, and worked mainly in the areas of commercial buildings, shop fittings and various kinds of business signs. However, few designs actually got built, the Phillips building in Stockholm being the sole work of importance produced during the period of this collaboration. After a few years, Lewerentz would buy out his partners.

The 1930s were a period of intense work for the architect, with projects ranging from complex urban planning and landscaping to furniture, from graphics to various technical aspects of building and construction. Each waking hour was dedicated to work, and Lewerentz literally burnt up his assistants. However, this decade was also one of disappointments. The bitterest of all was that encountered with the Woodland Cemetery project, but then there were also the difficulties with the project for the Malmö City Theatre. The fact that he was judged incapable of actually carrying out the work—in spite of his excellent study proposal and his victory in two stages of the design competition—was a severe personal blow. However, with a certain sense of solidarity, he accepted the proposal put forward by the Building Committee and agreed to work on " An Architectural Study for the City Theatre" together with David Helldén and Erik Lallerstedt, who had won the second prize.

Many other works in this period did not get beyond the production of designs on paper and blueprint. A lot of this was due to Lewerentz's intransigence over the problems that might arise. He was obstinate and in no way willing to change his mind once he had made a decision. However, in spite of all this, some of his designs did make it beyond the drawing-board. For the Marmaverken company in Söderhamm he designed production facilities and workers' housing; with the Skoghallsverken company he began a collaboration that would last a good twenty-five years; for the Stockholm Exposition he produced various works: from illuminated signs to the large mainmast; from graphics and posters to display cabinets and upholstery; from boats to furniture; from the Gröna Caffè to an apartment and small-scale workers' accommodation (exhibited at the Housing Exposition). During this period he also won the State Public Works competition to build the new headquarters of the Social Security Administration, with a design that blended functionalism with classicism. The offices and warehouses for the Swedish branch of Phillips, built around this time, were even more "functionalist" in design.

Towards the middle of the 1930s Lewerentz began to work with the wholesalers Bröderna Edstrand of Malmö for the sale of IDESTA window frames. For the Edstrand family themselves he designed a holiday home at Falsterbo—a commission that gave him the opportunity to try out various theories and ideas about the expressive forms that could be used in construction work. Here, he abandoned the abstractions of the drawing-board and worked directly to mould the house-in-progress, visually composing the materials at his disposal to establish the rhythm of the construction. Brickwork surfaces and the play in the fitting-together of components became essentially important. Steel girders were left bare; welding and bolts were no longer hidden; he also experimented with new types of door and window frame. The result was a sort of striptease—a "neo-brutalist" construction *avant la lettre*. Lewerentz had found his way forward. This is clear, for example, in the designs of the twin chapels for the Eastern Cemetery in Malmö, where the architect makes full show of his rich knowledge of building techniques. Each detail is handled with precise care: the granite stones in front of the entranceway; the woodwork in the ceiling of the atrium; the sheets of copper and marble; the window fittings, the quality of the plasterwork; the influx of daylight.

The Factory Period

After the war, Lewerentz concentrated on the manufacture of products he had designed himself. He had bought an old factory at Eskilstuna—moving there in 1943—and there set up a top-floor apartment for himself and his wife Etty and a "workshop", as he preferred to call it, which employed a total of thirty men. Now, finally, the meticulous architect could exert complete control over the production process.

Even during this "factory period", however, Lewerentz worked on an architectural project that was destined to last for years: the restoration of the Uppsala cathedral. The project began with a design purchased in a public competition and an outright victory in the competition which followed. Based on the original layout of the fourteenth-century Helge Zetterwall cathedral, his proposal was greatly admired by his fellow architects. The building by this stage had a number of technical problems: the water drainage system, for example, was so complicated that it had led to damage of the walls and decorations. Lewerentz resolved these problems in a very convincing way: modifying the layout of the roof, he created simple and well-articulated drainage channels. He also removed masses of brickwork from the western side of the church, thus re-emphasising its Gothic character. The proposal, however, was blocked by the church authorities, who said they did not want a "drain-church".

Things having ground to an impasse, here—as in other cases—the matter had to be resolved by an enquiry. In the end, Peter Celsing, after being put under great pressure by the head of the Institute of Public Works, Gunnar Wejke, agreed to take on the work, but only on condition that he could work in collaboration with Lewerentz.

The enquiry eventually produced four alternative and one main proposal, but none of them was accepted. The discussion that ensued were really only so much window dressing, and the entire question was ultimately shelved. Celsing/Lewerentz had carried out their task; and nothing more was said about the possibility of continuing with the work.

Grand Finale

At the age of seventy Lewerentz was still working full-time. He was invited to enter the competition for designs for a church and presbytery in Björkhagen, which he won; the resulting buildings made his name known well beyond the limited circle of architects. The designs marked a return to the Helsingborg brickwork of his youth, with no regular system of bricklaying. The bricks seemed to "swim" freely in the surrounding mortar—resulting in a visual image that echoed the dark marks on the white bark on the surrounding birch trees.

Off his own bat, Lewerentz then presented a controversial proposal for a remodelling of the Helgaandsholmen and Normalmstorg; his aim being less to provide the facilities required by the new single-chamber Parliament than to provide a sharper image for the area. His idea seemed to be that, architecturally, the Royal Palace would achieve full significance only if the surrounding buildings were reduced in scale and modified in appearance.

Lewerentz's last works show a further simplification in approach, with the adoption of a leaner language that verges on the poetic.

The Church of St Peter's in Klippan was written in cement, Helsingborg brick, Höganäs clinker, Töreboda wood, stainless steel and soundproof glass. Lewerentz used the light to weave together these materials, claiming to have drawn his inspiration from the brickwork architecture of Ancient Persia.

Yet whilst the Klippan church marked the "grand finale" of his career, there was a *da capo* in the late 1960s with the two cement Chapels and Flower Kiosk in Malmö's Eastern Cemetery (unfortunately the kiosk was later ruined by an amateurish extension).

By this stage Lewerentz was eighty-five years old; and with the passage of time work took ever longer to complete. However, the eternal competitor, he did manage to take part in the competition for the church of Växjö; his designs being one of those purchased. He also designed various chairs in laminated wood and steel tubing (paying particular attention to the design of the backrests). During the autumn of 1975 Lewerentz's strength gradually began to fail him, and he died on 29 December of that year.

(from J. Ahlin, *Lewerentz*, exhibition catalogue, Milan 1987, pp. 6–15).

Skogskyrkogården

Fredric Bedoire

It was clear from the very beginning—that is, from the time of the First World War—that the Skogskyrkgården Cemetery to the south of Stockholm would turn out a masterpiece. And this recognition —and ambition—would make itself felt in the further work carried out there in the period between the two world wars. The artistic value of the site has been confirmed by whole generations of architects from all over the world, for whom the cemetery has become a veritable place of pilgrimage. Today, Skogskyrkogården is recognised as one of the most important parts of the country's artistic heritage—together with Drottningholm Castle, it has been included in the UNESCO list of monuments to be preserved in the event of war.

Much has been written and said about the symbolic significance and artistic value of Skogskyrkogården; but, like all other masterpieces, it continues to invite analysis and description.

The central question tackled by all cemetery design is how to give form to that moment of passage from life to death. Here, the architects have managed to create a celestial landscape, where atmosphere, beauty and a sense of the eternal lift us beyond the immanent. There is a beauty here that speaks to one and all of us; a perfect harmony is established between the discrete forms and details of the buildings and the natural landscape in which they are set. The architecture presupposes the participation of humankind, providing pathways through the woodlands for processions, plus pine copses, open spaces and chapels for prayer and contemplation. The very beauty of the place was envisaged as something that could serve to attenuate the harshness of human sorrow.

The question that automatically arises to mind is what it is precisely that enables Skogskyrkogården to develop those features that have made it famous throughout the world. What were the situational, cultural, political or economic particularities that contributed to its success? What were the aims and inspirations of the architects who created it? What role did the idea of death play in their project? And what role was played by aesthetic considerations?

One should point out that, from the very beginning of the twentieth century, questions relating to graveyards and cemeteries were—at least as far as Stockholm was concerned —seen as being the province of a local government department, a special "Cemeteries Commission" whose statute envisaged the presence of an architect. Throughout the nineteenth century, the city's growing need for burial space was met by the Noora Cemetery at Solna; but towards the end of the century, its role was taken over by Sandsborgskyrkogården in Enskede. In 1911, the Cemeteries Commission noted the shortage of burial space in the areas to the north of Stockholm, envisaging that the city's future burial needs would necessarily require the expansion of Sandsborgskyrkogården. At the time, the Stockholm City Council had already acquired a sizeable area of building land at Enskede, which was earmarked for the construction of a slaughterhouse and private housing. Within this zone it was decided to allocate 75 hectares for the expansion of the cemetery.

In 1912 a first study plan for the new cemetery was drawn up, even if there was no detailed research of the terrain (a gravelly ridge with sandy areas and tall vegetation). With the further assistance of the City Building Office and the Parks and Gardens Department, the project might swiftly have been put into effect—if, that is, people had been satisfied with simply following the tried-and-trusted procedures. Had that happened, the result would simply have been a larger version of the already existing Sandsborgskyrkogården.

During the nineteenth century, nearly all cemeteries had been modelled on a standard schema, with slight rare concessions to changing tastes. However, now a different approach was adopted, due largely to a revision of existing canons of beauty and the influence of such artistic talents as Ellen Key and Ragnar Östberg.

Ellen Key championed a creed of "beauty above all else" and claimed that harmony of form could instil joy and happiness. Ragnar Östberg was at the time working on the building of the City Hall, a design that reflected the architectural ideals of the day. In urban architecture the gridwork layout of the nineteenth century was being replaced by something else; as the little-known contemporary Larkstaden pointed out: aesthetic considerations were sometimes more important than economic. One can see a new approach in the design of cemeteries emerging when, on New Year's Day 1913, the seventy-year-old architect Dahl was replaced by the distinguished young architect Gustaf Wickman, himself a member of the city authorities and head of the modern slaughterhouse at Enskede (as well as of the hospitals of Soderby and Kangbro). As a member of the Building Committee, he helped Östberg in producing his architectural masterpiece by making available funds on a scale enjoyed by no other construction company. We cannot be absolutely sure that the arrival of this new architect was the decisive factor in the change of approach in cemetery design, but we do know that in February 1913 he had already called a competition of "architects and gardeners" in order to achieve "burial places that were more satisfactory from the aesthetic point of view". The city authorities were not used to seeing this importance given to the construction of public buildings, and objected that council gardeners and the City Building Office were already sufficient to the task. After further shilly-shallying, funds were made available for a competition open to architects from Sweden and abroad. Such competitions have never been a means to achieve great aesthetic results—at least, not in the eyes of those for whom the artistic quality of their own work is of great importance. The Cemeteries Commission, however, took this competition as a starting-point from which to exert pressure on the city authorities—emphasising that the creation of the new cemetery was an economic and cultural—as well as aesthetic—matter. In the years before this date, the question of cemeteries had been a topic of discussion not only amongst those who belonged to the new-born movement for the promotion of cremation, but also among a wide variety of architects, who had taken part in numerous competitions (for example, in such German cities as Berlin, Bremen and Mainz). The main problem was that of finding a solution to the difficulties posed by the fact that cremation lay outside the usual cycle of death and decay (the young Lewerentz, for example, had been attracted by a project for a crematorium that was exhibited at the 1914 Baltic Exposition). In the end, because of the number of such projects in Germany, the Cemeteries Commission decided to call an international competition that would be judged by a German who was an expert in the field. The result was the very first international architectural competition held in Sweden.

The Jury was to comprise a German Cemetery Director from Stettin, the architect Wickman of the City's Cemeteries Commission, the well-known expert of public parks, Rudolf Abelin, and two other figures chosen from the National Association of Architects: Lars Israel Wahlman and Ragnar Östberg. When the competition was first called the First World War had just broken out, and yet a total of sixty-three projects were received (many of them from German architects). The Jury agreed in assigning the First Prize to a design that was not only simple but also took most advantage of the natural woodland setting. And thus the prize went to two of the most gifted architects in Swedish history: Asplund and Lewerentz.

It is clear that the dark days of impending war had had some influence on the way the architects tackled the main theme of the competition: how to give form to our encounter with death. However, another important factor was a renewed religious sensibility that had made itself felt in the country as a whole.

The two architects set about their task with great commitment and sense of responsibility. In a detailed report on the realisation of the work—dated 1917—it is clear that both architects aimed to extend the area concerned well beyond the walls enclosing the new cemetery; they envisaged that a perimeter some thirty metres wide should be left unbuilt (even though that land was part of a site earmarked for housing).

The two young man had considered every single detail of what should be done with Sandsborgskyrkogården; careful tests and site checks were carried out; nothing was left to chance. At the same time, the architects drew up detailed sketches of the private chapels that would be included in the cemetery. In 1921, at the consecration of the first chapel—The Woodland Chapel—Asplund and Lewerentz were commissioned to design an even bigger chapel in the southern part of the cemetery; this new structure, built to designs by Lewerentz in 1925, was the Chapel of the Resurrection. A comparison between the two buildings immediately reveals the difference between them, with the more bucolic poetics of the former giving way to a more idealistic and monumental approach.

The Cemeteries Commission immediately called highly-qualified experts to evaluate the work of the two architects: these included professors Erik Lallerstedt and Sigurd Curman from the Stockholm Art School, and Gustaf Wickman (whose place was taken in 1916 by Lars Israel Wahlman).

The chapel was relatively small in size, and the most interesting part was the entrance, incorporated into the enclosure of the cemetery. Lewerentz alone had been responsible for this design.

The architects had managed to create great continuity in the development of the cemetery and were at this point ready to carry out the work on the large main chapel of the Crematorium.

A City Council ruling of 1927 recognised the growing popularity of cremation and the need for a crematorium to the south of Stockholm; but its sole consequence was the construction of a provisional facility in the Sandsborg Chapel. In 1930, however, Asplund and Lewerentz submitted their project for a large chapel, characterised by a spare functionalism that was in deliberate contrast with the gentle landscape of the site. It seems that the Commission was rather critical of the plan, having hoped for something closer to traditional, classicist canons. The discussion when on into 1931, when the functionalist Sven Markelius resigned as Consultant Architect to the Commission; and three years later, in 1934, when the building should have already been completed, the Committee found a way of rejecting it totally and calling another competition. However, this decision was, in its turn, rejected by the City Council under Yngve Larsson, who in 1935 officially commissioned Asplund to carry out the work. Konrad Elmeus, an architect who had been a member of the Cemeteries Commission since 1920, objected strongly to this, asking in vain for Asplund and Lewerentz to "work out a design together". The resulting cultural and political bagarre could well have caused the total failure of the entire project. It was not only a conflict between council departments and city officials, but an aesthetic dispute: functionalism had already given rise to heated debate within the Council Works Department, where Asplund (assisted by Lewerentz himself) had worked as head architect; one of the most determined opponents of the movement was Ragnar Östberg.

In effect, the three experts called to evaluate the project in 1931—Lars Israel Wahlman, Ragnar Östberg and Sigurd Curman (Director General of the Heritage Ministry)—were all opponents of Functionalism. The latter two were, in fact, at time working on a project that was very far from embodying functionalist tenets: the Sjöhistorika Museet [Marine History Museum]. By excluding Lewerentz, who was more severely "tainted" with that approach, Yngve Larsson clearly hoped that things would develop along less functionalist lines. In effect, it was during this period that Gunnar Asplund was working towards a less extreme, more traditionalist, architectural language, and Larsson left him carte blanche with regard to the project. At which point, the Cemeteries Commission too had its say on architectural matters.

It was now clear that the outcome of the work on Skogskyrkogården would be something truly extraordinary, and pressure built up for things to get underway. And in 1935 Wahlman, Östberg and Curman were fulsome in their praise when called upon to evaluate Asplund's final design for the main chapel: "An extraordinary construction, part of a remarkable and excellent design project which over the years has developed to embrace the whole of Skogskyrkogården; the principal part of which is the graceful building that the visitor encounters immediately upon passing through the main entrance."

One minor point that now exercised a large group of figures from the world of the arts was where, within the project, one could find a worthy site for John Lundqvist's sculpture *Resurrection*, a work which had excited great interest when shown at the Stockholm Exposition, the same year in which the Fine Arts Committee proposed its final location should be within Skogskyrkogården. Asplund and Lewerentz had already envisaged their own sculptural group, arising from the base of a tall obelisk placed opposite the entrance to the cemetery. Eventually, in 1935, the Lunqvist group was set up where Asplund suggested: in the open air near the large chapel.

In November of that year forty-five influential figures from the world of the arts presented the City Council with criticism that concerned purely technical aspects of the project (given that, under Yngve Larsson, the Cemeteries Commission had mainly concerned itself with aesthetic considerations). The principal technical problems arose from the creation of the crematorium itself. When work started on the chapel building in 1934, the Commission sent a delegation throughout Europe to study existing crematoria; and those in Prague, Basel, Hanover and Hamburg were eventually taken as models.

By spring 1936 work at Skogskyrkogården was so far advanced that it was decided to complete it as planned, with Yngve Larsson having to defend the continually mounting costs (amongst the numerous criticisms made were those regarding the need for such a large and costly chapel).

By spring 1936 the question had come before the courts, where Larsson did manage to defend the ambitious project and the high costs it involved. The critics of the project argued that the funerals could still have been held in the city's churches, thus obviating the need for such imposing and expensive chapels. Obviously this question did not affect the more affluent classes in the city (because they continued to have their own burial spaces within churches); but think, for example, of the funeral of a workingman: he was the representative of the entire workforce of a factory, and so his funeral might attract large numbers of mourners. Hence the need for large chapels (Larsson was, in fact, strongly opposed to the construction of those rather mean chapels in city's northern cemetery). This was the point of view upheld by the city council.

The following year new funds were allocated for a competition for the decoration of the interior of the chapels. The result was that the architectural achievement of the constructions themselves was worthily enhanced by such important masterpieces as Sven Frixon's frescoes in the Holy Cross Chapel and Otte Sköld's mosaics in the Hope Chapel.

At the official inauguration in 1940, Yngve Larsson could declare his satisfaction that "these great and glorious expressions of art speak to the afflicted with a language of beauty and peace that transcends our normal understanding".

It is likely that the man himself was slightly embarrassed at having excluded Lewerentz from the final phases of the project. In fact, in his book on his own experiences with the scheme he omits all reference to the building commissioned from Lewerentz (even if it is artistically the most significant and complete of the whole project).

Work on Skogskyrkogården began during the First World War and ended with the completion of the main chapel during the Second. Contemporary with the advent of universal suffrage in Sweden, the cemetery dates from a period when the country was going through a period of important democratic renewal. For all the economic crises and controversies that dogged its creation, the project is undoubtedly Swedish architecture's highest achievement of the inter-war years. The most distinctive characteristic of the entire cemetery is the equal care shown in handling both whole and individual details. Nothing was left to chance; each and every aspect of the project was worked on with the same loving care and attention.

(from *Arkitektur*, no. 4, May 1990, pp. 34–41)

Revealing Details
Lewerentz at Klippan

Peter Blundell Jones

The wall is rough brick, very rough with unusually wide joints. The pointing is not raked or trowelled as usual but "bagged off", crudely wiped with an old sack, causing the bricks to be smeared. From time to time this texture is relieved by another in acute contrast: a pure semireflective plane of glass with a perfect silver edge, evidently applied to the outside of the wall. Its delicate form is held in position by the crudest means: a bracket in each corner secured with two screws. This is a window in the St Peter's Church by Sigurd Lewerentz at Klippan, Sweden, of 1963–66. It is a favourite with architects, for once seen it is never forgotten; but it is only imitated by the brave.

First a brick hole is formed, a pure rectangular void surrounded by a pure brick edge. A thick layer of mastic is then applied to the outside face of the hole, and a sealed doubleglazing unit a few centimetres larger is pressed into place, the brackets screwed on to retain it. From inside there seems hardly a window at all, for the glass remains invisible and frameless, simply a brick hole in a thick brick wall. On the outside the precision and fragility of the glass contrast poignantly with the brutality of the brickwork. It is of course a fixed window, ventilation being supplied by other means.

St Peter's was Lewerentz's last major work, begun when he was seventy-eight years old. Its architectural language was a development of that employed at the slightly earlier church of St Mark at Björkhagen near Stockholm. Here too were rough brickwork, vaults, and much expressed construction; however at Klippan the language is more refined and more austere. Lewerentz spent a lot of time on site developing the details, and it is in the details that the building lives most profoundly. The crudeness, almost clumsy or ugly in places, one knows to be deliberate. It is an old man's building, and the weight of a lifetime's experience is somehow encapsulated, but in some ways this is more by renunciation that by quotation. In 1926, at the age of forty-one, Lewerentz had produced his Chapel of the Resurrection, one of the most powerful and sophisticated Neo-Classical monuments of the century. Yet at Klippan there are no orders, no clear axial progressions, little symmetry, and little in the way of an evident proportioning system.[1] Later, in middle age, Lewerentz almost stopped designing buildings altogether, turning his attention instead to details, to the door and window-frames produced by the IDESTA factory which he set up and owned.[2] Yet the famous windows at Klippan have no frame whatsoever: indeed they use some of the most advanced technology of their time—sealed units and mastic—just to avoid having one. It was perhaps typical of Lewerentz that in the age of Brutalism he produced what now seems the last word in that manner, but it was also in some sense a return to, and reinterpretation of, the tradition to which he had been exposed in his youth—National Romanticism, Sweden's Arts and Crafts Movement.[3] The sophistication of classical form and surface was rejected in favour of a poetry of construction.

The Church and Its Setting

St Peter's stands just east of the central area in the little town of Klippan, between a pair of converging roads leading out to the suburbs. Beyond it is a park, and the site initially suggested was nearer the middle of this, further to the east. However Lewerentz chose to anchor the church against the northern road from which it is approached, turning the area to the west—i.e. between it and the road junction, and facing the town—into a garden. The garden is the principal outdoor room of the complex, celebrating the west and principal façade of the church, that with the largest—and most ceremonial—doors, from which couples emerge together for the first time after being married. The space boasts the only piece of added sculpture, and also a large bricklined pool—a still nordic lake for reflection and reflectiveness, rather than the cooling fountain of the south.

The church is correctly orientated, so the altar stands opposite the west doors. It is square in shape, suggesting a more intimate ritual in the tradition of *circumstantes* (standing in a circle) in place of the more usual linear progression. This marks an attempt to return to origins: to the early Christianity of secret meetings in the catacombs. It is the religious equivalent of the search for the essential and primitive which runs so poignantly through the architecture. The church is entered via a side chapel off a tiny alleyway to the north, deliberately intimate and informal, for people arrive for religious observance one by one: it is only at the end of the service that, united by the experience, they progress out together through the west doors. The bells are placed to one side of this alleyway above the sacristy, so one is summoned by their music directly to the point of entry.

Behind the church to south and east is a lower L-shaped block of parish offices and meeting rooms, placed to make a larger square in plan with the church, on the same diagonal. This element is separated from the church by another outdoor room, a narrow street-like space onto which doors of the various facilities open, and which is closed at night by iron gates. At the north end, where it gives onto the main road, the entry to this street is partly screened by a skewed free-standing wall. The outer façades to the landscape on south and east are the most subdued and informal, but they also boast the largest windows—belonging to meeting rooms—and also the most domestic element—the expressed fireplace and chimney of the social hall. The organisation of the complex is clearly hierarchical, focusing appropriately on the central church.

Sacredness of Vaults

Vaults have long been associated with religious architecture. They are essential not only to the Gothic, but also to Romanesque and Byzantine building, and to Mosques. They make a skyscape (we also speak of "the heavenly vault"), they confer some order and rhythm on the plan, and they demonstrate inspiringly how the hardest and heaviest materials can be persuaded to defy gravity. Their use in the second half of the twentieth century is unusual and could seem archaic, were they not reinterpreted in a wholly modern manner. Lewerentz uses brick vaults, but what he does with them is only possible with the strength of iron, for they are layed between rolled steel joists. They are expressed externally by following their form directly with a copper skin, unlike the secondary roof of Gothic churches—another instance of the desire to return to essentials. The church vaulting runs towards the altar, so it is seen externally on the most important west and east ends. It rises towards the centre, both to provide a climax and to drain the rainwater to the sides, while it is lifted above the supporting structure by a series of minimal steel posts. This gives the impression that the vaults are floating above, rather than loading, the supporting structure. But they are in fact held up on a pair of great transverse beams carried on a cross-shaped central column. That this element has a more than purely structural, utilitarian, profane role, is underlined by it being asymmetrical when structural logic would demand symmetry. The shorter arm runs, as one might expect, in the direction of the altar. But though clearly symbolic, it remains T-shaped, without the upper arm of a true cross: for its meaning is evident enough, and must not be overstressed. The steelwork is not painted but left raw and rusty, ageing, and therefore a symbol of suffering. The welded joints, as throughout the building, are left unground, so the welder's work appears in all its naked simplicity.

The vault idea was first tried at St Mark's Björkhagen (1960), where vaults were used for all parts of the complex. At St Peter's they occur more hierarchically: just for the church, side chapel, and the council chamber at the corner of the L-shaped block. Only the church vaults are visible externally, other parts of the complex having more profane low-pitched copper-covered timber roofs. And while roof edges of vaults are finished as flush as possible, the profane buildings have overhanging eaves which project, displaying their timber structure and the way it is strapped to the walls. These roof projections are oblique in several places, exaggerating the need to bring the rainwater to an outlet at the lowest point, but also providing additional protection over doors. The general effect is a lively profile quite unexpected from the orthodox looking plan.

Crazy Brickwork

Brick is used everywhere at St Peter's, a rough dark brick, between brown and purple in colour. In the church it forms the walls, the vaulted roof, the altar and pulpit, and of course the floor. This is broken only by the baptismal trough, a primeval slot, a water-filled fissure in a cave, the edge of which swells up mysteriously. The effect of all this brick is dark and hard and earthy; it generates a space which is almost invisible until one's eyes adapt to the gloom, echoing with the drip of water from the tropical shell used as a font. On the outside there is much play with different bonding patterns in the brickwork, most notably at the end of the street-like space to the east of the church, where alternating vertical and horizontal coursing suggests a huge chequerboard, reminding one also of the decorative games played with brick infill on old timber-framed houses.

Lewerentz seems to have imposed one unorthodox rule at the start: a brick should never be cut. This is not in the interests of time-saving and modular construction, indeed it is almost an ironic comment on that idea—made at a time when it was in force. For Lewerentz does so many difficult irregular things with his bricks that his rule clearly creates more problems than it solves. So why? Is it out of respect for the brick and what it "wants to be", as Louis Kahn put it? Or is to create a discipline of construction which will inform the design—an aesthetic derived from and founded in technique? Perhaps both.

To avoid cutting bricks there are sometimes enormous joints. At the edges of sloping roofs for example, are triangular wedges of mortar as deep as a brick, and this was only achieved by bulking out the mortar with ground slate. The effect is crude and messy, almost shockingly so in places, and carried through with utter ruthlessness. Internally, floor tiles are subject to the same discipline, and all irregularities are taken up within the pattern in which they are laid, producing some unusual arrangements.

Joinery

We began with the windows. The doors too, with notable exceptions, are applied to the front of a brick hole, bolted on and sealed with mastic. The exceptions are the most sacred, most hierarchically important doors. One is the main entrance down the little side alley, the only door in the entire complex to be placed at the back of its brick hole rather than on the face. Also exceptional are the two doors of the west front, which are placed flush in their façade rather than onto its face. The larger double door is also taller in keeping with its status. It would be all too easy, by concentrating on traditions and crafts, to produce an olde worlde and sentimental image. Lewerentz avoids this completely by reinterpreting ancient techniques, and also combining them with the latest technology. The doors and their frames are made of laminated timber, with the glued joints visible. Externally they are left as sawn, with the slight ridges produced when the strips of wood did not quite lie flat in the glueing clamp, but internally they are sanded off to give a smooth surface. This slight difference of texture is the only concession to the increase in civilisation between the front and rear faces of the door,[4] for both are finished in the same dark stain. The construction of the doors is stated in a somewhat minimal way, for though they are essentially formed of frame and panel elements, the panel is flush and continuous with the side pieces of the frame, with only a simple groove and change in direction of grain revealing the joints with the top and bottom of the frame. Running vertically down the centre of each door is an expansion slot between the two sides of the panel, producing a clear vertical stripe.

Expressed Construction – or Something More?

At first sight it seems that all materials and techniques are exposed and expressed: brick and its bonding, timber and its assembly, the fragility of glass, the unground welds of steel. Yet on further reflection it becomes obvious that this expression is neither wholly consistent nor complete. Comparison with the expressive brickwork of the nineteenth century, with that of Butterfield or Berlage, for example, reveals a big difference. The openings are treated quite differently. For while an architect like Butterfield[5] would give considerable attention to arches over doors and windows, and to restraining arches in the wall above, Lewerentz takes bricks across the head of an opening apparently unsupported. This allows his brick holes to be treated in the same way on each side, asserting their geometrical purity, but it denies any expression of the way that the forces of gravity make a head fundamentally different in nature to a sill.

The construction is achieved, presumably, by laying steel reinforcing bars between the brick courses where tension forces are felt. But all this is concealed! It is certainly not brick construction in the traditional sense, indeed it could almost be interpreted as a concrete building, with the bricks as aggregate.[6]

The expression of functional requirements can be equally selective. All the way around the subordinate buildings the disposal of rainwater becomes a conspicuous element, and on the back of the church—the east face—is an elaborate arrangement of copper gutters and downpipes draining the vaults. On the west front, however, there is no visible apparatus of this kind, although the roof discharges just as much water. It disappears, apparently, in a series of downpipes concealed in the walls. I have no doubt that this was the right decision, for it liberates the most sacred face from profane considerations, and helps differentiate it from the hierarchically less important east face—in fact I find the decision most poignant. In terms of pure construction or convenience, however, it makes little sense, and in terms of functional expression it might be called dishonest.

From Fact to Fiction: Reconstructing Modernism

The strength of the Modern Movement surely lay in its attempt to escape the repetition and consequent devaluation of applied styles, refounding architecture instead in use and in construction. Unfortunately, this was generally done at too literal a level, due often to an excessive belief in pseudo-scientific objectivity. Use was defined in the narrowest and meanest way—for example in terms of *existenzminimum*, while construction techniques were allowed to dominate for their own sake or in pursuit of spurious economic arguments.[7] There was a quite unwarranted certainty about the whole enterprise, and when passed down as dogma at third or fourth hand, the results were depressing.

So-called Post-Modernism rejected all this, and brought back in a new guise the applied styles that Modernism had tried to abolish—but these were merely added as surface ornament. The building underneath continued to be designed according to precisely those impoverished concepts of use and construction that had killed the Modernist idea. They just went underground and became part of the implicit way of doing things, remaining unchallenged in the vast majority of current work.

For oddly enough, pure use and pure construction turn out to be chimeras: the more one pursues them, the more evasive they seem to become. They are not objectively sustainable, for they are always subject to interpretation according to a particular world view or version of reality. Reality is not hard and fast, but socially constructed.[8]

Use and construction, if undefinable in a pure or absolute state, are the fundamental themes of architecture. In their spatial relations and formal articulation, buildings say things about the way they might be used, and also encourage certain kinds of use. Buildings have to be made, and tell us (or lie to us) about how they were made, if we can read them. Functionalism and Constructivism might thus be considered fictional themes: the building telling stories about itself, relating to its ancestors and retelling its myth of origins. That is what I think St Peter's Klippan is about: it shows the poetry that lay at the heart of Modernism before it became prosaic.

[1] There is evidently a geometrical system in the plan, but it does not seem to run through consistently in three dimensions, whereas the Chapel of the Resurrection has a clear proportional system visible in the drawings.

[2] These components were used by many Swedish Modernists including Asplund and Markelius.

[3] Lewerentz, along with Asplund, was one of the pupils at the breakaway Klara school, taught by Östberg and Westman. Östberg, architect of Stockholm City Hall, was the leader of the National Romantics in Sweden.

[4] It seems to be a widely accepted convention that buildings be smooth inside, rough without, like a coconut, expressing internally an increased degree of control and refinement, a transition from the raw to the cooked, from nature to artifice.

[5] William Butterfield was a Gothic Revival architect working in the middle of the nineteenth century, and known particularly for his bold use of polychromatic brickwork. Famous works are All Saints Margaret Street, London, and Keble College Oxford.

[6] I owe this reading to Florian Beigel.

[7] The purest expression of this point of view is Hannes Meyer's manifesto *Bauen* at the Bauhaus of 1928. Here he states unequivocally that there are twelve and only twelve functions to be considered in designing a house, and gives a list of parameters that need to be measured in order to allow the whole thing to be objectively and quantitatively done.

[8] Supporting arguments for this statement are beyond the scope of the essay. The reader is referred to *The social construction of reality* by Peter Berger and Thomas Luckmann.

(from *Spazio & Società*, no. 53, January–February 1991, pp. 88–97)

The Spiritual Possibilities of Landscape

Caroline Constant

"To live one day eternally, one must give oneself over to death many times." (Caspar David Friedrich)

Werner Oeschlin traces "the modern history of the cemetery as an architecturally defined locality, as an ideal synthesis of architecture and landscape"[1] to Quatremère de Quincy. In his 1788 article "Cimetière" the French encyclopedist elucidated the principle of the unity of art and nature based on the concept of the Elysian Fields, which he located in the necropolises of Pozzuoli and Arles. If twentieth-century artistic avant-gardes strove instead to achieve the unity of art and life, Swedish architects of the period formed a more complex understanding of the total work of art. In the modern cemetery they aspired to fuse art with nature, death with life. The immediacy of religious experience sought by Martin Luther during the sixteenth century was replaced by the modernist ambition of attaining unmediated experience per se. Landscape's very indeterminacy made it a salient vehicle to reanimate the social dimension of art. By severing familiar correspondences between form and content, modernism laid bare the issue of meaning, an issue made more poignant in cemetery design by the breakdown of traditional religious values. If the nineteenth-century suburban cemetery conceived as a park-like urban adjunct reflected the void engendered by that spiritual crisis, early twentieth-century Swedish architects responded by imbuing their cemeteries with a more fundamental spiritual content that was grounded in psychological realities and experiential rituals rather than doctrinal symbolism. The history of Asplund's and Lewerentz's collaborative efforts at the Woodland Cemetery reveals their persistent suppression of the competition proposal's overt symbolism—its primordial forest teeming with burial mounds of pagan inspiration and tombs of Neoclassical provenance—in favour of using palpable experience in support of the ineffable and the imagined. Although historical references permeate their design, the cemetery landscape resists definitive analysis in historical terms; its meaning cannot be completely deciphered. Indeed, such amplification of the symbolic through recourse to unmediated experience characterized all of Asplund's and Lewerentz's cemeteries, in which landscape is sensed as much as it is viewed.

While these cemeteries have numerous precedents within Swedish landscape traditions, their spiritual essence originates in German Romanticism, particularly in the paintings of Caspar David Friedrich, which Lewerentz may have encountered during his apprenticeship in Berlin and Munich. From Romanticism Asplund and Lewerentz derived their general aim of creating an art that was both nonconventional and intelligible, personal and objective, in which forms of nature could express ideas and sentiments without the mediation of history.

According to Joseph Koerner's analysis, Friedrich forged a radical reconception of the relationship between art and self, wherein in the structure of the image is governed by accommodation of the viewer, located in experience. Koerner's interpretation is indebted to late nineteenth-century developments in German aesthetic theory, ideas that were familiar to both Asplund and Lewerentz, particularly Theodor Lipps's theory of empathy. Contemporary German aestheticians elaborated on such psychological currents by focusing on the enabling relationship between art and life. As Lipps argued in his *Aesthetic* (1903–06): "Art can draw out and make us understand that which is human, or better, that which is positively human: life, power, work, the industriousness of the will—activity, in a word. And all this, all of this life, can find an echo in us and satisfy our nostalgia—indeed, every nostalgia that we feel can be reduced to a single thing: the nostalgia for living." By projecting the domain of the cemetery's expression into the realm of the social and the political, however, Asplund and Lewerentz avoided the solipsism associated with contemporary aesthetic concerns.

The noted Viennese art historian Alois Riegl, frequently cited by Worringer, anticipated the broader social implications of artistic practice. Reacting against the purely subjective focus of empathy theory and, indeed, of modern art, Riegl posited his concept of attentiveness, denoting the contemplating subject's potential interaction with the work of art, not as the formal means, but as the ethical purpose of art. Margaret Olin characterizes Riegl's theory as "an attempt to preserve communication while circumventing the issue of representation." Granting humanity a common basis in communication involves both political and religious dimensions, as Olin elaborates:

"Clearly Riegl thought attentiveness, and all it entailed, not only an effective way to unify a picture, but an admirable way to lead one's life, in concord with one's fellow man. It meant respect (or regard), democracy, equality."

The association of aesthetic theory with civic virtue was not unique to Riegl, as Terry Eagleton demonstrates in *The Ideology of the Aesthetic*. He cites Friedrich Schiller and Jean-Jacques Rousseau, among others, in arguing that "the category of the aesthetic assumes the importance it does in modern Europe because in speaking of art it speaks of these other matters too, which are at the heart of the middle class's struggle for political hegemony. The construction of the modern notion of the aesthetic artefact is thus inseparable from the construction of the dominant ideological forms of modern class-society, and indeed from a whole new form of human subjectivity appropriate to that social order." Thus, while it is unlikely that Asplund and Lewerentz would have encountered Riegl's writings directly, their Woodland Cemetery embodies similar motivations. Rather than embrace the solipsism of Friedrich's paintings, threatening the viewer to subsume the world into himself and remain alone, the architects posited mutuality, the possibility of overcoming isolation through human fellowship. This humanitarian quality derives as much from the convergence of social, political and artistic forces in early twentieth-century Sweden as from the architects intentions.

While the search for the spiritual and ineffable that arose during the early decades of the twentieth century in opposition to positivist and materialist philosophies was an influential force in modern painting, its effect on landscape design has been relatively unacknowledged. For certain proponents of the architectural avant-garde, such as individuals associated with De Stijl, the Deutsche Werkbund or the Bauhaus under Walter Gropius, the spiritual was a device for empowerment, authorizing the artist/architect as the privileged interpreter of the modern world. Swedish architects of the period were more humble in their aspirations. Focusing on the *humane* rather than the human, they made their appeal to the inner life, seeking to enhance the spiritual essence of daily life. As Gunnar Ekelöf has argued, "One of the most important things in all art: Leave a respectable part up to the reader, the observer, the listener, the participant. There shall be an empty setting at the ready-laid table. It is his."

(from C. Constant, *The Woodland Cemetery: Toward a Spiritual Landscape*, Byggförlaget, Stockholm 1994, pp. 134–35)

Beyond the Wall of Hadrian's Villa Parrhasius' Veil: Lewerentz's Journey to Italy

Luis Moreno Mansilla

Fortunately, among the boxes containing the material of Sigurd Lewerentz (1885–1975) in Stockholm's Arkitekturmuseet, there appeared, wrapped in paper brittle with age, some photographic negatives of some images from Italy. In their manner of portrayal, these photographs, in which little could be recognised, contained the suggestion of a very peculiar view of Antiquity, and perhaps a key that allows us to shed further light on so complex an oeuvre as that of Lewerentz. The photographs, each particular in their point of view, are enigmatic even in their framing. Or perhaps one of us, photographing a mosaic, would have aimed his camera at the constellation of monochrome tesserae, avoiding the figures, displacing from the centre those forms that to Lewerentz seemed to mean almost nothing: only a few agile legs, trapped forever in a fragmented yet uniform surface.

In fact, we know little or nothing about Lewerentz's trip to Italy. A few sparse photographs and uncertain dates remain as mute witnesses to his sojourn in the Mediterranean. However, ever since Zola described art as a corner of nature seen through a temperament, we have been losing our yearning for an abstract, perfect fidelity in reproduction; thus art begins to be a representation of our own form of understanding and seeing reality through the eyes of the artist. The crucible in which the Classical was cast has cracked. Since then, the manner of travelling, the manner of drawing and photographing, or definitively, the manner of representing, changed into a manner of seeing, and thus into a form of thinking. Therefore the photographs taken by Lewerentz during his visit to Italy become documents of inestimable value for a man given to few words: for they bring us closer, not only to his way of seeing and understanding the past, but above all, to an understanding of the intimate character of his work. This collection of photographs perhaps constitutes his sole architectural testament.

The Wall of the Pitti Palace

What did Lewerentz see in Italy? Can we capture from these old negatives what it was that gave his work such a peculiar character? Just as in the case of the mosaic's photograph, where he avoided content, focussing on nothing but texture, Lewerentz stood before the Pitti Palace in Florence and again aimed his camera away from the centre. He ignored the imposing façade, and was captivated by the powerful, uncomposed wall of huge stones, moulded by light; almost nothing but *texture*. Indeed it is only from the windows, that appear accidentally in the background, that we know of Lewerentz's visit to Florence.

The photograph of the sheep's legs, taken at disturbingly close range, again eschews form: it is not really a relief that is being photographed, but only the texture thereof, in which the stones almost seem like tears.

It seems curious that Lewerentz did not photograph the façade of the Pitti Palace, yet his failure to photograph any façades at all is more surprising. All the views are taken at close range, avoiding form and composition; they portray fragments of pavements, bases of columns, details, surface, almost exclusively *textures*. This observation is not without significance for anyone who has purposefully visited the work of Lewerentz: Lewerentz's façades resist being photographed, and surprisingly, any photographs one takes of his work inevitably acquire the same character. The architecture of Lewerentz is never seen from afar, as if the construction can only be seen and understood at close range, where surface and texture predominate, and the building may be touched and almost felt.

Exaggerating, Lewerentz portrayed himself as a master respectfully caressing textures, indicating that it is not the form of the object itself that is important, but rather its precise effect, its surface, its scale, its shadow. Now, to say that Lewerentz's interest in the classical method of façade composition is minimal suggests that his way of making architecture is far removed from that of ideal composition, in which, whilst maintaining integrity, a whole is divided simultaneously by certain rules and is closer to a process of aggregative composition of affiliated pieces, more by means of texture and intuition than a geometrical composition, or overall regulation of the design.

It is difficult to understand the architecture of Lewerentz as an "unicum", because the works are only seen at close vicinity, never in their entirety. The concept of a façade, of an architectural plan composed according to abstract rules, whether ancient or modern, does not exist.

This somewhat radical assertion derives not only from his fragmentary photographs, or from my own personal experience of his works: it is definitively confirmed, at least as far as we know, by the sets of project drawings of his work, consisting of a multitude of partial drawings for each project, in which the various parts of the building are studied separately. As the work advances, the various parts are progressively defined and modified on revised general layouts. General elevations are not to be found among the designs of the later churches: there are only drawings of the sundry parts of the building, a corner, a chimney; defining with absolute precision all the bricks thereof, one by one. Paradoxically, the general plan of the façade has virtually no importance; but each and every brick has its intention, and on site. Lewerentz himself was wont to explain tirelessly how each one was to be placed.[1]

The fragments, designed with a rigorous but unapparent geometry, were assembled naturally; the bricks were laid one upon another, with the apparent randomness of tombs in a columbarium, each one peering out at us from its immense solitude. This reality, unitary in its feeling but tremendously fragmentary in its composition, is never perceived as a whole.

The Church of St Mark, in the suburbs of Stockholm, situated in a small hollow, is hidden amid nature. Here it may be said that Nature imitates

Art, for the bricks and mortar take on the same aspect as the surrounding screen of birches with their rough bark. The approach is always sideways, thwarting the observer's view, and the small pool situated between the two wings of the building obliges us always to move close to the building, touching it, caressing it. Furthermore, the pergolas at the entrance to the building again deny us an overall perception of the ensemble; advancing towards the pool and throwing a perpetual shade on the façade which, with its doors and windows confused, tells us nothing of what is inside. The entrance to the church itself is hidden in the folds of the wall, removing any idea of hierarchy.

Something similar occurs in the approaches to the twin chapels of the Malmö cemetery. Separated by high hedges, one never sees both of them at once, and each chapel is glimpsed only when one is already very close. As one arrives at the entrance, the ground rises sharply, as though the chapel had been built first and the natural ground had adapted itself to the situation. Once again, the freestanding portico which increasingly resembles the surrounding trees, veils our view of a nonexistent façade and with its shadows, hampers our understanding of what is happening behind.

In the small chapel situated behind those of St Knut and St Gertrude, the door, composed of narrow planks of wood, is flush with the brickwork, and the upper part of the enclosure continues this disposition; the door as such disappears and the façade loses its scale, the expanse of wall becoming a mere surface without depth.

At another scale, in the Edstrand Villa, the door of the garage and that of the house are confused in an almost continuous plane, compositional elements being reduced to a minimum. In different circumstances, Gunnar Asplund used the same gesture in the Snellman Villa. Entry to the house is by way of a hall, in which the front door and those of the surrounding cupboards are identical; the visitor is disconcerted by his failure to discern the exit, and is trapped in the intimate world of the Swedish master's architecture.

In the Church of St Peter in Klippan, the narrowness of the space between the two structures and the sinuous routes that take us to the chapel, reinforce that concept of immediacy and fragmentation so dear to Lewerentz.

Perhaps it is not yet time to speak of how Lewerentz's fragmentary composition and the dominance of texture is somehow a clear reflection of the multiply dented plate that constitutes a more modern vision of culture—contrary to the classical version, where a perforation caused by hammering at a single central point represents architecture as remaining consistent.

One may however agree that the loss of the sense of language or of words, heralded by the deconstructionists, corresponds more to a loss of the sense of form as organizer of an architectural language, than to a loss of the sense of structural rationalism, because language, like form, is an invention of the mind, while structure belongs to the physical world, and is thus independent of mental processes. It is my understanding that the "end of the line"[2] does not concern the question of structural instability or its representation,[3] but rather the absence of artificial form.

The work of Lewerentz, rooted in formal minima and oblivious to pretensions, humbly ministers to a desire to offer distilled concepts, renouncing forms that are unnecessary. This attitude, so much in accord with the contemporary spirit, is not only the ultimate reason for present-day interest, but also perhaps an unexplored path for a now disoriented architectural culture.

The Wall of Hadrian's Villa

In this document, it is of little importance if the photograph of the sepulchral way in Pompeii, with the wall in front of it hiding the tombs, contributed more or less than that of Asplund to the elaboration of the Woodland Cemetery project, south of Stockholm.[4] Nor is it of much importance that the photo of the approach to the wall of Hadrian's Villa bears an extraordinary resemblance to the access to the Chapel of the Resurrection. What is important from our point of view, is an attempt to discover the influence upon Lewerentz of that visit to antiquity, the ideas that arose from amongst those powerful ruins. The photograph that Lewerentz took of the villa is of an almost metaphysical simplicity. A wall of handsome *texture*, a surface that through time has acquired a patina, with its immense length so veiled by trees that it is quite hidden, and a great hole: or perhaps it would be better to say, and only a great hole. A wall that separates, an opening that joins two distinct spaces. Throughout his career, the echo of this simple and moving vision was to give life and character to part of his work.

The Resurrection Chapel contains, *in nuce* and costumed in an apparently classical language, many of the ideas that inform the later architecture of Lewerentz.

A view of the entire chapel, like that of the wall of Hadrian's Villa, is only possible when one is very near to the outside columns, a space that brings to mind another space photographed in Pompeii. The notion of passing through a wall, of placing behind us the frontier between the natural and built worlds, led Lewerentz to treat exterior and interior as two distinct spaces. The proximity of the walls, from without or from within, thus imposes diverse rules.

We are in the presence of two distinct worlds, with their own geometrical rules, with their own *textures*, their own spirit. The thick wall of the chapel thus becomes a mere filling between two planes, two surfaces, that are the true protagonists and have a real existence. The photograph in which a smiling child, symbol of curiosity, appears before that immense wall in which, on account of their distance apart, the front and rear planes have nothing in common, and that magnetic balcony looking out over nothing, may help us to outline this idea.

The thickness of the chapel walls disappears in its imposing massiveness, as it is merely a consequence of the creation of two distinct spaces.

Some of this also happens at the Church of St Peter in Klippan. The thickness of the walls varies throughout the length of the chapel, as if to underline the different unfolding of the interior and exterior spaces as the most important element. The master, like the narrator of the *Thousand and One Nights*, carries us sagely from outside to inside, almost imperceptibly constructing time with skill. Slowly, fragment by fragment, the chapel appears in the way that short narrations succeed one another incomprehensibly in the oriental tale, fragments strung together only by *texture*. The absence of composition in the traditional sense of the word, the notion of proximity to a texture, and the mystery represented by the division between nature and architecture, is that which in our understanding, may be observed in the background of the photographs taken in Italy.

When, displacing art from reality for the observer, Zola enriches the window of Alberti, he speaks of the famous classical, romantic and realist glasses. Before which of these visions does Lewerentz stand? Would he not rather contemplate that veil that Parrhasius painted, in competition with Zeuxis, and which Luca Pacioli, a personality no doubt dear to the architect, narrates in his book, *De divina proportione*?[5] Zeuxis beguiled the birds with a basket of fruit that he had painted. Parrhasius, with precision, fooled the master painter, by firmly representing not a real object but a concept. He drew the first abstract picture, the first white on white, nothing. He painted what existed between the classical picture and the spectator; almost a sentiment, a curiosity. He covered the surface of the canvas with *texture*, renouncing form, which is as much as to renounce the theme, the word; a *texture* reducing space to planar nature.

The mystery of what is behind the Veil of Parrhasius is the mystery that moves us as we wonder what lies behind the walls of Lewerentz, behind the rear pediment in the portico of the chapel of the Resurrection, or simply, beyond the immense wall of the fragmentary Hadrian's Villa.

[1] J. Ahlin, *Sigurd Lewerentz. Arkitekt*, Byggförlaget, Stockholm, 1985.
[2] S. Alenius, "La Iglesia de Björkhagen con Roma como referencia", *Sigurd Lewerentz arquitecto*, exhibition catalogue, Madrid 1987.
[3] A. Vidler, "Después del fin de la linea", *Arquitectura*, no. 270, Madrid, February, 1980.
[4] Johnson and Wigley, *Deconstructivist Architecture*, The Museum of Modern Art, New York 1988.
[5] L. Pacioli, *La Divina Proporción*, Editorial Losada, Buenos Aires 1959.

(from *9H-On Continuity*, 1995, pp. 1–10)

Lewerentz-Klippan

Pierluigi Nicolin

In their confirmation of the exhaustion of one mode of relating architecture to the world, and going beyond the variant that meets a need for contextualization to reestablish a channel of communications between subject and the external situation, Lewerentz's last works tackled the central problem of the architecture of the second half of the twentieth century—that of responses to the opening of a breach—in a manner that was absolutely ahead of its time.

All this is easier for us to understand after three decades of the architectural debate have made us aware that the optimistic assumptions of the first half of the century are no longer applicable. At a certain moment—the origin of which would be difficult to pinpoint and which would be easier to describe as the "beginning of impossibility"—a breach opened up in the system of architectural representation, and the effect of this on the language of architecture meant there was a tendency to lose touch with reality. This is a development that was certainly linked to the abrupt termination of the architect's social mandate, but was, nonetheless, implicit in the epistemological fractures of the twentieth century.

From a certain point onward, therefore, Lewerentz's architecture was invested with a centrifugal force stemming from an extremely ideological relationship with reality, which prevented a complete reunion of the language with the vision of the world to be represented and therefore forced the former into a radical self-contextualization and a painful self-demolition.

From his perilous traversal of the events of the first half of the century, which saw him first as protagonist, along with Asplund, of a celebrated phase of Nordic Classicism and later immersed in the programs of the New Objectivity—and therefore of the most confident version of the programmatic contents of the modern movement—to the point of interpreting the new concept in terms of production (for a fairly long period Lewerentz devoted himself to making building components with a company of his own: door and window frames, prefabricated panels etc.), Lewerentz seemed to develop an awareness, in his old age, of the wounds and alienation that had been inflicted by the history of architecture. This conviction led him to begin a sort of retracing of steps in search of a free zone in which none of the contradictions that had been experienced and suffered had yet arisen, with a determination that had no equals in its boldness and consequentiality anywhere in the architecture of the contemporary world. This return to the origins of language and meaning meant moving progressively down through the sediments of language as far as the magma of primordial matter in which both the meaning and its expressive formalization are still totally undecided, seeking an area of operation in which the project had not yet introduced the distinction between subject and object. The idea of starting from blocks of material, while waiting for something that would cause it to jell, served to put him in a condition where he could bring to the fore the primary function of the significant, the original datum of the formulation of language. This entailed making the significant absolute in some way and providing fields of action, chiefly in the form of brickwork, where even before any intervention of the subject and by virtue of an autonomous operation of the mechanism that was set in motion (like that of not permitting the cutting of the bricks from which the building is constructed), a "truth" was found solely by the force of the meeting-collision between formal elements. This assumption of the language as ontology, the tendency to consider language a dimension totally independent of reality, so as to eliminate the distinction between object and its representation, ended up by challenging the formal code developed by the modern European tradition, for instance that of Nordic Empiricism.

The rejection, so evident in certain aspects, of a merely discursive logic, or a descriptive one in the manner of Aalto, and the presence of surreal and hermetic elements seem to be aimed at bringing out the separate "truth" of the language. Thus the combinations of materials, the early Christian etymologies, and certain of the constituent syllables of the church at Klippan—the building on which these considerations are based—result in the appearance of momentary epiphanies, cloaked in a space of semi-darkness but shot through with unprecedented, dazzling figures.

The adoption of subversive techniques at the level of the significant, the simultaneous presence of action (and the labour of the builder) and writing as representation (the rigorous design theorem of the architect) produce a different and unknown space. In this procedure the architecture is shifted onto a terrain that is unattainable from the world he had so awkwardly ventured into during the phase of production-oriented optimism in the thirties: now the space of the birth of meaning is produced by a slow settling of the tectonic masses whole inscrutable movements are coupled with those of the psychic masses of the unconscious.

As a consequence of the way that they are assembled, the walls of the church of St Peter at Klippan present surfaces in which the dark bricks of Helsingborg appear to stand out from the white bed of mortar in which they float. "He let the brick swim freely in the mortar, obtaining a result similar to the dark spots on the white bark of the surrounding birches," wrote Janne Ahlin, using an analogy with the organic world to suggest a particular location in space and time. For his part, the architect claimed, with a subtle propensity for anachronism, to have been inspired by ancient Persian architecture in brick (we cannot fail, at this point, to observe how Lewerentz was prefiguring what would become more pressing among contemporary architects and could be described as that rupture or dislocation of time, that disjointing of the present, that makes it no longer contemporaneous with itself).

Separated by an unusual thickness of mortar, the bricks are arranged in *patterns* that hint at a range of subtle emotions.

From one drawing, *Detalj till fönster i rum*, it can be seen precisely how the laying of that elementary sign represented by the brick recalls the radical procedures adopted by people like Carl Andre, Joel Shapiro or Agnes Martin in their research not so much into minimal conditions as into, exclusively, the necessary conditions of art.

By this unorthodox use of an orthodox language, like that of the patterning of a brick wall, an effect is produced that brings into question the conventions of the visual perception of a wall.

In it is represented the slowness of construction, the act of setting the line of each brick, one after the other, so that matter and geometry produce the emotional content of Abstract Expressionism. In it we can see the heroic aspect of construction, the moral experience of a ritual gesture repeated endless times, as it were a vehicle capable of bringing revelation. From this point of view the building emanates an Oriental sense of religion, close to the spiritual messages of Buddhism or Taoism.

It displays a restricted geometric vocabulary in which the grid tends not so much to dematerialize the surface as to become the actual object of our vision. In this there is also, if we can put it this way, a sort of abstraction, which brings the construction of these grids close to the spiritual experience that modern painting attributes to its geometrical patterns.

So what we see taking place here is a radical annihilation of the difference between material and surface, between construction and decoration. In this perfect coincidence of the two traditional components of the wall, in this attempt to find a non-hierarchical and non-relational equilibrium of the surface, is represented that state of the formulation of language in which the hierarchies are not yet preestablished and it is possible to come into contact with the primary function of the significant.

In this backward movement there is no longer any room for the ego of the architect and, parodoxically, this building so full of traces remains anonymous, or rather, shows a residual presence of the subject through the natural imperfections of manual work. If the details of the material and the illusory sequence of *textures* stand out from close-up, a second crucial moment of perception takes place as soon as we move further away. The walls become opaque, the structural mass of the building regains its normality and, from this distance, a new element appears. The building recedes into the background, is reduced to a neutral wall on which hand mir-

rors that reflect images of the surrounding nature.
We experience a total sense of exteriority in the face of this opaque and impenetrable wall, which bounces back luminous images of the atmosphere from the places where its windows should be. Fixed simply, and brutally, from the outside, the sheets of double glazing of the windows look like reflecting surfaces that instead of commenting on the continuity of the wall—as in so many elegant contemporary versions of the façade—stand out by contrast from a dark mass: seen from this distance and the outside, the brickwork of the building becomes a mineral background for an installation of mirrors *à la* Robert Smithson.
From this distance the view from outside, with its explicit invitation to catch glimpses of the landscape through the multiplicity of "takes" thrown back by the reflective windows, conveys an idea of nature as mere image or apparition.
It is a proposal to consider the truth of nature as an illusion, preparing for the abrupt transition to the view of the textures of the material from close-up and, subsequently, the atmosphere of an early Christian catacomb that we find inside. Such mutable modalities of appearance bring into play the unease of an uncertain relationship between architecture and world. Yet it is precisely through this perennial self-questioning that the sequence from the "pagan" naturalism of the space outside to the mystical Christian semi-darkness of the interior is brought into existence.
Having abandoned the dream of modernist architecture to make the inside coincide with the outside—symbol of a transparency between nature and architecture and of a mirroring of objective structures—the only possibility left to architecture is to proceed through a risky interpretation of heritage and origins. The representation of the space inside is also involved in this procedure.
This, at first sight, presents itself as a space cloaked in a deep semi-darkness that prevents an immediate grasp of the surroundings. If this darkness conjures up a possible connection between violence and the sacred, the subsequent adaptation to the dim light produces a gradual unveiling of the liturgical space as a familiar place, as if to evoke the process of "secularization" introduced by Christianity, in opposition to any violent interpretation of the sacred: a process that in fact separates modern civilization from its sacred origins. As soon as we enter, a wan and cold light from the windows in the outside walls and the narrow slits in the roofing vaults just allows us to make out the confines of the hall, which remains steeped in shadow. As our eyes adjust the space is slowly revealed by a dim light, almost like that produced by candles, given off by hanging lamps.
Once we have overcome the doubts and uncertainties of the initiatory moment, we can move cautiously into the space and expect the unexpected. The apparent disorder awaits a ritual that will give meaning to the accidental character of the interior, made ready, it seems, to house something that has not yet arrived.
Whence the organization of the space into an open structure, where no conclusion is wanted because nothing ends and nothing begins in a system of which we possess only immanent coordinates. Moving through this space, amidst the magic of the architect-wizard who lays out his symbols in a manner that is both instinctive and premeditated, observing the details of the construction, we are introduced to a technique of improvisation, which is a way of creatively forgetting technique, and which in the end represents for the architect the obtaining of a scripture.
Beginning in 1956 with the parish church of St Mark in Stockholm, Lewerentz's effort to dismantle the certainties and knowledge of a long career (the laborious reexamination of every architectural question from the foundations) came to its conclusion in the masterpiece of St Peter at Klippan, Scania, in southern Sweden. And since he then chose to remain silent, rather that speak, his figure became cloaked in an aura of mystery.
(from *Lotus international*, no. 93, June 1997, pp. 6–19)

Biography

Born in 1885 at Vasternörrland, in the north of Sweden, Sigurd Lewerentz first studied engineering at the Gothenburg Polytechnic and only later did he take architecture at the Fine Arts Academy in Stockholm. He then abandoned this course to attend the Klara Skola— a free school established, following the suspension of teaching at the academy, by Erik Gunnar Asplund and Osvald Almqvist, as well as by Lewerentz himself—where the lecturers included Carl Westman and Ragnar Östberg. After the experience of the Klara Skola, Lewerentz spent a period of apprenticeship in Germany, in Berlin and Munich, in the offices of a number of leading German architects—Bruno Möhring, Theodor Fisher and Richard Riemerschmid—where he came into contact with the ideas that were being developed at that time in central Europe.

When he returned to Sweden in 1911, Lewerentz opened an office together with Torsten Stubelius, from whom he separated in 1917, ending a partnership rich in ideas and reflections on architecture that were to be of use to him the rest of his life. From then on he worked alone, apart from a number of competitions or specific commissions, where he collaborated with colleagues or artists. Displaying great versatility at all levels, Lewerentz tackled a wide range of themes, including advertising graphics and landscape architecture, in his long career. His most outstanding achievements were in the field of landscape design, where he realized a number of great masterpieces, such as the Stockholm South Cemetery (with Erik Gunnar Asplund) and the Eastern Cemetery at Malmö.

As regards more conventional architectural projects, Lewerentz was most successful in the design of residential buildings, often undertaken in collaboration with Torsten Stubelius—see, for example, the various projects for workers' housing estates, such as those of Eneborg and Pålsjö, at Helsingborg (only partially realized), or the one for the Marma-Långrörs Sågverk at Marmaverken, on which he worked from 1915 onwards.

In 1929 he founded a small firm specializing in the production of illuminated signs and display stands —Stockholm Ljusreklam AB—and began, as an interior designer, a lucrative and intense activity renovating commercial premises, which occupied much of his time for nearly twenty years and also led him to take in interest in advertising graphics. He designed, for example, the posters and logo for the Stockholm Exhibition of 1930. Nonetheless, between 1930 and 1940— the year in which he opened a factory for the production of IDESTA door and window frames and metal fixtures at Eskilstuna—Lewerentz continued to work on competition projects for buildings and the design of new cemeteries. Having always been fascinated by the problems associated with the details of the project, he patented numerous fittings for the use of metal door and window frames in the same period. It was only in 1956 that he left the management of the IDESTA factory to his son and returned to devote himself, once again, exclusively to architecture. This date is especially significant because it is the year in which Lewerentz won the competition for St Mark's Church at Björkhagen, Stockholm. Published in the leading international architecture journals, the project earned him fame that was destined to grow enormously. This were the years when the now elderly architect, increasingly austere and less willing to compromise, produced his last works, in particular three masterpieces displaying extraordinary lucidity and perspicacity: the church of St Mark at Björkhagen, that of St Peter at Klippan and the flower stall in the Eastern Cemetery at Malmö. Lewerentz died in 1975, aged ninety, at Lund, where he had moved after the death of his wife Edith. This was only a few years after the completion of the flower kiosk in the cemetery at Malmö, the last addition to a project on which he had worked for a large part of his career, having won the competition for the design of the cemetery in 1916. Thus, by a strange quirk of fate, the long story of the architect can be said to have started and finished in the same place.

Professional Associations and Awards

Member of the Svenska Slöjdföreningen (Swedish Society of Arts and Crafts, 1914.

Honourable mention at CIAM XII in Brussels, 1930.

Member of the Kung. Akademien för de fria konsterna (Royal Academy of the Liberal Arts), Stockholm, 1936.

Prince Eugene medal, 1950.

Member of the Kunstakademiet of Copenhagen, 1954.

Member of Die Bayerische Akademie der schönen Kunst of Munich, 1960.

Awarded the *hederskub* of the Svensaka Akitekters Riksförbund (National Association of Swedish Architects), 1961.

Honorary doctor of the Kungl. Tekniska Högskolan of Stockholm, 1962.

Tessin Medal, the Kung. Akademien för de fria konsterna, Stockholm, 1962.

Awarded the first Kasper Sahlinpriset by the Svensaka Akitekters Riksförbund, 1962.

Awarded the Olaf Höbergplaketten, Norrlandsförbund (Association of the Nordic Countries), 1965.

Honorary member of the Svensaka Akitekters Riksförbund, 1967.

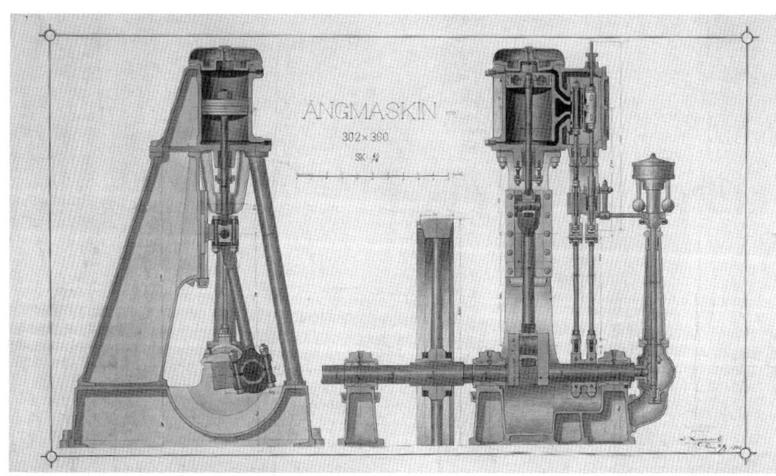

Chronological List of Works

1909.1
Project for a Summer Residence, 1909
School Project (under the guidance of Prof. C.A. Grundström).

1910.1
Project for a Naval Museum at Kastellholmen, Stockholm, 1910 (1)
School project (prepared while studying at the Klara Skola)

1910.2
Project for a Residential Building, Norrköping, 1910–11
(prepared while studying at the Klara Skola)

1911.1
Competition Project for a Mixed School, Nässjö, 1911, with T. Stubelius

1911.2
Project for the Restoration of the Church of Ytterlänä, Ångermanland, 1911

1911.3
Project for Workers' Housing at Eneborg and Pålsjö, Helsingborg, 1911–18, with T. Stubelius

1911.4
Working-Class Housing at Karlshäll, Luleå, 1911–13, with T. Stubelius, partially demolished

1911.5
Furnishings, 1911 onwards

1912.1
Villa Gustav M. Ericsson, Lidingö-Brevik, 1912, with T. Stubelius

1912.2
Boathouse for the Canoes of the City Rowing Club, Stockholm, 1912, with T. Stubelius

1912.3
Project for Residential Building, Norrköping, 1912

1912.4
Building with Shop and Flat at Näsby, Finspång, 1912

1912.5
Participation in the Nationalföreningen mot emigrationen exhibition, Stockholm, 1912

1912.6
Lamps for ASEA and Böhlmarks, with T. Stubelius

1912.7
Furnishings for NK (Nordiska Kompaniet), 1912, with T. Stubelius

1912.8
Project for Managers' Houses for Sandö Sågverk AB, Sandö, 1912–13, with T. Stubelius

1912.9
Workers' Houses for Skånska Kolbrvtnings AB, Nyvång, 1912–13 with T. Stubelius, project partially realized

1913.1
Competition Project for a Primary School, Kalmar, 1913, motto "Per"

1913.2
Competition Project for the Liljevalch Art Gallery, Djurgården, Stockholm, 1913

1913.3
Renovation of the *Corps de Logis*, Ånhammer, 1913, with T. Stubelius

1913.4
Restoration of the Church of Bro, Uppland, 1913

1913.5
Carpet for Göteborg Tapetfabrik, 1913, with T. Stubelius

1913.6
Glass Objects for Färe Glasbruk, 1913, with T. Stubelius

1913.7
Holiday House for Olle Hjortzberg and Project for a Housing Scheme at Kummelnäs, Värmdö, 1913–14, with T. Stubelius, demolished

1913.8
Renovation and Extension of the Axel Villa, Drottningholm, Stockholm, 1913–14, with T. Stubelius

1913.9
Project for the Extension to the Baltic Separatorer AB Factory, Södertälje, 1913–14, with T. Stubelius and Industribyrån AB

1913.10
Conference Hall for Färe Glasbruk, Sibbhult, 1913–14, with T. Stubelius, demolished

1913.11
Project for Tombstones and Funerary Monuments, 1913 onwards

1914.1
Villa Ahxner, Djursholm, Stockholm, 1914, with T. Stubelius (extension and renovation of attic, 1926-27)

1914.2
Project for the Villa of K.J. Beskow, Helsingborg, 1914, with T. Stubelius

1914.3
Villa Solsidan and Project for a Housing Scheme at Saltsjöbaden, Stockholm, 1914, with T. Stubelius

1914.4
Project for a Crematorium at Bergaliden, Helsingborg, 1914, with T. Stubelius

1914.5
Project for a Housing Scheme at Bergaliden, Helsingborg, 1914, with T. Stubelius

1914.6
Project for Houses for the Workers and Engineers of Forsbackabruk, Forsbacka, 1914, with T. Stubelius

1914.7
Exhibition of the Baltic Nations, Malmö, 1914, with T. Stubelius,

1914.8
Summer Restaurant at Pålsjö, Helsingborg, 1914, with T. Stubelius, completely rebuilt

1914.9
Villa Ramén, Helsingborg, 1914–15, with T. Stubelius

1914.10
Forsbacka Cemetery, 1914–22, with T. Stubelius

1914.11
Project for the Development Plan of Brantevik, 1914–29

1915.1
Project for the Villa of Erick Banck, Helsingborg, 1915, with T. Stubelius

1915.2
Competition Project for Buildings for the Swedish Navy at Skeppsholmen, Stockholm, 1915, motto "till Skepps"

1915.3
Renovation and Extension of the

Corps de Logis at Högsbo, Sandviken, 1915

1915.4
House and Shop in Kungsgatan, Stockholm, 1915

1915.5
Illustration for *Teknisk Tidskrift*, 1915

1915.6
Project for the Town Hall of Storängen, 1915

1915.7
Project for the Tomb of L. Forsber, Stockholm, 1915

1915.8
Competition Project for the Extension to the Stockholm South Cemetery at Enskede, Stockholm, 1915, with E.G. Asplund, motto "Tallum", first prize

1915.9
Valdemarsvik Cemetery, 1915–16, interior of the chapel altered in 1942

1915.10
Works and Projects for Marma-Långrörs Sågverk, Marmaverken, Söderhamn, 1915–16, partially with T. Stubelius

1915.11
Various Versions of the Project for the Stockholm South Cemetery at Enskede, Stockholm, 1915–19, with E. G. Asplund

1916.1
Project for the Tombstone of N. and M. Cronstedt, Stockholm, 1916

1916.2
Project for the Tomb of the Grub family, Stockholm, 1916

1916.3
Project for a Housing Estate at Eneborg, Helsingborg, 1916–18, with T. Stubelius, partially realized

1916.4
Rud Cemetery, Karlstad, 1916–19, partially realized, later considerably altered

1916.5
Competition Project for the Eastern Cemetery at Malmö, 1916, motto "Ås", first prize

1917.1
Project for the Cemetery of Nynäshamn, 1917

1917.2
Project for Workers' Houses at Öjervik, Rottneros, 1917

1917.3
Renovation of the *Corps de Logis*, Rottneros, 1917

1917.4
Renovation of the *Corps de Logis*, Öjeby, Rottneros, 1917

1917.5
Project for the Tomb of the Bernström Family, Stockholm, 1917

1917.6
Competition Project for the Reconstruction of the Götaplatsen, Gothenburg, 1917–18, motto "Sköll", first competition

1917.7
Workers' Houses and Project for the Houses of the Engineers of Marma-Långrörs Sågverk, Marmaverken, Söderhamn, 1917–20, with T. Stubelius, demolished

1918.1
New Layout of Eskilstuna Cemetery, 1918

1918.2
Extension to Sundsvall Cemetery, 1918

1918.3
Competition Project for the Urban Design of the Area around Saltsjöbaden Station, Stockholm, 1918–19, motto "Tre", second prize

1918.4
New Version of the Project for the Eastern Cemetery at Malmö, 1918–20

1919.1
Competition Project for the Design of a Prototype of a Tombstone for the Stockholm South Cemetery at Enskede, Stockholm, 1919, with E.G. Asplund

1919.2
Tomb for the Belfrage Family, Stockholm, 1919

1919.3
Project for a Cemetery at Pålsjö, Helsingborg, 1919–20

1919.4
Wallpaper Factory at Undersås, Gothenburg, 1919–20, demolished

1919.5
Project for the Resurrection Chapel (various versions), Waiting-Room and Mortuaries in the Stockholm South Cemetery, 1919–22

1919.6
Extension to Stora Tuna Cemetery and a Cemetery with a Chapel at Kvarnsveden, Borlänge, 1919–24

1920.1
Förening Verkstad Exhibition, Djurgården, Stockholm, 1920, realization of a domestic interior

1920.2
Various Proposals for the Main Entrance to the Stockholm South Cemetery, 1920–23, with E.G. Asplund

1920.3
Project for a Cemetery at Ljungby, 1920–23

1920.4
Realization of the Service Buildings in the Eastern Cemetery at Malmö, 1920–23

1921.1
Project for Urban Renewal of the Norrmalm District, Stockholm, 1921

1921.2
Project for an Extension, Långsele Cemetery, 1921–22

1921.3
Competition Project for Gävleån Cemetery, 1921–22, motto "Efter ån"

1921.4
Cemetery and Chapel at Kvarnsveden, Borlänge, 1921–24, a crematorium has been added to the chapel

1921.5
Tomb for the Malmström Family, Stockholm, 1921–30

1922.1
Project for Single-Family Houses at Rostorp, Malmö, 1922

1922.2
Exhibition at the Liljevalch Art Gallery, Djurgården, Stockholm, 1922

1922.3
Pavilion for the National Exhibition, Gothenburg, 1922–23

1922.4
Realization of the Open-air Ceremonial Area in the Eastern Cemetery at Malmö, 1922–25

1923.1
Competition Project for Students' Residences and the Students' Union at the University of Uppsala, 1923, with O. Almqvist and B. Hedvall, motto "Futurum"

1923.2
Project for a Cemetery with a Crematorium, Gothenburg, 1923

1923.3
Furnishings for the Förening Verkstad at the Gothenburg Exhibition, 1923

1923.4
Competition Project for the Furnishing of an Office for Åtvidaberg, in the Förening Verkstad Section at the Gothenburg Exhibition, 1923, with O. Almqvist

1923.5
New Version of the Project of Eastern Cemetery at Malmö, 1923

1923.6
Project for the Main Chapel in the Eastern Cemetery at Malmö, 1923–4

1923.7
First Project for the Crematorium in the Eastern Cemetery at Malmö, 1923–5

1923.8
Resurrection Chapel (final version) in the Stockholm South Cemetery, 1923–25

1923.9
Realization of the Chapel of St Birgitta and the Adjacent Mortuary in the Eastern Cemetery at Malmö, 1923–6

1924.1
Design for a Candelabrum, 1924

1924.2
Project (1924–27) and Competitions (1933 onwards) for the Malmö Theatre, 1924 onwards

1924.3
Various Schemes for the Main Entrance to the Stockholm South Cemetery, 1924–31

1925.1
Project for an Extension to the National History Museum, Stockholm, 1925

1925.2
Project for the Djurskola, 1925–30

1926.1
Project for a Work of Art in a Square, Stockholm, 1925–26, with I. Johnsson, project purchased

1926.2
Competition Project for Kviberg Cemetery, Gothenburg, 1926–27, motto "Finis", third prize

1926.3
Extension to Villa H. Ahxner, Djursholm, Stockholm, 1926–27

1927.1
Furnishings for the Dining-Room of G.J. Versteeghs's House, Söderhamn, 1927

1927.2
Project for a Tomb for Häradshövdingen, Stockholm, 1927–28

1927.3
Industrial Building for Ljusnans Sulfatfabrik and Workers' Houses, Marmaverken, Söderhamn, 1927 onwards, partially altered

1928.1
Competition Project for the Urban Renewal of a Block in Jönköping, 1928, with O. Almqvist, first, second and third prizes and a fourth project citation

1928.2
Competition Project for the Katarina Middle School, Stockholm, 1928, with O. Almqvist, motto "Aula"

1928.3
Competition Project for a Nursing Home and Old People's Home, Uppsala, 1928, motto "Fyrisvalls gård"

1928.4
Competition Project for the Urban Renewal of the Area around Lund Cathedral, 1928

1928.5
Hill of Remembrance (final version) in the Stockholm South Cemetery, 1928

1928.6
Project (1928) and Competition (1930) for the Office Building of the Riksförsäkringsanstalten (Social Security Administration), Stockholm, 1928 onwards

1928.7
New Version of the project for the Eastern Cemetery at Malmö, 1928

1928.8
Second Project for the Crematorium in the Eastern Cemetery at Malmö, 1928–29

1929.1
Design for a Malmö Spårväger bus, 1929

1929.2
Wallpaper for Göteborg Tapetfabrik, 1929

1929.3
Tombstones of Edit and Sigurd Lewerentz, Utterö, 1929

1929.4
Tomb for the Holming Family, Gothenburg, 1929–30

1929.5
Offices for Philips AB, Stockholm, 1929–30, rebuilt

1929.6
Tomb of T.A. Bergen, Utterö, Stockholm, 1920

1929.7
Renovation of the Marabou shop, Gothenburg, 1929–34, demolished

1929.8
Factory Building for Uddeholms Sulfatfabrik at Skoghallsverken, Karlstad, 1929 onwards

1929.9
Pavilions and Other Buildings, Furnishings, Objects and Graphics for the Stockholm Exhibition of 1930, Djurgården, 1929–30

1929.10
Renovation Project Executed by Stockholm Ljusreklam AB, AB BLOKK and AB IDESTA, 1929 onwards

1930.1
Project for a Factory Building for Östrands Sulfatfabrik, Sundsvall, 1930

1930.2
Sigurd Lewerentz's Speedboat, Stockholm, 1930

1930.3
Renovation of the Diners de Paris Restaurant, Stockholm, 1930, demolished

1930.4
Project for the Interior Design of the Hotel Eden, Stockholm, 1930

1930.5
Enköping Cemetery, 1930–32

1930.6
Invitation Competition for a Project for the Headquarters of the Riksförsäkringsanstalt (National Insurance Institute), Stockholm, 1920–32, first prize (1930 competition)

1930.7
Project for the Renovation of the PUB Department Store, Stockholm, 1930–34

1930.8
Renovation of Filips Confectioner's, Stockholm, 1930–34, demolished

1930.9
Project for the Main Chapel, the Crematorium and the Entrance Area of the Stockholm South Cemetery, 1930–34, with E.G. Asplund

1931.1
Project for a Standard Holiday Chalet, 1931

1931.2
Participation in the 46th Exhibition of the Architectural League of New York, New York, 1931

1931.3
Project for the Shop Front and Sign of an Ironmonger's, Stockholm, 1931

1931.4
Renovation of the Husmodern Department Store, 1931, demolished

1931.5
Renovation and Interior Design of the Stockholm Skofabrik, Stockholm, 1931, demolished

1931.6
Renovation and Interior Design of the Regina Magazinet, Stockholm, 1931

1931.7
Project for the Renovation and Interior Design of the Rivoli Cinema, Stockholm, 1931

1931.8
Competition Project for a Girls' High School, Stockholm, 1931–32, with O. Almqvist, motto "Balk"

1931.9
Project for the Renovation of the Italien Storre Department Store, Stockholm, 1931–32

1931.10
Realization of the Chapel in the Eastern Cemetery at Malmö, 1931–32

1932.1
Competition Project for Malmö City Museum, 1932, with O. Almqvist, E. Wettergren and A.G. Hedberg, motto "Anno 1932", citation

1932.2
Competition Project for the Town Plan of the Nedre Norrmalm District, Stockholm, 1932, motto "5881"

1932.3
Furnishings for the Koux Family's Bedroom, 1932

1932.4
Project for the Renovation of the Livsmedelsbutik Shop, Stockholm, 1932

1932.5
Olssons Car Showroom, Stockholm, 1932, demolished

1932.6
Renovation of the Centralvarhus, Stockholm, 1932, demolished

1932.7
Renovation of AB Arkimedes Baekmans, Stockholm, 1932, demolished

1932.8
Renovation of the Helios & Henkel Department Store, Stockholm, 1932, demolished

1932.9
Project for a Chapel with an Adjacent Crematorium in Djursholm Cemetery, Stockholm, 1932–33

1933.1
Project for a Power Station at Djursholm, Stockholm, 1933

1933.2
Project for a Residential Area at Djursholm, Stockholm, 1933

1933.3
Project for a Warehouse at Frihannen, Stockholm, 1933

1933.4
Project for the Division of Land into Plots at Aludden, Djursholm, Stockholm, 1933

1933.5
Project for Gudmundrå Cemetery, 1933

1933.6
Project for an Industrial Building, Hammarby, 1933

1933.7
Project for a Crematorium, Kramfors, 1933

1933.8
Renovation of the Centrum Shop, Stockholm, 1933, demolished

1933.9
First Competition for the Malmö Theatre, 1933, motto "43", first prize

1933.10
Project for an Extension to the Headquarters of the Riksförsäkringsanstalt (National Insurance Institute), Stockholm, 1933–34

1933.11
Villa Edstrand, Falsterbo, 1933–37

1933.12
Competition Project for the Church of Johannesberg, Gothenburg, 1933–34, motto "Svart och vitt"

1934.1
Competition Project for Bromma Airport, Stockholm, 1934, citation

1934.2
Project for Norberg Cemetery, 1934

1934.3
Interior Design of a Number of Rooms of the Förening Sällskapet, Stockholm, 1934

1934.4
Project for the Tomb of R. Dymling, Stockholm, 1934

1934.5
Funerary Monument for C.D. Ekman, Northfleet, England, 1934

1934.6
Internal Fixtures and Entrance Door of the Museum of Technology, Stockholm, 1934, demolished

1935.1
Project for Manhem Cemetery, Falun, 1935

1935.2
Second Competition for the Malmö Theatre, 1935, motto "1625", first prize

1935.3
Building for Bröderna Edstrand AB, Malmö, 1935–36, altered and extended

1935.4
Realization of the Chapel in the Eastern Cemetery at Malmö, 1935–36

1935.5
Project for and Realization of the Bell-Tower, the Chapels of St Gertrud and St Knut and the Extension to the Crematorium in the Eastern Cemetery at Malmö, 1935–43

1935.6
Final Project for the Malmö Theatre, 1935–44, with E. Lallerstedt and D. Helldén

1936.1
Competition Project for an Extension to the Karolinska Institutet, Solna, 1936, with David Helldén, motto "abc"

1936.2
Extension to Fönsterfabric AB, Eskilstuna, 1936, demolished

1936.3
Renovation of the Façade of the Meeths Shop, Stockholm, 1936, demolished

1936.4
Project for an Extension to the Headquarters of the Riksförsäkringsanstalt (National Insurance Institute), Stockholm, 1936

1937.1
Project for St Sigfrid Griftegård Cemetery, Borås, 1937

1937.2
Project for an Extension to Berns Salonger, Stockholm, 1937

1937.3
Proposals for Finishings for the Stockholm South Cemetery, 1937–40

1938.1
Competition Project for the Factory and Offices of Åhlrén & Åkerlunds, Stockholm, 1938, motto "Nu"

1938.2
Project for a New Building in Valhallavägen for the Headquarters of the Riksförsäkringsanstalt (National Insurance Institute), Stockholm, 1938–39

1939.1
Project for Bonnierhuset, Stockholm, 1939

1940.1
Renovation of a Factory, Eskilstuna, 1940 onwards, demolished

1940.2
Various Works and Projects for IDESTA, Eskilstuna, 1940–56

1942.1
Proposed Project for Sködvde Cemetery, 1942

1943.1
Realization of Lewerentz's Flat on the Top Floor of the IDESTA Factory, Eskilstuna, 1943, demolished

1944.1
Competition Project for a Work of Art in Vasa Torget, Linköping, 1944, with I.R. Nilsson

1944.2
Extension to Villa Edstrand, Falsterbo, 1944

1947.1
Competition Project for the Renovation of Uppsala Cathedral, 1947–55, motto "med fasta rötter"

1947.2
Project for the Conservation of Nianfors Chapel, Hudisvall, 1947

1948.1
Renovation of the North Wing of the *Corps de Logis* at Broxvik, 1948

1949.1
Competition Project for the Uppsala City Hall, 1949, invitation competition, motto "Miljo", project purchased

1949.2
Competition Project for the Interior Design of a Flat, for Svenska Slöjdföreningen, 1949, motto "Rör"

1949.3
Second Competition for the Conservation of Uppsala Cathedral, 1949, motto "reflexion", first prize

1950.1
Various Alternative Proposals for the Conservation of Uppsala Cathedral, 1950–55, with P. Celsing

1951.1
Project for an Extension to the Headquarters of the Riksförsäkringsanstalt (National Insurance Institute), Stockholm, 1951–52

1952.1
Competition Project for a New Layout for the Kungsträdgården, Stockholm, 1952, motto "Kul"

1952.2
Storerooms and Service Buildings in the Stockholm South Cemetery, 1952–61

1955.1
Project for and Realization of the Chapel of Hope in the Eastern Cemetery at Malmö, 1955–56

1956.1
Renovation of Lewerentz's House at Skanör, 1956

1956.2
Competition Project for Students' Residences and the Students' Union at the University of Uppsala, 1956, motto "UBBO VI", citation

1956.3
Competition Project for St Mark's Parish Church at Björkhagen,

Stockholm, 1956–64, invitation competition, motto "Mellanspel"

1958.1
Place of Remembrance in the Stockholm South Cemetery, 1958–61

1961.1
Project for Stadsgård Square, Arboga, 1961 onwards

1962.1
Project for another house near the Villa Edstrand, Falsterbo, 1962 onwards

1962.2
Project for the Town Plan of Helgeandsholmen and Gustav Adolfs Torg, partially with P. Celsing (1962–64) and Competition for an Extension to the Parliament Building, partially with Bernt Nyberg (1969–71), Stockholm

1962.3
St Peter's Church at Klippan, 1962–66

1968.1
Project for and Realization of the Flower Stall and Custodian's House in the Eastern Cemetery at Malmö, 1968–71

1969.1
Competition Project for an Extension to the Parliament Building, Stockholm, 1969–71, partially with B. Nyberg (1969–71), motto "Genom samma port"

1971.1
Waiting-room and Place of Remembrance in the Stockholm South Cemetery, 1971

1972.1
Project for and Realization of Gates in the Eastern Cemetery at Malmö, 1972–74

1974.1
Competition Project for a Parish Church and Adjacent Buildings at Växjö, 1974, with B. Nyberg, motto "Circondare", citation

1974.2
Chair in Metal and Laminated Wood, 1974

1975.1
Project for a Display Stand for the Bricks of Helsingborg Tegelfabrik on the Premises of the Svensk Byggtjans, Stockholm, 1975

Works and Projects Lacking Precise Dates

0.1
Project for Slottshagen, Helsingborg, n.d. (attribution uncertain)

0.2
Study for a Column, n.d.

0.3
Seaside Villa (other details lacking)

0.4
Renovation of the Interior of the Röska Applied Art Museum, Gothenburg, n.d.

0.5
Flooring of the Bergslaget Museum, n.d.

0.6
Project for a Funerary Chapel at Hotagen, n.d.

0.7
Project for the Furnishings of a Bedroom, n.d. (1910–30)

0.8
Project for an Altar, n.d. (second decade of twentieth century)

0.9
Lovön Pavilion at Drottningholm, Stockholm, n.d. (second decade of twentieth century)

0.10
Project for the Interior Design of a Cinema, Stockholm, n.d. (second decade of twentieth century), with T. Stubelius

0.11
Project for the Tomb of M. Tisell, Stockholm, n.d. (second decade of twentieth century)

0.12
Various Projects for Tombstones, n.d. (second decade of twentieth century)

0.13
Various Projects for Tombstones, n.d. (1920s)

0.14
Competition Project for the Bekå Department Store, Malmö, n.d. (1930s)

0.15
Project for Various Items of Furnishing (1930s)

0.16
Various Projects for Tombstones, n.d. (1930s)

0.17
Project for the Feith Cafeteria, Stockholm, n.d. (1930s)

0.18
Renovation of a Shop in Storgatan, Stockholm, n.d. (1930s)

0.19
Project for the Renovation of a Shop in Oslo, Norway, n.d. (1930s)

Bibliography

1913

Almqvist, O., "Täflan angående ny folkskolan i kalmar", in *Teknisk Tidskrift: Arkitektur*, no. III, March 1913, pp. 29–38.

Bergsten, C.G., "Några fabriksmässigt framställda föremål", in *Teknisk Tidskrift: Arkitektur*, no. V, May 1913, pp. 57–61.

1914

Bergsten, C.G., "En rjekterad krematorieanläggning för Helsinborg", in *Teknisk Tidskrift: Arkitektur*, no. X, 1914, pp. 111-118.

"Sommarstugor vid Kummelnäs", in *Teknisk Tidskrift: Arkitektur*, no. IX, 1914, pp. 105–08.

1915

Blanck, N., "Der Wettbewerb", in *Die Garten Kunst*, September 1915a, pp. 113–15.

Blanck, N., "Täflan om utvidgning av Stockholms Södra Begrafningsplats", in *Teknisk Tidskrift: Arkitektur*, no. VI, 1915b, pp. 43–68.

Lewerentz, S., "Kyrkogård, kyrka och gravkapell för Forsbackabruk", in *Teknisk Tidskrift: Arkitektur*, no. III, 1915, p. 28.

1916

"Skeppsholmstäflingen", in *Teknisk Tidskrift: Arkitektur*, no. I, 1916, p. 25.

"Tävlingen till Malmö Östra kyrkogård", in *Teknisk Tidskrift: Arkitektur*, no. V, 1916, p. 72.

1917

Fisker, K., "Svensk nogle spredte indtrik," in *Arkitekten*, no. 6, November 1917, pp. 49–55.

1918

Ahlberg, H., "Der Neue Sudliche Begrabningsplats von Stockholm", in *Die Gartent Kunst*, June 1918, pp. 73–78.

"Götaplatsen", in *Teknisk Tidskrift: Arkitektur*, no. VIII, 1918, pp. 111–23.

1919

Asplund, E.G., "Saltsjöbadtävlingen", in *Teknisk Tidskrift: Arkitektur*, no. III, March 1919, pp. 33–41.

Lewerentz, S., "Ingenjör H. Axners bostad Djursholms–Ösby", in *Teknisk Tidskrift: Arkitektur*, no. XII, December 1919, pp. 149–51.

1920

Åkerlund, J., "Verkstadens utställning", in *Tidskrift för Hembygdsvård*, 1920, pp. 1–11.

Bergsten, C.G., "Möbler och interiörkonst på verkstadens utställning", in *Svenska Sjödföreningens Tidskrift*, no. 13, 1920, pp. 59–81.

Wahlman, L.I., "Rumkonsten på Verkstadens utställning", in *Teknisk Tidskrift: Arkitektur*, no. XII, December 1920, pp. 157–68.

1923

Ahlberg, H., "Konstindustribyggnaderna på Göteborgsutställningen", in *Byggmästaren*, no. 5, 1923, p. 286.

Asplund, E.G., "Bilder med randanteckningar drån Konstindustribuggnaderna på Göteborgsutställningen", in *Byggmästaren*, no. 5, 1923, pp. 277–85.

Blanck, N., "Göteborgsutställningen", in *Teknisk Tidskrift: Arkitektur*, no. 19, October 1923, pp. 339–45.

Lewerentz, S., "Verkstadens avdeling", in *Byggmästaren*, no. 5, 1923, pp. 286–87.

1924

Ahlberg, H., "Tävlingen om byggnad för Uppsala studentkår", in *Byggmästaren*, no. 1, 1924, pp. 1–10.

Friberger, E., "Teatertävlingen och Götaplatsen", in *Byggmästaren*, no. 8, 1924, pp. 97–105.

Rasmussen, S.E., "Hanstholm", in *Teknisk Tidskrift: Arkitektur*, no. 7, April 1924, pp. 97–112.

1926

Lewerentz, S., "Helsingborgs stads egna hem", in *Byggmästaren*, no. 4, 1926a, pp. 25–28.

Lewerentz, S., "Nyare byggnadsverk i Skåne", in *Byggmästaren*, no. 2, 1926b, pp. 22–24.

Lewerentz, S., "Uppgifter rörande Skogskykogårdens Uppståndelsekapell med tillhörande byggnader", in *Byggmästaren*, no. 20, 1926c, pp. 238–41.

Markelius, S., "Uppståndelsekapellet", in *Byggmästaren*, no. 20, 1926, pp. 233–37.

Pauli, G., *Daneliustävlan*, *Byggmästaren*, no. 13, 1926, pp. 150–56.

1927

Friberger, E., "Den nya begravningsplatsen i Göteborg", in *Byggmästaren*, no. 4, 1927, pp. 41–45.

1928

Blanck, N., "Gammal och ny kyrkogårdskonst i Skåne", in *Byggmästaren/Arkitektupplagan*, 1928, pp. 181–87.

Lewerentz, S., "Östra kyrkogården i Malmö", in *Byggmästaren/Arkitektupplagan*, 1928a, pp. 188 ff.

Lewerentz, S., "Stora Tuna Norra begravningslats", in *Byggmästaren/Arkitektupplagan*, 1928b, pp. 18–19.

"Några kapell och staplar: Stora Tuna Norra begravningslats", in *Byggmästaren/Arkitektupplagan*, 1928, pp. 20–25.

Sundahl, E., "Tävlingen om Katarina Real", in *Byggmästaren/Arkitektupplagan*, 1928, pp. 81–88.

Sundbärg, G., "Tävlingen av Uppsala Ålderdomshem", in *Byggmästaren/Arkitektupplagan*, 1928, p. 29.

"Tävlingen till Uppsala", in *Byggmästaren/Arkitektupplagan*, p. 141.

"Två tävlingar: Bebyggandet av visst kvartersområdet i Jönköping", in *Byggmästaren/Arkitektupplagan*, 1928, pp. 141–45.

1929

Schamalensèe, K.V., "Tävlan om ordnandet av trakten kring Lunds Domkyrka", in *Byggmästaren/Arkitektupplagan*, 1929, pp. 28–29.

1930

"Stockholmsutställningen 1930", in *Byggmästaren/Arkitektupplagan*, special issue, 1930.

1931

Olsson, T.W., "Norrmalmstävlingens program", in *Byggmästaren/Arkitektupplagan*, 1931, pp. 161–62.

1932

Bartning, H., "Holzhausbau in Schweden", in *Werk*, no. 2, February 1932, pp. 52–60.

Lewerentz, S., "Riksförsäkringsanstaltens nybyggnad", in *Byggmästaren 32/Arkitektupplagan 11*, 1932a, pp. 191–200.

Lewerentz, S., "Svenska Aktiebolaget hilis nybyggnad i Stockholm", in *Byggmästaren 32/Arkitektupplagan 11*, 1932b, pp. 201–06.

Lindström, S., "Tävlingen om Malmö Museum", in *Byggmästaren 38 /Arkitektupplagan 13*, 1932, pp. 223–36.

Romare, B., "Tävlingen om högre allmänt Läroverk för Flikor i Stockholm", in *Byggmästaren 5/Arkitektupplagan 2*, pp. 30–31.

1933

Curman, J., "Tävlingen om Malmö Stadsteater", in *Byggmästaren 35/Arkitektupplagan 12*, 1933, pp. 178–92.

1934
"Arkitekttävlingen om flystationsanläggning vid Bromma", in *Byggmästaren 32/Arkitektupplagan 11*, October 1934, pp. 197–205.
Markelius, S., "Norrmälmstävlingen", in *Byggmästaren 3/Arkitektupplagan 2*, 1934, pp. 20–34.
Olsson, T., "Trafikkommiten och Norrmälmstävlingen", in *Byggmästaren 14/Arkitektupplagan 5*, 1934, pp. 79–82.
Zimdahl, H., "Tävlingen om Johannesbergskyrkan i Göteborg", in *Byggmästaren 14/Arkitektupplagan 5*, pp. 67–78.

1935
Ahrbom, N., "Den andra tävlingen om Malmö Stadsteater", in *Byggmästaren 29/Arkitektupplagan 10*, 1935, pp. 161–72.

1937
"Tävlingen till utbyggnad av Karoliniska Institutet i Solna", in *Byggmästaren*, no. 13, 1937, pp. 135–46.

1941
Ahlsèn, E., "Sigurd Lewerentz' Villa Edstrand, Falsterbo", in *Byggmästaren*, no. 25, 1941, pp. 313–16.

1942
"Malmö stadsteater", in *Byggmästaren*, no. 10, 1942, pp. 130–42.
Skogskyrkogården och Heliga korsets Kapell i Stockholm, Stockholm 1942.

1943
Zevi, B., "Crematoria in the Forest Cemetery of Enskede, Stockholm", in *The Architectural Review*, no. 94, September 1943, pp. 63–67.

1944
Lallerstedt, E. *et alii*, "Malmö stadsteater och konserthus", in *Byggmästaren*, no. 22, 1944, pp. 398–422.
Renius, L., "Ny Teater", in *Byggmästaren*, no. 22, 1944, pp. 395–97.

1945
Ahlberg, H., "Sigurd Lewerentz", in *Byggmästaren*, no. 19, 1945, pp. 359–60.
Jacobsen, A., "Kapel og krematorium i Malmö", in *Byggmästaren*, no. 19, 1945, pp. 360–79.
Lewerentz, S., "Några data från bygget", in *Byggmästaren*, no. 19, 1945, pp. 380–82.

1947
Reinius, L., "Uppsala Domkyrkas Yttre Restaurering", in *Byggmästaren*, no. 8, 1947, pp. 117–32.

1948
Lewerentz, S., "Takvåning i Eskilstuna", in *Byggmästaren*, no. 1, 1948, pp. 2–7.

1949
Reinius, L., "Stadshus i Uppsala", in *Byggmästaren*, no. 23, 1949, pp. 493–503.
"Tävlingen till Uppsala Stadshus", in *Tävlenbadet*, no. 3, 1949, p. 25.

1950
Lewerentz, S., "Osvald Almqvist", in *Byggmästaren*, no. 11, 1950, p. 240.
Reinius, L., "Domkyrkan", in *Byggmästaren*, no. 7, 1950, pp. 125–32.
"Tävlingen till Kungssträdgården", in *Byggmästaren*, no. 13, 1950, p. 275.

1951
L. Reinius, "Uppsala Domkyrka, en permanent skandal?", in *Byggmästaren*, no. 4, 1951, p. 67.

1956
Lind, S.I. *et alii*, "Uppsala domkyrkas restaurering", in *Byggmästaren*, no. 35, 1956, pp. 117–21.
"Tävlingen till studentbostader och kårhus", in *Byggmästaren*, no. 40, 1956, p. 156.

1961
Celsing, P., "Hur en kyrka blir till. Kyrkan bygger 1960–1961", in *Stockholm*, 1961, pp. 29–39.
Johansson, B.O.H., *Skogskyrkogården i Enskedek*, Uppsala Universitet, Uppsala 1961.

1962
Lind, S.I., "A Poem in Fact", in *Kontur*, no. 11, 1962a, pp. 10–19.
Lind, S. I., "Kyrkorum i vår tid", in *Form*, no. 2, 1962b, pp. 71–79.
"Tegel og arkitektur", in *Tegel*, no. 6, 1962, pp. 10–17.
Uhlin, L., "Skaparen av kyrkan i Björkhagen", in *Vår Tid*, no. 25–26, 1962, pp. 5–18.

1963
Ahlberg, H., "Sigurd Lewerentz", in *Arkitektur*, no. 9, September 1963, pp. 201–44.
Almqvist, O., "Markuskyrkan i Skarpnäck", in *Arkitektur*, no. 9, September 1963, pp. 246–54.
Fisher, K., "Markuskyrken i Björkhagen", in *Arkitektur DK*, no. 1, February 1963, pp. 1–17.
Knutsen, K., "En Mesterarkitekt i Norden", in *Byggekunst*, no. 3, 1963, pp. 68–71.
Lewerentz, S., "Biörkhagen church near Stockholm", in *Architectural Design*, no. 3, March 1963, pp. 137–38.
Lind, S.I., "Om kvalitet i kyrkobyggndet", in *Skarpnäcks kyrkfrämjandet*, no. 1–2, 1963, p. 5.
Lund, K., "Det glomda språket", in *Byggekunst*, no. 3, 1963, pp. 61–67.
Naucler, J., "Tegel balkar", in *Tegel*, no. 2, 1963, pp. 26–31.
Olsson, P.–O., "Fenomenent Lewrentz", in *Arkitektur*, no. 9, September 1963, pp. 255–56.
"Sigurd Lewerentz", in *Arkitektur*, no. 9, September 1963, monographic issue.

1964
Olsson, P.–O., "Arkitektuppdrag", in *Arkitektur*, no. 3, March 1964, p. 41.
Celsing, P., "Om Helgeandsholmen", in *Arkitektur*, no. 3, March 1964, pp. 42–48.

1965
Linn, B., *Markuskyrkans arkitektur*, Nyköping 1965, brochure.

1966
"Brevväxling om Sergelstorg av Sigurd Lewerentz", in *Arkitektur*, no. 12, December 1966, p. 143.
Exner, J., "Kirken i Klippan", in *Kirkens Verden*, no. 4, 1966, pp. 105–14.
Sykes, C., "Biörkhagen Church", in *The Brik Bulletin*, no. 4, May 1966, pp. 2–5.

1967
Hård af Segerstad, U.H., "Kyrkobygglia betraktelser", in *Arkitektur*, no. 4, April 1967, pp. 160–61.
Olsson, P.–O., "Kyrka i Klippan", in *Arkitektur*, no. 4, April 1967, pp. 162–63.

1968
Friberg, P., "Karlstads förra Kirkogård", in *Tavlingsblad*, no. 8, 1968, p. 21.
Jackson, J.B., "The Vanishing Epitaph", in *Landscape*, 17, no. 2, 1967–68, pp. 165–69.
Lind, S., "Kyrka i Klippan", in *Arkitektur*, no. 5, May 1968a, pp. 2–13.
Lind, S., "Kirka i Klippan", in *Arkitektur DK*, no. 3, October 1968b, pp. 217–27.
Nordenström, H., *Strukturanalys Sigurd Lewrentz Uppståndelskapellet på Skogskykogårdeno. En arkitekturteotisk studie*, STH, Istitutionen för Arkitektur, Stockholm 1968.
Nyberg, B. (ed.), *Sigurd Lewerentz 1968*, Lund 1968.
"Sct. Petri Kirke i Klippa", in *Tegl*, no. 2, 1968, pp. 12–19.
"The Church in Klippan, Sweden", in *Mobilia*, no. 150, 1968.

1969
Arlock, E., *St. Petri kyrka i Klippan*, Klippan 1969.

1970
Högmässa i Klippan, St. Petri, Klippan 1970.
"Markuskyrkan 10 år", in *Skarpnäcks församlingsblad*, no. 1, 1970, pp. 6–7.

1971
"Tävlingen till nytt Riksdagshus på Helgeandsholmen", in *Tävlingsbladet*, no. 7, 1971, p. 44.

1972
"Riksdagshus tävlingen", in *Arkitektur*, no. 3, 1972a, pp. 28–29.
"Riksdagshus tävlingen", in *Arkitektur*, no. 10, 1972b, p. 22.

1973
Lewerentz, S., "Betonghus på Östra kyrkogården i Malmö", in *Arkitektur*, no. 2, 1973a, pp. 4–9.
Lewerentz, S., "Om–och tillbygnad av krematoriet", in *Arkitektur*, no. 2, 1973b, pp. 10–13.
Olsson, P.–O., "Arkitekt i vår tid", in *Arkitektur*, no. 2, 1973, p. 3.
Rappe, K., *Markuskyrkan, Skarpnäck församling i Stockholm*, Uppsala Universitet, Uppsala 1973.
"Riksdagshus tävlingen", in *Arkitektur*, no. 1, 1973, p. 2.

1974
"Circondare", in *Tävlingsbladet*, no. 6, 1974, p. 19.
Debatten om Uppsala Domkyrkas restaurering, Stockholm 1974.
Konfeldt, I.-H., *S:t Petri kyrka i Klippan*, Lunds Universitet, Konsthistoria Istitutionen, Lund 1974.
Wretholm, E., "Där den yttersta enkel-heten segrat", in *Vecko Journalen*, no. 41, October 1974, pp. 14–17.

1976
Anshelm, K., "Sigurd Lewrentz's last house", in *Arkitektur*, no. 2, May 1976, p. 3.

Codrington, J., "Sigurd Lewrentz 1885–1975", in *The Architectural Review*, no. 950, April 1976, p. 223.
Gonzalez, G.A., "Om Skogskyrkogarden", in *Arkitektur*, no. 8, December 1976, p. 27.
Nyberg, B., "Sigurd Lewerentz's last house", in *Arkitektur*, no. 2, May 1976, p. 2.
Roth, N., "Sigurd Lewerentz och Markuskyrkan", in *Skarpnäcks församlingsblad*, no. 1, 1976, pp. 5–8.
"Sigurd Lewrentz in Memoriam", in *Arkitektur DK*, no. 3, February 1976, p. 55.

1977
Porphyrius, D., "Reversible faces", in *Lotus international*, no. 16, 1977, pp. 35–41.

1981
Uhlig, H., *Klippano. Lewerentz kyrka*, Konstakademiet, Copenhagen 1981.

1982
Ahlin, J., "Tidigt om Lewrentz", in *Arkitektur*, no. 10, 1982, pp. 14–21.
Bedoire, F., "Den moderna klassicismen", in *Arkitektur*, no. 2, 1982, pp. 12–15.
"Fyra klassiker", in *Arkitektur*, no. 2, 1982, pp. 9–11.
Johansson, B.O.H., "Skogskyrkogården och den sanitaria estetiken", in *Arkitektur*, no. 2, 1982 / vol. I, no. 8, 1982, pp. 26–28.
Knight, S., "Swedish grace", in *International Architects*, vol. I, no. 8, 1982, pp. 8–43.
Mårtelius, J., "Arkitekturens klassiska språk", in *Arkitektur*, no. 2, 1982, pp. 4–5.
"Swedish neo-classicism of the 1920s", in *Arkitektur*, no. 2, 1982, special issue.

1983
Edman, B., "Sigurd Lewerentz", in *Spazio & Società*, no. 23, September–December 1983, pp. 98–105.
Lovén, Å., "Lewerentz' racer", in *Arkitektur*, no. 2, 1983, p. 40.
Porphirios, D., "Classical, Christian, Socialdemocrat: Asplund and Lewerentz's funeraary architecture", in *Lotus international*, no. 38, 1983, pp. 59–70.

1984
Rubino, L., "Where does Lewerentz come in?", in *Spazio & Società*, no. 28, December 1984, pp. 112–19.
Smithson, A., "The landscape that can survive and the Lewerentz connection", in *Spazio & Societa*, no. 25, March 1984, pp. 78–85.

1985
Ahlin, J., "Sigurd Lewerentz", in *Arkitektur*, no. 6, July–August 1985a, pp. 19–29.
Ahlin, J., *Sigurd Lewerentz arkitekt*, Stockholm 1985b (London 1987).
Alenius, S., "Björkhagen Kyrka med Rom som referens", in *Arkitektur*, no. 6, July–August 1985, pp. 30–34.
Eriksson, E., "Asplund & Lewerentz", in *Arkitektur*, no. 6, July–August 1985, p. 2.
Schöenbenck, G., *Sankt Petri kyrka i Klippan*, Göteborg 1985.
Sigurd Lewerentz, 1875–1975, Stockholm 1985.

1986
Ákos, M., "Emlékező modernizmus", in *Magyar Épìtómúvészet*, no. 4, 1986, pp. 51–53
Alenius, S., "Nel centenario di Sigurd Lewerentz", in *Casabella*, no. 528, October 1986, pp. 42–51.
Caldenby, C., "El nordico solitario: Sigurd Lewerentz", in *Quaderns*, no. 169–170, April–September 1986, pp. 120–143.
Gustafsson, C.-H. (ed.), *Sankt Petri Kyrka*, Klippan 1986 (brochure).
Helin, P., "Elämänja kuoleman huoneeti Sigurd Lewerentzin pitkä tie", in *Arkkitekti*, no. 4, 1986, pp. 68–72.
Lindvall, J. (ed.), *Sigurd Lewrentz*, Arkitektmuseets årbok, Stockholm 1986.
Schönbeck, G., "Boken om Lewerentz", review, in *Arkitektur*, no. 4, 1986, pp. 48–49.
Thelaus, E., "Att skriva om arkitektur", review, in *Arkitektur*, no. 9, 1986, pp. 38–39.
Treib, M., "Woodland Cemetery: a dialogue of design and meaning", in *Landscape Architecture*, no. 2, March–April 1986, pp. 42–49.
Vindum, K., "Skogskyrkogården", in *Skala*, no. 6, October 1986, pp. 16–17.

1987
Buchanan, P., "Exhibiting architecture", in *Architectural Review*, no. 1084, June 1987, pp. 4–6.
"Details", in *Techniques & Architecture*, no. 373, special issue, August–September 1987, pp. 62–70.
Hultin, O., "Lewrentz årsbok, recensione", in *Arkitektur*, no. 5, 1987, p. 56.
Lewerentz, exhibition catalogue, Milan 1987.
Linde, G., "Lewrentz da capo", in *Arkitektur*, no. 1, 1987, pp. 60–61.
Sharp, D., *Unsung hero. Sigurd Lewerentz*, review of the exhibition, in *Building Design*, no. 853, September 1987, pp. 26–29.
Sigurd Lewrentz, 1885–1975, exhibition catalogue, Madrid 1987a.
"Sigurd Lewerentz", review, in *AA Files*, no. 16, Autumn 1987b, pp. 104–05.

1988
Andersson, H.O., "Sigurd Lewrentz", in *Classicismo nordico*, Milan 1988 (Helsinki 1982), pp. 123–25.
Markuskyrkan, Stockholm 1988 (brochure).
St John Wilson, C., "Masters of Building: Sigurd Lewerentz", in *Architects' Journal*, no. 15, April 1988a, pp. 32–43.
St John Wilson, C., "Sigurd Lewerentz and the Dilemma of the Classical", in *Perspecta*, no. 24, 1988b, pp. 50–77.
"Swedish architecture", review, in *Society of Architectural Historians' Journal*, no. 2, June 1988, pp. 205–07.
"The box and the forest", review, in *Design book review: DBR*, no. 14, Spring 1988, pp. 52–53.
Uhlin, L. (ed.), *Markuskyrkan*, Stockholm 1988.
Williams, E., "Sigurd Lewerentz", in *Architects' Journal*, no. 15, April 1988, pp. 46–52.

1989
Brawne, M., "Monumental ambivalence", in *Architects' Journal*, no. 7, February 1989, p. 85.
Ortelli, L., "Die Arkitektkten einer idealen Landschaft: Der Südfrienhof in Stckholm von Asplund und Lewerentz, 1915–1940", in *Werk, Bauen + Wohnen*, no. 4, April 1989, pp. 56–60.
Pimlott, M., "Assessing a classic modern: the career of Sigurd Lewerentz", in *Building Design*, no. 925, February 1989, pp. 32–34.
Schmidlin, H., *Herausgeber, Sigurd Lewerentz*, Basel 1989.
Smithson A. and P. (eds.), *Sigurd Lewerentz 1885–1975: The Dilemma of Classicism*, exhibition catalogue, London 1989.
"Truth and beauty: Sigurd Lewerentz 1885–1975. The crisis of classicism", review of the exhibition, in *Architects' Journal*, no. 4, January 1989, pp. 74–75.
Wang, W., *Sigurd Lewerentz: Detail and Reflexion*, Cambridge 1989.

1990
Ahlberg, H., "Sigurd Lewerentz 1885–1975: The Dilemma of Classicism", in *AA Files*, no. 19, Spring 1990, pp. 82–90.
Bedoire, F., "Skogskyrkogården", in *Arkitektur*, no. 4, May 1990, pp. 34–41.
Göran, C., "Le chiese luoghi di aggregazione", in *Abitare*, no. 287, July–August 1990, pp. 184–85.
Jones, B.P., "Mauereröffnungen: Lewerentz' Fenster und Türen bei St Peter in Klippan", in *Architese*, no. 6, November–December 1990, pp. 22–28.
Lund, N.-O., "Kravet om ægthed", in id., *Nordisk Arkitektur*, Copenhagen 1990, pp. 90–92.
Santi, C., "Il parco della meditazione", in *Abitare*, no. 287, July–August 1990, pp. 164–71.

1991
Blundell Jones, P., "Revealing Details. Lewerentz at Klippan", in *Spazio & Società*, no. 53, January–March 1991, pp. 88–97.

1992
Bedoire, F., "Kontorshus: Granne med Lewerentz och Östberg", in *Arkitektur*, no. 5, 1992, p. 59.
Architecture, no. 405, December 1992–January 1993, pp. 92–96.
"Kirkebænke og salmesang", in *Arkitekten*, no. 13, October 1992, p. 384.
"Lewerentz e la Svezia", itinerary no. 83 of *Domus*, in *Domus*, no. 742, October 1992, pp. V–X.
Porro, R., "Retour a la trascendance: cimitiere au sud de Stockholm", in *Techniques et architecture,* no. 405, December–January 1992–93, pp. 92–96.
St John Wilson, C., "Sigurd Lewerentz: The sacred Buildings and the Sacred Sites", in *Architectural Reflections*, London 1992, pp. 110–37.
Wang, W., "Sigurd Lewerentz: Riksforsäkringsanstalten, Stoccolma 1930–1932", in *Domus*, no. 742, October 1992, pp. 74–80.

1993
Edman, B., "Lewerentz muratore", in *Spazio & Società*, no. 64, October–December 1993, pp. 76–83.

1994
Constant, C., *The Woodland Cemetery: Towards a Spiritual Landscape*, Byggförlaget, Stockholm 1994.
Dahle, E., "Sankt Petri Kyrkan i Klippan", in *Mur*, no. 4, 1994, pp. 30–31.

Johansson, L., "Det mest moderna", in *Form*, no. 2, 1994, pp. 60–64.
"Sverige på engelske", review, in *Arkitektur*, no. 7, October 1994, pp. 62–65.
Treib, M., "Constructing significance", in *Landscape Australia*, no. 1, February 1994, pp. 26–31.

1995
Mansilla, L.M., "Beyond the Wall of Hadrian's Villa", in *9H-On Continuity*, 1995, pp. 1–10.
"Sigurd Lewerentz: la neutralidad del orden", in *A&V*, no. 55, September–October 1995, pp. 42–45.

1996
Hart, V., "Sigurd Lewerentz and the 'half-open door'", in *Journal of Architectural History*, vol. 39, 1996, pp. 181–96.
Johansson, B.O.H., *Tallum*, Stockholm 1996.
Wærn, R., "Götaplatsen", in *Tävlingarnas tid*, Stockholm 1996a, pp. 108–38.
Wærn, R., "Kalmar Folkskola", in *Tävlingarnas tid*, Stockholm 1996b, p. 219.
Wærn, R., "Liljevalchs Konstutst; allningensbyggnad", in *Tävlingarnas tid*, Stockholm 1996c, pp. 223–24.
Wærn, R., "Nybyggnader för Kung. Flottan", in *Tävlingarnas tid*, Stockholm 1996d, p. 219.
Wærn, R., "Malmö Begravningsplats", in *Tävlingarnas tid*, Stockholm 1996e, p. 232.
Wærn, R., "Stockholms Södra Begravningsplatsen", in *Tävlingarnas tid*, Stockholm 1996f, p. 229.

1997
Caldenby, C. (ed.), *Architect Sigurd Lewerentz*, Stockholm 1997.
Nicolin, P., "Lewerentz-Klippan", in *Lotus international*, no. 93, June 1997, pp. 6–19.
Postiglione, G., "L'ultimo progetto di Lewerentz", in *Lotus international*, no. 93, June 1997, pp. 20–33.
Sigurd Lewerentz. Two churches, Stockholm 1997.

1998
Postiglione, G. (ed.), "Il cimitero Est di Malmö. Sigurd Lewerentz architetto", in *Casabella*, no. 659, September 1998, pp. 38–65.

1999
Postiglione, G., "Sigurd Lewerentz. La chiesa di S. Pietro a Klippan", in *Costruire in Laterizio*, January–February 1999, pp. 44–51.
Ridderstedet, L., *S. Lewerentz och P. Celsing sakral arkitektur*, Uppsala 1998.
Rudberg, E., *The Stockholm Exhibition 1930*, Stockholm 1999.

2001
Cornoldi, A. (eds.), *Le case degli architetti*, Venice 2001, pp. 226–27.

Monographs
Skogskyrkogården och Heliga korsets Kapell i Stockholm, Stockholm 1942.
Johansson, B.O.H., *Skogskyrkogården i Enskedek*, Uppsala Universitet, Uppsala 1961.
Nordenström, H., *Strukturanalys Sigurd Lewrentz Uppståndelskapellet på Skogskykogårdeno. En arkitekturteotisk studie*, STH, Istitutionen för Arkitektur, Stockholm 1968.
Nyberg, B. (eds.), *Sigurd Lewerentz 1968*, Lund 1968.
Arlock, E., *St. Petri kyrka i Klippan*, Klippan 1969.
Rappe, K., *Markuskyrkan, Skarpnäck församling i Stockholm*, Uppsala Universitet, Uppsala 1973.
Konfeldt, I.-H., *S:t Petri kyrka i Klippan*, Lunds Universitet, Konsthistoria Istitutionen, Lund 1974.
Uhlig, H., *Klippan. Lewerentz kyrka*, Konstakademiet, Copenhagen 1981.
Ahlin, J., *Sigurd Lewerentz arkitekt*, Stockholm 1985 (London 1987).
Schöenbenck, G., *Sankt Petri kyrka i Klippan*, Göteborg 1985.
Lindvall, J. (ed.), *Sigurd Lewerentz*, Arkitektmuseets årbok, Stockholm 1986.
Gustafsson, C.-H. (ed.), *Sankt Petri Kyrka*, Klippan 1986 (brochure).
Sigurd Lewerentz, 1885–1975, exhibition catalogue, Madrid 1987.
Lewerentz, exhibition catalogue, Milan 1987.
Markuskyrkan, Stockholm 1988 (brochure).
Smithson, A. and P. (eds.), *Sigurd Lewrentz 1885–1975: The Dilemma of Classicism*, exhibition catalogue, London 1989.
Constant, C., *Towards a Spiritual Landscape*, Stockholm 1994.
Johansson, B.O.H., *Tallum*, Stockholm 1996.
Sigurd Lewerentz. Two churches, Stockholm 1997.
Caldenby, C. (ed.), *Architect Sigurd Lewerentz*, Stockholm 1997.
Ridderstedet, L., *S. Lewerentz och P. Celsing sakral arkitektur*, Uppsala 1998.

Photograph Credits

Arkitekturmuseet Bildarchiv, Stockholm, Sweden
Canadian Centre for Architecture, Montréal, Canada
Giovanni Chiaramonte, Milan
Nicola Flora, Paolo Giardiello, Gennaro Postiglione, Milan Polytechnic
Kyrkogårdsförvaltningen, Malmö, Sweden
Martin Charles, Hounslow, United Kingdom
Tiofoto AB, Stockholm, Sweden